West Germany and the Iron Curtain

West Germany and the Iron Curtain

the Iron Curtain

Environment, Economy, and Culture
in the Borderlands

———◆◆◆———

ASTRID M. ECKERT

OXFORD
UNIVERSITY PRESS

OXFORD
UNIVERSITY PRESS

Oxford University Press is a department of the University of Oxford. It furthers
the University's objective of excellence in research, scholarship, and education
by publishing worldwide. Oxford is a registered trade mark of Oxford University
Press in the UK and certain other countries.

Published in the United States of America by Oxford University Press
198 Madison Avenue, New York, NY 10016, United States of America.

CIP data is on file at the Library of Congress
ISBN 978–0–19–069005–2

Contents

Acknowledgments

EVERYTHING ANYONE HAS ever said about writing one's second book is true. It takes much longer than you think, and in the end you are indebted to a team of medical professionals for having kept you going. I thus acknowledge with profound gratitude the skills of my eye surgeons at the Emory University Eye Center, Drs. Beck and Jain. They enabled me to finish this book.

Several grants and fellowships made this project possible. A Leibniz Fellowship at the Center for Contemporary History in Potsdam (ZZF) set me on the right path to do the necessary research for the chapter on border tourism. The ZZF's journal also published my early work on the subject. Summer research fellowships from the German Academic Exchange Service (DAAD), the American Philosophical Society, and Emory's College Research Grants in Humanistic Inquiry supported my archival work. The book took shape conceptually during my first full leave, supported by Emory's University Research Committee (URC) Award and the American Academy in Berlin. At the American Academy, I benefited greatly from the input and joviality of my fellow fellows, and I thank Pieter M. Judson in particular for his friendship and generosity. Most of the writing of this book was supported by Alexander von Humboldt Foundation fellowship. I thank the late Axel Schildt and his colleagues, who hosted me at the Hamburg Forschungsstelle für Zeitgeschichte, for a fabulous year. I am grateful to the Department of History and Emory's College of Arts and Sciences for underwriting my research leaves. The deans generously added a decisive completion leave semester at the very end that served the purpose it was designed to do.

I have benefited from the expertise of numerous archivists and librarians who supported my wide-ranging research. At the top of my list is Marie Hansen who, before her well-deserved retirement, served at Emory's

Inter-Library Loan Department and managed to procure even the most obscure publications; she never flinched even if the requested title made me seem like a nuclear physicist. I also wish to thank the archivists and staff at the Bundesarchiv in Koblenz (particularly Kerstin Schenke), Berlin-Lichterfelde, and Freiburg who accommodated my many visits, sometimes at short notice. Thanks also to the archivists at the state archives in Wiesbaden, Munich, Hannover, Wolfenbüttel, and Schleswig. Rainer Hering at the Landesarchiv Schleswig-Holstein made an unprocessed collection of customs records available to me, and this gave me valuable leads at an early stage of my research. Herr Dziomba at the Stasi archive accommodated many twists and turns in my efforts to query the black box that is the BStU. Herr Heiko Fischer hosted me at the Archive of Lower Saxony's State Parliament and scanned protocols not available elsewhere. Peter Krüger in Lüchow generously opened the county archive at times that accommodated my schedule. The most memorable day of archival work was the one that I spent at the Green Belt Project office in Nuremberg, where I read files while sitting in a beautiful garden.

My debt to colleagues, friends, and perfect strangers is so wide and deep that chances are high I will inadvertently forget to mention someone. People have answered my queries, taken my calls, shared memories and materials, and commented on my work. In alphabetical order, I wish to thank Ralf Ahrens, Reinhold Albert, Frank Altrichter, Hermann Behrens, Dieter Bieberstein, Hendrik Bindewald, Andrew Blowers, Peter Boag, Fritz Dieterich, Axel Doßmann, Ernst Eberhardt, Bryan Falgout, Bernd Friedrich, Alon Gelbman, Helmut Hammerich, Winfried Heinemann, Michael Heinz, Ingolf Hermann, Ulrike Jureit, Axel Kahrs, Bernd Katzer, Melanie Kreutz, Markus Leibenath, Thomas Lekan, Gunnar Maus, Alfred Milnik, Karsten Mund, Bernd Nicolai, Andrea Orzoff, Otto Puffahrt, Gerhard Sälter, Rainer Schenk, Ralf Schmidt, Detlef Schmiechen-Ackermann, Thomas Schmitt, Lu Seegers, Hasso Spode, Marita Sterly, Hartmut Strunz, Christoph Strupp, Maren Ullrich, and William Glenn Gray. Sigurd Müller and Harry Wieber granted me permission to use their photos.

Particular thanks go to my interview partners, who took considerable time out of their busy schedules to meet with me. I had the privilege of learning a great deal from the conservationists with whom I talked. My thanks to Karl Berke (Ilsenburg), Wolfram Brauneis (Eschwege), Kai Frobel (Nuremberg), Martin Görner (Ranis), Lebrecht Jeschke (Greifswald), Ralf Maaß (Mustin), and Hubert Weiger (Berlin).

I had the great fortune to work alongside colleagues who were conducting their own research on the Iron Curtain. The fact that my book is the last to come out from our loose group of five means that I benefited the most from everyone's work. I thank Edith Sheffer, Sagi Schaefer, Jason B. Johnson, and Yuliya Komska for their support and for their books.

As the project was taking shape, I had the chance to gather feedback in several *Forschungskolloquien*, a venerable German academic tradition in which works-in-progress are thoroughly discussed. I thank all discussants at each venue, as well as Muriel Blaive and Thomas Lindenberger (Vienna), Ute Frevert (Berlin), Christof Mauch (Munich), Martin Sabrow (Potsdam), Dirk Schumann (Göttingen), and Hermann Wentker (Berlin) for inviting me. Over the years, the participants of the annual South-East German Studies Workshop (SEGSW) found themselves on the receiving end of multiple short papers related to my project. This gem of a workshop provided a wonderful opportunity to polish ideas still rough around the edges, and I thank everyone for their input.

At Emory, I benefited from collegial support in the History Department and across campus more generally. As chair for five years, Jeffrey Lesser advocated for my leaves and wrote many letters on my behalf. I learned a great deal from my two co-teachers, Sander Gilman and Matthew Payne, who sustained me with their insight, wit, and tremendous knowledge. I also thank Becky Herring, Kelly Richmond Yates, and Allison Rollins for having my back. Even at the busiest of times, Allison Adams's "Sit Down and Write" group refocused me for at least an hour per week.

Some friends and colleagues went the extra mile and read sections of the manuscript and provided invaluable feedback at times when their own desks were already crowded. I wish to thank Joe Perry, Adam T. Rosenbaum, Stephen Milder, Andrew S. Tompkins, Sandra Chaney, Stefanie M. Woodard and Sean Wempe, as well as the Emory colleagues in Devin Stewart's faculty writing workshop, the graduate students in the European borderlands seminar at Emory, and the graduate students at Berkeley's *Der Kreis* group. I may not have managed to follow each and every one of their suggestions, and any resulting shortcomings are clearly my responsibility.

I am deeply indebted to the anonymous reviewers of the book proposal and the manuscript. Their constructive and helpful comments allowed me to wrap up this project. I am grateful to my language editor, Ulrike Guthrie, who went over my English and made this book a better read. At Oxford University Press, Alexandra Dauler and Macey Fairchild expertly guided me through the assessment and production process and came through when I needed them the most. They assigned me the best copy editor one can ask for, and I am grateful to Mary Becker for her diligence.

My close friends and family have heard more about this project than can be good for anyone. My parents still reside in the former West German borderlands and were the reason why I chose to write this book. I also thank Judy and Richard, Kelly, Suanne, George, Karen, Solveig, Polly and Daniel, Keno and Kora, Markus, Tanja, Knud, Katrin and Bob, Will, the Schwerins in Koblenz, and the Weinbergs in Efland for their friendship. I dedicate this book to the other two history PhDs in my family—Eike and Brian.

West Germany and the Iron Curtain

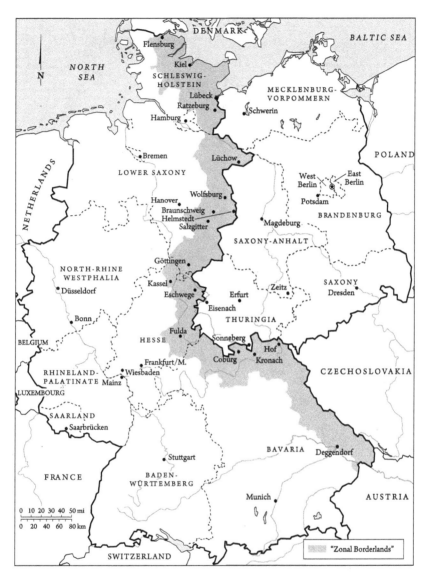

MAP I West Germany's "zonal borderlands"

Source: Bill Nelson

MAP 2 Lakes, rivers, and mountain ranges along the inter-German border
Source: Bill Nelson

MAP 3 The county of Lüchow-Dannenberg and Gorleben
Source: Bill Nelson

Introduction

ON AUGUST 3, 1984, a truck bearing the identity of the fake but cleverly named Friedemann Grün (or Peaceman Green) company carried Greenpeace activists into the compound of the coal-fired power station Buschhaus near Helmstedt. Within minutes, the protesters assembled a ladder, climbed a cooling tower, and unfurled a banner denouncing the plant as a major polluter (Figure I.1). Buschhaus became the object of an acute political crisis in the Federal Republic because it was slated to open without desulfurization filters at the height of public anxiety about acid rain and forest dieback. Although the West German government had passed a directive in 1983 that required such filters, Buschhaus had been authorized years earlier and was about to be grandfathered in without them. Its supporters cited the jobs the plant would provide, its opponents the pollution it would emit. The discord over Buschhaus entered the annals of West German environmental history as a classic conflict between economy and ecology and as an indicator of West Germany's newly developed ecological consciousness.[1]

Yet what amplified the conflict was the coal power plant's location. Buschhaus had been built in the West German borderlands right on the Iron Curtain. It belonged to a company, the Braunschweigische Kohle Bergwerke (BKB), whose coal mining fields had been sliced in half by the inter-German border in 1952. Without access to all the coal deposits, the long-term viability of BKB was at risk; its staff therefore regarded Buschhaus as a new lease on life. In the political economy of the Federal Republic, the regions along the border, the "zonal borderlands" where the BKB was located, had acquired preferential treatment as depressed areas. State subsidies flowed into the border counties to create and retain industrial jobs, hence regional political leaders' dogged support for the smoke-belching project. The border also magnified the environmental dimension of Buschhaus because it was instantly cast as a transboundary issue. At a time when the Federal Republic was chiding East Germany for its unparalleled sulfur dioxide emissions, allowing a coal power plant to go online without filters right on their shared border, and upwind of the German Democratic Republic (GDR), was diplomatically unwise. The environmental activists picked up on the transboundary cue. On June 17, 1985, the federal holiday celebrating German unity, the organization Robin Wood staged a protest on the border. Its banner hovered over the demarcation line, and a GDR watchtower formed the backdrop (Figure I.1). The conflict over Buschhaus was much more than a clash between economy and ecology. It was shaped by the presence of the inter-German border and reminded everyone that Germany remained a divided country.

This book examines the consequences of the volatile inter-German border for West Germany. It takes a fresh look at the history of the "old" Federal Republic and the German reunification process from the spatial perspective of the West German borderlands that emerged along the Cold

FIGURE I.1. On June 17, 1985, the environmental activists of Robin Wood staged a protest against the Buschhaus coal-fired power station right on the demarcation line against the backdrop of a GDR watchtower.
© Ullstein Bild—Ali Paczensky

War demarcation line. The 1,393-kilometer-long border between the two German states was part of the Iron Curtain that divided postwar Europe into West and East. Unlike its urban sibling, the iconic Berlin Wall, the inter-German border meandered mostly through rural landscapes, often in the form of a fence running through fields. Yet the western border counties were also home to cities such as Lübeck, Wolfsburg, Braunschweig, Salzgitter, Göttingen, Kassel, Fulda, Coburg, and Hof. These borderlands did not merely mirror some larger developments in the Federal Republic but helped to shape them. Acknowledging my debt to the late Daphne Berdahl, one of the first scholars to address Iron Curtain borderlands after 1990, I consider these border regions to be "fields of heightened consciousness" and argue that they formed the most sensitive geographical space in West Germany.[2] Throughout the lifetime of the "old" Federal Republic, this area constituted a laboratory where West Germany had to wrestle in concrete ways with its ideological adversary, socialist East Germany. If the new western state was to be successful, the blessings of its economic, political, and social order—the very countermodel to the GDR—had to reach into every corner of West Germany in order to unfold their integrative force. In the borderlands, state authorities had to address the practical consequences of partition in order to firmly integrate these liminal regions into the state territory. These consequences affected the local economies and infrastructure, manifested themselves as ideological competition in the realm of culture as long as the border was still permeable, and, as the Buschhaus episode indicates, became tangible in environmental relations.

To gauge the consequences of the Iron Curtain for West Germany and throw the border-centered interactions between West and East into sharp relief, this book employs topical chapters. Two chapters address the economic consequences of the inter-German border for the Federal Republic. They make the case that the West German borderlands coalesced as a spatial unit due to economic processes and the lobbying work of those affected by them. From the perspective of the eastern periphery, they trace how the Federal Republic adjusted to its postwar economic geography. A chapter on tourism to the Iron Curtain explores West German ways of seeing the border and follows the narrative arc from the 1950s into the 1990s, when some of the same locations that used to put partition on display switched to commemorating a country once divided. Three chapters engage environmental themes, such as transboundary pollution, border-induced landscape change, and the planned nuclear industrial site at Gorleben that, like Buschhaus, was meant to bring jobs to the borderlands. Together, these chapters constitute the first environmental history of the German Iron Curtain. The book thus examines the history of West Germany and the inter-German border from several perspectives, each of which considers the narrative beyond the 1990 caesura and thereby integrates the "long" postwar era with the postunification decades. Much historical scholarship on postwar Germany remains wedded to a 1945–1990 timeframe, leaving postunification history grossly understudied. The study of unification itself is strongly driven by anniversaries.[3] There is diminishing justification for the 1990 caesura, and this book provides a model of how to write across it.

Recent scholarship on the German Iron Curtain has shown that the divide was profoundly shaped by the interactions between both German states and Germans on each side, by the give and take that unfolded in "high" politics as well as in local encounters.[4] As the border solidified discursively and materially, it created borderlands on both sides. In the East, military authorities demarcated a 5-kilometer-deep security zone in 1952 that was off limits to nonresidents and became an integral part of the border fortifications. As Thomas Lindenberger has argued, the ripple effects of the GDR border regime proved constitutive for the East German dictatorship.[5] In the West, residents of a county-deep strip along the demarcation line turned to the state for support to compensate for the economic disruptions the border was causing. State support was slow in coming, but once aid measures took shape, these areas came to be known in West Germany as "zonal borderlands" (Zonenrandgebiete). Including the "wet border" on the Baltic in the North and the border between Bavaria and Czechoslovakia in the South, the regions officially recognized as adversely affected by the Iron Curtain amounted to almost 20 percent of the Federal Republic's territory and were inhabited by almost 12 percent of its population.[6]

Zonenrandgebiete: the awkward name of these border regions was itself an artifact of the early Cold War. It contained a dismissive slur against socialist East Germany. By referring to the German Democratic Republic as "the Zone," West Germans implied that despite the founding of an independent East German state in 1949, the GDR remained a Soviet puppet regime not much different from the Soviet military occupation zone that it had once been. Calling the West German regions along the demarcation line "zonal borderlands" served as a reminder that they were a product of partition.[7] This book explains how the conditions of the Cold War helped create these West German borderlands, elucidates the many ways in which they mattered throughout the history of the "old" Federal Republic, and shows how their afterlives continue to reverberate in reunified Germany. The border regions thus stand at the center of inquiry. Yet they also serve as a lens through which to regard the history of the Federal Republic, its relations to the GDR, and the process of reunification.

As Eagle Glassheim reminds us, the borderlands created by the Iron Curtain have little in common with the lively contact zones and culturally hybrid spaces that animate much of borderland scholarship.[8] Although the inter-German border was never hermetically sealed, as its moniker "Iron Curtain" implied, it was fully intended to separate adversarial ideologies and inhibit migration. It moved from being fluid and porous to becoming increasingly restrictive and static.[9] East and West German border guards policed their respective sides, and Allied troops reserved the right to maintain military outposts on the demarcation line and to patrol it whenever they saw fit.[10] From its early days, the inter-German border gained notoriety as a deadly structure; according to the latest figures, the East German border regime claimed up to three hundred lives there before it was dismantled.[11] Throughout its existence, the inter-German border remained a contested political boundary and retained its symbolic power as the frontline of the global Cold War.

Fueled by this symbolic valence, the Iron Curtain magnified all activities and occurrences within its orbit. For example, East German border authorities perceived Sunday outings by ordinary West Germans who came to see the border as a centrally orchestrated psychological warfare operation to challenge the existence of the GDR. Similarly, the pollution of rivers in the borderlands was not just an environmental problem like any other but turned into a hot-button issue in inter-German relations because the pollutants swept into the Federal Republic from the GDR. Transboundary air and water contamination subsequently brought some locations in the West German borderlands into disrepute during the 1970s and 1980s, yet the same decades also marked the "rediscovery" of the borderlands as allegedly authentic rural spaces and "intact" landscapes. Since accelerated modernization during the postwar reconstruction years had passed these regions by, their less developed status now turned from an economic liability into a tourist asset. As this book shows, a borderland perspective provides a unique vantage point on the environmental histories of East and West Germany, in terms of both pollution and landscape change. Finally, the borderlands also assumed a key role in determining Germany's energy future when they were chosen in 1977 as the site of a nuclear waste reprocessing and storage plant that was thought to be essential to the nuclear industry's development. However, instead of securing the industry's ascendency, the choice of the village of Gorleben in Lower Saxony triggered a lasting protest movement that amalgamated with and furthered similar anti-nuclear protests elsewhere in the country, ultimately putting a stop to nuclear energy use in Germany. In all these respects, the periphery became central to West German history, even as remoteness and peripherality continued to undergird borderland residents' claim to state support throughout the postwar decades.

As a historiographical subject, the inter-German border is finally moving out of the shadow of the better known Berlin Wall. Recent works have explored particular locales along the German Iron Curtain, adding significantly to our understanding of how the evolving border regime affected the communities it divided. On the basis of her microstudy of the adjacent towns Neustadt in Bavaria (West) and Sonneberg in Thuringia (East), Edith Sheffer argues that the border "was not simply imposed by the Cold War superpowers but was also an improvised outgrowth of anxious postwar society."[12] Daily interactions along the demarcation line solidified it before it was ever physically fortified: before a border was visible on the ground, it was becoming real in people's minds. In rural areas, however, the dynamic sometimes differed. In the Eichsfeld region, where the social fabric was often tied to landholdings through which the border now ran, border residents could act only "within limits determined in constant interaction with state" authorities. Sagi Schaefer found that "individual agency diminished over the decades" as state structures in East and West, and thereby the border itself, grew stronger.[13] Jason B. Johnson, by contrast, follows the more familiar narrative that the GDR regime pressured border residents into compliance. In his study of the divided village of Mödlareuth on the border between Bavaria (West) and Thuringia (East), those dwelling on the eastern side found themselves in a hyper-surveilled environment where "the Iron Curtain descended with a top-down nature, a process in which villagers saw the state as an external force imposing division."[14]

The German Iron Curtain not only consisted of the Berlin Wall and the inter-German border, but also contained a stretch between Bavaria and Czechoslovakia that had long served as a state border and that had been drawn into nationality conflicts between Germans and Czechs during the interwar period.[15] After 1945, most ethnic Germans from the former Sudetenland were expelled across the Czech–German border.[16] Yuliya

Komska and Friederike Kind-Kovács show how those expellees who now resided in West Germany subsequently appropriated the Bavarian–Czech section of the Iron Curtain to commemorate their lost homeland. Whereas the inter-German border turned into a cruel symbol of the Cold War, the Bavarian–Czech section of the Iron Curtain carried the additional burden of memory relating to wartime suffering.[17] Works on the Iron Curtain outside of Germany further confirm the uneven development of the Cold War divide, the importance of local contexts, and the relevance of prior experiences of living with state borders in the encounter with Europe's postwar partition.[18]

Collectively, these various approaches to the *"local* Iron Curtain" (Kind-Kovács) serve to de-essentialize the border by peeling off the layers of Cold War propaganda that have dominated its perception ever since Winston Churchill's famous "Iron Curtain" speech in March 1946. "In many ways," writes Edith Sheffer, "the Iron Curtain was a boundary like any other."[19] Despite posturing on each side that blamed the respective other for the militarization of the border and attributed to the ideological adversary the responsibility for its victims,[20] the border itself remained a shared burden that triggered and necessitated interaction. This dynamic is best captured by the observation that Cold War Germany was politically "divided, but not disconnected."[21] The emerging border had predictable consequences with which borderland scholars are well familiar. Any fresh border, especially one enforced in a modern state with well-developed infrastructural networks and sophisticated interregional divisions of labor, would disrupt the flow of people, labor, and goods. It would alter economic, social, and—as this book shows—ecological conditions in its adjacent regions, and possibly even further afield.[22] That the new border was ultimately sealed so tightly, and with increasing military force, made its effects in the abutting border regions all the deeper.

This book explores the development of the borderlands on the western side of the inter-German border. Chapter 1 introduces the economic heterogeneity of the borderlands through snapshots of the port city of Lübeck on the Baltic, the rural county of Lüchow-Dannenberg on the Elbe River, the city of Braunschweig in Lower Saxony, and the industrial town of Hof in Upper Franconia. As the tightening demarcation line made itself felt, a broad coalition of borderland advocates—elected officials in local, state, and federal parliaments, as well as civil servants and representatives from business and commerce—joined forces to pressure the federal government to help prevent their regions from turning into economic backwaters.

These lobbying efforts revealed that borderland residents cared less about living in the shadow of the Iron Curtain than about living in the shadow of the "economic miracle" that, from their perspective, was partially achieved at their expense. In their pitch for state aid, borderland advocates declared their regions to be economically, socially, and politically more vulnerable than other parts of the country and came up with the "brand name" *Zonenrandgebiet*, which enlisted Cold War parameters to imbue their demands with more urgency vis-à-vis regions that had "merely" been damaged by the recent war. Their efforts yielded the "zonal borderland aid" program (*Zonenrandförderung*), which soon became an integral part of the border regions' economic and cultural life.

Chapter 2 explains how borderland aid became an ongoing feature of the West German subsidy landscape. By continuing to depict these regions as "victimized" by the Iron Curtain, borderland advocates succeeded in turning ad hoc aid measures into a regional aid law, but they also inadvertently transformed the border regions into "the East of the West" in the process: the "zonal borderlands" acquired the image of being behind and underdeveloped. Once firmly established by law in 1971, borderland aid benefited from a path dependency that insulated it against criticism even in the face of subsidy abuse. The persistent support for borderland aid across political parties left only the European Commission as a credible challenge to this regional aid program.[23] Pushing beyond 1990, the chapter addresses the economic consequences of the fall of the border and the widespread hope that the erstwhile periphery would turn into the new "center" of Germany and Europe, an expectation prefigured by decades of advocacy that depicted the border as the root cause of economic decline. The borderlands turned into places where the postunification "cotransformation" was instantly felt.[24] The toolkit of economic aid that had been employed to prop up the borderlands now moved a few miles farther east, across the former border: *Zonenenrandförderung* turned into Aufbau Ost (Reconstruction East), the program charged with rebuilding the economic capacity of East Germany along capitalist lines. The two chapters on the regional economy along the border not only uncover the strategies of borderland advocates to bring about and defend an aid package for their regions. More important, they historicize these discourses and show how they helped to construct the borderlands as such.

Chapter 3 considers tourism to the Iron Curtain as a way that West Germans and their visitors sought to make sense of the global Cold War through local activity. Already in the 1950s, the Iron Curtain attracted curiosity seekers and eventually turned into a well-developed tourist attraction. Sightseeing at the border began as a grassroots activity that the state eventually harnessed and transformed into political education. An elaborate tourist infrastructure emerged on the western side of the inter-German border that allowed visitors to peek into East Germany from lookout towers, travel the Elbe River on pleasure boats, and collect colorful postcards depicting fences and watchtowers. The frontline of the Cold War was put on display in a way that provoked the East German border authorities into seeking opportunities to render Iron Curtain visits less attractive for western tourists. Especially during the 1950s and 1960s, border tourism offered an outlet for West German anti-Communism and was frequently framed as a demand for German unity. The chapter argues, however, that this activity did little to overcome partition but rather stabilized the political and territorial status quo. Border tourism helped West Germans become accustomed to partition.

Chapter 4 moves into environmental history and addresses a typical borderland problem—transboundary air and water pollution. During the 1970s and 1980s, rivers carried eastern industrial waste and sewage into West Germany; the wind blew sulfur dioxide both ways. Their environmental interdependency forced both German states to the negotiating table, eventually producing the ineffectual Environmental Accords of 1987. The western encounter with eastern pollution through the interface of the inter-German border confronted West German authorities with early signs of East Germany's dissolution. While they failed to grasp this message, their experiences with East German pollution and the futile diplomatic efforts to curb it nonetheless gave rise to knowledge about the nature and extent of the GDR's environmental problems that became the prerequisite for the post-1990 ecological restoration of East Germany, a task that turned into the "most elaborate environmental protection project in the world."[25]

Chapter 5, in turn, investigates the consequences of the border regime for landscape and wildlife. The ecological impact of the inter-German border has become widely known through a postunification conservation project referred to as the Green Belt, which seeks to preserve the swath of land once occupied by the border and which is frequently presented as the beneficial outcome of an otherwise nasty situation. As is worth remembering, however, the Iron Curtain was first and foremost a military installation with a political function that encroached on Central European landscapes which had themselves been shaped by human interference for centuries. The chapter not only looks at the ecological footprint of the Iron

Curtain from its end in 1989 but also considers the effects of the border regime on landscape over time. It argues that the border's effects were neither purely detrimental to nor exclusively beneficial for nature and wildlife; hence neither a narrative of decline nor a narrative of creation adequately captures the dynamic influence of the border regime. This chapter introduces the term "transboundary natures" to refer to the landscapes shaped by the border, a concept that highlights the role of the border in landscape change, regardless of whether these changes were embraced by contemporaries as advantageous for or rejected as deleterious to nature.

Chapter 6 explores the implications of the fact that the village of Gorleben in the border county of Lüchow-Dannenberg was nominated in 1977 as the potential site of a nuclear waste reprocessing and storage facility. The nuclear plant would have become West Germany's most costly industrial project to date. It was planned on the assumption that nuclear energy would allow Germany to move beyond fossil fuels and gain proximate energy independence. In view of discursive patterns conceived in the 1950s that framed the border regions as areas in need of state aid and industrial development, the borderland location of Gorleben precipitated its nomination. The presence of the border shaped and magnified every aspect of the Gorleben siting controversy. The Gorleben decision endowed county officials with leverage over the federal government, a newfound power they exercised along the lines of the well-established borderland lobby work. The immediate proximity of Gorleben to the inter-German border also drew the GDR into the siting dispute, thereby ratcheting up an already raging political controversy. The border itself was enlisted for anti-nuclear protest activities. So were the landscapes it had created: in the plans for the nuclear facility, Gorleben opponents perceived the seeds of destruction of a rural idyll. Gorleben turned the periphery into the center of the longest-lasting anti-nuclear protest of the Federal Republic and changed its energy future, albeit not in ways that proponents of nuclear energy imagined in the 1970s and 1980s.

Although this book was crafted with an intentional emphasis on the role of the borderlands on the western side of the German Iron Curtain, it is nonetheless deeply rooted in the historiography of the Federal Republic *and* the GDR and draws on archives from both. It is based on East and West German materials from nineteen federal, state, and municipal archives, as well as several private collections and some American diplomatic records. It also relies on newspapers and periodicals and various government-issued publications, including ephemera like fliers, brochures, and postcards, some of which I obtained at online auctions where Iron Curtain–related materials are still being hawked. A limited number of interviews and correspondence with contemporary witnesses and actors round out the source base.

These western borderlands were where I grew up. Born in a rural county in Lower Saxony in the 1970s, I thought it normal that the country roads ended some half hour to the east. When I walked to school and past the local train station, I often sidled past military vehicles waiting to be loaded onto cargo trains. They were Dutch, French, or British. On an outing through the woods, I stumbled upon dugouts with camouflaged soldiers inside who raised their heads and signaled that I should remove myself from their war games. In the mid-1980s, we took our exchange students from France to the border and showed off the Iron Curtain. I cannot remember why we did this or what they thought about it; probably it was simply one of the few things we could do in our region that might impress teenagers from Paris. I crossed the inter-German border frequently to visit relatives on the other side. Each time I wondered why we were pulled over and searched or otherwise held up by East German border personnel, until I figured that it must have something to do with the pro-NATO bumper sticker on my father's car. When we met up with family members in the GDR, my brothers and second cousins compared notes on their military training and joked about who would reach the other's base first. This book is thus also my effort to understand the absurdities with which I grew up, and why I didn't find them absurd then.

I

The Making of the West German Borderlands, 1945–1955

IN THE DEPTHS of the winter of 1957, the journalist Barbara Klie traveled to Upper Franconia, the northern edge of Bavaria. The Bohemian winter winds wrap the region in a chill that spawned the nickname "Bavaria's Siberia." By the time of Klie's visit, Upper Franconia, once a busy trade hub that boasted vibrant textile, porcelain, and beer brewing industries, found itself smack up against the Iron Curtain. Klie's assignment was to take the pulse of those who dwelled in the borderlands from Hof in Upper Franconia to Travemünde on the Baltic. Her subsequent stories for the conservative Protestant weekly *Christ und Welt* display a range of tropes that were well established in West Germany by the mid-1950s. It was at the border that "all roads ended," that the soil on the other side remained uncultivated, that people left, depopulating the region one by one.[1] A script had emerged that depicted the borderlands along the Iron Curtain as the end of the West, at once the last outpost of freedom and yet desolate and underdeveloped—the poorhouse of the otherwise prospering Federal Republic.[2]

So it was that Klie came upon a population with a confused sense of belonging. Borderlanders felt forgotten by their compatriots. The mayor of a small town alerted her to how his people related to the country in which they lived. "Have you noticed how they talk here?" he asked. "When they refer to Frankfurt or Essen, they speak of 'West Germany'—as if we were not living in West Germany ourselves but in the Zone! When they say 'over there' (*drüben*), they're not referring to the Zone but to the rich western Germany beyond the mountains that shares so little of its wealth with us."[3] Their new state appeared to so alienate these townspeople through material exclusion that socialist East Germany—despite being pejoratively referred to as the "Zone"—became a potential alternative for their allegiance.

The young Federal Republic had a problem at its eastern periphery. Since the late 1940s, the emerging Iron Curtain had given birth to borderlands where there had been none before. During the early 1950s, the counties adjacent to the nascent inter-German border were still overflowing both with German refugees expelled at war's end from Eastern and Central Europe and with migrants from East Germany. For the established residents in these counties, already competing for scarce resources, the transformation of their home region into a borderland only created further insecurity. Local officials were quick to argue that economic hardship among natives and destitute new arrivals could easily translate into political instability, a situation the socialist neighbors on the other side of the demarcation line were said to be waiting to exploit. During the early Cold War, West Germans began to buy into the notion that they could not afford such ambiguity and brittle allegiances among borderland dwellers. And thus, by 1953, an economic aid program began to take shape, a program designed to cope with the local consequences of partition and prop up these border areas in order to provide their residents with the sense that they were invited to partake in the economic recovery of the country.

This chapter explores the economic consequences of the budding inter-German border, from the early effects of the demarcation lines between the Allied occupation zones to the establishment of the borderland aid program. It argues that the emergence of the West German borderlands along the Iron Curtain was first and foremost a function of economic processes and some heavy lobbying work of those affected by them. The German economy at midcentury, heavily reliant on mining, construction, and industrial production, had developed a sophisticated interregional division of labor.[4] Any border would necessarily constitute a hindrance to the flow of labor, supplies, and goods. As the following portraits of Lübeck, Braunschweig, Hof, and the rural county of Lüchow-Dannenberg reveal, these border locations were indeed hampered by the disruption of established economic patterns and, depending on their respective economic profile, developed specific deficiencies as a result. At times, the people in these locations also managed to "game" the new conditions, although such gains tended to be short-lived. All border regions were deeply affected by the introduction of a new western currency in June 1948; the appearance of the deutsche mark (DM) created a currency dualism along the demarcation line that fanned a shadow economy of smuggling and low-wage labor. Least expected, however, were the detrimental consequences of the "economic miracle" for the border counties. As the engines of economic recovery on the Rhine and the Ruhr began to crank into gear, they sucked capital, business, and labor out of the borderlands. Before West German industry recruited workers from abroad, the border regions, with their abundance of expellees and refugees, constituted the labor reservoir of the Republic.[5] As the counties lost skilled labor and even whole companies to relocation bids from farther inland, borderland residents felt that economic growth farther west put them under "friendly fire."

In response, the border counties—tellingly at first represented by the regional chambers of industry and commerce—petitioned the newly constituted federal government to launch a comprehensive aid package to offset the negative consequences of their redefined location. This demand joined the already highly audible chorus of similar expectations directed toward the state within the reconstruction landscape that was West Germany.[6] In view of such competition for state attention and resources, advocacy for the border regions necessitated an increasingly systematic approach. This lobbying constituted a crucial step in the formation of these regions into one spatial unit that soon acquired its own brand name—"the zonal borderlands." Whereas other regions suffered "only" from war damages and run-of-the-mill structural weaknesses, the border regions could point to, and actively enlisted, the ideological parameters of the Cold War; theirs were problems caused by Communist aggression. In their quest to be recognized as disadvantaged by the hardening border, those who spoke for the borderlands developed a visual and rhetorical language of partition that fixed the demarcation line on the mental map of their compatriots even *before* East German authorities famously escalated the border regime and locked down the demarcation line in May 1952. When an aid package finally materialized as a product of electoral exigency in the first federal elections of 1953, it was borderland advocates themselves who defined the spatial dimension of the borderlands. A 40-kilometer-deep strip from the Baltic in the North to the Bavarian Forest in the South was slated to benefit from an economic aid program designed to cope with the local consequences of partition. Together with aid to West Berlin, "zonal borderland aid," or *Zonenrandförderung*, became the most enduring regional aid program in West German history. Not only had West Germany thus acquired a borderland, it had also designated almost 20 percent of its state territory as a space created by the Cold War.

Economic Life with Demarcation Lines

Germany's new borders were determined by the outcome of World War II and Allied postwar planning at the conferences of Tehran, Yalta, and Potsdam, although its territorial shape after 1945 remained uncertain for years as the former Allies improvised their policies.[7] Once Allied troops occupied Germany, local commanders negotiated last-minute adjustments to their demarcations to incorporate an outlying village or a vital road; a sizable enclave in the Erzgebirge (Ore Mountains) in the Soviet Zone even remained militarily unoccupied, sandwiched between American and Soviet lines.[8] On July 1, 1945, American, Soviet, and British troops withdrew to their respective zones, while France, the "late victor" that had not participated in the postwar planning conferences, received territory carved out of the American and British zones in the southwest of Germany. Until the British and American military governors merged their zones into the Bizone (January 1947) and, through French accession, into the Trizone (March 1948), each military governor oversaw his respective zonal economy as he saw fit. The Allied pledge at the Potsdam Conference of August 1945 to treat occupied Germany as one economic unit never materialized.

Aside from the political imponderables that resulted from inter-Allied disagreements, the destruction of traffic infrastructures, the dislocation of workers, the food shortage, and the demarcation lines greatly hampered any economic activity in the immediate postwar period.[9] Since the occupying powers decided to police and, to varying degrees, enforce their demarcation lines instead of simply treating them as an administrative matter, the lines began to serve in effect as political borders and generate issues that suddenly required regulation. Mundane activities like going to work, for instance, could acquire an "interzonal" quality that the Allied Control Council sought to regulate—although locals tended to ignore such regulations whenever possible.[10]

Goods took the form of exports if they were destined for a location beyond the originator's zone.[11] Legal interzonal trade itself, however, was at first impossible and, once addressed by the Allied Control Council, became heavily regulated and easily turned into a pawn amid rising political tensions between the occupying powers. Even companies that obtained the coveted paperwork (*Warenbegleitpapiere*) could be turned away under unpredictable pretexts. Since individual companies could barely jump through the necessary hoops, the re-established German states (*Länder*) and even individual cities made barter trade agreements with each other: Bavaria delivered beef cattle, Saxony reciprocated with seed potatoes; Lübeck delivered cookware and horses, Mecklenburg responded with wood and straw.[12] To describe Germany's economic regression, contemporary commentators felt compelled to recall the days predating the 1834 Customs Union.[13]

With legal exchanges almost impossible, Germans turned to illegal means: smuggling and black marketeering. The volume of illegal trade was at least double that of legal trade.[14] Many Germans already had plenty of experience maneuvering within a shadow economy, the material shortages of the late war having provided ample opportunity. Black market activities remained a characteristic feature of the German rubble society during the immediate postwar years and especially flourished along the demarcation lines, Germany's outer borders, and between the four sectors of Berlin.[15] Disparities in economic opportunities along political boundaries have always attracted enterprising individuals. "You can live from the border on the border," reported the warden of a hostel in Schöningen (West) near Helmstedt on the Soviet line of demarcation who provided beds to smugglers and other boundary crossers. The particular commodity for smuggling in his vicinity was herring. Traders from Saxony carried barter goods to Bremen and Bremerhaven, where they stocked up on herring. The sale of the fish back in Saxony netted enough cash and new barter wares to finance the next trip. The train connection via Schöningen became known as the "herring train" (*Heringsbahn*) because of the smell in the railcars.[16] As long as smuggling and "procuring" did not turn into professional profiteering, Germans took a benign view of it: a nuisance perhaps, but also a matter of survival.[17]

Postwar Germans quickly developed differentiated perceptions of the boundaries within and around their country. The demarcation lines between the British, American, and French zones disappeared in the spring of 1948, yielding an entity that Germans called "Trizonia." But the lines controlled by the French and the Russians remained trouble spots. The demarcation line between the Saarland and Rhineland-Palatinate, for instance, rapidly turned into a strictly policed boundary, overseen by 1,200 customs officials who searched for contraband and refused entry to anyone without identity papers. The boundary cut into the economic fabric of the region and separated manufacturers from production supplies and markets. Its purpose was to unhinge the Saarland in order to incorporate it into France, but neither the British nor the Americans approved of this plan. After some twelve years as part of the French economy, in 1959 the Saarland territory joined West Germany.[18]

The border triangle west of Aachen in the Eifel region was another notorious postwar boundary. It rose to prominence as the "hole in the West" famous for smuggling. Between 1945 and 1953, smugglers imported some one thousand tons of coffee from Belgium. Every third cup in the Rhineland was brewed with smuggled beans until the Bonn government finally lowered the coffee tax in 1953, abruptly ending the profitable trade. Until then, slipping through the hole in the West remained a lucrative but dangerous occupation. German customs officials killed more than fifty smugglers in shootouts. But Rhinelanders had no intention of criminalizing the bootlegging across the Siegfried Line, not least because they had a stake in it.[19]

Although the situation along all the remaining demarcation lines was still contingent, the line along the Soviet zone was depicted differently. The journalist Josef Müller-Marein traveled along all the borders of Trizonia in late 1948 and published his impressions in the weekly *Die Zeit*. He described the eastern demarcation line in highly charged terms. His past as a Nazi propagandist may have influenced his word choice when he held that this line "cut through the *Lebensraum* of a *Volk*." It was here that "two world views, two forms of life" collided, forming a "border of mistrust right across Germany." He recounted tales of murder and mayhem in which Russian sentries shot border crossers, and self-appointed guides mugged and killed their clients instead of providing them safe passage. It was only the demarcation line along the Soviet zone that Müller-Marein thought was rubbing off on the people living on either side. By 1948, he already had the impression that "the zonal border had created new types of Germans: eastern and western types." The easterners felt abandoned by the westerners, while the westerners tried to fend off the easterners wherever possible.[20] Summarizing his tour, he concluded that "in the West, it's the bootlegging that endangers Trizonia, in the East, it's the ever-growing stream of refugees."[21] The West was hope; the East was fear.[22] From the West people smuggled much-needed commodities; from the East they smuggled only themselves. Unlike any other boundary that the postwar Germans encountered, the Soviet demarcation line had begun to produce difference.

Two events contributed significantly to the growing divergence between Trizonia and the Soviet zone and profoundly altered the rules of engagement of legal and illegal trade along that demarcation line: the western currency reform of June 1948 and the Soviet response, which was to block all transit routes to West Berlin. Soviet authorities had already increased border security and tinkered with the transit routes before the western Allies introduced the deutsche mark in Trizonia, and they continued to do so after the Berlin blockade was officially terminated in May 1949.[23] When the western Allies replaced the worthless reichsmark currency with the new deutsche mark in the three western zones in June 1948, the Soviets retaliated by first blocking all rail transportation to West Berlin, followed by all roads and waterways.[24] Much to the dismay of West German trade officials, the western Allies responded in July 1948 with a lesser-known counterblockade and prohibited all deliveries into the eastern zone, beginning with coal and steel. The interplay of blockade and counterblockade made the time from March 1948 to May 1949 so devastating for legal trade across the eastern demarcation line.[25] Anyone who had obtained the elusive permits to ship goods into the Soviet zone now found them null and void. Braunschweig's chamber of commerce informed its members that there was no point in even trying to dispatch merchandise.[26] Supplies and barter goods from the Soviet zone destined for western recipients were equally undercut. Interzonal trade that had been on the upswing in the first half of 1948 took a drastic nosedive.[27]

Illegal exchanges filled part of the vacuum again, yet the stakes had risen. Trizonia and the Soviet zone entered a dicey phase of currency dualism dominated by the allure of the western deutsche mark. When the Soviets sealed the demarcation line in mid-1948, they also did so to prevent the now worthless reichsmark from flooding East Germany, where it was still in circulation.[28] The dynamic along the demarcation line underwent a sea change. After a spike in unemployment, the introduction of the western currency laid the foundation for economic recovery in the West.[29] In retail, long-hoarded commodities and foodstuffs moved out of the shadow market and into the stores. The fortunate Germans who called this new money their own now had less need to engage in black marketeering. Small-scale barter exchanges—eastern silk stockings for western herring—collapsed. Yet cross-border smuggling rose exponentially and now turned into a predominantly eastern preoccupation. Selling goods on the western side not only netted deutsche marks; their exchange into eastern marks also profited from a rate gain.[30] Smuggling became increasingly criminalized as profiteering, a stigma that now affected mostly easterners although westerners were also involved in such transactions or benefited from them.[31]

A practice called *Grenzgängertum*, or border crossing, increased as well: eastern workers without permits crossed over and accepted work for a pittance as long as they were paid in the coveted western currency. Both western and eastern authorities battled *Grenzgängertum*, at times collaborating happily. Western officials fought it because it put additional pressure on already tight labor markets in the border counties and undercut the earning potential of western workers. Besides, workers from the West who commuted into the East could not live on their eastern wages and requested compensation payments from western public authorities.[32] Eastern officials fought it because it underscored the weakness of the eastern currency and, by extension, the socialist economy. They stigmatized eastern border crossers as "parasites" for living in a subsidized socialist economy on capitalist money.[33] The flow of smugglers and border crossers included a sizable number of migrants who intended to stay on the western side. The currency reform constituted a new impetus for migration from the East to the West, a movement that had been going on since the end of the war. Tellingly, western authorities refused to consider these migrants as "real refugees," accusing them of coming for economic reasons.[34]

The demarcation line had been disregarded and infringed upon ever since its inception in the summer of 1945, but the currency reform made these infringements increasingly one-sided. Germans on the western side grew ever more protectionist of "their" local economy. Contrary to popular memory, it was *western* police, customs officials, and British and American troops who stepped up border controls and erected barriers to stem the smuggling and enforce the counterblockade.[35] Müller-Marein's observation that the line was creating "eastern and western types" of Germans is echoed by Edith Sheffer, who argued that "westerners already expected easterners to appear needy, and easterners were already well aware of it." Early East–West stereotypes therefore "formed not just from ideology but also from material disparity."[36] Thus, the currency reform of 1948 marked the moment when the eastern demarcation line morphed into a "DMark-ation Line," and growing economic asymmetry turned it into a border.[37] This was also the moment when the West became "golden."

Early Consequences of the Eastern Demarcation Line for Local Economies

How did this hardening demarcation line affect the local economies on its western side? As the following brief portraits show, the regions abutting the Iron Curtain were economically diverse. The port city of Lübeck relied greatly on Baltic trade, while Hof in Upper Franconia prospered thanks to the textile industry but drew its supplies predominantly from Saxony and Thuringia. The exchange of goods between the territories that turned into West and East Germany used to be significant: in 1936, the western part sent 36.5 percent of its products eastward and received 39.9 percent of its goods from there.[38] Not only did the border halt such trade; it also divided the brown coal fields near Helmstedt (West) as well as the potash and shale mines along the Werra River between Hesse (West) and Thuringia (East). Yet for many miles, the demarcation line traversed purely rural regions. Here, it often separated farmers from their fields and cattle from their barns.[39] Especially mountain ranges like the Harz Mountains, the Rhön region, and the Bavarian Forest on the border with Czechoslovakia had long been considered economically weak and peripheral.[40] With few exceptions, such as silver and ore mining in the Harz, industrialization in these parts barely made it beyond the level of cottage industries. The mid-nineteenth-century folklorist Wilhelm Heinrich Riehl made "Rhön poverty" proverbial in Germany. The nascent border exacerbated the issue, but was never its root cause. The following snapshots give a sense of the economic heterogeneity of the counties, towns, and municipalities along the Iron Curtain and indicate the range of problems they experienced.

Lübeck on the Baltic

The city of Lübeck is an old Hanseatic port, the riches of early modern trade reflected in its architecture, the vagaries of prosperity immortalized in Thomas Mann's *Buddenbrooks*. Before 1945, Lübeck was an important Baltic port for transshipments of wine, grain, timber, fish, salt, ore, scrap metal, and pharmaceuticals. Across the Baltic, its corresponding ports were located in Scandinavia, Russia, Poland, and modern-day Latvia, Lithuania, and Estonia. Though thanks to a network of rivers and canals, wares from Lübeck reached well into the south of Germany, Lübeck was predominantly oriented to Northern Europe. As a trading hub, Lübeck had to deal with a string of setbacks that severely curtailed its reach. In 1913, Hamburg surpassed Lübeck in its core business of Baltic trade because the Kiel Canal, opened in 1895, had granted Hamburg access to Lübeck's home waters. While the Allied blockade of World War I hit all German ports equally, the declining trade with Russian and Baltic harbors after the Russian Revolution affected Lübeck in particular. Wholesale business also suffered during the Great Depression, and Lübeck did not return to its pre-1914 trade volume until 1938. By that time, it had slipped from sixth to tenth position among the Baltic ports. At the close of World War II, Lübeck's port was a regional one. Industrialization during the second half of the nineteenth century had made up for the gradual loss of trade-related work. By 1907, shipbuilding, manufacturing, and processing industries provided almost 60 percent of all jobs. Lübeck was turning from a port into an industrial city, albeit a provincial one.[41]

The inter-German border ushered in a new chapter in Lübeck's decline. In the early 1950s, Lübeck's chamber of commerce painted a dark picture of the border's effects on its district.[42] Each industry had lost vital hinterlands: key Baltic ports moved into the orbit of the Soviet Union, turning Scandinavian harbors into Lübeck's main correspondents. The reduced Baltic trade meant that related industries such as shipbuilding and repair, as well as the work of professionals like shipping agents, also declined.[43] Not only did international shipping fall, but Lübeck's role as an inland port was likewise affected. The Elbe-Lübeck Canal, which the city had completed at its own expense in 1900 to make up for the competition by the Kiel Canal, connected Lübeck with Lauenburg-on-Elbe. But after the Elbe east of Lauenburg disappeared behind the Iron Curtain, the canal no longer brought in the bulk of the city's production supplies. At great expense, Lübeck's industry had to transfer much of its incoming and outgoing cargo from inland waterways to rail.[44]

What was more, Lübeck's wholesale business had lost key markets in Mecklenburg, Western Pomerania, and beyond. After the lifting of the Berlin blockade, Lübeck's traders briefly harbored hopes that they could reestablish their ties to merchants on the other side, only to find that interzonal connections remained fickle and former partners were no longer free to make business decisions.[45] As a consequence, the wine trade, for instance, a signature commodity in Lübeck, fell by 50 percent, for some wholesalers even by 80 percent. Efforts to develop new markets succeeded for only a few commodities and were otherwise blocked by traders in the south and west of Germany who now retaliated against Lübeck's past protectionism of its erstwhile markets.[46] The government of Schleswig-Holstein felt compelled to compare Lübeck's situation to that of Trieste and Hong Kong, its economy to one placed under a "blockade."[47] As if having suffered a stroke, the city was said to be "quasi-paralyzed on its right side."[48]

Lüchow-Dannenberg County on the Elbe River

The presence of expellees and refugees became a signature feature of the nascent borderlands. At the end of the war, expellees from the lost German eastern territories either had halted their march once they found themselves just west of the demarcation line or had been directed into these predominantly rural areas where, unlike in the cities, the housing stock was still intact. As long as the demarcation line remained permeable, the border counties received further migrants from the Soviet occupation zone.[49] The county of Lüchow-Dannenberg, also referred to as the Hanoverian Wendland, was no exception. Nestled in the bends of the River Elbe in eastern Lower Saxony, the county grew from 41,399 residents in 1939 to 73,106 in 1950, or by 76.5 percent.[50] The influx of migrants overwhelmed the predominantly agricultural economy; the unemployment rate in 1951 rose to 25 percent.[51]

The Wendland had rarely known prosperous times. Agriculture had long been the economic backbone of this county, but its farmers competed for their livelihood with the waters of the Elbe and Jeetzel Rivers that frequently flooded croplands and grazing areas.[52] The cultivation of flax for the production of linen brought a brief respite in the late eighteenth and early nineteenth centuries until cheaper cotton took over by midcentury.[53] With few exceptions, industrialization passed the county by because the railroad passed it by. Since Lüchow-Dannenberg ended up in the blind spot of the Hamburg–Berlin–Hannover rail triangle, its own connections remained decisively regional.[54] Economic stagnation propelled rural exodus; by 1910, the county had lost some thirty thousand people. On the eve of World War II, two-thirds of the remaining population still worked in agriculture; others found employment in dairies, brickworks, sawmills, or furniture factories. The war turned some of the peasants into munitions workers, but by the time the expellees arrived, the county had only about a thousand industrial jobs.[55]

The tightening demarcation line dramatically exacerbated Lüchow-Dannenberg's poor traffic connections. Destroyed by an air raid, the Dömitz bridge across the Elbe was not rebuilt until 1992; the rail

connections to Salzwedel and Wittenberge on the eastern side were
no longer of any use; and the only checkpoint for car traffic in Bergen-
Dumme was closed in June 1952. The county was surrounded on three
sides by the Iron Curtain; it had effectively become a dead end.[56] There
was not much to gain from the inter-German border other than a customs
office in Schnackenburg-on-Elbe and tourists who eventually came to see
the fences on the eastern side during boat tours on the Elbe. In 1951, before
any talk of systematic federal aid for the "zonal borderlands," the county
had already become the target of regional work-creation schemes. Once
federal aid kicked in, government subsidies helped to attract some industrial jobs in the early 1960s.[57] Yet despite such efforts and investments of
between DM 120 million and 150 million (1951–1968) to support ailing agriculture, drain marshlands, and develop tourism, Lüchow-Dannenberg
continued to lose more of its population, eventually becoming the county
with the lowest population density in the Federal Republic. Residents
commuted out for work and young people moved away to pursue educational opportunities.[58] With local politicians agilely demanding more
government support, the county in 1977 became the proposed site of West
Germany's most expensive industrial project to date, budgeted at more
than DM 11 billion and slated to create some four thousand jobs: a nuclear
complex consisting of a reprocessing plant, a fuel fabrication plant, and a
waste-disposal facility.[59] But as we shall see in Chapter 6, instead of creating durable jobs in and around the village of Gorleben within spitting
distance of the border, the plans produced the longest-lasting anti-nuclear
protest movement in German history.

Braunschweig in Lower Saxony

The city of Braunschweig and its environs constituted one of the industrial centers in Lower Saxony, the second largest federal state after Bavaria
with a predominantly agrarian orientation. During the war, Braunschweig
played a sizable role in armaments production, which made it a target for
Allied air raids. At war's end, 90 percent of its inner city lay in rubble;
52 percent of the housing stock was destroyed. Despite the destruction,
Braunschweig turned into a temporary intersection of several population movements: former forced laborers and concentration camp inmates
sought to leave, while demobilized soldiers and residents displaced by the
bombing raids tried to return. In addition, the city had to absorb the characteristic influx of expellees and refugees.[60] Braunschweig's industries had
to undergo peacetime conversion and dismantling as part of the Allied

reparations program. The former Hermann Göring Works in Salzgitter-Watenstedt bore the brunt of the dismantling and released its workers to join the unemployed in Braunschweig's vicinity.[61]

Braunschweig's traditional industries resumed production relatively quickly. Its leading companies belonged to the metalworking and food-processing sector; others engaged in vehicle construction (Büssing), mechanical engineering, and machine building or produced leading optical brands such as Voigtländer and Rollei. As in the case of other manufacturing regions, the hardening demarcation line presented Braunschweig with a loss of its hinterland. The chamber of commerce estimated that 60 to 70 percent of the district's prewar economic relations had been directed toward the territory that was becoming the GDR. The food canning industry alone had sold 40 percent of its products there and depended on eastern Germany for half of the produce that went into the cans.[62] But Braunschweig entrepreneurs also suffered from poor geographical knowledge of their compatriots and felt shunned by their business contacts farther west. Brunsviga, a calculator manufacturer, decided to write to its clients, explaining where to find Braunschweig: "It's neither located in the U.S.A. nor behind the Iron Curtain. [. . .] Purchases from Braunschweig do not require [British] authorization nor do they constitute an import transaction."[63] In short, buying in Braunschweig did not require engaging in interzonal trade—"So why aren't you buying?" was the not-so-subtle pitch.

Yet no company found its fate more closely tied up with the border than Braunschweig's coal mining company (Braunschweigische Kohle Bergwerke, BKB), located in Helmstedt. The demarcation line divided its production facilities: the company's power plant, a briquetting plant, and two open-pit mines ended up on the eastern side. Since both the British and the Soviets had a vital interest in BKB's supply of electricity and coal, production resumed swiftly and remained unimpaired for a few years, despite the fact that the Soviets socialized the eastern parts of the company.[64] Production came to an abrupt end on May 26, 1952, when Soviet and East German troops closed the border. On that one day, BKB lost more than DM 30 million to the GDR's new border regime because much of its machinery and 60 percent of its brown coal deposits were stranded on the eastern side.[65] One of the many ripple effects of BKB's calamity hit Helmstedt County; along with BKB's losses, the county lost DM 3.2 million in corporate taxes.[66] As borderland companies suffered, so did their municipalities.

Braunschweig's chamber of industry and commerce alerted the state government in Hannover to yet another dimension of the borderland location: Communist infiltration. Eastern authorities, the chamber reported, frequently invited skilled workers and their families from Braunschweig to spend their vacation in East Germany and then seized the opportunity to train these individuals in Communist agitation. Back on their Braunschweig shop floors, these workers disseminated the propaganda they had absorbed. Worse, the GDR also targeted children from areas with high unemployment such as Salzgitter-Watenstedt. These "uncritical kids" were then "stuffed with effective Communist propaganda" and sent back into their depressed home regions. The borderlands, the chamber warned, were all the more receptive to such infiltration the less they participated in the budding economic recovery.[67]

Hof in Upper Franconia

The town of Hof in Upper Franconia was located in the triangle formed by the Federal Republic, the GDR, and Czechoslovakia. Hof's industry produced two major commodities: textiles and beer. As elsewhere in Western and Central Europe, textiles had propelled industrialization in the nineteenth century. Growing out of Hof's early modern drapery trade, its textile production had developed from a cottage industry into machine-based industrial mass production. In the process, Hof diversified regionally, becoming a town of spindles and looms from which yarn, twine, and staple fabric moved into Saxony for the production of lace, knitwear, bedding, and garments.[68] Hof's brewing industry likewise depended on the Northeast for its malting barley and the sale of its beer. The network of licensed pubs, wholesalers, and shops amounted to 75 to 90 percent of the breweries' market in Saxony and Thuringia.[69] Another relevant site of the sale of beer was the train station, where the brew was sold on the platforms. Hof was a major railroad hub for both passenger and freight traffic, serving Berlin, Munich, Dresden, and Frankfurt, with one train every eleven minutes.[70]

As the demarcation line tightened, Hof's industries lost their markets and suppliers, just like those in Lübeck and Braunschweig. Their efforts at reorientation toward the West faced the same challenges experienced by other borderland locations: established entrepreneurs defended their turf. But Hof quickly became the leading example of increased transportation costs for incoming and outgoing cargo. Although all borderland locations suffered from this new disadvantage, towns in Upper Franconia found themselves shut off not only in the East (CSSR, Saxony/GDR) but also in the North (Thuringia/GDR). By prewar standards, the flow of traffic was reduced to a trickle. The weakening connections first made themselves felt in the supply of brown coal from the CSSR and Saxony. As the vital supply of energy became spotty and unreliable, Hof's textile mills had to buy coal from the faraway Ruhr area, with a concomitant 30 percent increase in transportation costs. Similarly, the distance to the port of Bremen where Hof's cotton arrived grew from 481 to 675 kilometers since traffic had to be routed around the Thuringian "knob."[71]

Advocates for Hof and Upper Franconia vociferously emphasized the very real damage that the region had sustained because of the inter-German border.[72] They did not, however, find much to say about the damages that the undoing of traditional economic ties was causing on the other side in Saxony and Thuringia, where private businesses were additionally subjected to nationalization efforts; nor was it politically feasible to mention how Hof or Coburg temporarily benefited from the border. Many manufacturers actually relocated from Saxony and Bohemia to Hof and its vicinity. The former counted as refugees, the latter as expellees, and both drove Hof's economy into a brief resurgence: instead of the standard 90,000 jobs in industry that the town had offered in 1939 and again after the war, by 1951 it featured 145,000 such jobs, an increase of 61 percent.[73] The arrival of these manufacturers allowed the textile industry in and around Hof to close the production cycle and turn out finished products instead of delivering commodities like yarn and fabric to be finished elsewhere.[74] The border also had the welcome side effect of eliminating competitors. Especially the manufacturers of toys, Christmas decorations, and baby carriages in and around Coburg and Neustadt, not far from Hof, benefited from the disruption of delivery routes. The basketmakers around Coburg, hitherto producing only infant cots, would never have considered producing entire carriages had the main plant in Zeitz (East) not been cut off.[75] Such benefits were quickly forgotten; more relevant to contemporaries became the fact that, by 1954, every third bankruptcy in Bavaria occurred in Upper Franconia.[76]

Borderland Formation: The Early Articulation of Economic Interests

In 1949, the federal minister for transportation, Hans-Christoph Seebohm (of the Christian Democratic Union, CDU), delivered a speech to the Braunschweig chamber of industry and commerce about "Braunschweig as a borderland." This was a remarkable topic to choose since, as Seebohm correctly stated, "Braunschweig has never been a borderland." Rather, the town was located several hundred miles away from any of Germany's outer borders. Due to the Berlin blockade and the recent interruptions of trade and travel, however, Seebohm perceived the chamber's district as slipping into economic desolation, since its industries now found themselves "pressed against a dead border." For the time being, he considered the situation "irremediable"; contingency planning was the only option.[77] Up and down the inter-German border, chambers of commerce sprang into action and began polling their members about the consequences of the fickle boundary. Reports poured in over the course of 1950.[78] The timing of this activity suggests that the confluence of the experience of the Berlin blockade and counterblockade, the reunion of the economies in the three western zones, and the political founding of the Federal Republic of Germany in 1949 made it an opportune moment to take stock. Especially the establishment of the West German state constituted a prerequisite for engaging in interest politics since it clarified political responsibilities. Representatives of the borderland economy now knew where to lodge their claims.

Interest politics coalesced on three levels: the chambers of industry and commerce (IHK), the counties, and the federal states adjacent to the border all convened working groups that articulated their positions.[79] Between 1950 and May 1952, these entities directed a barrage of petitions (Denkschriften) at the federal government and attuned their message both to the realities of West Germany's reconstruction society and to the evolving workings of West German federalism.[80] Individual towns and regions crafted their own petitions, adding to the multitude of cries for help.[81]

The first of these petitions, issued by the chambers of commerce in late 1950, aggregated the reports from all chamber districts along the border to highlight the fallout of the demarcation line for the local and regional economies. It diagnosed a "disharmony of economic composition and economic intensity" in the new Federal Republic, manifested by a west-to-east gradient of decreasing economic activity and a realignment of traffic flows that bypassed the border regions.[82] Since economic relations depended heavily on transportation, the petition put a particular focus on traffic and freight. By October 1950, West–East routes had been reduced to twelve rail crossings, twelve main roads, and three waterways. The loss of established lines of communication saddled any company still wanting to conduct business with eastern partners with increased transportation costs since the distance to the next border crossing had grown. A westward reorientation came at increased cost, too. In the past, companies in Braunschweig had found all necessary business contacts within a distance of 150 kilometers, but only in the eastern direction. Within the same distance to the North, West and South, however, the offerings were slim: businesses from Braunschweig would only reach Hannover or Bielefeld. As the companies had to pay more to bring in coal and other production supplies, the cost of the final products rose accordingly and rendered the firms uncompetitive once they offered their products and services farther west. The spatial reach of the economies along the border was shrinking as a result, all the more since federal rail (*Bundesbahn*) had greatly increased freight rates after the currency reform.[83]

To make matters worse, the chambers noted, those federal states burdened with these newly sidelined regions happened to be the very states that had taken in the largest number of expellees and refugees. The sudden influx of labor had overwhelmed local, often agricultural labor markets, and the simultaneous distress of industry and trade offered no relief. The municipalities, in turn, had to make do with reduced income from corporate taxes but faced increased welfare costs owing to high unemployment and a large number of destitute new residents. All in all, the analysis by the chambers of commerce pointed strongly to imminent pauperization and "desolation" (*Verödung*) of the border regions, some of which, such as the Bavarian Forest and the Rhön, already counted among the traditionally underdeveloped areas.[84]

To address these problems, the chambers of commerce offered a range of policy proposals. First and foremost, they hoped that the federal government would acknowledge the scope of the problem, which, they argued, was neither limited nor regional but affected the entire national economy. The dilemma was that "[o]ur industrial potential lies in the West, our labor potential resides in the East [. . .]. Should labor come to industry or industry to labor?"[85] The Federal Republic as a whole, the chambers held, required a spatial realignment, including a reorientation of its major traffic axes. New north–south routes needed to complement the established east–west arteries, with adequate connections into the borderlands. The petition thus tossed a major issue toward spatial planners, a group of policy advisers who were assuming an influential role in Bonn during the early 1950s and had been tasked with determining aid measures for distressed regions.[86] Further, the chambers asked for priority in any federal reconstruction and economic stimulus program. The

borderlands needed fresh investments and capital, new industrial development, and affordable loans for established companies. The petition
also demanded a more equal distribution of expellees and refugees, not
only those of prime age and health but also those who would likely depend on welfare, as well as more money for the construction of housing
for those who stayed.

To make up for the competitive disadvantages that borderland companies were already enduring, the petition demanded that federal rail establish subsidized freight rates. The Bundestag had, in fact, already taken
up this issue and voted to grant financial support to address it, but the
chambers of commerce considered this measure a short-term fix and
asked for a major reform of rail tariffs.[87] Next, the petition suggested various tax breaks for individuals, companies, and municipalities in the borderlands. Not only should taxes be in line with economic strength (or lack
thereof), they should also consider the added expenses brought about by
the border. Among the reductions, the chambers pleaded for an exemption
from the solidarity tax for West Berlin (*Notopfer Berlin*). Bonn had introduced this surcharge in late 1948 to support West Berlin's economy during
the blockade, but the chambers argued that it defied reason to ask one
distressed area to help another. Finally, the petition defined the regions
that were intended to benefit from any federal support and suggested uniformly recognizing them as depressed areas.[88]

However, in a country recovering from war, mass migration, and military occupation, depressed regions were not exactly in short supply. No
one contested the difficulties experienced by the eastern border counties, but their claims for federal aid competed with those of traditional
depressed regions (*Notstandsgebiete*) and areas ravaged by war like the
heavily bombed cities or the "Red Zone" in the Palatinate. In fact, advocates for the Red Zone—counties bordering Belgium, Luxemburg,
Saarland, and France—had not missed a beat in eliciting federal aid.
Many villages in the Red Zone had been devastated during combat in
early 1945, their residents evacuated, their livelihoods destroyed. The
government in Rhineland-Palatinate, one of the federal states formed
in 1948, found the distress in the Red Zone beyond their means. In
September 1949, the month that the Bundestag convened for the very
first time, emergency relief for the Red Zone immediately moved onto
the political agenda. By January 1950, an aid package was signed and
sealed.[89] Subsequently, a Borderland Fund (Grenzlandfonds) received
DM 25 million, but despite its name, it was internally understood that

the western borderlands would be given priority in the distribution of the funds.[90] This is not to say that the federal government overlooked the regions along the Iron Curtain, but that its attentions were selective. Before May 1952, the state of Schleswig-Holstein, the town of Salzgitter-Watenstedt, and the Bavarian Forest region received funds—not due to their borderland location but because of the large number of expellees and the excessive unemployment in those areas.[91]

Cognizant of the competition from other depressed regions, representatives of the borderlands realized that they had to emphasize what made them unique in the West German reconstruction landscape: the Iron Curtain. The ideological imperatives of West and East Germany collided on this particular border and tied the abutting regions to the political storms of the day. In early 1952, a ministerial official from Lower Saxony identified the weak spot of the previous aid solicitations: thus far, he noted, everyone had mostly argued in economic terms, which made the problems of the regions along the border to the GDR indistinguishable from those of other depressed areas. Basing claims on economic indicators would also bring to the fore that some municipalities did fairly well, at least better than some depressed regions outside the border area. In order to establish a priority, he advised that borderlanders argue in political terms in order to "thwart" any objections Bonn might raise. Such efforts should begin with a brand name for the afflicted regions: "zonal borderlands."[92] The term merged Cold War fears with a dismissive slur on the socialist neighbor (the "Zone"), added an established aid category ("borderland"), and fused these elements into a moral claim on the state. By increasingly voicing their needs in concert and finding a common label, the heterogeneous regions along the Iron Curtain made conscious efforts to coalesce into one recognizable spatial unit that shared important characteristics.

Yet what did "arguing in political terms" entail? The *Länder* abutting the GDR implemented this new approach in May 1952 with a new petition to the federal government. They released it just ten days before the GDR closed the inter-German border.[93] Like the previous *Denkschrift* of the chambers of commerce, the *Länder* petition drew attention to the economic problems on the demarcation line and defined the afflicted areas as a 40-kilometer-wide strip that included the stretch between Bavaria and Czechoslovakia, as well as the "wet" border, that is, Schleswig-Holstein's eastern coast.[94] The petition's innovation consisted of its focus on the political fallout of these economic problems that the border was said to have caused. Put differently, it coated economic and social distress

with Cold War rhetoric. For instance, unemployment in the borderlands
mattered not because it was high, but because the unemployed masses
became easy targets for Communist propaganda. If the West did not
offer the destitute some work, they might turn to the East, where the
prospects of full employment beckoned. This aspect resonated well in
the press; an article in the weekly *Die Zeit* eagerly seized on the idea that
persistent hardship bred political radicalization, which, as the author
claimed, meant that eastern agents made good progress in building and
financing Communist groups, infiltrating expellee organizations, and
fogging the minds of youth.[95]

The *Länder* petition reminded Bonn that the regions along the border
would have an important role to play once the East and West German
states reunified. Since reunification was the constitutional mandate of
West German politics, it followed that Bonn had to ensure that the regions
were in a position to play that role in "political, psychological and economic" terms. This would work only if the residents proved immune to
eastern advances and strong enough to motivate their relatives and friends
on the other side to fight for unification from within the socialist system.
In view of multiple familial ties across the border, the borderland residents
were, in fact, the natural ambassadors for the western cause, an opportunity West Germany could not afford to waste. Yet the residents on both
sides of the demarcation line were said to have reasons to feel written off, a
sentiment the GDR could easily exploit. The *Länder* memorandum argued
that the borderlands had to become the "display window of the Federal
Republic," showcasing reconstruction, not neglect. Economically healthy
borderlands were therefore a "prerequisite" for reunification.[96]

Despite the talk about reunification and local ties to the GDR, the cover
image of the *Länder* petition sent a very different message (Figure 1.1).
It visualized the demarcation line as a solid, impermeable wall running
from the Baltic in the North to the southeastern tip of Bavaria. Given the
map's scale, the wall appeared disproportionately high. It cast a shadow
exactly over those regions that were asking the government for aid, reinforcing the notion that people there were literally living in the shadow
of the wall. While West Germany had a distinct shape on this map, East
Germany appeared frayed, a hatched area with no outer borders. The cover
image showed Germany effectively divided, with East Germany indeed
written off.

In the early articulations of economic interest, the advocates of borderland aid presented their regions as victimized by the Iron Curtain and

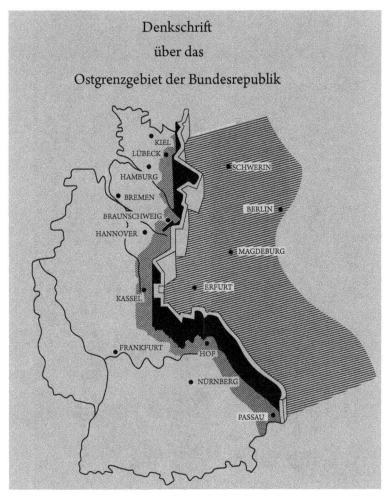

FIGURE 1.1. Before the GDR introduced the border regime on May 26, 1952, a West German petition already depicted the inter-German border as a solid wall that overshadowed the counties on the western side.

Source: Denkschrift, May 1952

used dramatic language and visual props to get their message across (Figure 1.2). This rhetoric and imagery in support of borderland aid was fully in place before the GDR even closed the inter-German border in May 1952. Although the efforts of borderland advocates clearly built momentum and reached the intended audiences in Bonn, the yield remained modest; impatience and frustration continued to rise.[97] In this situation, the escalation of border trouble in May 1952 proved productive for the counties on the western side. In retaliation against the West German signature under

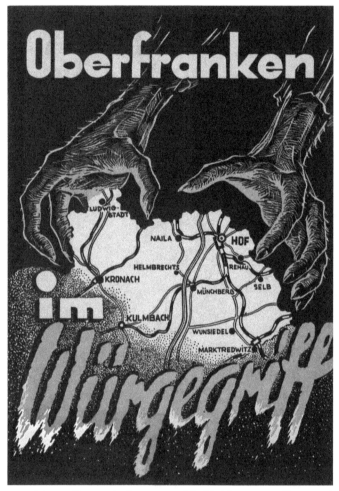

FIGURE 1.2. Upper Franconia in a stranglehold. The cover of a 1950 brochure about economic difficulties in the region illustrates the threat with red "socialist" hands ready for a land grab in the western borderlands.

Source: Arno Behrisch, *Oberfranken im Würgegriff* (Hof, 1950)

the General Treaty, a key element of Adenauer's westernization strategy, the leadership of the Socialist Unity Party (SED) abruptly closed the remaining border crossings, deported allegedly unreliable residents to the hinterland, and triggered a wave of migration into the West. The western borderlands now finally received the political attention they needed to advance their cause. As the East German measures were decried as totalitarian, political support for "zonal borderland aid" grew immensely, although its implementation remained contested.

The Fallout of Border Closure in 1952

Despite the frequent tinkering with border opening and closure, a writer for Frankfurt's *Neue Zeitung* in late 1951 still considered it practically impossible to close the demarcation line along the full stretch of its 1,393 kilometers.[98] Yet in May 1952, GDR authorities tried just that. In response to Adenauer's move toward western integration, the GDR's leadership received orders from Moscow to seal the border and establish a border regime modeled on Soviet precedent. Previously passable checkpoints were closed, and commuter permits revoked; the border turned into a militarized zone. Specifically, the order to establish a "special border regime" called for the creation of a 5-kilometer-deep prohibited zone that only residents and authorized personnel could enter and a 500-meter security strip that came under the direct administration of the border authorities. The demarcation line itself was turned into a 10-meter control strip cleared of all structures and vegetation that marked the border for the time being.[99] Residents within the prohibited zone were henceforth deprived of avenues of public sociability—no more pubs, concerts, cinemas, or church services.[100] As part of the new eastern border regime, allegedly unreliable residents of the prohibited zone were deported to the hinterland. This forced removal of almost 8,400 people unfolded over the summer of 1952 under the dehumanizing code name "Action Vermin"[101] and rippled into the western borderlands as some 4,500 refugees arrived from the adjacent eastern counties.[102] Another less sweeping wave of deportations unfolded after the building of the Berlin Wall in August 1961, but the shock that accompanied the introduction of the new border regime in the summer of 1952 had already conveyed the message that henceforth the threat of deportation hovered over borderland residents. This reality subsequently helped foster a culture of compliance and self-policing.[103] East Germans bore the brunt of these measures as they lost property, faced deportation, and came under intense surveillance, including from their own neighbors.[104] In view of the life-changing events that eastern border dwellers endured, the fallout of border closure on the western side was an inconvenience in comparison, some of which, however, proved costly to fix.

The East German escalation of border control dashed all remaining hopes that the western borderlands would be able to maintain the already reduced economic ties to their former hinterlands. The number of official crossing points fell to six rail lines, four major roads, and two waterways.[105] Basic communication with the other side suffered further when eastern authorities clipped local phone lines.[106] The last cross-border working arrangements collapsed too: at the brown coal mines near Helmstedt, the potash mines on the Werra, and some porcelain factories in Upper Franconia, hundreds of people could no longer get to work and lost their jobs. Farmers with fields on the other side of the demarcation line realized that, come summer, they would not be able to bring in the harvest. Communities nestled in one of the many bends and pockets along the demarcation line found themselves almost cut off from roads and rail. Henceforth, daily commutes included endless detours.

Another new and costly border problem related to utility services. As eastern border guards cordoned off the demarcation line, the delivery of water, electricity, and gas and the treatment of sewage became unreliable. Easterners and westerners missed each other both as customers and as suppliers of such services. In some communities, the lights went out.[107] In other cases, it seemed to be only a question of time before power was cut, as with a hydroelectric plant on the Werra where the pertinent part of the river lay in the West but the power plant in the East.[108] To regain control over vital utility switches, each side tried to disengage from the other by duplicating the respective services, a cumbersome and expensive process.[109] West Germany rose to these challenges and, through its newfound economic muscle, resolved the immediate local and regional problems caused by partition, thereby eliminating any practical need for reunification.

The western border counties also experienced the arrival of new East German refugees. Many fled to preempt deportations and arrived on the other side with only the shirts on their backs. They then often utilized familial relations to find a temporary home.[110] On the federal level, the new border escalation induced a reassessment of refugee politics. In their (futile) efforts to prevent the further influx of people into West Germany, authorities had thus far distinguished between "real" refugees, who fled for political reasons and deserved support, and mere economic migrants, who should be convinced to stay where they were.[111] The border crisis of 1952 offered an excellent opportunity for West German authorities to use the refugee issue to denounce the devious machinations that the SED regime carried out on behalf of its Stalinist masters. Not only could the East now be accused of single-handedly deepening Germany's division, the refugees from the GDR provided living proof that the SED's rule lacked legitimacy. These newcomers therefore assumed a new political significance in the propaganda war between both German states as refugees from totalitarianism. Since West Germany sought to embody the opposite values, it now readily offered them refuge, thus demonstrating its own political superiority. The rhetoric shifted from damning illegal border crossers to referring to them as "the new guests from the borderlands of the eastern zone."[112]

On the ground in the borderlands, however, their arrival triggered well-established reflexes against further influx. The idea that the boat was full had undergirded the expellee and refugee policy of the "refugee states" since 1947, when the occupation authorities had initiated the first redistribution and resettlement schemes between states.[113] The members of the Hessian state cabinet reminded themselves that, in view of interstate agreements, they were not obligated to keep more than 5 percent of the incoming refugees. Yet they also had the needs of the Hessian economy in mind and resolved to retain any potash miners as well as those farmers who owned land on the Hessian side. These desirable migrants should be allowed to stay, even beyond Hesse's 5 percent quota; the excess should simply be charged against later arrivals.[114] Western officials had engaged in such "cream-skimming" strategies since the late 1940s, when British occupation authorities ran a short-lived program that used planes sustaining the Berlin airlift to relocate East German arrivals in West Berlin to the Ruhr mines.[115] On a smaller scale, the city government of Neustadt in Upper Franconia (West) made major efforts to fend off "illegal" cross-border migration from neighboring Sonneberg in Thuringia (East), yet was simultaneously contemplating "moving allowances and accommodation for important skilled workers from the East Zone" in order to entice the useful ones to move over.[116]

Since 1950 and increasingly after border closure in 1952, however, borderland representatives realized that they were in no position to skim off the cream. The migrants crowding into the borderlands did not remain static. As the West German economy sputtered into a higher gear around 1950 and labor needs increased in the industrial centers farther west, more and more skilled workers from the ranks of the newcomers moved on to seize opportunities there. These were the very people the border regions needed for reconstructing and sustaining their own economies. The first petition for federal aid had already set forth the demand that the resettlement programs be comprehensive, that is, cover whole families including the elderly, not just those of working age.[117] One county director called it "irresponsible" that a state like North Rhine-Westphalia would welcome only "physically capable skilled workers," thereby stripping the borderland economy of its labor assets and turning the region into "a nursing home and poor house."[118] With an eye to public finances, county officials thus distinguished between people who could support themselves and those who depended on welfare. Regardless of whether paid work was actually available in the borderlands, the distinction ultimately hinged on productivity. The officials' assessments were couched in denigrating terms, the kinder versions of which referred to women, children, the sick, and elderly as "social baggage" (*Sozialgepäck*), whereas the blunter terms depicted them as those who could no longer face the "struggle for life" or simply as "less viable people" (*die Lebensschwächeren*).[119] One may or may not detect traces of eugenic thinking in both the focus on productivity and the language employed to describe these demographics; the sharp distinction between locals and newcomers testified not only to the strained solidarity in the counties along the demarcation line but also to growing anxieties about losing out on the increasing competition for labor necessary to partake in economic recovery.

Finally, border closure bore yet another major consequence for the western borderlands: it prompted many entrepreneurs who had been vacillating about their redefined location to move their companies farther west. Such decisions were bad enough for borderland communities, yet what incensed local politicians in particular was the fact that western cities actively targeted promising companies in relocation bids. Such enticements may have existed before May 1952, but they reached a critical mass only thereafter.[120] The mayor of Kiel singled out the city of Mainz for approaching a company in such a fashion even though the owner had not even considered relocation.[121] The chief administrator of Braunschweig found an offer from "a southwestern state" barely legal and politically "unbearable" since said state offered plots of land for one deutsche mark per square meter and asked for this token amount only to conceal the fact that it would also give the plots away for free.[122] Frankfurt ran advertisements praising its business-friendly climate. The ads as such were not objectionable, but as Lübeck's mayor knew all too well, ensuing inquiries quickly turned into conversations that allowed Frankfurt's office for business development to recite the city's advantages.[123] Business owners then picked up the phone and asked their home municipalities how they intended to counter the outside offer.[124] Typically, the borderland community lost out in the ensuing bidding war. The head of the Association of Cities and Towns (Deutscher Städtetag) appealed to its members to refrain from such practices. It could only damage the national economy, he argued, if one municipality faced "ruin" by losing a vital company while another municipality gained that company only by waiving taxes for years.[125] The federal minister of finance heartily agreed but found no way to curb this activity other than ordering the regional tax authorities to keep an eye on the matter and appealing to everyone's sense of solidarity.[126]

Pitted against market principles, however, solidarity was hard to come by. Before 1952, some borderland economies, indeed the West German economy as a whole, benefited from the disastrous policies of the SED that drove businesses across the border and into the fold of the capitalist market economy. One scholar estimates that 20 percent of all companies relocating from the GDR settled in the western borderlands. Their owners assumed that the country's division would not last and that a borderland location would allow for an easy return.[127] The evidence remains spotty, but western companies in border towns and farther inland appear to have facilitated such relocations. East German anti-entrepreneurial policies obviously encouraged businesses to leave, but a town like Neustadt in Upper Franconia had no qualms about actively recruiting companies from Sonneberg that nicely complemented its own industrial portfolio. Neustadt's mayor had drawn up elaborate plans in 1950 to "transfer [. . .] important and desired enterprises from the East Zone" while "keeping away unwanted and unreliable companies."[128] The border closure of May 1952 put an end to all that. Western communities could no longer draw on their eastern equivalents in such a fashion. Instead, the closed demarcation line solidified their status as a borderland, and their own economy was suddenly up for grabs. They now had done unto themselves what they had done to others. The borderlands became the East of the West. As the western industrial hubs skimmed the cream off the borderlands' workforce and drew manufacturers into their orbit, its representatives now decried the lack of solidarity in the new West German state. They intensified their efforts to prompt the federal government to rein in the invisible hand of the market and, if that proved impossible, to make up for the various competitive disadvantages. The much-maligned escalation of the border regime provided the ideal occasion to draw public attention to the borderlands and build political momentum for an aid package.

In the Shadow of the "Economic Miracle": Federal Aid for the Borderlands

After the dramatic events of late May 1952, developments at the demarcation line briefly moved up the political agenda for the first time and became the topic of a Bundestag debate. The opposition parties rolled out the well-known list of problems and demanded to hang Communism out to dry by eradicating poverty in the borderlands. The goal, a deputy from Hof argued, was to confront "the dead strip of the Soviets with a living strip on our side."[129] The combative politician Herbert Wehner of the Social Democratic Party (SPD) expected more than a "Band-Aid" from the Adenauer administration and called for the development of the Federal Republic "up to the last centimeter" of the border.[130] Adenauer himself responded and seized the opportunity to "solemnly protest" the "terroristic measures of the Soviet zonal forces" and accuse the GDR of deepening Germany's division. Yet he had no intention of uniformly declaring that the borderlands were areas experiencing an emergency (*Notstandsgebiete*). Rather, he wanted to wait until someone could quantify the damage caused by the new GDR border regime and apply aid according to demonstrated need. He counted on the spatial planners to develop a coherent program for depressed regions that would include borderlands where necessary.[131]

Of course, Adenauer's government could not ignore the Cold War escalation on its eastern boundary. The chancellor's words raised expectations.[132] After the Bundestag debate, an ad hoc committee reviewed emergency aid to the counties where the refugees from the GDR arrived and where alternatives to severed connections—from roads to utility lines—were desperately needed. The committee's deliberations betrayed just how far Bonn's assessments diverged from that of the border states. After the border regions had already argued for two years that the economic consequences of the demarcation line and the refugee situation were exhausting their means, the committee's insistence that the affected states and regions were expected to pitch in 15 percent to any federal aid measure was unlikely to be well received. The federal committee not only cited frugality to justify such a copayment but deliberately inserted it as a way to keep the petitioners at bay.[133] On the whole, the border situation was depicted as a temporary malaise, and already at the committee's first meeting, the representative of the federal rail service reported that "deficits" in passenger traffic had been "fixed" by replacing trains with buses.[134]

It was such quick fixes that the federal minister of finance, Fritz Schäffer of the Christian Social Union (CSU), in particular would have preferred. The cabinet approved DM 6 million to address the most pressing utility problems and some DM 30 million to aid refugees. Yet the additional demands of the border states for acute damages amounted to DM 106 million, not to mention the fact that they wanted a comprehensive borderland aid package. Schäffer, known for his aversion to public spending and any "entitlement" expressed by organized interests,[135] considered releasing a mere 5 million to be broadly distributed along the border. Before providing any additional funds, though, he forced the border states to define their own contributions and accused them of trying to modernize their utility systems at federal expense.[136] In view of such haggling, Bonn's smattering of aid evaporated politically on the way to its destinations. Before long, the federal government became the target of increasingly impatient pleas that no longer followed party lines. Even deputies of the CDU and Free Democrats (FDP) chided the Adenauer administration for committing too few resources and accused Schäffer of stalling.[137] As the Federal Republic entered its first election campaign, the pitches grew sharper and aid for the borderlands turned into a campaign issue that the SPD opposition appeared to handle with more aplomb than the chancellor.

Recognizing the hesitation of Adenauer's government, the SPD inundated it with propositions and motions in parliament.[138] In early July 1953, still feeling the impact of the failed uprising of June 17 in the GDR, the Bundestag debated borderland aid a second time. At issue were no longer merely emergency measures but "a long-term program for the zonal borderlands" that addressed structural shortcomings. The political line of argumentation that the borderland advocates had developed in their own petitions now won out completely: the borderlands, the main speaker held, suffered from a "political development" that required a political answer, not a region-by-region needs assessment. Indeed, propping up these regions now turned into a "national-political task."[139] Deputies from both the opposition and government parties outdid each other in their advocacy of borderland aid, the latter clearly in an attempt to regain the initiative. They reached consensus that not only the regions abutting the GDR but also the "wet border" on the Baltic shores of Schleswig-Holstein and the Bavarian stretch bordering on Czechoslovakia needed help. For a second time, the Bundestag voted in favor of borderland aid.[140]

Suddenly, things could not move fast enough. Vice Chancellor Blücher (FDP) urged the Ministry for Economic Affairs to finalize plans for borderland aid in order to allow the federal government to announce them "two weeks before election day" on September 6, 1953. The cabinet based its spatial definition of the "zonal borderland strip" on the 1952 memorandum of the border states. It covered the towns and counties within a 40-kilometer zone along the entire length of the German Iron Curtain, including the Baltic coast. The state secretary from the Ministry of Labor raised the concern that the strip would include regions that were far from destitute. But practicality and simplicity won out: 40 kilometers it was—and remained so until 1994. In the rush, differentiation no longer mattered; Bonn's "interest in [. . .] utmost speed" muffled all further discussion.[141] By 1953, West Germany had thus defined almost 20 percent of its state territory as a borderland. Some 12 percent of its population now lived in a space officially recognized as affected by the Cold War, a status West Berlin had held since the Federal Republic's founding.[142] Adenauer's CDU party won the 1953 elections by a wide margin. When the chancellor mentioned the borderlands in his postelection address to parliament, the political will to come to their rescue was no longer in doubt.[143] The federal budget of 1954 featured a special DM 120 million borderland fund in addition to other resources on which these regions could draw, such as tax breaks, access to credit, freight subsidies, as well as preferential treatment for government contracts and for the rebuilding of traffic infrastructure.[144] Although the volume of the special borderland fund remained modest, the commitment as such held out the prospect of more aid in the future. Communities outside of the 40-kilometer strip suddenly pushed for inclusion: the much-maligned border location had turned into a resource worth fighting for.[145]

Despite Bonn's apparent commitment to the borderland region, political haggling was far from over. The finance minister refused to release the DM 120 million unless the *Länder* agreed to an unrelated tax proposal.[146] Worse, word got out that the money was intended as a onetime measure, and some additional DM 25 million earmarked for the support of cultural activities and schools never materialized.[147] To ordinary residents, aid measures such as freight subsidies and adjusted tax schedules were not visible anyway, but even corporate recipients lamented the ongoing red tape. The state governments seized the opportunity to highlight federal inactivity, and in two further Bundestag debates, Adenauer's cabinet, especially Ministers Erhard (Economy) and Schäffer (Finance), came in for much of the blame, although Schäffer eventually produced the promised borderland funds.[148] Amid the controversy, Adenauer tried to calm the storm by appointing a special borderland envoy with the rank of a federal minister. He asked Waldemar Kraft (BHE) to embark on a fact-finding mission and draft a memorandum on the borderland situation.[149] Since the closing of the border in May 1952, politicians had made a point of visiting the demarcation line in order to be "present in crisis." More often than not, they had heartily agreed with locals that something needed to be done to aid the borderlands, yet from the perspective of those visited the increased interest in their plight met with no tangible outcomes. By October 1952, the border states were incensed about the numerous visitors from Bonn who made promises but then left the state governments to deal with inflated expectations.[150] Kraft's appointment therefore did not strike anyone as a good idea. Even members of Adenauer's CDU complained that "we don't need further memoranda from anybody, not even [. . .] from a member of the cabinet."[151] After almost two years of federal involvement, an official from the Ministry for Economic Affairs reported in March 1955 that "the complaints from the zonal borderlands have not abated."[152]

If anything, the mood in the borderlands had deteriorated since 1952 because the impression of residents that they lived in a forgotten and forsaken part of the country was compounded by another development: during the early 1950s, the West German economy as a whole experienced processes collectively known as the "economic miracle." A period of "stormy economic growth" (Abelshauser) unfolded at an unexpected pace, aided by the political-economic framework created by the currency reform of 1948, the end of price control on (most) commodities, as well as the Marshall Plan, spurred by armament-oriented export and massively supported by a continuous stream of qualified migrants into West Germany.[153] Yet while the economic miracle became a staple of government publicity, its material blessings remained unevenly distributed.[154] The economy might have been booming on the Rhine and Ruhr, but in the borderlands its effects looked different: companies received relocation bids, skilled workers migrated west, and unemployment remained high.[155] The period until 1955, especially the time of apparent inactivity in Bonn, therefore solidified a calamity discourse within and about the borderlands. Observers predicted that the regions along the inter-German border would turn into depopulated, desolate wastelands. Young people packed up to move into the "golden West," a term that was said to hold the same promising ring in the borderlands as it did across the demarcation line.[156] A mayor in eastern Bavaria reported that borderlanders "finally want to catch up with the standard of living in the west. [. . .] The Ruhr is the particular object of envy."[157] Borderland residents cared less about living in the shadow of the Iron Curtain than about living in the shadow of the economic miracle. They felt that recovery was passing them by. They saw a gap opening up between themselves and the western parts of the country where the economy, they thought, was recovering not least by cannibalizing the borderlands. By the mid-1950s, *Zonenrand* residents thus defined their distress relative to western parts of the country. Such comparisons made their plight look worse. Inadvertently, however, such an "eye on the West" also signified a slow but crucial spatial reorientation of the borderland population. West Germany was coming into its own.

Culture to the Rescue

Borderland advocates found some of their most poignant arguments for federal support in the ideological competition between East and West Germany. After the founding of both German states, the inter-German border turned into a propaganda site where each side pitched its social and economic order as superior to the other. Not unlike Berlin, yet with less public attention, the borderlands became a space where the ideological competition between both German states played out.[158] In the early 1950s, West Germans developed a strong sense that their socialist neighbors conducted this propaganda war with greater resources and in a fashion that actually entailed the threat of success. The Federal Republic, to be sure, was not an ingenuous bystander in this battle for allegiances. The difference was that the GDR was called out for issuing "propaganda," while West Germany perceived itself as disseminating "information." This self-perception explains the hue and cry when, periodically, West German methods came to light that did not differ from GDR activities along the border, for instance the distribution of anti-socialist leaflets using balloons.[159]

Communist infiltration, real or imagined, took many forms. The government felt compelled to warn its citizens of "Trojan horses," organizations that purportedly facilitated contacts between East and West Germans only to propagandize and instigate discontent among the latter.[160] The borderlands appeared particularly vulnerable as a "gateway for subversive forces."[161] East German authorities conducted frequent forays into the neighboring territory. Some of these breaches were simply criminal, for example when eastern forces abducted critics of and refugees from the GDR.[162] Others undermined West German security, when eastern authorities sent spies over or tried to plant rumors to unsettle the borderland population.[163] The West German government initially also struggled to control the flow of news at the country's edge. In analogy to the interrupted traffic infrastructure, the existing broadcasting technology left parts of the borderlands with only weak radio reception that was easily overpowered by eastern stations.[164] Subversion could take yet other, seemingly innocent forms and play out in the fields of theater, sports, and other leisure pursuits. In the pervasive anti-Communist climate during the early years of the Federal Republic, the opinion of Bundestag deputies that "the battle against the East will be won [. . .] above all through cultural superiority" was not a far-fetched position.[165] Borderland advocates employed the East German propaganda activities to heighten the sensitivity of policymakers to the border regions' plight. In the competition for state funding, being the target of eastern propaganda efforts set these regions apart from traditional distressed areas that suffered "only" from structural economic deficiencies.

Throughout the 1950s, the border remained permeable enough for visits back and forth, especially whenever the GDR leadership decided that such exchanges furthered its political goals. One of the better-known incidents was related to the World Youth Festival of the SED's Free German Youth (FDJ). Staged during the Pentecost weekend in East Berlin in 1950, the festival drew some ten thousand youth from West Germany. As these teenagers returned home, western border police intercepted them at the Lübeck-Herrnburg border crossing. The border police attempted to collect their names and addresses, and since they had slept on Communist straw mattresses during their visit, doctors were on hand, allegedly to check them for communicable diseases. A standoff ensued as western border guards denied the western teenagers re-entry; the tired youngsters eventually conceded.[166] The playwright Bertolt Brecht immortalized the incident in his *Herrnburger Report*: "Germans / were caught by Germans / because they ventured from Germany / to Germany."[167] The Bonn government remained concerned about such western–eastern ventures and cited offers for free summer camps in the GDR for western children as an example of the GDR's "Trojan horse" strategy. The Braunschweig chamber of commerce had been among the first to warn against such invitations, which also extended to skilled workers and their families.[168] Between 1954 and 1957, the West Germans offered counterprograms that drew about a hundred thousand youth from East Germany.[169]

Locked in a race for the more successful reconstruction effort, the GDR devoted particular resources to cultural offerings in its borderlands. In Lübeck (West), officials gained the impression that their counterparts in Mecklenburg (East) based their programs on an analysis of Lübeck's shortcomings in order to make the city look as pinched as possible to its own residents. As they pointed out, "[T]he Iron Curtain is simply not as tight as not to allow for comparisons between here and there." And these comparisons, they warned, were not necessarily to the Federal Republic's advantage.[170] Worse, in an inversion of the feeling of superiority that West Germans had enjoyed shortly after the introduction of the deutsche mark, the GDR's largesse in the field of culture made them feel like the poor relations of their eastern neighbors. Whether for choir concerts or soccer games, the eastern municipalities dispatched buses to pick up western visitors and made a point of wining and dining them. Whole soccer teams came home with new track suits and other equipment. For the return visits that decorum and tradition required, the western municipalities had to scrape up resources from their already besieged budgets.[171]

The GDR took advantage of another vacuum when it encouraged its own choirs, folk dance ensembles, and theater companies to seek engagements in the western borderlands.[172] For each guest performance that theater companies could secure in the West, they would receive a bonus of 2,000 eastern marks. Smaller towns without their own theater company traditionally booked itinerant shows to populate their cultural calendars. In 1956, the Thuringian State Theater from Eisenach (East) thus sponsored 60 percent of all performances in northern Hesse (West). Ensembles from Altenburg, Erfurt, and Gera toured the area as well and proved cheaper than western ones.[173] For the All-German Ministry in Bonn, the range of GDR activities only showed that the "potentates" on the other side were trying "to create the impression that a thriving, Communist cultural life was developing behind the dividing barbed wire."[174] Although the Ministry implied that this was certainly a false impression, the attention that it began to pay to cultural affairs in the borderlands indicates that officials were not sure whether local residents could see through the ruse. What if the have-nots in the borderlands came to the conclusion that East Germany was the better Germany after all?

Time and again, commentators singled out the unemployed as susceptible to eastern propaganda and potentially willing to accept money for spying.[175] Every dip in the western borderland economy, even in individual sectors, was said to be seized upon as an object of eastern propaganda. As long as borderland residents retained the feeling that they had been written off by the rest of the country, to serve only as "cannon fodder in the Cold War," the other side had an easy time impressing them.[176] The only antidote lay in the "mental armament" and the "strengthening of the ideological immune system" of the borderland population, which, however, could be effected only through economic security.[177] The question of culture in the borderlands thus amounted to a struggle for the allegiance of the local population that was at times perceived as wavering. The talk about strengthening the resolve of the borderland residents moved cultural efforts into the realm of national defense. The link flowed naturally from the contentious debates about rearmament that preoccupied the West German public during the 1950s, an issue that also provided ample propaganda opportunities for the GDR. In the combative diction of the federal minister for transportation, Hans-Christoph Seebohm, the borderlands had to become "a bulwark of freedom against slavery" by putting residents on "mental-political 'defense alert.' "[178] Financial support for the borderlands thus turned into a defense contribution and, as one Bundestag deputy suggested, might as well come out of the defense budget.[179]

Advocates of borderland aid continuously cultivated and refined the argument that the border regions had to become the "display window" or "business card" of the Federal Republic in order to convey to eastern Germany the "superiority of the West."[180] West Berlin provided the model for this line of argument, turning the borderlands into another concrete example of the "magnet theory." That theory, or rather hope, prominently expressed by the chairman of the SPD, Kurt Schumacher, held that prosperity in West Germany would become an "economic magnet" for East Germany. The steady force of the Western "magnet" would overcome the illegitimate power exercised by the SED; economic success would prove stronger than propaganda promises, thus paving the way for unification.[181] Of course, the magnet theory had an obvious flaw: it did not square with the initial hostility toward "economic migrants" from East Germany who had followed the magnet's force. Nor could it accommodate the fact that, as the GDR enhanced border fortifications, fewer and fewer East Germans could see, let alone experience, this "window to the West." The theater festival in Bad Hersfeld (West) on the Hessian border, for instance, accepted its subsidies with the justification that it would light a "cultural bonfire for the SBZ." Yet when East Germans actually appeared at the performances, as was still possible throughout the 1950s, they were all but ignored.[182]

Despite cross-party consensus about the urgency of the issue, money for cultural activities was initially hard to find. The aid package that parliament adopted in 1953 featured DM 25 million for cultural affairs, but the amount did not pass muster with the finance minister. Only in 1955 did the Ministry for All-German Affairs offer 2 million for the first time.[183] The building of schools enjoyed priority during the 1950s to accommodate expellee and refugee children. But libraries, theaters, concerts, choirs, museums, exhibitions, community spaces, and public pools qualified for federal subsidies as well. In 1960, the Ministry was pleased to announce that cultural life in the borderlands showed a "vitality such as had never existed before"[184]—not a surprising claim in a government publicity brochure dedicated to good news, yet also a tacit acknowledgment that some municipalities had been endowed with cultural offerings and institutions that they had never had before and that they had acquired simply because of their border location.

By 1987, the annual budget for cultural and social affairs in the borderlands had ballooned to DM 173 million. The money helped restore churches, fund concerts and festivals, create track fields, tennis courts, and soccer fields, support adult education and public libraries, facilitate exhibitions, and build new town halls, kindergartens, and retirement homes—a wide range of worthy causes.[185] But how, exactly, did these projects prepare the country for reunification? In the mid-1980s, no one was even trying to answer this question anymore, but even in the early 1950s, it elicited rather nebulous answers. Apart from the magnet theory that assigned the borderlands the role of displaying the successes of reconstruction and, by extension, of the sociopolitical order of West Germany, arguments were hard to come by at a time when the Adenauer administration was emphatically pursuing western integration. To patch over the contradiction between actual policies and trite unification rhetoric, Seebohm and other borderland advocates paradoxically argued that a vital culture and economy would provide jobs and adequate living conditions for *East* Germans at the moment of unification. Reconstruction, he loftily implied, was thus almost a selfless act of altruism; it did not occur "for our own sake or for the sake of material affluence."[186] The ultimate test for this argument would come in 1989.

More to the point, however, was the observation of a Bundestag deputy that culture, broadly conceived, constituted a distinct locational advantage. Many workers migrated westward not because the jobs near Frankfurt, Mannheim, or Darmstadt necessarily paid better but because those cities offered secondary schools, cultural events, and other opportunities.[187] For the chambers of commerce, economic and cultural aid had therefore been two sides of the same coin all along.[188] As far as causalities can be construed at all, the dearth of "culture" in the borderlands probably had less to do with the border as such than with traditional contrasts between rural and urban life. The leverage toward the state, however, had everything to do with the border. Unlike the traditional distressed areas that suffered "only" from structural economic deficiencies, the eastern border regions could activate Cold War fears to support their cause. By blending "economic self-interest and Cold War rhetoric," borderland advocates had found a powerful tool to gain and retain political attention.[189]

Conclusion: "Real" Borders Produce Borderlands

West German propaganda and subsequent narratives have frequently depicted border closure in May 1952 as a major step in the development of Germany's partition. At that time, GDR authorities blocked traffic, undercut cross-border trade, prevented workers from reaching their jobs, deported allegedly unreliable residents on the eastern side, and erected fences. For the development of a West German borderland, however, June 1948 is the more pertinent date.[190] For one, the decision to launch the deutsche mark as an independent western currency triggered the Soviet blockade of West Berlin and the Allied counterblockade. It was arguably the blockade experience that dealt the local economies along the demarcation line a crippling blow.[191] Additionally, the new money itself established a currency dualism and turned the early border into an economic divide. Since the line now demarcated territories of diverging economic opportunity, it destabilized the border regions by increasing cross-border labor migration (*Grenzgängertum*) and smuggling, turning both practices, hitherto considered acceptable forms of labor and survival, into unwelcome and illegal activities. Despite a multitude of close familial ties across the boundary, the currency reform contributed significantly to deteriorating relations between Germans on either side.[192] Its impact unfolded in the borderlands with such force because it was along the demarcation line that the strong and the weak currencies collided without a buffer. The next chapter indicates how, four decades on, the currency dualism would haunt the borderlands again. After November 1989, the open border once again pitted western against eastern money and re-created conditions already known (and vilified) in the late 1940s and early 1950s. The stark disparity created significant pressure to seek a currency union in 1990 and, ultimately, hastened unification.

The emergence of the borderlands and their geographical and metaphorical location as the East of the West stands for the larger spatial alignment of the new postwar state. Most of Silesia was becoming Polish, while the hopes of East Germany's planned economy rested on the industrial triangle of Magdeburg–Halle–Leipzig. Reduced by the eastern territories and with the "rump" cut in two, western Germany was thus forced to develop an adjusted economic geography. The hub of its industrial gravity shifted to the Rhine and Ruhr region and the orbit of cities like Frankfurt, Stuttgart, Ludwigshafen, and Mannheim, slicing the Federal Republic somewhat diagonally into a more industrially developed southwestern part and a more agriculture-oriented northeastern part. Neither in political nor in economic terms did the federally constituted West German state ever produce an obvious center.[193] Despite the lack of such a clear center, however, it is legitimate to refer to the borderlands as a periphery. At the risk of stating the obvious: Rhenish capitalism had a clear spatial dimension, compounded over the years by the progress of European integration that further marginalized the periphery.[194] Nowhere does this adjustment became more visible than from the perspective of the borderlands, where the interaction between postwar economic recovery and borderland formation (or periphery production) became tangible. As the next chapter shows, the perception of persistent peripherality actually created an image problem for the borderlands as "underdeveloped" areas, a disadvantage its representatives accepted since they needed to draw on the periphery argument to institutionalize borderland aid for good.

Early borderland aid was the product of dogged lobbying work and electoral exigency. The aid program owed its existence to the Cold War and the skills that borderland advocates had developed in harnessing the related anti-Communist rhetoric. Beyond the launch of an early aid package and the official recognition that economic and infrastructural challenges existed along the demarcation line, the greatest success of the regions' advocates undoubtedly consisted of the spatial definition of the borderlands as a 40-kilometer-deep strip. To define almost a fifth of West German territory as eligible for federal support was rather generous; it did not even require the beneficiaries to be located within view of the demarcation line. After initial hesitation, even the "wet border" of Schleswig-Holstein's Baltic coast from Flensburg down to Lübeck was included, although only Lübeck actually touched the border.[195] The expansive extent of the recipient regions suggests another dimension of the program that is revealed in Herbert Wehner's demand to develop the new country "up to the last centimeter" on the border.[196] His plea indicates that "zonal borderland aid" constituted an integral part of the territorialization processes of the young Federal Republic. Territorialization, defined by Ulrike Jureit as the creation of political spaces that most commonly unfolds alongside state-building processes, is of central importance to new states with fresh borders.[197] That the GDR pursued territorialization along its western border with more brutality than the Federal Republic does not mean that territori-alization did not take place in West Germany as well; it only took different forms, such as the alimentation of the borderlands. The confused allegi-ances of borderland residents that Barbara Klie reported in 1957 indicated that these regions were still veritable liminal spaces with the potential to oscillate between West and East. Territorialization became urgent because infringements from the other side were perceived as threatening to the West German state-building project.

"Zonal borderland aid" soon became an integral part of the borderland's economic and cultural life. State support did not focus solely on retaining and creating jobs; it also tried to generate educational and recreational opportunities to enhance the overall quality of life in the border coun-ties. This approach contrasted sharply with the intentional depopulation and lack of development of the borderlands on the GDR side. Where East Germans allowed their borderlands to "die," West Germans wanted theirs to "live." Without state support, western observers in the early 1950s pre-dicted a successive "desolation" (*Verödung*) of the border counties, a process that contemporary economic geographers and spatial planners considered inevitable along "real" borders: "real" borders produced borderlands, and borderlands were understood as areas of desolation or even desertification (*Versteppung*).[198] Since the Adenauer administration did not consider the GDR a legitimate state but rather a Soviet puppet regime, the border of the GDR obviously could not be recognized as a legitimate political border either. In official parlance, it therefore continued to be referred to as a "de-marcation line" in order to tie it to the occupation period as a time of total political dependency, while school maps represented it as a dotted line to underscore its impermanence and illegitimacy.[199] If only "real" borders produced borderlands, the federal government could not possibly allow overall decline and especially depopulation to unfold in the counties along the inter-German border: an acceptance of the borderlands sliding into desolation would have made the GDR border "real." Until the mid-1960s, economic support for the border regions was therefore another manifesta-tion of the West German policy not to recognize the western border of the GDR and, by implication, the East German state as such.

2

The East of the West

AN ECONOMIC BACKWATER AT THE BORDER

AFTER THE LATE 1940s, the borderland regions abutting the GDR became West Germany's most sensitive geographical spaces. They constituted a proving ground where West Germany had to wrestle in concrete ways with its ideological adversary, socialist East Germany. It was here that the Federal Republic had to address the practical consequences of the border, in particular its economic and infrastructural challenges. To ensure the new western state's consolidation and acceptance, the benefits of the Federal Republic's economic, political, and social order had to reach the border regions, too, in order to integrate them into the new state. This was not just a political necessity born of contemporary exigency: spatial planners within the government considered it a constitutional mandate to create "comparable living conditions" across the land.[1] The relevance of these regions explains why the borderlands remained sites of intense politicking throughout their existence.

This chapter explains how borderland aid became a steady feature of the West German subsidy landscape and managed to withstand various challenges to its status as a preferred region within federal aid schemes. Once Bonn acknowledged political responsibility for the border regions in the early 1950s, borderland officials set their sights on a new goal: making federal support *permanent*. This was not an easy task, since the permanence of borderland aid flew in the face of the still prevalent reunification rhetoric. Ongoing aid implied the persistence of the very border that the West German Constitution expected politicians to overcome. Although much of the reunification rhetoric during the Adenauer years rang hollow,[2] its continued use was a prerequisite for holding Soviet and East German intransigence responsible for the deepening division of the country. How could West Germany begin to treat support for the borderlands as a permanent feature and simultaneously demand that the border disappear? The strategies employed by borderland advocates to square this circle and enlist ongoing government support indicate their vested interest in essentializing the special status of their regions and fixing that status as an unassailable reality, an approach that was directly tied to material resources. Overall, their efforts were successful. In 1965, borderland aid appeared in a federal law for the first time, namely in the Spatial Planning Law. However, borderland advocates wanted a law dedicated exclusively to their regions, analogous to the public commitment to West Berlin. Although it was a legal technicality that required the drafting of such a Zonal Borderland Aid Law in 1971, it was feted as the borderland lobby's great achievement. But along with unwavering state support, the borderlands also acquired an image problem. By the mid-1960s, the constant demands to rectify the economic consequences of the Iron Curtain had led many West Germans to believe that the borderlands were backward, poor, and overall unattractive. Particularly during the 1970s, after the seminal shift in inter-German relations induced by *Ostpolitik*, attempts to change this image were only mildly successful.

If borderland aid was indeed a piece in a larger political strategy to dispute the legitimacy of the East German state, as indicated in the preceding chapter, then Bonn's departure from its nonrecognition policy toward the GDR to a more pragmatic interaction with the socialist neighbor in the early 1970s had the potential to undermine political support for *Zonenrandförderung*. The transformation of inter-German relations under Chancellor Willy Brandt (SPD) made the very term "zonal borderland aid" stick out like a sore thumb.[3] However, by the time *Ostpolitik* yielded its most important contractual agreement between both German states in 1972 that could have triggered revisions of borderland aid, the program had become enshrined in a federal law. Not only had the claims of the border regions gained legal status, federal support since the early 1950s had created expectations in those regions. Like many subsidies in the Federal Republic, borderland aid had thus moved onto a path dependency that insulated it against criticism during the 1970s and 1980s and remained hard to break even when its core justification—the border—disappeared.[4] A credible threat to the program could thus come only from outside domestic politics, in this case the European Commission, which began to scrutinize national regional-aid programs in the mid-1970s and mounted the most potent challenge to borderland aid.

The fall of the Berlin Wall in November 1989 and the successive opening of crossings along the inter-German border predictably caused major upheaval in the borderlands. This chapter addresses the immediate and medium-term economic consequences of border opening, some of which amounted to a déjà-vu: phenomena from the late 1940s such as currency dualism and related activities like smuggling returned to the borderlands, causing frustration on both sides of the dismantled fence. The dissolution of the GDR and unification in 1990 finally also undermined the justifications for borderland aid; it was terminated in 1994. The chapter closes with a look at the afterlife of the regions that had been borderlands for almost four decades. *Zonenrandförderung* was irretrievably lost but Reconstruction East (Aufbau Ost) was just beginning. The federal subsidies saved by terminating borderland aid were earmarked for the reconstruction of the East German economy and infrastructure. Both figuratively and literally, *Zonenrandförderung* turned into Aufbau Ost. An economic divide consisting of a subsidy and wage gap thus continued to exist along the former demarcation line, creating what many former borderlanders from the western side now bemoaned as lopsided economic opportunities. Well into the 1990s, then, residents of the western borderlands who had for so long considered themselves to be living in the shadow of the Iron Curtain even now struggled to move out from under it.

Spatial Planning and the Entrenchment of Borderland Aid by Law

After GDR authorities introduced the harsh border regime in May 1952, western commentators denounced the new measures as inhumane, criminal, and even, in Adenauer's words, "terroristic."[5] However, to many observers in the 1950s, the phenomena of fresh borders and the ensuing emergence of borderlands were not as unfamiliar as the contemporary rhetorical outrage would suggest. Borderland advocates and political commentators, especially the nationalists among them, drew on a vocabulary that resonated with everyone who remembered the territorial losses after 1918. During the interwar years, the newly drawn borders of Poland and Czechoslovakia were frequently described with evocative organic metaphors and maps that depicted the "body" of the nation as "mutilated" and "bleeding."[6] Comparable metaphors returned in the 1950s and early 1960s. "Any body that sustains a wound," reads one example of this language, "throws all its defense and reconstructive capacities towards the edge of this wound. Unfortunately, the zonal border, this dangerous wound on the body of the German people (*Volk*), is experiencing that the defense and reconstructive capacities are fleeing from the edge of the wound."[7] Apart from dramatizing the situation of the border counties, tapping into the "bleeding border" rhetoric promised to trigger memories of the Weimar government's response to the challenge. That response had featured a borderland fund. Not surprisingly, calls that employed organic metaphors were also likely to reference erstwhile Osthilfe, or Eastern Aid, the program designed to sustain East Prussia and regions in western Prussia.[8] The Osthilfe of the late 1920s was in many ways an unhelpful reference, for it was geared toward sustaining agriculture and safeguarding the privileges of large landholders in the region and had ended in scandal.[9] Nonetheless, invoking Osthilfe allowed 1950s borderland advocates to underscore their demands for long-term federal aid. In their quest to distinguish the borderlands from other depressed regions and entrench federal support for the borderlands by law, they found allies among spatial planners, who played an influential role in the early Federal Republic as policy advisers and experts.

The way spatial planners approached the problems of the new borderlands also betrayed revealing continuities. Indeed, these continuities help explain why the *Zonenrand* became a prime concern for this profession. Postwar western Germany was in a condition that posed myriad challenges to spatial planners but also provided them with the opportunity to prove the worth of their profession. The freshly divided country had to adjust its economic capacities to a reduced space, process an unprecedented in-migration of expellees and refugees, and cope with massive war damage to housing, traffic infrastructure, and public works. Once postwar economic growth set in at an unexpected pace, the growth processes posed more challenges, since they unfolded in spatially uneven and "unhealthy" ways. The country was in obvious disarray, and spatial planners were perceived as experts who could restore order, a reputation that stemmed not least from their involvement with planning in war-occupied Poland. Like any other professionals in postwar Germany, spatial planners had been complicit in a range of Nazi policies. After the war, they adjusted to the new political conditions with relative ease and continued to advance some of their core visions of "order."[10]

Simply put, the ideal "order" consisted of an even distribution of people, economic resources, and economic activity within the remaining space of the bisected country, ensuring comparable living conditions across the land. Economic activity, especially industrial production and manufacturing, had to be decentralized across the country, not clustered within a few industrial centers. This, in turn, would lead to an even distribution of people, reduce stark differences between urban areas and the countryside, and ultimately lead to spatial harmony and equilibrium and social peace. Since the private economy did not appear to act according to the desired distribution principles—processes of economic agglomeration were still poorly understood at the time[11]—the state had to intervene within the parameters of the new social market economy.[12] Embedded in this vision of order were anti-modern and anti-urban ideological tenets that had accompanied spatial planning since its inception after World War I. Urban agglomerations of industrial production and people (*Ballung*), so the thinking went, exposed residents to the dangers of "massification" (*Vermassung*), which cut their ties to the soil and made them politically susceptible to Communist ideas.[13] Besides, many economically distressed regions, so-called *Notstandsgebiete*, were found in rural areas, a phenomenon that spatial planners of the 1920s and 1930s believed to be intrinsically linked to unchecked urbanization.[14] The plight of rural areas could be compounded if they were located along a border.

In the 1930s, leading planners like Gerhard Isenberg studied the economic effects of the new eastern borders drawn after 1919. Those borders severed established trade relations, the local economy lost its hinterlands, manufacturers faced increased distances to new markets, the traffic infrastructure was poor, and migrants from the "other side" crowded into the borderlands. At the time, Isenberg recommended that the state counter these developments with freight subsidies, low-interest loans and tax incentives for entrepreneurs, as well as a targeted development of the public infrastructure like roads and rail.[15] Confronted with the new postwar demarcation line, spatial planners thus had an established vocabulary with which to talk about fresh borders and emerging borderlands. The "zonal borderlands" quickly became regions of prime concern for spatial planners during the 1950s since they fell so squarely into familiar categories of thinking. Not least because of a strong continuity in personnel in this field, the basic precepts of spatial planning from the prewar decades informed postwar analyses, with some adjustments to the new political circumstances.

In 1950, the federal government established an interministerial committee known as IMNOS (Interministerieller Ausschuss für Notstandsgebietsfragen), and tasked it with identifying distressed regions that suffered from the consequences of war, especially high unemployment due to the influx of expellees and refugees. Chaired by a representative of the Ministry for Economic Affairs, the committee sought the advice of the nearby Institute for Spatial Research in Bonn-Bad Godesberg and even featured Gerhard Isenberg as a member since he was now employed by the Ministry of Finance. IMNOS became the main conduit for turning spatial planning analysis into policy, since IMNOS not only identified such regions but also made aid decisions. Indeed, the committee was laying the groundwork for regional development policy in the Federal Republic.[16] In the first years, IMNOS was primarily concerned with distressed regions in general, not the borderlands in particular, although many traditional *Notstandsgebiete* such as the Bavarian Forest, the Rhön mountain range, and northeastern Hesse were now located along the border.[17] Yet both the Bonn government and IMNOS remained reluctant to consider the borderlands as one spatial unit. Even after the GDR closed the demarcation line in May 1952, an event that bolstered borderland advocacy, IMNOS maintained that "the distress in some other regions of the Federal Republic is considerably higher than in the border strip along the Iron Curtain."[18]

Concerns for differentiation notwithstanding, the borderlands displayed many paradigmatic problems in which spatial planners were genuinely interested. The waxing and waning of borderland demographics kept spatial planners particularly engaged, not least because the shifts there—from overpopulation due to expellees and concomitant unemployment to the perceived population drain during the economic upswing and the ensuing threat of "desolation"—appeared to undermine the goals of "order" and equilibrium that they considered essential to social peace. The Cold War dimension of these problems constituted an important link between spatial planners and borderland advocates. Both groups heartily agreed that it was especially important for the Federal Republic to flaunt the success of its social and political order in the border areas. Leaving the borderlands to fend for themselves would amount to "closing the [western] display window" to the East.[19] Both parties also tended to stoke anxieties to advance their goals: borderland advocates activated fears of Communism, and spatial planners evoked the specter of a "disorder" capable of undermining the state.[20] Above all, borderland representatives benefited from the view among spatial planners that the goal of achieving comparable living conditions across the country was anchored in West Germany's Basic Law and was therefore a constitutional mandate. However, as Ariane Leendertz has argued, the connection between the general orientation principle (*Leitbild*) of comparable living conditions and the Constitution was one of legal interpretation. While a few articles did reference this goal, the Constitution provided spatial planners with a means of justifying their preconceived general principle but was not its self-evident source. Instead, Leendertz sees the origins of the enthusiasm for this *Leitbild* in the anti-modern quest for order of the 1920s and 1930s: comparable living conditions were the embodiment of spatial harmony.[21] In short, without explicitly reaching out to one another, spatial planners and borderland advocates argued in highly complementary ways.

As IMNOS worked to streamline regional aid for distressed areas, or redevelopment areas (*Sanierungsgebiete*) as they came to be called by the mid-1950s,[22] it integrated the borderlands into the first coherent West German regional development program. Launched in 1954, the program focused on war-ravaged areas but continued to adjust both its scope and methods. As war damages became less acute, eligible regions were redefined. Similarly, the early approach of allocating aid equally among recipients (the so-called *Gießkannenprinzip*) was replaced by Walter Christaller's Central Place Theory, according to which regional and local centers of economic activity should be propped up in the expectation that they would in turn elevate their immediate surroundings. Regardless of these shifts in scope and method, the border regions received special consideration and also featured prominently in the first federal spatial planning report of 1963.[23] That the "zonal borderlands" were thus pulling ahead of other distressed areas also became manifest in 1956 when Bonn negotiated the Treaty of Rome with its European partners. The Ministry for Economic Affairs ensured that an exemption for current and future borderland support would find a way into a draft of the competition rules for the Common Market.[24] In February 1957, the Common Market delegation approved the German request. The final version exempted "[a]id granted to the economy of certain areas of the Federal Republic of Germany affected by the division of Germany, in so far as such aid is required in order to compensate for the economic disadvantages caused by that division."[25] In an exegetical protocol, the German delegation specified that the paragraph pertained to West Berlin, the "zonal borderlands" (without defining their extent), as well as the Saarland and its neighboring counties. Since aid for the Saarland and its environs was assumed to run out in 1963, only

West Berlin and the *Zonenrandgebiet* were expected to benefit from the exemption in the long run. Borderland advocates considered the wording of this important treaty "a great success."[26] As explained later in the chapter, its true value would emerge in the 1980s when the European Commission set out to challenge borderland privileges.

By the early 1960s, however, borderland representatives felt they were falling behind vis-à-vis West Berlin. The latent competition between the *Zonenrand* and West Berlin for attention, status, and material resources was nothing new. Ever since the Soviet blockade of 1948, Berlin epitomized the Cold War to the western world. To raise funds for the beleaguered city, Bonn introduced a special solidarity tax called Notopfer Berlin, which became most visible as a two-pfennig stamp on every piece of domestic mail. In 1950, Bundestag also passed the Berlin Support Law. The building of the Berlin Wall in August 1961 finalized the division of the city. As West Berlin became an exclave, connected to federal territory by a few fickle transit routes, Bonn's material support for the "outpost of freedom" only increased. The Berlin Support Law was now put on a permanent footing. It offered federal debt guarantees, tax breaks, and other aid measures designed to prime West Berlin's economy, keep manufacturers in place, and provide the necessary jobs to prevent an exodus of the city's residents. By 1989, fully 51 percent of West Berlin's income came from federal sources.[27] This is not to suggest that aid to West Berlin was ever uncontested, but as borderland supporters were keenly aware, neither a tax nor a law had ever been designed for the *Zonenrand*. "Since the building of the Wall in Berlin," stated the director of Helmstedt County, Hans Walter Conrady, "the efforts of the federal government [have] focus[ed] almost exclusively on creating the prerequisites for Berlin's survival despite the Wall." He worried that this approach was reducing the German question to a Berlin question and would come at the expense of borderland support.[28] He therefore demanded a law whose name contained the word "borderlands" to show that Bonn "felt as obliged to the *Zonenrand* as it does to West Berlin."[29] All along the Iron Curtain, local politicians and county officials repeated the message to their visitors from Bonn.[30]

Several conditions in the 1960s proved conducive to the goal of entrenching borderland aid by law. First, the political landscape had changed profoundly. With the building of the Berlin Wall, Germany's partition had reached a state of finality. During the 1950s, borderland advocates still had to argue that long-term aid for their regions did not imply that East Germany had been written off.[31] After 1961, such rhetorical acrobatics were no longer necessary. Second, although borderland representatives often considered themselves to be competing for resources with West Berlin, they actually benefited from the status as the other space created by partition. West Berlin, where Germany's division had reached its dramatic climax, possessed the symbolic capital that kept Bonn and the *Länder* engaged in ensuring its well-being, political bickering about modalities notwithstanding. Borderland advocates' strategy of comparing their plight to that of West Berlin allowed the *Zonenrand* to ride on the coattails of the divided city. Third, borderland advocates benefited from what amounted to the refounding of the Federal Republic in terms of governance and fiscal policy during the "long 1960s." With an optimism dampened only by the recession of 1966–1967 but not yet checked by the "oil shock" of the early 1970s, the state, aided by a host of experts, engaged in a broad range of planning and reform projects designed to direct economic processes, ensure prosperity in a rational and "modern" manner, and expand the purview of state expenditure.[32] It was consistent with this climate of reform and the well-entrenched status of the *Zonenrand* among spatial planners that borderland aid made its first appearance in *any* federal law in the Spatial Order Law of 1965 (Raumordnungsgesetz, ROG). One of the defined goals of this law was to "give preference to the strengthening of the economic performance in the zonal borderlands in order to create in all of its parts living and working conditions as well as economic and social structures that are at least on a par (*mindestens gleichwertig*) with those in the whole federal territory."[33] Fourth, in the political context of the late 1960s, the borderlands were not hurt by the needs of other regions, although their advocates frequently assumed otherwise. To the contrary, the crisis of the coal mining sector in the Ruhr region triggered the reconception of regional aid in a program called Common Tasks, or Gemeinschaftsaufgaben. The program's creation was part of the major finance reforms of 1969 that redefined the allocation of revenue and the functioning of West German federalism.[34] It was the confluence of these factors that finally produced the Zonal Borderland Aid Law of 1971 (Zonenrandförderungsgesetz, ZRFG), which sealed the status of these subsidies as unassailable.

The penchant of borderland advocates to fear that any new aid program not directed at their regions might hurt them was visible again in the late 1960s during the Ruhr crisis. The decline of the mining industry in the Ruhr region inaugurated the end of West Germany's "economic miracle." Between 1958 and 1969, the issue dominated domestic politics and sent politicians scrambling for answers to structural processes that were larger than any one national economy.[35] As the minister for economic affairs, Karl Schiller (SPD), set out to support the ailing energy sector—and with it the entire Ruhr region—through the Coal Adaptation Law and the Ruhr Plan, he triggered anxieties that the SPD within the Grand Coalition was planning to focus structural policy exclusively on traditional SPD strongholds. Subsidies for the Ruhr region also violated long-standing conceptions of regional aid that, in keeping with the visions of spatial planners, had been geared toward industrializing and sustaining underdeveloped regions, and not supporting a highly industrialized region in adapting its industrial structure. What was more, Schiller intended to incentivize new industries in the Ruhr with a 10 percent premium on private investments. Such an investment premium (*Investitionszulage*) had thus far been reserved for West Berlin and the borderlands; granting it to another region constituted the most direct threat to their special status. The Ruhr, this object of envy of borderland residents during the 1950s that had enticed so many of them to leave, was thus about to become a national project just like the "political" regions West Berlin and *Zonenrand*.[36] A storm of protest from CDU politicians and borderland representatives led the SPD to a political solution that, in the words of the historian Christoph Nonn, amounted to nothing less than "structural policy for all."[37] Instead of fighting the political battle on behalf of the Ruhr region, it was easier to roll out comprehensive structural and regional aid programs that allowed everyone predictable access to federal funds. Put differently, as the Ruhr region joined the "club" of recipients of federal aid, the benefits of existing programs were increased accordingly to maintain the relative balance of financial allocations. The ensuing ballooning of federal spending was backed by a broad "expansion coalition" within West German politics that anticipated continued economic growth and agreed to finance the rising state expenditures with debt instead of tax increases.[38]

Yet Schiller's plans to support the Ruhr and pacify his critics raised a range of constitutional issues, since regional economic development was, strictly speaking, the purview of the federal states. Indeed, the cooperation between the federal government and the states, especially revenue equalization and co-financing, had been a gray zone since the founding of the Republic. Borderland aid, too, had operated in this gray zone and had amounted to an endless string of ad hoc and emergency measures, often instituted by decrees.[39] Regional aid and a range of other problems in the workings of West German federalism were finally addressed by the finance reform of 1969.[40] The idea that the federal and state governments would co-finance several Common Tasks became a key feature of the new "cooperative federalism" that the finance reform inaugurated.[41] Although the need to overhaul the financial relationship between Bonn and the states predated the Ruhr crisis, the Common Tasks program was the political answer to the criticism the Ruhr Plan had received. One of the Common Tasks was called "improving regional economic structures" and turned into the main venue of regional aid in West Germany.[42] Although regional development remained the duty of the individual *Länder*, the federal government shared 50 percent of the cost. In three-year plans (*Rahmenplan*), resources were allocated to admitted regions according to specific needs. The base assumption was that, ideally, aid would enhance the economic structure of a region to a point that it could be reduced and eventually terminated. Amid predictable political wrangling, regions therefore rotated in and out of each new plan.[43]

Having witnessed how aid for West Berlin, the coal mining industry, and regional aid through the Common Tasks program had attained legal status, borderland advocates feared that government subsidies were becoming leveled and egalitarian, turning borderland aid into one program among many.[44] They therefore renewed their push for a law that would enshrine the priority of borderland aid "*after* Berlin but *before* any other development region." They benefited from the technicality that the Common Tasks program had put an end to any previously existing regional aid schemes, thereby creating the legal necessity to codify borderland aid.[45] Although the borderland lobby thus pushed through an open door, they considered this law their "crowning achievement."[46] On June 17, 1971, the federal holiday commemorating the East German uprising of 1953, the Bundestag passed the Zonal Borderland Aid Law. It reaffirmed the spatial definition of the borderlands as a 40-kilometer-wide strip along the Iron Curtain and gave legal status to all previously employed financial instruments and administrative activities on behalf of these regions.[47] Borderland advocates were fully satisfied with the law, not least because they had written it themselves.[48] On the one hand, the law simply enabled the federal government to continue doing what it had been doing for the borderlands all along; on the other hand, it held real "cash value" because it required an amendment of the Common Tasks program. In the original version of the program, *Zonenrand* had not received any special attention. Since it had now been turned into a development region by law, however, Common Tasks needed to accommodate its special status. It did so by acknowledging the borderland's "politically induced special situation," admitting it in its entirety, and granting it preferential treatment vis-à-vis other regions. While other regions were assessed by economic indicators, received differentiated aid measures, and rotated in and out of the program, the *Zonenrand* was there to stay, regardless of economic performance.[49] Borderland advocates had good reason to believe that "zonal borderland aid" had become untouchable.

Image Problems: West Germany's Developing Country

The lobbying efforts in the 1950s and 1960s to obtain and entrench state support had a lasting impact on the image of the borderlands. Since these campaigns and related press coverage reiterated time and again that the border towns and counties were struggling to partake in economic recovery, the predictable result was that West Germans outside the borderlands, to the extent that they thought about it, began to perceive the *Zonenrand* as "poor people's land." Borderland residents discovered on their trips to the Rhineland and elsewhere that their fellow West Germans pitied them for having to live there, or seemed to believe that they passed the time complaining about their lot.[50] Their compatriots often did not even know whether a town in the general vicinity of the border was still in the West or already in the East. When a team from Helmstedt (West) traveled some seventy miles west to a swim meet in Hameln (West) in the spring of 1959, they were greeted as "guests from the other side of the Iron Curtain."[51] Indeed, as time went by, the borderlands seemed like faraway lands to some West Germans. They literally overestimated the spatial distance and travel time from their own location to a borderland location, for example from Munich to Hof.[52]

By the late 1960s, politicians and bureaucrats realized that the borderlands had an image problem that was hampering their very efforts to prop these regions up. As a ministry official from Hesse put it, "Constantly painting these areas as depressed is doing a disservice to the people who live [t]here and discourages entrepreneurs from coming."[53] Yet as people in Bonn's Ministry for Economic Affairs knew all too well, the press preferred to report on the most extreme cases, such as Schnackenburg-on-Elbe and Duderstadt near Göttingen, which only furthered perceptions about the border regions as the "poor house of the Federal Republic"—deserted and desolate.[54] The borderlands' image oscillated between that of "depressed areas" and that of "window to the West," neither of which represented the realities on the ground in the economically heterogeneous regions along the Iron Curtain.[55]

The post-Adenauer years saw a noticeable shift in the official representation of the borderlands, from an emphasis on problems to a focus on achievements. This shift coincided with the seminal reconception of inter-German relations (*Deutschlandpolitik*) collectively known as *Ostpolitik*, the German version of détente. No West German party was ever prepared to pull the plug on borderland subsidies. In fact, it was a signature of *Zonenrandförderung* that it had found a place above the political fray. Political bickering about the program lingered on nuances, not on substance. The *Zonenrand* image was an ideal venue for such bickering because it was perfectly inconsequential. Disputes regularly erupted when a government office published a brochure that highlighted the extent of government support and reflected on its achievements. For instance, in 1964 the conservative mayor of Fulda, Alfred Dregger (CDU), accused Heinz Kreutzmann of embellishing the record of the Hessian state government. Kreutzmann served as state commissioner for depressed regions and the zonal borderland. He had begun his political career in expellee politics but grew increasingly convinced that a less confrontational approach to inter-German relations was necessary; he became an SPD member and a staunch supporter of *Ostpolitik*. Dregger thought the brochure gave the impression that matters "weren't so bad after all" in the borderlands, whereas Kreutzmann refused to continue to paint the situation "as black on black," since this would ultimately repel both investors and tourists.[56] Such squabbles over the borderlands' public representation neatly split along partisan lines, identifying them as proxy debates about policy, notably *Ostpolitik*.[57]

However, some local representatives, regardless of party affiliation, were opposed to an overly positive representation of the borderlands. They had the most to gain from an ongoing perception of their regions as having a legitimate need, since that status translated into an influx of material resources. They therefore clung to variations of the victimization discourse of the 1950s that reappeared in various guises well into the 1980s, arguing in 1983, for instance, that "the zonal borderlands still bear, for all of us, the burdens of the lost war and the downfall of the Reich."[58] This kind of rhetoric emphasized the ongoing obligation of the state that the state itself found impossible even to modify, not least because postwar suffering broadly construed had customarily underwritten a great deal of the Federal Republic's financial assistance to groups and individuals.[59] Borderland representatives anxiously protected the moral capital that underpinned their claims and resisted, for example, any suggestions of abandoning the very term "zonal borderland," even though polls suggested that the term *Zonenrandgebiet* triggered negative associations. Although the federal government replaced the term with the more neutral "borderlands adjacent to the GDR," local politicians continued to rely on the term's name recognition, which carried a reminder of how and why the borderlands had come about, thus reaffirming their status as disadvantaged through no fault of their own.[60] An episode from the late 1970s throws this dynamic into sharp relief.

Like other players in borderland politics, the Federal Ministry for Inter-German Relations under Egon Franke (SPD) was trying to change its tune. Attempts to reinvent the image and also the self-perception of the border regions culminated in a "confidence" exhibition in 1978, which the Ministry sent to forty-five borderland locations under the telling title "Our home region is something to be proud of" (*Unser Zuhause kann sich sehen lassen*).[61] The federal government wanted to highlight how much it had already done for the borderlands and change the calamity mentality that it had helped to create in the 1950s. The exhibition confronted that mentality wherever it showed up. In Braunschweig, for instance, the city's mayor held the "demarcation line" responsible for the area's lack of attraction to investors. Without state support, which, he argued, had to be "higher than for other assisted areas," the disadvantages could not be evened out. In response, the Ministry's state secretary, Egon Höhmann, took the risk of pointing out that some of the border regions were doing much better than some depressed areas in other parts of the country.[62] Höhmann had done his homework: the Ministry had prepared summaries of the economic situation for each location the exhibition would visit. For Braunschweig, the summary duly noted the recent setbacks that local companies such as the camera manufacturer Rollei had suffered over the past eight years. Unlike the local authorities, though, the Ministry explained these setbacks not in terms of the borderland location but as managerial ineptitude. Rollei, for instance, had diversified its product line at an inopportune time and underestimated Japanese competition.[63] Clearly, Braunschweig's industries, like those elsewhere, were suffering from the structural crisis of the 1970s that affected the southeast of Lower Saxony earlier and somewhat more sharply than regions farther west.[64] However, in the presence of a federal representative, no local politician or entrepreneur would engage in a sober macroeconomic analysis lest he damage the moral basis for the region's claim on federal aid.

When the exhibition rolled into Lüchow, the seat of the rural county Lüchow-Dannenberg, the official tasked with delivering the opening speech received a similar briefing from the Ministry. In 1978, the county was torn over government plans to build a nuclear reprocessing and waste storage plant at Gorleben, right on the border with the GDR—a topic addressed in greater detail in the final chapter. Locals also feared the termination of unprofitable rail lines, which would worsen the county's situation as a traffic blind spot. The county director's standard complaint, though, was Lüchow-Dannenberg's continuing loss of population. The figures were dramatic indeed. From 72,741 inhabitants in 1950, the county's population had declined to 51,271 by 1967.[65] But as the Ministry did not fail to point out to its exhibition speaker, the calculations of the county director, Wilhelm Paasche, always started in 1950, when the area was bursting with expellees and refugees. It had been state policy to move and resettle these populations, a policy welcomed by locals who had not necessarily embraced the destitute new arrivals. Taking prewar population statistics into account, ministry officials came up with a very different calculation: in 1978, the county was home to 25 percent *more* residents than in 1939.[66]

Each side knew how to read the arguments of the other. As another speaker put it, "It has long been considered a communal duty (*kommunale Pflicht*) to reiterate the distress of the municipalities and counties along the inter-German border even when there was nothing to complain about."[67] The pattern persisted. Wherever the exhibition appeared, local officials seized the opportunity to ask for more aid. Punning on the exhibition's title, their motto clearly was "Our home region is something of which we could be even prouder."[68] While this persistence could suggest that nothing ever changed in the borderlands, federal subsidies repeatedly came under fire during the 1970s and 1980s. West Germans had grown accustomed to partition, and "zonal borderland aid" seemed no longer to be in step with the times.

Challenges to the Status Quo: The 1970s and 1980s

"You aren't promising anything this time?" The glossy magazine *Stern* depicted the city director of Duderstadt as flabbergasted when a fact-finding mission, traveling on behalf of the West German parliament, came through town in the mid-1970s without announcing any new funds for it. "The city director," *Stern* claimed, "is used to the fact that any[body] coming from Bonn is bringing money."[69] The presentation of the borderlands in the magazine's provocative piece was anything but flattering. It portrayed the *Zonenrand* as a bottomless pit in which millions seeped away without anyone in Bonn being able to say where exactly the money came from and went to. It provided examples of federally funded projects, emphasizing how small communities ended up with an inflated and disproportionate infrastructure. It pointed out that one of West Germany's wealthiest communities—Wolfsburg with its VW plant—happened to be located in the borderlands. It compared small towns along the border with equivalent towns farther inland that struggled with similar problems, from an aging population to the lack of specialized medical care. And it hinted strongly that "investors" regularly abused Bonn's generosity by availing themselves of the various investment premiums and tax incentives without actually creating any jobs.

Such mishandling of "zonal borderland aid," especially in real estate, became an issue during the 1970s. Real estate developers discovered the potential value of vacation spots in the borderlands and kicked off a major building boom along the Baltic coast in Schleswig-Holstein, in the Harz Mountains, and in the Bavarian Forest. Outsized hotel and apartment buildings soon dotted the landscape, pitched to individual investors as a safe path to tax savings and capital returns. Borderland privileges made the calculation inviting indeed. Combining various incentives,[70] the state picked up some 10 percent of the investment or purchase price and offered 30 percent special depreciation on immovable and 50 percent on movable goods. For the builder, the plots and credits came cheap, the *Länder* governments proved amenable to backing major loans, and the municipalities paid for development costs such as utility connections and streets. Between 1969 and 1973, thirty-six such complexes sprouted in the borderlands, increasing the number of beds on the Baltic coast by 43 percent and in the western Harz by 44 percent.[71] West Germans were familiar with these kinds of vacation complexes from their visits to Mediterranean beaches, but would they work in less favorable climes? Hoteliers on the Baltic hoped in vain to turn overcast weather into sunshine. Introducing the yearlong season proved elusive. The overall economic climate did not cooperate either; interest rates began to climb and the recession of the 1970s settled in.[72] Besides, the building boom created overcapacities. The press followed these developments with a critical eye beginning in the early 1970s.[73] Born of sheer affluence, these projects no longer had anything to do with the initial idea of showcasing economic superiority in the borderlands or preparing the regions for possible reunification. To the contrary, a local official in Sierksdorf (West) on the Baltic actually worried that "one day, Ulbricht might open the border and the beaches, and then everyone will go over there since it's cheaper there."[74] A few years later, the bubble burst, cementing the reputation of *Zonenrandförderung* as a misguided flow of taxpayers' money.[75]

Developments like the "resort bubble" deepened the divide between federal states on the receiving end and those who had to underwrite the program without benefiting from it. These divides went back to the creation of "zonal borderland aid" when the nonrecipients wanted to restrict federal support to payments for damages directly caused by border closure in May 1952. Representatives of Hamburg and North Rhine-Westphalia argued at the time that all of West Germany, not just the border regions, had to reckon with tectonic shifts in the economic landscape due to partition.[76] For the city-state of Hamburg in particular, borderland aid turned into a major nuisance. The port city itself did not qualify for this kind of support, but a semicircle of counties on Hamburg's eastern outskirts did. In a reversal of the dynamic during the reconstruction years, the counties began to compete with Hamburg during the 1970s and 1980s. They promoted themselves as advantageous business locations: not only could they offer immediate proximity to the metropolis, borderland aid also reduced much of the entrepreneur's cost.[77] Hamburg's politicians woke up to this threat in 1972 when the machine-building company Bran & Lübbe announced its move to adjacent Norderstedt, taking along some 360 jobs and an annual business volume of DM 50 million.[78] In the ensuing skirmish with the government of Schleswig-Holstein, a Hamburg senator referred to borderland aid as a "misallocation of public funds."[79] Yet the issue was never resolved, and the relocation of businesses beyond the city limits continued. Hamburg's Senate thus demanded the introduction of economic indicators to determine which parts of the borderlands qualified for aid, but to no avail.[80]

By the late 1970s, Hamburg was no longer alone in its call for more accountability of "zonal borderland aid."[81] The program had come to stand for handing out monies to all and sundry, not least because its advocates refused to (re)consider both its spatial scope and the introduction of economic indicators for the allocation of funds. Even the chairman of the Parliamentary Committee on Inter-German Relations, Olaf von Wrangel (CDU), who, by definition, was obliged to advocate for borderland aid, pleaded for more differentiation in the funding structure. Wrangel's own electoral district, Stormarn, was one of the counties in Hamburg's subsidized outskirts. He knew he would damage his political career if his electorate perceived him as speaking against federal support for his own district. His solution to the dilemma shows how little the subsidies had to do with the consequences of partition or proximity to the GDR: instead of excluding economically strong areas of the borderlands from the program, he suggested giving the weak regions more money.[82] For Wrangel, at least, there was no way out, only up.

In view of such mindsets, a lasting solution to Hamburg's woes was unlikely. In 1986, the city thus launched its own investment aid program to counter the advantage of the surrounding counties. It expended more than DM 27 million to keep thirty-seven companies in town, only to see its aid scheme declared illicit under European competition law.[83] In 1987, after another wave of business relocations,[84] Hamburg's Senate finally exercised its most potent option and introduced a bill into the Bundesrat for a substantial reform of borderland aid. The bill did not even move beyond committee level.[85] Representatives from the state of North Rhine-Westphalia could have predicted this outcome. A few years prior, they had tried to abolish *Zonenrandförderung* altogether. At the time, their initiative had been shot down, as one politician put it, by the "concerted Zonenrand mafia."[86] After the fall of the Wall in November 1989, Hamburg's politicians wasted no time demanding an end to borderland subsidies.[87]

The strongest and most persistent challenge to the borderland program, however, emanated from the European Commission (EC) in Brussels. Unaffected by national election cycles and shifting government coalitions, the EC Directorate-General for Competition, or DG IV, pursued the issue throughout the late 1970s and 1980s. The intervention of DG IV actually caught the West German government by surprise. It had relied on the exemption for borderland aid that the Adenauer administration had slipped into the 1957 Treaty of Rome.[88] Bonn had taken the pertinent article to mean that the program would not be subject to EC state aid control. However, since 1970 the DG IV had been monitoring the extent of West German regional aid as a whole.[89] In 1978, no less than 61 percent of West German territory received aid within the Common Tasks structure.[90] In its overall goal to curtail the extent of West German regional aid, DG IV targeted borderland aid in particular since it was a large, permanent, and unquestioned beneficiary of Common Tasks monies. Despite German efforts to prevent Brussels's scrutiny, the Commission publicly "expressed reservations" about *Zonenrandförderung* in 1979 and opened an investigation.[91]

At the heart of the ensuing dispute stood the interpretation of the article exempting the borderlands from European aid control. While Bonn emphasized that "certain areas [. . .] affected by the division of Germany" were cleared for any kind of aid, the EC insisted that the article pertained only to aid "required in order to compensate for the economic disadvantages caused by that division."[92] Like the Hamburg Senate, Brussels criticized *Zonenrandförderung* for defining state aid recipients by location rather than by quantifiable need based on economic indicators. It proved unwilling to accept the generous German spatial definition of the borderlands that the Treaty of Rome had never endorsed in the first place and wanted to remove counties with strong labor market statistics from borderland aid.[93] Above all, the EC insisted that the exemption covered only aid that addressed consequences of partition, which, as DG IV saw it, required a certain specificity.[94] The German reference to the *potential* economic development that these regions could have undergone *if* partition had not occurred was, in Brussels's view, counterfactual and therefore not empirically verifiable.[95] The EC found Bonn's assumed causal connection between the border and the economic performance of adjacent regions particularly difficult to accept three decades after Germany's division. Pressing for clarification, the Commission thus asked Bonn to produce a report outlining the economic developments in the borderlands since the end of the war.[96] The EC challenge cut to the core of the rationale and justification of *Zonenrandförderung*. By asking how local and regional economies were still suffering from partition and how, specifically, state subsidies were addressing those disadvantages, the EC's investigation demonstrated that, as far as Brussels was concerned, partition had become the new normal.

The federal government was caught in a bind. Internally, officials at Bonn's Ministry for Economic Affairs concluded that the spatial definition of the borderlands would not hold up at the European level and, more important, that their own claim that partition was *causal* to ongoing economic disadvantages within the border regions was weak.[97] Still, for domestic political reasons, government officials circled the wagons and defended the ongoing need for *Zonenrandförderung*.[98] In its first response to the EC, Bonn flatly denied that economic indicators could serve as the basis for determining the border regions' needs and questioned the very methods the EC had applied to gather such data.[99] The disagreement over data collection was not just a quibble; it constituted a real threat to the borderlands. Ever since the European Commission had ventured into its own regional aid program in the early 1970s, it had made efforts to map the economic performance of member regions by economic indicators.[100] Common economic indicators made disadvantaged European regions comparable— that was the point. In view of West Germany's overall prosperity, though, such a comparison made its borderlands look satisfactory on a European scale. Borderland advocates had initially even believed that their regions might become beneficiaries of the European Regional Development Fund (ERDF).[101] They now realized that within ERDF, *Zonenrand* was up against the "much worse conditions in the Mezzogiorno, Ireland, and Scotland," an insight that domestic opponents of borderland aid such as those in Hamburg might seize with glee.[102]

For the federal government, the only way out of potentially damaging disputes about economic indicators was therefore to redeploy the argument that borderland aid was a *political* program: the regions received preferential treatment in pursuit of the constitutional mandate to effect reunification. If, then, the program was not an economic development scheme, comparing economic data became unnecessary. In response to Brussels's request for a report, Bonn sent a document that acknowledged the borderland's economic heterogeneity, only to declare this aspect irrelevant to the discussion at hand. Regardless of current indicators, the Germans argued, the entire borderland suffered from "consistent and permanent damage" (*gleichmässiger Dauerschaden*) that justified equally consistent support.[103] Borderland advocates repeated this line of argument wherever they could. Under pressure from the EC, they lashed out at other federal programs—from subsidies for the steel industry to development funds for other regions—to safeguard the extent of their own.[104]

With both sides unlikely to budge, the dispute between Bonn and Brussels was set to continue for the long haul. Instead of undertaking the futile attempt to make the federal government abandon its position, DG IV decided instead to challenge borderland aid on a case-by-case basis and litigate specific items at the European Court whenever it suspected that sectoral subsidies were hiding behind the smokescreen of borderland aid. In a 1986 decision against aid to a synthetic fiber company, the Commission made explicitly stated that it had "never considered the Zonal Border Areas of [. . .] Germany to be automatically exempt from the monitoring of State aid to industrial sectors."[105] It reiterated that the Rome Treaty exemption from competition rules pertained only to consequences of partition, and when Bonn could not prove a causal connection between partition and a resultant disadvantage, aid was declared illicit. Members of the Bundestag took the pressure from Brussels seriously enough to start rumors only a few months before the Wall fell that the EU Commission intended to ask the federal government to terminate borderland aid altogether.[106] In the end, only the one event for which this program had allegedly prepared the border regions—the disappearance of the border through unification—could put an end to the largesse. Even then, however, borderland advocates did not intend to go quietly.

Open Border and New DMark-ations

When the Iron Curtain famously burst open on November 9, 1989, the first East German citizens crossed the border not in Berlin but at the Marienborn-Helmstedt checkpoint on the inter-German border.[107] Over the coming weeks, existing border checkpoints opened and local communities pressed for new crossings in their vicinity. By February 1990, the inter-German border featured 192 crossing points, including five ferry routes across the Elbe River.[108] Each new border opening prompted festive celebrations as long-estranged communities reached out to each other for the first time in decades. With only limited means of travel, GDR citizens made West German border towns the destinations of their first excursions to the other side. Residents there soon began to struggle with clogged city centers, where the main thoroughfares were packed with the ubiquitous East German Trabis. Town halls, banks, and post offices were likewise overwhelmed with East Germans collecting the DM 100 "welcome money" provided by the West German government. The money was often spent the same day in western shops and supermarkets, leaving those equally crowded.

Such was the dynamic in Mellrichstadt in Lower Franconia. Like other borderland residents, the 5,000 citizens of Mellrichstadt cheered the arrival of the first East Germans even though they found themselves outnumbered from the start. On November 10, the town recorded 7,000 visitors. It was all fun and games for the first few days, but before the month was out, Mellrichstadt had hosted no fewer than 330,000 visitors. The town's administration began to wonder who would foot the bill for the food and services offered to the Thuringians. Finding himself caught between happiness and despair, Mellrichstadt's mayor wrote to the governor of Bavaria in search of support. However, to officials in Munich, safely removed from the practical challenges on the ground, the conditions amounted to the "best possible borderland aid," and they did nothing.[109]

Such an assessment likely stemmed from the assumption that East Germans would instantly want to satisfy pent-up consumer demand, not least by drawing on the western welcome money. Between November 10 and December 31, 1989, the federal government disbursed some DM 2 billion before discontinuing the practice.[110] In the days and weeks after the border opening, the welcome money contributed significantly to the collapse of the infrastructure in western border towns and municipalities. On November 10, some 2,000 East Germans queued at administrative offices in Braunschweig to collect the welcome money. That same day, the city of Duderstadt handed out half a million deutsche marks but was out of cash by evening. In Lübeck, too, cash reserves quickly ran low. The city then borrowed money from a local bank until it ran out of funds as well, whereupon a department store helped out. A circular cash flow had been born: the department store sent money to the issuing city offices, which handed it to East German visitors, who, in turn, carried it back into the department store.[111] As East Germans were seen flocking to western stores, the value of the leading retail chains briefly shot up on the stock market.[112] Yet East Germans were not necessarily going on a mindless shopping binge, as the western press liked to suggest at the time. The welcome money itself was not sufficient to purchase the most coveted consumer goods like electronics anyway but was more often spent on groceries. Retailers in Hamburg soon realized that East Germans were wandering through the shops out of curiosity rather than with the intent to purchase anything. On November 12, a Sunday, when shops in many borderland towns remained open, retailers in Hamburg therefore decided to stay closed.[113]

The open border threw the economic disparities between West and East into sharp relief. Its most poignant and immediate outcome was the return of a currency dualism that led to conditions and practices typical in borderlands with lopsided economic capacities, and already familiar on the inter-German border from the time period after the introduction of the deutsche mark in 1948. The welcome money symbolized this dualism and quickly became a flashpoint for the material discrepancies between East and West that the open border laid bare. Suddenly small-scale currency speculation, nicknamed "ruble-ization" (*Umrubeln*), became a profitable pastime. None other than Chancellor Helmut Kohl himself explained to US President George Bush how it worked: "If, for instance, a couple with three kids travels to the West," he said, "they receive 500 DM in welcome money. If they spent 200 DM with us and exchange [the remaining] 300

DM into the GDR's eastern mark at a rate of 1:20, they basically carry home six average monthly wages in cash."[114] Since many East Germans had been unable to spend their savings on consumer goods in the socialist economy, an unfavorable exchange rate did not deter them for long. Driven by fear that their precious savings might be wiped out in an anticipated currency union, they preferred to spend them in the West.[115]

Smuggling returned to the border as well. Instead of converting their hard-earned money into western currency at a loss, some GDR citizens took to selling material assets instead. Antiques, stamp and coin collections, china from Meissen, glass from Jena, Zeiss optical equipment, and even subsidized eastern groceries and textiles were sold across the border and in West Berlin.[116] A baker from Ilsenburg (East) in the Harz Mountains sold an ornamental nineteenth-century cast-iron oven, traditional to the area, and replaced all the windows in his house with the proceeds.[117] Not only consumer goods could be turned into cash: the Federal Ministry for the Environment grew alarmed about the sale of protected species. Rare animals, stuffed or alive, were peddled at flea markets and pet shops and via classified ads. Native raptors and exotic birds were trapped or stolen from zoos in order to be sold on the black market for western currency.[118] Finally, another phenomenon of the late 1940s returned to the borderlands: the *Grenzgängertum*, or border crossing for work. Those who did not have money to convert or assets to hawk could still try to sell their labor in the West.[119] Either way, proximity to the open border could be leveraged as a resource, at least for a short time.

The winners of the currency dualism were the West Germans. They either exchanged money at the official rate of 1:3 or went straight to the black market for an even higher rate. Thus fortified, westerners could find bargains on foraging trips to the other side, not only because they paid with "cheap money" but also because the GDR heavily subsidized common foods and certain consumer goods. Eastern authorities noted that West Germans showed up "as regular customers in [eastern] border communities" to do their weekly family grocery shopping. In particular, they stocked up on "bread, rolls, pasta, sugar, flour, carps, trout and other foodstuffs."[120] When a supermarket in Sonneberg in Thuringia offered bananas for the first time, the manager was stunned to find westerners in the queue.[121] By December 1, 1989, GDR Trade Ministry officials estimated that western "tourists" had already spent about 2 billion eastern marks for merchandise worth some 3 to 4 billion, since their production had been subsidized.[122] Westerners also went after gasoline. Not only did they fill up their car tanks, they also brought along jerrycans or, in one blatant case, a 200-liter barrel, for diesel. "Sonneberg," an eastern resident commented with bitterness, "is nothing but a huge rummage sale for them."[123]

The currency dualism left lasting strains on the relations between western and eastern borderlanders. The euphoria over the opening of the Iron Curtain eventually gave way to misunderstandings, antipathy, and resentment. Westerners expected easterners to be grateful, and easterners experienced westerners as patronizing; for a while both sides were trapped in "a colonial dynamic."[124] It was, again, the welcome money that captured the changing mood. While thankful at first, GDR citizens soon sensed the implications of the well-meaning DM 100. As the mayor of Mellrichstadt reported, they began to see the money "more and more as a humiliation, as charity; they don't feel good receiving it."[125] The welcome money carried the hurtful message of the GDR's economic inferiority.

From Periphery to Center?
Unification and the End of Borderland Aid

Despite waning euphoria on both sides, the fall of the border created high expectations among western borderland advocates and residents. Exposed for decades to rhetoric proclaiming that the border had *caused* the decline of an erstwhile bustling center of Germany into a sleepy periphery, the disappearance of the fence raised hopes that the periphery would slide back into the center.[126] If the "sudden" peripherality was indeed the root cause of economic decline, as government propaganda had frequently suggested,[127] then the end of being the East of the West should be the first step toward recovery, an assessment that was sustained by a short-lived "unification boom" in the borderlands. Three decades after unification, however, the picture has become more differentiated. The preceding section identified the renewed currency dualism as the immediate outcome of the Iron Curtain's opening, but how did the fall of the Iron Curtain affect the borderland economy in the longer term?

The most significant change the border regions had to reckon with was the phaseout of borderland aid. Unification had made these expenses politically untenable, and the federal government decided in May 1990 to cut "partition-related liabilities" (*teilungsbedingte Lasten*).[128] This was not only common sense but also a financial necessity in view of the enormous costs of unification. Chancellor Helmut Kohl singled out borderland aid in particular as funding by habit rather than by need.[129] The first cut to *Zonenrandförderung* was the elimination of freight subsidies: in 1989 still expended at DM 65.6 million, they were gone by January 1991.[130] The government also expected quick results from the reduction of the various tax incentives in West Berlin and the borderlands. For 1991, it projected an extra 500 million in tax revenue and in 1992 even 2.3 billion.[131] Support for cultural and social measures was reduced as well. While cultural funding had actually increased over the course of the 1980s (DM 158.2 million in 1983 to DM 180.5 million in 1989), it declined dramatically after unification and was reduced from DM 120 million in 1991 to DM 20 million in 1994, when it ended.[132] On the whole, however, the Kohl administration initially contemplated a rather spacious transition period of seven years for the phaseout of borderland aid, a plan that elicited sharp criticism from the Council of Economic Advisers.[133] Not surprisingly, borderland advocates had pushed for such a leisurely pace and had also come up with reasons why their regions now needed support more than ever, including the argument that companies in the new federal states might produce at lower cost than in the former West.[134] The news magazine *Der Spiegel* suspected that Minister of Finance Theo Waigel (CSU), a politician from Bavaria, was acting as a borderland advocate himself since a 400-kilometer stretch in his home state benefited from the monies. Waigel was also considered the culprit when it turned out in 1993 that the law abolishing the tax incentives within borderland aid had left loopholes for two additional years.[135] In the early 1990s, Bundestag representatives from borderland districts inundated the government with queries about money for projects like funding orchestras and building track fields, which were often the most visible measures for their constituents. They also pressed for possible ersatz programs for their regions, especially for eastern Bavaria since the border to Czechoslovakia was obviously still in place.[136]

In view of Bonn's dilatoriness, it was the European Commission that ultimately pulled the plug on borderland aid. Since its directorate for competition (DG IV) had already tried for years to trim the extent of West German regional aid, unification presented a welcome opportunity to press the issue. In a dramatic meeting between the minister of economic affairs, Jürgen Möllemann (FDP), and the commissioner for competition, Leon Brittan, in early 1991, Möllemann agreed to cut the extent of regional aid within the Common Tasks program, amounting to an end to borderland aid by 1994. Regions within the borderlands would henceforth be subject to individual need assessments like any other area that sought Common Tasks support. In return, Brittan agreed that the new federal states, that is, the former GDR, would get a priori clearance to receive the highest support within Common Tasks for five years, a privilege formerly held by the border regions. Not only the cash saved on borderland support but also the entire toolbox used to incentivize investments was slated to move farther east. Bonn and Brussels both wanted a clear subsidy gap (*Fördergefälle*) between the old and the new federal states in order to move Reconstruction East (Aufbau Ost) forward; they simply disagreed about how to achieve this goal.[137] The Kohl administration actually tried to revive the Treaty of Rome exemption that it had traditionally used to defend borderland aid against EC challenges. It argued that East Germany as a whole should now be treated as "affected by the division of Germany."[138] The EC did not openly challenge this convenient interpretation, and the fact that the exemption article stayed on the books even after the 1992 Treaty of Maastricht led many legal commentators to conclude that the EC agreed with the German view. However, the EC remained remarkably consistent. Aid addressing obvious consequences of partition, like that earmarked for the rebuilding of an interrupted rail line between Bavaria and Thuringia, went unchallenged. Aid to specific companies and sectors beyond agreed ceilings, by contrast, was struck down, such as subsidies for a VW plant in Chemnitz in 1996.[139]

The borderlands experienced a brief "unification boom" until 1992–1993. The boom unfolded predominantly in construction, retail, skilled crafts (*Handwerk*), and tourism and led to a noticeable spike in employment.[140] Construction and skilled crafts capitalized on the backlogged demand for the modernization of private homes, public buildings, and other public works projects, including road and rail construction. In retail, too, pent-up demand among East German consumers benefited the western border regions more than the national average. As Daphne Berdahl has argued, East Germans had been culturally conditioned to desire western commodities, so that their sudden availability after November 1989 redefined social relations and hierarchies. For about two years, "anything purchased in the West had to be better because it was not from the East."[141] The moment such attitudes became paired with spending capacity, retail in the western borderlands profited simply because it was the closest incarnation of "the West" to satisfy such demand. In that sense, the borderlands finally, albeit only temporarily filled the role of the display window of western prosperity, although this role now no longer served the purpose of undermining the socialist project—the GDR had already dropped dead. Predictably, the retail boom in western shops abated once new shopping opportunities became established in the new federal states.[142] The adjacent cities of Sonneberg (Thuringia) and Neustadt (Bavaria) famously created a shopping center standoff right on the former demarcation line: each built a mall because they could not agree on a *common* facility.[143] The newly segregated shopping experience may well have been a consequence of the humiliation East Germans felt in the western consumer world in the winter of 1989–1990.

The unification boom in the western borderlands petered out as the 1990s wore on. By the mid-1990s, the most relevant difference in economic terms between the two former borderlands was the subsidy gap created by the termination of borderland aid in the West and the introduction of comparable state support in the East. In 1996, the subsidy gap had reached its full extent. Combining the various financial tools of regional aid, an eligible large company in the Thuringian Eichsfeld (East) could theoretically claim incentives up to 35 percent of its investment, a small or midsized company even up to 50 percent. Companies in neighboring Duderstadt (West), by contrast, could claim only 18 percent if they were large and 28 percent if they were small or midsized.[144] Some businesses therefore followed the money and moved their operations a few miles farther east into the zone with higher subsidies. Since the distance of such moves was often small, these companies did not run the risk of forfeiting established clients, an aspect of particular importance to skilled crafts entrepreneurs. Duderstadt lost seven companies with 120 jobs to neighboring Thuringia; Helmstedt lost five businesses and some 250 jobs in similar fashion to Saxony-Anhalt.[145] As painful as these losses were, however, the companies willing to relocate for subsidy's sake were likely those that had arrived in the western borderlands for that very reason in the first place. With company headquarters outside of the borderlands, they provided low-skilled jobs like mechanical assembling and were not tied to specific locational requisites, hence their mobility.[146] These companies were easily sucked into the globalizing trends of the 1990s and did not think locally or even regionally about their location decisions. With the Iron Curtain gone, producing in Eastern Europe became a distinct possibility. Both Duderstadt and Helmstedt were actually hurt more by relocations to Eastern Europe than by local moves across the former demarcation line.[147]

Another common phenomenon along the former border was the founding of branch offices of western companies on the eastern side, which provided indirect access to subsidies while extending the market reach. Such expansions, however, could take the form of simply building a warehouse.[148] By the mid-1990s, especially small and midsized companies in skilled crafts and construction felt the pinch from competition with the East, where lower wages allowed for lower bids. Losing a bid to a recently relocated "local" company was considered especially frustrating.[149] These various processes, different as they were for specific sectors, led to a rapid, albeit somewhat asymmetric integration of the borderlands: western companies "diffused" into the eastern borderlands, East Germans commuted into the western borderlands for work, and some West Germans moved into the eastern borderlands for cheaper housing.[150]

Spatially speaking, the fall of the Iron Curtain did indeed move the borderlands into the center of Germany again. In fact, the geographic center of unified Germany lies somewhere near Bad Hersfeld in Hesse. In 1999, Amazon built its then-largest European distribution center there, a decision the company would obviously not have made had the nearby border endured.[151] However, many hopes and aspirations held by local and state politicians tied to the spatial shift did not materialize. Since 2000, the western borderlands have experienced growth rates below the average in the old Federal Republic. Between 1999 and 2009, only seven of the former thirty border counties enjoyed increased employment; Upper Franconia and the Harz region in particular were lagging.[152]

As the unification boom abated, the old economic heterogeneity of the border regions once again came to the fore. Press reports about the former borderlands, often triggered by a unification-related anniversary, reflected this heterogeneity. Articles vacillated between alarmist reports about decline, on the one hand, and stories of entrepreneurial success in the "new center," on the other.[153] Some made a point of arguing that any recovery east of the former demarcation line was achieved at the expense of the former Zonenrand, and they decried the Aufbau Ost–related incentives as equivalent to a new "subsidy border" (Fördergrenze)—without acknowledging, of course, that borderland aid had once created a similar "subsidy border" within the old Federal Republic.[154] In its quest to find out how the former border regions were faring, the press coverage could only be contradictory because these regions themselves had always been so. As borderland aid faded away, it became increasingly obvious that the spatial unit once called the "zonal borderland" had been an artificial region. Today Lübeck is on the Baltic again and Hof in Franconia.

Conclusion: Justifying Subsidies

The various strategies of borderland advocates to obtain and retain a substantial aid program revealed them as lobbyists for their regions; borderland aid at times seemed a West German version of pork-barrel politics. Trying to secure support for their regions and defending the level of such support was, however, a perfectly rational approach for local businessmen, trade and industry representatives, as well as elected officials; not creating or going after these opportunities would have made for poor regional politics.[155] Overall their efforts were successful. Borderland representatives managed to institutionalize their claim on the state and fend off undue scrutiny. This was no small feat given that the borderlands were by no means the only "needy" regions in West Germany, especially as the former engines of reconstruction—coal and steel—began to sputter and skid into a seemingly perpetual structural crisis in the 1970s.

In their quest for a substantial aid program, borderland advocates benefited from overlapping interests with spatial planners who, for their part, reached an influential position as policy experts during the 1950s and especially in the 1960s. Their guiding principle of ensuring comparable living conditions across the country had an obvious appeal to regions that feared staying or falling behind. Yet neither the role nor the principles of spatial planners remained static. The oil price shock of 1973 checked much of the planning optimism of the late 1960s. With the local government reform of the 1970s, planning experts were confronted with larger and more confident municipalities, undermining any remaining attitudes that the spatial organization of the country could be effected at the drawing board. The environmental movement of the 1970s and 1980s led to an "ecologization" of spatial planning during the 1980s, indicating that the profession had to make an effort to maintain its relevance. The new guiding principles, enshrined in the Federal Spatial Order Law of July 1989, now placed the free development of the individual, the protection of natural resources, and the open-ended use of spaces alongside the established goal of creating comparable living conditions.[156] Another profound challenge occurred in 2004 when Federal President Horst Köhler (CDU) stated in an interview that differences in living conditions had to be accepted, prompting spatial planners' renewed engagement with the concept.[157] Köhler's words sparked opposition from governors of states in the former East Germany who quite rightly felt he had addressed them, although his musings equally affected former borderland counties like Lüchow-Dannenberg, Werra-Meissner in northern Hesse, and Rhön-Grabfeld in Lower Franconia.[158] For some parts of the former borderlands as, indeed, for rural regions more generally, this debate may prove consequential in the long run, since it elicits the normative question of whether sparsely populated regions should maintain an infrastructure of schools, hospitals, and public pools that is comparable to those of more densely populated areas.[159] In response to demographic change and increasing debt, some municipalities have entertained plans to merge in order to co-fund their infrastructure.[160] This discussion affects some former border regions not because they were borderlands but because they are rural. It serves as a reminder that economic and demographic developments in the borderlands were never an exclusive function of a more or less closed border but that they experienced larger structural trends, such as the decline of agriculture, that had nothing to do with the Iron Curtain.

From its beginnings in the early 1950s, the "zonal borderland aid" program had a self-serving ring to it. The tightening demarcation line surely *did* have economic and infrastructural consequences for the western border counties, but it had a much greater impact on the eastern side of the Iron Curtain. To argue, as the federal minister for transportation had done in 1955, that reconstruction in the borderlands would create jobs for *East* Germans at the time of (eventual) unification was therefore to add insult to injury.[161] Officials like him had justified borderland aid over the years with the dual argument that the program was conceived to compensate the local economies and municipalities for disadvantages caused by partition and that the economy and infrastructure in these regions needed to "shine" eastward across the border and stand at the ready for unification. Even if one considers these comments to be aspirational goals that could neither be measured nor reached, the fact remains that even contemporaries struggled to construct a tenable link between specific aid measures and these goals. The criticism of the European Commission targeted precisely this missing link. However untenable in practice, the justifications for *Zonenrandförderung* from the early 1950s nonetheless remained in active use as political arguments and were deployed, and therefore regularly reaffirmed, whenever borderland aid came under fire. Yet if the claim that borderland aid was furthering the goal of unification was already questionable at its inception, then it could only grow weaker as West German society as a whole settled into the reality of living in a divided country. In autumn of 1964, fully 42 percent of West Germans asserted that they had grown used to partition; in 1967, the figure rose to 61 percent. This was the time when West Germans thought that Germany was doing better than ever before. This was also the time when West Germans began to say "Germany" and mean the Federal Republic.[162] Aside from its beneficiaries, borderland aid had no supporters left by the 1980s because its advocates continually justified it with arguments from the 1950s, casting the region as a relic of the early Cold War.

But how exactly did West Germans became accustomed to partition? Amid the general stabilization of both German states and the coming-of-age of a generation born into the divided country, a quirky cultural practice relating to the inter-German border had a share in defining partition as the new normal. As the next chapter shows, tourism to the Iron Curtain provided West Germans with the opportunity to disavow the competing ideology and affirm their own circumstances, thus inscribing the dividing line onto their mental maps as a postwar fact.

3

"Greetings from the Zonal Border"

TOURISM TO THE IRON CURTAIN

WHEN AN ASSIGNMENT took the writer Rolf Schroers to the border in northern Hesse in 1962, he thought he felt enmity emanating from the fence. Looking across, he thought that on the other side lay a place where "hostages live in enemy hands." When he conversed with locals, he found them guarded, subdued, and resigned to the presence of the border. What a surprise when into the "gloom of this place" a group of Latin American visitors traipsed spryly toward the demarcation line and broke off pieces of rusty barbed wire from the old fence to take home as souvenirs. Schroers had stumbled upon border tourism. "That, too, is the border," he thought. "A sight like the Eiffel Tower in Paris, the Tower of London, the Acropolis in Athens, the ruins of Hiroshima, or the cathedral in Cologne."[1] The tensions of the early Cold War brought about a peculiar kind of battlefield tourism in which the war's principal frontline, the Iron Curtain, was the main attraction.

Border tourism started at the grass roots. People simply went to see the site that played a key role in early Cold War politics and hence featured often in the news media. Ever since Winston Churchill's famous speech in Fulton, Missouri, in 1946, the term "Iron Curtain" had come to symbolize the partition of Europe into East and West and, significant for this chapter, structured expectations of how the divide actually looked.[2] By the mid-1950s, border tourism was in full swing. Especially on Sundays, crowds jostled toward select spots and overwhelmed the western customs officials who tried to guide them.[3] A local observer felt that the border near Lübeck had turned into a "fairground for travel parties."[4] The activity soon grew into a sizable phenomenon: in 1965, some 1.65 million people came to see the border; in 1978, the number had reached 1.84 million.[5] Yet because these visitors were dispersed across the entire length of the Iron Curtain and over the course of the year, they were not necessarily perceived as descending upon the border en masse. Indeed, East and West German border guards regularly commented on the seasonal fluctuations in the stream of visitors. The trips peaked during the summer months, particularly on June 17, when West Germans commemorated the GDR workers' uprising of 1953.

Border tourism was made up of many actors: West German and foreign tourists came to see the border. Local communities hosted them, with varying degrees of interaction between the visitors and the visited. Western border guards and customs officials turned into tour guides as they tried to ensure the visitors' safety at a site that was notorious for violence. Federal and state agencies provided the funds that enabled the tourism infrastructure—from guidebooks to lookout towers—to expand during the 1960s. Elected officials at the local, state, and federal levels tied hopes for economic development to the influx of visitors. And representatives of the East German border regime sought to undercut this activity, which they perceived as a large-scale provocation orchestrated by the West German government. Border tourism, then, was a complex field of social and political interaction in which each party sought to shape the visits, define the meaning of trips, and harness them to its own advantage.

Visits to the border unfolded along the entire German Iron Curtain and took various forms. Devoted to national traditions of hiking, a teacher from Eutin near Lübeck, sought to turn the "borderlands into hiking lands" by developing a trail from Lübeck to Passau.[6] Some communities built such trails to acquaint visitors with the local incarnation of the Iron Curtain; others erected lookout platforms and towers.[7] Bus operators drove travel parties to select spots along the border, then took them on to local inns and cafes. After 1990, a hotelier from the border triangle formed by Hesse, Bavaria, and Thuringia recalled that "busloads of people came from Holland, from the Ruhr area and peeked over the German–German border."[8] In the 1970s, when the Border Commission tackled the problem of the disputed course of the border along the Elbe River, mariners from Hitzacker (West) began to offer cruises on the Elbe for the sole purpose of showing passengers the border. At peak times, their boats made five trips a day. The tourists "all wanted to see the border and the [eastern] patrol boats," reported one mariner. "If one of those drove by, everyone suddenly ran to one side of the boat. You needed to be careful that the ship didn't capsize."[9] Yet this kind of travel triggered a certain unease among border-land residents and other contemporaries because the border did, after all, represent a national tragedy. The above-cited hotelier therefore referred to the phenomenon as *Gruseltourismus*—tourism that gives you the creeps—pointing to one of several tensions that this chapter seeks to address: tensions between the visitors and the visited, between expectations about the site and its actual appearance, between local and federal officials, between West and East.

As the term "creepy tourism" suggests, the attraction of the inter-German border did not consist merely in its prominence as the Iron Curtain in Cold War politics; it was also a site of danger, death, and sorrow. During the unsettled postwar years, the demarcation line acquired a reputation as a place of violence and insecurity, of escapes, kidnappings, and shootings that made the headlines.[10] Border visitors themselves frequently stepped into risky situations through ignorance, carelessness, or bravado and were arrested or seriously injured as a result. The very danger of the border and its perception as a place that generated grief and invited mourning formed part of the attraction of an Iron Curtain visit. Aspects of these visits therefore fall conceptually into the category of "dark tourism," defined in its earliest analysis as the "consumption of real or commodified death and disaster sites."[11] Much of the dark tourism literature, however, focuses on sites that used to be related to death and danger at some point in the past, some of which were purposefully developed for tourist consumption.[12] The inter-German border, by contrast, became such a destination while still in active use, a feature it shares with the Demilitarized Zone (DMZ) between North and South Korea.[13] Yet while tourism to the inter-German border clearly contained dark elements, it did more than generate a morbid chill. It allowed visitors to make sense of world politics through local activity. It confronted western travelers with a political, social, and economic order that was an alternative to their own, providing them not only with a place to indulge in the anti-Communism so typical of the 1950s and 1960s but also to embrace their own half of Germany as the superior one. Sightseeing at the border had tangible political benefits as well: carting foreign dignitaries to the Iron Curtain allowed the West German government to bolster its credentials as a reliable partner in the western alliance. Besides, in its most banal incarnation, border travel was simply an easily available activity in rural areas short on tourist attractions.

Sightseeing at political borders is a well-known phenomenon within tourism studies. Border poles painted with national colors, fences, and

welcome and warning signs frequently form the backdrop for tourist photography. Such markers, usually intended to delimit state territory and jurisdiction, can also be erected with tourism in mind, as in the case of the
Southernmost Point Buoy in Key West or the Four Corners Monument,
where the states of Arizona, Colorado, New Mexico, and Utah meet. As
with famous monuments and sites, the geographical location of border
markers is unmistakable; tourists are thus able to "collect places" in the
form of snapshots, postcards, and souvenirs.[14] The inter-German border
was certainly not the only part of the Iron Curtain to attract onlookers.
The Berlin Wall became a fixture in West Berlin tourism, and the city as
such, despite its complicated status, became a destination for state visits
from 1956 onward.[15] Tourists also flocked to the border between Finland
and the Soviet Union to see part of the Iron Curtain and to pay homage
to a mythical Karelian landscape imagined as the cradle of the Finnish
nation-state.[16] After the fall of the Wall, sites associated with the former
Iron Curtain continued to attract tourists, this time as Cold War heritage
destinations.[17] In some cases, sightseeing simply relied on the pre-1989
border tourism infrastructure like the information centers that were re-
vamped as museums, but it also developed new forms, such as the much-
criticized photo ops with actors wearing the uniforms of border guards
at Checkpoint Charlie in Berlin and the re-enactment of the "Cold War
border experience" on the Finnish–Russian border.[18]

This chapter explores the phenomenon of tourism to the inter-German
border in its various manifestations as sightseeing, state-sponsored political education, and borderland travel. The emergence of a tourist infrastructure, regardless of how haphazardly it came about, created an uneasy
mix of propaganda, information, consumption, leisure, and politics.

The Infrastructure of Border Tourism, or How to View the Border

A tourist exploring the inter-German border around 1970 encountered a
well-established infrastructure devised to enhance the visit, ensure the
visitor's safety, and present the border in a way that emphasized its un-
just character. Depending on where visitors approached the sight, they
might park their car in a lot especially provided for border trips, enter a
viewing platform, pick up fliers and brochures, visit an exhibition about
the fortifications, query a border guard about his duties, snap pictures

with border warning signs in the background, and mail a postcard of the scene back home.

This section analyzes the role of postcards, lookout points, and travel guides in border tourism, typical elements of tourism that share a focus on *viewing* and underscore that a visit to the border was indeed tourism. What visitors saw at the border depended on their motivation for making the trip, on their preconceived notions about the Iron Curtain, and on the presentation of the sight. Postcards, lookouts, and guidebooks were relevant for the encounter but never exclusively shaped the experience, since border visits remained embedded in the political discourses of the day. Yet thanks to their confluence over time, postcards, lookouts, and travel guides helped standardize the visits and indicated what to look for and how to regard it. They preconfigured tourist expectations and established a hierarchy of sights along the border by advertising or depicting some spots in preference to others. When visitors came to see for themselves where Germany and Europe were divided, they found a sight that had been prepared in multiple ways for their viewing and that they had likely encountered in some form even before arriving.

The picture postcard gained currency as a tourist device in the late nineteenth century and became a popular medium closely tied to modernity and reflective of the rise of tourism beyond the Grand Tour.[19] Its visual composition was highly constructed, and retouching, photomontage, and other techniques created a certain hyper-reality, especially if elements were either added to or removed from the scene. To anchor such idealized motifs geographically, postcards could include text that identified the location of the depicted site. The serial production of postcards and their visual message eventually generated what Sándor Békési calls the "iconic freezing" of a motif. In combination with other tourist media, postcards standardize a sight to a point where they are often dismissed as kitsch.[20] At the same time, the cards depict the "correct" view of an attraction, which tourists regularly try to reproduce in their snapshots, measuring the original sight against preconceived mental images.[21] Like guidebooks, postcards serve as visual aids that provide orientation, (re)produce recognition of a sight, and help determine "what ought to be seen."[22] Once cards are mailed with a personal message, the tourist turns them into status markers by producing them as evidence of a successful trip and inadvertently further advertising the sight.[23]

Postcards were, in fact, the first indication of a budding interest in the Iron Curtain as a tourist site. The earliest card with an Iron Curtain theme that I could identify dates from 1951. It features an inn at the border crossing in Helmstedt (West) and follows touristic conventions by offering "Greetings from the zonal border."[24] Helmstedt was not just any crossing. The road from Checkpoint Alpha in Helmstedt (Figure 3.1) to Checkpoint Bravo in Dreilinden on the outskirts of Berlin was the shortest transit route to West Berlin and a vital supply route for the city, including the garrisons of the western allies. This route rose to prominence during the Berlin blockade in 1948, and for countless transit travelers or visitors to the GDR, Helmstedt signified either the beginning or the end of an anxiety-ridden journey through East Germany.[25] Because postcards depicting the checkpoint at Helmstedt were frequently mailed during the 1950s and 1960s, the motif was well known and easy to decode as part of the Iron Curtain.[26] Other postcards from the 1950s, however, were not yet equally explicit in their representation of the Iron Curtain.

Although the years leading up to the building of the Berlin Wall in 1961 were pervaded by Cold War fears, the early postcards could not yet visually capture this anxiety or convey the symbolic meaning of the Iron Curtain because its fortifications were not (yet) commensurate with its

FIGURE 3.1. A postcard of the border checkpoint "Alpha" at Helmstedt (West), late 1950s.
© Hans Hartz/DHM

Cold War significance. This is not to say that no images of the border existed; yet unlike government brochures and films in which images appeared with directing text or voiceovers and could be aggregated for effect, picture postcards were more dependent on one or very few meaningful shots.[27] The visual anemia of the early cards is evident in a postcard from the western Harz Mountains that depicts a family on an outing to the demarcation line. They are coming off a sand path and are standing on short grass, looking at weeds about 4 feet high. Within the tall grass, barely visible, are poles that may or may not support barbed wire. The transition between short and tall grass presumably constitutes the line between West and East. The only clue in the photo to the location is a signpost set up by the western Consortium for an Undivided Germany (Kuratorium Unteilbares Deutschland), which advocates for German unity. To rule out any remaining ambiguity about where the family is standing, a printed caption identifies the town as Hohe Geiß at the "zonal border." Without these additions, the card would be visually mute, reduced to a depiction of a family contemplating an overgrown meadow.[28]

Other postcards from the late 1950s might feature a road interrupted by a red and white barrier or a meticulously harrowed security strip, yet still require a caption identifying the location of the scene at the "zonal border." The reference to the "zonal border" justifies the very existence of these cards, which would otherwise be devoid of a sight worth seeing. The dilemma between the desire to convey the political drama of the location and the scarcity of elements with which to do so is well captured by a card with the cutline "View into the Zone" from around 1960 that offers three shots from Bavaria into Thuringia near the town of Blankenstein (East) (Figure 3.2). Although the photos feature barbed wire affixed to concrete poles and what appears to be a GDR propaganda billboard, the dramatic effect is enhanced by graphically inserted wire with menacing barbs that runs across the black background of the card, as well as a font for the caption that would have reminded contemporaries of crime coverage in newsreels. By making barbed wire the dominant element, the card tapped into the most potent visual code associated with the Iron Curtain in western propaganda.[29]

After the GDR ramped up the border fortifications during the 1960s, the postcards of the 1970s and 1980s gained a much larger range of recognizable motifs and were no longer ambiguous about conveying what they pictured. These mass-produced colored cards frequently showed multiple locations at the border, combining four, eight, or even ten photos

FIGURE 3.2. "View into the Zone." A postcard from around 1960, depicting Blankenstein in Thuringia (East), is enhanced with barbed wire.
© Drechsler, Bad Steben

on one card (Figure 3.3). The images predominantly focused on easily recognizable elements of the fortifications, such as observation towers, fences, and GDR border poles, as well as the western barriers and signs that had been erected to prevent tourists from accidentally strolling across the demarcation line. The border postcards were either mailed or kept as souvenirs. Due to their serial production and the repetition of motifs, the cards echoed and reinforced the visual arsenal relating to the inter-German border and helped produce the "iconic freezing" of some motifs that came to stand for the border as a whole.

Border viewing was also shaped by lookout platforms and towers. Seeking out vistas and consuming landscapes from natural elevations like mountains or from constructed viewing points such as lookouts had become a staple of the traveler's experience since at least the late eighteenth century. At lookout towers, the scenery was often presented in a structured, panoramic view through viewing maps on the railing of the lookout balcony. The tourist gaze was thus guided toward landmarks that visitors might know from the ground, offering them a new perspective on familiar objects but also a sense of visual control as the landscape divulged

FIGURE 3.3. Mass-produced colored postcards from the 1970s and 1980s emphasized blocked roads and dead ends.

© Harry Wieber, Flieden

its geological structure unintelligible from the ground.[30] The lookout towers along the inter-German border followed nineteenth-century conventions in that they were erected at locations that promised a sublime view of the landscape. However, what distinguished these towers from constructions that exclusively overlooked romantic vistas was that some of them were also conceived as monuments (*Mahnmale*) designed to mourn partition. Among these were towers like *Thüringerwarte* in Lauenstein (1963), *Bayernturm* in Zimmerau (1966), and the "Monument to German Division" in Bodesruh near Kleinensee (1961–1964).[31] Tellingly, all were built at a time when the SED regime massively expanded the fortifications, thus inadvertently giving purpose to these towers by providing *something to see*.

If viewing from traditional towers offered some sense of visual control of the scenery, this sentiment constituted the very goal of the lookouts along the border. They were built for the explicit purpose of exhibiting the GDR border fortifications and placing them at the center of the panoramic view. The East German Stasi fully understood this intention when its agents reported that the windows of the Lauenstein tower provided "visual sectors" (*Blicksektoren*) that were trained on the fortifications and allowed a view some 15 kilometers deep into GDR territory.[32] As will be discussed in more detail later, the growing number of tourists along the border was a major provocation for East German authorities and led to the introduction of various measures to obstruct the view: the less the western visitor could see, the better. The aerial view from a tower on the western side, however, foiled any such efforts. It demystified the fortifications by allowing the visitor to fully take in their intricacies, seeing beyond the impenetrable wire mesh of the metal fences and discerning the deeply layered structure of the Iron Curtain. What was forbidden knowledge for East Germans was openly displayed on the western side. The extent to which these lookouts were implicated in the mission to expose the border fortifications became amply clear after 1990 when, having accomplished their duty, some lookouts were demolished.[33]

The lookouts on the Iron Curtain itinerary were further popularized by border travel guides. The first of these guides, published in 1964 by the Ministry for Expellees and Refugees in Lower Saxony, introduced the state as an emerging player in border tourism. The Ministry printed this initial guide not to entice more visitors to the area but in reaction to existing public demand, underscoring again that border tourism started out as a grassroots phenomenon. The press considered the guide a touristic travel book, referring to it as a "Baedeker's [guide] to the zonal border."[34] By referencing the most renowned German travel guide, the nickname conferred the Baedeker's stamp of reliability on these new booklets.[35] Their foremost function was to direct tourists to spots along the border that were considered worth a visit and to keep them out of trouble once they were there. Since tourists and onlookers traditionally travel in order to see *something*, the guides highlighted locations where the Cold War frontline appeared most gripping and ruthless. The goal was to depict the border as an "unnatural" divide. Featured locations thus included Zicherie (West) and Böckwitz (East) near Gifhorn in Lower Saxony, where a wall separated two villages with close historical ties.[36] A similar wall, erected in 1964, divided the tiny village of Mödlareuth and its fifty inhabitants, separating farms from their fields and, at times, even cattle from their barns.[37] The border could be even more disruptive, running right through a house, as in the case of the printing shop of the Hossfeld family in Philippsthal on the Werra. After hauling the machines into the western part of the building to prevent confiscation in 1951, the family was no longer allowed to enter the eastern part of the house. The idea of a divided house with a neatly renovated western half that contrasted sharply with a dilapidated eastern half—an image that corresponded well with West German propaganda about material scarcity under socialism—was too inviting to pass up: "This side of the building," a news article reported, "appears well-kept; here people live and work. The other side breathes decay and destruction." The Hossfeld printing shop thus featured regularly in border guides.[38]

Finally, the brochures contained practical tips about where to stay in the vicinity and how to contact the local customs or border guard (BGS) office to request expert guidance at the demarcation line. Customs officials and border guards had been engaged in visitor security ever since onlookers had started to flock to the demarcation line. The travel guides, however, institutionalized the option to book a uniformed official as a tour guide.[39] One of the key tasks of the border guards, however, was still to prevent tourists from causing incidents at the demarcation line.

The Dangers of Border Visits

Visiting the border could be dangerous. Border tourists, behaving either carelessly or recklessly, were regularly arrested and even shot by East German border guards for stepping over the demarcation line and infringing on GDR territory. It was, in fact, the mental image of the border among visitors that contributed to the hazard. Nurtured by government publications and West German media, not least by its very name, the casual visitor expected to see an Iron Curtain—in the literal sense. A reporter who came upon a tourist in Schnackenburg-on-Elbe in 1964 surprised her with the news that the GDR lay right across the river. "Why," she remarked, "there is no iron curtain!" What did she think such a curtain would look like? the reporter asked. She clearly expected "a fence, or a wall and the mine strip."[40] Ignorance about the exact location of the demarcation line stood at the center of numerous incidents involving border tourists. In the early years, the meticulously harrowed 10-meter-strip marked the divide. During successive rounds of securitization after 1961, however, the border's fences, ditches, tripwires, and minefields were moved deeper into GDR territory; the 10-meter strip was abandoned and became overgrown. The first fence visible from the western side was now some 50 or 100 meters away from the demarcation line, always depending on the terrain. Mistaking the fence for the demarcation line, camera-wielding tourists regularly strolled right onto GDR territory, where eastern border troops arrested them. If lucky, they were interrogated at length, kept for a night or two in a Stasi cell, and deported at the nearest checkpoint within forty-eight hours.[41] If they were less lucky, they were shot and at times seriously injured.[42] Such incidents occurred throughout the existence of the Iron Curtain, but they appear to have peaked after the building of the Berlin Wall. Until the mid-1960s, eastern border troops proved particularly trigger-happy toward western onlookers.[43] One travel guide was therefore explicit in its warnings: "The misery of our people," it stated, "is not a stomping ground for ignoramuses."[44]

Yet for some tourists, the danger was part of the thrill of a border visit, and they deliberately invited it. To that end, some stepped across the demarcation line to brag that they had been in the GDR, shouted curses and obscenities at GDR border guards to provoke a reaction, or threw trash and rocks across the border. Others stole from the border poles the metal plates bearing the GDR's hammer and sickle emblem, wanting them either as a political statement or as a souvenir.[45] Youths frequently dared each other to engage in such activities just for the fun of it.[46] This disorderly behavior defied the rules of both eastern *and* western authorities. Eastern guards perceived it as part of a larger West German strategy to mock East German sovereignty, whereas western guards feared for visitors' security and even pressed criminal charges in response to property damage and theft of GDR border poles.[47] The consequences, however, could be dire, as three high-schoolers found out near Witzenhausen in northern Hesse in April 1964. Thinking it a good idea to walk directly along the double fence, they were targeted by fifteen shots. The most heavily injured boy lost an arm as a result.[48]

In order to protect the life and limb of the visitors, West German border authorities started marking the demarcation line to make it visible on the ground. At high-traffic places, the BGS erected wooden or metal barriers. The western troops dotted the landscape with poles and warning signs to keep visitors out of trouble. Yet even well-intentioned railings were a sensitive issue in Cold War politics. To prepare for the "summer season" in 1956, for example, customs officials in Lübeck set up a wire fence at a popular spot to hold back the expected crowds on the western side. They were promptly criticized for sending the wrong political message in view of ongoing demands for reunification. Five years later, the installation of a chain on the divided Priwall Beach near Lübeck prompted similar complaints; the customs office had to defend its actions by arguing that the chain cable did not undermine demands to "open the Gate."[49] Over the years, the BGS and customs officials produced a veritable forest of signage along the inter-German border that changed the appearance of the border for western tourists and frequently dominated their snapshots. Unwittingly, then, border visitors themselves had triggered the changing appearance of the sight they had come to see.

Navigating the border remained tricky not only because it meandered arbitrarily through the landscape but also because the exact location of the demarcation line remained contested in some places. Territorial exchanges in the immediate postwar period, lack of alignment with old administrative borders, and local bickering about land ownership left parts of the border in dispute.[50] At such spots, tourists might well have thought they were still on the western side, but if eastern border guards disagreed, the interlopers inadvertently produced another incident. To eliminate sources of ongoing political friction, in 1972 as part of the Basic Treaty both German states agreed to form a border commission. Such commissions were an established instrument of high politics to create consensus about the location of political borders, especially when natural resources were disputed.[51] The first task of the German-German Border Commission was to delimit and demarcate the exact course of the border. When it finished in 1978, only the disagreement about the border along the Elbe River remained unresolved.[52] On the whole, however, the Commission had successfully stabilized and pacified the border. This stabilization was part and parcel of *Ostpolitik,* and the pacification consisted in no small part in reducing incidents involving western tourists. However, it was during the Commission's delimitation work that the inter-German border actually became even more deadly. Beginning in 1970, East German border authorities installed antipersonnel splinter mines, proving that pacification on the western side and increasing danger on the eastern side could inhabit the same space and time.

Border Travel as Political Propaganda

Border tourism started at the grass roots, but the activity was eventually harnessed by interest groups and state agencies. State-sponsored and politically motivated tourism to fresh borders was not without precedent in German history and was a common feature of German irredentist and nationalist campaigns in the 1920s and 1930s. The new borders imposed by the Versailles Treaty, which ceded German territory, were the subject of vitriolic protests; the territorial adjustments benefiting Poland and Czechoslovakia proved particularly potent in that regard. Both the

Prussian and Reich governments financed such eastern border tours. In related propaganda materials, state-issued or otherwise, the border was metaphorically depicted in organic terms as a wound, inflicted by external powers, that hurt the body of the nation; politically induced border tourism was constantly rubbing salt into this wound. Other than keeping alive and well the sense of injustice over the loss of Eastern territories after 1919, ready to be tapped in September 1939, the border traffic also aimed to generate income for the economically weak borderlands and foster bonds between interior and borderland dwellers of Germany. By the mid-1930s, "Strength through Joy" (KdF) tours shifted their focus from social integration toward national integration and sent travelers into communities, including borderlands, that had seen virtually no tourists before.[53]

These interwar practices of political border travel were the available template for early visits to the Iron Curtain. The unbridled nationalism of the interwar years, discredited by the recent German past and unacceptable to West Germany's new allies, was supplanted by anti-Communism, which served as the main integrating ideology in the young Federal Republic.[54] The concern that West Germans might actually grow accustomed to partition was most tangible in the work of the Consortium for an Undivided Germany (Kuratorium Unteilbares Deutschland). Founded in 1954 in reaction to the failure of the Berlin conference of foreign ministers to effect German unity, the Consortium sought to be an all-German popular movement that advocated for unification. Its leadership valued German unity over western integration and in so doing contravened Adenauer's political priorities. It thus had to make do without the chancellor's support but predictably attracted a fair number of Adenauer opponents instead.[55] Through its regional and local branches, the Consortium launched numerous activities that are frequently misremembered as having been initiated by the government itself: placing candles in windows at Christmastime in remembrance of the "brothers and sisters" in East Germany; wearing Brandenburg Gate lapel pins with the slogan "Open the Gate!"; setting up Brandenburg Gate replicas in West German cities to show support for West Berlin; or placing Christmas trees along the demarcation line.[56] Mobilizing West Germans to visit the Iron Curtain was central to the Consortium's activities. True to its larger political agenda, the local volunteers of the Consortium framed border visits as demonstrations of German unity and as an expression of unwavering commitment to the Germans on the other side of the fence.

In their search of support in dealing with the many visitors to the demarcation line, local officials found the Consortium more responsive than the state. Because Helmstedt was attracting so many guests from abroad, the county director, Hans Walter Conrady, requested two full-time staff members as early as 1956. His suggestion of turning the unguided border tourism into political education was not yet gaining traction in Hannover or Bonn. He therefore collaborated with the Consortium instead.[57] It was also the Consortium and not a state agency that set up the first border information centers in Zicherie (1960) and Offleben (1961) near Helmstedt.[58] Other communities followed suit and established information booths at town halls, municipal centers, churches, schoolrooms, and the headquarters of the resident border guard regiment. Maintained and curated by dedicated individuals, these centers exhibited regional maps, models of the border fortifications, border guards' uniforms, and, if available, even their weapons. The 1960s exhibitions commonly juxtaposed western freedom with eastern captivity.[59] Lower Saxony, the federal state that shared the longest stretch of border with the GDR (544 kilometers), responded to the local demand in the first half of the 1960s and began to support these initiatives, as well as set up new information centers. The state's involvement was a response to the growing number of visitors who were taxing the time and patience of local officials.[60] By 1978, Lower Saxony supported twenty-seven such centers, Bavaria maintained fifteen, Hesse fourteen, and Schleswig-Holstein ten.[61]

Like the volunteers of the Consortium for an Undivided Germany, federal and state officials seemingly assumed that border travel had a rather linear political effect. "The closer one lives to the Iron Curtain," a reporter for *Neue Zeitung* noted in 1951, "the more its danger serves as [political] stimulation."[62] Seeing the border or living near it, the reasoning went, would shake up West Germans and turn them into politically literate and engaged citizens, ready to defend West Germany's political order against the hostile ideology next door.[63] An analysis of the travel guides that state agencies made available to border visitors confirms this presumed stimulus-response pattern. Although some travel guides advocated nurturing contacts with Germans in the GDR, those published in the 1960s were completely fixated on the fortifications and the logistics of the visit. The political message was straightforward: whoever saw the border, a Bavarian booklet stated, would instantly grasp the "horrible consequences of the Second World War for our people." Being confronted by "a Communist system" (mention of the GDR was carefully avoided) "allows us to appreciate the value of our freedom of movement."[64] The juxtaposition of freedom in the West and captivity in the East was an ongoing theme in these brochures and thus capitalized on one of the main tropes in western Cold War propaganda.[65] The guidebooks also left no doubt about the blame for the current conditions. The GDR was portrayed as the "outpost of Soviet desires for expansion" where "the Communist regime in the unfree part of our fatherland does its utmost to make the separation of Germans from Germans even harder, ever more unrelenting and inhumane."[66]

A border visit was expected to become a transformative experience. A 1964 guide from Hesse assumed the trip would shake visitors out of their "pervasive lethargy," which was probably an unintended acknowledgment that many West Germans had already become quite used to partition. Once travelers saw the border fortifications, sensed the binoculars of GDR border troops following each of their movements, and realized that "German people [on the other side] put their life on the line by simply waving at us [. . .] the visit would cease to be a leisurely getaway."[67] A guide from Lower Saxony published two years later presumed that by seeing minefields and barbed wire, visitors would find the courage to fight "injustice and violence" in favor of "justice and freedom." To do so was the "great national task" that the brochure, and by extension the border trip, sought to serve.[68] Not surprisingly, such trips were considered particularly beneficial for high school students. Even in the late 1970s, the Bavarian minister of the interior still thought that an encounter with the border fortifications would inoculate them against "Communist infiltration."[69]

Government publications not only addressed domestic audiences but were also printed in various foreign languages in anticipation of tourists.[70] In fact, the Adenauer administration explicitly enlisted the border as a foreign policy asset and initiated a border program for foreign guests coordinated by the Auswärtiges Amt in Bonn. Acquainting audiences from abroad with the inter-German border allowed the West German government to boost its anti-Communist credentials and present itself as a reliable partner in the western alliance. By seizing the opportunity to warn the western world about the "new totalitarianism" across the Iron Curtain, this strategy also conveniently de-emphasized the recent Nazi dictatorship. By the late 1950s, a routine for such border visits was well established: in cooperation with the state authorities in Kiel, Hannover, Wiesbaden, and Munich, the Auswärtiges Amt tailored itineraries for travel parties ranging from British ladies' clubs, to foreign correspondents, military units, diplomats, and heads of state.[71] A West German diplomat would accompany the foreign dignitaries and report their reactions back to the Auswärtiges Amt. The arrangement usually proved highly satisfactory. The visitors confirmed that they had never seen such an "inhumane demarcation line";[72] a French member of parliament declared in Helmstedt that he had now seen "a new Germany";[73] and Latin American bishops experienced a "confrontation with militant atheism."[74]

On at least one occasion, the choreography of such a trip combined a visit to a concentration camp with a stop at the border. In November 1959, former Belgian resistance fighters asked to visit Bergen-Belsen and continue on to see the border. The request resonated with the established visual language about the border that was dominated by barbed wire and implied prison or concentration camp imagery.[75] Linking Belsen with Helmstedt moved the visitors in time and space from the recent German past into the West German present. The accompanying diplomat was keenly aware of this transmutation. "The visit to the memorial at the former concentration camp Bergen-Belsen on a foggy and dim November day," he wrote in his report, "provided a transition for the visit to the border with its barbed wire and watch towers that could not have been more impressive. Time and again the participants declared that they believed themselves at the fence of a gigantic concentration camp."[76] By implying that East Germany amounted to a vast concentration camp, observers depicted the GDR as another manifestation of totalitarianism. This theme continued as the Belgian *résistants* moved on to West Berlin, which Mayor Willy Brandt called "a city of resistance." Deeply impressed by how Berlin residents braved their circumstances, the spokesman of the group, Hubert Halin,[77] declared that Berlin "displays the same spirit of resistance against totalitarianism that had animated [us]" against the Nazis.[78] If former resistance fighters against German military occupation granted the holy status of *résistance* to their former occupiers, the Auswärtiges Amt could safely consider the trip a success.

Yet while the blatant anti-Communism of border visits went uncontested in the late 1950s and after the building of the Berlin Wall, the consensus on what the trips should achieve began to crumble by the mid-1960s. The borderland commissar of Hesse, Heinz Kreutzmann, reported after a fact-finding trip in 1965 that Lower Saxony had invested in information centers not only to unburden local officials but also because "unqualified people had frequently taken over the supervision of the ever growing number of zonal border visitors." The border protection forces in particular, the BGS, were said to use the audiences for recruitment pitches and to convey veritable "Cold War propaganda," which presumably amounted to the pointed anti-Communism cultivated around 1960. The goal in Lower Saxony was therefore to provide "judicious" (*vernünftig*) information focused not exclusively on the "barbed-wire situation" but also on the consequences of partition for the western borderlands.[79] Attention was thus redirected from the fellow Germans in the GDR to the West Germans borderland dwellers, a focus that grew stronger during the 1960s. When Kreutzmann requested federal funding in 1968 to set up information centers in Hesse as well, the emphasis had all but shifted to bringing visitors to the borderlands lest its residents felt forgotten.[80] Kreutzmann's request also followed the Lower Saxon model in that he sought to allow his state government to exert "certain influences on the work of these information centers."[81]

The gradual and uneven departure from crude anti-Communism in border travel over the course of the 1960s mirrored the transformation of West German politics from Adenauer's confrontational stance toward the GDR to Brandt's brand of *Ostpolitik*. As the political parameters shifted, border travel became the target of bickering along party-political lines. The head of the Parliamentary Commission on Inter-German Relations, Olaf von Wrangel (CDU), claimed in 1974 that the trips were instrumentalized "to propagate the politics of the current [SPD] administration in a one-sided fashion."[82] Conversely, the Social Democratic head of the Agency for Political Education in Hesse accused the CDU-led states of Lower Saxony and Bavaria of using border visits to undermine the politics of the SPD-led federal government.[83] In the meantime, educators at the information centers warned that border trips were degenerating into "state-funded outings (*Vereinsausflüge*) replete with straw hat and beer can." Indeed, by 1971 the VW production plant in Wolfsburg proved a greater tourist draw than the nearby border.[84] There were further indications that the framing of border visits as a desire for German unity had run its course. The founder of the information center at Offleben, the dedicated Waltraud Buchholz, withdrew in 1971, ushering in the center's decline. Soon thereafter, Helmstedt County no longer wanted to bear the maintenance costs, the janitor was let go, and the exhibit was frequently vandalized. It was closed in 1976.[85]

Within less than two decades, then, border travel had moved away from the original impetus of the Consortium for an Undivided Germany of harnessing the grassroots interest in the Iron Curtain in order to protest partition and demand unification. As the glue of anti-Communism gradually lost its adhesive power, the accusatory rhetoric of government brochures and travel guides abated as well. Guides from the 1980s still chronicled the expansion of the fortifications but refrained from attacks on the GDR and even contained information about towns on the other side of the fence, an aspect absent from earlier guidebooks.[86] One brochure from 1987 expressed the desire to uphold a rudimentary sense of the cultural "unity of the German nation," yet without demanding territorial unification. It even contained fifty pages about the "cities and landscapes along the inter-German border" on both sides, thereby essentially erasing the border, at least for armchair travelers. But since there was no information about cross-border travel *into* the GDR, these pages ultimately directed the traveler into the *western* borderlands and the "popular vacation landscapes" there.[87] The change in overall tone and approach did not mean, however, that people no longer went to see the border; it remained a popular sightseeing destination until its fall. In fact, throughout the 1980s during the tenure of Governor Ernst Albrecht (CDU), Lower Saxony invested significantly in restoring and refurbishing its border infrastructure. It also opened ten new information centers, the last one in Bad Bodenteich near Uelzen in 1988.[88] However, border visits and their handling by state agencies had become habitual and formulaic, the border itself a fixture in the mental and physical landscape. Lower Saxony had barely concluded setting up the ten new visitor centers when a ministry official recommended closing them again for lack of visitors.[89]

The Visitors and the Visited

The steady stream of visitors did not mean that border communities embraced this kind of tourism unambiguously. In fact, sightseeing at the border led to certain tensions between the visitors and the visited. For the visited, the border was an everyday reality, whereas the visitors approached it with sentiments ranging from fear, curiosity, solemnity, and mischief to a certain casualness. These attitudes, in turn, could offend locals, who perceived in them a sense of ignorance about their living conditions. Whereas sightseers arrived with preconceived notions of the Iron Curtain and expected to have them confirmed, residents expected a degree of propriety during the guests' stay in their communities. Each side wanted to shape the border visits, and indeed over the years a distinct script emerged according to which these trips unfolded. The script reflected how borderland residents wanted visitors to behave and what, in turn, the visitors sought to experience. By the mid-1960s, when the tourist infrastructure was well in place, the script also reflected the hand of the state. Though visitors came to "see for themselves," they actually encountered a sight that was very deliberately staged for them. Some travelers to the border, especially organized groups of expellees and refugees, contributed to the sight's presentation by embellishing the demarcation line with interpretative signs and structures.

As border tourism got under way in the 1950s, local officials, state representatives, and the federal Ministry of All-German Affairs frequently objected to the way these unguided visits were conducted. Officials expected border visitors to take into account that East Germans on the other side of the "attraction" were oppressed and that fellow West Germans were living on the frontlines of the Cold War. The very term "tourism" did not sit well with the Ministry, for it was increasingly associated with crowded Mediterranean beaches and thus implied leisure and consumption. The Ministry preferred to see trips to the border framed as educational travel.[90] The director (*Landrat*) of Fulda County denounced "coffee trips to the zonal border with an ensuing dance event" as being in bad taste; companies advertising such border trips, including the federal railway (*Bundesbahn*), were cited for their lack of political tact.[91] Locals officials like the director of Helmstedt County, Hans Walter Conrady, felt a sense of political obligation that came with living on the frontline of the Cold War, combined with the desire not to be forgotten. He therefore tirelessly endured busloads of visitors and welcomed foreign dignitaries.[92] Others accepted the obligation as well, or could not escape it, but rejected any kind of commercialization of their border location. The mayor of the divided village Zicherie reported in the mid-1980s that he had always insisted that "the border would not be turned into a fairground. [. . .] We prevented the arrival of postcard racks and the running of hot dog stands. We want that just as little as the selling of [pieces of] barbed wire."[93] Clearly, neither sensationalism, nor commercialization, nor a too obvious intermingling of the trip with leisure and "fun" was welcome.

Yet of course such demands had developed because all of the above did in fact occur. Already in the late 1950s, a newspaper from Lübeck questioned the appropriateness of a campground next to the demarcation line. Beneath a photo of a VW Beetle, a symbol of newfound prosperity, the paper mused about "camping next to barbed wire. One gazes across but creates an otherwise cozy (*gemütlich*) environment with a car, chairs, table, with coffee and cake." The paper found the leisurely Sunday outing to the border equally offensive. Under the photo of two women primly dressed in petticoats, it wrote: "A snapshot for the family album. Mom takes the pic. The watchtower forms the backdrop—interesting setting. And when it gets dark, everyone drives home again."[94] The tourists further alienated locals by engaging in behavior that was quintessentially "touristy," like carving their initials into the wooden barriers that had been erected to keep them at a safe distance from the demarcation line.[95]

The commercialization of border tourism unfolded as well, albeit on a rather modest and episodic scale. In August 1969, for example, a family of nine escaped East Germany near Helmstedt. The tabloid *Bild* ran a series on the Oborny family that drew crowds to the location of their escape over the ensuing weeks, to which enterprising Helmstedters responded with sausage stands and beer carts.[96] In its marketing materials, a local inn touted its "quiet location" (*ruhige Lage*) and the border view from its guest rooms. Such inns also typically sold border postcards, which were, as we have seen, widely available.[97] Knick-knacks with border motifs, on the other hand, remained rare.[98] The Latin American visitors observed by Ralf Schroers, as described at the opening of this chapter, had broken off pieces of barbed wire precisely because no other mementos were readily available. Only a few typical souvenirs made it into circulation. The border museum in Helmstedt displays an ashtray and a demitasse from the 1950s that feature the notorious checkpoint in town. In Duderstadt, tourists could buy stickers and T-shirts sporting a pun that turned the letters *DDR* into *DuDeRstadt*.[99] On the whole, however, the rarity of such items indicates that locals like the mayor of Zicherie managed to enforce a kind of respect with regard to residents' situation and to prevent an uneasy commingling of overt consumption and the tragedy of the border.

Yet what appears to have bothered borderland dwellers the most were visitors who arrived to confirm their hinterland stereotypes about the Iron Curtain and disturbed the community by behaving in unacceptable ways. Whereas locals had to endure the border's depressing presence on a daily basis, tourists mostly knew it from media representations and expected it to live up to its reputation as a Cold War hotspot. However, while border visits could indeed become dangerous if tourists violated the demarcation line, the trips more typically remained perfectly unspectacular. Embedded mainly in rural settings, the inter-German border featured few spots that oozed drama, such as divided houses or villages. A group of students from Denmark who came to see the border near Lübeck in May 1961 ended up disappointed. "No shootout, no incidents—for the [Danish visitors] this is all rather boring. They crawl back into the leather seats of their bus."[100] In view of such lack of action, some visitors decided to enhance the border experience. A team of American photo journalists, for instance, tried to trigger some land mines on the eastern side by throwing rocks across the border in order to capture some "realistic" images.[101] The files of the East German border units are replete with reports of attempts by West Germans to damage the border fortifications, trigger mines, steal border poles, and shout insults at border guards.[102] Not all of these activities involved visitors; inebriated locals did their share. But by 1969 a western border guard had grown jaded about "these leisure Germans, border gapers, and souvenir hunters who steal the GDR emblem off the black-red-golden border poles."[103] Some locals reacted to the frequent intrusions by trying to ignore the outsiders or remaining cautious in response to their inquiries.[104]

Who were the border tourists and how did their visits unfold? Among the core border travelers were expellees from former German territories in East Central Europe and refugees from the GDR. For both groups, the Iron Curtain was not only an ideologically charged Cold War border that separated NATO from Warsaw Pact states but a barrier that separated them from their former homes. The border was deeply intertwined with their migration history: crossing the demarcation line into the western zones of occupation or, after 1949, into the Federal Republic signified arrival after a traumatic journey, stood for a successful escape, or meant greater economic opportunity. As the first points of arrival, the border counties absorbed a relatively large number of expellees and refugees until economic recovery enticed many of them to move on. The recent migrants were thus tied both to the border and to the borderlands in complex ways that defined their relationship to the Iron Curtain as different from that of nonmigratory West Germans. As Friederike Kind-Kovács and Eagle Glassheim have argued in the case of Sudeten Germans, these expellees recoiled from the Iron Curtain not as an act of solidarity with western anti-Communists but because the border invoked a deep sense of trauma and fear; the people on the other side were perceived not merely as Cold War adversaries but as inhabitants of their former homes and poor stewards of their erstwhile land.[105] For such recent migrants, trips to the border amounted to communing with their lost homeland, or *Heimat*, which lay just across the Bavarian–Czech border. Countless *Heimat* newsletters and yearbooks recounted the tales of these trips.[106] For expellees from regions farther east who could not gaze directly into their former *Heimat*, the border nonetheless represented the closest point to their homeland, at least until the fruits of *Ostpolitik* eased travel restrictions for trips to Poland.[107] Barred from memorializing their homeland at authentic places, expellee *Landsmannschaften* frequently chose the borderlands to construct "surrogate *Heimat* spaces" as commemorative sites.[108] *Landsmannschaften* planted large crosses at sites close to the border, widely visible monuments that became incorporated into the annual activities of expellee organizations, drawing crowds for outdoor church services, reunions, as well as group tours and hikes.[109] As Yuliya Komska has shown for the Bavarian–Czech border, Sudeten Germans produced a veritable "prayer wall" of icons, crucifixes, and (replica) chapels along the border. By saturating the western side with Christian iconography, this particular constituency turned border visits into pilgrimages.[110] With a dual impetus for undertaking border trips—to mourn the lost *Heimat* and to contemplate partition—expellees were early, numerous, and steady Iron Curtain visitors.[111]

Refugees from the GDR were another such group. They participated in border-related activities through the Consortium for an Undivided Germany and various associations that operated under the umbrella of the Alliance of the Germans from Central Germany (Bund der Mitteldeutschen) in 1969. To commemorate the failed uprising of June 17, 1953, these organizations convened large gatherings along the inter-German border, putting the East German forces on high alert each year.[112] East German border authorities were particularly piqued by these associations because their core demand was unification. Well into the 1960s, the territorial contours of the desired unification still included the lost eastern territories; East Germany thus featured as "Central Germany" in the Alliance's name, implying the continued existence of a German East. Like the expellee *Landsmannschaften*, these groups did their part to post signs and erect memorials on the demarcation line in order to remind visitors that "over there is Germany, too," that "Germany remains indivisible," or that a Germany divided into three parts remained unacceptable (*"Dreigeteilt? Niemals!"*).[113] Both expellee and refugee organizations thus created destinations for trips to the demarcation line and mobilized their rank and file to visit individually or partake in sponsored borderland group activities, turning the border into one of their preferred spheres of activity. With the advent of *Ostpolitik* in West German politics, however, these efforts seemed to fall out of step with the political spirit of the time. A reporter for the liberal weekly *Die Zeit* mocked the use of the border as a "relic for mythical stagings. A multi-purpose backdrop for May Day rallies, for leaping over bonfires, and deep sighs during border hikes."[114] As the reports of East German border troops indicate, however, these activities continued unabated through the 1980s.[115]

Other identifiable border travelers were high school students, recruits of the Federal Armed Forces (Bundeswehr), and Allied soldiers stationed in West Germany. Each of these groups may be classified as "captive audiences" since the border trip was offered by their school or unit. For military personnel, the study of the terrain along the border, its layered fortifications, and the military equipment of the other side was part of their military training.[116] In their intelligence reports, East German border guards meticulously counted anybody in uniform and tried to identify insignia. Groups of young men aged around eighteen to twenty-one, even if in civilian clothes, were usually also counted as recruits on the assumption that they were merely "disguised."[117]

For high school students, trips to the border or an excursion to West Berlin were often part of the curriculum as civic education "on site." At the Freiherr-vom-Stein school in Frankfurt, a dedicated teacher, Dr. Willi K., regularly organized three-day trips to the borderlands in order to acquaint the students with the current status of the German question. Visits to the border were considered conducive to this educational goal and were therefore sponsored by the Hessian Bureau for Political Education. After the trip, the students wrote reports, adorned with their own photographs and drawings. The 1961, 1962, and 1968 scrapbooks show that the students experienced, or at least depicted, the border as a threat; the accompanying West German border guards thus appear less as tour guides than as bodyguards. The students emphasized the absurdity of the border that made nearby villages and buildings unreachable and "separate[d] Germans from Germans," thereby echoing the government brochure *In the Heart of Germany*, which was most likely used to prepare them for the trip. Behind the Iron Curtain reigned "fear and mistrust," they wrote. East German citizens were forced to remain silent about the oppressive conditions in their country, culminating in the rhetorical question: "They have to be silent, but should we, who enjoy the security and freedom of the West, also remain silent?" In the students' observations, the border fortifications held center stage: the meticulously harrowed 10-meter strip, observation towers, barbed wire, mines, watch dogs, and cutoff roads or tracks impressed upon them "how absurd the forceful division of Germany" was and caused feelings of trepidation. Such sentiments were reinforced by lectures that emphasized the brutality of the East German border guards, their lack of "fair play" when they pursued refugees and snatched them back even from western territory, as well as the impact of the border on everyday life in the borderlands. Judging by the scrapbooks, Dr. K's school trips were exemplary border visits. Even if we take into account that the scrapbooks were a homework assignment, the reports reflect an already established script for such border trips that identify highlights such as divided roads and houses, portray West German border guards as travel guides, and draw on local expertise to collect anecdotes about border incidents and life on the Cold War frontline.[118]

The individual visitors, however, who traveled outside of organized groups, left only random traces. Those involved in border incidents made the files of the border troops in the West or East. A few others became known because they staged their visits in some extraordinary way, like the man who reported in 1964 that a religious apparition required him to turn the "zonal border" into his Via Dolorosa and carry a large wooden cross from Hof in the South to Lübeck in the North.[119] Regular private visitors, however, came and went without a mission. According to an intelligence report by GDR border troops, such individual travelers actually accounted for a large part of the border tourists.[120] It appears that borderland residents took their personal guests to the border since it was one of the few attractions in these predominantly rural areas. Touring the border became almost an obligation if those visitors came from outside Germany. "When we had visitors from abroad," wrote a Sudeten German expellee residing near the Czech border, "we went to the border and looked at it, how it actually was. [. . .] Silberhütte was always a destination if you had guests from Vienna or wherever. They always wanted to see it."[121]

Twenty-three-year old Peter Boag, an American traveling in Europe in the summer of 1984, was one such guest. He stayed with a German family in Windsbach southeast of Nuremberg. As part of an outing, his hosts drove Boag to the border at Neustadt near Coburg, where the elaborate border fortifications with their "technological gizmos" left a deep impression on him: "It was simply amazing the border patrol they have. Through binoculars I was able to look into the guard towers & I saw them looking right back at me with binoculars, & taking pictures of us w[ith] zoom lenses. They also took notes of our movements & perhaps of what we said—I [was told by the host family] that the whole area was bugged." Boag could not resist the temptation to step onto GDR territory, "so I can say I have been to East Germany." Probably influenced by the way his host family introduced him to the border, Boag perceived the Iron Curtain as the dividing line between Communism and freedom that was patrolled by sinister-looking border guards.[122] Boag's border experience of the mid-1980s is thus very much in line with the choreography of the 1960s school trips, suggesting that the standardization of border travel and perception was well in place and passed along by local hosts. As Maren Ullrich argues, it was established to such a degree that it endured well beyond 1989 and influenced how the border would become memorialized.[123]

As the visitors and the visited engaged the border and each other and thereby shaped the character of border visits, one group had no voice in the process: the residents of border communities in the GDR. After 1990, East German borderland dwellers reflected on the western tourists and, not surprisingly perhaps, related that they made them feel "angry because we were stared at like 'monkeys in a cage.'"[124] At the inception of border tourism, contemporaries had already noted the absurdity of eyeballing each other, of staring "like wild animals in the zoo."[125] As the zoo metaphor suggests, however, the eyeballing had been a one-sided glare from the beginning, where power lay with those staring into the "cage." The unease about the gaze at "other people's misery" was picked up by the British punk band Sex Pistols in a 1977 song mocking Wall tourism in Berlin. It also features in the popular comedy film *Sonnenallee* (1999), which opens with a scene of western tourists staring from a viewing platform down on "ossies" (or easterners) like animals in a zoo—"feeding prohibited," says the voiceover.[126] Even those East Germans who knew that it was their own western relatives looking in on their village life felt the need to reappropriate the gaze after the border had fallen. One of the first things a resident of Kella (East) did after the border opened was to go to the "exact spot where my western relatives would have stood when they came to look at Kella."[127]

East German Responses to Border Tourism

The development of tourism to the Iron Curtain remained a major provocation to East German authorities throughout the existence of the GDR. The visitors saw what the SED regime sought to deny: the border had been fortified to lock people in, not to keep "fascists" and "imperialists" out. Border tourism thus posed a major image problem for the GDR leadership, not only when there were violent border incidents but on an almost daily basis.[128] How, then, did the East German authorities react to the gradual establishment of a tourist infrastructure on the western side that made a spectacle of the border fortifications, including the border guards policing it?

The issue surrounding western onlookers had already bothered border troops and local representatives before the building of the Berlin Wall. The deportations of allegedly unreliable inhabitants from the security strip in 1952 had left homes and farmsteads in immediate proximity to the demarcation line abandoned. Settling new residents was usually not an option; rather, further deportations occurred after August 1961, sometimes as a punishment for political nonconformity. The abandoned buildings predictably decayed, a process hastened by local residents, who gutted them for building materials, or through wanton destruction by border troops.[129]

That dwellings and villages visible from the West provided ample visual material for anti-eastern propaganda became a growing concern for local East German officials. Indeed, early West German propaganda about the border such as the popular brochure *In the Heart of Germany* emphasized the property crimes of socialism and mocked the waste of arable land along the demarcation line.[130] Formerly well-maintained and profitable farms, such western mockeries went, were now a pitiful sight, testifying to the economic and moral depravity of socialism. The lifelong labor of industrious folk crumbled in front of their very eyes. The brochure skillfully tied productive labor to private ownership of the means of production, thereby condemning the recent collectivization of farms on the eastern side.[131] The art historian Maren Ullrich argues that the visual language of this particular brochure exercised a strong influence on how West Germans imagined the border.[132] A year after the first edition, East German officials began to refer to the western visitors as a nuisance. They noted "a strong flow of visitors from the western side who come to see what it looks like 'behind the curtain.'"[133] West German bus tour operators organized whole "tourist parties [. . .], who are carted to the border from the hinterland, and these [dilapidated] houses are made to stand for the conditions in the GDR" as a whole.[134] The East German officials' interpretation of western intentions was perfectly apt. Just as the brochure *In the Heart of Germany* had been conceived to contrast West German reconstruction with East German decay and to elicit a strong negative response to the eastern system, such trips were designed to allow visitors to feel indignant about the GDR. A visit to the border pushed them to transform the resultant chill into an affirmation of their own state and life circumstances.

The logical response of eastern authorities to such western objectives was to remove the evidence of decay and thus undermine western self-affirmation. In 1959, border communities were therefore asked to report abandoned buildings, which were subsequently either torn down or renovated. Not only the condition of a building but its visibility from the West decided its fate. If the sight of it "was negative for the image of the GDR in West Germany," the building had to go.[135] Whole villages were razed due to border security and image concerns.[136] In order to spruce up the objects of western vilification, in the mid-1960s the Stasi suggested "initiating a beautification contest among border villages."[137] It is unknown what became of the idea, but villages in the security strip were privileged recipients of scarce construction materials, enabling them to beautify at least the facades of buildings facing west and to turn themselves into a kind of "Potemkin village."[138]

The Stasi's suggestions were part of a larger 1964 analysis of the "provocative [western] border visitations." In view of the ever-growing phenomenon, the Stasi felt compelled to figure out who offered such trips, where participants came from, and which locations attracted the most gawkers. The Stasi perceived border tourism as part of western psychological warfare and considered itself ill-prepared to counter these efforts.[139] The report recommended devising effective "counterpropaganda" tailored to the border situation. Highly frequented locations should be equipped with "visual agitation" (Sichtagitation), or billboards, that would provide continuously updated "information about the progress in the GDR and illustrate to the West German people our standard of living."[140] The report further suggested that on particularly busy days, like June 17 and August 13, when West Germans were likely to take border trips, loudspeakers be used to disrupt speakers and tourist groups.[141] With these suggestions, the Stasi merely expanded on efforts already under way in border guard units. The chief of the border troops had issued elaborate instructions a year prior on how to distract the Western gaze during construction work on the fortifications. Smoke machines were to produce enough fog to cloud the view and prevent photography and filming while loud music or announcements about socialism's progress were intended to unnerve unwanted visitors.[142] Troops also shot leaflets across the border, informing tourists that their own government was using them in a propaganda ploy.[143] To get a sense of the conversations that border visits provoked, the National People's Army even installed bugging devices near lookouts and other points where tourists gathered.[144] Indeed, the years 1963 and 1964 appear to have been a period of concerted efforts to fend off western sightseeing. At that time, East German authorities experimented at least once with tourist visits of their own, carting large groups to the border in June 1964 to gaze at the West. Western border guards interpreted the group's behavior as "sightseeing" and noted its novelty.[145]

Activities targeting western border tourism did not stop at the demarcation line. In fact, the Stasi considered a 30-kilometer-deep strip on West German territory to fall within its purview and tried to monitor NATO and Bundeswehr activities there as well as movements of western border troops. A special unit within the Stasi's Border Troop Command was in charge of reconnaissance within this zone of interest to spy on western military installations and other entities.[146] These surveillance efforts targeted the western infrastructure that supported border travel, especially information centers. Through informants and agents, the Stasi sought to identify staff and volunteers involved in educating tourists about the border and learn more about the composition of visiting groups.[147] Prominent individuals like the county director of Helmstedt, Hans Walter Conrady, and the head of the information center at Offleben regularly appeared in these Stasi reports. Tourist sites such as lookout towers featured as "enemy objects," and it particularly galled the Stasi to learn that East Germans—either former GDR citizens or retirees who were allowed to travel—were among the frequent visitors to such sites.[148]

Yet regardless of how much the Stasi knew about the information centers and lookout towers, this knowledge had no bearing on the number of visitors who came to see the Iron Curtain. Rather, any banal activity along the fence enhanced the experience for border tourists. A West German cyclist who biked along the entire border in 1985 made fun of a cluster of visitors who stared intently at farmhands bringing in the harvest on the other side of the Werra River "as if they were observing the seventh wonder of the world." Similar scenes that unfolded on western fields, he contended, would not turn anyone's head, but "since these were the farmers from a [GDR] collective, they received undivided attention."[149] This incident may serve as a reminder that tourists and onlookers more generally travel or pause in order to experience something out of the ordinary; they travel to see *something*. While GDR authorities obviously could not prevent them from coming to the border in the first place, they could nonetheless influence what these visitors would get to see, hence the demolition and beautification efforts referenced above.

The continuous modernizations of the border fortifications after the building of the Berlin Wall offered another opportunity to address what western visitors would see. To be sure, the main goal of any enhancement of the fortifications was to prevent escapes. To that end, the infrastructure of the Iron Curtain increased, was moved farther inland, and became more deadly. The entire border regime was adjusted in order to capture potential escapees already in the hinterland and avoid any drama within eye- or earshot of western witnesses. Although the construction required to make these "improvements" provided an additional opportunity for onlookers to watch and rant, the net outcome was that they would ultimately see less activity. After the overhaul, the only "Iron Curtain" a western observer could lay eyes on was a mesh-wire fence up to 200 meters away from the line. The old 10-meter control strip that used to be harrowed so meticulously was abandoned. Already by 1963, it had become quite overgrown.[150] Indeed, in some areas shrubbery was allowed to sprout and eventually obstructed the view of the fence.[151] The overall goal, defined by the Stasi in the mid-1960s, was to provide "a clean appearance along the border [that] would deprive the enemy of certain arguments in his diatribes."[152] The greenery pacified the demarcation line, making it appear harmless, especially to visitors from abroad.[153]

The border-guarding routine was adjusted to fit the new fortifications. Regular troops now stayed on the eastern side of the fence and were thus out of view to western observers. On the western, or "enemy," side of the fence, only politically reliable reconnaissance troops (*Aufklärer*, or GAKs) were allowed to patrol, making ample use of observation bunkers and dugouts that often did not betray their presence.[154] To encounter a border patrol in action thus became unpredictable and increasingly rare.[155] By and large, the GDR border command had thus managed to withdraw from view western visitors' favorite photo object. When GAKs did appear, they refused to become the object of the tourist gaze and returned it with their own binoculars and cameras.[156] The thrill of irregular GAK appearances notwithstanding, during the 1970s and 1980s eastern border authorities sought to manage the border as a fait accompli that was not worth visiting. While the beautification projects of the late 1950s acknowledged that Westerners were watching, later strategies were aimed at making border visits uneventful and boring. The Bavarian border police understood the intention perfectly well. "Where the border is visible," they stated in their 1986 annual report, "nothing is meant to happen."[157]

Borderlands as Travel Lands: Vacationing on the Iron Curtain

In view of the economic challenges in the border counties, the Iron Curtain as a sightseeing destination held out the not unreasonable hope that tourism could boost the local economy. Once the shock and fear about border closure in 1952 had abated and guests returned to established destinations such as the Harz Mountains, some borderland representatives began to contemplate the expansion of tourism. The idea of developing peripheral regions for tourism was hardly original, and contemporary spatial planners even envisioned sparsely populated peripheries offering respite for worn-out city dwellers.[158] Yet while tourism was considered a substitute for "real" industry in some rural border regions during the 1950s and 1960s, a major shift occurred over the course of the 1970s, fanned by an environmental "awakening" in the Federal Republic. The lack of industry that constituted the much-bewailed disadvantage of the border counties during the first decades turned into a major selling point amid a new zeitgeist: unindustrialized landscapes turned into an asset.

In the early 1950s, the Iron Curtain proved detrimental to leisure tourism. When the GDR sealed the border in May 1952, the established Harz resorts (*Kurorte*) on the western side felt the impact immediately. Fearful of an impending military clash, guests canceled their reservations, reducing business in Hohe Geiß, for example, by 60 percent.[159] The resort director of Braunlage detected a "zonal border fear" in the cancellation letters that amounted to a veritable "psychosis."[160] Officials in Goslar and Bad Harzburg even struggled with people's false assumptions that their towns were situated in the GDR.[161] Trying to prevent their image as sites of relaxation and recuperation from becoming associated with the dangers of the Iron Curtain, some resorts made efforts to downplay their proximity to the border in advertising materials and travel guides.[162] Others, however, eventually lost their hesitation and addressed the problem head-on. The resort director in Braunlage supported the building of a gondola lift to the Wurmberg, the highest mountain in the western Harz. He enlisted well-established rhetoric about partition by saying that he wanted to turn the mountain into "something like a 'look-out tower' on Germany's bleeding border. Visiting it [. . .] would drive home the realization of the veritable laceration (*Zerrissenheit*) of our country."[163] The lift opened in 1963. That very year, however, an escapee was shot in Hohe Geiss and died just a few yards from the demarcation line, in plain view of western spa guests. The memorial cross for the victim quickly became a sight in itself, drawing busloads of visitors.[164] During the 1970s and 1980s, trips to the border became an integral part of tourist programming in the Harz resorts. Twice a month, a free bus took guests along the fortifications in the southern Harz.[165]

While the western Harz Mountains had an established hospitality industry, rural border regions in particular had none. During the 1950s, the federal state of Hesse systematically tried to develop tourism in the borderlands. Hesse was the only state that instituted a full-time State Commissariat for Distressed Areas and the Border Counties.[166] The first incumbent in that office, Wilhelm Ziegler, was particularly interested in enlisting federal aid to boost tourism. His plans were geared toward a postwar society that was slowly regaining disposable income and increasingly acted upon pent-up leisure demand to recover from "the efforts of war and postwar reconstruction."[167] The new West German prosperity found expression in growing car ownership but also in the gradual introduction of the five-day work week during the 1960s, significantly expanding leisure time.[168] The State Commissariat therefore counted on the development of weekend travel and adopted the slogan of Alfred Töpfer's nature park movement to provide recreational "oases of tranquility" (Oasen der Ruhe) for stress-afflicted urbanites who were considered to be in dire need of escape from their congested and noisy surroundings. The urban centers of Frankfurt, Kassel, and especially West Berlin with its "trapped" residents seemed to hold endless potential for borderland tourism in Hesse.[169] In 1955, Ziegler announced a five-year investment package of up to DM 4 million per year for tourism in those regions.[170] For Ziegler, the package was not only about economic development but also about political appearances. His efforts were another expression of West Germany's window-dressing politics (Schaufensterpolitik). Ziegler subscribed to the idea that the border regions had an "all-German" duty to fulfill. "The inhabitants of central Germany [i.e., the GDR] must get a view into a well-stocked display window that reveals the achievements of economic prosperity in the Federal Republic. The borderlands must not show any signs of poverty." Therefore, investments in the tourist infrastructure were well justified because tourism was not only strengthening the local economy but "also had a political role to play."[171] Like countless other officials in the West German state bureaucracy of the 1950s, Ziegler, himself a man of the past,[172] was more likely than not to draw on models of state-sponsored nationalist travel that were familiar from the 1920s and 1930s.

In order to direct the weary urban masses into the rejuvenating border-lands, Ziegler's office offered federally subsidized loans to farmers willing to convert chambers in their farmhouse into guest rooms, thus developing bed-and-breakfasts as a new branch of the home economy. Established inn-keepers and owners of small hotels were likewise encouraged to expand. Thanks to such incentives, the capacity for overnight stays in Hesse rose from 28,848 to 69,817 beds between 1950 and 1958.[173] A border county like Rotenburg-on-Fulda, with little industry but many beautiful landscapes, increased the number of overnight visits from 45,439 in 1956 to 64,726 in 1957. The town of Hilders, east of Fulda, increased the number of guest-nights from 10,000 in 1957 to an astonishing 70,000 in 1969.[174]

Postwar travelers, however, wanted to leave the deprivations of the rubble years behind and developed certain expectations in terms of com-fort. "Inns without running cold or hot water are no longer in demand."[175] Similarly, serene scenery alone, of which the border counties had plenty, would not suffice. Hoping to make a splash, the Hesse state government therefore invested heavily in a leisure infrastructure, including public swimming pools. Fourteen new *Badeanstalten* were built in Hesse's border counties from 1954 to 1956, again drawing on subsidies from Bonn.[176] The subsidy flow into the borderlands allowed even small communities to ramp up their public infrastructure to an extent that would not have been feasible on their own steam. The little town of Tann in the Rhön Mountains built a public pool, too, and also featured a sanatorium and ten family vacation homes. The town council established trails, added a com-munity center with Kneipp facilities, a public library, a bowling alley, and a day-care center for senior citizens. Federal subsidies thus aided in almost doubling guest nights in Tann from 25,742 in 1960 to 45,859 in 1967.[177]

Ziegler's successor, Heinz Kreutzmann, continued the focus on tourism to the borderlands. His hope: "Every citizen of the Federal Republic should vacation in the borderlands at least once."[178] Yet by the time the Hessian border counties were ready to accommodate larger numbers of tourists, the postwar travel boom had begun to drift abroad. Not the edge of the pool in Eschwege but the beaches of Rimini were becoming the chosen destination of affluent West Germans for the most valuable weeks of the year.[179]

The push for leisure tourism in the borderlands was backed by the growing realization that mere sightseeing at the Iron Curtain, while briefly bringing in a large number of visitors, hardly affected the bottom line of local communities. The divided village of Zicherie, with about 200,000 visitors per year, did not manage to cash in on its popularity: "[The tourists] pull up in the free parking places beside the burgermaster's house, walk to the border, read the placards, take some snapshots and drive away without spending a pfennig."[180] Obersuhl, on the border be-tween Hesse and Thuringia, experienced the same phenomenon. In 1965, about 70,000 visitors stopped by to see the border, but the village had no need to expand its overnight capacity of thirty-five guest beds.[181] The municipality of Kleinensee in Hesse offers a similar cautionary tale. This community erected the lookout tower Bodesruh in 1963 and renovated a nearby inn to accommodate visitors. Despite federal support, by 1970 the municipality was still stuck with the loan for the construction work. The project never broke even.[182] Local officials nonetheless hoped that the Iron Curtain would serve as a conduit to acquaint visitors with the re-gion. In the mid-1960s, the mayor of Bergen-Dumme in Lower Saxony was confident that "of a hundred visitors to the local [border] informa-tion point, ten return for a vacation."[183] Similarly, SPD members of parlia-ment concluded during a borderland visit in 1970 that "the distribution of travel parties to all border counties caused a considerable increase in the number of visitors to economically weak areas." The ensuing "striking increase in tourism to those communities [had] led to notable economic advantages in several localities."[184] The villages within the nature park of the Lauenburg lake region were among the beneficiaries. Farmers could make more money on vacationers from nearby Hamburg than on cattle. Accommodated in converted barns, these new guests flocked to the shores of Lake Schaalsee simply because they could no longer reach the lake dis-trict in neighboring Mecklenburg.[185]

Leisure tourism to the borderlands experienced a modest breakthrough during the 1980s that was closely tied to West Germans' newfound appre-ciation of unindustrialized landscapes. The fact that accelerated moderni-zation during the 1950s and 1960s had bypassed much of the borderlands was now discovered to be a boon for tourism. As one travel writer noted as early as the mid-1960s, "What constitutes economic misery for people in this region translates into tranquility and relaxation for us: seemingly never-ending forests, dreamy villages, quiet roads."[186] Two decades later, a cyclist who pedaled from Priwall Beach in the north to Hof in the south during the summer of 1985 confirmed that he "had never experienced the Federal Republic more beautiful, remote, sleepy and natural" than here.[187] Realizing that villages considered "remote" and "sleepy," shunned in the 1950s and 1960s, had turned into a draw for certain demographics, border communities seized on the trend and pitched their very remoteness as a major plus. The locational disadvantage of the reconstruction years was turned on its head. Up and down the border, peace and quiet, "intact" landscapes, and moderate prices were enlisted to attract tourists. Indeed, catering to a diffuse sense that something authentic had been lost in the focus on economic growth, the borderlands were marketed as places where "the world was still in good order."[188] Once bemoaned as backward and obsolete, unaltered village structures and the persistence of time-honored crafts now appeared to allow for a comforting "glimpse into the past."[189] A journalist for the *Frankfurter Allgemeine* detected a dialectic element in this new perception of the borderlands and concluded that these more remote provinces benefited from the "environmental destruction in the metropolitan areas and the overly developed holiday regions."[190] Put differently, the keener the sense of loss in the hinterland, the greener the borderlands appeared. The changing perception was even reflected in the border travel guides issued by government agencies. Initially focused exclusively on the Iron Curtain's fortifications, they now also highlighted the "recreational value" of the charming landscapes in the border regions.[191] Via tourism marketing and travel writing, the borderlands were thus turned into a window onto the German past that was cast as a rural idyll, a trend that connected with the rediscovery of *Heimat* and a pronounced embrace of regional identities during the 1980s.[192]

The tourism breakthrough of the 1980s was aided by another phenomenon. Over the course of the 1970s, the border counties became a popular location for second homes.[193] Low real estate prices and tax-saving schemes made the acquisition of a vacation home affordable there. Especially space-strapped West Berliners used the borderlands to escape the confinement of their island and fanned out into the deltas of their transit routes. Four autobahns connected the city with the Federal Republic and motivated many West Berliners to choose their weekend homes in the vicinity of Lüneburg, Braunschweig, and Göttingen, as well as in the Harz Mountains and Upper Franconia. For leisure and recreation, the borderlands thus constituted West Berlin's new hinterland.[194]

Nowhere else did these two developments—the yearning for "intact" landscapes and the second-home phenomenon—become more evident than in the county of Lüchow-Dannenberg. West Berliners in particular streamed into the dead-end triangle on the Elbe River. Of all property sold to "external" buyers in 1978, West Berliners made up half of the clients, followed by buyers from Hannover (27 percent) and Hamburg (23 percent). By the early 1980s, West Berliners owned 3,024 second homes in a county with only 48,000 permanent residents. In most communities within the county, external owners held between 10 and 30 percent of real estate.[195] The county thus experienced a major urban infusion during the 1970s and early 1980s that affected the demographic makeup of this rural area, since a sizable number of those who became acquainted with it via short-term stays moved there for good. While many of these new residents were retirees,[196] contemporaries noted a distinct influx of intellectuals and artists: professors, poets, painters, and potters introduced "alternative life-styles" to a county otherwise known for its political conservatism and reno-vated traditional farmsteads as part of a larger West German movement to preserve a romanticized rural past.[197] As many of these intellectuals had ready access to the leading West German newspapers, Lüchow-Dannenberg was written up throughout the 1970s as a place where "picture book vil-lages still dot the landscape," essentialized as "the most curious corner of Germany," and hailed as a "modern Worpswede" in reference to the fin-de-siècle artist colony near Bremen.[198] As the last chapter will explain, the relocators in the Wendland villages were to become an essential element in the county's "agrarian–leftist alliance"[199] that fueled the protest against government plans to build a nuclear reprocessing plant in Gorleben. It was borderland tourism—the weekend trips from West Berlin, Hamburg, Hannover, and Göttingen—that had brought them there.

Conclusion: A Postunification Memorial Landscape

Sightseeing at the Iron Curtain started out as an unguided grassroots ac-tivity that quickly grew into a sizable and persistent phenomenon. Visitors came to see for themselves where the Cold War had divided Germany and Europe and encountered a sight that continuously changed its ap-pearance and that both West and East German authorities staged for their viewing. As visitors congregated at the demarcation line, various actors sought to shape the time they spent in the West German border-lands and influence their interpretation of the space they encountered. Since the Iron Curtain constituted the obvious place where partition be-came tangible, and since partition was framed as a national tragedy, lo-cals expected tourists to approach it with a certain earnestness, hence the frequent quibbles whenever this activity commingled too openly with leisure and consumption.

The Consortium for an Undivided Germany arranged border visits as demonstrations of unity and solidarity with the Germans on the other side. Intended to maintain ties with East Germans and thereby counter the very purpose of the border, this plot amounted at best to a skewed form of communication between West and East. Precious few people in the GDR, namely residents in direct proximity to the border, were aware that the Consortium staged these efforts to reach out, and even these few targets of the Consortium's "dialogue" disappeared behind ever more fences, turning the conversation into a western monologue. State agencies joined the efforts of the Consortium only in the early 1960s after partition had reached a degree of finality with the construction of the Berlin Wall and, as Simone Derix suggests, after the Federal Republic had stabilized its own sovereignty sufficiently to join the chorus demanding unification.[200] The Federal Ministry of Inter-German Affairs and *Länder* governments came to subsidize border trips for civic education on site and used the GDR as the negative foil that gave western democratic values and institutions purpose and legitimacy. The subsidized trips also aimed at reassuring borderland residents that they were not "forgotten." By sponsoring border trips and the related travel infrastructure, the state sought to mark the borderlands as an integral part of West German territory and not a space apart from the hinterland.

Yet border tourism related uneasily to the intentions of those who sought to direct it. Members of the Consortium, local officials, and state agents were united in emphasizing the "unnatural" and brutal character of the border and blaming the SED regime, the Soviet Union, or simply Communism for its existence. These characterizations of the border as something out of the ordinary appear to have contributed to the very attraction of the sight, drawing streams of curiosity seekers to the Federal Republic's territorial edge to inspect the monstrosity. The rhetoric about the Iron Curtain also structured expectations about the encounter with it that were not always met, especially once East German authorities sought to pacify and "green" the demarcation line in order to render it boring for visitors from the western side.

Putting partition on display through border trips also seems to have produced a number of unforeseen consequences. The Consortium certainly intended to highlight unity and a common Germanness on both sides of the demarcation line, but the very infrastructure of border tourism encouraged visitors to juxtapose "here" and "there," a distinction that easily translated into "us" and "them." Border tourism thus likely had its share in creating difference and reinforcing otherness.[201] Similarly, diffuse

hopes that trips to the demarcation line would fuel resentment about partition and nurture the desire to strive for reunification came to nothing.
During the Adenauer years, border tourism undoubtedly provided anti-
Communism with a concrete focal point, as indicated by Adenauer's famous quip that "Asia begins at the Elbe River."[202] A border trip surely
afforded visitors the opportunity to bristle at the competing ideology. Yet at
the same time, border viewing inscribed the border on the mental maps of
those who came to see it. Regardless of the occasion for the trip, whether
visitors came to condemn it, learn about it, or gaze into a lost homeland,
border tourism likely contributed to West Germans' slowly adjusting to
the fact that the border was there to stay. Supported by an infrastructure
geared toward easing border visits, the trips unwittingly contributed to the
growing realization and eventual acceptance that partition was an element
of a new and enduring postwar reality in Germany. Seeing the border and
its ever-growing fortifications did nothing to overcome partition but rather
tended to underwrite the political and territorial status quo. Time was not
on the side of those who wished to keep the German question open. The
underlying motivations to encourage or undertake border travel became
more formulaic as the years went on, pointing to the oft-noted process
during which West Germans became accustomed to partition, accommodated their country's predominant western orientation in terms of politics,
culture, and consumption, and were consequently flabbergasted at the dissolution of the GDR in 1989.[203]

After 1990, border communities hastened to dismantle the deadly
fortifications that had separated them. Only two communities, namely
Hötensleben (East) and the divided village of Mödlareuth, had the fore-
sight to preserve an original stretch of the border intact with the goal of
turning it into an outdoor museum.[204] Other villages had to reconstruct
parts of the fortifications at a later date once they had reached a consensus
that the existence of the defunct Iron Curtain within their community
should be remembered. In addition, a range of local memorials and art-
works celebrating unification and commemorating the victims of the Iron
Curtain adorn the border strip today.[205] In 2009, the *Länder* ministries for
transportation added road signs at each spot where the border opened in
the winter of 1989–1990.[206] Numerous museums and exhibitions along
the demarcation line now document the border's history, drawing between
80,000 and 100,000 visitors each year.[207] Some of these sites are actually the very information centers that once catered to border tourists and
then adapted their exhibitions to the new conditions. As Maren Ullrich has

argued, this continuity reproduced the western perception of the border and the western historical explanation for its very existence.[208] The disappearance of the border finally canceled out the reservations about its commodification; souvenirs are now available, although still on a modest scale.[209] In short, the former border strip has been turned into a memorial landscape. Border tourism thus continues, albeit framed as commemoration of partition overcome.

4

Salts, Sewage, and Sulfurous Air

TRANSBOUNDARY POLLUTION IN THE BORDERLANDS

FOR MONTHS AFTER the fall of the Berlin Wall, media coverage both stoked and confirmed the worst fears about pollution in the GDR. Alarming reports about poisoned rivers, scarred landscapes, toxic soils, and dying forests conveyed the conclusion that in ecological terms, the GDR was "a failed state."[1] Preliminary scientific studies seemed to confirm that the SED regime had committed ecocide,[2] saddling the newly unified Germany with the responsibility of launching "the world's largest environmental protection operation" to clean up socialism's mess.[3] To a cadre of western experts on inter-German relations, however, the ecological cost of the socialist planned economy was hardly news. For years, the wind had blown sulfur dioxide, fly ashes, and herbicides across the border into western territory; and the rivers had carried heavy metals, fertilizers, and sewage into the Federal Republic. Finding itself on the receiving end of pollution emanating from GDR industry, the Bonn government throughout the 1970s and 1980s had tried to engage its East German counterparts in environmental diplomacy. An environmental historical perspective throws into sharp relief that Cold War Germany may have been divided but was never disconnected.[4] Environmental ties bound the two sides together: issues of water management ranging from the drinking water supply for West Berlin and Duderstadt (West) to waste water and sewage treatment; the maintenance of dykes along the Elbe River and dams in the Harz Mountains; disaster control measures for nuclear installations and forest fires; rabies prevention and bark beetle control in border forests; and shared resources such as natural gas and lignite, salt, and potash mines that at times were even connected subterraneously. Unencumbered by the ever-perfected border regime, the inter-German border and the Berlin Wall remained environmental contact zones between both German states.[5] Indeed, it was the border itself that generated some of the problems that cross-border diplomacy then needed to address.

Pollutants and waste crossed the border in both directions, a fact that was all but buried by the 1990 "discovery" of East German environmental iniquities in 1990. Throughout the 1980s, West German municipalities and public corporations had exported household and hazardous waste to the GDR, choosing the dump in Schönberg (East) as a cheap solution to western disposal regulations.[6] Environmental activists therefore reminded the West German public in 1990 that efforts to keep the Federal Republic "clean" had resulted in making the GDR "dirty."[7] West German industries likewise released sulfur dioxide that the wind carried into East Germany. Yet the GDR emitted sulfur dioxide at much higher rates, not least due to its dependency on lignite for energy production. During the 1980s, East Germany had the highest sulfur dioxide emissions in Europe.[8] When it came to water contamination, the Federal Republic was the almost exclusive recipient of East German pollution for the simple reason that most rivers along the inter-German border flow westward. Positioned downstream, the Federal Republic received significant quantities of various salts, sludge, untreated sewage, agro-chemicals, and other pollutants.

While the Bonn government thus had genuine cause for complaint, it also seized on these incidents to exert political pressure on the GDR. The Stasi warned the SED leadership that West German negotiators were trying to squeeze the GDR economically since "environmental protection would require enormous expenditures which would put the GDR [. . .] into a difficult position."[9] At the same time, the Politburo feared negative western news coverage about its environmental sins.[10] When the GDR's environmental ministry instructed subordinate agencies in 1981 to avert environmental damages, the order was not motivated by any concern for the environment but by a potential public loss of face. Spills as such were not the issue; only those that would provide Bonn with further leverage constituted a problem.[11] This attitude was matched by complementary thinking among West German officials for whom East German pollution was a concern only if it crossed the border. What both countries thus shared throughout their engagement about pollution was the fact that the natural environment was never a value as such, only a bargaining chip in the larger context of their complex relations.

Although the negotiations over transboundary pollution had many aspects specific to the context of divided Germany, they fit into a larger pattern of environmental politics between the "blocs" during the Cold War. It was not only West Germany that tried to make East Germany adhere to the emerging Polluter Pays Principle in international law. The Scandinavian countries held stakes in the Baltic Sea that they shared with the Soviet Union, Poland, and the GDR. The Elbe River not only straddled both German states for some hundred kilometers but originated in Czechoslovakia. The effects of the Chernobyl disaster of 1986 reached from Soviet Ukraine deep into Western Europe. The GDR itself suffered atmospheric contamination from the petrochemical plants in northern Bohemia. As Robert G. Darst has pointed out, before 1989 most western environmental experts assumed that the main obstacle to effective environmental protection in eastern bloc countries was the lack of political will. Only gradually, and most clearly after 1990, did they realize that the problems were systemic.[12] In fact, the "revelation" of the ecological balance sheet of East German socialism to West German media audiences in 1990 has hindered the historical contextualization of the GDR's environmental record. The verdict was too clear, the evidence seemed too obvious.

This is not to say that the environmental problems in East Germany upon unification were not massive—they were. Yet the verdict concerning East Germany's environmental record was also shaped by West Germany's own eco-anxieties, which it had nurtured since the late 1970s,[13] and a certain self-satisfaction about a better environmental record that had, however, been achieved only over roughly the decade preceding the collapse of the GDR. As Frank Uekötter notes, the eastern and western paths in terms of environmental protection had not yet clearly diverged in the 1970s.[14] Put differently, West Germany's own green conscience was a rather recent acquisition. One reason the idea of socialism's ecocide had proved so appealing and has been reiterated many times since 1990 may lie in the fact that it meshed so well with an overall triumphalist post-Wall narrative in which "the West" had won the Cold War.[15] To provide historical explanations for East Germany's environmental record, however, requires moving beyond merely chronicling the SED regime's environmental turpitude.

Pollutants know no boundaries. This truism has made transnational perspectives in environmental history a necessity. While the respective economic systems and environmental policies of any given modern state shape the use of natural resources within national borders, the consequences of these political and economic systems for the environment cannot be contained by those borders. In view of "the interconnectedness of all parts of the planet in matters ecological," as J. R. McNeill writes, environmental history advances global histories, a scale that is particularly plausible for pressing concerns such as the history of climate change.[16] Yet even in environmental history, where the need for transnational, global, and even planetary approaches is obvious, calls to leave national frameworks behind are more easily issued than heeded.[17] What is more, as imperative and instructive as it is to write across modern national boundaries in order to lay bare the ecological interconnectedness that McNeill addresses, it also pays to retain a focus on the actual border that pollutants and biota were crossing. The political functions and symbolic meanings of a border, and the power asymmetries that these meanings often signify, bring questions of agency and power to the fore and are therefore an integral part of transboundary environmental entanglements. In Nancy Langston's words, "[M]any pollutants ignore national borders but the effects of exposure are still mediated by those borders."[18] The degree of a state border's visibility on the ground, its fortification or nonfortification, reflects the political relationship of neighboring states.[19] The nature of this relationship subsequently bears on any engagement over the damage of environmental goods, from the infringement of fishing rights to the release of sulfur dioxide plumes or spills into transboundary waters. Putting the border "back in" need not result in a "mere" political environmental history. Rather, the challenge consists of integrating the biological and physical environments alongside the political wrangling over natural resources.[20]

    This chapter focuses on transboundary pollution along the interGerman border during the 1970s and 1980s.[21] It contributes to the ongoing revision of East Germany's environmental history by exploring on what led to the very negative West German perception of the GDR's environmental record in the early 1990s. It covers the entanglement between the two German states regarding water and air through case studies of the Werra River, which was rendered ecologically dead by chloride salts, and of sulfur dioxide emissions from a paper factory in Thuringia that affected the air in Hof (West) and stands *pars pro toto* for the air pollution held responsible for acid rain in the 1980s. Both countries reacted to pollutants infringing on their territories, a reaction exacerbated by the political and symbolic meaning of the very border that these pollutants crossed: this was the Iron Curtain, after all. Over the course of the 1970s and 1980s, some locations within the "zonal borderlands" thus gained another characteristic: they became places with poisonous rivers and sulfurous air. In the 1950s, the Adenauer government had felt the need to defend the borderlands against Communist infiltration. In the 1980s, the infiltration had become environmental. The indisputable environmental interdependency forced both German states to the negotiating table and eventually produced the Environmental Accords of 1987. The chapter argues that the western encounter with eastern pollution through the interface of the inter-German border confronted West German authorities with early signs of East Germany's dissolution. As the East German economy declined, its industries decayed and exuded pollution. While western observers failed to recognize this message, the encounter nonetheless produced the knowledge about the nature and extent of the GDR's environmental problems that became the prerequisite for the post-1990 ecological restoration of East Germany.

A River Runs Through It

Most rivers, canals, and creeks that crossed the inter-German border drained westward into the territory of the Federal Republic.[22] During the 1970s, these waterways carried an increasing load of pollutants. Yet the GDR considered rehabilitation measures for these waterways only if the water quality became so poor that it impaired industrial production. Even such minimal efforts the GDR deemed superfluous for transboundary rivers in particular, "since the[se] waters usually leave the GDR after short stretches and therefore the pollution of these waters does not result in any restrictions on water use within GDR territory."[23] Farther downstream, this very attitude defined West Germany's woes. The pollutants that the rivers carried into West Germany mirrored the different kinds of environmental problems that confronted the GDR. Although West German government agencies monitored the various pollutants, they did not realize that they were tracking the GDR's economic decline. Increasingly squeezed by foreign debt, the SED leadership would rarely make any investments in the modernization of basic public infrastructure and industrial equipment, and so wore out the substance of the GDR's economy.[24] In the process, the failing industries were "bleeding" pollution. The accelerated decline of the GDR economy during the 1980s was the overriding structural cause of the increase in the GDR's free-riding incentives on its downstream neighbor. What kind of pollution reached the Federal Republic, and what environmental damage did these pollutants represent?

For one, the rivers carried simple household waste from poorly secured trash dumps into West Germany. In principle, East German consumers produced less packaging waste than their western counterparts due to lower consumption levels and a well-developed system of scrap recycling.[25] Yet garbage and even industrial waste regularly ended up on illegal dumps, from which it could find its way into streams.[26] Although the removal of solid waste from rivers was generally an easier task than the cleanup of any chemicals, the garbage not only was a nuisance but also could cause tangible economic damage. The Steinach River regularly carried trash from the Köppelsdorf landfill in Sonneberg County (East) into Kronach County in Upper Franconia. After light flooding in April 1975, the electricity company Weiss in Mitwitz (West) had to shut down its power station on the river and rid the water of cans, plastic bottles, rubber tires, boxes, chairs, and various wooden objects. Weiss even fished the corpse of a pig out of the station's grate.[27] The Weiss company repeatedly alerted county officials to the problem, but even a complaint that the Border Commission filed with East German authorities did not ameliorate the situation. After four years of entreating the local government without success, the company turned to the federal Ministry of Justice in Bonn to demand progress in the matter, yet to no avail.[28]

Agricultural production in the GDR was another source of water pollution. Fertilizers, pesticides, herbicides, liquid manure, and wastewater from food-processing industries like abattoirs, dairies, and breweries as well as agrochemical plants affected transboundary streams. To be sure, industrialized agriculture developed in both German states and led to environmental degradation in both, but in West Germany civil society at least had the opportunity to protest the excesses of agrobusinesses.[29] Both sides also engaged in ruthless land improvement schemes to clear surfaces for agricultural use. They removed hedges and small wooded areas, straightened the course of rivers and creeks, and drained wetlands in order to enlarge fields and accommodate larger machinery.[30] The decision to separate livestock farming from crop production in the early 1960s proved particularly problematic for East German agriculture. Intensive mass animal farming yielded corresponding amounts of liquid manure that was usually distributed on land near animal factories.[31] At the same time, plant production went chemical and increased the use of mineral fertilizers, pesticides, and herbicides. In the deployment of fertilizers, however, West German agriculture was even more damaging than that in the East; because of its lesser purchasing power in foreign currency, East

German agriculture used less high-end fertilizer and retained some agriculture practices that had become outmoded in West Germany.[32]

By the early 1970s, GDR agriculture found itself in a vicious cycle. The erosion and contamination of soils, the decline in the groundwater table levels, the eutrophication of surface waters, and the expansion of open lignite pits reduced the amount of land available for agricultural production. To make up for the reduction of land, production cooperatives (LPGs) tried to increase soil quality through the use of more fertilizer and fresh rounds of land improvement. Behind this drive for high production rates stood the political imperative to retain low food prices. Efforts to break out of this cycle around 1980 did not gain traction with individual LPGs.[33] By the time the GDR collapsed, agricultural land was devastated and worn out. In a phrase analogous to that applied to contaminated industrial plants, the ecologist Michael Succow referred to these landscapes as "brownfield sites."[34]

On the western side, East German industrialized agriculture manifested itself in transboundary rivers. In the smaller streams like the Föritz, Kreck, Itz, and Milz in Franconia, fish populations regularly went belly up—literally. The western representatives on the inter-German Border Commission tried to hold the GDR liable for such property damages. Yet rarely did the East German representatives concede that the incidents had originated in GDR territory.[35] More often, they insisted that their own watershed authorities found no cause for the pollution that their western interlocutors had alleged.[36] With the GDR dodging liability, the damaged parties turned to western agencies to file for compensation. In 1970, the Bavarian State Chancellery still expected most border-related damages to result from displaced eastern mines that subsequently exploded on western territory. By 1976, however, the damages for which citizens sought compensation related chiefly to dead fish in transboundary streams.[37]

Another kind of water contamination stemmed from untreated municipal sewage. In 1983, fully 90 percent of East German households were connected to the central drinking water supply, but only 70 percent to public canalization and 53 percent to sewage plants.[38] Untreated municipal sewage was either deposited in landfills, released into rivers, or irrigated on wastewater farms (*Rieselfelder*). Sewage sludge was also deposited on cultivated fields.[39] Insufficient maintenance and general wear and tear reduced the cleaning capacity of municipal sewage plants, which were often equipped with only the primary (mechanical) treatment unit but lacked the secondary (biological) and tertiary (chemical) means to purify the water.[40] In 1987, the problem caught up with a major sewage plant in Dresden-Kaditz that served 520,000 people. Kaditz suffered an outage when the Elbe River flooded the plant. Overwhelmed by the floodwaters, the electricity supply broke down, the seventy-year-old pumps stopped working, and the entire pumping station suffered irreparable damage. With the Kaditz plant completely incapacitated, for the next five years all the sewage from Dresden and the adjacent municipalities poured untreated into the Elbe.[41]

The first two inter-German environmental agreements addressed municipal sewage plants, indicating just how pressing this problem was for the West Germans downstream. In 1982, both sides agreed to modernize three plants in East Berlin, to which the Federal Republic contributed DM 68 million in the hope of improving the water quality of West Berlin.[42] The second agreement in 1983 pertained to the river Röden between Thuringia and Bavaria. Since the city of Sonneberg did not have a sewage plant for its 28,000 residents, the sullage, including abattoir refuse, went directly into the river. Between Sonneberg (East) and Neustadt (West) the Röden was a cesspool.[43] The condition of the river was well known in the GDR's Ministry for Environmental Protection and Water Management. An internal report of 1983 noted that

> due to the discharge of wastewater the Röden is a particularly contaminated river that takes on the character of a sewage canal at times of low water levels. Downstream from Sonneberg and well beyond the state border to the BRD, the use of water from the Röden is impossible. The high levels of contamination lead to putrefaction and a permanent unpleasant odor. The hygienic conditions are alarming. There is a danger of epidemics.[44]

However, since 1982 such disturbing results had been classified information in the GDR.[45] On the Bavarian side, though, the official secrets of the GDR were public knowledge. The Bavarian government first tried to treat the river's waters at a purification plant in Neustadt-Wildenheid, yet the plant was soon overwhelmed.[46] After lengthy negotiations, both sides agreed to build a modern sewage plant in Sonneberg itself. The Federal Republic contributed the environmental technology as well as DM 18 million, which the GDR even received in freely convertible currency.[47] The plant was operational in 1987.[48]

If the contamination of rivers with sewage already constituted a major strain, the pollution caused by industrial wastewater moved many streams toward the tipping point. The thorough cleaning of industrial wastewater would have required major investments in environmental technology, which the East German authorities considered only if a river's water quality rendered it unusuable even for industrial cooling purposes and therefore hampered industrial production.[49] Commonly, however, the wastewater was only subjected to primary clarifiers that removed solids and skimmed off floating oils and greases. Thus treated, the effluent was released into a river, where, according to GDR officials, the stream's "natural self-cleansing abilities" would finish the job.[50] The idea that a river was an organic machine that could take care of itself was rooted in the river disputes of the industrial era.[51] During the 1980s, however, the Elbe River and its tributaries had no magical "self-cleansing abilities" left. The pollution of the Elbe started in Czechoslovakia and gained further traction over the course of its 588-kilometer run through the GDR. During negotiations over the state of the Elbe in 1983, GDR diplomats insisted on a "considerable self-cleansing stretch" between Magdeburg (East) and Boizenburg (East) and argued that the Elbe was "not unduly polluted" when it crossed the border into the Federal Republic.[52] The West Germans estimated, however, that the river carried 80 percent of its polluting load by the time it reached federal territory in Schnackenburg (West).

When unified Germany issued the first all-German water quality atlas in 1990, the Elbe required the introduction of a new category to describe its state: category 8—ecologically dead.[53] What was true of the Elbe was true also of almost every stream that crossed the inter-German border. Yet it was not the mighty Elbe River between Dresden and Hamburg that prompted the federal government to engage in environmental diplomacy with the GDR, but the Werra, a river with a long history of pollution from potash mining.

Potash Mining along the Werra River

The Werra has its source in the Thuringian Schiefergebirge (Shale Mountains). The middle part of its course between Thuringia (East) and Hesse (West) meandered to and fro across the inter-German border. After a 298-kilometer run, the Werra merges with the Fulda River at Hannoversch Münden (West), creating the Weser River, which runs through Bremen and into the North Sea. Salt seams stretch along the banks of the Werra on both sides. These deposits became the basis of potash mining in the middle of the nineteenth century.[54] By 1900, potash mining was the most important industry in the region. The mines drew upon the available natural resources as a matter of course. The river thus not only provided the potable and irrigation water for agriculture but also absorbed the wastewater generated by mining. Yet potash mining soon contaminated the river to such a degree that other water users complained about the infringement of their own water rights. In 1911, opponents of potash pollution—fishermen, farmers, factory owners, and municipal representatives—staged the first organized protest against the disposal of saltwater solutions and other waste products. It soon became clear that the success of the entire potash industry hinged on the question of its effluents.[55]

Ensuing efforts at cooperation brought about a Prussian-Thuringian Potash Wastewater Commission. Its task was to regulate the amount of brines entering the Werra in order to keep the river's chloride concentration under control. Yet concentrations between 500 and 1,500 milligrams per liter (mg/l) remained common, well above the 250 mg/l considered acceptable if the river was still to provide potable water. Experts predicted that seashore vegetation would develop along the river if such high salinity persisted. In 1925, the river experienced its first "water bloom," a mass growth of saline-tolerant freshwater diatoms and a subsequent fish kill, because the algae had monopolized the water's oxygen.[56] Since 1912, the city of Bremen, located downstream on the upper Weser, had protested the increasing chloride concentration in its drinking water. Bremen demanded that the Reich Health Office enforce a maximum concentration of 250 mg/l, yet to no avail. In the 1930s, Bremen gave up on its protest. The potash industry had muffled the city's complaints by offering to dispatch part of its exports via the city's port. In addition, Bremen received a 200-kilometer-long water pipe from the Harz Mountains for its drinking-water needs.[57] Then, during World War II, the war effort overrode all competing concerns. The permissible chloride level was raised by decree to 2,500 mg/l. What was intended as a temporary exemption to boost wartime production became the new normal after the war.[58]

The Werra's salinity had long been detrimental to the river's ecology. A chloride concentration of 250 mg/l makes water "hard" and no longer potable. Water with a 650 mg/l concentration is not suitable for irrigation and animal use. Freshwater organisms have different levels of salinity tolerance: 500 mg/l kills native crawfish, 2,000 mg/l wipes out crustaceans like freshwater mussels (Unionidae) and waterbugs (*Asellus aquaticus*), and 2,500 mg/l destroys most native freshwater fish, of which even the hardy eel (*Anguilla anguilla*) perishes in a 4,000 mg/l concentration.[59]

Under pressure from various stakeholders, the potash industry entertained several alternatives to address the plight of the river. One of those alternatives, conceived in 1912, was a pipeline that would transport the sharp brines from the mining region and deposit them near the mouth of the Elbe and Weser Rivers for release into the North Sea. This idea was dismissed as too expensive.[60] Instead, the industry considered the geological conditions of the mining region suitable for injecting brines into the ground. Beginning in the mid-1920s, the liquid waste was therefore discharged either into decommissioned mine shafts or into wells that were sunk for this purpose (*Schluckbrunnen*). By the 1950s, readily available cavities were becoming rare, so that the industry sought to maximize the underground dolomite formations through pressurized deep-well injections (*Verpressen*). Compared to weathering the brines directly into the river, this method may have been the lesser of two evils; yet it was never without its problems. Shortly after the industry had turned to deep-well injections, reports poured in that the pressurized brines were resurfacing and contaminating fields. The underground wastewater also pushed up the water table and contaminated the groundwater. Back on the surface, the flora adapted to the new salinity. Near Heringen (West), for example, a swath of the Werra floodplains developed salt marshes replete with coastal vegetation, just as had been predicted decades prior. In 1979, this curious strip was placed under nature protection.[61]

Although the pollution of the Werra therefore had deep historical roots, it reached its apex during the years of German partition. In 1947, the Potash Wastewater Commission assigned waste contingents for the last time. The Thuringian mines received two-thirds of the contingent, the Hessian mines one-third. As of 1951, East German representatives no longer attended the Border Commission meetings and did not provide information about the amounts discharged from the Thuringian mines. Yet a major fish kill in 1953–1954 based on a chloride concentration of 6,000 mg/l indicated just how active the eastern mines were. By the early 1960s, the salt concentration in the Werra prevented its waters from freezing in winter.[62] In 1968, the Thuringian mines abandoned any deep-well injection of brines because they had run out of underground cavities. The injections had also contaminated the drinking water of Eisenach (East) and agricultural areas in the vicinity.[63] With no further options for underground storage, the Thuringian mines released the brines directly into the

Werra. As a consequence, the fish now also died downstream in the Weser River; in the Werra itself, freshwater organisms were already long gone.[64]

Henceforth, the contamination of the Werra reached ever new heights. As the news magazine *Der Spiegel* explained to its readers, "If you wanted to transport the salt in the Weser's riverbed by federal rail, you would need a freight train with 40 cars carrying 15 tons each, and then run a train every 55 minutes toward the North Sea."[65] Indeed, the Werra had become "saltier than the North Sea."[66] The river reached its highest chloride concentration in 1976 with 40,000 mg/l, which manifested itself downstream in Bremen as 2,400 mg/l. Fish in the Weser died at regular intervals, causing incidents at the Würgassen nuclear power plant in 1971 and 1976 when tons of fish cadavers blocked the water cooling intake pumps.[67] In 1982, Bremen abandoned all efforts to extract potable water from the Weser; it was not even clear whether the water was safe for agricultural use.[68] The aggressive brines caused tangible harm to technical equipment and structures along the river, as they gnawed on turbines, pipes, bridges, and ships. In 1988, the damages due to corrosion were estimated at DM 65 million per year.[69] A leading official in the environmental ministry of Lower Saxony commented in 1980 that the contamination of the Werra and its downstream watershed "presently constitutes the most pressing environmental problem between the GDR and the Federal Republic."[70]

The Context of Inter-German Environmental Diplomacy

Until the collapse of the GDR in 1989–1990, the Werra River saw no relief. Lack of knowledge was not the issue. Just as GDR authorities had all the pertinent information about the contamination of the Röden, they also knew full well the state of the Werra. In an internal assessment drawn up in 1971—some three years after the Thuringian mines had moved to dumping all brines into the stream—experts listed all actual and potential damages resulting from this disposal method. East German authorities were fully aware of the harm to fisheries, drinking water, and process water, as well as the spatial reach of the problem through the Mittelland Canal all the way to Münster in Westphalia.[71] Yet although each side had the relevant data on hand, East and West German officials came to fundamentally different conclusions about the issue and were unable to reach any agreement to relieve the maltreated river. What, then, were the factors that made inter-German environmental diplomacy such a futile exercise?

For one, the starting points of each German state were simply incompatible. The Federal Republic maintained that the GDR was causing the environmental damage and was therefore responsible for introducing protective measures that would reduce contamination. The West German representatives thus argued along the lines of what became known as the Polluter Pays Principle (PPP). In the early 1970s, when the Bonn government first tried to engage the SED leadership in environmental matters, however, the PPP itself was still very much in gestation as a legal principle in international law and nowhere near universal acceptance.[72] The GDR, by contrast, insisted that the Federal Republic would benefit from any environmental improvements; hence *it* should cover the cost. Given this mindset, the East German attitude is best described as the "beneficiary pays principle" although such a term did not exist in international environmental law.[73]

These incompatible starting positions were themselves a function of the complex web of inter-German relations where tension was ever present. Under Chancellor Willy Brandt, the relationship of the two German states underwent a major overhaul, culminating in the Basic Treaty of 1972. Although relations in general had thus moved in a more constructive direction, the GDR nonetheless refused to discuss *any* environmental issues between 1974 and 1980. The refusal was an attempt to retaliate for the "illegal" founding of the Environmental Federal Agency (Umweltbundesamt, or UBA) in West Berlin in 1974. Unlike the GDR, West Germany did not have an environmental ministry but sought to create a federal agency for environmental affairs modeled after the US Environmental Protection Agency (EPA).[74] The federal government decided to locate this new agency in West Berlin to increase the federal presence in the divided city. The East German government, traditionally hypersensitive about any federal activities in West Berlin, accused Bonn of breaching the Four Power Agreement on Berlin of 1971. In the East German reading of the Agreement, West Berlin was not an integral part of the Federal Republic; hence Bonn was not within its rights to place any federal agencies there.[75] In the short run, the GDR vented its displeasure about the UBA by tinkering with the transit routes to West Berlin.[76] In the long run, however, it blocked any environmental talks. As a consequence, the environmental agreement originally slated to follow on the coattails of the Basic Treaty did not materialize as planned in 1973 but only in 1987.

The Werra was brought to the brink of disaster because it got caught up in the tug of war about the UBA. Ever since the Thuringian potash mines had ceased injecting brines into the ground in 1968 and instead discharged them directly into the river, the contamination of the Werra had become a pressing issue for the Federal Republic. At first, lower-ranking officials tried to address the problem directly with their East German counterparts, yet the GDR had rejected such low-level contacts since the late 1950s as insufficiently official. It was determined that any conversations other than at the highest level would be avoided in order to effect an official West German recognition of East German sovereignty. For its part, the federal government was withholding recognition under the "Hallstein Doctrine," which considered West Germany the only legitimate German state.[77] In a first legal assessment about transboundary pollution in 1971, East German attorneys concluded that Bonn could hold the GDR liable for damages only if it recognized it as a subject of international law. Yet "as long as West Germany maintains its presumptuous principle of sole representation, it cannot press these kinds of demands."[78] Not finding any local channels of communication, the federal government sought to address environmental problems in the context of the Basic Treaty.[79] The 1972 treaty envisioned future topical agreements, including those in the realm of environmental protection, "in order to contribute to the prevention of damages and dangers for the respective other side."[80] In the ensuing preparations for an inter-German environmental agreement, the ever-increasing salinization of the Werra quickly took center stage, yet these preparations were cut short by the tussle over the UBA. The GDR terminated the environmental talks in 1974, and the brines continued to pour into the river.[81]

This could have been the end of it had it not been for the brine injections of the *western* potash mines. Although the GDR refused to address its own waste disposal methods, it wanted to talk about those on the western side of the river. In February 1975, engineers at the Thuringian Karl Marx mine found brine seepage in one of its shafts. In addition, the drinking water in Unterbreizbach (East) showed increased salinity and brines were resurfacing in the vicinity. On June 23, the Karl Marx shaft collapsed. The GDR government decided to hold the pressurized deep-well injections by the western Hattorf and Wintershall mines responsible for this "seismic event" and demanded damages of 80 million valuta marks (VM), the agreement currency between the two German states.[82] The Bonn government rejected these claims outright and produced an expert opinion that mistakes in the Thuringian mines were responsible for the damage.

Specifically, the report charged that the carnallite pillars that had held the shaft's ceiling had been clipped too much in order to increase the mining of this mineral.[83] The West Germans also disputed the claim that western brines had resurfaced on GDR territory.[84] Yet since pressurized brines were known to have resurfaced on the western side as well and altered biotopes where they did, the GDR most likely had a justified complaint in that regard.[85]

Günter Mittag, the secretary for the economy of the Central Committee of the SED, held no expectations that Bonn would accept the GDR's claim for damages. He nonetheless urged Erich Honecker to authorize negotiations over cross-border mine safety.[86] At stake was nothing less than the integrity of East German state territory, since the West German brines were literally undermining the border.[87] The SED leadership was convinced that the western mines were injecting their brines into GDR territory in order to comply with "obligations of environmental protection issued by BRD agencies at the expense of the GDR."[88] They realized, however, that any approach of western officials on the issue of potash mining would inevitably prompt the Federal Republic to address the condition of the Werra. Indeed, the GDR's environmental minister, Hans Reichelt, concluded in 1977 that the international trend pointed toward the need for cooperative and even contractual solutions to issues of transboundary pollution, a trend from which the GDR could not abstain indefinitely. He predicted that the cheap method of discharging all brines into the river could not be "maintained for an extended period of time," since it would "seriously" damage relations with the Federal Republic. On the other hand, he reasoned, the mineral deposits along the Werra were finite, expected to be exploited by 2020. Until then, however, Reichelt advised holding onto the "economically convenient disposal method for the GDR of draining [wastewater] into the Werra." This goal determined the strategy that Reichelt suggested adopting for the Federal Republic. The point was to "postpone the beginnings of [any] negotiations about the salinization of the Werra or other environmental questions" as long as possible.[89]

Concessions, however, became inevitable. After four years, the West Germans succeeded in using the issue of cross-border mine safety that the GDR *did* want to address to introduce the topic of the Werra's contamination, which the GDR *did not* want to address. The first tangible success that the Bonn delegation managed to achieve was the agreement of its East German counterparts to allow a public statement that preliminary conversations about the Werra were indeed taking place. As of April 1980, the Werra was finally an official item on the inter-German diplomatic agenda.[90]

Cum Grano Salis: *The Werra Talks*

The ensuing Werra talks are a prime example of the dogged nature of inter-German diplomacy. From the perspective of the river, their net outcome was nil. The East German negotiators entered the talks with a set of instructions that did not bode well. It was their declared goal to address only the transgressions of the West German industry but not to allow a conversation about the discharge of brines from the Thuringian mines.[91] They also made clear that whatever the West Germans desired to do, "[t]here must not be any cost for the GDR."[92] This demand reflected the narrowing margins of the GDR economy. East German authorities themselves were painfully aware that as early as the mid-1970s the free-riding behavior of the Thuringian mines constituted "the only possible method within the economic parameters [of the East German command economy] to continue potash production according to plan."[93] They were willing to turn the preliminary conversations they had agreed to in April 1980 into something resembling negotiations only if a "concrete commitment [by the Federal Republic] to financial cost-sharing" was forthcoming.[94] Besides insisting on their "beneficiary pays" attitude, the East German representatives also developed the ecologically fantastic argument that the entire issue of the Werra's salinity was merely a "transit problem": "The waters [. . .] are only directed through the Federal Republic until they finally reach the North Sea."[95] In short, the approach of the GDR negotiators was to talk about the problem without actually engaging it.

If the starting position of the GDR was actually a nonstarter, why did the SED leadership agree to meetings in the first place? The reason has to do with another characteristic of East–West environmental diplomacy during the Cold War. The GDR leadership was hoping to gain access to western environmental technology through these negotiations. It sought to enlist the West German interest in reducing the chloride contamination of the Werra to modernize its own production technology. If the Federal Republic delivered this technology, the not-so-subtle hint went, its goal of reducing the ongoing pollution of the Werra would move within reach. During the years of silence after the UBA debacle, the West Germans had first considered possible technical solutions to the problem on their own. Naturally, the states that Werra and Weser traversed—Hesse, Lower

Saxony, and Bremen—had the strongest interest in a timely solution. Their governments revisited the old idea of a wastewater pipeline that would conduct the brines from the mines to the North Sea. Yet such a 400-kilometer-long pipeline would have been prohibitively expensive; at DM 1.3 billion, it would have become West Germany's most expensive environmental project. Politically not feasible, the idea was buried in 1981.[96] When the GDR signaled interest in western equipment, the Federal Republic offered flotation technology that separated kieserite (magnesium sulfate) from halite and generated less brine in the process. This technology could have been installed within two years. The offer also included retention ponds that withheld the brines when the river ran low and released them when the stream carried enough water to dilute the effluent. In their desperation, West Germans even considered trying to entice the East Germans to simply stop producing kieserite by providing them with however much of the mineral they needed on the assumption that the western mines would produce it with less pollution.[97]

Yet the East German experts had very clear ideas about which western technology they intended to obtain. They wanted to install a newly developed electrostatic separation process called ESTA, invented by the western company Kali & Salz (K&S) in Kassel and used since 1980. The procedure recovered potash from the mineral ore in a dry process. Its waste product was therefore not brines but salt tailings. The tailings were then piled up into stacks that were growing into widely visible "mountains" in the landscape. This elaborate separation method that internalized the environmental cost explained why potash production in Hesse was more expensive than in Thuringia.[98] However, ESTA was not a bargaining chip the federal government could play at will. K&S held the patent. Although the K&S management was willing in principle to share the technology, they expected in return that the GDR would commit to not selling kieserite on the world market since it would predictably offer it at lower prices than K&S, not least because of its environmental sins. The western delegation was not keen on offering ESTA anyway because it undermined the Polluter Pays Principle, would take longer to install than flotation technology, and was also much more expensive, given that it carried the additional cost of the K&S patent. As usual, the GDR leadership indicated that it was "not willing to pay either for the patent or for the [ESTA] pilot installation and expected the Federal Republic to cover all costs."[99]

Six years into the Werra talks, the river was comatose and the West German side showed clear signs of attrition. In 1980, 160 kilograms of chloride were dumped into the stream *per second*; by 1986, the amount had risen to 180 kilograms per second. Every day, the river thus carried some 35,000 tons of chloride along, of which 90 percent was said to originate in the GDR.[100] Time was on the East German side: the ongoing pollution of the Werra increased the desperation among the West Germans and hence their willingness to accommodate.

The GDR also reached its goals in the field of mining safety. As explained, the eastern delegation wanted the deep-well injections of brines in Hesse to stop. Since K&S had turned to ESTA in 1980, the need for injections had decreased anyway because this was a dry beneficiation method—the GDR's demand had taken care of itself without the opportunity for the West Germans to gain any concessions in return.[101] In 1984, both sides signed agreements that addressed two further GDR grievances, namely territorial disputes relating to the potash mines along the border and coordinated rock blasting.[102] Western observers had long detected a one-way pattern here: whenever the GDR was pursuing its own interests, negotiations had quick results, but not the other way around.[103] Not even the spectacular publicity stunt that Greenpeace staged in East Berlin in 1986 could shame the GDR into action. Under the heading "Return to Sender," the NGO dumped a hundredweight of Werra salt in front of the East German environmental ministry.[104] All that the western negotiators had to show for their efforts was an agreement that the eastern mines would give retention ponds a try. The permanent installation and use of such ponds, however, the GDR tied to the well-known demand that the Federal Republic cover all related costs.[105]

The West German delegation was left with only two bad options: to allow the continuing contamination of the river or to pay up. A leading bureaucrat in the Ministry for Inter-German Relations asserted that "in the interest of Germany [as a whole] and the Germans living in the GDR, the 'rich' Federal Republic [. . .] [should be] open to and capable of financial contributions to environmental protection in the GDR."[106] Once all West German stakeholders were on board with such an approach, the federal government offered the GDR a package in September 1988 consisting of access to ESTA technology and financial support of DM 200 million to install it.[107] At this point, the GDR could no longer afford to see the talks fail. After the Chernobyl disaster of 1986, the OECD countries made efforts to further entrench the Polluter Pays Principle as well as country liability for environmental damage. Even Günter Mittag, the Central Committee's economic secretary, now considered it "inevitable that the GDR also make material [i.e., financial] efforts to reduce the salinization" of the Werra. This concession, however, came with a complaint that the West German offer of DM 200 million was too low.[108] Clearly, both sides had to give during the Werra talks. The Federal Republic scored a victory by forcing these negotiations on the GDR at all, yet the GDR then used the talks to extract a major financial commitment from West Germany. There might not have been a winner in this constellation, but there surely was a loser all along—the river.

Something in the Air

In the autumn of 1979, Anneliese H. from Lichtenberg in Upper Franconia took her horses to a meadow to graze. When she retrieved them in the evening, she was shocked to find that their nostrils showed signs of chemical burn. Alarmed at the injury to her animals, she lodged a complaint with the Bavarian environmental ministry. For H., the cause of the injury was easily identified: the cellulose factory VEB Rosenthal in Blankenstein (East) in neighboring Thuringia (Figure 4.1).[109] While the state government of Bavaria had been well aware of sulfur dioxide plumes emanating from this particular factory, the burnt nostrils of the grazing horses marked the beginning of Bavaria's efforts to combat the emissions of VEB Rosenthal.

Yet air pollution in Upper Franconia never stemmed from one source alone. The pungent smell that hovered over the region during the colder season and that the press graphically described as resembling cat urine (*Katzendreckgestank*) drifted in from the industrial centers in northern Bohemia in Czechoslovakia. What assaulted the residents' olfactory senses in the border triangle was not sulfur dioxide but mercaptan, which resulted from a chemical combination of sulfur and crude oil during coking. The town of Hof (West) in particular became tied up with *Katzendreckgestank*. As one reporter put it in retrospect, Hof "wasn't exactly a climatic spa" during the 1980s.[110] The air pollution in this region was not just a smelly inconvenience. As the 1970s progressed, forestry officials in Bavaria and elsewhere grew alarmed about a new kind of damage to conifer forests that went beyond the well-known effects of sulfur dioxide. The news magazine *Der Spiegel* famously articulated the issue in 1981: acid rain caused forest dieback (*Waldsterben*). The environmental challenge of the 1980s was born.[111]

As *Waldsterben* began to dominate the press and Bavaria besieged the federal government to address emissions drifting in from across the Iron

FIGURE 4.1. The paper factory VEB Rosenthal in Blankenstein (East) on a winter day in January 1984.
© BayHStA

Curtain, air pollution became the second priority of the Federal Republic in its environmental diplomacy with the GDR.[112] Negotiations over emissions took on a different character and tone than those over rivers. First, whereas the flow path of the streams from eastern into western territory inevitably put the GDR on the defense, the situation was less clear-cut with air pollution, where the exchange of pollutants worked both ways and prevailing west–east winds deposited most of East Germany's transboundary emissions in Poland. While the GDR was one of the world's worst sulfur dioxide polluters, the Federal Republic was not the exclusive recipient as it was in the case of the Werra.[113] Second, negotiations over air pollution not only were an inter-German issue but were embedded in a larger European framework. Since the late 1960s, the Scandinavian countries had pushed for international recognition of damages caused by airborne pollutants and used the forum of the 1972 UN Conference on the Human Environment in Stockholm to that effect. Although the GDR did not attend the 1972 conference, both German states took part in the ensuing Stockholm process, a string of meetings aimed at understanding and curbing the acid rain phenomenon. Commitments made in this international framework then reflected back on their mutual engagement.[114] Third, the issue was a quintessential borderland problem. Among the West German federal states, Bavaria considered itself most seriously affected by East German air pollution. The GDR, in turn, found itself on the receiving end of pollutants from industries in northern Bohemia, which, incidentally, also reached Bavaria. In this triangular relationship, the GDR pursued similar goals toward its socialist neighbor Czechoslovakia (CSSR) as Bavaria did toward the GDR, in both cases to little avail.[115]

Reacting to strong complaints from residents in Upper Franconia, Bavarian authorities began measuring the air quality along the Iron Curtain in early 1977. They concluded that *Katzendreckgestank* must be related to coking processes in the Czech hydrogenation plant in Sokolov (Falkenau) and that it became particularly intense during the winter months when it encountered sulfur dioxide (SO_2) emissions.[116] Politically, this was important information. It meant that the mercaptan from the CSSR and the SO_2 from the cellulose factory in Blankenstein reinforced each other—the air above the border triangle had turned into a chemical lab of sorts. For the Bavarian state government, the air in Upper Franconia mattered not only because pollution was problematic anyway, but because the affected region was the "zonal borderland" that Bavaria had tried to prop up since the 1950s. The plumes puffing out of the VEB Rosenthal's chimney drifted into the highest political quarters. In August 1980, Governor Franz Josef Strauss implored Chancellor Helmut Schmidt to address the paper factory in his next meeting with Erich Honecker to safeguard the investments Bavaria had already pumped into the region. The unpleasant odors around Hof threatened to undo economic development in the borderlands, leaving the region to "continue to struggle for a positive image."[117] Borderland communities that had embraced leisure tourism for economic development felt especially undermined by air pollution from the other side.[118] Unnerved by the lack of progress, the city of Hof issued an "environmental resolution" in May 1986. In clear reference to the economic downturn of the 1950s, it contended that the city's viability was victimized "a second time": first by the border itself, now by pollution emanating from across the border.[119]

There were specific macroeconomic reasons for the increase in air pollution in the GDR during the 1980s. The East German economy had long benefited from cheap crude oil deliveries from the Soviet Union that covered its domestic energy needs and allowed it to produce a trade surplus, especially through the sale of various oil derivatives. For a few years, Soviet oil shielded the East German economy from the oil price crisis of 1973. Until 1976, the GDR paid only 50 percent of the world market price for crude oil, but the price among socialist friends was rising as well and reached 80 percent in 1978. In 1981, the Soviet Union went a step further and began to reduce those oil deliveries that were still below market, offering the GDR the rest of its required quantities at world market price.

The SED leadership was thus confronted with the decision to cover the GDR's oil needs either by paying realistic prices or by reducing the domestic consumption of oil.[120] It opted for the latter. East German industry therefore returned to the only fossil fuel available domestically, namely lignite. Burning lignite for electricity production, however, resulted in high SO_2 emissions. The switch to lignite would therefore have required massive investments in environmental technology like flue gas desulfurization. These, however, the SED leadership would not provide, although party leaders were neither ignorant about nor indifferent to the problem. Although the East German environmental ministry took the right steps to plan for desulfurization, the person who mattered the most in this context, SED's secretary for economic affairs, Günter Mittag, was dismissive of ecological concerns and excised most of the desulfurization investments in the planning documents of the mid-1980s.[121] Mittag's decisions, in turn, reflected the accelerating and irreversible tailspin of the East German economy by the mid-1980s. They were decisions nonetheless.

There were also specific microeconomic reasons why pollution at VEB Rosenthal had already increased in the 1970s. In line with a central planning decision of 1971, the factory was to raise its production from 90,000 to 140,000 tons of cellulose per annum. The Swedish equipment imported to meet the new quota was functional by 1977.[122] In keeping with the widely accepted idea that it was possible to dilute flue gas by releasing it from significant heights, Rosenthal also received a new 175-meter smokestack. In reality, however, the factory merely dispersed its SO_2 even farther than before, turning initially localized pollution into a regional problem. Before long, the Bavarian neighbors found out. Northeastern winds carried the smoke into Upper Franconia, and colder inversion weather pressed the polluted air down. Leaves turned yellow, grass and pines tested high for sulfur, and the nostrils of Anneliese H.'s horses were burned. The Bavarian forestry district south of Blankenstein reported 300 hectares of damaged spruce forest, and border police in Hof found white foam descending on western meadows.[123] Rumors about conditions in Blankenstein soon ran rife. Borderland residents in Franconia claimed to have already been aware in 1976 that the factory's acrid fumes had burned the finish on cars parked nearby, all of which had to be resprayed. Fruit trees in Blankenstein had allegedly died. The interior of the new smoke-stack was said to have corroded after only two years of use, and the smoke-stack might even have to be decommissioned.[124]

As in the case of the Werra, East German officials had all the relevant data about VEB Rosenthal's footprint in hand. The Ministry for Environmental Protection commissioned a study about the effects of SO_2 emanating from Blankenstein in the hope of gathering material to refute West German complaints and liability demands. Yet the internal study proved the West Germans right. Between 1976 and 1979, SO_2 emissions had risen by 46 percent. The factory caused most of its damage on GDR territory, where the Bleiloch dam had turned into a cesspool and the rolling hills along the Saale River were denuded of trees, including a rare stock of hundred-year-old pines. The East German scientists drew all the correct conclusions from the depressing results and suggested modernizing the factory's energy production and use.[125]

For the East Germans, too, the border location of VEB Rosenthal magnified the problem politically. Because the cellulose factory was so very exposed to the west and allowed the Bavarian state government to measure its emissions rather accurately, the factory management decided to modernize select aspects of the production process in an attempt to silence Bavarian protest. The smokestack was outfitted with a demister in 1980, and an outdated boiler house was decommissioned. Once these changes were made, western observers found the smokestack to be operating according to western environmental standards. As Bavaria's environmental minister conceded in 1984, the updates cut SO_2 emissions by 25 percent; citizens no longer reported plants withering in the vicinity.[126] The investments in Blankenstein fit into the established pattern of GDR authorities trying to avoid giving Bonn further leverage in environmental questions.[127]

The improvements benefited East German residents as well but they were not the intended targets, since environmental damage on GDR territory itself was allowed to fester. When polluting east of the demarcation line, VEB Rosenthal found it easier to pay fines than to adapt its production methods. Between 1977 and 1989, the company paid DM 30.3 million to East German environmental authorities for contaminating the Bleiloch dam instead of introducing a tertiary (chemical) stage at their water purification plant.[128] Similarly, ground-level odors that presumably had already bothered residents in Blankenstein in the 1980s were not addressed until 1991.[129] And yet the interesting point is that VEB Rosenthal *did* introduce environmental updates at a time when the GDR as a whole was beginning to be severely strapped for cash. The decision to allocate resources to this particular factory stemmed from its borderland location.

For VEB Rosenthal represented a regional problem at a time when transboundary air pollution was becoming part of a larger European framework. In 1968, the Swedish soil scientist Svante Odén argued that sulfur compounds could travel long distances from the source of emission and were responsible for acid rain in Sweden that damaged lakes, fish, and soil. Odén's paper marked the beginning of an accumulation of knowledge about the atmospheric flow of pollutants, the composition of air pollution, and the effects of individual toxins. For years, the causes of *Waldsterben* were far from clear, yet the long-established recognition of SO_2 as an industrial pollutant made it an obvious starting point in international environmental diplomacy.[130] The 1972 United Nations Conference on the Human Environment in Stockholm included airborne pollutants on the European agenda for the first time and formulated the general principle that activities carried out in one country must not cause environmental harm in another, or to the global commons. Affirmation of and reservations regarding this principle were determined by whether a country was an importer or exporter of emissions, which related as much to polluting activity as to wind currents and atmospheric conditions. Two of the damaged parties, Sweden and Norway, predictably pressed for the reduction of sulfuric emissions, while main emitters like Great Britain and the Federal Republic squirmed. The Stockholm process nonetheless moved forward, not least because the Soviet Union under Leonid Brezhnev threw its weight behind the idea of cutting SO_2 emissions, albeit for political reasons within the larger context of détente.[131] In 1979, thirty-three countries, including both German states, signed the Convention on Long-Range Transboundary Air Pollution (CLRTAP) in Geneva. The Convention did not yet contain concrete targets but provided the framework for future protocols and tasked each signatory with developing domestic policies for pollution control.

West Germany's transformation from "laggard to leader" (*Wettestad*) triggered another leap forward. The growing anxiety about *Waldsterben* led the Bonn government to introduce caps on SO_2 emissions in 1983 in what constitutes a major turning point in West German environmental history.[132] Spurred by the policy change in West Germany, a "30 Percent Club" of ten states emerged in 1984 that pledged to reduce 1980 levels of SO_2 emissions by 1993. At the follow-up conference in Munich in 1984, both the Soviet Union and the GDR joined the 30 Percent Club, a step that was made official when twenty-one states signed the Sulfur Protocol in Helsinki in July 1985 under the auspices of the UN Economic Commission for Europe (ECE). By this time, the discussion no longer centered only on SO_2 but also on nitrous oxide (NO_x) and so-called volatile organic compounds (VOCs).[133]

Although the GDR never ratified the Helsinki Protocol, it had nonetheless committed on the international stage to curbing its emissions.[134] As welcome as the pledge was, West German observers had serious reservations about whether the GDR could ever deliver on its promise. The western think tank German Institute for Economic Research (DIW) had documented the GDR's return to lignite since the early 1980s and considered the SO_2 reduction it aspired to technically possible but financially out of reach for the GDR.[135] Why, then, did the GDR box itself in at highly visible international conferences? Scholars have frequently pointed out that the general secretary of the SED, Erich Honecker, in charge since 1971, craved international recognition and status.[136] Besides, following the lead of the "big brother" was safe enough politically. Yet unlike the Soviet Union, the GDR did not have the option of meeting the quota by switching from oil to natural gas and nuclear energy.[137] Its economy had been chained to lignite ever since the Soviet Union had restricted its bargain offer on crudes.

Tobias Huff directs attention to a third, internal development: the Stockholm process allowed the minister for environmental protection, Hans Reichelt, to angle for political relevance within the GDR government. Once it became clear that *Waldsterben* also affected East German forests and thus threatened a resource of central importance to the country's economy, Reichelt's proposals for desulfurization gained traction. With each international conference, he managed to increase his standing, yet his room for maneuvering remained politically restricted.[138] To give but one example, in 1979 East German scientists developed the first reliable model for calculating the long-range atmospheric diffusion of pollutants under varying weather conditions in order to assess how much domestic SO_2 was reaching neighboring countries. As it turned out, Poland received 69 percent of the GDR's SO_2 emissions, Scandinavia 18.1, Czechoslovakia 6.7, and the Federal Republic 6.2 percent.[139] The study itself constituted a breakthrough in fluid mechanics, but since its results were detrimental to the GDR's standing in the Stockholm process, the environmental ministry kept the study mum, wasting the lifetime achievement of several scientists along the way.[140]

Most severely, however, Reichelt's ambitions were circumscribed economically. In 1983, the minister announced a plan to desulfurize industrial plants and power stations in urban areas. Observers in Bonn found the plan "astonishing" because it refrained from blaming pollution on capitalism and was unusually forthcoming about air quality in the GDR.[141] Various pilot projects for desulfurization had been under way since 1981, well ahead of the West German policy change of 1983. Technically, however, the GDR could afford only a dry flue gas desulfurization process based on lime that promised some reductions but was never a match for the increased emissions from lignite combustion. The elaborate filters and wet desulfurization processes used to retrofit West German power plants and factories were available only for hard western currency and hence beyond reach. Only in one case did the GDR purchase western technology in Great Britain to modernize a power plant in East Berlin.[142] With an unanticipated increase in crude oil prices in 1985, however, Reichelt's muscle atrophied as quickly as it had formed. Although a good number of functionaries within the SED and the state bureaucracy were convinced of his program's necessity, Günter Mittag cut most of Reichelt's projects out of the planning documents. Instead of reducing SO_2 emissions, after 1985 the GDR could not even hold them steady.[143] Indeed, when the East German delegation signed the Helsinki Sulfur Protocol in the summer of 1985, the SED leadership was fully aware that it was set to renege on the international 30 percent promise. To keep up appearances, the GDR government therefore submitted falsified data to the monitoring body in Oslo. Measuring stations were placed in rural areas far away from the emitters, and emission figures were knowingly reported as lower than they were.[144]

When the GDR engaged with West Germany over air pollution in the early 1980s, the same factors that made it falter on the international stage also determined its stance in talks with the Federal Republic. The Stockholm process promised only immaterial gains like prestige that Honecker clearly cared about. Negotiations with West Germany, by contrast, might yield what the GDR needed the most to combat its own sulfurous air: western currency and technology. As in the Werra talks, transboundary air pollution became a vehicle for the GDR to rope in western subsidization of its own deteriorating industrial infrastructure. The timing of environmental diplomacy throws this dynamic into relief: talks about the Werra began in the spring of 1980, conversations about air quality in 1983.[145] Environmental diplomacy with West Germany was thereby turning into a new arena of activity for the SED leadership at the very time when the GDR's liquidity crisis was pushing it into a growing dependency on West German loans and other transfers.[146] For the GDR, this new field in inter-German relations was thus instantly burdened with, and subordinated to, the expectation to generate foreign currency income, or valuta. The West German interest in environmental protection looked like a possible new income stream, and any issues that the western negotiators wanted to discuss were appraised according to their potential cash value. When Mittag instructed Hans Reichelt in 1984 to devise a directive for future environmental agreements, the priority was "valuta income," followed by access to West German technology, which would save the GDR research and development costs.[147] The same spirit informed the negotiations over the Environmental Accords, which were signed during Honecker's visit to Bonn in 1987.[148] The instructions for the GDR delegation defined the goal of these meetings as the "exchange of scientific-technological information and experiences that promise to increase economic effectiveness as well as improve the environment and the quality of life for the population in the GDR."[149] Not surprisingly, the preparations for the Accords stalled when the West Germans did not make concrete offers to provide desulfurization technology to the GDR.[150] The drive on the GDR side to obtain such technology as part of the Accords could only increase once Günter Mittag dashed Reichelt's desulfurization projects.

On the West German side, the Werra talks had already driven home the point that an asymmetry in vulnerability was at play, which the GDR sought to exploit with its argument that the beneficiary of environmental improvements should pay. The federal government resisted this logic for a good while because it undermined the Polluter Pays Principle. As the GDR's economy dissolved over the course of the 1980s and drove up transboundary pollution as a result, however, more and more western representatives came to value progress over principle. This dynamic is best explained with an example from West Berlin. Stranded within GDR territory, the city was directly exposed to the emissions from several GDR power plants and regularly suffered from smog during the 1980s when the winds blew from the southeast.[151] In 1985, West Berlin's electricity company, Bewag, announced an investment package of DM 2 billion in order to reduce its own SO_2 emissions by 40,000 tons. The very same amount invested in the GDR, however, would most likely cut emissions at East German power plants by several hundred thousand tons and benefit West Berlin's air quality to a much greater extent.[152] From West Berlin's perspective, it was therefore cost-effective to subsidize the GDR. Predictably, the city's representatives advocated for any scheme that would reduce emissions in the GDR, even if that meant building a whole new power plant there at western expense.[153] For West Berlin, asymmetrical vulnerability thus overrode the Polluter Pays Principle.[154]

The Bavarian state government eventually went down the same path. Since the Stockholm process brought no relief to Bavaria's trouble with VEB Rosenthal, the state government in Munich pressured Bonn to pursue an itemized deal with the GDR that would target this factory specifically, analogous to the Röden agreement of 1983, which had also addressed a local problem. The Munich government had initially thought it could fix the problem on its own because its relations with the GDR were excellent. Governor Franz Josef Strauss had famously brokered major western loans for the GDR in 1983 and 1984 that restored the country's international credit rating and may have averted its insolvency at the time.[155] It was no coincidence that Hans Reichelt visited Bavaria in October 1983 in what became the first official visit of a GDR minister to a federal state.[156] During the visit, the minister fell over himself praising Strauss as having single-handedly improved inter-German relations. "Governor Strauss," Reichelt proclaimed, "has achieved more with his one visit [to the GDR in July 1983] than others have in years."[157] Bavaria's environmental minister, Alfred Dick, returned the visit in May 1984 to confer further about air pollution, flue gas desulfurization, and *Waldsterben*.[158] Dick came home with the assurance that those industries whose emissions affected northern Bavaria would be given priority in the installation of desulfurization filters.[159] After the visit, his ministry also received a detailed response about VEB Rosenthal's efforts in environmental protection, although the GDR was known from other talks to be extremely cagey about the release of this kind of information.[160] The unusual complaisance not only was a bonus for Strauss but also coincided with Reichelt's "strong period" in East Berlin.

Yet conversations collapsed in 1984. Under pressure from the Soviet Union, Erich Honecker canceled a visit to Bonn that was initially planned for that year and was subsequently rescheduled for 1987. Preparatory meetings on the Environmental Accords were interrupted accordingly.[161] It did not help the West German position that Lower Saxony authorized the operation of a coal-fired power plant, Buschhaus, near Helmstedt (West) that was slated to start production in 1984. Not only did Buschhaus open at the height of anxiety about *Waldsterben* in the Federal Republic, it turned into a major scandal because it had received its permits *without* flue gas desulfurization filters.[162] East German authorities did not miss a beat and installed measuring devices to capture Buschhaus's emissions and collect "evidence" that West Germany was freeloading on the GDR.[163] Although preparations for the Environmental Accords had already resumed in 1985, bilateral talks between Bavaria and the GDR did not. Bavaria had to wait for the Accords to materialize before a deal concerning VEB Rosenthal was possible. In view of the Röden experience and the ongoing Werra talks, the politicians in Munich had no illusions about what such a deal would look like. Improvements could be achieved only if the Federal Republic delivered the technology and paid a significant share for its installation.[164] The VEB Rosenthal agreement in the spring of 1989 proved them right: West Germany committed DM 6 million to refurbish some of the factory's environmental technology, a process projected to be concluded in 1994.[165] As in the Werra talks, the GDR did not last long enough to see the consummation of the deal. Yet these late-breaking environmental agreements between both German states had not only generated detailed knowledge about East Germany's environmental conditions, but at times also produced rather accurate templates to fix them.

Conclusion: Pollution Without Frontiers

Inter-German diplomacy relating to transboundary pollution shaped the West German perception of the GDR's environmental situation in important ways. As engagement intensified during the 1980s, West German media not only covered the various talks and the emergence of the Environmental Accords, but also intensified the coverage of East Germany's increasingly hapless struggle with industrial pollution.[166] There is no indication that anyone on the West German side understood the escalating East German pollution as a hint regarding the ongoing dissolution of the GDR. Rather, representatives from Bonn perceived the demands of the eastern delegation in these talks as a pattern of extortion that enlisted West German environmental concerns for East German economic gain. This perception manifested itself one last time during negotiations over the contamination of the Elbe River in early 1989 when the West German delegation reported its impression that the GDR had agreed to meetings only to find ways to modernize its industries along the river at the expense of the Federal Republic.[167] What the western delegates did not appear to have grasped, however, was the fact that the East German negotiators no longer had any choice. Having worn out much of its industrial infrastructure, the SED leadership was not in a position to invest or modernize, let alone innovate. Because the two German states were joined at the border by numerous streams, West Germany involuntarily shared the consequences of the GDR's unraveling. In retrospect, it is easy to see that conducting environmental diplomacy as if the GDR still had the ability to hold up its end of *any* agreement became increasingly futile as the 1980s progressed. In July 1989, both German states concluded one last agreement. West Germany committed to investing in protective measures for chemical and pharmaceutical factories on the Saale and Elbe Rivers.[168] It is not much of a counterfactual to spin this trajectory forward: had the Wall not fallen, western activities to prevent pollution in the GDR would only have increased over time.

The inter-German border magnified the political meaning of pollution for both German states. Both reacted to the territorial intrusion of pollutants from across the Iron Curtain, whether those arrived by air, in rivers, or even subterraneously through geological formations. Atmospheric conditions and flow paths decided who was on the receiving end. Because the Iron Curtain was a highly symbolic and contested border, these infringements drew outsized political attention. As early as 1977, the GDR's environmental minister, Hans Reichelt, warned Günter Mittag that nonengagement with respect to the Werra had the potential to spoil relations with the western neighbor, with dire consequences for other aspects of the uneasy German symbiosis.[169] Especially during the 1980s, when the GDR had grown increasingly dependent on West German financial transfers, this was not an appealing prospect. Of the few major investments in environmental protection that the GDR did undertake in the 1980s, a noticeable number were located in the borderlands or had transboundary effects. Günter Mittag confirmed this connection in his postunification justifications and fondly remembered the sewage plant on the Röden River in particular.[170]

Due to its border location, VEB Rosenthal was one of those investment targets. Whereas the major expenditures at the factory in the early 1970s had the goal of increasing production capacities, later updates were aimed at curbing the very pollution that the Bavarian state government was complaining about. Ultimately, the ongoing investment activity at VEB Rosenthal through the 1980s saved the company after 1990. To be sure, the years after unification were a rollercoaster ride for the (new) management and the factory's employees. The accumulated wrath of Blankenstein residents finally hit VEB Rosenthal in ways that had not been possible before 1990.[171] Although the factory's environmental iniquities continued to antagonize its neighbors, the first post-*Wende* manager credited the investments of the 1980s as the company's strong "bones." To address the factory's SO_2 emissions and production odors, the management could even draw on the deal with Bavaria from the spring of 1989. The DM 6 million pledged by West Germany a few months prior to the collapse of the GDR still went toward the designated purpose.[172] Thus, VEB Rosenthal was spared the strategy frequently employed during the ecological restoration of the former GDR, namely to shut down the polluter. Rebranded as Zellstoff Rosenthal (ZR), the factory found a Canadian investor in 1994, weathered the 1990s, and is still in production.

The environmental dimension of German unification remains grossly underexplored among historians.[173] The State Treaty of July 1, 1990, which created the Monetary, Economic, and Social Union, also gave birth to the little-known Environmental Union (EnvU). The EnvU extended West German environmental law to East Germany and sought to create comparable environmental conditions in the new federal states by the year 2000.[174] Gone was the tiresome to and fro of inter-German diplomacy that allowed only for closely monitored baby steps. The early agenda for ecological restoration featured many projects that had already been part of the West German demands of the 1980s. There was not only continuity in projects and goals such as the creation of smog warning systems and the rescue of the Elbe River. As the case of VEB Rosenthal indicates, the inter-German environmental talks had generated the very knowledge that was required to pursue the ambitious agenda of the EnvU at the envisaged pace. The environmental diplomacy of the 1980s thus shares significant characteristics with the international Stockholm process, which took its time to arrive at concrete reduction targets and protocols but along the way significantly furthered scientific knowledge about acid rain, air pollution, and climate change.[175] For a brief moment, the EnvU also forced West

Germans to consider their own part in transboundary pollution during the 1970s and 1980s. With the GDR's collapse and impending unification, the self-exculpatory pointer toward the ecological sins of East German industry was no longer available. Western industries had contributed to the pollution of the Elbe and the Werra all along but conveniently ducked under the widely shared assumption that pollution swept in from the East. West German municipalities and corporations also lost the option of exporting household and hazardous waste to eastern dumps that were now considered to be unsafe. As one news report aptly put it, "[T]he times of cheap trash disposal are over."[176] It is impossible to assess the cost of the EnvU because it was inseparable from the restructuring process of the East German economy. In 2010, speeches for the twentieth anniversary of unification referenced the cost as DM 15 billion. The environmental historian Joachim Radkau estimates it at DM 80 billion.[177] The truth may lie not somewhere in between but well beyond.

If addressed by historical scholarship at all, the ecological restoration of East Germany is framed as a success story that cleaned the air, saved the rivers, created national parks, and turned lignite pits into lake districts.[178] It did all that. In contemporary discourse, however, the EnvU was intrinsically linked to the western "discovery" of the GDR's environmental record in 1990. To quote the *New York Times*, the West was getting "ready to scrub the East's tarnished environment." Put in even catchier terms, "the orderly and scrubbed half" was about to "help clean up the disheveled and polluted half."[179] Yet the redemption narrative of the postunification "cleanup" is merely the twin of the teleological account of the GDR's ecocide. Where the ecocide account runs toward the "dirty" climax of 1990, the redemption narrative takes that climax as a starting point and moseys off toward "green deliverance." To counsel caution for future work on the history of ecological restoration in East Germany is not to deny that significant and even astonishing progress has been made. The issue is, however, that the above-mentioned emplotments do not take the natural environment as a measure, only the degree of human pollution. A last dip into the Werra clarifies this trap.

In the short term, the Werra looked like a winner of unification. Between 1990 and 1996, the chloride concentration dropped some 70 percent.[180] The cause of the reduction was the shutdown of the potash mines Merkers (Ernst Thählmann) and Bischofferode (Thomas Müntzer) in Thuringia. Like most of the early successes of the ecological restoration of East Germany, the immediate relief for the Werra was thus achieved through the shutdown of polluters, or deindustrialization. In 1993, the remaining Thuringian mines were sold to the western competitor K&S in Kassel in a secret contract between K&S and the federal *Treuhand* trust agency; this arrangement externalized environmental costs related to the closed mines to the state of Thuringia.[181] During the subsequent consolidation process of the K&S corporation, the company invested in environmental technology for the remaining Thuringian mines, closed two mines in Lower Saxony, and became a global player in the fertilizer industry.[182]

Yet chloride levels in the river remain high, and the polluter is now the "western" K&S alone. Since the late 1990s, the chloride concentration has hovered around 2,500 mg/l, the level that had been introduced in 1941 as a wartime exemption. A 2012 agreement between K&S and the state of Hesse prescribed a chloride reduction from 2,500 mg/l in 2015 to 1,700 mg/l in 2020.[183] However, even at 1,700 mg/l, the river would hardly qualify as a freshwater stream, and at 2,500 mg/l, biologists consider life for native freshwater fish to be precarious.[184] In order to argue the opposite, K&S commissioned a study and announced to the press in 2014 that the bullhead (*Cottus gobio*), a kind of sculpin that thrives in brackish waters, could reproduce in the Werra.[185]

The loss of the transboundary dimension and the politics associated with it thus bring the genuine environmental consequences of potash mining to the fore again. Potash mining as such was never a subject of discussion during the inter-German Werra talks, which had been fixated on the eastern contamination of the river that had made western pollution look relatively benign in comparison. The ESTA process that K&S invented and applied after 1980 was no doubt superior to the GDR's wet beneficiation method, yet it necessitated the stockpiling of salt tailings, the waste product of ESTA. These "salt mountains" continuously release chloride as rain runoff and will do so for generations to come. In the 1990s, K&S also resumed deep-well injections and still discharges brines directly into the Werra. The quantity of brines is lower than it used to be in GDR times, and they are released at intervals that correspond to the water level of the river in order to dilute the wastewater.

Yet it is exactly this before-and-after comparison that entails a perspective that easily muddies the assessment of the postunification ecological reconstruction: just because conditions before 1989 were worse does not mean that conditions after 1990 were good. Put differently, the excesses of pollution in the GDR were such that *any* abatement seemed like a satisfactory development. The Werra's highest chloride level reached 40,000 mg/

l in 1976, so that 2,500mg/l in 2015 sounds good enough. But despite this indisputable abatement, the Werra remains the river with the highest salinity in Europe. A descent from the levels of GDR pollution and ecological viability are simply not the same.

With the ideological lid removed, concerns about the Werra reverted back to a traditional conflict between the potash industry and various disadvantaged parties, just as it had been around 1910. Now K&S held regional politicians hostage with a reminder that 4,300 jobs were on the line. Other stakeholders, including municipalities with contaminated drinking water and environmental NGOs, eagerly seized the European Water Framework Directive of 2000 that tasked European Union member states with restoring surface waters to an ecologically good status by 2015. The chloride concentration of ecologically "good" in the Directive translated into the German classification as 200 to 400 mg/l.[186] Attempts at finding consensus in round-table negotiations failed, the old idea of a wastewater pipeline was still considered too expensive, and a 2014 plan to phase out the discharge of brines projected a return to freshwater conditions in the Werra for 2075, or, as the NGOs saw it, until the cows came home.[187] To break up what opponents of K&S considered a collusion between the industrial giant and bureaucrats who dutifully extended wastewater permits, eighteen aggrieved parties enticed the European Commission to open treaty violation proceedings against Germany about the condition of Werra and Weser.[188] In early 2016, state prosecutors in Thuringia also opened proceedings against the K&S management for illegally injecting brines into the ground of the municipality of Gerstungen in Thuringia.[189]

Clearly, the conflict over potash mining is far from over. The SED leadership projected exploiting the mines along the Werra until 2020; K&S now plans to do so until 2032 (for Unterbreizbach) and 2060 (for Philippsthal). Even if the mines were to close tomorrow, the Grimm Brothers fairyland along the Werra would remain a brownfield site. The legacy of more than a hundred years of potash mining has changed the region's landscape forever. It is now dotted with salt mountains, grows seaside flora, and sits on an underground lake of injected brines nearing the size of Lake Constance.[190] For the riverine ecology of the Werra, the difference between socialism and capitalism was one of degree, not of substance.

5

Transboundary Natures

THE CONSEQUENCES OF THE IRON
CURTAIN FOR LANDSCAPE

ONE DAY IN March 1982, a red telephone rang at the East German Border Control Office in Salzwedel (East). The phones had been installed nine years earlier, a byproduct of the 1973 inter-German Border Commission, and allowed for emergency communication between West and East German border guards. Conversations unfolded according to a strict protocol; the caller began by saying, "I have some information for you," to which the respondent gave the curtest of answers. Not even a "Good day" crept into these austere exchanges. The call in March was no exception. A border guard in Uelzen (West) asked his Salzwedel counterpart to postpone a scheduled mine detonation until late June. The explosion, the Western officer explained, would disturb the breeding grounds of cranes (*Grus grus*). The East Germans consented, not without noting that "requests [. . .] pertaining to bird sanctuaries in this area have not been made before."[1]

In truth, no official bird sanctuary existed, though an accidental one was flourishing. By the time the red phone rang, the border infrastructure was at its most mature and restricted human activity in its immediate vicinity. From the western side, visitors could approach the demarcation line, leaving a swath of land between the line and the first fence untouched. Westerners often wrongly referred to this strip as a "no man's land," although it was an integral part of GDR territory. Only eastern reconnaissance troops (*Aufklärer*) known to be politically reliable patrolled this area; regular border troops remained behind the fence and covered the hinterland. Hence, in this no man's landscape, as I call it, foot traffic was rarely encountered. Ground-breeding birds were the prime beneficiaries of the new ecological regime in the immediate border area.

This chapter investigates the ecological footprint of the inter-German border and the consequences of the militarized border regime for landscape, wildlife, and humans. Researchers from various disciplines have taken note of how fortified borders inscribe themselves on landscapes and affect adjacent ecosystems as well as wildlife migration.[2] The Iron Curtain appears to have captured the imagination of scholars and a broader public alike as an example of a successful conversion of an abhorrent military structure into a nature conservation project. When the border opened in late 1989, environmental groups rushed to preserve the ecologically valuable biotopes that the border had sheltered for many years. What started as a German undertaking turned into a European-wide effort along the entire stretch of the defunct divide from Finland to the Adriatic Sea in the early 2000s.[3] Where this deadly Cold War border once meandered, a European-wide conservation project, the Green Belt, now seeks to protect the landscapes it created.

Like other military-to-wildlife conversions, the Green Belt acquires curiosity value from the paradox that military activities and infrastructures, commonly coded as "destructive," coexisted with wildlife and even protected sensitive ecosystems by preventing civilian use and development.[4] The Iron Curtain is thus frequently discussed alongside the demilitarized zone (DMZ) between North and South Korea, where military conflict created a buffer zone within a former battlefield that is off limits to both sides. What is a no-go area for humans allows wildlife to thrive.[5] Since both the Iron Curtain and the DMZ originated during the Cold War, the conversion of the border in Central Europe into a green belt has inspired the idea of creating a "peace park" at the DMZ in the event that the two Koreas improve their neighborly relations or even reunify.[6] As the geographer Jeffrey Sasha Davis observes, "Military activities do not just destroy nature, they also *actively produce it.*"[7]

Yet what kind of nature the Iron Curtain produced, and how, frequently remains vague even in scholarship.[8] In marketing materials and related press coverage, the Green Belt is celebrated as the end result of an almost miraculous transformation of a "death strip" into a "lifeline."[9] To explain the noteworthy biodiversity within the (former) border strip, the conventional Green Belt narrative references a thirty-year respite, or breathing space (*Atempause*).[10] Nature is said to have been on a "40-year holiday."[11] Such metaphors, to be sure, are deployed for public consumption to aggregate complex processes. However, they also stick in significant ways and project a narrative of human noninterference with the land that is deeply ahistorical because it treats the border as static. As Brandon Larson reminds us, metaphors in environmental science—from "alien species" to "ecological integrity" and "ecosystem service"—influence our perceptions, guide our inquiries, and catalyze particular outcomes.[12] The Iron Curtain was, after all, a military installation with a political function. It was placed into Central European landscapes that had themselves been shaped by human influences for centuries. The political objectives of this border dictated how the land was managed.

Before any respite settled over the Iron Curtain, the expansion of border fortifications degraded the landscape. In the name of security, eastern border troops denuded forests and kept weeds short. Contemporary western observers in the 1960s likened the border to a scar on the landscape.[13] "From the air," noted a British travel writer in the early 1980s, "the border looks like earth that has just been prepared for a new road, much lighter than the surrounding ground of fields and forests." Watchtowers cast a pall on the scenery "like the gibbets in a landscape by Brueghel."[14] As the fortifications evolved, so did their consequences for wildlife. Animals, rarely recognized in conventional historical writing, emerge as agents in this chapter if by "agency" we mean animal activities that led to human responses, in this case adjustments of the border fortifications.[15]

The political economy of the borderlands further influenced the landscapes along the border. In the hyper-surveilled eastern 500-meter-deep security strip, agriculture and forestry work were hampered. In the 5-kilometer-deep restricted zone, industrial development was prohibited. In the western "zonal borderlands," by contrast, development was encouraged and subsidized, yet to little avail. Low population density was forced by deportations (East) or came about as the result of weak job markets (West). In myriad ways, either direct or indirect, the border regime thus altered the natural environment adjacent to the border. I suggest that the resultant landscapes are best understood as *transboundary natures*: they transcended a politically and socially constructed barrier, which is of course a truism in environmental studies. However, the term also identifies the barrier itself as an agent in this process. Not the fact that a border runs *through* a landscape, but the consequences of the border *for* landscape are captured by this term and shape this chapter.

Over the course of the 1970s, conservationists, local residents, and even some politicians discovered the transboundary natures along the

Iron Curtain and began to appreciate them as an unintended consequence of the East German border regime. This appreciation was conditioned by increasing environmental sensibilities and the growing awareness that the postwar affluence West Germans had come to enjoy came with increased pressure on land use and contributed to the overall pollution of water, soil, and air. During the 1980s, West German officials and environmental NGOs initiated attempts to persuade GDR authorities to participate in the establishment of transboundary nature preserves. Parts of the Lauenburg lake region in the north, the Drömling wetlands east of Wolfsburg, and the Rhön mountain range straddling the border between the states of Hesse, Bavaria, and Thuringia anchored these efforts. None of these little-known projects came to fruition before 1990. They were ultimately lost in the maze of unsuccessful inter-German environmental negotiations addressed in the preceding chapter. Although these endeavors failed at the time, they prepared the way for the Green Belt conservation project that materialized on the heels of the GDR's collapse and that this chapter seeks to historicize. By asking how, exactly, the border shaped landscapes over time, under which circumstances these changes came to be appreciated, and how the Green Belt conservation project came about, the chapter seeks to avoid the "redemptive stories" that have come to be associated with the Green Belt.[16]

Border Fortifications and No Man's Landscapes

As early as the 1960s, the border regime began to produce unintended ecological consequences. These consequences differed according to landscape type and species. The border snaked through a cross section of German landscape types such as cultivated landscapes and open space (552 kilometers), woodlands and forests (535 kilometers), as well as lakes, wetlands, and rivers (225 kilometers). For 58 kilometers it ran through towns, villages, and hamlets.[17] Over time, the border infrastructure assumed an increasing amount of space and even changed location by moving farther inland. During peak periods of development, the natural environment along the border was altered significantly. In view of the differing terrain, neither the border infrastructure nor its upkeep was ever uniform or fully standardized; the same was true of its ecological consequences.

The first round of interventions came with the introduction of the border regime in May 1952. The land on the East German side was dissected into a 500-meter security strip and a 5-kilometer-deep prohibited zone. These areas were intensely policed, their residents monitored or selectively deported, public life and sociability reduced to a minimum. At the same time, military authorities ordered locals to clear a 10-meter-deep strip of land and harrow it twice a year to keep it free of vegetation. Even asphalt was ripped up or covered with sand. No one was allowed to cross this strip in either direction, and those who did cross in defiance of the injunction would be fully exposed. This control strip, as it was called, was not an obstacle in itself, but it alerted border guards to the frequency of crossings, allowing them to adjust their patrols accordingly. A barbed-wire fence was set up on the demarcation line, although it took years to cover the entire length of the Iron Curtain with even such a simple fence.[18]

The next major escalation of fortifications unfolded after the construction of the Berlin Wall in August 1961. The inter-German border saw a buzz of activities aimed at making it impenetrable and consequently littering the landscape with more "hardware": higher fences, at times erected in parallel rows (*Doppelzaun*), along with watchtowers, observation bunkers, anti-vehicular ditches, minefields, dog runs, floodlights, and patrol roads. Walls were built in some villages like Vacha and Mödlareuth to prevent visual contact with the western side. Border troops also increased the policing of the restricted zone; checkpoints now regulated entry from the hinterland. Some villages in the security strip even found themselves sandwiched between two fences: one toward the west, the other toward the hinterland. Well into the 1980s, whole dwellings, even villages and hamlets, were razed if the border authorities considered them a security hazard.[19]

The final push toward a fully militarized Iron Curtain began in the late 1960s. The barbed-wire fences were replaced by galvanized steel mesh fence panels more than 3 meters high that were bolted to reinforced concrete posts. Many sections of the border were equipped with parallel fences enclosing land mines or dog runs. Beginning in 1970, the border troops also mounted tripwire-activated antipersonnel shrapnel mines, the infamous SM-70s, on the westernmost fence.[20] With the front to the west now reliably deadly, the focus of the border regime shifted toward policing the eastern hinterland and thwarting escapes well before anyone even reached the security strip. The number of escapes over the inter-German border subsequently fell below one hundred in 1974.[21]

During these successive rounds of border construction, the most obvious intervention into the landscape entailed the clearing of land to set up the fence, to lay minefields, or to make the terrain more visible to the

guards. Swaths of land were cleared of forest and undergrowth along select stretches of the border. Resistance to such measures was extremely
rare, but Walter Elmer, a forester in the Harz Mountains, notably tried in
1961 to save an old-growth beech forest located in a landscape protection
area from being denuded in the name of border security. In retaliation,
he and his family were deported to Thuringia, where his career suffered
a setback.[22]

With the improved fortifications in place, border troops continued to
regulate the vegetation. Growing corn in the restricted zone was prohibited because the tall crop could provide cover for an escapee.[23] Certain
areas, such as the control strip, the minefields, and the patrol roads, were
kept entirely free of vegetation. During the 1950s, local farmers were conscripted to harrow the control strip, but in later years the border troops
simply applied herbicides to the areas where they needed a clear view. At
times, the wind carried the baneful mist onto western fields, causing crops
to wither.[24] While the loss of vegetation already had adverse effects on insects, insects also became the explicit target of border troops. Beginning
in 1963, intelligence units placed microphones on the demarcation line
to record conversations among tourists and western border personnel.
The humming of insects often made the recordings inaudible, prompting
the National People's Army (NVA) to apply insecticides around the microphones.[25] After the fall of the Berlin Wall, rumors surfaced within border
communities that the NVA had practically poisoned the border strip,
leaving the soil deeply contaminated.[26] Amid news of environmental
degradation throughout East Germany, such rumors rang true, but unlike many alarming discoveries after the GDR's demise, this one at least
proved unfounded.[27]

One key development in the emergence of transboundary natures,
however, was the gradual repositioning of the entire border infrastructure
farther inland, away from the actual demarcation line. The original fence
and control strip were abandoned, new versions thereof erected farther
east. The land between the demarcation line and the new fence, the alleged no man's land, was more or less abandoned.[28] By 1963, western authorities reported that the old control strip that had previously been kept
bare became overgrown with weeds, followed by shrubs and birch trees.[29]
These no man's landscapes would assume key importance for the Green
Belt conservation project.[30]

Only in rare cases did GDR land on the "enemy side" of the fence remain
in agricultural use. Allowing farmhands to work beyond the westernmost

fence required intense surveillance by border troops, since the workers on this strip were separated from the West only by their desire to return to their families at night. The fear that this desire might be lacking and the fact that even the most banal activities tended to draw crowds on the western side thus influenced the use of the land beyond the last fence. If the land was touched at all, the border authorities allowed only activities like grass mowing and irregular maintenance work.[31]

Yet this low-key maintenance created and preserved meadows and neglected grasslands and proved beneficial for the recovery of a flora and fauna increasingly displaced elsewhere in both German states by high-intensity farming. Unlike farmland, these meadows remained unfertilized. The insect-rich, often moist meadows attracted rare birds, such as the European nightjar (*Caprimulgus europaeus*) and the northern lapwing (*Vanellus vanellus*), while ground-breeding birds like the bluethroat (*Luscinia svecica cyanecula*), the corn bunting (*Emberiza calandra*), the stonechat (*Saxicola torquata*), and the whinchat (*Saxicola rubetra*) benefited from the lack of foot traffic. These birds actually integrated the border fortifications into their habitat. The sloping sides of the anti-vehicular ditches provided ideal nesting grounds, since these birds prefer to nest on an incline. The metal fence and border poles were the perfect height for song posts and perching.[32] Indeed, a whinchat perched on one of the black-red-and-yellow GDR border poles later became the marketing symbol of the Green Belt campaign.

Animals and the Iron Curtain

While birds found ways to benefit from the Iron Curtain, the situation was different for mammals. As long as the border fortifications consisted of a simple barbed-wire fence, wildlife had no trouble coexisting with it. The first generation of fences, erected after May 1952, posed no hurdle for small animals; they could slip through the wire. If a fence blocked an established deer passage, the animals could run alongside the barrier until they found an opening. And mature stags could easily clear an early fence, which stood less than 5 feet high. As the SED regime sealed off Berlin in August 1961, however, the fence grew ever more effective in deterring human migration, undercutting mammal migration as well. The worst development for wildlife at this juncture was the installation of minefields. Border troops were ordered to bury land mines, a treacherous job that occasionally claimed the life of a conscript. Though they were intended to blow up refugees, even hares and foxes could trigger these deadly devices. Thus began the wildlife massacre of the 1960s.[33]

In the Harz Mountains, land mines were installed in the winter of 1962. By mid-1963, western forestry personnel had counted six hundred dead animals. Officials in the county of Lauenburg (West) near Lübeck estimated the loss of some one thousand deer in the two years since the mines had been laid.[34] An East German hunter residing in the security strip recalls there being "cadaver fields" along the fence.[35] Local newspapers described the fate of maimed creatures in the same dramatic language usually reserved for reports on escape attempts: "One of the strongest stags of the southern Harz," one paper wrote, "a 14-point buck, stepped onto a mine in a deer crossing. The wounded animal managed to drag itself to the West."[36] Another stag, a splendid specimen, received his coup de grâce from a western ranger after it became caught in barbed wire. In the struggle to free itself, the animal pulled some 20 kilograms of barbed wire into its antlers.[37] By the mid-1960s, West German customs personnel in the Harz Mountains were convinced that the population of roe deer had already been decimated by the mines.[38] Yet there was no feasible way to keep the animals off their century-old deer passages and away from the border. Building a fence on the western side was out of the question for political reasons; East German propagandists would have had a field day if "the West" had erected fences, too. Some thought was given to a chemical fence whose odor would deter the animals, but such an expensive solution was never implemented.[39] The despair among western foresters and hunters over the border's senseless cruelty undoubtedly ran deep, yet the main killer of wildlife during the 1960s was not the GDR border regime but the West German symbol of newfound prosperity—the car.[40] Road kill, however, was less politically charged than the dramatic death of animals at the Iron Curtain.

Clearly, change could come only from the eastern side, and eventually it did. Not concern for wildlife but worries about escalating costs prompted action. For one, the need to prevent migrating deer from reaching minefields and damaging signal fences provided a shameful excuse to shoot them. Under the pretext of military necessity, high-ranking officers of the border troops would convene hunting parties and go for the kill.[41] These "hunts" flouted all the rules and proud traditions of German huntsmanship. Animals were shot while feeding, in the closed season, in the glare of floodlights, or within corrals. Anything that moved was fair game: gravid does, fawns, and wild sows with litters. The hunts were supposed to be top secret, but residents in the security strip usually realized what was going on.[42]

Since large-scale extermination of wildlife was not practical, keeping the animals away from the expensive minefields was factored into the next round of enhancements to the border fortifications. After a brief experiment with nets, the construction of double metal fences in the second half of the 1960s proved effective in reducing the carnage. Two parallel 10-foot fences enclosed the minefields, making them inaccessible to deer. Animals still migrated along the fence in search of passage, though. At some locations, border troops cut holes into the bottom of the fence to allow at least hares and foxes to cross at unmined spots. And indeed, by the early 1970s, western newspapers were reporting that the death of wildlife at the border had abated. But they also noted the end of biological exchange. The gene pool of German deer was now effectively divided.[43]

Another deadly innovation was introduced to the inter-German border at the same time: SM-70 antipersonnel mines. These devices were connected to three wires; two wires were designed to keep away deer and birds, the third triggered the shrapnel.[44] Thus, while some thought had been given to preventing the mines from discharging toward animals—again, solely for cost reasons—some animals were nonetheless at the mercy of this new weapon, this time as guinea pigs. During a testing period, animals were driven toward the devices, which exploded, confirming their deadly effectiveness. An officer reported that "wild boars, deer, and winged game [were] mostly (72 percent) mortally wounded" by these weapons.[45]

It was not only wildlife that suffered such fates at the inter-German border; service animals also fared poorly. To improve security, border authorities deployed service dogs that filled traditional roles such as patrolling, tracking, pursuit, and detention. Like their West German counterparts, GDR border troops considered the German shepherd the most suitable breed for such duties, but they also employed Rottweilers, Airedales and other terriers, and schnauzers. The best animals served with the elite reconnaissance troops. Yet a chronic shortage of valuable breeds forced border guards to turn to dogs of similar sizes, provided they proved their worth during training. If a dog lacked adequate skills, it was treated as waste and assigned to watchdog duties in dog runs amid the border fortifications, a cruel fate exceeded only by the use of dogs for target practice.[46]

Beginning in 1968, some difficult-to-guard stretches of the border were equipped with dog runs and dog trails. The use of guard dogs increased after 1983 when, in response to international pressure, the GDR began to dismantle the SM-70 shrapnel mines.[47] On these trails, dogs were attached to steel cables with individual leashes. Dividers on the cables prevented them from reaching each other and defined the space in which they were to patrol. Some dogs strangled themselves on their leash. Within the perimeter created by the leash stood a simple hut and a food bowl that was attached to the ground. Once hooked up to the cables, the animals were more or less abandoned. A border guard would drive by once a day and hurl some food at the unfortunate creatures from the back of an army truck. If the food landed outside a dog's perimeter, the animal endured a day without food. In the Harz Mountains, heavy snow could prevent border guards from reaching the animals in winter. Weakened by the lack of food, the dogs would eventually freeze to death. Yet it did not take extreme weather conditions to torture the animals. Without any meaningful contact with humans, most of the dogs slowly went mad. Western observers depicted the dogs on border duty as particularly aggressive and bloodthirsty specimens, trained to fell a refugee.[48] More accurately, however, they were extremely unfortunate and abused animals.[49]

Nothing underscores this more acutely than the fate of the dogs on Lankow Lake. During one particularly hard winter—witnesses differ in their recollection of which year it might have been—the lake between Schlagsdorf (East) and Ratzeburg (West) froze solid. To prevent people from escaping across the lake, a dog trail was installed on the ice. No one attempted to escape, and so the winter passed until the ice grew thinner. The officer in charge was not on site but decreed from afar that the ice still held strong. The dogs therefore had to stay put. The local border guards, however, knew better and no longer dared to approach the animals with food. The heaviest dog in the middle broke through the ice first, his body weight pulling on the steel cable to which he was attached. One by one, his canine comrades went down into Lankow Lake, sharing his fate. Only one collie mix survived because he had been tied up close to the shore and was rescued by a compassionate border guard.[50] Some 6,500 service dogs were still in use in the GDR border regime when the Berlin Wall fell; 2,500 were reassigned to western customs and police officials. Another 1,500 dogs were taken in by East Germans, but for the remaining 2,500, the future would be grim. The West German Humane Society mounted an adoption campaign for the "Wall dogs," as they came to be called. Most of them could be placed in private homes.[51]

Wetlands and Waterways

The inter-German border not only shaped the natural environment within its immediate vicinity; it also had ecological consequences well outside the fortifications, for instance in the Drömling wetlands. The Drömling is a fen of some 320 square kilometers located east of Wolfsburg and Braunschweig. As David Blackbourn has shown, much arable land in Germany had emerged over the centuries from fens, moors, and marshes that were drained, dammed, and diked. These lands required continuous hydrological management lest dams become silted, dikes porous, or ditches overgrown.[52] The draining and melioration of the Drömling started during the reign of Frederick II of Prussia in order to settle colonists on the moors. The rivers Aller and Ohre became part of a complicated system of drainage ditches, dams, locks, ship hoists, and bridges: the Drömling turned into a "land of a thousand trenches." In 1933, the Drömling acquired its biggest "trench" when the Braunschweig segment of the Mittelland Canal opened. In order to maintain fields in drained wetlands, German farmers formed cooperatives that collectively financed and provided the labor for their upkeep. In the case of the Drömling, the Aller-Ohre Cooperative saw to this work.

After the war, the demarcation line split the moors, giving some 6,000 hectares to Gifhorn County in Lower Saxony and three times that to the GDR district of Magdeburg.[53] Much reclaimed land on the western side belonged to farmers east of the border who could no longer gain access to their fields. Collective maintenance of the Aller-Ohre Cooperative collapsed as well. Near the demarcation line and within the security strip, many ditches silted up.[54] Not surprisingly, the waters in the divided Drömling no longer drained in the way they were engineered to do but reverted to their more natural ways, in this case flowing westward and submerging fields and pastures in Gifhorn County during spring floods. Plans to pump the water into the Mittelland Canal were dismissed as too costly.[55] By the late 1960s, officials and farmers concluded that the Drömling fields, once wrenched from the waters, should be returned to them. Not only were the fields small and not profitable, even under ideal drainage conditions and much melioration the soils were considered poor.[56] The collapse of the wetland's complex hydrological management due to the border thus prompted the rethinking of the Drömling's future. Arable fields were given up and allowed to revert to wet-pasture meadows.

Conservationists quickly realized that these border-induced changes presented an opportunity to preserve the Drömling. The ornithologist Rudolph Berndt of Braunschweig suggested designating the entire western part of the Drömling as an area for nature protection and study. The wetland was home to a broad range of vegetation: extensive reed beds, autochthonous pines, spruces, and gray alders, marine vegetation alongside boreal flora. Wildlife was similarly diverse. Berndt pointed out that the Drömling had become the last refuge for many species dislodged by high-intensity farming elsewhere. Yet an argument based solely on biodiversity would not suffice to effect a political decision to designate a protected area. Berndt therefore attuned his proposal to the political realities of a divided Europe and promoted it to a local population containing a significant number of expellees and refugees. In terms of climate and flora, he depicted the Drömling as a transplanted landscape: "It is East Prussia in Lower Saxony, East Germany in West Germany or Siberia in Western Europe—north Eurasian 'taiga' in central European deciduous forests." Such landscapes had disappeared behind the Iron Curtain, Berndt continued, beyond the reach of the Western European naturalist and hiker. The Drömling thus provided people the chance to experience a piece of Eastern Europe in the west. Especially refugees from the GDR who now lived in the Federal Republic would appreciate the preservation of these wetlands, Berndt argued. Here was "the only opportunity to hike in a landscape, to observe and experience nature that shows a striking semblance to home."[57]

Yet things got worse before they got better. Berndt's project of a grand wetland reserve had to await unification. Despite the fact that the Drömling experienced seasonal flooding, the overall trend during the 1970s and 1980s indicated that its desiccation was due to the sinking water table. Farming collectives on the eastern side clamored for continuing melioration and draining to boost their production. But the West Germans had even more potent means of damaging the wetlands. The city of Wolfsburg drew its drinking water from the Drömling and was intent on increasing its extraction. Not that Wolfsburgers were suddenly drinking more, but Drömling water contained less nitrate than the groundwater in areas with intensive farming and fertilizing. The city's suppliers thus hoped to sell Drömling water to other utility companies that needed to dilute their more contaminated waters. And because the water table was sinking, the remaining fields and pastures in the Drömling suddenly needed irrigation that, counterproductively of course, drew on groundwater.[58]

In view of the competing interests of agriculture, water users, and nature protection, the preservation of the western Drömling remained piecemeal despite the major efforts of West German advocacy groups.[59] It is therefore interesting to note that the conservationists in East Germany, who had to proceed with political wit and caution, nonetheless managed to protect the wetland. Under the leadership of Giselher Schuschke, the founder of the Society for Nature and the Environment (GNU) in the Magdeburg District, regional conservationists founded a Drömling association and promoted the protection of the landscape in order to "increase its recreational value for the working class."[60] The association's greatest success was preventing the further enlargement of the River Ohre in 1986. Much to the chagrin of the Stasi, the members of the association were speaking Bolshevik so well that the Stasi could not prove any "activities in an adversarial and negative sense" or any "abuses" of the causes the GNU was allowed to pursue.[61]

As the example of the Drömling shows, the border regime proved instrumental in bringing about landscape change by returning fields to wetlands. All activities that kept the border functional and that this militarized strip prevented or necessitated contributed to the emergence of transboundary natures, that is, landscapes shaped by the border. On both sides of the demarcation line, observers began to notice these changes. Although such observations were few and far between, they are worth recording since they cultivated an awareness of the border strip's ecological value that became the basis for the efforts to transform it into a conservation project after 1989.

Watching the Grass Grow: Nature Observation along the Iron Curtain

When and why did Germans actually notice that the border strip was taking on a life of its own? Many West Germans were well familiar with the monstrosity on their country's edge thanks to countless media reports and border tourism. Yet whereas news coverage and visits to the Iron Curtain tended to focus on the fortifications and ideological dimension of partition, a new element entered the perception of the inter-German border over the course of the 1970s—nature. The "discovery" of nature in the border strip at that time was no coincidence. Scholars commonly regard the 1970s in West Germany as the decade when concerns for the environment moved to the political mainstream. The environmental cost of reconstruction and the increasing pressure on land use turned into a point of concern around 1970, and the environment consequently emerged as a new field of civic and political engagement.[62] The fact that conservationists in the 1970s discovered the border areas as ecologically intact and particularly rich in biodiversity was thus predicated on a growing sense of loss. Familiar landscapes and species that used to be common fell victim to industrialized agriculture and urban sprawl. The border, usually vilified in West German political discourse for its violence, turned into the unlikely mirror of these developments.

Random observations surfaced as early as 1958 when residents of Lübeck took note of the "wonderfully secluded opportunities for hikes where the wanderer encounters wild boars, roe deer, and pheasants" east of town along the demarcation line.[63] In the nearby Trave Bay, Buchhorst Island (West) was in the midst of an ecological transformation by 1964. Since the bay and its inlet, Dassow Lake, were difficult to police, GDR border authorities fortified the shores of Dassow Lake. On the eastern side, the lake could no longer be used for fishing or water sports.[64] However, through Trave Bay the inlet remained accessible to West German boats: only the shores were off limits. In view of the frequent incidents that this confusing situation created, Buchhorst Island was abandoned and no longer used even as pastureland. The island's characteristic maritime vegetation flourished, and with it came migratory birds and Nordic waterfowl, "a unique constellation in the Lübeck area," as one observer noted.[65] The state of Schleswig-Holstein turned Dassow Lake into a nature preserve in 1983, and Buchhorst Island became officially off limits even to West Germans.[66]

By the late 1970s, the ecological value of the "the longest biotope" along the demarcation line was becoming an insider tip among naturalists.[67] On the border between Schleswig-Holstein and Mecklenburg, Thomas Neumann of Ratzeburg represented the World Wildlife Fund (WWF) and lobbied in particular for the protection of cranes (*Grus grus*) and the white-tailed eagle (*Haliaeetus albicilla*). During the 1980s, Neumann could count on support from the state and federal governments. Some people did, after all, consider the white-tailed eagle the heraldic symbol of the Federal Republic. It was ubiquitous on official seals and flags, yet all but missing in nature; only a handful of breeding pairs were known to nest in West Germany, although around a hundred bred in the GDR.[68] This was a common pattern among several endangered species, such as the autochthonous Elbe beaver (*Castor fiber albicus*), cranes, and white storks (*Ciconia ciconia*). These animals might put in an appearance in the West but settled on the quieter eastern side to breed. Neumann gathered such information from conservationists in Mecklenburg (East) whom he visited within the framework of the 1972 Inter-German Travel Agreement. Neumann also recruited customs officers to monitor crane populations and trained them how to interact with people who might interfere in breeding areas of rare birds.[69]

In Hesse, the Association for Ornithology and Nature Protection (HGON) was the leading player among the conservationist NGOs. One of HGON's board members, Wolfram Brauneis, was the driving force behind the designation of several nature preserves near the border and monitored the landscapes along the Werra where the river meandered across the demarcation line.[70] Brauneis made it his life's mission to reintroduce the peregrine falcon (*Falco peregrinus*) to Hesse. The population had collapsed due to the heavy use of pesticides in agriculture.[71] Started in 1978, the reintroduction program lasted fifteen years. Many of the released birds migrated into the GDR and nested, for instance, on the face of Heldrastein cliff immediately across the border. In 1981, East German ornithologists began to report sightings of the tagged falcons to their western colleagues. Transboundary cooperation would have made Brauneis's work much easier, but official collaboration was out of the question. Only the seditious border crossings of the falcons created a bond between eastern and western birders.[72]

Another ornithologist who began to pay attention to the transboundary natures was Kai Frobel, a member of the NGO Bund Naturschutz in Bavaria (BN), who would become one of the founding fathers of the Green Belt project. As a teenager in the mid-1970s, he mapped the whinchat (*Saxicola rubetra*) around Coburg County in Upper Franconia. The resulting map showed the rare birds' nesting sites right on the dividing line between the two German states; the dots for each breeding pair mirrored the contours of the demarcation line (Figure 5.1). Frobel published the results and included a message to policymakers: it apparently took the morally repugnant death strip to preserve species that should have been common in Germany but had fallen victim to industrialized agriculture.[73] Frobel's frequent appearances along the border, his accidental presence at a secret gate used to smuggle East German agents into Bavaria, and his first visits to the GDR to meet East German birders triggered Stasi surveillance of

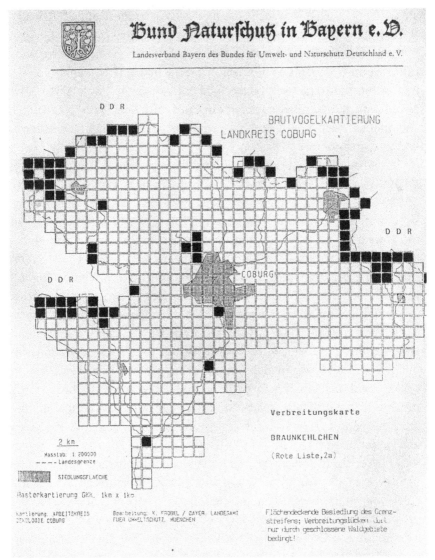

FIGURE 5.1. The ornithologist Kai Frobel mapped the whinchat (*Saxicola rubetra*) in Coburg County (West) in the mid-1970s. The recorded nesting sites mirrored the contours of the demarcation line.

© Bund Naturschutz in Bayern

this rather unassuming ornithologist.[74] On the basis of Frobel's mapping work, the BN in 1982 began to purchase select tracts of land on the demarcation line. Thomas Neumann did the same on behalf of the WWF in the Lauenburg lake district.[75]

A broader public learned about all creatures great and small in the border strip from the work of the filmmaker and conservationist Heinz Sielmann. Sielmann produced the popular prime-time series *Expeditions into the Animal Kingdom*. In 1988, he dedicated one show to "animals in the shadow of the border." Like Frobel, Sielmann had nothing good to say about the border as such, but he realized the value of the habitats that it protected. The closing words that he broadcast into German living rooms almost sound like a prophecy today. The landscapes along the border, he suggested, would make a tantalizing transboundary conservation project between the two German states. A national park stretching from the Baltic to the Thuringian Forest would be the most fitting monument to German unity once the border was overcome, he said.[76]

Observing the no man's landscapes on the demarcation line was relatively easy for western naturalists but next to impossible for East German ecologists. Still, the very first report about bird life in the border strip was filed by an East German ornithologist. Helmut König of Halberstadt monitored birds in Lenzer Wische, a wetland in the triangle formed by the towns and villages Dömitz (East), Lenzen (East), and Gorleben (West) on the Elbe River. Beginning in April 1965, König had observed the grasslands of Lenzer Wische for weeks at various times of day and night. He soon found himself "on a first-name basis" with each breeding pair in his control area. König was a border guard. He enlivened his patrols with birdwatching; binoculars were part of his equipment anyway. While he did not mention his official mission in his avifaunistic publication and chose his words carefully, any reader from the region would have had a clear sense of where he had been.[77]

It appears that birdwatching among GDR border guards had become somewhat more common by the late 1970s. Bernd Katzer, an amateur ornithologist conscripted into a motorized infantry regiment near Sonneberg in Thuringia, still remembers the heavy traffic of pheasants (*Phasianus colchicus*) and partridges (*Perdix perdix*) in the Muppberg cemetery on the western side that he could observe from his post. Serving not out of conviction but by necessity, Katzer tried to stay out of trouble during the notorious inspections of lowly border guards by superior officers. He therefore enlisted the common blackbird (*Turdus merula*), going on alert whenever the bird's warning call announced that "danger," or rather an officer, was approaching.[78] Another border guard recounts that for someone interested in ornithology and herpetology, "every shift turned into an excursion." Bernd Friedrich spent his military service between 1981 and 1983 on the border in Eisenach County and rediscovered the eagle-owl (*Bubo bubo*) as a breeding bird. Curiously, he published his findings in a West German ornithology journal in 1987.[79] Others stuck to the publications of their home associations and remained vague about their exact locations.[80] One ornithologist from the Harz region even suspected that male naturalists were deliberately drafted for border duty because they came with proven outdoor and observation skills.[81]

For a few years, the districts of Erfurt, Gera, and Suhl even dispatched a professional conservationist into the border strip. In the spring of 1984, the Institute for Landscape Research and Nature Conservation (ILN) received a phone call from a Thuringian border guard unit that reported "a strange black bird with red feet that flew back and forth across the metal fence."[82] The Institute sent the ornithologist Martin Görner to investigate the sighting. Near Wurzbach in the Franconian Forest, beyond the last fence and thus within reach of West German territory, he discovered a pair of black storks (*Ciconia nigra*) tending to a nest. The black stork had not been recorded as a breeding bird in Thuringia for the previous 170 years. Among ornithologists, the discovery caused a minor sensation.[83] The sharply meandering demarcation line, especially in southern Thuringia, created deep pockets and enclaves in the restricted zone. This terrain, for instance in the Grabfeld region, now moved onto the radar of GDR conservation officials. The ILN dispatched Görner for regular inspection trips. Görner received an entry permit for the restricted zone and the security strip. For his annual inspections, the border guards even opened the gate in the last fence and let him roam unsupervised in the no man's landscape.[84]

A Western Idea the GDR Did Not Want:
Cross-Border Nature Preserves

With environmental sensibilities on the rise, the biodiversity of the border strip became relevant to western politicians as well. Uwe Barschel, the CDU governor of Schleswig-Holstein, was the first to develop a significant policy initiative to preserve landscapes in the border county Herzogtum Lauenburg (West).[85] In 1985, Barschel launched a program geared toward the southeastern edge of his state, which shared 132 kilometers of border with the GDR. The language of the program was not unlike that of later conceptions of the Green Belt: the partition of Germany, it noted, resulted in "enforced tranquility" around Lauenburg and Ratzeburg and thereby created "spaces of refuge and retreat for those plants and animals endangered in other regions." Besides protecting these areas, the program envisioned paying farmers to switch to extensive use of fields and meadows, as well as supporting ecotourism in the counties adversely affected by the border.[86]

The state government earmarked DM 20 million for the program. The initiative was well received among conservationists.[87] However, Barschel was at pains not to allow anyone to perceive the initiative as a recognition of the GDR and its border regime. In fact, the program referred to the border between Schleswig-Holstein and Mecklenburg in order to avoid mentioning the GDR. Yet the key to the program was nonetheless the idea of creating cross-border nature preserves in cooperation with the GDR. With the same biota on both sides of the fence, Barschel was hoping the SED leadership would prove amenable to designating as protected areas the corresponding eastern sections. He intended the divided Schaalsee Lake to become the first such transboundary project.[88] The transboundary natures thus received the political assignment of pacifying the border and starting a conversation between its neighbors.[89]

For Barschel, this was not just a regional initiative: he was jockeying to become a player in inter-German relations, both in upcoming state elections and presumably to build his reputation in the hope of attaining federal office.[90] He tied his foray into nature conservation to the vague promise to the GDR that economic advantages might ensue if the SED leadership went along with his ideas.[91] His move was in sync with the *Deutschlandpolitik* of the 1980s. Unencumbered by the change of administration from Chancellor Helmut Schmidt (SPD) to Helmut Kohl (CDU) in 1982, inter-German relations continued to be geared toward pragmatic cooperation.[92] Aided by the GDR's increasingly precarious economic situation, West German politicians managed to engage the SED leadership in a host of policy initiatives that eventually led to a string of high-profile inter-German agreements. One of these was the Environmental Accords of 1987. As explained in the preceding chapter, West Germany had sought such an accord since 1973 to address issues such as transboundary pollution, but the GDR refused to participate in any environment-related talks until 1980. The breakthrough came in the context of Erich Honecker's desire to visit West Germany in order to showcase the extent of the GDR's acceptance as a sovereign country. During his visit to Bonn in September 1987, he signed several

agreements that were hailed as signs of progress in inter-German relations.[93] The Environmental Accords, however, did not commit its signatories to any concrete action, only to further talks. Hence, the paper was
paired with a voluminous agenda for further consultations, to be carried
out by various working groups.[94] As the fourteen working groups gathered to address *Waldsterben*, air pollution, and waste management, the
smallest one was tasked with discussing nature conservancy.

When Barschel alerted Chancellor Kohl and federal agencies to his
initiative on cross-border nature preserves, he encountered the ongoing
preparations for the Environmental Accords.[95] As early as July 1984, the
Bonn government had approached the GDR with a proposal for an agreement about landscape and nature conservation. However, the federal proposal had deliberately skirted the issue of cooperation across the border,
assuming that it would only elicit a negative response. Since the GDR
never specifically reacted to this first federal proposal, it was folded into
the general negotiations for the Environmental Accords instead.[96] While
Barschel's regional program forged ahead on the western side around
Lauenburg,[97] his plan for cross-border nature preserves became part of the
federal efforts. In fact, when queried, Bavaria, Lower Saxony, and Hesse
all contributed potential transboundary conservation projects. Bavaria
nominated the Lange Rhön, a mountain range straddling the border of
Bavaria, Thuringia, and Hesse. Lower Saxony had five candidates, including the Drömling. Hesse drew attention to the efforts to reintroduce
the peregrine falcon, and Schleswig-Holstein added all the ideas that had
been part of Barschel's initiative, including the protection of sea eagles,
cranes, cormorants, gray geese, and otters.[98] Undergirding these federal
efforts was, of course, the work of environmental NGOs on the ground.
Several of Schleswig-Holstein's propositions bore the signature of Thomas
Neumann's work; Hesse's contributions drew on Wolfram Brauneis's
HGON group. The HGON was indeed fully prepared for the day when the
GDR might agree to cross-boundary conservation. The plans to extend the
western HGON preserves beyond the border were ready and waiting well
before November 1989.[99]

Yet none of the transboundary projects materialized before 1990,
though not for lack of effort on the West German side. Barschel, for one,
scheduled a visit to the GDR for December 1985 and managed to secure
appointments with the Politburo member Günter Mittag and the GDR's
environmental minister, Hans Reichelt.[100] He pursued these talks not

only to entrench himself further as a player in inter-German relations but also to deflate accusations by Social Democrats in his state that his transboundary ideas amounted to hot air.[101] He returned from the excursion announcing that he had found his interlocutors receptive to the idea of nature preservation. Indeed, an ordinary newspaper reader might have gained the impression that the designation of Schaalsee Lake as a preserve was imminent.[102] However, Hans Reichelt had only listened politely to Barschel's suggestions and pointed to the pending negotiations over the Environmental Accords before any further details could even be considered. He also declined Barschel's invitation to visit Schleswig-Holstein until the Accords were ratified.[103]

Once the 1987 Environmental Accords were signed, western representatives intensified their advocacy for cross-border nature preserves. The Drömling wetlands became Bonn's priority in the hope that it would blaze the trail for other projects like Schaalsee Lake. During the environmental consultations envisioned in the Accords, the GDR certainly took pride in showcasing some of its own prestige conservation projects, such as the Vessertal biosphere reserves in Thuringia, Steckby-Lödderitzer Forest in the Elbe plains, and the hatchery and reserve for great bustards (*Otis tarda*) near Rathenow.[104] The participants in the working groups—leading ecologists, forestry personnel, biologists, ornithologists, and so on—enjoyed the opportunity to compare notes, exchange literature, and reestablish old ties. The highest forestry official in the GDR, Rudolf Rüthninck, even reported in June 1988 that the "conclusion of the Accords had been a good thing," claiming that western representatives had, on several occasions, come around to East German views.[105]

Yet on the issue of cross-border preserves there was no progress. The Politburo considered the exchange of information and the coordination of certain preservation measures within the existing working groups sufficient for East German purposes. Creating preserves straddling the border remained out of the question.[106] The idea that a West German conservationist might be traipsing through the security strip on mapping or inspection trips, perhaps in plain view of the border fortifications, made this issue a nonstarter. To undercut any further West German efforts to advocate for a transboundary Drömling, for example, GDR authorities made sure their own nature preserve in that area, the 320-hectare Oebisfelder Stadtforst, would at no point align with the territory of the planned West German Kaiserwinkel preserve.[107]

The GDR's Last Stand: Encroaching
on the Security Strip

As western NGOs and politicians tried to protect select border landscapes, the GDR moved in the opposite direction and began to consider them as untapped resources. During the 1980s, the GDR's abysmal economic situation was patched over for the duration by West German loans. While western support might have granted the GDR a stay of execution, it did not lessen the desperation with which the SED leadership tried to mobilize the already shattered socialist economy. Along the border, this desperation manifested itself in attempts to draw on unclaimed natural resources. Whereas border security had thus far regularly limited the option to cultivate the forests and fallow land in the security strip, these were no longer necessarily considered off limits as the 1980s progressed. What is more, even the terrain between the demarcation line and the first fence—the no man's landscapes—now moved into the realm of possibilities. If that land had been touched at all, it was predominantly for maintenance purposes. Any work beyond the last fence immediately turned into labor-intensive deployments, since the logic of border security demanded close surveillance of workers so near to the unfortified demarcation line. The shifting plans in forestry work throw this development into sharp relief.

Wood was one of the few natural resources the GDR had at its disposal and managed with great care.[108] The woodlands of the GDR were divided into seventy-seven state forest districts, twenty-three of which extended into the restricted zone, the security strip, and even beyond the metal fence. Theoretically at least, these twenty-three districts managed a total of 40,000 hectares of woodland on both sides of the fortifications. These border forests ranged in size from 250 to 4,400 hectares.[109] In practice, however, the woods in the security strip and beyond the fence were inaccessible to forestry personnel, and even access to the 5-kilometer-deep restricted zone posed problems since it required a permit. A 1974 agreement between the Ministry for National Defense and the Ministry for Agriculture, Forests and Food Supply (MLFN) stipulated that the border troops would be in charge of any terrain within and adjacent to the border fortifications. The role of the forestry officials in the ministry was reduced to nominating suitable staff members and workers for any maintenance work, providing technical equipment, and ultimately paying for the upkeep. But the initiative for any maintenance work rested with the border troops.[110]

For forestry professionals, this was a vexing state of affairs. Like agriculture, forestry in the GDR was pressured into producing high short-term yields and fulfilling quotas defined in production plans.[111] Any district with border forests was disadvantaged from the outset in the "socialist competition" with other districts because it could not draw on its entire inventory to meet its quotas. As one forester complained, "The restricted zone was created without consultation and participation of [this forest district]. A normal management [of these woods] is barely possible."[112] Obtaining entry for forestry personnel was slowed by endless red tape and coordination with the bureaucracy of the border troops. The section patrolled by Border Regiment 23 in the Magdeburg District contained woods belonging to three different forest districts. Each one would have to petition Regiment 23 for access.[113] For security reasons, maps of the security strip and restricted zone were withheld, leaving the foresters with outdated information.[114] Over the years, they simply lost track of the stock and condition of forests on the periphery of their districts. Small wonder, then, that foresters disliked inaccessible and therefore unproductive woods in their districts. The director of the Schleiz forest district in southeast Thuringia repeatedly tried to divest himself of the unproductive forests under his purview and pass them along to the National People's Army.[115]

Since initiative and awareness of forestry concerns were usually lacking among the border troops, the border forests were for the most part left to themselves unless they got in the way of new infrastructure. When border troops began to create minefields in the early 1960s, for instance, they cut aisles into the forests. Throughout the 1970s, the border forests untouched by such security measures posed problems of a different order. The predominant coniferous monocultures—pine and spruce—were prone to wind and snow damage. In the border forests, toppled trees were not cleared, inviting invasions of the bark beetle. Once these invasions turned into calamities, as they did in 1976–1977, the pest infested heretofore healthy and productive adjacent woods. Such incidents finally warranted interventions, even in the security strip.[116] For old-school forestry professionals, productive forests required management. Bark beetle infestations therefore constituted a sure sign of neglect. Overseeing border forests that were practically off limits must have been a thorn in the side of these foresters.

But neglect could have unintended consequences. The forest was no longer under scientific management and was allowed to follow its natural life cycle. The head forester of Schleiz described some 336 hectares of woods in his district that appeared to have contained the underbrush, deadfalls, and snags so vital to biodiversity: "Directly on the state border, and visible from the side of the Federal Republic," he wrote, "the nasty state of the forest is dominated by uncleared trees broken by wind, ice, and snow. There are dry trees of all ages and sizes, snags, partly toppled over, in various stages of decay lying around by themselves or in clusters."[117] For the Schleiz director, this was a dreadful scenario. His letter was directed to regional superiors to drum up support for the bureaucratic fistfight with the border troops to gain access to these woods, hence the description of a forest in immediate need of intervention. Reading his words from a conservationist perspective, however, it becomes clear that, unwittingly, concerns over border security had created spaces akin to the core zone of a national park where a policy of noninterference leaves the forest to itself, allowing it to complete the life cycle, which necessarily includes "various stages of decay." Thus, some border forests, too, turned into transboundary natures. The border regime proved causal in guiding such development.

In 1982, GDR authorities rediscovered the more or less untapped wood reservoir in the border area. The ministries representing the border troops and the forest officials arrived at a new agreement that shifted emphasis *from maintenance* in order to maximize border security *to management* in order to increase wood production. Even woodlands on the western side of the last fence were included in this effort to tap into hitherto unexploited resources.[118] The shift began with inventory and mapping work in the hope that the "lost" border forests could be reintegrated into regular management plans by 1985.[119] However, the woods refused to go along with the new plan. Years of neglect meant that the foresters had to play catch-up, a situation rendered even more severe by snow breakage during the harsh winter of 1981–1982.[120] Besides, the lofty goal of harvesting forgotten pockets of trees did not mean that the leadership of the border troops would relax security. As in the past, each forestry worker had to undergo a background check for political reliability and obtain an entry permit for the restricted zone. Permission to enter the security strip was even more complicated and required careful scrutiny, thus tying down personnel from among the border troops. Manpower was lacking on both sides—forestry and army— for this desperate push to save the East German economy. One way to reduce the need for surveillance of forestry personnel was to turn the border troops *into* forestry personnel: in the district of Suhl, army conscripts thus received chainsaw training and were sent off into the woods.[121] Whether the sudden activities in the border forests were successful by any measure remains unclear. Most likely, the considerable efforts in 1984–1985 never amounted to forest management but only to salvage harvests.[122]

Similarly desperate attempts occurred in agriculture to gain fresh arable land. East German agriculture had long been caught in a vicious circle: geared toward maximum yields, GDR production methods had led to the erosion of topsoil, the contamination of soil and groundwater, the lowering of the water table, and eutrophication of surface waters.[123] Declining yields were addressed with more fertilizers, new rounds of melioration, and the mobilization of the last resources of whatever fallow land could be found in the border strip. In 1985, observers registered increasing agricultural activity in the security strip near Lübeck (West) and heard rumors that farming collectives on the eastern side intended to recultivate some no man's landscapes.[124]

The expansion of agricultural land along the border continued until the eleventh hour. In August 1989, less than three months before the fall of the Berlin Wall, alarming petitions reached West German authorities, this time from Franconia. East German melioration squads began to encroach on fallow land in the border strip. In the cases reported in the summer of 1989, habitats sheltering a range of red-listed species, mostly birds and frogs, were ploughed under. Pipes were installed up to 30 meters from the demarcation line to drain wetlands. Hectares of valuable reed vegetation were lost, and it horrified ornithologists in particular that "melioration" work was conducted during breeding season.[125]

On November 9, 1989, of all days, the West German minister of the environment, Klaus Töpfer, dispatched a letter requesting that the intrusions be stopped.[126] By the time the letter reached Töpfer's counterpart in East Berlin, Hans Reichelt, history had overtaken it. The scale of the task had shifted during that historic November night: not only the preservation of biotopes along the inter-German border was now at stake, the ecological restoration of the entire GDR became a burning task for the soon-to-be unified new German state.

November 1989: Of Jubilant Crowds and Endangered Species

The day Töpfer wrote to Reichelt, the postwar era in Europe drew to a close. The euphoria that greeted the fall of the Berlin Wall on November 9, 1989, was repeated up and down the inter-German border over the ensuing weeks as holes were cut into the metal fence and communities along the border, estranged by separation, reached out to each other for the first time in decades. The border was open. All over East Germany, citizens without (much) prior experience in political office took on responsibility, supported by the established West German parties and bureaucracies. In March 1990, East Germans flocked to the polls for the first democratic elections in their state's history. Until unification day on October 3, 1990, a freely elected GDR government under Lothar de Mazière (CDU) had some six months to prepare the country for accession to the Federal Republic.[127] It was a time of great expectations, once-in-a-lifetime opportunities, and early disappointments.

Change was rushing through the borderlands. The open border quickly caused friction between border communities, each of which was trying to seize a piece of the historic moment as it saw fit. The combustible mix of opportunity and unclear jurisdictions contributed to a feverish gold rush. Where Chancellor Helmut Kohl projected "prospering landscapes" (blühende Landschaften) all across East Germany, borderland officials filled in the blanks and imagined what the end of their communities' peripherality would bring: new roads, resort hotels, industrial jobs. Before such dreams were checked by reality, they posed serious threats to the transboundary natures that the Iron Curtain had created. The stage was set for a collision between advocates of economic development and nature conservationists. The latter hoped to preserve "the longest biotope" as a green belt from the Baltic to the Bavarian Forest, just as Heinz Sielmann had prophesied. But the conservationists' efforts appeared to stand counter to the rush toward national unification, which acknowledged no place for the border and, much to the chagrin of some border communities today, wanted to eradicate the dividing line as quickly as possible.

For starters, improvised border crossings along the inter-German border sprung up in the days after the events in Berlin. On November 11, crowds of people forced down the fence in Stapelburg (East) to cross the river Ecker into Bad Harzburg (West). The very steel panels that had formed the border fence now turned into a bridge.[128] At other places, heavy-construction vehicles were called in to lift the fortification elements. Wherever a new hole was poked in the Iron Curtain, people streamed across, forming jubilant masses any time of day. In a matter of days, such holes widened and became much-frequented semi-official border crossings. The crossing near the village of Mustin east of Ratzeburg (West), for example, was opened at first only to pedestrians, yet in May 1990,

4,500 cars—on peak days well over 10,000—inched across every day.[129] Crossings tended to spring up where roads and bridges had once connected communities before 1952, but they also popped up in open fields. Either way, any opening suddenly drew crowds into the no man's landscapes that had barely seen foot traffic for years.

The traffic infrastructure on either side was instantly overwhelmed. Single-lane roads that most recently had led nowhere now had to accommodate throngs of cars. Traffic rules were abandoned; cars were parked in meadows and forests, on lake shores, and in nature preserves (Figure 5.2). Trains did not provide a serious alternative. Too many cross-border tracks had been abandoned, leaving precious few crossings. Westbound travelers who caught one of those rare trains had to put up with cramped conditions aboard. Even a train hijacking was reported: East Germans blocked the tracks of the Rostock–Munich express in Reichenbach, Saxony, and demanded extra cars for those who had not made it on.[130]

With trains of only limited use, the car remained the preferred mode of transportation in the winter of 1989–1990. West German borderland dwellers were quick to complain about exhaust from Trabis, the two-stroke-engine cars that East Germans drove.[131] Images of Trabi jams

FIGURE 5.2. After the border opening, an improvised parking lot sprang up on a meadow near Ratzeburg (West) in northern Germany, November 1989.

© Sigurd Müller, Archiv Bundespolizeiabteilung Ratzeburg

with their bluish exhaust clouds contributed to the widely shared assumption among local and regional politicians that the traffic infrastructure in the borderlands needed immediate attention. In late 1989,
no one knew yet where the momentous political developments were
heading, but regardless of whether they led to a confederation of the
two German states or to unification, old roads still needed paving and
"building bridges" had to become more than a metaphor. The Bavarian
government hoped to close a 16-kilometer gap in the autobahn between
Hof (West) and Plauen (East) within weeks. Many local officials had
their own ideas for bypasses, parking lots, and autobahn access roads
that might well have been on their agenda for some time.[132] The Trabi
jams pointed not only to a real need but also to a unique opportunity
to push such ideas forward. The infrastructure projects merged with
the hope that the erstwhile periphery would become the new center of
a larger Germany, even the gateway to an enlarged Europe. Predictably,
the pleas of environmental NGOs to shift the focus from the building of
roads to the reopening of East–West rail tracks met with a hostile reception within the construction lobby.[133]

East Germans were not the only ones traveling. On November 13, 1989,
the GDR rescinded the control of access to the border strip.[134] The wave
of visits that had lapped westward beginning on November 10 was now
sloshing eastward, although the number of visitors was smaller. During
the spring and summer of 1990, the hospitality industry, local officials, and
concerned East Germans alike expected that millions of West Germans
would take advantage of the open border to explore the GDR. Depending
on their perspective, they either welcomed this as a source of revenue or
dreaded it as an onslaught. For the western tourism industry, the GDR
looked like a blank slate, ready for development.[135] Rumors about plans
for golf courses and resort hotels ran rife in communities that boasted
a lake, coastline, or mountain range. Advocates of slow and sustainable
development had a hard time, especially around Berlin. Two million West
Berliners were ready to venture away from the island that had housed
them for twenty-eight years. "We can obviously not leave the Berlin Wall
in place only to protect the surrounding area," argued even the West Berlin
senator for the environment.[136]

The formerly restricted zone held pride of place for East and West
Germans alike. Barred by their own government from getting anywhere
near the inter-German border, the ring around West Berlin, or stretches on
the Baltic coast, East Germans wanted to break the spell of the structures

that had walled them in for so long. Heading out to lakes, woods, and coastlines that had been beyond reach became an expression of their new-found freedom. For West Germans, the GDR borderlands formed part of a day trip, close enough for visitors to make it back at night when excursions deeper into the country were still hampered by the lack of tourist accommodations. From whatever direction they were coming, "from the Baltic to the Frankenwald, the excursionists are chugging and traipsing through an almost intact flora and fauna."[137] They shared a sense of transgression, perhaps even of conquest: "The hikers stroll through the restricted zone animated by the feeling of legally doing something forbidden."[138] Yet what exercised ornithologists about these strolls was that, come the spring of 1990, they would coincide with breeding season. In the weeks and months after the border's opening, conservationists time and again encountered the human inclination "to boldly go where no man had gone before." Without legal protection of the areas in question, the conservationists could only appeal to visitors' better nature to show restraint.[139] But restraint was hard to come by in a revolution that had been fueled by cries for freedom. The most prominent mountain of the Harz, the Brocken, exemplifies this dynamic.

Ever since the Romantic era, the Harz had held a particular allure for Germans. Heinrich Heine visited it, Caspar David Friedrich painted it, Johann Wolfgang von Goethe immortalized it in his play *Faust*. Goethe hiked to the Brocken summit three times, taking a particular route subsequently called the Goethe Path.[140] The inter-German border had cut through the Harz Mountains, assigning the Brocken to East Germany. In 1952, the villages at the foot of the mountain became part of the restricted zone: tourists needed a special permit to gain access to the villages and the Brocken. In August 1961, however, the mountain was turned into a prohibited zone, out of bounds for anyone but Soviet and GDR military personnel. The Soviets built their westernmost listening post on the mountain plateau; the East German Stasi operated another. A wall enclosed the installations, and the Brocken plateau within these walls was partially paved over.[141] For naturalists, the Brocken had been an object of study for centuries, but like everyone else they found themselves shut out. News about the condition of the mountain's unique subalpine flora and fauna rarely surfaced.[142] On December 3, 1989, more than two thousand people hiked up the mountain and demanded an end to all restrictions on the Brocken. With banners proclaiming "Free Citizens! Free Brocken!" they assembled in front of the gate to the walled-in plateau. In reference to the

Brandenburg Gate in Berlin, they demanded, "Open the gate!" until the guards finally complied. Today, a memorial with the inscription "Brocken free again!" reminds hikers of that sunny day in December 1989.[143]

Once "liberated," the Brocken continued to draw thousands of people every day. Since the mountain did not have a tourist infrastructure to speak of, the hikers trampled down their own trails, left trash behind, and followed nature's call in the great outdoors.[144] Ornithologists were quick to note a drop in the population of sensitive species such as the ring ouzel (*Turdus torquatus*).[145] But for locals, the mountain was their only asset. A development faction was soon pitted against a nature faction. The former wanted tourism and detected "western arrogance" in the pleas for preservation; the latter called for restraint and tried to prevent the reopening of the traditional mountain railroad, *Brockenbahn*, which would cart in even more people. When a piece of the tracks went missing two days before the reopening of the narrow-gauge railway, locals suspected that western conservationists had engaged in a form of ecoterrorism.[146]

Not only was the subalpine vegetation on the Brocken in danger of being loved to death, by early 1990 alarming reports reached environmental NGOs from all directions. Motocross enthusiasts were running races in the border strip, even in the Drömling.[147] Farmers, predominantly from the West, took advantage of the ambiguous jurisdiction during the transitional period of the GDR and expanded their fields into the no man's landscape and security strip. Grassland that had not been touched for decades was suddenly ploughed.[148] At the Heldrastein cliff, where the HGON had reintroduced the peregrine falcon (*Falco peregrinus*) into the wild and was hoping to protect the eagle-owl (*Bubo bubo*), investors planned a sports hotel with a climbing center. While conservationists from Hessen and Thuringia managed to fend off the hotel, they could not prevent masses of people from hiking up to the shell limestone rock. Hiking enthusiasts also erected a snack shack on the mountain plateau despite the fact that local GDR authorities had already designated Heldrastein as a nature preserve.[149]

Sensitive aquatic biotopes likewise came under siege. With the same order that rescinded control of access to the restricted zone, GDR authorities opened all lakes along the border to water sports. While this news might not have been of immediate interest in mid-November, it did not bode well for the spring of 1990. Indeed, the winter of 1989–1990 gave the hospitality industry enough time to plan for cross-border excursions of their expected clientele. At Dassow Lake near Lübeck, for instance, an entrepreneur planned a regular ferry crossing between Travemünde (West) and Dassow (East).[150] With the fall of the fences, both the Lauenburg and Mecklenburg lake districts suddenly lay bare.[151] It was the fate of Schaalsee Lake that received the most attention in the press, not least because it exemplified the clash between the interests of nature conservationists, residents of the formerly restricted zone, leisure-seeking urbanites, and western carpetbaggers.

Schaalsee Lake lies within easy reach of Hamburg and Lübeck. On the western side, it had long served recreational purposes; a campground was located there. On the eastern side, however, it had been off limits as part of the security strip. Not surprisingly, waterfowl and rare species such as the European otter (*Lutra lutra*) regularly elected the more tranquil eastern shore for breeding. Within days after the border opening, the lake became a destination for explorations into the restricted zone. A Hamburg newspaper enticed its readers to drive to the small town of Zarrentin (East) to have a look at Schaalsee from its eastern side.[152] Western newspapers' descriptions of romantic cobblestone avenues and idyllic brick houses with thatched roofs promised a long-lost nativeness and simplicity that West German travelers were presumed to be seeking. Many of the early travel reports on the East German borderlands share the theme of travelers experiencing the trip as a return to the landscape of their youth.[153]

Whatever the residents of the formerly restricted zone might have been thinking about such traveling West Germans, tourism promised both an end to their isolation and a steady source of revenue. The mayors of Zarrentin and neighboring Lassahn resolved to build the necessary infrastructure. They started by issuing permits for pleasure boats, more than two hundred in Zarrentin and some sixty in Lassahn. Boats need docks and landings, and these were constructed amid the reed vegetation on the shore. Trees were felled to make room for the trailers carrying the boats. And since these trailers would be pulled by cars, a parking lot became an inescapable consequence of the boating permits. Conservationists quickly mobilized higher authorities and at least managed to thwart the plans for the parking lot. The mayors responded by forming the "Schaalsee Interest Group" to counter the conservationists. As in the Brocken situation, the mayors' development faction had strong arguments on its side. How, they asked, could the conservationists justify imposing fresh rules on residents who had been ruled through and through for decades, who had been restricted in their movements, who had lost educational and professional opportunities because of the location of their houses, who had lived under observation and had themselves been denied access to their lake?[154] The nature faction, on the other hand, tried hard to convey that their intention was not to restrict the residents but to prevent an invasion of city slickers from Hamburg.

Their fears were well founded. Western real estate speculators descended upon the GDR almost immediately after the Wall came down. Although it was still illegal for West Germans to buy property in the GDR, such deals were conducted through shell vendors. The bait for East Germans was quick access to western currency at a time when the terms of a potential monetary union between the two German states were still unknown.[155] While the property sharks showered much attention on East Berlin, lake properties held a particular allure, whether around Berlin or within driving distance of Hamburg. Jürgen Hinz, an SPD representative in the Schleswig-Holstein parliament, was one of many who decried attempts by Hamburgers to buy up land on the eastern shores of Schaalsee Lake.[156]

The white-tailed eagle did not wait for the parties to resolve their conflict. The two known breeding pairs on Schaalsee Lake were reported missing by May 1990. Rumors ran high about who or what had ultimately driven them out. Was it the couple from Hamburg who stood under the nest, clapping their hands until the birds finally took off? Was it the "bird lover" who hired a helicopter to inspect the nest from above?[157] Residents of the Mecklenburg lake district were left with the disturbing sense that their landscapes were being ransacked.[158]

Tying the Green Belt: Nature Conservation during Transformative Times

The opportunities that the transboundary natures offered for conservation went beyond the obvious fact that they provided refuges for endangered flora and fauna. West German conservationists had long wrestled with the traditional paradigm of nature protection that focused on the preservation of aesthetically pleasing cultural landscapes but proved ineffectual in halting the decline of biodiversity.[159] Having left behind the conservative nature-as-*Heimat* approach that sought to freeze cultural landscapes in time in order to preserve their familiar appeal, the question remained as to which methods would prove effective for restoring and protecting ecological processes in the natural environment. "Our nature preserves," lamented the activist Horst Stern, "are hopelessly isolated, trapped between chemically contaminated landscapes of intensive use and therefore ineffectual for migratory species and their essential genetic exchange."[160] To counter the insular character of nature reserves, much larger protected areas would have been one answer. But West Germans remained hesitant about opening expansive national parks given the lack of space in a relatively densely populated country, and the efforts to establish the first one in the Bavarian Forest in the late 1960s proved a major struggle.[161]

If national parks in highly developed Western Europe were not an easy option, the idea of biotope networks appeared to be a solution that would still allow for conservation in vast areas (*auf der Fläche*). The concept of biotope networks gained currency in the late 1980s and became a new paradigm in nature conservation.[162] At that time, the European Union was developing a Europe-wide network of nature protection areas—this program came to be called Natura 2000 and was adopted in 1992.[163] The transboundary natures that the Iron Curtain had created and Natura 2000 were an obvious fit: the GDR border regime had unwittingly produced a 1,393-kilometer-long north–south corridor that connected different landscape types. The West German environmental ministry eagerly seized on the idea of the border as a green belt as the German contribution to the EU agenda.[164]

Apart from coinciding with policy initiatives, the Green Belt's marketing narrative resonated profoundly on the German and European levels in the early 1990s. The metaphors deployed to generate popular and political support for this conservation project—"from death strip to lifeline," "borders separate, nature unites"—harnessed the Cold War history and symbolic valence of the Iron Curtain. The Green Belt marketing slogans gave literal meaning to the words ascribed to the former German chancellor Willy Brandt, "Now what belongs together will grow together," which contained yet another organic metaphor.[165] The Green Belt turned into the conservation project befitting the post-Communist era because it mirrored in compelling ways the political project of German unification and European integration.[166]

In view of the range of threats caused by the border opening, West and East German conservationists immediately reached out to each other. A host of regional cross-border alliances sprang up: in Hesse and Thuringia the group Nature Conservation in the Borderland (Arbeitsgruppe Naturschutz im Grenzland) planned to turn the Hohe Rhön mountain range into a transboundary preserve. In addition, the HGON now resurrected its plans for the Werra plains and found competent partners in the district of Suhl.[167] In the Lauenburg lake district,

Thomas Neumann of the WWF collaborated with the professional conservationists in the Mecklenburg border counties. In Lübeck, professional and voluntary conservationists from both sides met in January
1990 and demanded that the border strip in the vicinity be put under
preliminary protection.[168] Whereas the various regional actors focused
on particular landscapes within their purview, the Bund Naturschutz
in Bayern (BN, Association for Nature Protection in Bavaria) and the
German Friends of the Earth (BUND) proposed merging these projects
along the entire length of the former border. They convened a meeting
with East German ecologists in Hof (West) on December 9, 1989, where
some four hundred attendees adopted a resolution that called for the
conservation of the border strip as a "green belt" that was to become the
"ecological backbone of Central Europe." To avoid any misconceptions,
the group added that such a demand "does not constitute a retroactive
justification of the border."[169] In addition, environmental NGOs as well
as private citizens inundated western federal and state offices with requests to put sections of the border under preliminary protection and
develop long-term plans for their preservation.[170]

Regardless of their many local and regional initiatives, the environmental NGOs needed the cooperation of the state, or rather *both* German
states. The goal was to put as much of the land along the border as possible under official nature protection and call the area the Green Belt.
Doing so while the GDR was coming apart turned into a race against time
and constituted both a challenge and an unprecedented opportunity. As
the GDR continued its ever-accelerating tailspin, it unleashed an unforeseen dynamic for change that East German ecologists funneled into nature conservation. The Central Round Table that served in lieu of a freely
elected parliament until the elections of March 1990 supported ecological
reforms. In addition, the GDR environmental ministry underwent a favorable realignment: Minister Hans Reichelt resigned and the biologist
Michael Succow assumed the post of deputy minister.[171]

At no time in the history of German nature protection did conservationists achieve as much as they did in 1990. Two days before unification,
on October 3, the GDR's ambitious National Park Program (NPP) went
into effect. Consisting of five national parks, six biosphere reserves, three
nature parks, and several areas slated for protected status, it encompassed
no less than 10 percent of the state's territory. The NPP shows what East
German nature conservationists, once liberated from SED tutelage, were
capable of.[172] The NPP matters for the history of the Green Belt because

landscapes in the borderlands became part of this historic conservation windfall. The NPP included a national park in the Harz Mountains, a biosphere reserve along the Elbe in today's Saxony-Anhalt, a biosphere reserve in the Thuringian Rhön, and nature parks in the Drömling and at Schaalsee Lake. The activism in East Berlin rippled into the respective districts (*Bezirke*) and on into the counties. Each county suddenly boasted one or two professional conservationists.[173] Along the border, their very first task was to put "ecologically valuable areas within the 5-km-zone" under preliminary protection. To that end, the West German NGOs and a pool of East German volunteers undertook the essential work of mapping the habitats in various areas.[174] By February 1990, the East Berlin ministry was able to produce a list of more than fifty planned nature preserves; a month later, they were officially secured.[175] If the West German government had been disappointed by the lack of cooperation from the GDR in previous years, it could now barely keep up with the flurry of activities unleashed on the other side. In Bonn, the minister for the environment, Klaus Töpfer, quickly latched onto the East German National Park project. He publicly supported not only the NPP but specifically the border-related conservation activities and signed off on the memorable line: "In 1990, no reasonable and well-developed project will fail for want of funding."[176]

The astonishing pace of events, however, produced various misunderstandings between East and West. When the East Germans said "national park," the West Germans heard "nature park."[177] Among the many protection categories, "nature park" was the weakest in West German environmental law since it was explicitly geared toward recreation and tourism.[178] The mere mention of "nature parks" provoked immediate protest from the environmental NGOs, which referred to such plans as "false labeling."[179] Yet the categories mattered not only in terms of the level of protection they would provide but also in terms of funding. In principle, the protection of nature in the West German federal system fell within the purview of the individual states. However, in 1979, the federal government had reaffirmed its own role by establishing a program that offered funds for the designation of large reservations of "national importance."[180] Töpfer was determined to fill this role in 1990, support Succow's NPP, and define "national importance" as broadly as possible. Yet he had to tread carefully. The GDR was still an independent country. Calls for a "third way" of socialism had not yet abated, and the first experiences with West German capitalism had already led many East Germans to fear an "annexation" or "colonization" of the East by the West. Continuously pressured by the western

NGOs to put the border strip under protection, Töpfer felt compelled to re-mind them that "we must not oblige the GDR to implement more nature protection [than we do] only because she has ecologically valuable areas to do so."[181] The situation for the Bonn bureaucracy became clearer on July 1, 1990, when, parallel to the Monetary Union that brought the deutsche mark to East Germany, the Environmental Union went into effect as well. In anticipation of unification, the EnvU extended West German environ-mental law into the GDR. By this time, the NPP was not yet reality but was well on its way.[182]

As valuable as Töpfer's political support was, the large transboundary projects were not possible without the West German federal states. Those projects that had been part of the pre-1989 West German transboundary park efforts stood the best chance of succeeding because preliminary work such as biotope mapping on the western side was already well advanced. Yet political will and the ongoing pressure of the NGOs remained essen-tial. Bavaria and Hesse linked up with the district of Suhl (after October 1990 the state of Thuringia) to create the Rhön biosphere reserve.[183] In Schleswig-Holstein, the bureaucracy was ready to roll out a conservation initiative that built on Barschel's 1985 program. However, bickering be-tween the SPD and CDU in the state parliament held up the designa-tion of Schaalsee Lake as a nature preserve. In the meantime, the eastern border counties put their part of the lake under preliminary protection.[184] In the end, Schaalsee Lake as well as the Drömling emerged only as "nature parks" since the stricter category "nature protection park" that Succow had tried to create had no basis in West German environmental law. The state of Mecklenburg continued to advance protection measures on the eastern part of Schaalsee and gained the coveted UNESCO status as a biosphere reserve in 1998. In a late commentary on Barschel's 1985 policy initiative, Schleswig-Holstein did not follow Mecklenburg's lead.[185] Lower Saxony, in turn, proved obstinate and blocked the extension of the Harz national park into its territory, citing the 1990 deadline as too tight. More likely, the preference of the CDU-led state government was for developing tourism.[186] In October 1990, a 5,900-hectare Harz national park came into being. It was located exclusively on the eastern side of the former border and was the smallest national park within the NPP. Under a new SPD/Green-led administration, Lower Saxony did eventually create a 16,000-hectare western equivalent, yet it took until 2006 for this last aspect of German unification to materialize: the unification of the eastern and western Harz national parks.[187]

Acceptance for the conservation of ecologically valuable landscapes is a complex proposition at the best of times. Economic and conservationist interests collide in various constellations, the clash between tourism and conservation representing only one of many. Restrictions on land use and on public access to core zones within preserves tend to fuel anxieties among local residents, who often perceive such measures as undue interference from "outsiders."[188] The fact that the land in question was the border strip exacerbated such anxieties. East German residents from the formerly restricted zone had the moral capital on their side when they expressed fears about new restrictions. The allegation that the conservationists intended to create a new "green border" constituted a potent argument. In its most aggressive form, the allegation came with the sarcastic suggestion of re-creating minefields to protect birds.[189] For locals, the old and alleged green borders meshed even further when administrative offices for protected areas moved into buildings of former GDR authorities. The first agency for the Drömling occupied offices near Calvörde (East) that had previously been used by the Stasi. The building was once even vandalized; indeed, protection for the Drömling's core zone had to be enforced at first with the help of a private security firm.[190]

One of the more devious mockeries of the Green Belt project came from Friedrich Karl Fromme, an editor of the conservative daily *Frankfurter Allgemeine Zeitung*. In a front-page editorial, "The GDR as a Nature Preserve?," he referenced the romanticized impression of travelers that the GDR was a long-gone Germany where "almost everything was as it used to be." He accused ecologists of pursuing the "sentimental wish" to preserve the GDR as some sort of "Old German *Heimat* museum," selfishly disregarding the economic prospects of the majority of East Germans who actually lived there. Especially the residents of the formerly restricted zone, Fromme wrote, "don't want to live on a new kind of reservation, if possible, as indigenous people in local costume who occasionally get toured upon." The residents wanted tourism, Fromme claimed, and the role of conservationists was merely to prevent developmental excesses (*Stilwidrigkeiten vermeiden*).[191] Yet six months later, Fromme's own paper had to acknowledge, somewhat incredulously, that what once sounded like a crazy vision was becoming reality—the conservationists were tying a Green Belt.[192]

During the early 1990s, two more major hurdles threatened the existence of the Green Belt, both of them deeply related to the history of the inter-German border: mine clearing and restitution claims. Between

1961 and 1985, some 1.3 million land mines had been buried along the border. In the mid-1980s, GDR border guards cleared the mines after the SED leadership had accepted western financial incentives to do so. On the basis of NVA maps, the Federal Ministry for Defense determined after unification that mines still posed a danger along some 190 kilometers of the border. It therefore contracted private companies to carry out demining. The contractors ploughed through the border strip with heavy bulldozers and other equipment, leaving it in a state that made it attractive for agricultural use.[193] The Bund Naturschutz protested immediately, especially since mine clearing began during breeding season in 1991.[194] The issue again allowed for easy attacks on the conservationists, accusing them of valuing wildlife over human life. Yet the conservationists simply demanded that demining be stopped in areas that never had minefields in the first place and that less invasive methods be used.[195] The Defense Ministry in Bonn, however, declared everything in order and informed the ecologists that nature regenerates quickly.[196] In February 1994, the search for mines was extended once more into areas previously considered safe. In fact, the issue has never been resolved; some thirty thousand mines have never been found.[197]

The other threat to the Green Belt related to questions of landownership since much private property had been expropriated from its rightful owners over the course of the GDR's existence. Whenever the ever-expanding fortifications along the border and around West Berlin required more terrain, the SED dictatorship simply confiscated it. Not surprisingly, after 1990 previous owners demanded the return of the so-called Wall Land Plots. In 1996, the Bundestag enacted a law that allowed owners to buy their former property back well below market price. A year later, the federal government had received 4,053 such claims.[198] The law also stipulated that the Federal Ministry of Finance divest the government of the remaining land in the border strip and pass on the proceeds to the new federal states in the former GDR.[199] Whether the old/new owners would cooperate with the NGOs in upholding the Green Belt was anyone's guess. Besides, the law had created a paradoxical situation in which one federal ministry (Finance) was preparing to sell land that another federal ministry (Environment) had pledged to protect.[200] The breakthrough came in 2002 when the SPD and the Greens, about to form their second coalition government under Chancellor Gerhard Schröder, acknowledged the Green Belt in their coalition agreement and pledged to sell any ecologically valuable land only to nature preservation agencies and organizations.[201] In 2005, the federal government declared the Green Belt to be part of Germany's "national nature heritage" (*Nationales Naturerbe*), further securing its status.

The numerous initiatives of the environmental NGOs after 1989 had secured 177 square kilometers of land, or 85 percent of the original border strip. The remainder was considered degraded, although efforts are currently under way to close the gaps in the Green Belt.[202] Thanks to a federally funded mapping effort, ecologists found 109 different habitat types within the Green Belt in 2002. Almost half of those are considered endangered; hence it came as no surprise that of the 160 animal and plant species in these habitats, half were endangered as well, 8 even on the verge of extinction.[203] A spot check of the inventory in the Coburg area where Kai Frobel began his mapping efforts in 1979 appears to confirm the trend: by 2011, the corn bunting (*Emberiza calandra*) and the European nightjar (*Caprimulgus europaeus*) had disappeared, and the populations of the common snipe (*Gallinago gallinago*), the whinchat (*Saxicola rubetra*), and the northern gray shrike (*Lanius excubitor*) were drastically reduced.[204] One reason was natural succession: these birds needed open grassland, but scrubs and birch trees were growing in areas where the GDR border guards would have kept vegetation low. The Green Belt therefore seeks to replicate this low-key maintenance work and maintain open spaces.[205] Another reason, however, is the fact that the conservationists never did create a new "green" border.

Conclusion: The Historicity of Landscape

This chapter has sought to clarify the ways in which the Iron Curtain and all activities that kept it functional directly or indirectly caused changes in the natural environment adjacent to the border. When the consequences of the border regime are studied in their historical context and over time, it becomes apparent that they were neither purely detrimental to nor exclusively beneficial for nature and wildlife. Hence neither a narrative of decline nor a narrative of creation captures the dynamic influence of the border regime. What I call "transboundary natures" emerged as a result of the evolving presence of the Iron Curtain's "hardware" on the ground, as well as border policing and decreased economic activity and population density in the borderlands on each side. By the 1970s, the changes that the border regime brought to certain kinds of landscape were beginning to be perceived as beneficial for nature. The ornithologist Rudolph Berndt may have been the first to recognize that the border provided an argument for opportunistic conservation in the Drömling wetlands, but he was followed by a number of conservationists in different regions who came to see the ecological value of various habitats along the border. These shifting perceptions were undergirded by a growing sense of loss of familiar landscapes and their resident biodiversity in the rest of the country and marked the beginning of the narrative that at least something good came out of the otherwise tragic situation.

Although the emergence of the transboundary natures was clearly an unintended consequence of the border regime, their eventual recognition as a beneficial outcome of unfortunate circumstances was a conscious move. West German conservationists embraced the transboundary natures as a refuge for endangered plant and animal species not only because that is what they had become, but also because they constituted a vehicle for raising awareness about ecological degradation in the rest of the country.[206] West German politicians enlisted them as an opportunity to engage the GDR in further environmental negotiations and even objected when East German authorities, at the eleventh hour, came to think of the transboundary natures as untapped natural resources. Well before the border fell, multiple observers had thus noticed the ecological value of the border area. Even before 1989, the trajectory in the Federal Republic pointed toward the creation of nature preserves along the border. By the fourth decade of partition, the inter-German border thus followed the global trend that buffer zones of "nature" tend to emerge alongside political boundaries, particularly contested ones.[207] This development, however, is not necessarily redemptive. It is worth remembering that the transboundary natures inhabited the same time and space as the pollution outlined in the preceding chapter.

Visitors to the Green Belt already have trouble discerning where the border infrastructure once stood. Interpretative plates and historical markers have increased accordingly and guide tourists through the terrain.[208] The landscapes produced by the Iron Curtain did not remain static once the removal of the fortifications allowed for different land use. The conservation efforts themselves contribute to the changes. Fields that were (illegally) extended during the transformative times after 1989 have been reconverted into open grassland. Perching posts have been erected in places in the grassland where birds would have rested on the abundant fences. Particular species, such as the Eurasian lynx (*Lynx lynx*), are being (re)introduced and radio-tracked. Brooks and rivers have been renaturalized and ponds created from scratch. The very effort of managing the transboundary natures alters them. Something new emerges in their stead that is shaped by preservation and restoration ecology.[209] Central European landscapes have been formed by cultural techniques for centuries: Europeans, too, "have historically known nature through work."[210] The activities that maintain and protect the Green Belt themselves constitute another cultural technique that bears on the landscape and on "nature." As Jedediah Purdy reminds us, "[E]ncounters with nature are themselves not natural; they are cultural."[211]

As this chapter has shown, the genealogy of the Green Belt is more complex than many accounts to date acknowledge. It consists not only of the material changes in the natural environment that the border regime wrought but also of the contemporary perceptions and appropriations of those changes. Pressing for a more nuanced genealogy of the Green Belt does not devalue the achievements of the conservation efforts. As the geographer David Havlick observes, "[F]ew would prefer a militarized death strip over a series of reserves dedicated to recreation and conservation."[212] Whether the historicity of the landscape can be preserved in the longer term will depend on whether, and how, its history continues to be told.

6

Closing the Nuclear Fuel
Cycle at Gorleben?

WEST GERMANY'S ENERGY FUTURE
IN THE BORDERLANDS

DURING A PRESS conference on February 22, 1977, Ernst Albrecht stepped up to a wall-mounted map. His right hand appeared to be moving toward Berlin but halted at the Iron Curtain, settled below the Elbe River, and pointed at a speck called Gorleben. The governor of Lower Saxony had just nominated the tiny hamlet in the border county of Lüchow-Dannenberg as the site of West Germany's most ambitious and costly industrial project to date. Gorleben was located in a thinly populated area atop a deep salt dome. This is where the Federal Republic intended to complete the nuclear fuel cycle by building a nuclear fuel reprocessing plant and a final waste repository to store the highly radioactive refuse that was the price of nuclear power. Gorleben in the borderlands thus turned into the linchpin of West Germany's future energy supply as conceived in the mid-1970s. It also became a sensation in the global nuclear community because it seemed that West Germany was about to build "the world's first fully integrated 'fuel cycle park.'"[1] This nuclear waste disposal center, or "fuel cycle park" (*Nukleares Entsorgungszentrum*, NEZ), was to include storage ponds for nuclear rods, a plant to reprocess some 1,400 tons of spent nuclear fuel per year, a related reactor-fuel fabrication facility to turn the plutonium (a byproduct of reprocessing) into new power plant fuel, a vitrification plant to encase high-level radioactive waste in glass, and a salt mine where the encased waste would find its final resting place. In short, the facility would combine all back-end processes of the nuclear fuel cycle in one location. The NEZ was expected to cost around DM 11 billion and take about fifteen years to build.[2] The siting decision instantly split the residents of Lüchow-Dannenberg County into those who saw Gorleben as a boon to industrial development and those who objected to the risk posed by nuclear technology. Instead of the predicted deference to government plans, state authorities encountered persistent local opposition that joined with similar anti-nuclear protests elsewhere in the country. Out of the borderlands thus emerged the longest-lasting anti-nuclear protest movement in (West) German history.

The importance of Gorleben for the history of Germany's energy history cannot be overstated. The plans for a nuclear "fuel cycle park," indeed the very idea of closing the fuel cycle, reflect the optimism about nuclear energy use in the 1970s.[3] The term itself projects the illusion that the nuclear fuel cycle was a closed system, suggesting an infinite process of recycling with minimal wastage when, in fact, reprocessing of spent nuclear fuel generates a large volume of radioactive byproducts.[4] As such, Gorleben was a typical project of high modernity.[5] Politically, the conception of a national *Entsorgungszentrum* that was to be built at Gorleben was closely linked to the experience of the first oil price shock in 1973 and the efforts to diversify the West German energy supply by increasing the share of nuclear energy over fossil fuels in order to avert an anticipated energy shortage and ensure continued economic growth.[6] In 1976, the licensing of new nuclear power plants became tied to evidence of their provisions for the disposal of spent nuclear fuel and all related wastes, thereby implementing the Polluter Pays Principle in the production of nuclear energy. The utility companies were thereby nudged in the direction of reprocessing, which at the time was considered superior to direct disposal (without reprocessing) of spent nuclear fuel.[7] While anti-nuclear protest had cut its teeth at individual power plant projects in the early 1970s, Gorleben as initially conceived was in a different category. The 1976 link between licensing and evidence for waste disposal turned Gorleben into the primary target of anti-nuclear protest. Opposing it, let alone preventing it, promised more leverage over energy policy than protesting against any individual nuclear power plant ever could, as disturbing as each of those may have been for their host communities.[8] Through decades of protest, Gorleben became the very symbol for Germany's use of nuclear energy.

This chapter investigates the ways in which the inter-German border and the borderland location shaped the conflict over Gorleben. The fact that Gorleben was located a mere 3 kilometers from the Iron Curtain mattered in various contexts. For officials in Lüchow-Dannenberg, the Gorleben decision was tied to hopes of economic development in a county that had learned to "play the border card" in its pursuit of state subsidies. The NEZ facility promised industrial jobs, an influx of new residents, and a steady stream of state investments and corporate taxes that would allow the county to address many of the woes that borderland advocates had traditionally blamed on the border. More than two decades of vying for state aid as part of the *Zonenrand* region had not only influenced the relationship of this rural county to state and federal agencies; it made local officials receptive, even eager, to turn the county into a nuclear community that accepted nuclear risk in exchange for affluence.[9] In terms of transboundary environmental connections, Gorleben's proximity to the inter-German border predictably triggered the involvement of the GDR, raising the specter of lengthy negotiations with the volatile neighbor. The border location therefore became a bone of contention between Governor Albrecht (CDU) and Chancellor Helmut Schmidt (SPD), who also worried about the security of weapons-grade plutonium that was generated during reprocessing right next to the Iron Curtain. Finally, the border influenced the anti-Gorleben protest, both in its methods and its composition. The protest movement, a coalition of urban intellectuals and local farmers, emerged from clusters of alternative culture that had formed in the borderlands precisely because these regions had been bypassed by postwar modernization and were romanticized for their alleged authenticity. Gorleben, in short, was deeply intertwined with the history of the inter-German border in ways beyond its geographic location. The conflict over this nuclear site once more shows the borderlands as West Germany's most sensitive geographic spaces where political conflicts became magnified by the presence of the Iron Curtain and what it represented.

Neither a reprocessing plant nor a final nuclear waste storage facility was ever built in Gorleben. In fact, the Gorleben project turned into a high-profile and costly failure.[10] Faced with massive protests and under the shadow of the nuclear incident at the Three Mile Island power plant in Harrisburg, Pennsylvania, Governor Albrecht withdrew political support for the reprocessing plant in May 1979. The subsequent attempt to build a reprocessing plant in Wackersdorf in Bavaria encountered adamant protest as well and was scrapped in 1989.[11] In the meantime, the German nuclear industry paid for reprocessing capacities in France (LaHague) and the United Kingdom (Sellafield) but remained contractually obligated to take back the high-level wastes that reprocessing generates. The industry therefore invested in exploring interim storages sites (*Zwischenlager*) and expanded at-reactor storage capacities. It also intensified research and development of transportation technology and means of storage, such as suitable containers. Ultimately, Gorleben received only an above-ground waste storage facility, conceived as an interim solution until an underground cavern was ready. To that end, explorations of the salt dome proceeded as well. Gorleben also received a pilot conditioning plant, never put to use, that would have prepared wastes for terminal storage.[12] Protests delayed each step of the development of Gorleben and its environs for nuclear purposes. West Germany's nuclear waste storage policy thus inadvertently morphed from the aspiration of a central repository into a decentral direct storage reality.[13]

Gorleben not only mirrored but shaped the (West) German nuclear energy policy beginning in 1977 and across the unification caesura of 1990. Instead of becoming the place where the Federal Republic closed the nuclear fuel cycle, Gorleben evolved into an unintended monument to the nuclear optimism and ambition of the 1970s and is emblematic of the unresolved problems of long-term nuclear waste storage. To gauge the enormity of the Gorleben project as initially conceived, the following section provides a brief overview of the assumptions and expectations that shaped the West German perception that a nuclear waste disposal center was a necessity.

The Global Dimension of Gorleben

At the time of Governor Albrecht's site announcement, the reprocessing of spent nuclear fuel and terminal waste storage marked the frontier of nuclear energy production worldwide. Although nuclear reactors contributed to the energy supply in the United States, Canada, the Soviet Union, Great Britain, France, West Germany, and elsewhere, none of these countries had yet mastered the challenges of large-scale reprocessing and terminal waste storage. Each country, for reasons of its own, had focused on the "front end" of the fuel cycle while neglecting the "back end" that reprocessing and waste storage represented.[14] With the issue of final waste disposal unresolved and commercial reprocessing piloted on only a modest scale, the announcement of a West German nuclear waste disposal center at Gorleben was a bold move indeed, designed to attract global attention.[15] The facility's magnitude as initially conceived reflects contemporary German assumptions about the future of nuclear energy, namely the expectation of its growing domestic relevance as an energy source, the export value of nuclear technology, as well as an eventual worldwide shortage of uranium as reactor fuel. In a confluence of political, technological, and commercial considerations, these mid-1970s assumptions appeared to necessitate reprocessing of spent nuclear fuel and propelled plans for a nuclear disposal center forward.

The West German development of a nuclear industry unfolded in the 1950s and 1960s, a period of general euphoria in the Cold War West over the possibilities of the "peaceful atom" and within an international context where the leading nuclear countries, above all the United States, provided technological expertise, possibilities for cooperation, but also commercial competition. Debates about the most prudent choice of reactor technology and fuel types reached a high point during the 1960s. The positions of nuclear scientists vacillated between advocacy of heavy-water- and light-water-moderated reactors that were powered by either natural or enriched uranium. Although the German preference lay with the heavy-water process and natural uranium, the relatively affordable American light-water reactor that ran on enriched uranium spearheaded the commercial expansion of nuclear energy during the 1960s.[16] German scientists, however, continued to think of the "first-generation" light-water reactor only as a stepping stone to the development of the "second-generation" fast breeder reactor, which they considered technologically superior.[17] During the energy-producing fission process, a breeder reactor would generate fresh plutonium by transmutation of the uranium so that it would "breed" slightly more plutonium over time than it burned, hence its name. A breeder also used uranium fuel more efficiently, an aspect that gained growing importance once prices for uranium rose after the oil crisis of 1973. At that time, nuclear energy received a boost as an alternative to fossil fuels, thereby increasing worldwide demand for new commercial reactors. Uranium prices rose accordingly, now coupled with predictions that supplies might eventually run out.[18] The reliable availability of uranium as reactor fuel thus became the perceived weak link in future energy production. This, in turn, strengthened the advocates of the fast breeder reactor, since this technology was said to be uranium-efficient and held out the prospect of stretching the global supply for decades.[19] Fast breeder reactors and reprocessing were inextricably linked, so that the assumption that breeder technology would carry the expansion of nuclear power in West Germany set the nuclear industry on a certain path. To benefit from the plutonium that a breeder accrued, the element would have to be recovered through a chemical process that separated it from the spent nuclear fuel and reprocessed it for renewed reactor use. Put differently, the successful use of breeder reactors would necessitate reprocessing technologies. Projecting an energy future based on fast breeders, as was the case in West Germany during the mid-1970s, thus put reprocessing front and center. Indeed, it was the breeder reactor that had given rise to the very thinking in terms of a "closed nuclear fuel cycle" in which spent nuclear fuel was reprocessed and reutilized. What sounded vaguely like "recycling," however, in fact produced large amounts of high-level radioactive liquid wastes that would require safe and perpetual storage, alongside other complex waste products.

However, the transgenerational liability of high-level nuclear waste and spent nuclear fuel had been underestimated and neglected ever since the atom had been put to civilian use.[20] In retrospect, this neglect was particularly acute in the 1960s, when the production of nuclear energy was expanding. The physicist Carl Friedrich von Weizsäcker reflected a common assumption when he stated in 1969 that the waste problem would remain limited. "I've been told in Karlsruhe [at the nuclear research center] that the entire nuclear waste that will exist in the Federal Republic by the year 2000 would fit into a box, a cube some 20 meters long. If the box gets closed and sealed well and stuck into a mine shaft then one may hope that the problem is solved."[21] Ten years later, such optimism had dwindled and the moral implications of relying on nuclear energy had become the subject of debate. "To what extent [. . .] is it right," asked the British physicist Brian Flowers, "to go on accumulating wastes in the hope that everything will turn out all right?"[22]

The fact that high-level wastes were indeed accumulating reflected the unresolved dilemmas on the back end of the nuclear cycle. In the United States, where such waste was also being generated by nuclear weapons programs, waste management, viewed as "a solvable problem" in the 1950s, was subsequently seen in the 1960s as "a huge and ever-increasing problem."[23] Reprocessing was considered part of the solution. By separating out uranium and plutonium for renewed use as reactor fuel, it reduced the amount of spent nuclear fuel that required safe storage.[24] This still left unresolved the question of ultimate disposal. Dumping radioactive waste into the ocean met with increasing resistance over the course of the 1960s. Sending it into space or burying it beneath the Arctic ice thankfully remained a pipe dream.[25] Storing it in geological formations such a granite and salt, however, was discussed in Western Europe and the

United States as a safe option. As early as the 1950s, consensus emerged among nuclear scientists that salt deposits were the most suitable geological formation for dumping high-level nuclear waste because these deposits occur in areas of low seismic activity, conduct heat in ways that promised to prevent overheating, and were expected to be free of groundwater.[26] American engineers studied the potential of salt formations as waste disposal sites for the first time in the mid-1960s in an abandoned salt mine near Lyons, Kansas.[27] The West German government acquired the deactivated rock salt mine Asse near Wolfenbüttel in 1965, purportedly for low- and medium-level waste to study nuclear waste storage as such.[28] Although the Asse mine has since turned into a major liability and safety risk, its acquisition was originally promoted as a step toward solving backend problems.[29]

Between 1974 and 1976, the SPD-led federal government inserted itself vehemently into debates on reprocessing and terminal storage. At that time, Bonn still expected nuclear energy's share of the total West German energy supply to increase.[30] The government developed an "integrated waste management concept" to ensure the safe disposal of spent nuclear fuel and related wastes. The concept privileged reprocessing over direct storage of spent nuclear fuel. After a permissible period of interim storage, the spent fuel had to be reprocessed, preferably at home to avoid transportation.[31] Detecting hesitation among the utility companies to embark on the enormously costly endeavor of building a reprocessing plant, parliament amended the Atomic Law in 1976. It now tied the issuance of operating licenses for new nuclear power plants to tangible progress on a facility for reprocessing. The government thus applied significant pressure on the nuclear industry to tackle the back end of the fuel cycle before allowing further expansion of the front end, a move that was perceived as placing a de facto moratorium on the expansion of nuclear power.[32] Not without astonishment, observers at the American Embassy in Bonn monitored the consequences of this provision, which they saw as seriously hampering the development of the German nuclear program.[33]

Yet while the law was certainly intended to propel the nuclear industry into action, industry representatives, too, considered a reprocessing plant vital.[34] After an incident at Windscale in 1973, it remained undetermined when the British would again provide reprocessing services. A year later the European pilot facility Eurochemic in Mol (Belgium) was taken out of commission, as scheduled. At the same time, it turned out that French reprocessing capacity was lower than expected.[35] When reprocessing abroad again became an option, the Germans winced at the cost. As the American Embassy reported in 1977, industry leaders preferred to construct interim storage facilities at home until German reprocessing replaced foreign management of German spent nuclear fuel abroad. The cost of the foreign reprocessing contracts was considered "enormous compared to the estimated total investment [. . .] for the German national reprocessing center."[36] Besides, the option of reprocessing waste abroad was said to expire in the mid-1980s.[37]

Just as the West Germans embarked on a strategy that centered on reprocessing, the United States abandoned the technology for good in the spring of 1977. After India had successfully detonated an atomic bomb in May 1974, the White House launched a review of American nuclear policy, especially reprocessing. The plutonium in the Indian bomb had come from a civilian reactor in Canada. Initiated by President Gerald Ford, the shutdown of commercial reprocessing in the United States was finalized by President Jimmy Carter through the withdrawal of federal funds. A plant in Barnwell, South Carolina, slated to open in the mid-1980s, was abandoned as a result. Carter's decision stemmed from concerns about proliferation. Since reprocessing yielded weapons-grade plutonium, Carter considered the line between civilian and military use of the material too thin to hold, as proved by the Indian bomb.[38] However, the American move only hardened the resolve among German officials and industry representatives to pursue their envisioned path. In fact, at the 1977 German Atomic Forum (Reaktortagung), the head of the fuel cycle department at the Federal Ministry for Research and Technology, Manfred Hagen, now considered reprocessing more important than ever. Since the United States had abandoned the option of producing any uranium through reprocessing or fast breeders at home, he reasoned, the Americans would have to satisfy their needs for reactor fuel on the world market, where they stood to consume more than 50 percent of the available uranium resources over the coming three decades. The United States, Hagen predicted, could well sweep the world market of uranium over the next few years, hence the need for countries with fewer energy resources like West Germany to generate some reactor fuel themselves to ensure its future availability.[39]

Last but not least, the perceived necessity to pursue a nuclear waste disposal center tied into the export ambitions of the German nuclear industry. The oil price shock of 1973 increased the demand for nuclear reactors, particularly in the Global South. One of the leading West German suppliers, the Kraftwerk Union (KWU), needed to sell four to five reactors per year to remain profitable. The West German market itself was limited; export was the avenue toward growth, and French and German companies had successfully established themselves on the market.[40] Even before a site for the NEZ was announced, the West German nuclear industry had displayed its confidence of mastering the fuel cycle by selling it in its entirety to Brazil in the spring of 1975. The deal to deliver four to eight nuclear reactors as well as reprocessing and uranium enrichment tech-nology to Latin America was the "largest single export order in German history."[41] Although the purchase was never consummated, because the Carter administration objected on grounds of proliferation concerns, the *Brasiliengeschäft* underscores the commercial potential of the Gorleben NEZ. If West Germany could successfully close the nuclear fuel cycle at Gorleben, it would not only make itself independent of commercial repro-cessing services offered only in the United Kingdom and France; it would also credibly demonstrate that the technology was safe, ready for further exports.

The confluence of political, technological, and commercial consider-ations described here indicates that the NEZ at Gorleben was not only of crucial relevance to West Germany's energy future as perceived at the time. With the challenges of commercial reprocessing and terminal waste storage unresolved worldwide—incidentally, to the present day—it was also a project with global significance among nuclear states who closely observed the West German efforts. Before a single plot of land was purchased at the designated site, the Gorleben project was already over-wrought with expectations. The stakes were high. It was this complex pro-ject that Ernst Albrecht dropped into a tiny hamlet in the West German borderlands on that fateful day in 1977.

Site Fights: The Gorleben Conflict

Most residents of Lüchow-Dannenberg learned of the Gorleben decision from the governor's press conference on February 22, 1977. Although earlier media coverage of the site search had provided an inkling that the county was in the running,[42] the announcement nonetheless caught most locals off guard. County officials had not been notified in advance, let alone involved in the search. As Andrew Blowers points out, Gorleben was an "exemplar of the Decide-Announce-Defend Approach" that was fashionable at the time.[43] When and why Gorleben was chosen over other

sites instantly became the subject of intense debate. Where government
and industry officials called the process responsible, scientific, and hence
objective, Gorleben opponents decried it as technocratic, untransparent,
and ultimately undemocratic.[44] Although the government of Lower Saxony
emphasized that the site was merely being explored to determine its
suitability, the lack of trust—not least inspired by the government's top-
down approach—made local opponents fear that a fait accompli was in
the works. Following templates established by anti-nuclear protests elsewhere, questioning the siting process itself became an integral part of
the anti-Gorleben protest. If it could be shown that the decision of Lower
Saxony's cabinet in favor of Gorleben had been motivated by criteria
other than geological, seismological, and meteorological suitability, then
Albrecht's government not only would be embarrassed but surely would
need to reconsider. This aspect of the site fight descended into a scramble
for smoking-gun government documents, as each side tried to prove the
other wrong, accompanied by pertinent press coverage.[45]

The siting controversy retained its potency in the party-political arena
for decades, to the point that a suggestion in 2009 that political pressure
had been brought to bear on the engineers of West Germany's metrology
institute in 1983 in order to suppress their advice that another site be explored alongside Gorleben led to a political scandal that resulted in a parliamentary investigative committee (*Untersuchungsausschuss*, UA).[46] From
2010 to 2013, the commission investigated why Gorleben was pursued
over other options, scrutinizing the entire decision-making process with
the resources of a special investigation.[47] The parliamentary inquest accumulated some 2,800 document folders and interviewed more than fifty
witnesses.[48] Using the rich empirical base that the inquiry and the literature provide,[49] this section focuses on how the inter-German border played
into the Gorleben siting process and ensuing controversy. It argues that
the border location caused disputes that gave rise to the widespread interpretation that Gorleben was chosen for political reasons, an allegation that
hindered local acceptance of the facility.

Based on the federal government's integrated waste management
concept, a site search got under way in 1974, conducted by an industry
consortium called KEWA.[50] Since the nuclear facility was slated to combine reprocessing and terminal waste storage at one location, a list of
parameters guided the search that addressed above- and below-ground
suitability but singled out the existence of salt formations as a lead characteristic. Geologically, the northern German plains were predisposed to

meet the search criteria; hence the KEWA short list featured only loca-tions in Schleswig-Holstein and Lower Saxony. In the various KEWA in-vestigations, Gorleben rotated in and out of consideration. The quality of its salt dome was beyond reproach, but like a location in eastern Schleswig-Holstein—a village called Lütau—Gorleben was dismissed for some time due to its proximity to the Iron Curtain. Ultimately, KEWA found Gorleben's geological and seismological characteristics superior to those of other sites but considered them diminished by the "highly ques-tionable" location of Gorleben next to the inter-German border.[51] Once it became clear that KEWA was focusing on Lower Saxony, the state assem-bled its own search committee in August 1976 and, using the KEWA re-sults, looked at the sites identified so far. Geological suitability remained the lead criterion.

The noteworthy difference between Lower Saxony's search and the fed-eral KEWA search was that economic concerns and structural policy now entered the considerations.[52] On November 11, 1976, three federal minis-ters traveled to Hannover to sound out Governor Albrecht on his willing-ness to support the federal project of an integrated nuclear waste disposal center and to press him to nominate a suitable site within a week. Albrecht himself and his staff remember the envoys of Chancellor Schmidt as ex-erting undue pressure.[53] The meeting had "dramatic highpoints" and left each side disappointed in the other.[54] In the annals of the Gorleben con-flict, this meeting is critical since it revealed to the federal representatives that Albrecht favored Gorleben and, in return, gave Albrecht and his team a clear sense that Bonn opposed the location because of its proximity to the Iron Curtain.

Gorleben's border location led to a dispute between Schmidt and Albrecht that drew the siting process into party and electoral politics. To begin with, Chancellor Helmut Schmidt (SPD) had to rely on a Christian Democratic state governor, Ernst Albrecht, to implement the complex in-tegrated waste management concept that was perceived and depicted in both industry and government as a pressing need. The amendment to the Atomic Law in 1976 had yielded a hardly navigable web of interdepend-encies: the industry needed to file for a permit to build a reprocessing facility in order to free itself of constraints on the licensing of new power plants; the federal government needed to build a final storage repository for which deep salt formations were considered best; and a federal state with such geological prerequisites needed to provide a site and license the construction. This triangular relationship was precarious, to say the

least, and accorded Lower Saxony an indispensable role and hence political muscle vis-à-vis the federal government. In principle, Schmidt
and Albrecht agreed that nuclear energy was a necessity.[55] However, they
clashed badly over the Gorleben siting. Schmidt deemed the matter so important that he wrote to Albrecht twice to convince him to drop Gorleben
and acquiesce to a different site in his home state.[56] In view of the known
inclinations of the SED regime to use West German concerns and requests as leverage for material compensation, the federal government
dreaded lengthy negotiations with the GDR about security provisions for
the nuclear facility that would endow East Berlin with long-term ties to a
sensitive policy area. Schmidt also held strong reservations about placing
advanced nuclear technology and weapons-grade plutonium in immediate
proximity to the border, where it could be exposed to surprise attacks by
Warsaw Pact troops or fall into the hands of terrorists. Besides, Gorleben
was located on the Elbe River, where the demarcation line remained disputed. Moreover, the Gorleben salt dome extended underground beyond
the border; attempts to access the eastern part might have geological consequences in the western section.[57] With Schmidt still resisting the site
choice, Albrecht's government pressured Bonn to inform the GDR about
the impending selection of Gorleben.[58]

The highly publicized dispute between these two politicians contributed to the widespread interpretation that Gorleben had been selected
for political reasons and not according to objective scientific criteria. The
press reported the dispute in party political terms and credited Albrecht
with a clever tactical move to damage Schmidt.[59] In a shrewd maneuver,
Albrecht was said to have picked the one location that Chancellor Schmidt
was known to reject, thereby undermining the federal government's nuclear program and putting Schmidt at the mercy of the GDR leadership.
Albrecht's Gorleben announcement thus amounted to a nondecision, the
papers said, and was expected to be undone again by Schmidt, which, incidentally, would then relieve Albrecht of a major problem in his state before running for re-election in 1978. A high-ranking GDR representative
even congratulated Albrecht on this "smart move," which amounted to
applause from the wrong side that Albrecht swiftly rejected.[60]

The siting controversy was exacerbated by the fact that Governor
Albrecht never made any bones about preferring Lüchow-Dannenberg
for economic reasons. Both in contemporary interviews and in his
1999 memoirs, he consistently mentioned the county's location in the
Zonenrandgebiet and its lack of industrial jobs as underpinning his siting

decision. The nuclear facility, especially the reprocessing plant, was to provide the county "for the first time since 1945 with a real chance for good economic development."[61] Once Albrecht himself had withdrawn his support from the reprocessing plant in May 1979, however, he needed to adjust his argument. Henceforth, not jobs per se but "purchasing power" became the blessing that the reduced nuclear complex would supposedly provide. When the interim storage facility and the final waste repository became functional, he argued, the nuclear industry would still be the largest employer in the county and, through wages and corporate taxes, would inject major purchasing power into the borderlands that would benefit local retail, restaurants, and tradespeople.[62]

Albrecht's focus on the borderlands became apparent in another major siting decision. Shortly after the Gorleben announcement, he authorized the operation of a coal-fired power plant, Buschhaus, near Helmstedt (West), which was scheduled to start production in 1984. By that time, Buschhaus coincided with the West German *Waldsterben* angst and quickly turned into a political scandal because the plant lacked desulfurization filters. Here, too, Albrecht was willing to take a political risk in return for jobs in the borderlands.[63] Albrecht's initiatives were fully compatible with the long-standing rhetoric of borderland advocates who singled out the Iron Curtain as responsible for economic problems in their regions. As we shall see, Albrecht's political priority for jobs in the border regions found receptive counterparts in the county leadership of Lüchow-Dannenberg. Among Gorleben opponents, however, the emphasis on industrial jobs gave rise to the suspicion that the siting process was dominated by structural concerns to which scientific criteria were secondary.

Albrecht provided additional reasons for the choice of Gorleben that did not increase the general perception that the site search had been conducted neutrally. Aside from the priority given to jobs, Albrecht had expected that the acquisition of the land required for the above-ground reprocessing, fuel fabrication, and waste vitrification plants would be relatively simple, since much of the pertinent land belonged to the estate of Andreas Count Bernstorff of Gartow. Because Bernstorff was of crucial importance, Albrecht followed the Count's suggestion of convening an international symposium of nuclear energy experts, the famous Gorleben Hearing, to debate security aspects of the planned facility but also the more philosophical dimensions of nuclear energy use.[64] To Albrecht's chagrin, Count Bernstorff turned into an adamant opponent of the Gorleben project and refused to sell any land.[65] Albrecht also miscalculated potential opposition when he pegged the county's population as relatively open to or at least not predisposed against nuclear energy.[66] Finally, the governor went on the record with the remark that he considered the oddly shaped county easy to secure.[67] It was, after all, surrounded on three sides by the inter-German border. This remark gave rise to the suspicion that the county had been selected for ease of policing anti-nuclear protesters or, in case of an incident, for containing contaminated citizens. As we will see later, these apprehensions would influence the methods of the anti-Gorleben protest. Gorleben's border location thus played a distinct role during the siting process and triggered political disputes that contributed to undermining public trust in the search. Albrecht's obvious efforts to prioritize economic development seemed to elevate the *Zonenrand* location of Gorleben above more scientific concerns, and the quarrel between Schmidt and Albrecht moved the debate into a party-political framework. In fact, Gorleben's proximity to the border created a classic transboundary environmental problem that became magnified by the fact that this was not any old border but the Iron Curtain.

Gorleben and the GDR

Despite Helmut Schmidt's vehement objections to Gorleben, the chancellor accepted Albrecht's site choice in July 1977, some five months after the governor's first public announcement.[68] While Schmidt still hesitated, the Hannover government insisted that Bonn approach the GDR about the impending exploration of the Gorleben salt dome. The very timing of when and to what extent to inform the GDR became part of the dispute between Hannover and Bonn.[69] Despite the GDR's prominent role in Schmidt's concerns about Gorleben, the GDR's position on the nuclear facility remains largely unknown. Albrecht himself played down the issue, arguing all along that if the facility was safe for West Germans, it was safe for East Germans as well.[70] The historian Anselm Tiggemann reports that the SED regime lodged only "mild" protest against Gorleben.[71] This line was spun further still by Manfred Popp, a leading bureaucrat in the Ministry for Research and Technology at the time. Reminiscing in 2006, Popp stated that "one of the many oddities in the history of the [nuclear] waste disposal policy was [. . .] the fact that the GDR did not perceive the [Gorleben] decision as a provocation and at no time tried to construe it as an imposition for which it was entitled to compensation. The concerns of the federal government in this regard [. . .] turned out to be unfounded."[72] The contemporary impetus to minimize the GDR's interest in Gorleben left room for later sensationalist disclosures in the press that seemed to prove the opposite.[73] What, then, was the position of the GDR on Gorleben? Given how involved the SED regime was in other environmental questions that mattered to West Germany, it is safe to assume that the East German government observed the nuclear project next door with heightened interest. What did the GDR know about Gorleben and when? What did the SED regime do or refrain from doing and why?

The Bonn government need not have strategized about the moment when and how to share information about the plans for Gorleben with the GDR. For the East German authorities were well informed all along and knew almost in real time how the internal western decision-making process about the nuclear waste disposal center was evolving. In the summer of 1974, when the integrated waste management concept was taking shape in Bonn, the foreign intelligence arm of the Stasi reported for the first time plans for a West German reprocessing plant. Stasi agents determined that Gorleben would be the most comprehensive facility of its kind in Western Europe, make the neighbor autarkic in regard to the treatment of spent fuel, and allow its nuclear industry to sell not only nuclear power plants but to market the entire fuel cycle.[74] The Stasi also picked up on the siting process in Lower Saxony in 1976, albeit in a rather rudimentary form.[75] In January 1977, the head of the Stasi, Erich Mielke, provided the SED leadership with a first substantial assessment of the site selection process, the specs of the planned nuclear complex, its construction schedule, as well as a summary of the political dispute between Schmidt and Albrecht about the Gorleben site. The report was said to be based on "reliable internal information."[76] It dwelled in particular on the objections that Bonn anticipated from East Berlin, which, transposed into a GDR document, now read like a blueprint on how to aggravate the Schmidt administration the most. Even the communications strategy that Bonn intended to use toward East Berlin was already known: if Albrecht could not be convinced to drop Gorleben, the GDR was to be approached and made to believe that an open-ended search was under way in which Gorleben was one possible site among many.[77] Mielke's report concluded that the nuclear plant would constitute a "permanent source of danger for the GDR." Especially the reprocessing of nuclear waste on the intended scale would make Gorleben an "experimental ground for the nuclear industry of the FRG" for years to come.[78]

Until the collapse of the GDR, the Stasi continued to monitor the Gorleben issue, covering the political decision-making processes, any construction and exploration work, as well as the anti-Gorleben protests. It derived its information directly from within the West German "nuclear cabinet," an interministerial group in Bonn concerned with the peaceful use of nuclear energy. Although it is not clear who the mole in the nuclear cabinet was, the top-level Stasi reports on the issue reflect the minutes of the West German meetings almost verbatim.[79] The Stasi also benefited from indiscreet employees of the companies related to the construction site who disclosed information in semi-social settings, like the Hannover Fair.[80] Such instances, however, were only the bycatch of a much larger effort to keep tabs on the West German nuclear industry, independent of the Gorleben issue.[81] Finally, the Stasi monitored protest activities against the nuclear facility, as well as the respective countermeasures of West German authorities such as the deployment of the police and BGS units at demonstrations. The Stasi files contain information about protest marches, the journeys of Gorleben opponents from West Berlin to events in Lüchow-Dannenberg County, and even internal gatherings and plans of the protesters.[82] Three informal collaborators, or IMs, were active in Lüchow-Dannenberg County, yet more people must have been reporting from within Gorleben protest support groups in Hamburg, West Berlin, or Göttingen as well as from within BGS units.[83]

On the basis of the intelligence the Stasi gathered, the SED leadership developed and adjusted its views and positions about Gorleben. Initial assessments within the GDR government about the risks relating to the nuclear waste disposal center actually differed. The head of the East German nuclear security agency, Georg Sitzlack, thought that normal operations of the reprocessing plant and the storage facility posed a smaller risk than any regular nuclear power station. He also expressed confidence in the quality of West German technology.[84] By contrast, the minister for coal and energy, Klaus Siebold, emphasized the general hazard posed by the NEZ and recommended that the SED government adopt a negative attitude toward Gorleben.[85] As more information about the West German plans trickled in, the SED party leaders grew convinced that Gorleben had been selected to externalize the security risk of the reprocessing plant onto GDR territory and thus minimize West German opposition to the facility. They also believed that Lower Saxony had salt domes that were equally or even better suited for storing nuclear waste than the one at Gorleben.[86] Once approached by Bonn, the SED leadership intended to take the position that they would not object to the storage of low- and medium-level nuclear waste but that they had reservations about high-level waste. Although accidents were considered unlikely, they rejected the reprocessing plant entirely because the location and the climatic conditions were likely to saddle the East Germans with the risks posed by the facility.[87]

When the West German diplomats in the Permanent Representation in East Berlin first officially broached the issue in late March 1977, the information they conveyed was perfunctory at best.[88] Their East German interlocutors knew full well that they were being fed piecemeal information. The western policy experts for inter-German relations at the Permanent Representation would have preferred a more comprehensive approach and actually repeatedly pressed Bonn for more transparency toward the GDR lest Gorleben undermine other environmental negotiations that the Federal Republic sought to advance.[89] What the Schmidt administration wanted to avoid, however, was the GDR government taking any informatory approach to mean that they had a say in the matter or could expect compensation for good conduct. Therefore, Bonn emphasized that their information sharing was entirely voluntary and merely served the purpose of maintaining good neighborly relations.[90] When the West German diplomat Günter Gaus was allowed to bring up the subject again in early July 1977, his counterpart already signaled that the issue would cause "serious problems" for their relations.[91] Whatever Gaus conveyed, the GDR government did not base its views on official input from Bonn but drew its information from the Stasi. The approaches from the West German government were merely assessed alongside the information from clandestine channels to determine whether Bonn was trying to dupe its neighbor. To keep its options open, and in line with its standard behavior whenever it sensed a West German predicament, the SED regime took a position of generic opposition and declared that it would consider a decision in favor of Gorleben to be directed "against the interests of the GDR" since the location would effectively transfer the risk of accidents across the border.[92] Indeed, they called Gorleben the "worst possible site."[93] While prepared press releases condemning Gorleben as a "provocation" remained unused for the time being,[94] the West German diplomats realized that the SED regime was digging in its heels. Indeed, they classified the GDR's reservations as "massive."[95]

Given that the East German government clearly did protest the West German plans to build the NEZ, the question remains why to the present day the perception prevails that the SED regime barely objected to

Gorleben, a response that would have been completely out of character in view of the customary East German remonstration in matters far more minor than a huge nuclear facility on its state border. That the exchanges for the most part unfolded behind the scenes can be only part of the answer. More likely, the West Germans had identified a suitable pressure point that was making the SED leadership reconsider its approach.

By late 1978, the talks were indeed on a trajectory that might have turned Gorleben into another major sticking point in inter-German relations.[96] The East German government remained dissatisfied with the answers it received and was particularly vexed about West German media coverage that the GDR had never commented on Gorleben. In the spring of 1979, the SED regime therefore launched a report through its news agency, ADN, in which it sought to set the record straight and repeat its objections.[97] West German diplomats were well versed in identifying so-called news items in the East German press that were effectively proxy communications to the Bonn government. The fact that the SED leadership was resorting to this method seemed to indicate that they were ready to escalate the Gorleben situation. In order to forestall such an escalation, the West Germans now changed tack and considered addressing publicly the security risks of the Soviet-model nuclear reactors that were producing energy in East Germany. Any such discussion, for instance at the International Atomic Energy Agency (IAEA) in Vienna, would most likely be eagerly seized upon by the Scandinavian countries, which already suspected the GDR of contributing to air pollution.[98] To convey their warning, the West German diplomats did nothing more than request information on a planned nuclear power station in Stendal (East), and in particular about the GDR's own nuclear waste repository in Morsleben (East).[99] Now each side had a ball in its court and an interest in slowing down the game.

From the first moment that the SED leadership considered its options of how to react to Gorleben, they were determined not to provide their adversaries with any reasons to pressure them in return. The most obvious pressure point was Morsleben, the GDR's own nuclear waste repository in a former salt mine. Ironically, Morsleben was located in immediate proximity to the Iron Curtain as well.[100] Applying an obvious double standard, the East German government had not seen fit to inform its western neighbors about plans for this repository on the flimsy grounds that the underground elements of the facility did not extend beneath the demarcation line into western territory. Instead, the existence of Morsleben was accidentally revealed in March 1976 when a member of the East German nuclear security agency made reference to it in a paper delivered at the IAEA in Vienna.[101] Morsleben was projected to house only low- and medium-level nuclear waste. High-level waste customarily had been handed over to the Soviet Union for disposal. By the mid-1970s, however, the GDR could no longer count on the Soviet Union to accept East Germany's spent fuel; the storage of such material at Morsleben was thus becoming likely.[102] Aware of its own vulnerability on this point, the East German government prepared a press release in case the Schmidt administration endorsed Gorleben, in which they intentionally refrained from any "polemical comparison" of Gorleben and Morsleben.[103] Internally, government officials continued to argue that Gorleben and Morsleben were very different facilities that should not be compared in the first place; Morsleben, they correctly pointed out, had nothing to do with reprocessing spent fuel.[104]

Yet such technicalities were irrelevant in view of the potent political problem undergirding Morsleben. The real concern among SED officials was that GDR citizens might catch the anti-nuclear "protest bacillus" that was running high in Lüchow-Dannenberg and in West Germany more generally.[105] Not only had the SED regime tried to keep the waste repository secret from its western neighbors, it was not exactly forthcoming with its own citizens either, a strategy aided by the fact that Morsleben conveniently lay within the border security strip, where mobility and information were tightly controlled.[106] Citizen participation, open debate, and government accountability were not hallmarks of SED rule to begin with. Tellingly, the first mention of Morsleben in an East German newspaper did not occur until October 1988, ten years after the facility received nuclear waste for the first time.[107] While the SED regime was well equipped to control information about Morsleben at home, the spatial proximity to and western debate about Gorleben threatened to draw attention to their own facility. West German media began to mention Morsleben, and the very arguments that western protesters deployed against Gorleben could be easily applied to Morsleben, since both waste storage caverns were located in similar rock salt formations. Given that news regularly crossed the Iron Curtain due to East German consumption of West German media,[108] the SED regime would not be able to enforce an information embargo on the facility if western discussions about Morsleben increased. So intertwined did Gorleben and Morsleben become for the SED leaders that in a literary slip of tongue, several internal documents referred to "Gorsleben."[109] West German observers noticed this weak spot. Western newspapers commented on the conspicuous silence in the East German press about the violent protests against the nuclear power plant in Brokdorf (West). Similarly, Albrecht's announcement of Gorleben as the site of the nuclear complex was not acknowledged with a single line in eastern newspapers.[110] The head of the Permanent Representation, Günter Gaus, noted that the GDR had been uncharacteristically mum about the protest against nuclear energy in the west. "One may conclude," Gaus wrote, "that the GDR leadership wants to avoid any discussion about nuclear facilities at home."[111]

Among the facilities the GDR leadership sought to avoid discussing in public were also its own nuclear power plants. This was the other issue that West German diplomats considered highlighting publicly if the GDR decided to turn Gorleben into a protracted dispute.[112] East German nuclear energy stemmed from Soviet water-water energetic reactors (VVER), which, like the related western pressurized water reactors, used light water as a moderator and coolant and enriched uranium as fuel.[113] In the late 1970s, the GDR operated two nuclear power plants in Rheinsberg and Greifswald, with a third under construction in Stendal.[114] The Stendal plant was contested within the SED leadership itself because its location did not allow for a 25-kilometer security perimeter around the reactor. In the end, however, the pressing need for energy prevailed, and construction began in 1974.[115] According to a 1965 contract with the Soviet Union, the plant would run on imported ready-for-use VVERs from the Soviet Union. The technology for the East German nuclear program came from the Soviet Union all along, relegating the GDR industry to a supporting role.[116] As the historian Mike Reichert emphasizes, the Soviet Union did not prove a reliable partner for the GDR in this matter and caused construction delays and escalating costs. Indeed, East German nuclear engineers used to joke that the VVERs did not arrive ready for use, only ready for repair.[117] The nuclear power plant at Greifswald-Lubmin proved particularly prone to incidents, including a fire in late 1975 that brought one reactor close to a nuclear meltdown.[118]

The prospect of the West German government addressing East German nuclear security must have been a credible threat for the SED leadership, given that they were acutely aware of ongoing problems with Soviet nuclear equipment. Bonn's polite inquiry about Morsleben and Stendal mattered because it forced the SED to reckon with the widespread assumption among its citizens that western technology and consumer products were generally superior to eastern equivalents. If Bonn raised doubts about the GDR's nuclear security, the SED would need to convince its own citizens that eastern technology was safe despite the fact that West German protesters publicly questioned their own government's ability to control the risks of nuclear energy production. By carefully applying pressure on the SED leadership, Helmut Schmidt's government was, however, walking a fine line itself. At a time of growing concern about the commercial use of nuclear power, any discussion about the safety of eastern nuclear technology could easily backfire and feed the general insecurity about nuclear energy at home. The West German nuclear industry thus decided to tread carefully in regard to incidents at East German nuclear plants. According to a Stasi report, the Kraftwerk Union group, which built and operated nuclear plants for Siemens, had a commercial interest in pitching its nuclear technology as more secure than Soviet equivalents; yet it refrained from releasing alarmist reports about any incidents lest such revelations stoke the already strong anti-nuclear sentiment in West Germany.[119]

Around 1980, both sides had reached a stalemate and were exploring how to capitalize on the other's predicament. The SED government now considered whether it could turn the West German quandary into a business opportunity by offering to reprocess and store nuclear waste on East German territory in order to generate valuta and gain access to western nuclear technology. When Ernst Albrecht called off the reprocessing plant at Gorleben in May 1979, the West German plans to close the nuclear fuel cycle at home took a serious hit. For the time being, spent fuel could still be dispatched to La Hague in France for reprocessing, but those contracts were slated to run out in 1985. The West German nuclear industry thus moved toward a major reprocessing dilemma that would not quickly be resolved domestically. In 1980, Alexander Schalck therefore proposed to Günter Mittag that reprocessing services be developed for West German spent fuel. The idea had the obvious flaw that the GDR had neither the expertise nor the capacity to build the necessary facility. The plan thus entailed offering the West Germans the tantalizing opportunity to "export" a major political dispute at home by financing and building the reprocessing plant in East Germany, thereby ending ongoing acrimonious fights over the site. In a countertrade typical of East German relations with its capitalist neighbor, the GDR would then pay for the cost of the plant "in kind" by reprocessing West German spent fuel for years to come. This scheme had the added advantage that the GDR would be able to reprocess its own spent fuel, which the Soviet Union was no longer taking back, and could try to attract further customers among the Comecon countries, thus advancing its own image as a modern industrialized state. In the end, Schalck and Mittag dropped the plan, presumably because it too obviously lay beyond the GDR's capacities.[120]

The West German government, by contrast, responded to the Gorleben stalemate with efforts to move toward an institutionalized information exchange on nuclear security questions with the GDR. Its experts for inter-German relations at the Permanent Representation wanted to move away from insipid tit-for-tat conversations about each other's waste storage facilities and address nuclear security more broadly in an effort to learn more about the East German nuclear energy program.[121] A first meeting of experts convened in October 1983 and laid the groundwork for the 1987 Radiation Protection Agreement (Strahlenschutzabkommen).[122] The federal government also covered its bases in legal terms and explored liability questions.[123] Above all, it was intent on avoiding anything that might provide the GDR with grounds for complaint.

What, then, allowed for the relatively quiet resolution of the GDR's protestations against the Gorleben site? For one, Albrecht's objection to the reprocessing plant in May 1979 removed an element of particular concern to the GDR from the plans for the nuclear waste disposal center. Gorleben was thus downsized to a nuclear waste storage facility. Since the GDR ran its own nuclear waste dump across the border, the two sides reached a stalemate on that issue. From that point onward, escalating the protest became more likely to create problems for the GDR at home than to interfere in the plans of its capitalist neighbor, especially once the West Germans signaled an "interest" in the security of East German nuclear reactors. This interest, however, was merely a tactical move to quell further needling and ensure that Gorleben would not become another staple of inter-German environmental problems.[124] Indeed, the West German diplomats managed to channel the quarrel about Gorleben into another codification of inter-German relations in the Radiation Protection Agreement, which was signed alongside the Environmental Accords during Honecker's visit to Bonn in 1987. Both agreements, it is worth noting, had originated in border-related disputes about transboundary pollution and potential radiation.

A Place at the Bargaining Table: The County's Role

Controversial large-scale projects such as airports, dams, waste incinerators, and nuclear power plants tend to be relegated to geographic and economic peripheries with low population density and a presumed weak civil society where the new facility can quickly establish economic dependencies by becoming the main employer.[125] Although the rural county of Lüchow-Dannenberg has always displayed peripheral characteristics, the Iron Curtain had exacerbated its peripherality in economic and geographic terms, thinned out the population, and driven the county into a strong reliance on state subsidies. Like Boyd County in Nebraska, Yucca Mountain in Nevada, Ōkuma in Fukushima, and, most recently, Bure in France, Lüchow-Dannenberg thus fit the pattern of a "vulnerable" community almost paradigmatically, with the notable exception that civil society and hence adamant protest proved unexpectedly strong.[126] Once sustained opposition coalesces around a controversial facility, however, the state is likely to step up material incentives to ensure local acquiescence.[127]

What emerged with Albrecht's announcement in February 1977 was the prospect of turning Lüchow-Dannenberg County into a "nuclear community." That term goes beyond merely denoting the geographic location of a nuclear facility; it also addressees the social, cultural, environmental, and economic consequences that manifested themselves within a community where a nuclear facility took shape or, as in the cases of Hanford (US), Sellafield (UK), La Hague (France), and Ozersk (Soviet Union/Russia), took over.[128] Above all, the term refers to communities where consent to host and operate a nuclear facility would benefit residents through access to jobs, improved public infrastructure, better housing, and other material perks—in short, where nuclear risk would be tied to prosperity, or the promise thereof.[129]

The prospect of becoming a nuclear community fell on willing ears among county officials in Lüchow-Dannenberg because of the county's history as part of the borderlands, where it had become standard practice since the 1950s to argue for a causal link between the border and economic deficiencies. Lüchow-Dannenberg certainly had the numbers to prove its economic underperformance, yet its representatives had also perfected the art of relying on the Iron Curtain to justifiy any state support. This line of reasoning had been employed by all border regions for years, but Wilhelm Paasche, the county's leading administrator from 1962 until 1978, gave the argument an edge that he hoped would elevate Lüchow-Dannenberg's status above that of other border areas. In 1968, he criticized a new development program that would, as customary, treat all *Zonenrand* counties equally. This, he argued, "made a mockery of the *really* depressed areas within the zonal borderlands," namely his county. Paasche's argument thus undermined the spatial unity of the 40-kilometer-deep strip that borderland advocates had established so arduously over the years. The attempt to represent his own county as harder pressed and hence more deserving than others became an integral part of Paasche's efforts in the early 1970s to shake loose additional funds from the federal government in Bonn and the state government in Hannover.[130]

Where did the county stand before the Gorleben decision? During the 1960s, agriculture was undergoing structural adjustments. Competition within the European Community pressured farmers into modernizing agricultural production and drove the less profitable ones out of business.[131] The number of farms in Lüchow-Dannenberg declined from 3,900 in 1960 to 1,735 in 1985.[132] At the time of an official visit undertaken by a parliamentary committee in 1968, Lüchow-Dannenberg featured 42 residents per square kilometer. Paasche thought that 100 residents per square kilometer, or an increase of 20,000 people, would be necessary to sustain economic development. He bemoaned the aging population and high unemployment, which stood at 16 percent in the winter of 1967. In well-rehearsed lines, Paasche explained the county's woes with reference to the border. In view of agriculture's decline, Paasche saw the only way out of this "vicious cycle" to be the creation of industrial jobs. Most notably, he complained about lack of support "from above."[133]

Spurred by the threat of being forced to merge with the neighboring county of Uelzen during a major administrative reform in Lower Saxony, county officials increased their efforts at economic development in the early 1970s. These efforts bear traces of desperation. In order to enhance the county's potential for tourism, Paasche suggested building artificial ski slopes to draw skiing enthusiasts into this region of the North German plain, which had no ties to winter sports whatsoever.[134] In the meantime, Kurt Dieter Grill (CDU), a member of the state legislature, tried to keep the county in the running as the location of tracks that would be used to test the technology for a high-speed maglev train, the later Transrapid. This large project was eventually undertaken in the Emsland region in the 1980s, an equally underdeveloped district in Lower Saxony near Bremen.[135] County officials also pinned their hopes on a nuclear power plant in Langendorf-on-Elbe that an energy company from Hamburg intended to build.[136] In May 1975, Grill and Wilfried Hasselmann (CDU), another member of the state legislature, pressed the Hannover government to accept a Lüchow development plan that they believed to be in the works. Although no such plan existed, the state government reminded the representatives that in 1974 alone the county had received some DM 29 million in subsidies, loans, and state investments.[137] Yet since no new industrial projects appeared on the horizon, in October 1975 Paasche accused the authorities in Bonn and Hannover of "dismantling" the "zonal borderlands," in particular Lüchow-Dannenberg. The pointed criticism won him some traction in the press.[138] Among the officials thus criticized, however, an alternative reading of the county's economic history emerged over the course of the 1970s. Whereas Paasche persistently argued that the region had never recovered from the advent of the Iron Curtain and *therefore* had few industrial jobs, bureaucrats in Bonn rejected the idea that partition alone had caused the county's problems. Instead they contended that borderland aid had allowed the agricultural region to acquire industrial jobs for the first time.[139] Each side clearly knew how to counter the rhetoric of the other.

What matters here, though, is the fact that the complaints from within the county reached a crescendo in late 1975, thus coinciding with the beginnings of the search for a nuclear site in Lower Saxony. In view of the county's incessant complaints, Governor Ernst Albrecht had good reason to be confident that any initiative that would create industrial jobs there would be more than welcome, as indeed it was among those county officials who prioritized economic development. The Gorleben decision of February 1977 gave the county exceptional political leverage with respect to both the state government in Hannover and the federal government in Bonn. If the county would agree to house this nuclear facility and therefore ensure West Germany's energy future as it was conceived during the mid-1970s, its representatives held the not-so-unreasonable expectation that Hannover and Bonn would finally agree to the county's longstanding demands. Once Helmut Schmidt had acquiesced to Albrecht's site choice, the county could bypass established channels and claim direct and unprecedented access to the chancellor himself. In a first communication, Paasche's successor, Klaus Poggendorf, acquainted Schmidt with the county's structural problems in order to define the local expectations regarding federal authorities.[140]

Yet the prospect of a nuclear waste disposal center took a serious hit in May 1979 when Ernst Albrecht announced his solitary decision that a reprocessing plant at Gorleben was technically possible but politically not feasible.[141] The Gorleben project was thus reduced to the construction of a nuclear waste repository with adjacent interim storage and a conditioning facility.[142] The county's leadership had pinned most of their hopes for the creation of industrial jobs on the reprocessing plant, whereas waste storage was not expected to generate jobs. In light of the apparent loss of the promised job machine, the county representatives now pressed the federal government to deliver a comprehensive development program. Poggendorf argued that the burden on the county would be the same regardless of whether the full NEZ or only a waste repository were built. Lüchow-Dannenberg's name had already been inextricably linked to nuclear waste, damaging tourism and agricultural production alike.[143] What Poggendorf expected, then, was that the Bonn government would uphold its part of the nuclear community bargain, namely the promise of prosperity. In November 1979 a group of eight county administrators and elected officials took the train to Bonn to convey this view at the Chancellery.

Intent on drawing on their newfound political capital, the county's delegation entered the Chancellery meeting with a catalog of demands.[144] The list reflected long-standing hopes for, among other things, rail connections and new roads, especially a new transit autobahn that would connect Lüchow-Dannenberg directly to West Berlin and route the "islanders" into the region to enliven local tourism.[145] The list also betrayed the desire to gain the upper hand in determining the extent of state aid that the county deemed suitable for its needs. The most potent item was therefore the demand for an annual special allocation of DM 10 million over ten years in order to enhance the county's infrastructure and create jobs. Lest this special allocation be set off against the existing support that "zonal borderland aid" already provided, the wish list made it very clear that these positions were to remain untouched. During the meeting with Schmidt, county officials further specified their ideas. They wanted to host a BGS border police unit, as well as various federal agencies in the county. They also asked that the DBE company, which would eventually run the Gorleben facility, build its headquarters there instead of in nearby Peine. The delegation from Lüchow-Dannenberg further requested that the Federal Ministry for Research and Technology situate testing facilities for alternative energy production, such as an ethanol plant, in the county. Finally, they asked the federal government to pressure the electricity firm Preussen Elektra to pursue and prioritize its plans for a coal or nuclear power plant in Langendorf-on-Elbe.[146]

Although the county's demands were rather bold, Chancellor Schmidt sympathized with them in principle. He realized that it was necessary for the proponents of the Gorleben project to present a credible link between the nuclear facility and future affluence before the next election. If the Gorleben supporters could not be retained in public office, the strategically important issue of terminal waste storage would be reduced to interim solutions, endangering West Germany's entire nuclear energy program. Schmidt therefore encouraged the federal ministries to support the county and think along "unconventional" lines if necessary.[147] With the chancellor's backing, the Federal Ministry for Economic Affairs coordinated negotiations in 1979 and 1980 between federal, state, and county officials on a development package containing the county's refined wish lists.[148] Particular items on the wish lists met with different reactions. For instance, the Federal Ministry for Research and Technology quickly embraced the idea of investing in a plant that would experiment with producing ethanol from sugar beets because it was considered "important for the mood" of the county to receive not only nuclear waste but also something with a "positive effect."[149] The county officials' hope of getting a nuclear power plant in Langendorf-on-Elbe, by contrast, was quickly thwarted on ecological grounds. Bureaucrats in faraway Bonn had a clearer conception of the ecological value of the Elbe floodplains, where the power plant would have been built, than did the local officials from Lüchow-Dannenberg.[150] Unbeknownst to anyone in the county and apparently in Bonn, Preussen Elektra had dropped the Langendorf project long ago, in November 1976, when the company management learned of the Gorleben site, which, they concluded, deserved priority over other nuclear projects.[151]

The most contentious issue was the county's demand for a special annual financial allocation. The federal government had concluded a contract with Lower Saxony in February 1979 that specified Bonn's financial contribution in view of the duties that the *Land* had acquired by becoming the location of the national nuclear project. Per contract, Lower Saxony received DM 200 million between 1979 and 1982 from Bonn. The federal government, in turn, received those 200 million from the nuclear industry, namely the DWK company.[152] In the conversations with the county, Bonn took the predictable position that the county's cash needs in relation to Gorleben were covered in this contract, which slated 24.5 million for the county to provide the local infrastructure for the nuclear project.[153] Part of Poggendorf's problem was that Hannover took its time handing over the county's share.[154] His problems grew once Albrecht scrapped the reprocessing plant in May 1979. Since the reprocessing plant had been a project of private industry, the DWK company was now no longer obligated to pay 200 million to the federal government.[155] Several high-level officials in Bonn, including the chancellor himself, argued that the entire contract with Lower Saxony was now null and void since Albrecht "broke his word."[156] In the end, the federal government maintained the contract with Hannover and paid the 200 million in four annual installments, thus making up for the lost DWK contribution. In the intense internal negotiations within the Bonn government about this issue, the contours of the nuclear community became very tangible again. Despite Schmidt's apparent anger at Albrecht, the ministers of economic affairs and the interior, Otto Graf Lambsdorff and Gerhard Baum, convinced him to uphold the contract with Lower Saxony. Like it or not, they argued, the money "buys [the] further cooperation of Lower Saxony as well as the acceptance [of the nuclear project] in the region around Lüchow-Dannenberg."[157]

While the county thus managed to secure its share of the federal payments to Lower Saxony,[158] the point of the meeting at the Chancellery in November 1979 had been to entice the federal government to grant Lüchow-Dannenberg a special allocation *beyond* these contractual payments. Since the Ministry of Finance objected to any direct federal payment to a county on constitutional grounds, the idea arose to involve the DWK.[159] The opportunity to make the DWK pay for structural aid came in 1980 when the municipalities of Gartow and Gorleben agreed to house an interim storage facility (*Zwischenlager*) for nuclear waste that was needed as long as the suitability of Gorleben's salt dome as a final repository was being explored. Beginning in 1995, the interim facility received the first CASTOR containers with spent nuclear fuel. Since the waste facility would not generate much corporate tax for the municipalities, the contract between DWK and the municipalities (*Ansiedlungsvertrag*) was said to make up for this deficiency.[160] Although the county's demand at the Bonn meeting for a special allocation of DM 10 million over ten years was prima facie never granted, money began to flow nonetheless. Between 1979 and 1993, the county received DM 113 million from federal, *Land*, and nuclear industry sources, which, arithmetically speaking, amounted to some 8 million per year over fourteen years.[161] The county officials had thus surpassed their original goal of receiving 10 million per year as far as cash was concerned. In addition, the county obtained the commitment of federal and *Land* authorities for a range of development projects, from the upgrade of roads, retention of rail lines, and subsidies for agricultural projects to the relocation of police units and support for tourism.[162] County representatives regularly reminded *Land* and federal authorities over the course of the 1980s of their promises or submitted new development proposals.[163]

Despite this unprecedented flow of state aid, unequivocal acceptance of the nuclear project was not forthcoming. In what were probably the most closely observed local elections in West German history, the political makeup of the county began to shift in 1981. The governing CDU retained a 52 percent majority, but an independent group captured 18 percent, reflecting the division that had taken hold of the county and suggesting that the CDU majority was not unassailable.[164] Although the county leadership took the position that the material blessings tied to the nuclear project contributed to the welfare of all, opponents called any money that reached the county in the context of the nuclear facility "Gorleben monies" (*Gorlebengelder*). The involvement of the DWK seemed particularly dubious; its payments were attacked as bribes.[165] Various projects for which these monies paid also came under attack. The town of Gartow, for instance, built itself a thermal spa with the last-minute addition of a water slide. The slide itself was not a cost factor, but since it did not fit into the pool building, the entire roof had to be raised to accommodate it. Similarly, the county approved itself a new administrative building in Lüchow. Here, it was the copper mailbox for DM 18,000 that came in for particular scorn.[166] The five hundred residents of the village of Waddeweitz got a new shooting range that, curiously, featured a sauna.[167] These projects, easily depicted as frivolous, were grist for the mill to the Gorleben critics. What incensed the opponents, then, were the telltale signs of the county's transformation into a nuclear community.

Since the reprocessing plant was never built, the four thousand industrial jobs associated with the full nuclear waste disposal center never materialized. The county gained some six hundred jobs at the interim waste storage facility and in relation to the explorations of the salt dome as a final repository.[168] By the mid-1980s, the local SPD withdrew its support from the nuclear projects, thus ushering in a realignment of the political tectonics in Lüchow-Dannenberg. In the municipal elections of October 1991, the CDU lost its majority. United by their opposition to Gorleben, all other parties formed a "colorful coalition" to govern. In 1993, this coalition decided to forgo accepting further Gorleben monies. The projects that had been supported by this cash influx tumbled like dominoes; the follow-up cost of the infrastructure that had been expanded during the affluent years now ratcheted up debt. In 1994, the county could no longer balance its budget.[169] A think tank for public policy in Hannover concluded that the leadership had led the county into a one-sided dependency on the Gorleben monies, which had also ensnared local politicians in a "spending pattern that under other circumstances would have neither been financeable nor [politically] explicable."[170] By the late 1990s and despite a brief local economic boom after unification,[171] the county fell back into its well-known patterns of destitution. The period of subsidization as a nuclear community had created only specious prosperity. In 1999, the county parliament requested a development fund from Bonn and Hannover to bail it out.[172]

"Gorleben Shall Live": Protest Culture on the Border

Gorleben was a milestone in the West German anti-nuclear movement. Out of the borderlands emerged the longest-lasting anti-nuclear protest in the Federal Republic, one that joined with and inspired similar protest activities elsewhere. Opposition to the civilian use of nuclear energy had taken shape in the early 1970s when residents objected to individual power plants in their vicinity. The first such site fight, in Wyhl near Freiburg, is commonly considered the beginning of the West German anti-nuclear movement. Wyhl garnered widespread media attention when the construction site, after being occupied in early 1975, turned into a protest village that lasted nine months and ended peacefully when the state government of Baden-Württemberg made concessions that significantly postponed construction work. Ultimately, the Wyhl reactor was never built.[173] Similar attempts to occupy construction sites of nuclear reactors at Brokdorf (November 1976) and Grohnde (March 1977), however, ended in violent clashes between police and protesters and ushered in a growing split within the anti-nuclear movement over their protest tactics.[174] Once Gorleben entered the equation as the central site of a reprocessing and waste storage plant, the anti-nuclear movement identified it as the weak link in West Germany's entire nuclear program. Since the industry was required by law to present a plan for the disposal of spent fuel in order to obtain a license for any new nuclear power plant, by preventing Gorleben from going into operation the movement could potentially stall future power plants as well.[175] Awareness of and debate about the use of nuclear energy was initially decentralized and occurred locally wherever a facility was planned. Yet as opponents educated themselves about a subject hitherto reserved for scientific discourse, devised methods to challenge state power, and networked with each other, anti-nuclear protest developed on local, national, and transnational levels that interacted in ever-changing constellations. Scholars have regularly noted the transnational dimension of these protests, particularly in the borderlands between Germany and France, where Wyhl and a number of French nuclear facilities were located.[176] As Andrew Tompkins writes, "[A]nti-nuclear protests developed in parallel to, and in tandem with, one another at sites around the world."[177] According to observers in the Central Intelligence Agency, by the late summer of 1979 West Germany had developed "the most organized and aggressive nuclear opposition in the world."[178] Of the many aspects of the Gorleben protests that deserve exploration, this section addresses the influence of Gorleben's border location on the opposition to the nuclear site.[179] At times concrete, at times diffuse, this influence manifested itself in the makeup of the protesters, the perception of the county's landscape, and the chosen protest methods.

The government of Lower Saxony had clearly underestimated the opposition that the Gorleben decision would encounter in Lüchow-Dannenberg County. Governor Ernst Albrecht had reasons for assuming that the county's demographic and political characteristics, paired with the policy of its leadership to press for state aid and industrial jobs, would ensure a relatively swift acceptance of the NEZ project. Yet the site fights elsewhere in West Germany had raised skepticism about nuclear energy that expressed itself first in NIMBY (not in my backyard) attitudes and eventually in open opposition. The local pastor described the mood on the day of the Gorleben announcement: "We were in agreement that any other location would be better suited for the nuclear factory than our beautiful county. I have to admit, that was our first reaction in those days, we thought: Anywhere else but here."[180]

Besides, the county's demographic profile had developed a relevant new aspect. As explained in Chapter 3, the Wendland had experienced a modest urban influx from the second-home phenomenon precisely because of its borderland location. Among those charmed enough by the Wendland to relocate for good were intellectuals, artists, and freelancers like writers Nicolas Born and Hans Christoph Buch, sculptor Klaus Müller-Klug, engineer Peter Runde, journalists Kai Hermann and Sophie von Behr, editor Jürgen Manthey, and painter Uwe Bremer, who moved the artist collective Werkstatt Rixdorfer Drucke from West Berlin to the village of Gümse in 1974. The newfound seclusion was disturbed by news that a Hamburg power company intended to build a nuclear power plant in Langendorf-on-Elbe, right under the nose of relocators. The plans for

Langendorf sparked the initial anti-nuclear mobilization in the county. It was also in the context of Langendorf that activists formed the Citizen Action Committee for Environmental Protection in Lüchow-Dannenberg (Bürgerinitiative Umweltschutz Lüchow-Dannenberg, BI), which became the main player in the struggle against the NEZ in Gorleben under the leadership of Marianne Fritzen.[181] Albrecht's announcement of February 1977 thus encountered a dismayed but not fully unprepared group of people ready to oppose the nuclear facility.

Although the government of Lower Saxony had expected that Lüchow-Dannenberg would eventually accept the nuclear project, the experiences with violent protests at Grohnde and Brokdorf gave reason for caution. On the very day that Albrecht announced the Gorleben decision, the security authorities in Lower Saxony called on their counterparts in Bonn and the other federal states to support them in keeping tabs on suspected violent elements of the anti-nuclear movement.[182] They also started an inquiry into the budding local Bürgerinitiative and the "leftist intellectuals" supporting it.[183] To the surprise of the Hannover government, however, the "leftist intellectuals" were joined by local farmers whom officials had pegged as reverential toward state authority. Some farmers came under immediate pressure to sell land to the DWK; others had economic reasons to resist the Gorleben decision, since it would link their produce to a nuclear site. Similar to the situation in Wyhl, where winegrowers and farmers had locked arms with students from Freiburg and other external activists, the Gorleben protest was soon carried by an "agrarian–leftist alliance."[184]

The shock over Albrecht's announcement of Gorleben as the choice for the NEZ was magnified by the depiction and perception of the county as a timeless, idyllic backwater untouched by industrial modernity. When Langendorf loomed, the relocators portrayed the Wendland as a last refuge from West German consumerism and ecological destruction.[185] With the influx of Gorleben protesters, writing about the Wendland only increased.[186] Unrecognized perhaps, the descriptions of Lüchow-Dannenberg County fell into a tradition of writing about the "zonal borderlands" that had begun in the 1950s when borderland advocates demanded federal aid: the border regions were depicted as forgotten lands, bypassed by the "economic miracle" and abandoned by the young and able, left with only sparsely populated villages and towns that went into hibernation.[187] A key trope in the texts about the Wendland was thus the similarity of its villages and landscapes to the way "Germany used to be."[188] Verging on *Heimat* kitsch, the write-ups on the Wendland introduced readers to people who still knew the land through their labor, attached meaning to the seasons, and treated their livestock with respect. They made jam, pickled cucumbers, and cured ham from home-slaughtered pigs. At high noon, dogs trotted along the village main streets, where no traffic light was needed until 1979. Children turned reed stalks into blow tubes and gleefully shot elderberries at each other. In these parts, the Count still counted for something.[189] Even among leftist intellectuals who had long detested the conservative *Heimat* discourse of the organized expellees, the Wendland spawned memories of a lost German East. When one writer observed that cranes flew in from Pomerania, his own mere mention of "Pomerania" appears to have startled him.[190] Although left-leaning intellectuals had embraced German partition as the justified outcome of a war of aggression, even as the price that Germany had to pay for Auschwitz,[191] confrontation with the border fence could call into question a postnational identity believed to be secure. Hell-bent on mocking the provinces, one writer from Hamburg suddenly felt "how something all-German (*etwas Gesamtdeutsches*) [crept] up my back" when he sighted the border fence, turning the weekend foray to Hitzacker-on-Elbe into an unexpected identity struggle.[192] The encounter with the landscape of the borderlands teased out reflections on Germanness, leaving another writer to confess her newfound affection for the "fatherland."[193]

The romanticized depictions of the Wendland were part and parcel of larger struggles of the West German Left during the 1980s with the meaning of *Heimat*, Germanness, and the partition of the country.[194] Yet in the context of the prospective Gorleben nuclear site, these depictions also served the purpose of defining the stakes.[195] Set against the vivid backdrop of picture-book villages with flowering apple trees, a nuclear reprocessing plant and the infrastructure necessary to service it could only augur the destruction of paradise. The county did indeed feature an exceptional biodiversity that had benefited from the seclusion provided by the border. Thanks to the proximity of the Elbe River and its tributaries, the Wendland hosted a range of riparian biotopes such as wetlands and moors as well as long-standing nature preserves like the Lucie, a 1,800-hectare lowland forest under protection since 1951. The ecological significance of large parts of the county was no chimera, although land improvement schemes continuously altered its hydrological makeup.

Opponents of the nuclear site drew upon the Wendland's landscapes in their battle against the Gorleben plant. They did so in concrete ways by citing nature protection codes.[196] The Citizen Initiative sought to educate out-of-county protesters about the ecological treasures of the landscape and urged them to respect them when it organized its first anti-Gorleben demonstration in March 1977.[197] The writings about the Wendland did their part by maximizing the clash between high modernity, as exemplified by the nuclear waste facility, and a secluded rural idyll. The landscapes of the Wendland that had been preserved and shaped by the border represented much of what the local protesters defended at Gorleben. Differing views on the value of the landscape pitted opponents against proponents, since the latter explicitly pursued the nuclear project to modernize and industrialize the county. Therein lay the particular provocation when one of the leading Gorleben advocates, Kurt-Dieter Grill (CDU), simply dismissed concerns about the landscape, "since no one gives us a penny for the ecological integrity of Lüchow-Dannenberg."[198] Where proponents like Grill actively sought to turn the county into a nuclear community, Gorleben opponents were repelled by the very materialism that undergirded this development.

The proximity of the border also influenced the methods of the anti-Gorleben resistance. To be sure, by the time the Gorleben protest erupted in early 1977, an array of templates for site fights had already emerged in the protests against nuclear facilities elsewhere.[199] The Gorleben opposition selectively adapted available protest forms to local circumstances, for instance the tractor rally of March 1979, when over the course of a week farmers on some one hundred tractors made their way from Lüchow-Dannenberg to the state's capital in Hannover to join the Gorleben Hearing of international scientists, at least on the streets. Warning Governor "Albrecht, here we come!," the farmers borrowed slogans from the sixteenth-century Peasants' War to voice their displeasure with the Gorleben decision.[200] Spurred by anxiety over the nuclear accident at Three Mile Island in Pennsylvania that had occurred just three days before, the cavalcade culminated on March 31, 1979, in the largest anti-nuclear protest the Federal Republic had witnessed thus far.

Another adaptation within early anti-Gorleben activism drew upon the occupation of the construction site in Wyhl. In Gorleben, this took the form of a symbolic act of secession from the nuclear state (*Atomstaat*) that the Federal Republic in the protesters' view had become: the founding of the "Free Republic of Wendland."[201] Some of the those who had relocated to the Wendland had joked about independence as early as 1974,[202] an idea that toyed with sovereignty and territory and thus suited the liminal character of the borderlands. The Free Republic of Wendland finally came to life briefly in spring of 1980 when several hundred squatters occupied "deep boring site 1004," where test drillings into the Gorleben salt dome were scheduled to take place. Aided by excellent weather in May 1980, the occupation of the drilling site quickly expanded into an anti-nuclear village of about three hundred core occupiers and several thousand weekend residents who camped in tents and wooden huts, generated alternative energy, and organized grassroots communal life around a large "friendship house." As the American Embassy in Bonn observed, the German media provided sympathetic coverage of the occupation. "The image of the anti-atom village [. . .] was of an Aquarian community, filled with idealistic and harmless, if bizarre young people."[203] To mark the Age of Aquarius, the Wendland Republic issued passports to its residents that were "valid for the whole universe [. . .] as long as its bearer can still laugh," operated the station "Radio Free Wendland," and flew its own flag with the anti-nuclear sun logo. In an afterthought, the Republic even sprouted an "embassy" in Bremen on the grounds of the former American consulate.[204] On June 4, 1980, the anti-nuclear village was cleared by "an extraordinarily large number of riot-equipped police."[205] Although test drillings began, the state did not emerge as the exclusive victor in this power struggle. The American Embassy noted the significant "amount of attention Gorleben attracted from other political movements." The protesters had "reaped a media bonanza" from the short-lived anti-nuclear village, which, the Americans predicted, "may become the summertime fad for anti-nuclear protest" across the country.[206]

After the tractor caravan and the proclamation of the Wendland Republic, the Gorleben opponents had garnered a reputation for creative protest. They continued in that vein by staging the first anti-nuclear demonstration on GDR territory. On January 27, 1982, some sixty local protesters crossed the demarcation line near the villages of Kapern and Gummern, and squatted in the no-man's landscape between the demarcation line and the first fence, exactly in the interstitial space where careless or audacious tourists were frequently arrested or injured.[207] Not only did the occupiers want to draw attention to their demand to stop construction work at Gorleben, they intended to force western and eastern authorities to disclose their emergency protocols in the case of a nuclear accident. The shape of the county—a triangle poking into GDR territory—had long nurtured tales that if the Cold War ever turned hot, NATO forces would instantly abandon this unwieldy swath of land to its fate.[208] An analogous rumor held that in the case of a nuclear disaster at the NEZ, West German authorities would merely seal off the county from the hinterland to prevent presumably contaminated citizens from carrying radiation farther west. Yet fleeing eastward was not an option either, because residents would encounter the Iron Curtain. As one of their banners stated, the eastern escape route led only into minefields; the Wendland would become a trap.[209] While the protesters pitched their tents for a cold overnight stay, western police and BGS stood by powerlessly since they were not allowed to set foot across the demarcation line. At the same time, the squatters took pains not to provoke eastern border troops by clarifying that they were not protesting against the SED regime but against Gorleben. To pacify the border guards, one of the activists sounded the tune of the *Internationale* on a bugle.[210]

Including the border itself in the anti-Gorleben protest was a cunning move. It defied authorities in both West *and* East, drew attention to the implications of Gorleben's borderland location, and maximized media attention. In July 1983, some thirty-five protesters therefore re-enacted the stunt and crossed into GDR territory near the village of Wustrow, this time demonstrating against the adjusted government plan to build the reprocessing plant in Dragahn and otherwise repeating the demands of the first occupation to disclose emergency protocols for the county. As with the first occupation, it remained a major mystery to West German observers why the East German border guards did not intervene when they were known for using force to defend the integrity of their territory.[211] Some commentators used this lack of action to accuse the protesters of being in cahoots with the Honecker regime.[212]

The second occupation of the border strip was also noteworthy because it divulged the long-standing fissures among the anti-Gorleben activists. A finely chiseled hierarchy of natives, the relocators of the early 1970s, and those newly drawn into the county by the protest activities divided the movement. The Bürgerinitiative Umweltschutz Lüchow-Dannenberg had been founded by locals. As the resident voice and engine of the Gorleben resistance, the BI sought to control the political message of the protests.[213] Indeed, as Andrew Tompkins argues, anti-nuclear activists shared the belief that local protesters were essential to any site fight: "localness" lent the protest "authenticity," which translated into legitimacy.[214] The activists staging the second border occupation, however, were newbies from outside the county. Where the original protesters had frozen bitterly during their January occupation of the border strip, the newbies were sunbathing in the no-man's landscapes in July. Where the locals knew the border from having lived with it for decades, the outsiders displayed a somewhat casual attitude toward it, causing unease not unlike the tensions between the visitors and

Mitgeführtes Transparent, das am Ereignisort aufgestellt
wurde.
Text: "Wir demonstrieren hier gegen ein Atommüllager im
Landkreis LÜCHOW - DANNENBERG!"

Mitgeführter Wimpel, mit sich kreuzender Forke und Dresch-
flegel sowie Jahreszahl.
Rechts ein Filmreporter des NDR.

Kopie aus dem Bundesarchiv

FIGURE 6.1. Opponents of Gorleben invented a new protest form in January 1982: occupying the no man's landscape between the demarcation line and the first fence. East German border troops produced meticulous photo documentation of the incident but did not intervene.

the visited in border tourism. Since the occupiers had come to the county as participants in protest summer camps hosted by the BI, the BI leadership defended its prerogative to define the summer's activities, an assumption the newbies defied. Citing safety concerns, Undine von Blottnitz and Marianne Fritzen of the BI urged their out-of-county supporters to abort the occupation of the border strip, yet to no avail.[215] The second foray into the no-man's landscapes showed that Gorleben had long ceased to be an exclusively local concern. The BI could not prevent others from emulating them; it could only excise the 1983 event from the movement's annals.[216]

Inexplicably even to the protesters, the GDR border troops sat tight on both occasions. The Stasi had actually gotten wind of the first border occupation months in advance. In August 1981, it was warned that "smaller circles within the [Gorleben] protest movement were discussing the provocative plan of a spectacular occupation of the state border of the GDR." Yet instead of compiling instructions on how to react to such a provocation, the Stasi apparently did not share the information even with Border Regiment 24, which patrolled the stretch around Gorleben.[217] The postmortem analysis of the events by the regiment's leadership acknowledged that the situation created by the squatters was unprecedented. The officers then descended into ideological waffling that was most likely intended to cover up the fact that the protesters had caught the regiment off guard. The occupation of the border strip was depicted as yet another expression of the conflict between socialism and imperialism, devised to test the preparedness of the border troops. The report implied that the presence of West German news media was part of a larger plan to entice the border troops to take a heavy-handed approach to the demonstrators that would subsequently be used to damage the reputation of the GDR border troops. Not to intervene, the regiment leaders claimed, was therefore a conscious and wise choice to foil the enemy's ploy.[218] The eastern troops did not break up the second occupation in July 1983 either. They called their western counterparts multiple times on the red telephone, but they did not take any action beyond meticulously documenting the comings and goings of the anti-nuclear activists. Although they regarded the squatters to be "slobs" who lived in "communities considered asocial," the eastern authorities appear to have relished the fact that the western BGS more or less counted on them to clear the campsite. The safest way to annoy the BGS was therefore not to play the part.[219] The second occupation of the border strip thus unfolded the way it did because it was drawn into the tedious eastern–western tussle of border guarding.

As the Gorleben protesters borrowed ideas from site fights elsewhere, they generated multiple iconic protest events, such as the tractor caravan to Hannover and the rather humorous founding of the Republic Free Wendland. The occupations of the border strip in Lüchow-Dannenberg County in 1982 and 1983 should be part of the list. In their wake, the method of crossing the demarcation line to generate media attention became almost standard practice. For the remainder of the 1980s, activists throughout the border-lands crossed onto GDR territory to draw attention to a range of mostly environmental concerns, as they did in their protest against the Buschhaus power plant with which this book opened.[220] The anti-Gorleben squatters had thus invented a new protest form that was possible only in a divided Germany: occupying the border strip and toying with a Cold War incident.

Years of protest changed the county for good. Unlike nuclear reactor sites where demonstrations targeted one construction project and petered out once a final decision had been reached, the BI Lüchow-Dannenberg protest kept the opposition to Gorleben alive. The late 1990s were dominated by protests against the transport of nuclear waste containers to the interim storage site. The first such CASTOR container arrived in Gorleben in 1995. For the next three years, each new CASTOR transport triggered ever-growing opposition, nurturing the protest culture in the county and causing security costs for the state to escalate.[221] Over the years, the protest attracted new people to the county, some of whom decided to stay.[222] The struggle against nuclear energy not only expressed itself in more or less spectacular confrontations with the state but also induced lifestyle changes designed to bring political goals into line with personal (consumer) choices and to develop an "authentic self."[223] In Lüchow-Dannenberg County, the pursuit of "authenticity," a signature of the West German Left's alternative milieu during the late 1970s and 1980s, manifested itself in communal living, ecological farming, and a renaissance of crafts such as pottery and weaving. Several communes with county newcomers tried their hands at farming and holistic living, with mixed economic success but much influence on the county's image as a pioneering place in ecofarming.[224] That image was actually furthered by the plans for Gorleben because some of the perks intended to generate popular acceptance of the nuclear facility also funded the development of alternative fuel and energy sources. In this context, the federal government supported research into ways to turn the county into an "ecological model region."[225] Out of these efforts emerged, for instance, an early farm-to-table distribution network for organic foodstuffs.[226] The county thus acquired its "eco" reputation not exclusively in opposition to nuclear power but also *through* it. Its reputation as a site of protests, however, was exclusively tied to nuclear power and, like the Wendland's landscapes, has been romanticized to a certain degree.[227]

Conclusion: Forever Waste

The history of nuclear energy in Germany to a large extent has become a history of "past futures" (Radkau). It was dominated by assumptions, expectations, and plans for an energy future that did not materialize or turned out radically different than anticipated. The single-location nuclear waste disposal center at Gorleben had already become a past future in 1979 when Governor Albrecht dropped the reprocessing component. Similarly, the fast breeder reactor that had been expected to carry the expansion of nuclear energy in Germany never arrived. Only one such breeder was ever built, in Kalkar on the Dutch border, but it never went online. And since fast breeders did not become the technology of choice during the 1980s, their absence inevitably altered calculations about how much spent nuclear fuel would be slated for reprocessing. This, in turn, made reprocessing as such look increasingly inefficient for the nuclear industry. The industry abandoned efforts to build a reprocessing plant in Wackersdorf (Bavaria) in 1989 and never resumed the project. The legislature caught up with these shifting futures in 1994 when it abrogated the 1976 requirement for reprocessing and paved the way for the direct storage of spent nuclear fuel without reprocessing.[228] Beginning in 1998, the Red–Green coalition under Chancellor Gerhard Schröder (SPD) initiated the phaseout of nuclear energy use (*Atomausstieg*) since this was the long-standing goal, even the raison d'être, of the Green Party, which was now in government for the first time. Under the chancellorship of Angela Merkel (CDU), the life span of Germany's seventeen reactors was extended one more time in 2009, but the catastrophe at Fukushima in March 2011 sealed the fate of German nuclear energy use. Plants operative before 1980 were shut down immediately; all others are to be phased out by 2022.[229]

Nuclear futures may have turned into nuclear pasts, but the wastes remain forever. Germany's commercial use of nuclear energy was remarkably short-lived. The first West German reactor went online in 1962, the last in 1989.[230] When, according to government plans, the last nuclear power plant is shuttered in 2022, Germany will still not have a final repository for spent fuel. Indeed, the imperative of dealing with the radiating residues of nuclear power will last indefinitely longer than the benefits this form of energy provided for two generations, raising the philosophical, albeit historically moot question of whether the attempt was ever worth it. As this chapter has shown, the presence of the inter-German border and patterns that had developed between *Zonenrand* advocates and the state since the 1950s shaped the Gorleben conflict in multiple ways. It burdened the siting process with the suspicion that the selection criteria had been political, not scientific. This criticism could be deployed in various forms but always targeted a deficit in the transparency and legitimacy of the siting decision.[231] The decide-announce-defend approach that Governor Albrecht adopted in 1977 may well have triggered massive protests at other sites as well, as indeed early KEWA explorations between 1974 and 1976 already did wherever the government engineers showed up.[232] The point here is, however, that Gorleben's border location injected a dimension into the siting controversy that would not have been present at a location farther inland. As I have argued throughout the book, the Iron Curtain magnified political and economic conflicts in direct and more oblique ways.

The Gorleben controversy also left its footprint in Lüchow-Dannenberg County. There are the physical remnants: an excavated salt mine, an interim storage facility half-filled with CASTOR flasks, and a mothballed conditioning plant.[233] Yet the greater legacy of the efforts to turn Lüchow-Dannenberg into a nuclear community may lie in the immaterial traces. Selected for its economic and geographic peripherality, the county ironically turned into the center of anti-nuclear protest and a lasting symbol of the unresolved problem of long-term storage of high-level nuclear waste.[234] Just as this kind of waste is a transgenerational liability, so too opposition to the repository was transferred from the veterans of the protest movement to the next generation.[235] The anti-nuclear opposition might be deprived of its unifying target at this point, but the local civil society it relied on and strengthened emerged again during the refugee crisis of 2015, when the county made headlines for its civic engagement on behalf of refugees.[236] Yet not everything that looks like a legacy of anti-nuclear protest is born of the alternative anti-Gorleben milieu of the 1970s and 1980s. Neo-Nazis, so-called *völkisch* settlers, have moved into the Wendland, fly the anti-nuclear flag, send their children to Waldorf schools, and practice ecological farming.[237] The meaning of the "eco" reputation of the county, acquired from efforts to develop sustainable lifestyles, may well become a contested legacy.

The most relevant outcome of the Gorleben siting controversy for the future lies in the fact that Germany now has a finely honed site selection process—at least on paper. When the Red–Green coalition under Chancellor Schröder initiated the reactor phaseout in 1998, they also sought to press the reset button on the divisive issue of a final waste repository. To accomplish this, they formed a committee called AkEnd,[238] which was tasked with drawing up policy suggestions for the waste disposal dilemma. By the time AkEnd took up its work in 2000, several administrations had muddled through the issue without a coherent plan.[239] AkEnd acknowledged the siting process, unlike the Gorleben decision, to be a scientific *and* social endeavor. It reversed several assumptions that had accompanied Germany's commercial use of nuclear energy from the beginning. While it retained the requirement that storage capacity be sought in deep geological formations, it no longer considered salt the only permissible host rock. It also recommended a *comparative* site selection process with meaningful public participation and full transparency, a stipulation that was nothing short of a damning verdict on the erstwhile Gorleben decision. Although citizen participation might not guarantee success, the Gorleben controversy had convincingly demonstrated that nonparticipation spelled failure. To free any fresh start from the burdens of the past, the siting was to begin with a "white map" of Germany in which every location with a suitable geological formation would be eligible. However, AkEnd's work never went beyond a first report. The utility companies, having invested heavily in Gorleben, refused to consider any other site; and Gorleben opponents feared that a "white map" that did not explicitly exclude Gorleben from a future search would come full circle and end up including Gorleben yet again, since the salt dome now housed a semi-finished storage mine.[240]

It took the Fukushima catastrophe of 2011 to breathe new life into the process. The renewed decision to abandon nuclear energy production in Germany altogether holds out the prospect of finite amounts of waste and has uncoupled the search for a repository from the irony that such a site might encourage further expansion of nuclear energy.[241] In 2013, the German parliament passed a law to govern the site selection process.[242] A new commission set out to finish AkEnd's work and map out the siting requirements as well as a participatory process.[243] Just as the nuclear waste disposal center at Gorleben had been a project of global significance at the time of its inception, its failure on all fronts now bequeathed a legacy of equally global significance, namely the blueprint for a state-of-the-art siting process, designed to prevent a rerun of the acrimonious site fights of the 1970s and 1980s.[244] However, there are no signs that the beautifully devised process of citizen participation and transparency will be implemented any time soon. The federal government intends to conclude any prospective search by the year 2031 and store high-level wastes beginning in 2050. In the meantime, the utility companies have restructured themselves to undermine the Polluter Pays Principle and have reached the important goal of moving the entire responsibility for siting, building, and running a waste facility to the state. The 24 billion euro price tag for this move notwithstanding, a formerly private good has thus turned into a public bad.[245] In the end, the wastes will outlast all stakeholders.

Once Germany ceases nuclear energy production in 2022, the country will be littered with decommissioned nuclear facilities. The demolition of such structures is already part of a highly specialized (de)construction industry.[246] Those facilities like the fast breeder in Kalkar and the excavated salt mine in Gorleben that were never put to use, however, do not require demolition and safe disposal. Today, the grounds of the fast breeder in Kalkar are home to a "Wonderland" amusement park.[247] The only fission and fusion processes at Kalkar probably occur at the ice cream stand. Like the coal industry before it, the nuclear industry has thus already entered a postindustrial age in which production facilities are "reinvented" for leisure use. What's in store for the excavated caverns in the Gorleben salt dome? Will they be turned into an "adventure mine" like the potash mines at Merkers on the Werra?[248] Will they house a museum whose themes are postwar enthusiasm for the peaceful atom, imagined nuclear futures, and the efforts of civil society to thwart them? Or are they yet to become the national repository for Germany's high-level nuclear waste?

Conclusion

WEST GERMANY FROM THE PERIPHERY

THE "ZONAL BORDERLANDS" are gone. They remain most vividly on display in Wim Wenders's 1976 movie, *Im Lauf der Zeit*, and have enjoyed a faint afterlife in a few recent novels.[1] The Iron Curtain is gone, too. Its memory has been institutionalized in a number of museums, in a north–south ribbon of commemorative road signs, and last but not least in a national natural heritage project, the Green Belt. Yet if one were to look for a defining signature of the "old" Federal Republic, along with its bland executive architecture in Bonn, its unassuming foreign policy, and its grappling with the Nazi past, it might well be this former border region. Like West Berlin, it was a space created by the Cold War. It emerged with partition and disappeared with unification. It was remarkably large, amounting to almost a fifth of West Germany's state territory. As this book has argued, these borderlands constituted the Federal Republic's most sensitive geographical space, a space where it had to confront partition and its often peevish neighbor in concrete ways. The nature of the engagement changed over time, reflecting the well-known trajectory of the Federal Republic from its anti-Communist founding and affluent "miracle" years through the era of Cold War détente into a postmaterial, rather self-absorbed last decade. Each issue that arose in these borderlands—from economic deficiencies to border tourism, environmental pollution, landscape change, and the siting decision for a nuclear facility—was magnified by the presence of what became the most militarized political border of its day, which epitomized the Cold War partition of Germany and Europe. This book, however, has investigated the West German borderlands not just as a particular space, but also as a lens through which to view the history of the "old"

Federal Republic and the process of unification. Reading West German history from its geographic periphery does not detract from established narratives, but it does yield significant new perspectives.

In economic terms, the borderlands became the beneficiary of one of West Germany's longest-lasting regional aid programs. Citing proximity to the ideologically charged Iron Curtain, borderland advocates managed to develop a moral claim on the state for financial assistance that held strong until unification, despite major shifts in inter-German relations and structural adjustments in the West German economy. There is conflicting evidence about whether "zonal borderland aid" was ever effective for economic development,[2] but its introduction as a politically unassailable regional aid program had a major influence on the functioning of West Germany's financial federalism. Above all, however, it is within the economic sphere that the *Zonenrandgebiet* became most evident as a spatial unit. Although the borderlands were never marked on the ground, the economic woes of the border counties, woes that were indiscriminately blamed on the border, constituted this region for the duration. This is how the *Zonenrand* entered West German discourse and memory—as a laggard alongside the rest of the country's modernization and prosperity.

Ultimately, the western borderlands did play a key role during German unification, but not in the sense that borderland advocates in earlier decades had imagined when they argued that these regions needed to project western prosperity into the East. As immediate neighbors of the GDR, residents in the western borderlands evidently had front-row seats during the collapse of East German socialism in the fall of 1989 and the crucial interlude until unification in October 1990. Apart from Berlin, it was in the borderlands that numerous East and West Germans encountered each other again for the first time outside of state-regulated visitation schemes. It was here that much of the initial joy of the reunion was on display, but also where a good dose of mutual hurt was inflicted by the material disparity between the two sides. As in the early years of partition, the open border and the dualism of the western and eastern currencies once more offered short-term opportunities that were soon experienced as destabilizing and irritating to each side.

After unification, the borderlands turned into a pivotal space that allows us to consider the "cotransformation" of East and West Germany within a regional framework.[3] Although most West Germans expected that the western political, economic, and legal order would simply be extended into the former GDR, thereby placing the onus of adapting squarely on the East Germans, the subsequent efforts to turn the socialist planned economy into a market economy and modernize East Germany's public infrastructure had repercussions for western Germany that were instantly and keenly felt in the "zonal borderlands." The narrative that had been groomed for decades—that the border was responsible for the region's economic deficiencies—was not borne out. After a brief economic boom after unification, the borderlands soon lost their generous aid programs, only to see similar subsidy packages reappear a few miles farther east. Efforts to "follow the money" by moving companies to the former East or establishing branches there contributed to the uneven and haphazard economic integration of the former border regions. While West Germans in the hinterland could, if they chose, hold onto the illusion that their version of the Federal Republic persisted, this perspective was not feasible in the borderlands.

The border itself already proved to be a magnet for onlookers in the early 1950s even before there was much to see, a phenomenon that evolved into veritable border tourism. Visits to the Iron Curtain inevitably became politicized. Regardless of the visitors' intentions, the sight imbued even harmless Sunday outings with political meaning because the tourists became part of a larger, albeit skewed communication between East and West. To eastern border authorities, Iron Curtain tourists were the foot soldiers in a centrally masterminded provocation designed to question East German sovereignty. To western border authorities, the travel parties were a welcome audience for political education but also potential instigators of frivolous incidents. The continuous interest in paying a visit to the central frontline of the Cold War changed the way each side presented the Iron Curtain. Eastern authorities sought to render it uninteresting; western authorities purposefully developed it as a trip destination. Ultimately, the very presence of tourists changed the look of the sight they had come to see. Although border tourism was frequently framed as a lament about partition and a desire for German unity, it may well have achieved the opposite and inscribed the contested border as a fact on the mental maps of those who came to see it at a time when the Federal Republic, as a new state with fresh borders, was literally being remapped.[4] To peer at the increasingly fortified border, especially in its fully militarized incarnation in the 1970s and 1980s, hardly conveyed the sense that it was ready to crumble anytime soon. Hopes of turning this kind of travel into a significant economic boon for the borderlands proved similarly futile. Only in the 1980s did the borderlands experience a modest increase of leisure tourism because their erstwhile economic disadvantage—remoteness and underdevelopment—found a new appreciation among those West Germans who felt that economic growth had corroded the landscapes of their *Heimat*. The borderlands, never exposed to the full thrust of postwar modernization, were now hailed for their alleged bucolic authenticity.

In environmental terms, the border became the interface through which both German states encountered each other's pollution. The uncontrolled pollution that resulted from the decline of East German industry swept into West Germany through transboundary rivers and enveloped West Berlin in smog. Regardless of how impervious the Iron Curtain was supposed to be, it was environmental ties that bound the sides together and eventually forced them to the negotiating table. Transboundary pollution is a classic borderland problem that was exacerbated in the German case by the fact that it unfolded along a contested border and threatened to undo much of the efforts at economic development in the West German borderlands. In the 1970s, environmental diplomacy thus became a new element of already complex inter-German relations. It soon suffered from mistrust familiar from other aspects of these relations: West German negotiators perceived their eastern counterparts as engaging in blackmail, while eastern representatives feared that their western interlocutors would resort to shaming strategies on the international stage. At no time did the confrontation with East Germany's increasing pollution during the 1980s lead West German observers to realize that they were witnessing the dissolution of the GDR. As ineffectual as much of this environmental diplomacy proved to be during the 1980s, it nonetheless played a crucial role in the production of knowledge about the nature of the GDR's environmental damage, which helps explain why the postunification cleanup and ecological restoration in East Germany proceeded at the quick pace that it did. Yet neither the teleological narrative about the GDR's reckless pollution nor its twin, the story about unified Germany's successful cleanup operations, helps us understand the material environmental history of particular landscapes and biotopes. As I argued in the case of the Werra, the river's actual ecological viability was never central to the negotiations, and the demise of socialism, while providing relief from pollution, still did not return the river to an ecologically healthy state. In that sense, the difference between the impact of socialism and that of capitalism on the environment has been one of degree, not of kind.

The Iron Curtain also proved to be an agent of landscape change. The evolution of its military "hardware" on the ground and all the activities that enabled its political function left an ecological footprint: fields turned back into wetlands, patches of forest completed their natural life cycles, and birds and plant species endangered elsewhere found refuge. Yet the border also funneled wildlife into minefields and led to the razing of forests to make way for fences. I introduced the term "transboundary natures" to capture the impact of the Iron Curtain on wildlife, landscape, and humans. These transboundary natures were created by the political history of the Cold War that yielded material ecological consequences in Central European landscapes. By the late 1970s, the transboundary natures had been discovered by conservationists, who used them as control areas to raise awareness about the degree of environmental damage in the rest of the country.

The transboundary natures also attracted the attention of politicians, who enlisted them for political ends by promoting the idea of cross-border nature preserves to involve the GDR in yet another common project, as was the strategy in inter-German relations during the 1980s. Although the GDR leadership rejected this overture, the proposals were the direct precursor of the Green Belt conservation project, which took shape against great odds after the collapse of the GDR. One last time, the now-defunct Iron Curtain magnified any activity in its vicinity. Land use for conservation purposes is contested at the best of times. The Green Belt encountered such opposition not because the number of stakeholders was higher than usual but because the land in question, once inaccessible and considered peripheral, was suddenly perceived as central and valuable. It also caused unease because the symbolic valence of the space it occupied was high. It triggered fears about a new, "green" border among locals who had endured old, galvanized steel borders for decades. The Green Belt advocates managed to overcome severe opposition because their project was empowered by a unique moment in European history, one that equipped them with evocative metaphors of "greening" the violent past of the Iron Curtain and the social hardship that the post-Communist transformation had brought about.

Skillful marketing and European-wide cooperation has since made the Green Belt a darling of the national and international news media. Especially on the anniversary of the border's fall, the natural wonders of the former "death strip" make an annual, or at least quinquennial, comeback. Indeed, a government-sponsored publication in honor of the twenty-fifth anniversary of German unification, in 2015, documents the phenomenon of "growing together" with a cover photo featuring a lush green area of the Green Belt and, within it, a decommissioned watchtower.[5] Like the inter-German border before it, the Green Belt has proven perfectly photogenic. Nothing captures its character more vividly than aerial photographs of a green strip running through grain fields, because they are so evocative of earlier depictions of the border as a "scar." A cottage industry of coffee-table, hiking, and cycling books is sprouting, fueled by this imagery of the border-turned-nature, that echoes some of the "dark" curiosity that had inspired border tourism before 1990.[6] Barbed wire turned into biodiversity—the Green Belt is commonly framed as the happy ending of European partition.

The relevance of the "zonal borderlands" to the history of the Federal Republic before and after 1989 comes into full focus in the Gorleben controversy. After the 1977 decision to construct a nuclear fuel reprocessing and waste storage facility in the immediate vicinity of the inter-German border, the borderlands seemed to hold the key to West Germany's energy future as imagined in the mid-1970s. I have argued that the presence of the border shaped every aspect of the Gorleben siting controversy in profound ways. After almost three decades of lobbying for economic aid, borderland advocates had contributed significantly to the perception among elected officials that their regions would gladly accept *any* industrial development, including risk industries. The bargain on the table amounted to the transformation of the border county of Lüchow-Dannenberg into a "nuclear community": the county would accept the nuclear facility in return for sustained economic development beyond the nuclear plant as such. For the county's leadership, Gorleben looked like the chance to exceed the confines of "zonal borderland aid" and, at long last, catch up with the prosperity perceived in the rest of the Federal Republic. However, the presence and character of the inter-German border did not allow Gorleben to remain a domestic affair. The proximity of the site to the GDR added to the nuclear project a dimension that would have been absent in other locations. Not only did it fuel Chancellor Helmut Schmidt's early opposition to the site choice, thus increasing party-political tensions between Schmidt (SPD) and Ernst Albrecht (CDU); it also presented the SED leaders with an opportunity to insert themselves into a vital West German policy arena. Finally, the border also shaped the protests against Gorleben. The very makeup of the protesters within the county had been shaped by an influx of new residents who, for various reasons, had sought out the seclusion of the borderlands. The border itself provided rather spectacular protest opportunities; nowhere else could one better generate media attention by toying with a Cold War incident than in the no man's landscapes along the border's fence. In retrospect, it is evident that nuclear power has only been a "transitional energy source" for the Federal Republic.[7] The failed efforts to close the nuclear fuel cycle at Gorleben made it so.

In the first week of September 2015, several thousand refugees from Syria and elsewhere found themselves stuck at Budapest's Keleti train station. Desperate to move on to Austria and Germany, several hundred of them set out on foot toward the border, trailed by TV cameras that beamed the migrants' march along the autobahn into European living rooms. On the night of September 4, 2015, Chancellor Angela Merkel is said to have taken the lone humanitarian decision to "open" the borders and allow them in. Instead of being forced to walk, the refugees were carried by train from Budapest to Munich, where locals welcomed them at the station with applause, hugs, food, and toys. Knowingly or not, the well-wishers were re-enacting the opening of the inter-German border, and the media covered it as such. A year later, journalists reconstructed the events in minute detail in ways reminiscent of the recurring anniversary coverage of the fall of the Berlin Wall. September 4 took the place of November 9, Merkel's announcement of her decision was emplotted as Schabowski's press conference, and the refugees played the part of "liberated" East Germans.[8] Evidently, the fall of the Berlin Wall in November 1989, restaged in towns and villages along the inter-German border well into 1990, remains deeply imprinted in the German psyche and has become the origin story of unified Germany.[9] Yet the reference in 2015 to the events of 1989 was not just a media ploy designed to elicit emotions; it marked the moment when the significance of borders returned to German consciousness, a significance that Germans—right in the middle of the Schengen area—had had the privilege of disregarding for twenty-five years.

As the second decade of the twenty-first century draws to a close, governments are more likely to create new borders and reinforce existing ones than to eliminate them. Understanding the repercussions of borders seems more pressing than ever, certainly more so as I conclude this book than when I started it. The post-Wall optimism in European borderland studies that celebrated the disappearance of borders and the ensuing integration of borderlands as "Euro regions" has come to feel depressingly dated. However, the current period, when new borders are going up, existing ones are being fortified, and dormant ones revived, may well be the right moment to historicize the Iron Curtain. The Iron Curtain is such a compelling subject because it has come and gone. It is noteworthy not only for the extent of its brutality but also for its disappearance. It was a real-life experiment in partition that could unexpectedly be undone. As the border's former meaning fades from the landscape, this book may serve as a reminder of the multifaceted repercussions that borders and walls have in our lives.

Abbreviations

AkEnd	Arbeitskreis Auswahlverfahren Endlagersuche, Committee on a Site Selection Procedure for Repository Sites
ADN	Allgemeiner Deutscher Nachrichtendienst, General German News Service
AL	*Abteilungsleiter*, head of department
atw	*Atomwirtschaft* (journal)
Bay.	Bayerisch, Bavarian
BGS	Bundesgrenzschutz, Federal Border Security
BHE	Bund der Heimatentvertriebenen und Entrechteten, Bloc of Expellees and of those Deprived of Rights
BkAmt	Bundeskanzleramt, Federal Chancellery
BKB	Braunschweigische Kohle Bergwerke
BM	Bundesministerium, Federal Ministry
BMF	Bundesfinanzministerium, Federal Ministry of Finance
BMFT	Bundesministerium für Forschung und Technologie, Federal Ministry for Research and Technology
BMI	Bundesministerium des Innern, Federal Ministry of the Interior
BMJ	Bundesministerium der Justiz, Federal Ministry of Justice
BMU	Bundesministerium für Umwelt, Naturschutz und Reaktorsicherheit, Federal Ministry for the Environment, Nature Conservation and Reactor Safety
BMWi	Bundesministerium für Wirtschaft, Federal Ministry for Economic Affairs
BN	Bund Naturschutz in Bayern, Association for Nature Protection in Bavaria

BpB	Bundeszentrale für politsche Bildung, Federal Agency for Political Education
BT	Bundestag
BUND	Bund für Umwelt- und Naturschutz Deutschland, Friends of the Earth
CASTOR	cask for storage and transport of radioactive material
CDU	Christlich Demokratische Union, Christian Democratic Union
CSSR	Czechoslovak Socialist Republic, Czechoslovakia
CSU	Christlich Soziale Union, Christian Social Union
DG IV	Directorate-General for Competition
DIW	Deutsches Institut für Wirtschaftsforschung, German Institute for Economic Research
DM	deutsch mark (West German currency)
Drs.	Drucksache
DWK	Deutsche Gesellschaft für Wiederaufarbeitung von Kernbrennstoffen, German Company for the Reprocessing of Nuclear Fuels
DzD	*Dokumente zur Deutschlandpolitik*
EC	European Commission
EEC	European Economic Community
EnvU	Environmental Union
EPA	Environmental Protection Agency
ERAM	Endlager für radioaktive Abfälle Morsleben, Final Respository for Radioactive Waste [in] Morsleben [GDR]
ERDF	European Regional Development Fund
FDP	Freie Demokratische Partei, Free Democrats
FRG	Federal Republic of Germany
GDR	German Democratic Republic
Gorleben UA	Gorleben Untersuchungsausschuss, Gorleben parliamentary investigative committee
IAEA	International Atomic Energy Agency
IHK	Industrie- und Handelskammer, Chamber of Industry and Commerce
IM	*inoffizieller Mitarbeiter* [der Stasi], informal [Stasi] collaborator
IMNOS	Interministerieller Ausschuss für Notstandsgebietsfragen, Interministerial Committee for Distressed Areas

KEWA	Kernbrennstoffwiederaufarbeitungsgesellschaft, Spent Fuel Reprocessing Association
K&S	Kali & Salz (company)
KWU	Kraftwerk Union (company)
LBV	Landesbund für Vogelschutz, State Federation for the Protection of Birds
LT	Landtag, State Parliament
MELF	Ministerium für Ernährung, Landwirtschaft und Forsten, Ministry for Food, Agriculture, and Forestry
MfS	Ministerium für Staatssicherheit, GDR Ministry for State Security
mg/l	milligram per liter
MLFN	Ministerium für Land-, Forst- und Nahrungsgüterwirtschaft (DDR), GDR Ministry for Agriculture, Forests, and Food Supply
MUW	Ministerium für Umweltschutz und Wasserwirtschaft (DDR), GDR Ministry for Water Management and Environmental Protection
Nds.	Niedersachsen, Lower Saxony
NEZ	*Nukleares Entsorgungszentrum*, nuclear waste disposal Center
NGO	nongovernmental organization
NVA	Nationale Volksarmee, National People's Army
OJC	Official Journal [series] C [of the European Union]
OKD	*Oberkreisdirektor*, county director
PTB	Physikalisch-Technische Bundesanstalt, Federal Metrology Institute
ROB	Raumordnungsbericht, Spatial Order Report
ROG	Raumordnungsgesetz, Federal Spatial Order Law
SBZ	Sowjetische Besatzungszone, Soviet [Military] Occupation Zone
SED	Sozialistische Einheitspartei, Socialist Unity Party
SH	Schleswig-Holstein
SO$_2$	sulfur dioxide
SPD	Sozialdemokratische Partei Deutschlands, Social Democratic Party
StaeV	Ständige Vertretung, Permanent Representation
StB	Stenographische Berichte, Stenographic Protocols
StFB	Staatlicher Forstbetrieb, State Forestry Enterprise
StK	Staatskanzlei, State Chancellery

StS	Staatssekretär, State Secretary
UA	*Untersuchungsausschuss*, parliamentary investigative committee
UBA	Umweltbundesamt, Environmental Federal Agency
VEB	*Volkseigener Betrieb*, people-owned enterprise
VVS	*Vertrauliche Verschlußsache*, confidential classified document
WP	*Wahlperiode*, legislative period
ZRFG	Zonenrandförderungsgesetz, Zonal Borderland Aid Law

ARCHIVES

AHL	Archiv der Hansestadt Lübeck
BArch	Bundesarchiv, Federal Archives
BArch-MA	Bundesarchiv Militärarchiv, Federal Military Archives
BayHStA	Bayerisches Hauptstaatsarchiv München
BStU	Bundesbeauftrager für die Stasi-Unterlagen, Federal Commissioner for the Records of the State Security Service
HAEC	Historical Archives of the European Commission, Brussels
HAEU	Historical Archives of the European Union, Florence
HAT	Historisches Archiv zum Tourismus, Berlin
HHStAW	Hessisches Hauptstaatsarchiv Wiesbaden
LASH	Landesarchiv Schleswig-Holstein
NARA	National Archives and Records Administration
NLA HA	Niedersächsisches Landesarchiv Hannover
NLA WO	Niedersächsisches Landesarchiv Wolfenbüttel
PA/AA	Politisches Archiv des Auswärtigen Amtes

Notes

INTRODUCTION

1. Metzger, *Waldsterben*, 478–483; Wirsching, *Provisorium*, 367–371; Angela Grosse, "Im Lager der Aktivisten," *Hamburger Abendblatt*, Sept. 8, 2005.
2. Berdahl, *Where the World Ended*, 7.
3. Grossbölting and Lorke, "Vereinigungsgesellschaft," 15–18, esp. the revealing footnotes on pages 16–17. See also Allen, "Ending Myth."
4. This is discussed in more detail later in the introduction.
5. Lindenberger, "Grenzregime," 111–121; for an earlier version of the argument see Lindenberger, "Diktatur der Grenzen," 13–44, esp. 131–136. See also Lindenberger, " 'Zonenrand,' 'Sperrgebiet,' und 'Westberlin.' "
6. Ritter and Hajdu, *Innerdeutsche Grenze*, 83.
7. *Zonenrandgebiet* literally translates as "area adjacent to the (Soviet occupation) zone" or "zonal peripheral area." To avoid these clumsy terms and emphasize the character of these regions as borderlands, I use the translation "zonal borderlands." As a reminder of the contemporary derogative connotation of the term, I keep it (along with "zonal borderland aid") in quotation marks throughout. I also speak of border regions, border counties, or simply borderlands to refer to these regions.
8. Glassheim, *Cleansing*, 6; Readman, Radding, and Bryant, "Borderlands in a Global Perspective," 1–23.
9. Preventing East–West migration actually constituted the culmination of a century-long development, as Zahra, *Great Departure*, has recently argued. For trajectory terminology see Parker, "Borderland Processes."
10. Sälter, *Grenzpolizisten*; Sälter and Maurer, "Double Task"; Stacy, *U.S. Army Border Operations*; Eulitz, *Zollgrenzdienst*; Walter, "Bundesgrenzschutz"; Scholzen, *Der BGS*; Krüger, ed., *Fulda Gap*.
11. The figures remain contested. The state-sponsored study by Schroeder and Staadt, *Todesopfer*, recorded 327 victims along the inter-German border but has recently been criticized for inflated numbers. See Alexander Fröhlich, "Umstrittene Studie zu Mauertoten 'nicht verfügbar,' " *Tagespiegel*, Nov. 8, 2018. For the latest figures on the Berlin Wall see Sälter, Dietrich, and Kuhn,

Die vergessenen Toten; Hertle and Nooke, eds., *Victims at the Berlin Wall*. On the methodological challenges of determining the number of victims see Sälter and Hertle, "Todesopfer."

12. Sheffer, *Burned Bridge*, 4.
13. Schaefer, *States of Division*, 7.
14. Johnson, *Divided Village*, 9.
15. Haslinger, *Nation und Territorium*, 358–384, 438–439; Jaworski, "Grenzlage."
16. Zahra, *Kidnapped Souls*, 253–258; Glassheim, *Cleansing*, 42–66; Douglas, *Orderly and Humane*, 98–101, 185–193.
17. Kind-Kovács, "Memories of Ethnic Cleansing"; Komska, *Icon Curtain*.
18. Blaive and Molden, *Grenzfälle*; Paasi, *Territories*, esp. 120–136, 249–253; Komlosy, *An den Rand gedrängt*; Pittaway, "Making Peace"; Sluga, *Problem of Trieste*.
19. Sheffer, *Burned Bridge*, 9.
20. Best explicated in Ahonen, *Death*.
21. Lindenberger, "Divided, but Not Disconnected"; Bösch, "Divided and Connected."
22. Murdock, *Changing Places*; Komlosy, *An den Rand gedrängt*.
23. Eckert, "West German Borderland Aid."
24. Ther, *Europe after 1989*, 260–287; Bösch, "Divided and Connected," 7–8.
25. Radkau, *Ära der Ökologie*, 535.

CHAPTER 1

1. Barbara Klie, "Der unfruchtbare Acker: Die deutsche Binnengrenze von Hof bis Travemünde," part I, *Christ und Welt*, Christmas 1957, 20; "Wo alle Strassen enden: Die deutsche Binnengrenze von Hof bis Travemünde," part II, *Christ und Welt*, Jan. 2, 1958, 20.
2. Paradigmatic texts for this script are in the government brochure *Im Schatten der Zonengrenze*, issued by the Ministry for All-German Affairs in 1956. See also "Das Armenhaus der Bundesrepublik: Ostbayerische Grenzkreise greifen zur Selbsthilfe," *Helmstedter Kreisblatt*, May 22, 1954; " 'Zonenrandgebiete brauchen ständige Hilfe': Erneuter Appell an den Bundestag," *Braunschweiger Zeitung*, Oct. 29, 1954; "An der Grenze der Freiheit: Augenschein im westdeutschen Zonenrandgebiet," *Neue Zürcher Zeitung*, Dec. 28, 1957.
3. Klie, "Der unfruchtbare Acker." See also Müller, "Dorf am Eisernen Vorhang," 23: "Nicht nur in der Ostzone spricht man vom 'Goldenen Westen.' "
4. Spoerer and Streb, *Wirtschaftsgeschichte*, 210. Contemporary analysis in Gleitze, *Ostdeutsche Wirtschaft*, 5–10.
5. The contribution of the expellees and refugees to West Germany's economic recovery has long been noted by economic and social historians. See Wehler, *Gesellschaftsgeschichte*, 35–36, 59; Hoffmann, "Binnenwanderung und Arbeitsmarkt," 219–325; Ambrosius, "Beitrag der Vertriebenen."

6. The idea that the state was responsible for "backward" regions was established around the time of the founding of the German Empire in 1871. See Jones, "Prussia's Peripheries."

7. Harbutt, *Yalta*; Judt, *Postwar*, 100–128; Westad, *Cold War*, 58–69, 71–98; Applebaum, *Iron* Curtain, 205–237.

8. Ritter and Hajdu, *Innerdeutsche Grenze*, 28–33; Shears, *Ugly Frontier*, 29–31; Pritchard, *Niemandsland*.

9. Abelshauser, *Wirtschaftsgeschichte*, 59–82.

10. Amtsblatt des Kontrollrates in Deutschland Nr. 11, Oct. 31, 1946, 213: Direktive Nr. 42 bzgl. des Grenzübertritts . . . vom 24. Oktober 1946. Visits and commutes across the Soviet demarcation line without a permit remained common until 1952. See von Melis and Bispinck, *"Republikflucht,"* 33–35; Kufeke, "Durchlässigkeit," 34–38.

11. Abelshauser, *Wirtschaftsgeschichte*, 82–83.

12. Various such agreements in Kruse, *Wirtschaftsbeziehungen*, 16–22; Federau, "Interzonenhandel," 386–387; Lübeck example in Jan Molitor (alias Josef Müller-Marein), "Zu viele Fragezeichen an allen Grenzen: Rund um Trizonien III," *Die Zeit*, Dec. 2, 1948.

13. Eick, *Folgen der Zonengrenzen*, 25; on interzonal trade, 73–75.

14. Abelshauser, *Wirtschaftsgeschichte*, 83; Federau, "Interzonenhandel," 386.

15. Mörchen, *Schwarzer Markt*; Steege, *Black Market*; Zierenberg, *Berlin's Black Market*.

16. Quote in Jan Molitor (alias Josef Müller-Marein), "Zu viele Fragezeichen an allen Grenzen: Rund um Trizonien IV," *Die Zeit*, Dec. 12, 1948. See also Walther and Bittner, *Heringsbahn*.

17. Schubert, "Interzonengrenze," 79.

18. For political context, see Long, *No Easy Occupation*; see also "Die ungeliebte Grenze," http://www.saar-nostalgie.de/ (accessed Apr. 2018).

19. Trees, *Schmuggler, Zöllner und die Kaffeepanzer*, fig. 22; on shootings, 171–185; Eulitz, *Zollgrenzdienst*, 272–273; Jan Molitor (alias Josef Müller-Marein), "Zu viele Fragezeichen an allen Grenzen: Rund um Trizonien I," *Die Zeit*, Nov. 18, 1948.

20. All quotes in Jan Molitor (alias Josef Müller-Marein), "Zu viele Fragezeichen an allen Grenzen: Rund um Trizonien III," *Die Zeit*, Dec. 2, 1948; see also, part IV, *Die Zeit*, Dec. 9, 1948. At that time, Müller-Marein still published under a pseudonym to obscure his prior association with the Nazi Party newspapers *Völkischer Beobachter* and *Das Reich*. In 1956, he became the editor-in-chief of *Die Zeit*.

21. Jan Molitor (alias Josef Müller-Marein), "Zu viele Fragezeichen an allen Grenzen: Rund um Trizonien V," *Die Zeit*, Dec. 16, 1948.

22. Jan Molitor (alias Josef Müller-Marein), "Zu viele Fragezeichen an allen Grenzen: Rund um Trizonien I," *Die Zeit*, Nov. 18, 1948.

23. Transit obstruction before June 1948: Kruse, *Wirtschaftsbeziehungen*, 23; after
    May 1949: Dossmann, "Stimmungsbarometer"; "Die kleine Blockade," *Die Zeit*,
    July 21, 1949; "Creeping Crisis on the Autobahn," *Life* magazine, Apr. 10, 1950,
    21–22, 24.

24. Contemporary documentation in Information Services Division, CCG(BE), ed.,
    *Berlin: Das britische Weissbuch zur Krise—Eine Darstellung der Ereignisse, die zur
    Überweisung der Berliner Frage an die Vereinten Nationen führte* (Hamburg: Die
    Welt, 1948), 10–13. West Berlin was never sealed off from East Berlin or its hin-
    terland: Stivers, "Incomplete Blockade"; Lemke, "Totale Blockade?," 121–135;
    Steege, *Black Market*, 221–227.

25. The counterblockade is commonly overlooked in historiography, but see
    Fäßler, *Wirtschaftsbeziehungen, 1949–1969*, 43; Kruse, *Wirtschaftsbeziehungen*,
    24–25. Koop, *Kein Kampf um Berlin?*, 223–246, shows how unpopular the
    counterblockade was among West German trade officials and how they tried to
    bypass it through barter trade. Mitdank, "Blockade gegen Blockade," 52–53, em-
    phasizes that the counterblockade was nonetheless effective and detrimental to
    the Soviet zone. Mitdank was an East German diplomat.

26. Rundschreiben [der IHK Braunschweig] Nr. 19, Oct. 18, 1948, 14, and Nr. 20,
    Jan. 20, 1949, 6.

27. Federau, "Interzonenhandel," 402–403. After bumpy beginnings, trade be-
    tween the western and the eastern zones had reached a volume of 500 million
    reichsmark in 1947. The first months of 1948 indicated an upward trend that
    was cut short by the blockade. See also Koop, *Kein Kampf um Berlin?*, 227.

28. Steiner, *Plans That Failed*, 42–44.

29. Companies without a solid capital stock, often founded by expellees, did not sur-
    vive currency reform. They had floated on worthless postwar money that made
    wages easy to pay, especially since the Allies had continued the wage freeze intro-
    duced by the Nazis until November 1948. Schneider, "Wirtschaftsgeschichte
    Niedersachsens nach 1945," 810, 819, 852; on the wage freeze see Abelshauser,
    Wirtschaftsgeschichte, 128; Riedel, "Niedersachsen, 1945–1950," 115–138, on un-
    employment, 126–129.

30. On the rate gain see Federau, "Interzonenhandel," 386. Studies on postwar
    black market activities also emphasize the caesura of the 1948 currency re-
    form: Zierenberg, *Berlin's Black Market*, 187–194; Steege, *Black Market*, 186,
    205–207, 267–271.

31. Sheffer, *Burned Bridge*, 59–60. For a case study of a smuggling network see
    Schaefer, *States of Division*, 30–33.

32. "Grenzlandprobleme," *Mitteilungen der IHK Braunschweig*, no. 31 (Apr.
    1950): 93–94.

33. Sheffer, *Burned Bridge*, 61–65. In Berlin, *Grenzgänger* persisted until 1961. See
    Roggenbuch, *Grenzgängerproblem*; Hoerning, *Berliner Grenzgänger*.

34. Hoffrichter, "Uelzen und die Abgelehnten," 190–209; Ackermann, *Der "echte" Flüchtling*; Stokes, "Permanent Refugee Crisis."

35. Schubert, "Interzonengrenze," 81–82; Sheffer, *Burned Bridge*, 59–61.

36. Sheffer, *Burned Bridge*, 55, 56.

37. For the term "DMark-ation" see Schaefer, *States of Division*, 18; Schubert, "Interzonengrenze," 81.

38. Ritter and Hajdu, "East–West German Boundary," 335; Gleitze, *Ostdeutsche Wirtschaft*, 5–10.

39. Schaefer, *States of Division*, 58–66.

40. Jaworski, "Grenzlage," 242–247.

41. Ritter and Hajdu, *Innerdeutsche Grenze*, 172–180.

42. Memo, Die wirtschaftlichen, verkehrspolitischen und sozialen Auswirkungen, die sich als Folge der Grenzlage für den Wirtschaftsraum Lübeck ergeben, Mar. 9, 1950; Industrie und Handelskammer zu Lübeck, Der Wirtschaftsraum Lübeck als "notleidendes Grenzlandgebiet" an der Ostzonengrenze, Apr. 1952, both in AHL, IHK zu Lübeck Nr. 708.

43. Ritter and Hadju, *Innerdeutsche Grenze*, 182, suggest that Lübeck's port actually recovered at a faster rate than Hamburg's. Especially its better access to Scandinavia gave it an advantage. In 1950, Lübeck's port transactions stood at 69.4 percent (1936 = 100), Hamburg's at 49.9 percent. In 1955, Lübeck reached 132.5 percent, Hamburg 108.8 percent.

44. "Notstandsgebiet Lübeck," *Frankfurter Allgemeine Zeitung*, June 26, 1952. Hamburg's port also suffered from the fact that the Elbe turned into a border river, but it managed to reactivate trade with Czechoslovakia. See Jakubec, *Schlupflöcher*, 159–200.

45. Memo, Die wirtschaflichen, verkehrspolitischen und sozialen Auswirkungen, die sich als Folge der Grenzlage für den Wirtschaftsraum Lübeck ergeben, Mar. 9, 1950, AHL, IHK zu Lübeck Nr. 708.

46. Industrie und Handelskammer zu Lübeck, Der Wirtschaftsraum Lübeck als "notleidendes Grenzlandgebiet" an der Ostzonengrenze, Apr. 1952, AHL, IHK zu Lübeck Nr. 708; Ritter and Hadju, *Innerdeutsche Grenze*, 185.

47. Das kulturelle Zonengrenzprogramm des Landes Schleswig-Holstein: Zusammengestellt vom Schleswig-Holsteinischen Kulturministerium, Oct. 20, 1952, BArch B135/126.

48. Memo, Die wirtschaflichen, verkehrspolitischen und sozialen Auswirkungen, die sich als Folge der Grenzlage für den Wirtschaftsraum Lübeck ergeben, Mar. 9, 1950, AHL, IHK zu Lübeck Nr. 708; quote in Barbara Klie, "Wo alle Strassen enden: Die deutsche Binnengrenze von Hof bis Travemünde," part II, *Christ und Welt*, Jan. 2, 1958, 2.

49. In 1939, there were 39.4 million people living in the territory that would become West Germany. In 1950, this figure had grown by 8.3 million, or 19 percent, to

47.7 million. Of the 12 million expellees who survived migration, some 8 million settled in West Germany. Among the people who migrated from East to West Germany, many were expellees who had first stopped in the Soviet zone of occupation but decided to continue their westward journey. Between 1949 and 1961, some 3 million refugees arrived from the SBZ/GDR. In 1960, a quarter of the West German population consisted of expellees and refugees. See Wehler, *Gesellschaftsgeschichte, 1949–90*, 35, 43–45; on the overrepresentation of expellees in the eastern counties of West Germany see Schneider, "Wirtschaftsgeschichte Niedersachsens nach 1945," 816–817.

50. Waldeck, "Räumliche Strukturanalyse," 47.

51. Ritter and Hadju, *Innerdeutsche Grenze*, 244.

52. Puffahrt, "Entwässerungsmassnahmen," 75–83; Bellin, "Wasser," 21–27.

53. Ritter and Hadju, *Innerdeutsche Grenze*, 241.

54. The first rail connection linked Hitzacker and Dannenberg with Wittenberge in 1873; another connected Lüchow with Salzwedel in 1890. Ibid., 241.

55. Ibid., 241–242.

56. The county shared 144 kilometers of border with the GDR but only 42 kilometers with adjacent West German counties. Paasche, "Die Zonengrenze," 97; Winterhoff, "Verkehrswesen," 129–133. Paasche served as county director at the time.

57. "Conti errichtet Zweigwerk in Dannenberg. Zonenrandkreis jetzt industriell gesättigt. Auch dort keine echten Arbeitslosen mehr," *Aller Zeitung*, Aug. 25, 1960. By 1970, the county had 2,830 industrial jobs. See Ritter and Hadju, *Innerdeutsche Grenze*, 246.

58. Schwenke, *Förderung*, 109–121, 153; investment figures, 121.

59. Investment volume in Tiggemann, *Gorleben*, 93.

60. Figures in Glatzel and Hundertmark, *Braunschweig*, 14–15; also Schneider, "Wirtschaftsgeschichte Niedersachsens nach 1945," 815–816, 902. On the context of Braunschweig's wartime production see Niemann, "Wirtschaftsgeschichte Niedersachsens," 617–623, esp. 618–619. For the surrounding Braunschweig county see Landkreis Braunschweig to Präsident des Nds. Verwaltungsbezirk Braunschweig, Nov. 8, 1950, NLA HA Nds. 500 Acc 2/73 Nr. 375/5.

61. Schneider, "Wirtschaftsgeschichte Niedersachsens nach 1945," 820–821.

62. "Helmstedt—Vorposten der freien Welt," *Mitteilungen der IHK Braunschweig*, no. 60 (Sept. 1952): 303; Glatzel and Hundertmark, *Braunschweig*, 49.

63. Brunsviga Maschinenwerke AG, "Wo liegt Braunschweig? Grenzland Braunschweig," *Mitteilungen der IHK Braunschweig*, no. 59 (Aug. 1952): 245.

64. Mund, *Landkreis Helmstedt*, 156–176; Steffens et al., *Lebensjahre*, 100–112.

65. Vorstand Braunschweigische Kohle Bergwerke to BMWi, May 26, 1952, NLA WO, 4 Nds. Zg. 01/1981 Nr. 232; "BKB fordern ihr Eigentum zurück: Gesamtverluste fast 25 Millionen DM," *Handelsblatt*, Sept. 5, 1952; "Verlust am 26 Mai 1952: 32 Millionen: Generalversammlung der Braunschweig Kohlenbergwerke," *Braunschweiger Zeitung*, Helmstedt ed., Apr. 28, 1953.

66. Landkreis Helmstedt to BM Wirtschaft, Sept. 18, 1952, NLA WO, 4 Nds. Zg. 01/ 1981 Nr. 232.

67. Ballhausen, IHK Braunschweig to Nds. Min. Wirtschaft und Verkehr, Feb. 8, 1952, AHL, IHK zu Lübeck Nr. 721. See also Glatzel and Hundertmark, *Braunschweig*, 82.

68. Ritter and Hadju, *Innerdeutsche Grenze*, 199–202. For similarly interrelated processes in the production of dolls between Neustadt (Bavaria) and Sonneberg (Thuringia) see Sheffer, *Burned Bridge*, 61. Overview of regional economy from Saxon perspective in Murdock, *Changing Places*, 26–29. Maps indicating the region's textile and garment industries in Gleitze, *Ostdeutsche Wirtschaft*, 135–137.

69. Ritter and Hadju, *Innerdeutsche Grenze*, 210.

70. Ibid., 192–199; Barbara Klie, "Der Unfruchtbare Acker: Die deutsche Binnengrenze von Hof bis Travemünde," *Christ und Welt*, Christmas 1957, 20.

71. Ritter and Hajdu, "East–West German Boundary," 341; Ante, "Developing and Current Problems," 71.

72. Behrisch, *Oberfranken im Würgegriff*; later example, Gerhard Wacher, "Probleme eines peripheren Industriegebietes unter besonderer Berücksichtigung der Zonengrenzlage, dargestellt am Beispiel Oberfranken," paper presented at Konferenz über Fragen der regionalen Wirtschaft, Brussels, Dec. 6–8. 1961.

73. Figures in Ludwig Alwens, "Soziale Erosion in Oberfranken," *Die Zeit*, Mar. 19, 1953; see also Alwens, "Oberfränkische Textilindustriegebiet," 19.

74. Ritter and Hadju, *Innerdeutsche Grenze*, 212–214; Weight, "Standorte," 385, 395.

75. Weight, "Standorte," 398–400.

76. W. F. Maschner, "Enttäuschung in bayerisch Sibirien," *Stuttgarter Zeitung*, Sept. 1, 1954. On the brief economic boom in Upper Franconia until 1952 see also Angerer, "Oberfranken," 35.

77. *Braunschweig als Grenzland*, ed. Chamber of Industry and Commerce in Braunschweig (Braunschweig: Westermann, 1949), quotes: 1, 28.

78. A number of such reports in AHL, IHK zu Lübeck Nr. 721 and NLA HA Nds. 500 Acc 2/73 Nr. 376/5. The latter reports were directed to the president of the district (*Regierungsbezirk*) of Braunschweig.

79. Each level convened a working group, called *Arbeitsgemeinschaft der Grenzlandkammern, Ostrandausschusses des Deutschen Landkreistages*, and *[Länder] Arbeitskreis Ostgrenzgebiet der Bundesrepublik* respectively.

80. Although the Basic Law obviously covered the rights and duties of Bund vs. *Länder*, the constitutional realities, especially in fiscal terms, evolved during the early 1950s and beyond. See Grüner, *Geplantes "Wirtschaftswunder"?*, 210–216.

81. Examples: [IHK Würzburg], Denkschrift über die grenzwirtschaftlichen Verhältnisse im Bereich des Regierungsbezirkes Unterfranken und des Industrie- und Handelskammerbezirkes Würzburg, n.d. [1950]; Denkschrift über die wirtschaftliche Notlage in den ostbayer: Grenzgebieten und ihre

Minderung durch Steuervergünstigungen—Überreicht von den IHK Bayreuth, Coburg, Passau, Regensburg und Würzburg, n.d. [1950]; Industrie- und Handelskammer Lübeck: Der Wirtschaftsraum Lübeck als 'notleidendes Grenzgebiet" an der Ostzonengrenze, Apr. 1952, all in AHL Bestand 02.05 IHK zu Lübeck, Nr. 721.

82. *Die Auswirkungen der Ostzonen Grenze auf die anliegenden Gebiete der Bundesrepublik: Erkenntnisse und Vorschläge,* ed. Arbeitsgemeinschaft der Grenzlandkammern, Sitz Braunschweig (Braunschweig, Dec. 1950), 8.

83. Ibid., 10–11, 15; on Bundesbahn see Kopper, *Bahn,* 84, 87. Freight rates increased by 40 percent.

84. *Auswirkungen der Ostzonen Grenze,* 8.

85. Ibid, 26.

86. On spatial planning see Chapter 2, this volume.

87. The Bundestag voted to grant DM 30 million. BT, 1. WP 1949, StB, 72. Sitzung, June 23, 1950, 2618–2619. It appears that only 5 million were released by the finance minister. On the lack of the reform of freight rates see Kopper, *Bahn,* 126–135.

88. *Auswirkungen der Ostzonen Grenze,* 8–9, 14–16, 28–29, 51–52.

89. BT, 1. WP, Drs. Nr. 95, Sept. 30, 1949; Drs. Nr. 348, Nov. 29, 1949; BT 1. WP, StB, 27. Sitzung, Jan. 18, 1950, 851–852; see also Drs. 429, Jan. 20, 1950. Background: *Denkschrift des Landes Rheinland-Pfalz zu dem Antrag der Landesregierung auf Anerkennung der Roten Zone und des Oberwesterwaldes als Notstandsgebiet* (Mainz, Nov. 1950), BArch B106/5151; "Die Rote Zone im Lande Rheinland-Pfalz: Aus einem militärischen Wort wurde ein Begriff der Grenzlandnot—Die bisherigen Hilfsmassnahmen der Regierung," *Staats-Zeitung,* May 30, 1950.

90. Auszug aus dem Kurzprotokoll über die 87. Kabinettssitzung der Bundesregierung, July 28, 1950, BArch B106/5151.

91. On Salzgitter: Sondersitzung der Bundesregierung, Nov. 22, 1951, *Die Kabinettsprotokolle der Bundesrepublik* 4 (1951), ed. Bundesarchiv (Boppard/ Rh.: Boldt, 1988), 778–779; on Schleswig- Holstein in the same volume: 135. Kabinettssitzung, Mar. 13, 1951, 225–226. For the Bavarian Forest see Grüner, *Geplantes "Wirtschaftswunder"?,* 200–205, 210–211, who emphasizes Adenauer's reluctance to support eastern Bavaria.

92. Dr. Duschek, Vermerk für den zeitl. Ablauf der Besprechung über grundsätzliche Fragen der Zonengrenzgebiete am 9.1.1952 in Braunschweig, Jan. 5, 1952, NLA HA Nds. 500 Acc. 2/73 Nr. 378/3.

93. *Denkschrift über das Ostgrenzgebiet der Bundesrepublik,* Vorgelegt vom Arbeitskreis-Ostgrenzgebiete der Bundesrepublik der Länder Bayern, Hessen, Niedersachsen und Schleswig-Holstein. The petition was handed to Ludwig Erhard on May 15, 1952.

94. The decision about the extent of the borderlands coalesced in the first three meetings of the working group of the border states (*Arbeitskreis Ostgrenzgebiet der Bundesrepubik*) on January 9, 1952 (inclusion of Czech–Bavarian border, 40-kilometer strip), February 20 (naming of eligible counties within 40-kilometer strip), and April 23 (inclusion of wet border). Documentation in NLA HA Nds. 500 Acc 2/73 Nr. 378/3.

95. Walter Fredericia (alias Walter Pedwaidic), "Das sterbende Grenzland am Eisernen Vorhang," *Die Zeit*, Mar. 13, 1952. Pedwaidic-Fredericia was a former Nazi from Vienna. See also Ilse Elsner, "Im Schatten der Zonengrenze," *Die Welt*, May 14, 1952; "Denkschrift der Zonengrenzländer," *Braunschweiger Zeitung*, May 17, 1952.

96. *Denkschrift über das Ostgrenzgebiet der Bundesrepublik*, Vorgelegt vom Arbeitskreis-Ostgrenzgebiete der Bundesrepublik der Länder Bayern, Hessen, Niedersachsen und Schleswig-Holstein (May 1952), 6–8.

97. Handwerkskammer der Oberpfalz in Regensburg to Max Solleder (CSU), Sept. 24, 1951; Solleder to Hans Globke, BKAmt, May 29, 1952, both in BArch B136/693.

98. Kurt von Gleichen, "Kuriositäten an der Nahtstelle der Grenze: Kleine Reise längs des Eisernen Vorhangs im Herbst, 1951," *Die Neue Zeitung*, Nov. 16, 1951.

99. Sälter, *Grenzpolizisten*, 24–37; Ritter and Lapp, *Grenze*, 19–25. The orders establishing the "new border regime" are in Bennewitz and Potratz, *Zwangsaussiedlungen*, 251–265. For Soviet precedent see Martin, *Affirmative Action Empire*, 314, 329–330; Chandler, *Institutions of Isolation*, 75, 82; Blaive, "Border Guarding," 98–99.

100. Sälter, *Grenzpolizisten*, 29. Any public events had to be approved and were supervised.

101. Figure in ibid., 30–31, with discussion of figures in note 62. The deportations are well documented on the local level. See Bennewitz and Potratz, *Zwangsaussiedlungen*; Wagner, *"Beseitigung des Ungeziefers . . ."*; Kaltenborn, "Leben mit der Grenze," 58–61; Walther and Bittner, *Heringsbahn*, 257–289; Oschlies, *Entrissene Heimat*; Gentzen and Wulf, *Zwangsausgesiedelte*; Thies, *Zicherie*, 32–39; Johnson, *Divided Village*, 65–88; Sheffer, *Burned Bridge*, 97–117.

102. Figure in van Melis and Bispinck, *"Republikflucht,"* 37; Sheffer, *Burned Bridge*, 106–107, 112–116; Bennewitz and Potratz, *Zwangsaussiedlungen*, 84–86; Thies, *Zicherie*, 40–44.

103. Berdahl, *Where the World Ended*, 51–52, 66–70; Sälter, "Loyalität und Denunziation," 159–184; Sheffer, *Burned Bridge*, 142–163, 189.

104. Sheffer, *Burned Bridge*, 97–117; Johnson, *Divided Village*, 65–88.

105. Figures in Ritter and Hajdu, *Innerdeutsche Grenze*, 35; on consequences for infrastructure in general see *Die Sperrmassnahmen der Sowjetzonenregierung an der*

Zonengrenze und um Westberlin (Bonn: BMin Gesamtdeutsche Beziehungen, 1953), 19–23.

106. Plück, "Innerdeutsche Beziehungen," 2019.

107. "Die leidenden Landkreise an der Zonengrenze," *Die Selbstverwaltung* 7:1 (1953): 3–4; Sheffer, *Burned Bridge*, 130. For GDR communities see Pingel-Schliemann, *Die Grenze*, 19.

108. BT, 1. WP, StB, 219. Sitzung, June 18, 1952, 9639.

109. Some of these connections, such as water deliveries to Duderstadt near Göttingen, remained in place throughout the Cold War: Amt für den Rechtsschutz des Vermögens der DDR (AfR), Forderungen der DDR an Schuldner in der BRD wegen Nutzung des Grund- und Quellwassers der DDR und aus Trinkwasserlieferungen, VVS, Mar. 10, 1971, BArch DK 5/1498. For the similar situation in West Berlin see Moss, "Divided City."

110. Aktenvermerk. Besprechung der Ländervertreter über Unterbringung und Betreuung der Flüchtlinge aus dem Sperrgürtel der Ostzone am 17 Juni 1952 im BMin Vertriebene, June 18, 1952; Aktenvermerk zur Situation in den Kreisen an der Zonengrenze, July 11, 1952; Hess, Innenmin., Monatsbericht Nr. 5/52—Sonderbericht: Die Lage an der hessischen Grenze zur Sowjetzone, Oct. 1, 1952, all in HHStAW Abt. 508/3185.

111. Ackermann, *Der "echte" Flüchtling*, 65–111; Heidemeyer, *Flucht und Zuwanderung*, 27–34, 127–133, 190–192; Stokes, "Permanent Refugee Crisis."

112. Hans Ewers (DP) in BT, 1. WP, 219. Sitzung, June 18, 1952, 9636. The discursive shift was accompanied by a policy shift toward the refugees, especially in regard to illegal crossers. See Heidemeyer, *Flucht und Zuwanderung*, 133–146, with a focus on West Berlin.

113. Hoffmann, "Binnenwanderung und Arbeitsmarkt," 224–228; Bethlehem, *Heimatvertreibung*, 29–33; for boat reference see Ackermann, *Der "echte" Flüchtling*, 96.

114. Auszug aus dem Beschluss-Protokoll über die 73. Sitzung des Kabinetts, June 9, 1952, HHStAW, Abt. 508/3185.

115. Hoffrichter, "Arbeitskräftebedarf contra Wohnraummangel."

116. Sheffer, *Burned Bridge*, 63.

117. *Die Auswirkungen der Ostzonen Grenze auf die anliegenden Gebiete der Bundesrepublik. Erkenntnisse und Vorschläge*, ed. Arbeitsgemeinschaft der Grenzlandkammern, Sitz Braunschweig (Braunschweig, Dec. 1950), 27.

118. Landkreis Blankenburg to Präsident des Nds. Verwaltungsbezirks Braunschweig, Nov. 14, 1950, NLA HA Nds. 500 Acc 2/73 Nr. 376/5.

119. The term "social baggage" was common in this context. See, e.g., "Grenzlandprobleme," *Mitteilungen der IHK Braunschweig*, no. 31 (Apr. 1950): 92; "struggle for life" in "Die leidenden Landkreise an der Zonengrenze," *Die Selbstverwaltung* 7:1 (1953): 5; "less viable" in Paul Noack, "Kulturpropaganda und Abwanderung: Zwei Probleme der Zonengrenze," *Frankfurter Allgemeine*

Zeitung, Feb. 10, 1955. On denigrating language see also Ackermann, *Der "echte" Flüchtling*, 66–67.

120. The May 1952 *Denkschrift über das Ostgrenzgebiet der Bundesrepublik* does not identify solicitations as a problem yet, but less than a year later, Schleswig-Holstein, Lower Saxony, Hesse, and Bavaria produced a list of companies that had left. See BMWi to StS BKAmt, Dec. 11, 1953, BArch B136/697.

121. Herbert Fuchs, mayor of Kiel, to Waldemar Kraft, BMin w/o portfolio, May 24, 1954, BArch B135/127.

122. Lotz, Stadtdirektor Braunschweig, to Nds. Min. Wirtschaft und Verkehr, Dec. 9, 1953, NLA HA Nds. 100 Acc. 1/89 Nr. 596.

123. Mayor of Lübeck to Waldemar Kraft, BMin w/o portfolio, May 26, 1954, BArch B135/127. Ads appeared, e.g., in *Messe und Ausstellungen* 34 (1953): 33, 46, a journal about business fairs.

124. The lists of advantages ranged from the reimbursement of relocation costs, low-interest loans, tax waivers, move-in-ready factories and administration buildings, electricity at reduced rates and—of major importance in the early 1950s—sufficient housing for workers and employees. See Hermann Ahrens, Economic and Transportation Minister, Lower Saxony, to Waldemar Kraft, BMin w/o portfolio, July 15, 1954, BArch B135/127. Also *Mitteilungen der Industrie- und Handelskammer für Südhannover für ihre Firmen* Nr. 7, Sept. 1, 1951, 4; "Zonengrenzland braucht besonderen Schutz," *Aller Zeitung*, Jan. 6, 1955.

125. Otto Ziebill, Deutscher Städtetag, to member cities, Mar. 24, 1954, BArch B135/127.

126. 300. Kabinettssitzung, July 7, 1953, *Die Kabinettsprotokolle der Bundesrepublik* 6 (1953), ed. Bundesarchiv (Boppard/Rh.: Boldt, 1989), 387; see also 298. Kabinettssitzung, June 23, 1953, 360–361. Order to revenue offices in BMI, circular to interior ministers of federal states, July 7, 1954, NLA HA Nds. 100 Acc. 1/89 Nr. 596.

127. Hefele, *Verlagerung*, 119. Contemporary: "Das Sprungbrett an der Zonengrenze," *Nordwestdeutsche Rundschau*, Nov. 24, 1952.

128. For Neustadt see Sheffer, *Burned Bridge*, 62–66, quote: 63; Weight, "Standorte," 399–400. For the massive migration of medium-sized businesses (*Mittelstand*) from East to West Germany, including manufacturers of brands like Wella, Odol, and Chlorodont, see Hefele, *Verlagerung*, esp. 115–120; Petzina, "Standortverschiebungen," 111; popular account: Golle, *Know-How*.

129. Arno Behrisch (SPD), BT, 1. WP, StB, 219. Sitzung, June 18, 1952, 9631C.

130. Herbert Wehner (SPD), BT, 1. WP, StB, 219. Sitzung, June 18, 1952, 9648C.

131. Konrad Adenauer (CDU), BT, 1, WP, StB, 219, Sitzung, June 18, 1952, 9633D-35C.

132. "Adenauer verspricht Hilfe: Ein Streifen des Lebens entlang der Zonengrenze," *Braunschweiger Zeitung*, June 19, 1952; "Zonengürtel wird

Notstandsgebiet: Bundestag gegen 'Willkür- und Terrormassnahmen' in der Sowjetzone," *Hannoversche Allgemeine Zeitung*, June 19, 1952. These headlines were incorrect. The federal government did not intend to acknowledge the borderlands in toto as distressed areas. Adenauer's more differentiated position was reiterated by the minister for expellees, Hans Lukaschek, in the All-German Parliamentary Committee at its meeting on June 19, 1952. See *Sitzungsprotokolle*, Doc. Nr. 60, 340.

133. Sitzung des Interministeriellen Ausschusses für Sofort- und Sondermaßnahmen an der Zonengrenze, July 26, 1952, BArch B 136/695, 4. The underlying issue here was that the committee did not see the federal government's responsibility for the border regions as a constitutional one but only as a moral one.

134. Ibid., 3.

135. Nützenadel, *Stunde der Ökonomen*, 249; Ullmann, "Expansionskoalition," 408; Grüner, Geplantes *"Wirtschaftswunder"?*, 174.

136. 243. Kabinettssitzung, Aug. 29, 1952, *Die Kabinettsprotokolle der Bundesrepublik* 5 (1952), ed. Bundesarchiv (Boppard/Rh.: Boldt, 1989), 539; Sitzung des Interministeriellen Ausschusses für Sofort- und Sondermaßnahmen an der Zonengrenze, Oct. 23, 1952, BArch B 136/695; Vermerk für die Kabinettssitzung, Bereitstellung von Bundesmitteln für Sofort- und Sondermaßnahmen [etc.], Nov. 29, 1952, BArch B 136/697.

137. BT, 1. WP, StB, 264. Sitzung, May 6, 1953, 12913C-12915A, 12917A; BT, 1, WP, Drs. Nr. 4276.

138. A list of propositions (*Drucksachen*) in BT, 1. WP, StB, 279. Sitzung, July 2, 1953, 13955A; Grüner, Geplantes *"Wirtschaftswunder"?*, 217–218.

139. Hans Henn (FDP) BT, 1. WP, StB, 279. Sitzung, July 2, 1953, 13955C-D, 13959D. Henn chaired the Zonal Borderlands Subcommittee within the Bundestag's Committee on All-German Affairs (Gesamtdeutscher Ausschuss).

140. Ibid., 14007C-D. The vote constituted a resolution (*Entschliessung*), i.e., a nonbinding political volition. See Butz, *Rechtsfragen*, 15. Preparation of the resolution in *Sitzungsprotokolle*, 88. Sitzung, June 10, 1952, Doc. Nr. 87, 730–736.

141. Kabinettsausschuss für Wirtschaft, 39. Sitzung, Aug. 19, 1953, http://www.bundesarchiv.de/cocoon/barch/0000/x/x1951e/kap1_2/kap2_41/para3_2.html (accessed July 2018).

142. The territory of the Federal Republic amounted to 245,379 square kilometers, of which 46,755 (18.8 percent) were part of the "zonal borderland." Figures in Ritter and Hajdu, *Innerdeutsche Grenze*, 83.

143. BT, 2. WP, StB, 3. Sitzung, Oct. 20, 1953, 14C. See also BKAmt, Erlass an sämtliche Bundesminister, Nov. 30, 1953, BArch B135/131. The Chancellery reminded all federal ministries of the political importance of the borderland problem.

144. Early aid measures are listed in Plück, "Hilfeleistungen," 107–112.

145. BT, 2. WP, Drs. Nr. 401, Einbeziehung des Kreises Alsfeld (Hessen) in die Fördermassnahmen für Zonenrandgebiete, Mar. 25, 1954; Landrat, Kreis Ziegenhain (Hessen), to BMWi, May 10, 1954, BArch B135/127; Grüner, *Geplantes "Wirtschaftswunder"?*, 218–219.

146. "Der gefährdete Streifen," *Frankfurter Allgemeine* Zeitung, July 12, 1954; BT, 2. WP, 31. Sitzung, May 26, 1954, 1469B, 1472C. At issue was the distribution of corporate taxes (*Körperschaftssteuer*) and income taxes between Bonn and the federal states.

147. BMWi, BMF, Schnellbrief 85/54, June 12, 1954, BArch B135/130. The letter conveyed that "the provision of DM 120 million for the border districts is a onetime measure and cannot be repeated in coming fiscal years." See also BT, 2. WP, Drs. Nr. 808, Sept. 8, 1954. On the 25 million for culture see BT, 2. WP, Drs. Nr. 534, May 18, 1954, 6.

148. LT Nds., 2. WP, StB, 65. Sitzung, Mar. 10, 1954, 4171–4182; "Wenn die Eiertänze um das Geld monatelang weitergehen [. . .] kamen wir zu dem Ergebnis, dass in den Zonengrenzkreisen wieder nichts geschieht," *Isenhagener Kreisblatt*, Apr. 3, 1954; BT, 2. WP, 31. Sitzung, May 26, 1954; 51. Sitzung, Oct. 21, 1954. News about the release of the DM 120 million came during the Bundestag debate of May 26, 1954.

149. Adenauer to Waldemar Kraft, Apr. 8, 1954, BArch B135/126; on Kraft's assignment see also Einleitung 4. Die Ordnung der Wirtschaft im Innern. Kabinettsausschüsse—Wirtschaft, http://www.bundesarchiv.de/cocoon/barch/0/x/x1954e/kap1_1/para2_4.html (accessed Nov. 2015).

150. StS Westrick, BMWi, Vermerk, Oct. 18, 1952, BArch B136/695. See also "Der Grenzwirtschaft den Rücken stärken. Keine Kommissionen mehr, sondern praktische Hilfe," *Braunschweiger Zeitung*, July 4, 1952.

151. Dr. Else Brökelschen (CDU), BT, 2. WP, 31. Sitzung, May 26, 1954, 1493.

152. Dr. Wilhelm Giel, Vermerk, Mar. 9, 1955, BArch B135/130.

153. Abelshauser, *Wirtschaftsgeschichte*, 129–152, 283–295, quote: 292. On dual impact of currency reform and the end of price control see Spoerer and Streb, *Wirtschaftsgeschichte*, 216–218.

154. Spicka, *Selling the Economic Miracle*, 108–204.

155. Siemer, "Bestandsaufnahme," 424–433. Regardless of the dire picture painted by borderland representatives, Siemer concludes in this contemporary article that none of the border counties slipped below their population and employment levels of 1939. The figures were "significantly higher" (433) in 1957 than in 1939.

156. Müller, "Dorf am Eisernen Vorhang," 23.

157. Quote in W. F. Maschner, "Enttäuschung in bayrisch Sibirien," *Stuttgarter Zeitung*, Sept. 1, 1954; see also Jürgen Eick, "Im Schatten der Zonengrenze," *Frankfurter Allgemeine Zeitung*, June 26, 1954; "Im toten Winkel des Wirtschaftswunder," *Die Flüchtlingsstimme*, no. 7 (1955): 3; "Die irrsinnige

Grenze: Wie soll Deutschland wieder zusammenkommen," *Vorwärts*, Dec. 20, 1957; "Ist hier das Ende der westlichen Welt? Schnackenburg—die tote Stadt im toten Winkel," *Bonner Rundschau*, May 25, 1958; "An der Zonengrenze schlägt der Puls des Landes langsamer: Verkehr und Industrie weichen zurüc —Bevölkerung nimmt ständig ab," *Fuldaer Volkszeitung*, Mar. 4, 1959.

158. The ideological competition (*Systemkonkurrenz*) is ground well-trodden. For historiographical approaches and controversies see Möller and Mählert, eds., *Abgrenzung und Verflechtung*; Wentker, "Zwischen Abgrenzung und Verflechtung," 10–17. For recent studies see Lemke, ed., *Schaufenster der Systemkonkurrenz*; Wengst and Wentker, eds.: *Doppelte Deutschland*. On West German activities to undercut and counter East German propaganda efforts (*Wühlarbeit*) see Heitzer, *Kampfgruppe*; Creuzberger, *Kampf für die Eineit*; Creuzberger and Hoffmann, eds., *"Geistige Gefahr."*

159. Contemporary: Karl-Heinz Krumm, "Kulissenkampf um Propaganda-Ballons: Bundesverteidigungsministerium drohte Presse und Rundfunk mit Landesverratsverfahren," *Frankfurter Rundschau*, Apr. 29, 1965. See also Schindelbeck, "Propaganda," 213–234; Gordon, "East German Psychological Operations," 89–123. For context see Krämer, "Westdeutsche Propaganda," 333–371; Creuzberger, *Kampf für die Einheit*, 252–257, 483–488.

160. Expression "Trojan horse" in "Gegen kommunistische Unterwanderungs-versuche," in *Deutschland im Wiederaufbau*, ed. Presse- und Informationsamt der Bundesregierung (1954), 323–325; "Die kommunistische Zersetzungstätigkeit," in *Deutschland im Wiederaufbau*, ed. Presse- und Informationsamt der Bundesregierung (1955), 381–382. Contrary to western impressions, Amos, *Westpolitik der SED*, 60–67, 114–123, emphasizes the inef-fectiveness of these eastern efforts.

161. IHK Lübeck, "Der Wirtschaftsraum Lübeck als 'notleidendes Grenzgebiet' an der Ostzonengrenze" (p. 19), Apr.1952, AHL, IHK zu Lübeck, Nr. 721.

162. Muhle, *Menschenraub*; Böckel, *Grenz-Erfahrungen*, 115–116.

163. Schmale, "Heimlich, still und leise," 80–90.

164. BMGesamt, Vermerk, Aug. 4, 1954, BArch B135/128. The memorandum called for more relay stations. See also Franz Xaver Unertl (CSU), BT, 2. WP, 31. Sitzung, May 26, 1954, 1498A. For the context see Creuzberger, *Kampf für die Einheit*, 241–244.

165. Quote in Dr. Else Brökelschen (CDU), BT, 1. WP, 264. Sitzung, May 6, 1953, 12917C/D; similar: Hans Henn (FDP), BT, 1, WP, 279, Sitzung, July 2, 1953, 13959C; Egon Franke (SPD), BT, 2. WP, 51. Sitzung, Oct. 21, 1954, 2538D.

166. "West German Reds Fight Registration: 10,000 Youths Won't Comply with Police Rules on Return from East Berlin Rally," *New York Times*, June 1, 1950. Kahrs, "Grenze und Entgrenzung in der Literatur," 254–255. On the event in Berlin see Lemke, *Vor der Mauer*, 141–145. On the extent of western travel re-strictions relating to the festival see Rutter, "The Western Wall," 78–106.

167. "Deutsche / wurden von Deutschen / gefangen / weil sie von Deutschland / nach Deutschland /gegangen." Bertolt Brecht and Paul Dessau, *Herrnburger Bericht: Gewidmet der Freien Deutschen Jugend anlässlich der 3. Weltfestspiele der Jugend und Studenten für den Frieden in Berlin* (Berlin: Zentralrat der FDJ, 1951).

168. "Gegen kommunistische Unterwanderungsversuche," *Deutschland im Wiederaufbau*, ed. Presse- und Informationsamt der Bundesregierung (1954), 324; Ballhausen, IHK Braunschweig to Nds. Min. Wirtschaft und Verkehr, Feb. 8, 1952, AHL, IHK zu Lübeck Nr. 721. See also Glatzel/Hundertmark, *Braunschweig*, 82.

169. Plück, "Innerdeutsche Beziehungen," 2034–2035.

170. SH Kulturministerium, Das kulturelle Zonengrenzprogramm des Landes Schleswig-Holstein, Oct. 20, 1952, BArch B135/126.

171. Paul Noack, "Kulturpropaganda und Abwanderung: Zwei Probleme der Zonengrenze," *Frankfurter Allgemeine Zeitung*, Feb. 19, 1955; on buses see Kühn, " 'Kunst ohne Zonengrenzen,' " 202.

172. For folk art and choirs see Kühn, " 'Kunst ohne Zonengrenzen,' " 197–204.

173. "Zonengrenze: Prämien für Kultur-Kontakte," *Der Spiegel*, May 23, 1956, 44. The GDR's theater policies in West Germany have not yet been investigated, but see Meyer-Braun, *Löcher im Eisernen Vorhang*. For select figures on cultural contacts during the 1950s see Plück, "Innerdeutsche Beziehungen," 2032–2036. For the Berlin situation see Lemke, *Vor der Mauer*, 440–458.

174. BMGesamt, Bericht über kulturelle Massnahmen gesamtdeutschen Charakters im Zonenrandgebiet, June 2, 1961, BArch B102/13194.

175. Unemployed: Frank Seiboth (GB/BHE), BT, 2. WP, 51. Sitzung, Oct. 21, 1954, 2528C; Rudolf Freidhof (SPD), BT, 2. WP, 51. Sitzung, Oct. 21, 1954, 2531D; spying: Arno Behrisch (SPD), BT, 2. WP, 31. Sitzung, May 26, 1954, 1485D–1486A.

176. Term in "Zonengrenzhilfe von Flensburg bis Passau: In Kassel wurde ein Aufbauplan begonnen," *Lübecker Freie Presse*, June 18, 1953. The newspaper supported the SPD.

177. "Geistige Aufrüstung," in *Denkschrift über die Zonenrandgebiete des Landes Hessen: Vorgelegt vom Staatskommissar für die Förderung der hessischen Notstandsgebiete und Zonengrenzkreise* (Wiesbaden, Mar. 1954), BArch B135/126; "Stärkung der ideologischen Abwehrkräfte," in Paul Noack, "Kulturpropaganda und Abwanderung: Zwei Probleme der Zonengrenze," *Frankfurter Allgemeine Zeitung*, Feb. 19, 1955. See also Bundesminister für besondere Aufgaben Waldemar Kraft, Vorschläge für Massnahmen zur Förderung der Zonenrandgebiete, Aug. 1954, BArch B135/126.

178. Hans-Christoph Seebohm (CDU), "Zonenrandhilfe dient der Wiedervereinigung," in *Kreisblatt für Helmstedt. Sonderausgabe: 10 Jahre Zonengrenzkreis* (Dec. 1955), 14.

179. Paul Bleiss (SPD), BT, 2. WP, 31. Sitzung, May 26, 1954, 1473C; similar Behrisch (SPD), BT, 2. WP, 31. Sitzung, May 26, 1954, 1486A.

180. Quote in Hans Henn (FDP), BT, 1. WP, 279. Sitzung, July 2, 1953, 1395B. The "display window" rhetoric is ubiquitous in borderland and West Berlin debates and was also applied in other West–East contexts. See Fritsche, *Schaufenster des "Wirtschaftswunders."*

181. The magnet theory is usually attributed to Kurt Schumacher (SPD), but see Abelshauser, "'Magnet-Theorie'"; also Abelshauser, *Wirtschaftsgeschichte,* 402–404.

182. Stunz, *Das "hessische Salzburg,"* 50, 135–137; for a similar incident see Sheffer, *Burned Bridge,* 132.

183. "Die Zonen-Randgebiete," in *Deutschland im Wiederaufbau,* ed. Presse- und Informationsamt der Bundesregierung (1955), 380; the ministry doubled the amount by 1959: "Wirtschaftliche und kulturelle Hilfe für das Zonenrandgebiet," in *Deutschland im Wiederaufbau,* ed. Presse- und Informationsamt der Bundesregierung (1959), 527.

184. "Wirtschaftliche und kulturelle Hilfe für das Zonenrandgebiet," in *Deutschland im Wiederaufbau,* ed. Presse- und Informationsamt der Bundesregierung (1960), 453.

185. Amount in BMInnerdeutsch, *Soziale und kulturelle Fördermassnahmen der Bundesregierung im Zonenrandgebiet* (1987), 4. This publication listed the supported projects for each year. See also *Ratgeber Zonenrandförderung* (Bonn: BMInnerdeutsch, 1983).

186. Hans-Christoph Seebohm (CDU), "Zonenrandhilfe dient der Wiedervereinigung," in *Kreisblatt für Helmstedt: Sonderausgabe: 10 Jahre Zonengrenzkreis* (Dec. 1955), 13. Similar line of argument: IHK Lübeck, *Der Wirtschaftsraum Lübeck als "notleidendes Grenzgebiet" an der Ostzonengrenze* (p. 19), Apr. 1952, AHL, IHK zu Lübeck, Nr. 721.

187. Frank Seiboth (GB/BHE), BT, 2. WP, 51. Sitzung, Oct. 21, 1954, 2529C.

188. *Die Auswirkungen der Ostzonen Grenze auf die anliegenden Gebiete der Bundesrepublik. Erkenntnisse und Vorschläge,* ed. Arbeitsgemeinschaft der Grenzlandkammern, Sitz Braunschweig (Braunschweig: Dec. 1950), 29.

189. Sheffer, *Burned Bridge,* 65.

190. For a similar assessment see ibid., 50, 54; Schaefer, *States of Division,* 26.

191. This claim would benefit from some trade volume data, but unlike the extent of damage wrought by the Soviet blockade of Berlin, the amount of damage caused by the Allied counterblockade to the western borderland economy has never been quantified or at least estimated, presumably because it was not politically opportune to do so.

192. Best illustrated in Sheffer, *Burned Bridge,* 50–70; for the context see Westad, *Cold War,* 110–112.

193. Abelshauser, *Wirtschaftsgeschichte,* 59–87, 105–118; Petzina, "Standortverschiebungen"; on "center" see Wolfrum, *Geglückte Demokratie,* 144.

194. The term "Rhenish capitalism" customarily refers to the West German economic order, a form of state-regulated capitalism with institutionalized social partnerships. If and to what extent it may be considered a countermodel or alternative to the Anglo-American version of capitalism constitutes a point of debate. See Sattler, "Rheinischer Kapitalismus," 688–692, 694–695.

195. The comprehensive 40-kilometer definition was not least an attempt to patch over internal differences among the border's neighbors. Those living in earshot of the demarcation line, like residents of Lübeck and Lüchow Dannenberg, had little sympathy for those located farther away, like residents of Braunschweig.

196. Herbert Wehner (SPD), BT, 1. WP, StB, 219. Sitzung, June 18, 1952, 9648C.

197. Jureit, *Ordnen von Räumen*, 16.

198. The term "desolation" is common in this context. See, e.g., *Grenzland der Mitte: Dokumentarisches Bildwerk über Wirtschaft und Verkehr in Niedersachsen* (Hannover: Steinbock, 1963), 46. *Versteppung*, translated as "desertification" or, literally, as "becoming a steppe," was a highly charged term in West Germany during the 1950s, since the steppe was easily associated with the Soviet Union. The term indicated metaphorically that a territory was moving into the Soviet orbit of power.

199. Lehn, *Deutschlandbilder*, 366–369, 563–564; Lotz, "Gestrichelte Linien und schattierte Flächen," 53–69.

CHAPTER 2

1. Leendertz, "Gedanke des Ausgleichs," 210–225.

2. Doering-Manteuffel, "Innerdeutsche Grenze," 127–140.

3. In fact, Egon Bahr's East German interlocutor, Michael Kohl, objected to the ongoing use of the term, identifying it as a major provocation to the GDR. *Dokumente zur Deutschlandpolitik* (DzD), series VI, vol. 1 (1969/70), doc. Nr. 257, 1006; doc. Nr. 260, 1020; doc. Nr. 261, 1032.

4. On (failed) efforts to curb subsidies in the 1980s see Wirsching, *Provisorium*, 250, 251–255; Jákli, *Marshallplan*, 226–268, esp. 263–268.

5. See, e.g., the brochure *Unmenschliche Grenze / Inhuman Frontier* published in German, English, and French by Lower Saxony's Landeszentrale für Heimatdienst in 1956. Adenauer quote in BT, 1. WP, StB, 219. Sitzung, June 18, 1952, 9634A.

6. Chu, *German Minority*, 40–49; Conze, "'Unverheilte Brandwunden'"; Harvey, "'Bleeding Border.'" On the importance of cartographic representation in this context see also Jureit, *Ordnen von Räumen*, 179–208; Haslinger, *Nation und Territorium*, 12–16.

7. "Die leidenden Landkreise an der Zonengrenze," *Die Selbstverwaltung: Organ des deutschen Landkreistages* 7:1 (1953): 7.

8. Ibid. See also Wandschneider, "Pfahl im Fleische," 93–97; Behrisch, *Oberfranken im Würgegriff*, 7.

9. Braun, "Osthilfe, 1926–1937;" for the origins of state aid to rural regions see Jones, "Prussia's Peripheries."

10. Leendertz, *Ordnung schaffen*; Kegler, "'Begriff der Ordnung,'" 188–209; Briesen and Strubelt, "Kontinuität und Neubeginn," 15–54, esp. 23–24.

11. Klaphake, *Regionalpolik*, 57–62; Grüner, *Geplantes "Wirtschaftswunder"*?, 226–233.

12. Leendertz, *Ordnung schaffen*, 264; Grüner, *Geplantes "Wirtschaftswunder"*?, 369–370.

13. Leendertz, *Ordnung schaffen*, 262–268, passim; Grüner, *Geplantes "Wirtschaftswunder"*?, 367–378; Leendertz, "Ordnung, Ausgleich, Harmonie," 129–150.

14. Leendertz, *Ordnung schaffen*, 133–142.

15. Ibid., 136, 164–165.

16. Demand, "IMNOS," 1234–1239; Grüner, *Geplantes "Wirtschaftswunder"*?, 195–199, 207; Leendertz, *Ordnung schaffen*, 262.

17. The director of the Institute for Spatial Research (IfR), Erich Dittrich, published heavily on distressed regions, e.g., Dittrich, "Notstandsgebiete 1951"; Dittrich, "Aufgabe der Raumpolitik"; Dittrich, "Notstandgebiete in der Bundesrepublik." See also Wilhelm Röpke, "Notstandsgebiete," *Frankfurter Allgemeine Zeitung*, Nov. 15, 1952.

18. StS Westrick, BMWi to BKAmt, Aug. 28, 1952, BArch B136/695.

19. Erich Dittrich, 1963, cited in Leendertz, *Ordnung schaffen*, 332.

20. Leendertz, "Ordnung, Ausgleich, Harmonie," 138, 141.

21. Most clearly argued in Leendertz, "Gedanke des Ausgleichs." The goal of striving for comparable living conditions was based on a broad societal consensus and remained the orientation principle (*Leitbild*) of spatial planners well into the 1980s. See Gnest, *Entwicklung der überörtlichen Raumplanung*.

22. Karl J. Meyer, "Was sind Sanierungs- und Randgebiete?," *Die Zeit*, July 26, 1956. The terms for recipients of regional aid changed from "distressed areas" (*Notstandsgebiete*), "redevelopment areas" (*Sanierungsgebiete*), and "passive areas" (*Passivräume*) to "federally assisted areas" (*Bundesausbaugebiete*). See Ritter and Hajdu, *Innerdeutsche Grenze*, 84.

23. Karl, "Entwicklung und Ergebnisse," paras. 27–28; Butz, *Rechtsfragen*, 17–18. The geographer Walter Christaller was a controversial figure because of his role in Nazi-occupied Poland. See Barnes, "Notes from the Underground," 11–17; Erster Raumordnungsbericht, BT, 4. WP, Drs. IV/1492, Oct. 1, 1963.

24. Wilhelm Giel, who was in charge of borderland affairs in the ministry, was praised by borderland advocates for his role in negotiating the exemption article 92(2)c EEC. See Starke, "Entstehung des Zonenrandprogramms," 31.

25. Art. 92(2)c EEC. During the negotiations of the EEC in 1956–1957, the article still bore the number 44. For the approval see Conference Intergouvernementale pour le Marché Commun et L'Euratom, Comité des chefs de delegation, Feb. 22 1957, HAEU CM3/NEGO-238.

26. Conference Intergouvernementale pour le Marché Commun et L'Euratom, Groupe du Marché Commun: Protocol relatif à l'article 44, Feb. 17, 1957, HAEU CM3/NEGO-238. Quote is in Starke, "Entstehung des Zonenrandprogramms," 31.

27. Ahrens, "Teure Gewohnheiten"; Zschaler, "Bundeshilfen für Berlin"; Rott, *Die Insel*, 54–58; Lemke, *Vor der Mauer*, 279–286.

28. Conrady, Das gesamtdeutsche Problem: Nöte und Aufgaben an der Zonengrenze, Redemanuskript, [Aug. 1963], NLA WO, NL Conrady, 94 N Nr. 437; see also Bernd Nellessen, "Die Mauer steht auch bei Duderstadt," *Die Welt*, May 25, 1963; Gerhard Wacher, "Über Berlin Zonengrenzgebiet nicht vergessen," *Bayerische Rundschau-Kulmbach*, Apr. 7, 1964.

29. Hans-Walter Conrady, "Problematik der Zonenrandpolitik," in *Probleme am Zonenrand: Protokoll einer DGB-Tagung am 13. August 1963 in Helmstedt*, ed. Deutscher Gewerkschaftsbund, 8. See also "Zonengrenzland fordert mehr Hilfe von Bonn: 'Gleichstellung mit Westberlin,'" *Braunschweiger Presse*, Aug. 14, 1963.

30. Deutscher Bundestag: Ausschuss für gesamtdeutsche und Berliner Fragen, Bericht über die Studienreise I in das ZRG vom 25. bis 27. Mai 1964: Ausschuß Drucksache IV/34, 1 Juni 1964, BArch B136/7501.

31. "Die leidenden Landkreise an der Zonengrenze: Versuch einer komplexen Schilderung der Störungen und Schäden—Vorschläge für eine durchgreifende Hilfe," *Die Selbstverwaltung* 7:1 (Jan. 1953): 1.

32. Ullmann, "Expansionskoalition," 394–417; Ruck, "Kurzer Sommer," 362–401; Metzler, *Konzeptionen politischen Handeln*; Nützenadel, *Stunde der Ökonomen*, 307–343; Schanetzky, *Die grosse Ernüchterung*, esp. part III but also the discussion of the historical literature, 12–17.

33. Butz, *Rechtsfragen*, 19–25, quote: 20; Berg, *Zonenrandförderung*, 36–39.

34. Renzsch, *Finanzverfassung*.

35. Nonn, *Ruhrbergbaukrise*, 13; Abelshauser, *Wirtschaftsgeschichte*, 200–214.

36. Nonn, *Ruhrbergbaukrise*, 315–317.

37. Ibid., quote: 364. Criticism by borderland advocates of Ruhr support in BT, 5. WP 1968, StB, 161. Sitzung, Mar. 27, 1968, 8422C–8426C. Example of borderland advocacy in this context: Edwin Zerbe, "Kohleanpassungsgesetz und Ruhrplan: Modelle für die Förderung der Zonenrandgebiete," *SPD-Pressedienst* 23:69 (Apr. 10, 1968): 1–2. Zerbe was the director of the Hessian borderland county of Hersfeld.

38. Ullmann, "Expansionskoalition," 404–413; Nonn, *Ruhrbergbaukrise*, 364–373. For the rise of state expenditures on the federal, state, and municipal levels see Ullmann, *Steuerstaat*, 195–201; for the context see Abelshauser, *Wirtschaftsgeschichte*, 408–416.

39. Butz, *Rechtsfragen*, 26.

40. On finance reform see Renzsch, *Finanzverfassung*, 209–260; Ullmann, *Steuerstaat*, 193–195.

41. On the creation of the Common Tasks program see Renzsch, *Finanzverfassung*, 221–229; Nägele, *Regionale Wirtschaftspolitik*, 67–79. Summaries in "Gemeinschaftsaufgaben," in *Handwörterbuch der Raumforschung und Raumordnung*, vol. 1 (Hannover: Jänecke, 1970), 958–963; Klemmer,

"Gemeinschaftsaufgabe," 366–369; Karl, "Entwicklung und Ergebnisse," paras. 30–53. On "cooperative federalism" see Jeffery, "German Federalism," 172–188, esp. 172–177.

42. The Common Tasks were based on the Basic Law Art. 91a. Besides regional development, the Common Tasks were agriculture, coastal protection, and the construction and support of universities. After 1990, a new Common Task was Reconstruction East (Aufbau Ost).

43. Karl, "Entwicklung und Ergebnisse," paras. 44–66; Nägele, *Regionale Wirtschaftspolitik*, 80–93.

44. Vermerk, Teilnahme RegDir Dr. Albert und Dr. Mehrlaender an Sitzung des Arbeitskreises der Zonenrandländer in Bamberg, Mar. 27, 1969, BArch B102/81793.

45. In fact, the practice of granting tax privileges in the borderlands had been declared illicit by the Federal Finance Court in July 1970, requiring the legislator to put such programs on a legal footing. See Butz, *Rechtsfragen*, 26, 61–62. Quote in Minutes of the Meeting of the Lübeck Circle on Jan. 24, 1970, in Gersfeld (Rhön), AHL Bestand 04.01-0 Zentralamt—Hauptamt Nr. 111.

46. Hans-Jürgen von der Heide, "Zonenrandförderung: Eine Bilanz," *Der Landkreis* 44:5 (1974): 163.

47. Butz, *Rechtsfragen*, 26–38; Sander, *Zonenrandgebiet*, 30–33; Berg, *Zonenrandförderung*, 39–43.

48. In January 1970, representatives from chambers of trade and commerce as well as town and county officials from the borderlands drafted a law in Lübeck. It became the basis of the law that was introduced in both federal chambers. See Butz, *Rechtsfragen*, 26, n. 4. Archival documentation in AHL Bestand 04.01-0 Zentralamt—Hauptamt Nr. 111.

49. Butz, *Rechtsfragen*, 112–114; Berg, *Zonenrandförderung*, 43–46, quote: 44; Ziegler, *Regionale Strukturpolitik*, 16, 33–34.

50. "Selbstbehauptungswille an der Zonengrenze—Brome," *Isenhagener Kreisblatt*, Aug. 30, 1967; Felix Kolumne, *Isenhagener Kreisblatt*, July 24, 1979.

51. Bjarsch, *Landkreis an der Grenze*, 198.

52. Ante, "Developing and Current Problems," 82. Ante's results are based on a 1982 survey among Bavarians about the image of Upper Franconia. After 1990, psychologists found similar overestimations between West and East Germany, compounded by a negative attitude toward unification. See Carbon and Leder, "Wall Inside the Brain," 746–750.

53. "Studienfahrt an die Zonengrenze," *Hessische Allgemeine Zeitung*, June 3, 1969; Reinhard Scheele, Massnahmen und Planungen der Hessischen Landesregierung für die Wirtschaftsförderung an der Zonengrenze: Referat anlässlich der Studienfahrt 1969 der Vertreter der Zonenrandländer an die hessische Zonengrenze, n.d. [June 1969], HHStAW, Abt. 502/1076.

54. BMWi, Vermerk, Förderung des Zonenrandgebietes, n.d. [Sept. 18, 1964], PA/AA B38/162; see also Herold, "Zonenrandförderung," 2–3. Example of the criticized press coverage: "Ist hier das Ende der westlichen Welt? Schnackenburg: Die tote Stadt im toten Winkel," *Bonner Rundschau*, May 25, 1958; " 'Wir leben am Ende der Welt!': Schnackenburg hofft auf Touristen—Elbe-'Zollgetto' an der Zonengrenze," *Landeszeitung Lüneburg*, July 12, 1969.

55. In 1964, the Markus Verlag in Cologne contacted the government of Hesse, offering to publish a quarterly about the borderlands that would rectify the regions' image and pitch them to investors. The editor, Helmut Bohn, suggested the title "The Bridge." Hessian officials declined, and the magazine never materialized. The terms cited here stem from Bohn's 1964 analysis of the borderland image. Helmut Bohn to Heinz Kreutzmann, Oct. 23, 1964, HHAStW, Abt. 502, vol. 3614.

56. Alfred Dregger to Heinz Kreutzmann, June 30, 1964; Kreutzmann to Dregger, July 6, 1964, both in HHStAW Abt. 502/1082. Kreutzmann's political trajectory took him from the All-German Bloc / League of Expellees and Deprived of Rights (GB/BHE) via the All German Party (GDP) into the SPD. See Heinz Kreutzmann, "Neue Ostpolitik braucht alle Kräfte: Warum ich mich der SPD angeschlossen habe," *Sozialdemokratischer Pressedienst*, Jan. 26, 1967, 2.

57. *Zonenrandförderung—warum? wieviel? wofür? Die Bundesregierung zieht Bilanz* (Bonn: BMB, 1976); letter of Winfried Hasselmann (CDU) to Egon Franke (SPD), Aug. 26, 1976, printed in *Ostpreussenblatt*, Sept. 11, 1976, 4.

58. Heide, "Zonenrandförderung," 114.

59. Hughes, " 'Through No Fault of Our Own,' " 193–213. For a perceptive analysis of this kind of obligation rhetoric after World War I see Sammartino, *Impossible Border*, 96–119.

60. " 'Zonengrenze' auf den Müll: Ein Name verschwindet, eine Tatsache nicht," *Elbe-Jeetzel-Zeitung*, Dec. 6, 1973; "Bonn gibt wieder nach: Jetzt heisst es 'Grenze zur DDR,' " *BILD*, Mar. 23, 1973; renewed discussion of name change and reference to polls: Niedersächsischer Landkreistag, Ergebnisse der 36. Sitzung des Unterausschusses für Zonenrandfragen in Helmstedt, Mar. 24, 1982, Kreisarchiv DAN, OKD/Landrat Nr. 126/2. See also Butz, *Rechtsfragen*, 42–44.

61. All materials about this exhibition in BArch B137/7064.

62. " 'Unser Zuhause kann sich sehen lassen': Ausstellung über Zonenrandgebiet in Braunschweig—Höhere Förderung verlangt," *Braunschweiger Zeitung*, Oct. 28, 1978.

63. Memo on Braunschweig in BArch B137/7064. On Rollei see contemporary press coverage, e.g., "Photoindustrie: Rückzug aufs Kleinformat," *Der Spiegel*, Jan. 27, 1975, 58–60; Heinz Blüthmann, "Im Schlaf gestorben: Zeiss, Leitz, und Rollei haben gegen die Japaner keine Chance," *Die Zeit*, June 6, 1978.

64. Fiedler, "Ökonomischer Strukturwandel," 931–946; Schneider, "Wirtschafts-geschichte Niedersachsens nach 1945," 901–905.

65. Figures in OKD Wilhelm Paasche to Karl Schiller, Federal Minister for Economic Affairs, July 25, 1968, BArch B137/12604; Helmut von Schilling, "Ein verlassener Kreis wird noch verlassener," *Hannoversche Allgemeine Zeitung*, Nov. 1, 1975.

66. Memo on Lüchow-Dannenberg, Nov. 2, 1978, BArch B137/7064.

67. "Image vom Armenhaus hat katastrophale Folgen," *Fränkischer Tag*, Oct. 15, 1979. The article covers the exhibition's appearance at a fair in Lower Franconia.

68. Erwin Gnan, "Trotz guter Ausstellungsoptik stehen Wünsche offen: Unser Zuhause könnte sich noch besser sehen lassen," *Mittelbayerische Zeitung*, Nov. 17–18, 1979.

69. "Der Stadtdirektor ist gewohnt, dass alles, was aus Bonn kommt, Geld bringt." Cited in Werner Heine, "Warum ist es am Zonenrand so schön?," *Stern*, Aug. 7, 1975, 44–52, quote: 45.

70. Investors frequently combined investment incentives (*Investitionszulagengesetz*, 1969), loan guarantees from the state, cheap loans from the European Recovery Program (ERP) with the tools of borderland aid such as special depreciations and loss allocations. Investors could also count on eager local and regional politicians who did their best to "make things happen."

71. Ritter and Hajdu, *Innerdeutsche Grenze*, 236. See also "Bonbons für Geldgeber am Zonenrand," *Die Zeit*, Dec. 20, 1968. West Berlin experienced a similar building boom (Steglitzer Kreisel, Ku'Damm Carré, Bierpinsel, Neues Kreuzberger Zentrum at Kottbusser Tor) and endured a sizable number of real estate–related scandals. See "Berlin-Förderung: So exzessiv und schamlos," *Der Spiegel*, May 28, 1973, 38, 41.

72. Abelshauser, *Wirtschaftsgeschichte*, 392–396.

73. "Opas Ostsee ist tot: Feriencenter-Boom durch fehlgeleitete Steuergelder?," *Die Zeit*, Nov. 20, 1970; Klaus Broichhausen, "Goldgräberstimmung an den Küsten Schleswig-Holsteins," *Frankfurter Allgemeine Zeitung*, August 14, 1971; "Katastrophe im Wald," *Der Spiegel*, Feb. 7, 1972, 82; "Manhattan im Harz," *Der Spiegel*, May 5, 1972, 57–58.

74. "Ostsee-Bäder," *Der Spiegel*, Aug. 17, 1970, 70.

75. Rainer Burchardt, "Die Kolosse kollabieren: Die Steuerzahler büßen für die Fehler der Ferienmanager in Schleswig-Holstein," *Die Zeit*, Jan. 30, 1976; "Ferienwohnungen an der Ostsee: Sturmreif für kleine Käufer," *Die Zeit*, Aug. 19, 1977.

76. Niederschrift über die 69. Sitzung des Wirtschaftsausschusses des Bundesrats, Oct. 16, 1952, BArch B136/695.

77. A marketing brochure, issued by the state government of Schleswig-Holstein, offered a model calculation: by investing DM 2 million, an entrepreneur would receive a return of DM 417,550 via tax breaks and favorable interest rates. After

five years, the entrepreneur would have recovered 40 percent of the investment. Without borderland aid, he or she would recover only 17 percent. "Das bietet Schleswig-Holstein," *Hamburger Abendblatt*, Oct. 5, 1985.

78. "Senat kritisiert Zonenrandförderung," *Hamburger Abendblatt*, Aug. 10, 1972; "Wir wollen keinen Streit mit Hamburg," *Hamburger Abendblatt*, Aug. 11, 1972; "Der Senat mit Lübeck im Zwist," *Hamburger Abendblatt*, Aug. 16, 1972.

79. "Wir wollen keinen Streit mit Hamburg," *Hamburger Abendblatt*, Aug. 11, 1972; "Der Senat mit Lübeck im Zwist," *Hamburger Abendblatt*, Aug. 16, 1972.

80. "Hamburg ist benachteiligt," *Hamburger Abendblatt*, Nov. 18, 1977; "Abwanderung schwächt die Hamburger Wirtschaftskraft," *Hamburger Abendblatt*, Oct. 19, 1978.

81. Wiesemann, "Bedürftige und Förderungswürdige," 27–28.

82. [Wrangel], *Abgeordnete des Deutschen Bundestages*, 200.

83. European Union, *20th Report on Competition Policy, Comp. Rep. EC 1990* (Brussels: EU, 1991), part 310; Commission Decision of 18 July 1990 on aid granted by the city of Hamburg (91/389/EEC), OJ L215/1, Aug. 2, 1991, 541–550.

84. "60 Handwerksbetriebe verließen Hamburg," *Hamburger Abendblatt*, Oct. 4, 1986; "Der Fall Montblanc," *Hamburger Abendblatt*, June 16, 1987.

85. "Der Speckgürtel rund um Hamburg muß weg," *Hamburger Abendblatt*, Oct. 15, 1987; "Hamburg will Reform der Zonenrandförderung," *Hamburger Abendblatt*, Oct. 21, 1987; Hansestadt Hamburg, "Entwurf eines Gesetzes zur Steigerung der Effizienz der regionalen Wirtschaftspolitik," *Drucksache Bundesrat* Nr. 489/87, Nov. 13, 1987; without the Hamburg-specific context see also Berg, *Zonenrandförderung*, 24–25.

86. Quote ("geballte Zonenrand-Mafia") in Roland Bunzenthal, "Zonenrand heute: Nicht mehr Armenhaus, aber noch hintendran," *Frankfurter Rundschau*, June 20, 1981.

87. "Zonenrand-Förderung stoppen!" *Hamburger Abendblatt*, Dec. 22, 1989.

88. Art. 92(2)(c) EEC considered to be compatible with the common market "aid granted to the economy of certain areas of the Federal Republic of Germany affected by the division of Germany, in so far as such aid is required in order to compensate for the economic disadvantages caused by that division." After the Treaty of Amsterdam in 1999, the article was renumbered 87.

89. Aufzeichnung betr. Prüfung der deutschen Regionalförderung durch die EG-Kommission, Oct. 4, 1978, BArch B102/198711.

90. Klaphake, *Regionalpolitik*, 148–149; Karl, "Entwicklung und Ergebnisse," paras. 44–53.

91. Quote in European Commission, *Eleventh Report on Competition Policy, Comp. Rep. EC 1981* (Brussels: EC, 1982), part 226. The federal minister for economic affairs, Otto Graf Lambsdorff (FDP), negotiated with the commissioner for competition, Raymond Vouel, in October 1978 to prevent an official DG IV investigation (*Beihilfeprüfungsverfahren*) of borderland aid. See Aufzeichnung [defining goals of conversation between Lambsdorff and Vouel], Oct. 4, 1978; StS

Schlecht to Vouel, Oct. 24, 1978. On the opening of the investigation see Vouel
to Hans-Dietrich Genscher, Foreign Minister, Jan. 30, 1979. All documents in
BArch B102/198711.

92. Art. 92(2)(c) EEC.

93. Regionale Beihilferegelungen der Gemeinschaftsaufgabe von Bund und
Ländern, p. 4: Anlage zum Schreiben Vouel to Genscher, Jan. 30, 1979, BArch
B102/198711. The European Commission wanted to curb aid to the counties
east of Hamburg (Stormarn and Segeberg, p. 12), restrict aid to Wolfsburg,
Göttingen, Kassel, and Schweinfurt to two more years (pp. 19, 25, 30, 36), and
cut aid to Braunschweig (p. 23).

94. Freight subsidies, for instance, were acceptable because the longer distances from
border areas to western markets were clearly caused by partition and persisted.
BMWi, Abt. IC2, Aufzeichung betr. Prüfung der deutschen Regionalförderung
durch die EG-Kommission, Oct. 4, 1978, BArch B102/198711.

95. Regionale Beihilferegelungen der Gemeinschaftsaufgabe von Bund und
Ländern, pp. 2–3: Anlage zum Schreiben Vouel to Genscher, Jan. 30, 1979,
BArch B102/198711.

96. OJC/316/5, Dec. 4, 1981.

97. [BMWi], Leiter Abt. E [Rechtsabt.] an BMin über StS, Sicherung der
Zonenrandförderung im Rahmen der Beitrittsverhandlungen mit
Griechenland, Oct. 12, 1978, BArch B102/198711.

98. The Ministry for Inter-German Affairs was so incensed by the audacity of
the EC to request a report on the borderlands that it suggested refusing to
make such a report. See Vorbericht für die 36. Sitzung des Unterausschusses
für Zonenrandfragen am 24. März 1982, in Helmstedt, Kreisarchiv Lüchow-
Dannenberg, Bestand OKD/Landrat Nr. 125/2.

99. Mitteilung der Regierung der Bundesrepublik Deutschland an die Kommission
der Europäischen Gemeinschaften, Jan. 8, 1982, as attachment to Vorbericht
für die 36. Sitzung des Unterausschusses für Zonenrandfragen am 24. März
1982, in Helmstedt, Kreisarchiv Lüchow-Dannenberg, Bestand OKD/Landrat
Nr. 125/2. See also BT, 9. WP, Drs. 9/1449.

100. Since the EC needed data sets that existed in each member state in order to engage in any comparison, it turned to GNP per capita and labor market statistics.
Already at the time, economic geographers pointed out that the national data
sets were incompatible because the underlying spatial parameters differed. See
Ortmeyer, "Regionalpolitik," 131; Klemmer, "Raumgliederung," 87–99.

101. Vermerk über die Sitzung der Referenten der Wirtschaftsministerien der
Zonenrandländer am 8/9 Sept. 1977 in Bad Sooden-Allendorf. Kassel, Sept.
20, 1977, Archiv der Hansestadt Lübeck (AHL), 02.05: IHK zu Lübeck, vol.
1955. In this meeting, representatives of the economics ministries in the
Länder adjacent to the border were disturbed that the borderlands were not
featured in the EC's plan for regional development ("Orientierungsrahmen für

die Regionalpolitik der Gemeinschaft," June 1, 1977). See also Vermerk von Preuschen, BMWi, Die europäische Regionalpolitik und das Zonenrandgebiet, July 11, 1973, PA/AA B202/105690.

102. Vermerk über die Sitzung der Referenten der Wirtschaftsministerien der Zonenrandländer am 8/9 IX 1977 in Bad Sooden-Allendorf. Kassel, Sept. 20, 1977, Archiv der Hansestadt Lübeck (AHL), 02.05: IHK zu Lübeck, vol. 1955.

103. Bericht der Regierung der Bundesrepublik Deutschland über die Lage und Entwicklung des Zonenrandgebietes, [Feb. 8, 1983], BArch B102/330232. The study of Berg, *Zonenrandförderung*, is entirely conceived as support for the German position in this dispute.

104. Walter Giesler, "Hände weg von der Zonenrandförderung," *Kurhessische Wirtschaft* 7 (1982): 323; Ergebnisvermerk, Sitzung des Arbeitskreises der Zonenrandreferenten am 23 Nov. 1981 in Coburg, BArch B102/330232.

105. Quote in OJ/L300/34, Oct. 24, 1986. The Commission prohibited subsidies to a factory manufacturing synthetic fiber in Neumünster, Schleswig-Holstein (OJ/L/181, July 13, 1985, 42–46), a similar factory in Deggendorf, Bavaria (OJ/L300/34, Oct. 24, 1986), and, in a late decision, a steel company in Salzgitter, Lower Saxony (OJ/L/323, decision 2000/797/EGKS, Dec. 20, 2000).

106. BT-Drs. 11/5037, Aug. 4, 1989, Nr. 22: The Ministry for Economic Affairs denied the assumption implied in the inquiry of MP Böhm (CDU/CSU) that the EU Commission was planning to ask Bonn to terminate borderland aid by 1992.

107. The term "DMark-ation" is borrowed from Schaefer, *States of Division*, 18. Since the TV cameras were rolling elsewhere, though, the first breach of the border remains little known. See Lars Broder-Keil, "Die Ersten," *Die Welt*, Nov. 7, 2009.

108. Figure in "Tätigkeitsbericht des BGS 1989," *Zeitschrift des BGS*, 17:4 (Apr. 1990): 9.

109. Mayor Oskar Herbig, Mellrichstadt, to Bavarian StK, Dec. 1, 1989, BayHStA StK 19461 with handwritten response on document "beste Grenzlandförderung."

110. The welcome money had been introduced in 1970 and increased from DM 30 to 100 in 1988. It was intended to alleviate the shortage of western currency for eastern travelers, especially retirees, who faced disadvantageous exchange rates and currency export restrictions from their own government. In early December 1989, Chancellor Helmut Kohl estimated the amount disbursed as welcome money to stand at DM 1.8 billion. See DzD Special Edition 1: *Deutsche Einheit: Sonderedition aus den Akten des Bundeskanzleramtes 1989/90*, doc. Nr. 109, 601–602. When the welcome money was discontinued on January 1, 1990, the West German government subsidized currency exchanges for East German citizens. They could exchange 600 east marks into 200 west marks per year. With the introduction of the currency union in June 1990, this scheme became obsolete. See Grosser, *Wagnis*, 140.

111. On Braunschweig and Duderstadt: "Die Katastrophe ist da," *Der Spiegel*, Nov. 13, 1989, 131; on Lübeck see Meyer-Rebentisch, *Grenzerfahrungen*, 108.

112. Nikolaus Piper, "Von der Mark geschockt," *Die Zeit*, Nov., 17, 1989.

113. Kaminsky, "Konsumwünsche," 106. On Hamburg see editorial by "ds," *Hamburger Abendblatt*, Nov. 13, 1989. See also Sheffer, *Burned Bridge*, 240–257; Berdahl, *Where the World Ended*, 155–181.

114. Quote in DzD—Special Edition 1: *Deutsche Einheit*, doc. Nr. 109, 601–602.

115. Michael Sontheimer, "Schmuggler, Schieber, Spekulanten," *Die Zeit*, Dec. 1, 1989.

116. Ibid.; "Stasi an den Schlagbaum: Interview mit Henry Otto, Stellvertretender Leiter der Zollfahndung der DDR," *Die Zeit*, Dec. 1, 1989; "Ostmark zum Willkür-Kurs," *Der Spiegel*, Nov. 27, 1989.

117. Interview with Karl B., July 5, 2014, in Ilsenburg, Harz.

118. BMU to Oberste Naturschutzbehörden der Länder, Mar. 27, 1990, Betr. Illegale Einfuhren von geschützen Tieren und Pflanzen aus der DDR, BArch B295/20719.

119. Roland Kirbach, "Sonneberg: Die tägliche Demütigung," *Neue Presse* (Coburg), Mar. 10, 1990; also in *Die Zeit*, Mar. 9, 1990. West Germans were also concerned that East Germans might take up residence on the western side just to collect welfare. See Dirk Kurbjuweit, "Stunde der Schwindler," *Die Zeit*, June 15, 1990.

120. Steiner, "DDR-Volkswirtschaft," 124.

121. Roland Kirbach, "Sonneberg: Die tägliche Demütigung," *Neue Presse* (Coburg), Mar. 10, 1990; also in *Die Zeit*, Mar. 9, 1990.

122. Michael Sontheimer, "Schmuggler, Schieber, Spekulanten," *Die Zeit*, Dec. 1, 1989.

123. Roland Kirbach, "Sonneberg: Die tägliche Demütigung," *Neue Presse* (Coburg), Mar. 10, 1990; Sheffer, *Burned Bridge*, 243–247.

124. Sheffer, *Burned Bridge*, 244. See also Berdahl, *Where the World Ended*, 155–160.

125. Mayor Oskar Herbig, Mellrichstadt, to Bavarian State Chancery, Dec. 1, 1989, BayHStA StK 19461.

126. The theme of moving back into "the center" was ubiquitous around 1990. See, e.g., Berthold Kohler, "Aus dem oberfränkischen Grenzland soll wieder die gute Stube Europeas werden," *Frankfurter Allgemeine Zeitung*, Jan. 9, 1990; Tobias Piller, "Die Stadt Hof fühlt sich nicht mehr in 'Bayerisch Sibirien,'" *Frankfurter Allgemeine Zeitung*, June 6, 1990; "Mitte statt Ende der Welt," *Der Spiegel*, Jan. 1, 1990, 21–22.

127. For an analysis of the influential trope of the periphery becoming the center in the government brochure "*In the Heart of Germany—In the 20th Century*," see Ullrich, *Geteilte Ansichten*, 107–117.

128. Besides aid to West Berlin and the borderlands, the main items of partition-related liabilities consisted of transit fees imposed by the GDR for the use of

roads to West Berlin (*Transitpauschale*); money slated for the buyout of political prisoners from the GDR; support for migrants from the GDR (*Übersiedler*); and the currency exchange scheme that had replaced the welcome money in January 1990.

129. Helmut Kohl, Regierungserklärung zur 12. Wahlperiode, BT, 12. WP 1991, StB, 5. Sitzung, Jan. 30, 1991, 73B: "This is why state aids that have lost their initial justification and that have become a dear habit for many in the old Federal Republic cannot be extended in perpetuity. This holds in particular for zonal bordeland aid."

130. 13. Subventionsbericht der Bundesregierung (13th Subvention Report), BT-Drs. 12/1525, Nov. 11, 1991, App. 1, item 84, p. 116.

131. Ibid., 37 and Übersicht 17, 38–39. Figures for West Berlin and the borderlands were not reported separately; the bulk of the increase in tax revenue stemmed from the phaseout of tax incentives in Berlin.

132. On figures for the 1980s see Offer, *Zonenrandgebiet*, 80. The overall budget from 1991 to 1994 for cultural and social projects was DM 270 million. The money was slated to conclude projects already under way or in concrete planning stages. BT, 12. WP 1991, StB, 18. Sitzung, Mar. 21, 1991, 1195C/D.

133. Jahresgutachten 1990/91 des Sachverständigenrates zur Begutachtung der gesamtwirtschaftlichen Entwicklung, 151, 191.

134. Dirk Kurbjuweit, "Schatten über den Mauerblümchen: Der Umbruch in der DDR macht die Hilfen für das Grenzland langfristig überflüssig," *Die Zeit*, May 11, 1990. See also Andresen, "Finanzierung der Einheit," 376–377.

135. The law abolishing the tax incentives of borderland aid was the Tax Modification Law (Steueränderungsgesetz, StÄndG) of 1991. On Waigel's suspected role see "Die Rechnung kommt später," *Der Spiegel*, Sept. 3, 1990, 135; "Der ehemalige Zonenrand wird noch zwei Jahre länger gefördert," *Frankfurter Allgemeine Zeitung*, Sept. 22, 1993.

136. On social and cultural projects, e.g.: BT, 12. WP 1991, Drs. 12/160, queries 9-12, Feb. 22, 1991; on ersatz programs, e.g.: Drs. 12/4792, query 44, Apr. 23, 1993.

137. The so-called Brittan-Möllemann Compromise of 1991 held that regional aid within the Common Tasks program would be reduced to covering regions inhabited by 27 percent of West Germany's population. It built on an earlier agreement with a similar thrust (Sutherland-Bangeman Compromise, 1988) but now contained the condition that borderland aid and aid for West Berlin be phased out. See Nägele, *Regionale Wirtschaftspolitik*, 163–164; Schwengler, *Einfluss*, 23–24. Reference to the meeting as "dramatic" in BT, 12. WP 1991, StB, 8. Sitzung, Feb. 20, 1991, 303D.

138. Art. 92(2)c EEC.

139. Wössner, *Deutschlandklausel*, 103–106, 114–120; Wishlade, *Regional State Aid*, 25–28.

140. Bürkner, "Regionalentwicklung," with tables 285–286; term "unification boom," 285; Erdmann, "Ende der Welt."

141. Berdahl, *Where the World Ended*, 114–126, 132–139, quote: 136.

142. Bürkner, "Probleme der Regionalentwicklung," 287–288; Erdmann, "Am Ende der Welt."

143. Sheffer, *Burned Bridge*, 248.

144. Jung/Krüsemann, *Struktur- und Entwicklungsprobleme*, 79–80.

145. Ibid., 93, 110

146. Bürkner, "Probleme der Regionalentwicklung," 281. The phenomenon of the "extended workbench" (whereby toll manufacturers finish a product developed and preproduced elsewhere) was also common in West Berlin and in Austria's Waldviertel (Forest Quarter). See Ahrens, "Teure Gewohnheiten," 289, 296; Komlosy, "Waldviertel," 247–292.

147. Jung and Krüsemann, *Struktur- und Entwicklungsprobleme*, 92, 110. Duderstadt lost 700 jobs in the electrical and textile industries to Eastern Europe. Helmstedt lost one company that way and was hurt by the closing of another, losing 700 jobs as well. Similar processes unfolded in the Austrian Waldviertel. See Komlosy, "Auswirkungen der Grenzöffnung."

148. Jung and Krüsemann, *Struktur- und Entwicklungsprobleme*, 93–94, 110–111; Rosenfeld and Kawka, "Regionale Differenzierungen," 33. On the warehouse see Jones and Wild, "Opening the Frontier," 270.

149. Jung and Krüsemann, *Struktur- und Entwicklungsprobleme*, 96, 104–105, 113.

150. Rosenfeld and Kawka, "Regionale Differenzierungen," 27–33; Heller, "Grenzüberschreitende Beziehungen."

151. Carla Ihle-Becker, "Europas grösstes Logistikzentrum," *Frankfurter Rundschau*, Aug. 27, 2008.

152. Erdmann, "Am Ende der Welt."

153. Examples of alarmist reports: Tina Kaiser, "Zonenrand ist abgebrannt," *Die Welt*, Nov. 2, 2003; Sebastian Fischer, "Wie Wessis im Zonenrandgebiet ums Überleben kämpfen," *Spiegel online*, Aug. 10, 2007. Examples of stories about success: Jan Hildebrand, "Eine Bauchentscheidung für den alten Westen," *Die Welt*, Oct. 27, 2010; Claus Peter Müller, "Vom Zonenrand in den Mittelpunkt," *Frankfurter Allgemeine Zeitung*, June 29, 2011.

154. Examples: Ute Semkat, "Neid im früheren Zonenrandgebiet—auf den Osten," *Die Welt*, Apr., 8, 1997; "Mühen einstiger Zonenrandgebiete in Bayern: Die Grenzorte Unterfrankens leiden unter dem Aufbau Ost," *Neue Zürcher Zeitung*, Aug. 21, 2001; "Zeit, dass sich was dreht," *Der Spiegel*, Apr. 23, 2007, 56–58; Christopher Schwarz, "Mitten am Rand der innerdeutschen Grenze," *Wirtschaftswoche*, Oct. 25, 2009.

155. Ahrens, "Teure Gewohnheiten," 299, points out that what is disparagingly called a "subsidy mentality" is actually a rational economic approach even if it

leads to rent-seeking behavior, i.e., economic activity for the sake of collecting subsidies.

156. Gnest, *Entwicklung der überörtlichen Raumplanung.*

157. "Gleichwertige Lebensverhältnisse: Diskussionspaper des Präsidiums der Akademie für Raumfoschung und Landesplanung," *Nachrichten der ARL* 2 (2005): 1–3; Barlösius, "Gleichwertig ist nicht gleich."

158. "Ostdeutsche Politiker kritisieren Köhler," *Frankfurter Allgemeine Zeitung*, Sept. 13, 2004. The issue continues to be framed as an East German one. See, e.g., Martin Greive, "Wir müssen Wohlstandsunterschiede hinnehmen," *Die Welt*, May 5, 2014.

159. "Studie zur Landflucht: Interview mit Horand Knaup, *Spiegel online*, Jan. 13, 2015; Claus Christian Maltzahn, "Gebeutelte Provinz: Siechtum deutscher Dörfer," *Die Welt*, July 22, 2014; Katja Auer, "Bayerns Bruchbuden: Leerstand im ländlichen Raum," *Süddeutsche Zeitung*, Feb. 25, 2015; Lucia Schmidt, "Mittendrin und doch ganz am Rand," *Frankfurter Allgemeine Zeitung*, June 16, 2012, 3.

160. Examples of former borderland municipalities: Schulz, "Kommunal-Fusion"; Hessischer Landtag, 15. WP, Drs. 19/1741, Mar. 17, 2015; "Elbgemeinden-Fusion überraschend geplatzt," *Hamburger Abendblatt*, Nov. 13, 2009.

161. Hans-Christoph Seebohm (CDU), "Zonenrandhilfe dient der Wiedervereinigung," in *Kreisblatt für Helmstedt: Sonderausgabe: 10 Jahre Zonengrenzkreis* (Dec. 1955), 13.

162. Wolfrum, *Die geglückte Demokratie*, 286–287. On the growing accommodation of partition see also Wolfrum, *Geschichtspolitik.*

CHAPTER 3

1. Schroers, "Die Sackgasse (1962)," 72.

2. Wright, *Iron Curtain*, traces the emergence of the Iron Curtain as political metaphor.

3. "Zwischenfall an der Grenze," *Lübecker Nachrichten*, July 22, 1956.

4. Quote: "Rummelplatz für Reisegesellschaften," in "Vopo räumte alle Hindernisse ab. Abbau nur an der Lübecker Zonengrenze," *Lübecker Freie Presse am Morgen*, June 3, 1959.

5. 1965 figure: Besuch der Arbeitsgruppe Zonenrandgebiet der SPD-Bundestagsfraktion am 28./29. Mai 1970 im Zonengrenzbezirk Gifhorn-Lüchow Dannenberg, HHStAW Abt. 502/1080. 1978 figure: Verzeichnis der Informationsstellen an der Grenze zur DDR. Stand: Januar 1979, NLA HA, Nds. 380, Acc. 160/95 Nr. 1. On the counting of visitors see Eckert, "Greetings," sec. 1.

6. "Wandern an der Zonengrenze," *Lübecker Nachrichten*, Nov. 1, 1964.

7. Towers are discussed further later in this chapter. The map of a hiking trail near Helmstedt is printed in Eckert, "Zaun-Gäste," 244.

8. Krenzer, "Eßkultur und Agrarkultur," 39.

9. Cited in Eckert, "Zaun-Gäste," 245. After 1990, tourism in Hitzacker collapsed. See Jelena Pflocksch, "Für Hitzacker ist der Mauerfall ein Desaster," *Die Welt*, Aug. 17, 2009.

10. Sheffer, *Burned Bridge*, 34–49; Johnson, *Divided Village*, 29–64. On migration from West to East Germany see Stöver, *Zuflucht DDR*; on kidnappings see Muhle, *Menschenraub*.

11. Foley and Lennon, "JFK and Dark Tourism," 198. I applied the category of dark tourism in Eckert, "Greetings."

12. For an overview of the field and terminology see Seaton, "Thanatourism"; Skinner, "Introduction"; Rosenbaum, "Dark Tourism"; Frank, *Checkpoint Charlie*, 170–178.

13. Bigley et al., "Motivations for War-Related Tourism."

14. Timothy, "Collecting Places." On the practice of taking photos at the Korean DMZ see Hunter, "Visual Representation."

15. Standley, "Bulwark of Freedom," 105–118; Wolfrum, "Die Mauer," 552–568; Derix, *Bebilderte Politik*, 93, and on the display of partition in Berlin during the 1960s, 107–124.

16. Paasi, *Finnish–Russian Border*, 127–132.

17. Baker, "Berlin Wall"; Light, "Gazing on Communism."

18. Frank, *Checkpoint Charlie*, 129–146; Löytynoja, "National Boundaries," 42–43.

19. Békési, "Ansichtskarte"; Hoerner, "Ansichtspostkarten." On the history of European tourism see Withey, *Grand Tours*; Hachtmann, *Tourismus-Geschichte*.

20. Békési, "Ansichtskarte," 411.

21. Ibid., 412, 415; Thumer, "Tourismus und Fotografie," 23–40, esp. 27, 31.

22. Koshar, "Tourists' Guidebooks."

23. Békési, "Ansichtskarte," 416; Winiwarter, "Buying a Dream Come True," 451–455.

24. This was a so-called *Hauskarte*, produced by the owner or licensee of the inn as an advertisement. I found all cards discussed in this section in an online auction forum and either acquired or downloaded them. For further discussion of this postcard see Eckert, "Greetings," sec. 3.

25. Delius and Lapp, *Transit Westberlin*; Dossmann, "Stimmungsbarometer."

26. See a number of cards reproduced in Eckert, "Greetings."

27. Ullrich, *Geteilte Ansichten*, 100–101.

28. Card published in Eckert, "Greetings," sec. 4.

29. On the centrality of barbed wire see Ullrich, *Geteilte Ansichten*, 61–66; on reading postcards in the context of other media see Békési, "Ansichtskarte," 406.

30. Schmoll, "Ritualisierung," 183–198; Urry, *Tourist Gaze*, 32; Lèofgren, *On Holiday*, 44–46.

31. On the Lauenstein and Bodesruh towers see Ullrich, *Geteilte Ansichten*, 77–85. Towers along the Bavarian–Czech border served the primary purpose of allowing

views into the former *Heimat* of Sudeten Germans. See Komska, *Icon Curtain*, 207–212, 221–233.

32. Feindobjektakte "Thüringenblick," Außenstelle des BStU Suhl, XI/584/ 84. I thank Reinhold Albert, Sternberg, for sharing this file with me. Fifteen-kilometer reference: NVA, 13. Grenzbrigade, Unterabteilung Aufklärung, May 24, 1963, BArch-MA, GT 1057.

33. "Aussichtsturm verlor seine Bedeutung: Symbolträchtige Plattform abgerissen [. . .]," *Goslarsche Zeitung*, Jan. 18, 1990. See also Ullrich, *Geteilte Ansichten*, 153–155, 158.

34. *Zonengrenze Niedersachsen*, ed. Nds. Ministerium für Vertriebene und Flüchtlinge (1964; further editions 1966, 1968); Rolf Seufert, "'Baedeker' für die Zonengrenze: Auch Dokumentations-Zentren," *Die Welt*, Jan. 4, 1965.

35. On the history of Baedeker see Müller, *Welt des Baedeker*; Koshar, *German Travel Cultures*, 19–64; on guidebooks more generally see Koshar, "Tourists' Guidebooks."

36. Thies, *Zicherie*.

37. Johnson, *Divided Village*.

38. Quote in "Der Kreistag an der Zonengrenze," *Weilburger Tagblatt*, Aug. 10, 1965; Shears, *Ugly Frontier*, 182–183; Clute-Simon and Emmerich, *Haus auf der Grenze*. The eastern half of the building was returned to the owners in 1976 as a result of the work of the German-German Border Commission (Grenzkommission).

39. Hessische Landeszentrale für politische Bildung, ed., *Die Zonengrenzfahrt* (Wiesbaden, 1964); Bayerischer Staatsminister für Bundesangelegenheiten, *Zonengrenze Bayern*, n.d. [1970s]; *Die Grenze: Schleswig-Holsteins Landesgrenze zur DDR*, 3rd ed., ed. Innenminister des Landes Schleswig-Holstein (Kiel, 1985).

40. Heinz D. Stuckmann, "An der Elbe—an der Grenze," *Die Zeit*, Oct. 9, 1964. The article mocks border tourists and the town's officials as anti-Communist zealots. In 1994, Stuckmann (by then head of a journalism school in Cologne) was uncovered as a Stasi agent and convicted for treason. See Karl Wilhelm Fricke, "Bekenntnisse von IM Dietrich," *Deutschlandfunk*, May 29, 2006, http://www. deutschlandfunk.de/bekenntnisse-von-im-dietrich.730.de.html?dram:article_id=102658 (accessed Jan. 2018).

41. These incidents were meticulously documented in the daily and weekly reports of the West German BGS and Customs Border Service (ZGD). They were also covered in the local press. Example: "Englischer Pfadfinder war unvorsichtig: Er betrat den Zehnmeterstreifen bei Grüsselbach und wurde von Volkspolizisten festgenommen," *Fuldaer Zeitung*, Aug. 14–15, 1961; Customs Office Fulda to Regional Finance Office Frankfurt/M., Telex Nr. 105, Aug. 18, 1961.

42. Examples: BM Finanz, Grenzzwischenfälle und -nachrichten, Aug. 26, 1963, PA/ AA B38/51; "Neue Grenzzwischenfälle belasten Verhältnis zur DDR erheblich," *Hessisch-Niedersächsische Allgemeine*, July 26, 1976.

43. The "border situation reports" (*Grenzlageberichte*) issued by the Ministry of Finance aggregated reports from all customs offices along the border and indicate a peak of incidents for the years 1961–1965. The reports are, e.g., in PA/AA B38/50–52.

44. Hessische Landeszentrale für politische Bildung, ed., *Die Zonengrenzfahrt* (Wiesbaden, 1964), 14.

45. "Rowdys an der Grenze," *Lübecker Freie Presse am Morgen*, June 16, 1957; "Zwischenfall an der Grenze," *Lübecker Nachrichten*, July 22, 1956; "Grenzpfähle als 'Andenken' demontiert," *Lübecker Freie Presse am Morgen*, Feb. 19, 1957. GDR border guards meticulously documented each such incident. See Dokumentation über provokatorische Handlungen durch Beschmieren und Beschädigung einer Grenzsäule an der Staatsgrenze der DDR durch unbekannte Täter, July 22, 1977, BStU, MfS, HA I Nr. 6.

46. Kind-Kovács, "Local Iron Curtain," 213; Sheffer, *Burned Bridge*, 202–203.

47. Böckel, *Erlebnisse eines "West-Grenzers,"* 73. Western advocates of unification criticized the involvement of the BGS in such criminal charges. They argued that federal law was wrongly enlisted to defend the GDR's state symbols. See the file BArch B106/83948: Strafverfolgung bei Beschädigung oder Entwendung von Emblemschildern und Betongrenzpfählen an der Demarkationslinie, 1967–1971.

48. BM Finanz, Grenzzwischenfälle und -nachrichten (Mar. 1964), Apr. 2, 1964, PA/AA B38/52.

49. "1,5 Meter Zaun auf 1 Kilometer Grenze: Wege gesperrt—DDR-Gebiet schon diesseits des 'Todesstreifens,'" *Lübecker Freie Presse am Morgen*, June 15, 1956; Hauptzollamt Lübeck West to Mayor of Lübeck, June 25, 1961, Stadtarchiv der Hansestadt Lübeck, Bestand 04.01-0 Zentralamt, Hauptamt Nr. 154. See also "Dicke Ankerkette sorgt am Priwall für Sicherheit," *Lübecker Nachrichten*, May 21, 1983.

50. For maps showing postwar territorial exchanges see Ritter and Hajdu, *Innerdeutsche Grenze*, 29–33; on bickering about land see Schaefer, *States of Division*, 79–82, 109–116.

51. Jureit, *Ordnen von Räumen*, 89–117, 227–234.

52. On the Border Commission see Füsslein, *Grenzkommission*; Nass, *Vermessung*.

53. Harvey, "'Bleeding Border'"; Haller, "'Heilige Ostmark'"; Spode, "'Kraft durch Freude' Tourism."

54. Brief overview in Weitz, "Communism;" see also Creuzberger and Hoffmann, "Antikommunismus," 5–6. On the idea of anti-Communism as the new nationalism see Wolfrum, *Geschichtspolitik*, 108.

55. Wolfrum, *Geschichtspolitik*, 115–121; Meyer, *Doppelstrategie*, 18–19, 53–76.

56. On the Consortium's activities see Meyer, *Doppelstrategie*, 130–137, 159–180, 209–217, 303–311; on June 17: 143–158, 240–303, 409–435; Doering-Manteuffel, "Innerdeutsche Grenze," 135–138.

57. Hans Walter Conrady, Helmstedt, to Gerhard Schröder, BMI, Feb., 25 1956, NLA WO, NL Conrady, 94 N Nr. 438; Conrady to BM Geamtdt. Fragen, n.d. (June 1959), BArch B137/1475.

58. "Erstes 'Zonenrandhaus' eingeweiht," *Frankfurter Allgemeine Zeitung*, Mar. 2, 1960; Ullrich, *Geteilte Ansichten*, 59–60.

59. Ullrich, *Geteilte Ansichten*, 59–60.

60. Heinz Kreutzmann, Bericht über die Besichtigung von Informationszentren entlang der Zonengrenze in Niedersachsen, Aug. 6, 1965; Zonengrenzberatungsdienst Niedersachsen, Maßnahmen zur Förderung des Zonenrandbesuchs, Nov. 12, 1965, both in HHStAW Abt. 502/11108a.

61. Verzeichnis der Informationsstellen an der Grenze zur DDR, Stand: Januar 1979, NLA HA, Nds. 380, Acc. 160/95 Nr. 1.

62. Kurt von Gleichen, "Die Grenznähe macht politisch aufgeweckter: Kleine Reise längs des Eisernen Vorhangs im Herbst 1951," *Neue Zeitung*, Nov. 13, 1951.

63. Ullrich, *Geteilte Ansichten*, 49; Steinle, *Feindbild*, 169, 172, 190–191.

64. *Zonengrenze Bayern*, ed. Bayerischer Staatsminister für Bundesangelegenheiten, n.d. [1970s].

65. Zahra, *Great Departure*, 20–21, 223–224.

66. *Zonengrenze Niedersachsen*, ed. Niedersächsischer Minister für Bundesangelegenheiten, für Vertriebene und Flüchtlinge, 1966, 1.

67. *Die Zonengrenzfahrt*, ed. Hessische Landeszentrale für Politische Bildung, 1964, 3.

68. *Zonengrenze Niedersachsen*, 2. See also the 1968 edition, 2.

69. Voraus-Auszug aus der Niederschrift über die [Bayerische] Ministerratssitzung vom Dienstag, 3. Juli 1979, BayHStA, StK/19489. The Bavarian minister of the interior, Gerold Tandler, said that "border tours [. . .] could serve as preventive measures against communist infiltration of our youth if the young people could see the conditions along the border to the GDR."

70. *In the Heart of Germany—In the 20th Century* (Bonn: Federal Ministry of All-German Affairs, 1960); *En el Corazon de Alemania en Pleno Siglo XX: La Frontera con la Zona* (Bonn and Berlin: Ministerio Federal para Asuntos de Toda Alemania, 1965); *Unmenschliche Grenze: Inhuman Frontier—Omänskliga Gränser* (Hannover: Niedersächsische Landeszentrale für Heimatdienst, 1958). The first two titles are a version of the government publication *Mitten in Deutschland*. The Federal Ministry for Inter-German Relations also considered printing brochures in Italian and Turkish to cater to the increasing number of "guest workers" among the border visitors. See Ministry to all Information Points and Visitor Centers, Nov. 28, 1974, HHStAW Abt. 502/7516b.

71. A number of such itineraries and the cooperation with the Foreign Office are documented in NLA HA Nds. 50 Acc. 96/88 Nr. 156/1.

72. Delegation of the French European Movement, visit in Feb. 1960, NLA HA Nds. 50 Acc. 96/88 Nr. 156/1.

73. Ibid. The MP was Edouard Rieunaud of the Mouvement Républicain Populaire (MRP), a Christian Democratic party that promoted French–German reconciliation.

74. "Südamerikanische Bischöfe von der Zonengrenze erschüttert," *Die Parole*, Feb. 15, 1964, 12.

75. Ullrich, *Geteilte Ansichten*, 61–65; Steinle, *Feindbild*, 168–169. The apex of the western concentration camp analogy came with the building of the Berlin Wall. See Ahonen, *Death*, 27.

76. Legationsrat I Junges, AA, Ref. 991, Aufzeichnung, Reise einer Delegation des Comité de Liaison de la Résistance durch Deutschland und nach Berlin, Nov. 1959, NLA HA Nds. 50 Acc. 96/88 Nr. 156/2.

77. Halin was a Belgian socialist involved in sabotage during the German occupation. After the war, he became a professional resistance activist and an anti-Communist militant. See Lagrou, *Nazi Occupation*, 270, 282–284.

78. Legationsrat I Junges, AA, Ref. 991, Aufzeichnung, Reise einer Delegation des Comité de Liaison de la Résistance durch Deutschland und nach Berlin, Nov. 1959, NLA HA Nds. 50 Acc. 96/88 Nr. 156/2.

79. Kreutzmann to State Governor of Hesse, Bericht über die Besichtigung von Informationszentren entlang der Zonengrenze in Niedersachsen, Aug. 6, 1965, HHStAW Abt. 502/11108a. See also "Grenzbesucher werden beraten," *Lübecker Nachrichten*, Aug. 21, 1964; Steffens, *Lebensjahre*, 113–114, Ullrich, *Geteilte Ansichten*, 53.

80. Kreutzmann to StateSec Günter Wetzel, BM Gesamtdt. Fragen, Dec. 16, 1968, HHAStAW Abt. 502/7516a.

81. Kreutzmann to State Governor of Hesse Georg-August Zinn, Dec. 12, 1967, HHStAW Abt. 502/11108a.

82. Olaf von Wrangel to State Governor of Bavaria Alfons Goppel, Mar. 19, 1974, BayHStA, Bay. StK Nr. 19489.

83. Arnold, Director of the Hessian State Agency for Political Education, to Sprenger, Commissioner for Matters Relating to the Borderland to the GDR, Mar. 6, 1980, HHStAW Abt. 502/7527.

84. Landkreis Eschwege, Bericht der Informations- und Betreuungsstelle für Zonengrenzbesucher, Jan. 20, 1971, HHStAW Abt. 502/11109a; Nds. StK, Vermerk über den Besuch der Zonengrenze, Apr. 16, 1971, Nds. 50 Acc 96/88 Nr 157.

85. Brückner, Nds. Min. für Bundesangelegenheiten, to BM Gesamtdt. Fragen, Feb. 20 1976, NLA HA Nds. 380, Acc. 160/95 Nr. 1.

86. *Die Grenze: Schleswig-Holsteins Landesgrenze zur DDR*, 3rd ed., ed. Innenminister des Landes Schleswig-Holstein (Kiel, 1985); *Deutschland diesseits und jenseits der Grenze. Niedersachsen*, ed. Nds. Minister für Bundesangelegenheiten, 1982; *The Border between Hesse and the GDR: Brief Information for Visitors*, ed. Hessendienst der Staatskanzlei (1986).

87. *Die Innerdeutsche Grenze*, ed. BM Innerdt. Beziehungen (1987), 61–112, quotes 61, 62, 112.

88. Grenzinformationszentren in Niedersachsen, n.d. [May 1986], NLA HA Nds. 380, Acc. 160/95 Nr. 2; Nds. Ministerium für Bundes- und Europaangelegenheiten to Bezirksregierung Braunschweig, July 5, 1988, NLA HA Nds. 120 Lüneburg, Acc. 160/95 Nr. 4.

89. Memo for State Secretary, submitted for political decision, Oct. 27, 1989, NLA HA Nds. 380, Acc 160/95 Nr. 3.

90. Heinz Kreutzmann, Bericht über die Sitzung der Zonenrandländer und Bonner Ministerien im Gesamtdeutschen Ministerium in Bonn bezügl. der Errichtung von Info- und Beratungsstellen für Zonengrenzfahrten, Dec. 23, 1964, HHStAW Abt. 502/11108a. On West German tourism preferences during the mid-1960s see Spode, *"Reiseweltmeister,"* 145–150.

91. Quote in "Mobilisierung der Hilfen für das Zonenrandgebiet: Landrat Dr. Stieler fordert Planungen auf längere Sicht," *Fuldaer Volkszeitung*, July 15, 1964; on *Bundesbahn* see Stoll, *Grenze*, 120.

92. Owczarski, *Weihnachtsbasar*, 15–19.

93. Klaus von der Brelie, "Tag für Tag rollen die Busse an die deutsch-deutsche Grenze: Informationsdienst erläutert Besuchern das Zonenrandgebiet," *Hannoversche Allgemeine Zeitung*, June 18, 1984.

94. "Zonengrenze 1958," *Lübecker Freie Presse am Morgen*, July 16, 1958.

95. Dieter Hildebrandt, "Leben am Todesstreifen: Ein Bericht von der Grenze in Deutschland," *Frankfurter Allgemeine Zeitung*, June 16, 1960, 11.

96. "Die Flucht mit Lok 83," *Bild* series beginning Sept. 8, 1969; information on enterprising Helmstedters by Margrit Sterly, Director, Helmstedt Border Museum, June 2007.

97. Eckert, "Greetings," sec. 13; Schroers, "Die Sackgasse (1962)," 72.

98. I am correcting the impression I gave in Eckert, "Greetings," sec. 4.

99. Schaefer, *States of Division*, 152.

100. "Flaggen zum 1. Mai an der Zonengrenze: Skandinavische Fahnen grüssen jenseits der Schlagbäume—Grenze immer noch 'Sehenswürdigkeit' für Ausländer," *Lübecker Freie Presse am Morgen*, May 1, 1961.

101. Sepp Binder, "Die Narbe der Nation: Zwischen Touristen und Tretminen—Die Zonengrenze," *Die Zeit*, June 13, 1969, 8.

102. Example: Grenztruppen der DDR: Grenzkommando Nord, Aufklärungssammelbericht über die Handlungen des Gegners an der Staatsgrenze zur DDR gegenüber dem Grenzkommando Nord im Zeitraum vom 26.4.83 bis 25.5.1983, May 26, 1983, BArch-MA DVH 48, Nr. AZN GT 13647. In this case, someone had used a rock tied to a rope to set off an SM-70 antipersonnel mine.

103. Binder, "Die Narbe der Nation."

104. Bailey, *Edge of the Forest*, 63–64; Schroers, "Die Sackgasse (1962)," 68–70.

105. Kind-Kovács, "Local Iron Curtain," 199–222; Glassheim, "Unsettled Landscapes," 318–336. See also Eisch, *Grenze*, 276–284.

106. Komska, *Icon Curtain*, 133–136, 162–175; Glassheim, "Unsettled Landscapes," 321.

107. Demshuk, *Lost German East*, 185–231. *Heimat* tourism increased significantly after the treaty with Poland in 1970. That year, more than 25,000 West Germans traveled to Poland. In 1975, the number rose to 254,000. See Stennert, "'Heimwehtourismus,'" 83–94; see figures in Ossowski, "Ostpreußen," 117.

108. Term in Demshuk, *Lost German East*, 163; for the example of Brieg Tower in Goslar see ibid., 177–183.

109. Ullrich, *Geteilte Ansichten*, 66–72.

110. Komska, *Icon Curtain*, 66–124; Eisch, *Grenze*, 284–300.

111. "An der Zonengrenze: 325 Heimatvertriebene aus dem Untertaunuskreis am Stacheldraht," *Hersfelder Zeitung*, May 13, 1965. The article makes a point of noting that this group, arriving in eight buses, was the largest to visit the border in Hersfeld County (Hesse) to date. On high visitor volume see also Komska, *Icon Curtain*, 148–150.

112. Example: NVA, 5. Grenzbrigade, Aufklärungssammelbericht für die Zeit vom 1.3.63 bis 31.3.63, Apr. 8, 1963, BArch-MA DVH 32, GT 1083. On the centrality of the border for June 17 commemorations see Wolfrum, *Geschichtspolitik*, 111–112, 151–152. For the context see Amos, *Vertriebenenverbände*, 226–238.

113. Ullrich, *Geteilte Ansichten*, 50–61; Wolfrum, *Geschichtspolitik*, 155–164; Meyer, *Doppelstrategie*, 332–337.

114. Binder, "Die Narbe der Nation."

115. Example: Grenzkommando Nord: Aufklärungssammelbericht über die Handlungen des Gegners an der Staatsgrenze zur DDR gegenüber dem GKNord im Zeitraum vom 26.5.1983 bis 25.6.1983, June 27, 1983, BArch-MA DVH 48, AZN GT 13647. This report identifies an increasing number of sports events such as relay runs along the border.

116. Stacy, *U.S. Army Border Operations*.

117. The intelligence reports registered the number of civilians and visitors in uniform and assessed any rise or fall in visitor volume. They also noted efforts to speak to eastern border guards, to incite them to desert, and to "make contact" in other ways, such as throwing items across the demarcation line or depositing cigarettes and pornographic magazines. See, e.g., 5. Grenzbrigade, Aufklärungssammelbericht für die Zeit vom 1.12.1967-31.10.1968, BArch-MA, DVH 36, GT 8017.

118. Unsere Fahrt an die Zonengrenze (1961); Staatspolitische Bildungswoche Bad Kissingen (1962); Unsere Fahrt in die Röhn (1969). All three scrapbooks are in the possession of the author.

119. BM Finanz, Grenzzwischenfälle und -nachrichten, Jan. and Feb. 1964, both in PA/AA B38/52.

120. "Instructions for [large] travel and excursion parties were observed only in a few cases. The majority [of visitors] were individual civilians or small groups who came to the border, lingered for a short time, usually took photographs and then returned." NVA, 13. Grenzbrigade, Aufklärungssammelbericht, Sept. 1963, BArch-MA, DVH 32/117480.

121. Quote in Kind-Kovács, "Local Iron Curtain," 214.

122. Peter Boag, personal journal, entry for Sept. 4 and 5, 1984; cited with permission of the author. My sincere thanks to Professor Boag for sharing these personal notes.

123. Ullrich, *Geteilte Ansichten*, 33–34, 159–161, 292. See also Bailey, *Edge of the Forest*, 157, who points out that West German border guards offered "a certain repetition of facts and figures" regardless where one encountered them.

124. Schugg-Reheis and Bahr, *Grenzenlos*, 15.

125. "Der Schnitt in unser Fleisch: Notizen von der mitteldeutschen Grenze," *Deutsche Zeitung*, Aug. 20, 1952.

126. Sex Pistols, *Holidays in the Sun* (1977): "A cheap holiday in other people's misery! / . . . / I'm looking over the Wall and they're looking at me / . . . / Well they're staring all night and / They're staring all day / I had no reason to be here at all / But now I gotta reason it's no real reason / And I'm waiting at the Berlin Wall." *Sonnenallee*, dir. Leander Haussmann (1999).

127. Berdahl, *Where the World Ended*, 160.

128. The legitimacy battles between both German states over the victims of the Berlin Wall are best explicated in Ahonen, *Death*.

129. Kommando der Deutschen Grenzpolizei (DGP), Operative Abt., Protokoll, gez. Major Klinger, June 20, 1959, BArch-MA, DVH 27/131453.

130. *Mitten in Deutschland: Mitten im 20. Jahrhundert*, 2nd ed. (Bonn: Bundesministerium für gesamtdeutsche Fragen, Jan. 1959). The brochure saw eleven editions between 1958 and 1971. It was also published in English (Oct. 1960). See also Bayerische und Hessische Landeszentrale für Heimatdienst, eds., *Wie lange noch?* (Wiesbaden: Landeszentrale, 1957).

131. This is my reading of the brochure's images, esp. no. 75 (*Mitten in Deutschland*, 7th ed., July 1961), where an old woman stares at the ruins of her former farm. The caption emphasizes her status as the "proprietor" who saw years of hard work destroyed within hours. West German reports also emphasized decay and uncultivated, "wasted" land in the Czech borderlands across the Bavarian border. See Glassheim, "Unsettled Landscapes," 322–323.

132. Ullrich, *Geteilte Ansichten*, 107–117; Steinle, *Feindbild*, 167–172.

133. Kommando der Deutschen Grenzpolizei (DGP), Operative Abt., Protokoll, gez. Major Klinger, 20. Juni 1959, BArch-MA, DVH 27/131453.

134. Kommando der DGP, 4. Grenzbrigade, gez. Bär, to Kommandeur der DGP, 17. Juni 1959, BArch-MA, DVH 27/131453.

135. DGP, Dienststelle Schönberg, Kp. Schlagbrügge, Protokoll (Nr. 3) über die Besichtigung und Überprüfung eines in unmittelbarer Grenznähe stehenden, baufälligen Wohngebäudes im Bereich der Dienststelle Schlagbrügge (Grenzbereitschaft Schönberg), Aug. 28, 1959, BArch-MA, DVH 27/131453.

136. Villages and hamlets were razed well into the 1980s. The issue is covered mostly in local histories. See Hesse, *Befriedet*; Fuchs, *Billmuthausen*. See also Sheffer, *Burned Bridge*, 182–183; Johnson, *Divided Village*, 157–158.

137. HA I, Abt. Aufklärung, Kommando der Grenztruppen, Apr. 14, 1964, Analyse der provokatorischen Grenzbesichtigungen an der Staatsgrenze West der DDR, BStU, MfS, ZAIG, Nr. 10695, Bl. 204.

138. Berdahl, *Where the World Ended*, 150.

139. HA I, Abt. Aufklärung, Kommando der Grenztruppen, Apr. 14, 1964, Analyse der provokatorischen Grenzbesichtigungen an der Staatsgrenze West der DDR, BStU, MfS, ZAIG, Nr. 10695. See also Major Günter Engmann, "'Grenz-Touristik' mit Gruseleffekt," *Tribüne*, Aug. 2, 1966.

140. HA I, Abt. Aufklärung, Kommando der Grenztruppen, Apr. 14, 1964, Analyse der provokatorischen Grenzbesichtigungen an der Staatsgrenze West der DDR, BStU, MfS, ZAIG, Nr. 10695, Bl. 204. See also Böckel, *Erlebnisse eines "West Grenzers,"* 71.

141. HA I, Abt. Aufklärung, Kommando der Grenztruppen, Apr. 14, 1964, Analyse der provokatorischen Grenzbesichtigungen an der Staatsgrenze West der DDR, BStU, MfS, ZAIG, Nr. 10695, Bl. 203–204.

142. Befehl des Chefs der Grenztruppen Nr. 18/63, Mar. 28,1963, gez. Oberst Peter, BArch-MA, DVW 1/12914.

143. The border museum in Helmstedt exhibits some of these leaflets. One reads: "A border traveler listens [. . .] to noble speeches about humanity, mutual contacts, freedom and democracy and does the right thing [. . .] if he demands [that his own government] [. . .] finally initiate negotiations between the Federal Republic and the government of the GDR. Only such talks can lead to a policy of understanding." n.d. (ca. 1964). See also Gordon, "East German Psychological Operations."

144. BM Finanz, Grenzzwischenfälle und -nachrichten, July 2, 1963, PA/AA B38/51. The information about the bugging devices was provided by an escaped border guard. A conversation protocol from 1979 based on such eavesdropping in BArch-MA, DVH 48, GT 8429.

145. BM Finanz, Grenzzwischenfälle und -nachrichten, July 29, 1963, PA/AA B38/51. Visiting groups were reported by western border authorities in Lower Saxony and Hesse, both describing the phenomenon as "besichtigen" and emphasizing that it was the first time this had been observed.

146. The unit was called Hauptabteilung I beim Kommando der Grenztruppen (HA I/KGT). Neumeier, "Staatssicherheit [. . .] in Bayern"; *Niedersachsen und die Stasi*, ed. BStU; *Hessen und die Stasi*, ed. BStU.

147. See, e.g., Information Nr. 80/84 über ständige und zeitweilige Konzentrationsbereiche von Personen im unmittelbaren grenznahen Bereich der BRD zur DDR, May 8, 1984, BStU MfS HA IX, Nr. 4307.

148. Schätzlein and Albert, *Grenzerfahrungen*, 224–253, cite extensively from the "Enemy Object File" on the Bavaria Tower in Zimmerau, Franconia; reference to visitors from GDR, 242. See also the reports on the tower near Lauenstein in Kronach County (Franconia) and the "zonal border house" in Zicherie, Lower Saxony, both in BStU, MfS, ZAIG Nr. 10708, Bl. 212–214, 217–220.

149. Nobel, *Mitten durch Deutschland*, 191.

150. BM Finanz, Grenzzwischenfälle und -nachrichten, July 29, 1963, PA/AA B38/51.

151. Ullrich, *Geteilte Ansichten*, 103; Ritter and Hajdu, *Innerdeutsche Grenze*, 45.

152. HA I, Abt. Aufklärung, Kommando der Grenztruppen, Apr. 14, 1964, Analyse der provokatorischen Grenzbesichtigungen an der Staatsgrenze West der DDR, BStU, MfS, ZAIG, Nr. 10695, Bl. 205.

153. Albrecht Schreiber, "US-Schüler an der Grenze: Schon bald nachdenklich," *Lübecker Nachrichten*, June 2, 1984: The border in Lübeck-Eichholz "becomes more and more overgrown and barely allows for a glance across [. . .] And everything appears so harmless: lush and sprawling grass, silence all around, no demonstrations of military power on either side."

154. Ritter and Lapp, *Grenze*, 69; images of such bunkers, 59, 81. See also Ritter and Hajdu, *Innerdeutsche Grenze*, 43.

155. Stoll, *Grenze*, 128, citing an article from *Frankfurter Allgemeine Zeitung*, Jan. 2, 1967: "To encounter a 'people's soldier' [*Volksarmisten*] along the barbed wire has almost become a matter of luck."

156. For some photos of such scenes see Ritter and Lapp, *Grenze*, 63, 81, 84, 93.

157. Report cited in Manfred Präcklein, "Der Zaun ist völlig zu. Innerdeutsche Grenzanlagen werden jetzt noch perfekter gesichert," *Lübecker Nachrichten*, Aug. 1, 1986.

158. Christaller, "Tourism Location," esp. 104. The Christaller article still reflects the unease about urban agglomeration (*Ballung*) and the uneven distribution of people and industrial production that West German spatial planners shared in the 1950s. See also Chaney, *Nature of the Miracle Years*, 114–147. For a social science perspective on peripherality and tourism, see Timothy, *Tourism and Political Boundaries*, 41–90.

159. Gaststätten- und Fremdengewerbe to Bundesregierung, June, 30 1952, NLA HA Nds. 500, Acc. 2/73 Nr. 376/5.

160. Kurdirektor Thiem, Braunlage/Harz to Stadtverwaltung Braunlage, June 16, 1952, NLA HA Nds. 500, Acc. 2/73 Nr. 376/5.

161. Landkreis Wolfenbüttel to Präsident Verwaltungsbezirk Braunschweig, Nov. 13, 1950; Stadt Goslar to Präsident Verwaltungsbezirk Braunschweig, Nov. 15, 1950, NLA HA Nds. 500, Acc. 2/73 Nr. 376/5.

162. For the example of Hohe Geiß see Ullrich, *Geteilte Ansichten*, 97–98. For the example of Travemünde see Sepp Binder, "Die Narbe der Nation: Zwischen Touristen und Tretminen," *Die Zeit*, June 13, 1969.

163. "Schwebebahn am Eisernen Vorhang: Der Wurmberg soll 'Fenster nach drüben' werden—Baubeginn noch in diesem Jahr," *Hamburger Echo*, Mar. 24, 1959.

164. Ullrich, *Geteilte Ansichten*, 95–98. Busloads of visitors noted in East German intelligence report: 7. Grenzbrigade, Aufklärungsbericht Oktober 1963, Nov. 11, 1963, BArch-MA DVH 32/117481.

165. Klaus von der Brelie, "Tag für Tag rollen die Busse an die deutsch-deutsche Grenze: Informationsdienst erläutert Besuchern das Zonenrandgebiet," *Hannoversche Allgemeine Zeitung*, June, 18, 1984.

166. The state Commissariat (Staatskommissariat für die Förderung der hessischen Notstandsgebiete und Zonengrenzkreise) was established in 1953. As part of the state Chancellery, the commissar reported directly to the state governor (*Ministerpräsident*). The two key incumbents of the office were Wilhelm Ziegler (1953–1956) and Heinz Kreutzmann (1963–1969).

167. "Die Chancen des deutschen Fremdenverkehrs," *Wiesbadener Tagblatt*, June 3, 1958.

168. Dienel, "Freizeitverkehr"; Schildt, "'Die kostbarsten Wochen des Jahres,'" esp. 74, 78–79.

169. On Alfred Töpfer's Nature Park Society see Chaney, *Nature of the Miracle Years*, 114–126; for the local adaption of "oases of tranquility" see *Hessendienst*, no. 13, Nov. 1957; *Hessendienst*, no. 18, May 1962; on the marketing of "An Inexpensive Weekend in Hesse" see Bund Deutscher Verkehrsverbände, Übersicht über den Fremdenverkehr in Hessen, n.d. [1962], both in HHStAW Abt. 502/374.

170. *Hessenspiegel*, no. 214, Nov. 10, 1955, in HHStAW Abt. 502/374. The money was designated for the region Kurhessen-Waldeck.

171. Karl-H. Reccius, head of the tourist association for Kurhessen and Waldeck, to Ziegler, Nov. 19, 1955, HHStAW Abt. 502/374. Although this letter went from Reccius to Ziegler, previous correspondence shows that this is Ziegler's wording. The same reasoning prevailed in Bavaria. See Schlemmer et al., "Landesplanung in Bayern," 384–385, 406–407.

172. Wilhelm Ziegler (1891–1962) was trained as a historian. In 1933, he joined Goebbels's Ministry of Enlightenment and Propaganda and, in 1941, was appointed honorary professor of modern history, politics and "Jewish issues" at Berlin University. In 1943, he became deputy director of the Ministry's literature section (*Schrifttumsabteilung*) where he was also in charge of Jewish questions (*Judenreferent*). For biographical data see Gruner, ed., *Ermordung der europäischen Juden*, 121.

173. Bund Deutscher Verkehrsverbände, Übersicht über den Fremdenverkehr in Hessen, n.d. [1962], HHStAW Abt. 502/374. For the effects of the

federally subsidized low-interest loans see *Hessendienst*, no. 13, Nov. 1957, and *Hessendienst*, no. 18, May 1962, both in HHStAW Abt. 502/374.

174. Kreisausschuß Rotenburg-on-Fulda to State Commissariat, Jan. 21, 1958, HHStAW Abt. 502/374; "Einblick in die Probleme des hessischen Zonenrandgebiets," *Fuldaer Zeitung*, June 6, 1969.

175. Bund Deutscher Verkehrsverbände, Übersicht über den Fremdenverkehr in Hessen, n.d. [1962], HHStAW Abt. 502/374.

176. *Hessendienst*, no. 18, May 1958, HHStAW Abt. 502/374.

177. Heinz Held, "Halt! Hier Zonengrenze: Fragen, Antworten, Hoffnungen," *Merian: Vom Meißner zur Rhön* 21:11 (Nov. 1968), 36.

178. "Einmal Urlaub im Zonengrenzgebiet," *Hessische Allgemeine*, May 4, 1963.

179. By the mid-1960s, half of those West Germans who opted for a beach vacation traveled to the Mediterranean. Spode, *Reiseweltmeister*, 148. See also Schildt, "'Die kostbarsten Wochen des Jahres.'"

180. Shears, *Ugly Frontier*, 175–176. Bailey, *Edge of the Forest*, 64, considers the visitors "a big boost to Zicherie's frail economy" but does not point to any concrete impact other than their presence.

181. Roth, *Dorf im Wandel*, 74–75.

182. HHStAW Abt. 502/375/4108. For the history of this tower see Ullrich, *Geteilte Ansichten*, 77–81.

183. Brönstrup, *Stacheldraht*, 57–58. The number of overnight stays in Bergen rose from 2,500 in 1955 to more than 10,000 in 1965, although there is no way to prove a connection between the information point and the rising guest stays.

184. Besuch der Arbeitsgruppe Zonenrandgebiet der SPD-Bundestagsfraktion am 28./29. Mai 1970 im Zonengrenzbezirk Gifhorn-Lüchow Dannenberg, HHStAW Abt. 502/1080.

185. Ernst-Otto Maetzke, "Der alte Kahn und die Staatsgewalt," *Frankfurter Allgemeine Zeitung*, Aug. 10, 1966.

186. Heinz D. Stuckmann, "An der Elbe—an der Grenze," *Die Zeit*, Oct. 9, 1964.

187. Nobel, *Mitten durch Deutschland*, 245.

188. Bert Gendher, "Hier ist die Welt noch in Ordnung," *Bayernkurier*, Feb. 21, 1981; "Ferien direkt an der DDR-Grenze," *Hannoversche Allgemeine*, Mar. 23, 1983; Bernd Hummel, "Rauchlose Industrie im Zonenrandgebiet," *Die Welt*, Aug. 28, 1984.

189. Hans-Jürgen von der Heide, *Zonenrandförderung: Ist sie heute noch notwendig?* (Clausthal-Zellerfeld: Arbeitsgemeinschaft der Industrie- und Handelskammern im Zonenrandgebiet, n.d. [1987]), 38.

190. Konrad Mrusek, "Grüne Hoffnung am Zonenrand," *Frankfurter Allgemeine Zeitung*, Nov. 28, 1985, R5.

191. *The Border between Hesse and the GDR: Brief Information for Visitors*, ed. Hessendienst der Staatskanzlei, 1986, 2: "The peace and charm of its landscape and the hospitality of its people give it a high recreational value."

192. Paradigmatic contemporary text about the borderlands: Renate Just, "Deutschland: Am schönsten, wo es am ärmsten ist," *Zeit Magazin* (Aug. 1986), 6–21. See also Geisler, "'Heimat' and the German Left," esp. 34–41.

193. In 1968, West Germans owned 187,000 second homes and apartments. In 1973, the figure had risen to some 300,000 second homes. See Maier, "Zweitwohnsitze im Freizeitraum," 2; Gerhard Krug, "Wenn die Russen kommen . . . ," *Die Zeit*, July 27, 1973.

194. Schubert, *Hinterland für Berlin (West)?*, 187–194; Maier, "Zweitwohnsitze im Freizeitraum"; Steinmetz, "Berlins Hinterland."

195. Schubert, *Hinterland für Berlin (West)?*, 192–193. For similar trends in new construction see Quis, "Anteil der Großstädter," 123–124.

196. Waldeck, "Bevölkerungsentwicklung," 322.

197. Quis, "Anteil der Großstädter," 124; Manfred Sack, "Bevor sie zerstört werden: Der Versuch, die letzten Runddörfer zu erhalten," *Die Zeit*, July 10, 1970; "Stadtflucht der Dichter," *Der Spiegel*, Feb. 4, 1974, 118; "Da geht es links und rechts nicht weiter," *Der Spiegel*, July 12, 1976, 78–82.

198. On picture book villages see Thomas Schröder, "Ein Wochenende in der letzten Ecke: Hitzacker—Wiesen, Deiche und die Spaltung des Gefühls," *Die Zeit*, May 16, 1975, 47; on Lüchow-Dannenberg as the "most curious corner" see Horst Vetten, "Gleich hinter Gorleben: Entdeckungen im Landkreis Lüchow-Dannenberg, der vielleicht seltsamsten Ecke Deutschlands," *Geo*, no. 6 (1980): 38–60, quote: 48; Worpswede: "Stadtflucht der Dichter," *Der Spiegel*, Feb. 4, 1974, 118.

199. Term in Vetten, "Gleich hinter Gorleben," 56.

200. Derix, *Bebilderte Politik*, 92–93; Doering-Manteuffel, "Innerdeutsche Grenze," 127–151.

201. This is a classic argument about alterity already masterfully made in Sahlins, *Boundaries*. On the production of difference in the borderlands see also Sheffer, *Burned Bridge*, 118–141.

202. Franz, "Antikommunistisches Denken," 145–159.

203. Müller, *Another Country*, 20–63; Wehler, *Gesellschaftsgeschichte*, 251–253, 298–303, 326–327; Wolfrum, *Geschichtspolitik*.

204. Johnson, *Divided Village*, 206–207.

205. Ullrich, *Geteilte Ansichten*, 146–279; Becker, *Wie Gras über die Geschichte wächst*. Documentation of commemorative spaces and objects in *Orte des Erinnerns*.

206. The signs read, "Here Germany and Europe were divided until [date and time]." See *Die Brocken Erklärung: Geschichtsprojekt zu 20 Jahren Deutsche Einheit* (Ministerium für Landesentwicklung und Verkehr des Landes Sachsen-Anhalt, 2009).

207. Mahlke, *Zukunft der Grenzmuseen*, counted twenty-four museums in Lower Saxony alone. See also *Orte des Erinnerns*. For the figures see Dicke, "Memorialkultur," 224.

208. Ullrich, *Geteilte Ansichten*, 159, 292. Dicke, "Memorialkultur," 232, points out that most visitors to the border museums appear to have hailed from the former West.

209. Ullrich, *Geteilte Ansichten*, 289–291; Johnson, *Divided Village*, 207.

CHAPTER 4

1. Huff, "Umweltpolitik der DDR," 523.

2. [DDR-Ministerium für Naturschutz, Umweltschutz und Wasserwirtschaft, MNUW], Informationen zur Entwicklung der Umweltbedingungen in der DDR und weitere Maßnahmen—Basisjahr 1988: Zur ökologischen Lage [Jan. 1990], BArch B295/20492; MNUW, Konzeption für die Entwicklung der Umweltpolitk (Berlin, Feb. 2, 1990); Institut für Umweltschutz, Information zur Analyse der Umweltbedingungen in der DDR und zu weiteren Massnahmen (Berlin, Feb. 1990), both in BArch B295/20493; Gesellschaft für angewandte Sozialwissenschaft und Statistik, Die Umweltsituation der DDR im Urteil ihrer Bürger: Ergebnisse einer Befragung bei der Leipziger Frühjahrsmesse 1990 im Auftrag des BMU und des Umweltbundesamtes, 1990, BArch B295/20494; BMU, Eckwerte für die ökologische Sanierung und Entwicklung in den neuen Ländern (Bonn, Nov. 1990). Aside from these official assessments, see also Petschow, Meyerhoff, and Thomasberger, eds., *Umwelt-Report DDR*.

3. Radkau, *Ära der Ökologie*, 535.

4. Lindenberger, "Divided, but Not Disconnected."

5. The theme is also pursued in Grady, "Shared Environment," but not developed in great depth.

6. Park, *Müllkippe*, 84–90, 192–196; Judt, *Kommerzielle Koordinierung*, 67–76, 192–203.

7. "Die BRD ist auch [deshalb] so 'sauber,' weil die DDR so 'schmutzig' ist." Quote in Gemeinsame Erklärung von Umweltverbänden aus Ost und West anlässlich des Round-Table-Gespräches am 13.12.1989 bei Bundesumweltminister Töpfer, Archiv Bund Naturschutz in Bayern (Nürnberg), Ordner DDR PM PROe.

8. Contemporary figures in Berg, "Umweltschutz in Deutschland," 380; Huff, *Natur und Industrie*, 255.

9. Ministerium für Staatssicherheit (MfS), Information Nr. 112/84 [1984] über [. . .] Verhandlungen mit der DDR zum Umweltschutz, Bundesbeauftrager für die Stasi-Unterlagen (BStU), MfS HVA Nr. 29, part 1 of 2, fol. 042.

10. The GDR Minister for Environmental Protection and Water Management, Hans Reichelt, assembled materials for the planned visit of Erich Honecker in Bonn 1984 that were intended to showcase the environmental "achievements" of the GDR in order to refute the "defamations of West German media energetically and conclusively." See Reichelt to Günter Mittag, Oct. 10, 1984, BArch-SAPMO, Büro Mittag DY 3023/1435.

11. Weisung Nr. 36/81 (VS B161-71/81), Nov. 24, 1981, BArch DK5/1498. See also Information über den erreichten Stand bei der Beseitigung von Gefährdungssituationen im Bereich der Staatsgrenze zur BRD und zu Westberlin und Vorschläge für das weitere Vorgehen, n.d. [Mar. 22, 1984], BArch-SAPMO Büro Mittag DY 3023/1442.

12. Darst, *Smokestack Diplomacy*; Darst, "Bribery and Blackmail," 52.

13. Huff, *Natur und Industrie*, 8.

14. Uekötter, "Entangled Ecologies," 157–158. Huff, *Natur und Industrie*, 20.

15. Dominick, "Capitalism, Communism, and Environmental Protection"; Laakkonen, Pál, and Tucker, "Cold War and Environmental History," 384–388.

16. McNeill, "Observations," 31.

17. Ibid., 18. See also Taylor, "Boundary Terminology," 456, who notes that too often "*transnational* is [merely] a chic way to say *international.*"

18. Langston, "Thinking like a Microbe," esp. 595.

19. See Martinez, *Border People*, 5–10, for types of cross-border interaction that are determined by mutual relations. "Alienated borderlands" emerge along borders between hostile states.

20. I follow the distinction between material, cultural/intellectual, and political environmental history in McNeill, "Observations," 6–9.

21. Parts of this chapter are based on an article on transboundary river pollution that I published in German. See Eckert, "Grenzgewässer."

22. Erfassung der Interessenlage der DDR zur Aufnahme von Verhandlungen auf dem Gebiet des Umweltschutzes mit der BRD, n.d. [Nov. 6, 1973], BArch-SAPMO, Politbüro DY 30/J IV 2/2. This document had been prepared for purposes of environmental cooperation between both German states as laid down in the Basic Treaty of 1972. The cooperation did not come to pass, as explained further later in the chapter.

23. Ibid.

24. Steiner, *Plans That Failed*, 151–153, 171–183; Roesler, "Unterschiede."

25. Hartard and Huhn, "SERO-System"; Möller, "Ewiger Kreislauf."

26. Buck, "Müllentsorgung," 462.

27. Elektrizitätswerk Weiss, Mitwitz, to Landratsamt Kronach, Feb. 13. and Apr. 15, 1975, BayHStA StK/19538.

28. Elektrizitätswerk Weiss, Mitwitz, to Dr. Hans De With, Parl. Staatssekretär, BMJ, Aug. 21, 1979, BayHStA StK/19538. Weiss management argued that the Border Commission achieved no results. "What does it help us, for instance, that you have been negotiating with the GDR about environmental pollution if things do not get any better."

29. Bauerkämper, "Industrialization of Agriculture."

30. On land improvement (*Flurbereinigung*) in the Federal Republic see the contemporary interventions by Weiger, "Flurbereinigung," 3–6; "Was spricht

gegen Plastikbäume?," *Der Spiegel*, May 9, 1983, 80–98; and Bölsche, *Deutsche Landschaft stirbt*. On the GDR see Heinz, "Klassenkampf gegen Hecken"; Könker, "Standortmeliorationen," 45–58; Mohr, "Entwässerung."

31. Heinz, *Mähdrescher*, 314–332; Schmidt, "Landwirtschaft und Naturschutz;" Buck, "Umwelt- und Bodenbelastung," 432.

32. George, "Vogelwelt der Agrarlandschaft."

33. Individual LPGs continued to feel pressured by production quotas and thus did not embrace the idea of returning to smaller fields or reversing the clearing of cultural landscapes by replanting shrubs and trees. Heinz, "Klassenkampf gegen Hecken," 34–35; Steiner, *Plans That Failed*, 183–185.

34. Succow was the GDR's deputy environmental minister at the time. See BMU, Ref. N1, Protokoll [der] Besprechung der für den Naturschutz zuständigen Abteilungsleiter des Bundes und der Länder am 24. und 25.4.1990 in Bad Reichenhall, BArch B295/20493.

35. Polizeimeister Dürrbeck, Grenzpolizeitstation Rödental, Schlussvermerk [über die Verschmutzung der Effelder mit Waschmittel], Jan. 14, 1987, BayHStA StK/19497.

36. "Fischsterben in der Kreck," *Neue Presse*, July 2, 1976; "Fischsterben in der Kreck: DDR-Behörden lehnen Verantwortung ab," *Coburger Tageblatt*, July 2, 1976. When the Milz was polluted in 1981, the response to a western inquiry stated "that an investigation of the Milz conducted by the responsible agencies in the GDR 'did not reveal any exceptional changes.'" See Franz Josef Strauss, governor of Bavaria, to Johann Böhm (CSU), member of the Bavarian Landtag, Oct. 30, 1981, BayHStA StK/19539.

37. Bekanntmachung der Bayerischen Staatskanzlei Nr. 105-3-20, Jan. 15, 1970: Richtlinien für den Ersatz von Sachschäden, die im Bereich der DL durch Sperrmassnahmen der mitteldeutschen Behörden verursacht worden sind, BayHStA StK/19536; Bay. StK to Landratsämter, Re. On damages along the border not caused by the fortifications (i.e., mines), July 7, 1976, BayHStA StK/19535: "The kind of damage particularly frequent at the moment [. . .] is fish kill in transboundary waters as well as damages on our territory caused by herbicides sprayed in the GDR."

38. Figures based on the Statistical Yearbook of the GDR for 1983 cited in Berg, "Umweltschutz in Deutschland," 381. See also Würth, *Umweltschutz*, 233. For comparison, in 1983 fully 99.9 percent of West German residents were connected to the central drinking water supply and 90.7 percent to public canalization; 95.3 percent of the latter had a connection to sewage plants. Information provided by the Federal Statistical Office (Bonn), July 12, 2012.

39. Buck, "Umwelt- und Bodenbelastung," 435.

40. Würth, *Umweltschutz*, 231–248; Bernhardt, "Industrialismus," 376–378; Klapper, "Gewässerschutz," 234.

41. Böhm et al., *Stadtentwässerung*, 110.

42. The three plants were Münchehofe, Falkenberg, and Nord. See Berg, "Umweltschutzabkommen," 124. The water quality in West Berlin did improve as a result. See Jahn, "Berliner Gewässer," 28.

43. Sheffer, *Burned Bridge*, 210–211; Füsslein, *Grenzkommission*, 120–121.

44. "Entwurf eines Berichtes zu den Auswirkungen der Verschmutzung der deutsch-deutschen Grenzgewässer durch Einleitungen aus der DDR," n.d. [Sept. 1983], report assembled by order of Minister Reichelt, BArch DK5/5752.

45. Huff, *Natur und Industrie*, 241–244.

46. "Problemkatalog der Grenzkommission für das Gebiet des Freistaates Bayern. Stand: 1.1.1977," memorandum, BayHStA StK/19673; "Grenzen: Teuflische Dinger," *Der Spiegel*, July 1, 1974, 43.

47. Deals of this kind were usually conducted in agreement currency. Receiving the amount in freely convertible currency enabled the GDR to make the amount go further than expected since all costs for the Sonneberg plant were billed in the lower-value East German currency. Besides, money in hand, the GDR simply scaled back the project in order "to reach a significant reduction of the investment cost." See Ministerrat der DDR, VVS B2-B161, Beschluß über Maßnahmen zur Abwasserbehandlung der Stadt Sonneberg, Dec. 12, 1983, BArch DK5/1995. Among SED officials the "Röden model" was henceforth considered the gold standard for any such deals.

48. Presse- und Informationsamt der Bundesregierung, [. . .] Vereinbarung mit der DDR in der Grenzkommission über Massnahmen zum Schutz der Röden im bayerisch-thüringischen Grenzgebiet, in *Bulletin* Nr. 106, Oct. 13, 1983, 969.

49. This happened in the case of the Saale River. See Wensierski, "Umweltprobleme in der DDR."

50. Wensierski, *Von oben nach unten*, 141–147, quote 143; Würth, *Umweltschutz*, 236–240.

51. Rommelspacher, "Wasserverschmutzung," 50–51.

52. Quotes in BM Innerdt. Beziehungen, Vermerk betr. Expertengespräch mit der DDR über die Verschmutzung der Elbe, Feb. 2, 1983, BArch B288/113. The argument about the self-cleansing abilities of the Elbe beginning after passing Magdeburg was already presented in Erfassung der Interessenlage der DDR zur Aufnahme von Verhandlungen auf dem Gebiet des Umweltschutzes mit der BRD k. D. [Nov. 6, 1973], BArch-SAPMO, Politbüro DY 30/J IV 2/2, p. 4.

53. The German working group on water issues, LAWA, assesses water quality on a scale of I to IV, with additional subcategories that, as of 1990, amounted to eight total.

54. Deisenroth, "Salzlagerstätte," 7–24.

55. Eisenbach, "Kaliindustrie," 194–222; Büschenfeld, "Harter Kampf." See also Büschenfeld, *Flüsse und Kloaken*, 289–406; Mehnert, "Aufbau des Kalireviers."

56. Hübner, *Fließgewässerbewertung*, 27–28; on saline vegetation see Büschenfeld, "Harter Kampf," 87–89.

57. Büschenfeld, "Harter Kampf," 100; Büschenfeld, *Flüsse und Kloaken*, 377–400.

58. Eisenbach, "Kaliindustrie," 216.

59. G. Buhse, Versalzung der Werra und Oberweser und Abwässer der Kali-Industrie, NLA HA Nds. 600 Acc. 143/92 Nr. 11. See also Eisenbach, "Kaliindustrie," 219.

60. Büschenfeld, "Harter Kampf," 101.

61. Eisenbach, "Kaliindustrie," 207–210; Büschenfeld, "Harter Kampf," 101–103. The salt marshes are called *Rohrlache*. See http://www.widdershausen.de/rohrlache.html (accessed Apr. 2019).

62. Hübner, *Fließgewässerbewertung*, 24–34; Hulsch/Veh, "Salzbelastung"; Liersch, "Salz."

63. MUW, June 9, 1977, BArch-SAPMO, Büro Mittag DY 3023/1434. See also Eisenbach, "Kaliindustrie," 218.

64. Eisenbach, "Kaliindustrie," 216–220; Hulsch and Veh, "Salzbelastung," 367–377; Arbeitsgemeinschaft der Wasserwerke im Wesereinzugsgebiet (AAW): Trinkwasserversorgung von fünf Millionen Menschen im Wesereinzugsgebiet durch Weserversalzung beeinträchtigt, [Press Information, n.d., estimated 1980], NLA HA Nds. 800 Acc. 2001/090 Nr. 171.

65. "Dass der Fluss so krank ist," *Der Spiegel*, Sept. 27, 1976, 69.

66. "Umwelt: Lenkt die DDR ein?" *Der Spiegel*, Sept. 25, 1978, 18–19. The saltwater concentration in the Baltic is 11,000 mg/l, in the North Sea 19,000 mg/l. See Hulsch and Veh, "Salzbelastung," 371.

67. Uekötter, "Entangled Ecologies," 149; "Dass der Fluss so krank ist . . . ," *Der Spiegel*, Sept. 27, 1976, 72–73.

68. Liersch, "Salz," 642–647.

69. Damage estimate in Herbert Schäfer, "'Hier beginnt die Nordsee': Bonn und DDR streiten um verschmutze Flüsse," *Die Zeit*, May 20, 1988.

70. Vermerk MR Jürgen Hulsch, Jan. 25, 1980, NLA HA Nds. 800 Acc. 2001/090 Nr. 171.

71. Arbeitsgruppe II, Forderungen und Verbindlichkeiten der DDR aus der Instandhaltung und dem Ausbau sowie Probleme aus der Abwasserbelastung der Grenzwasserläufe, Mar. 10, 1971, BArch DK5/1498. This document was drawn up by East German legal experts to anticipate potential environmental liabilities that the Federal Republic might address. The working group (Arbeitsgruppe II, or AG II) had been convened by the Office for the Legal Protection of the Assets of the GDR (Amt für den Rechtsschutz des Vermögens der DDR, AfR). The document was shared with the head of watershed management, Johann Rochlitzer, in April 1971.

72. The PPP was devised by the OECD in 1972, appeared in the Stockholm Declaration the same year, and was globally endorsed in aspirational terms in

the Rio Declaration of 1992. In international law, the PPP and liability for envi-
ronmental damage are two distinct issues, although commonly conflated. See
Atapattu, *Emerging Principles*, 439–483, esp. 439–430, 470. See also Sadeleer,
"Polluter Pays Principle," 155–156.

73. International law knows the term "Victim Pays Principle" (VPP) as the negative
and undesirable counterpart to the PPP. The VPP is not a legal principle per se
but a description of a situation where the damaged party has no leverage over
the polluter but can no longer tolerate the ongoing pollution. In that situation
of asymmetrical vulnerability, the victim of the pollution agrees to pay for environmental improvements in the neighboring country, effectively subsidizing
the polluter. Darst, *Smokestack Diplomacy*, 38, argues that "for all the lip service
paid to the polluter pays principle, international environmental politics remains
a 'victim pays' world."

74. See the memoirs of the GDR diplomat Seidel, *Berlin-Bonner Balance*, 184–186.
The East German Ministry for Environmental Protection and Water Management
(MUW) was founded in 1971. The West German Ministry for Environmental
Protection, Nature Conservation and Reactor Safety (BMU) was founded in
1986, chiefly as a reaction to the Chernobyl disaster.

75. Wentker, "Bundespräsens," 241–262; *40 Jahre Umweltbundesamt, 1974–2014*
(Dessau: UBA, 2014), 23–28.

76. "Kneift gewaltig," *Der Spiegel*, June 24, 1974, 23–24; "Berlin: 'Schikanen auf
niedriger Ebene,'" *Der Spiegel*, Aug. 5, 1974, 17–19.

77. Gray, *Germany's Cold War*; Schaefer, *States of Division*, 89–109. Schaefer holds
the Federal Republic responsible for the breakdown of cross-border dialogue
between municipal officials.

78. AG II, Forderungen und Verbindlichkeiten der DDR aus der Instandhaltung und
dem Ausbau sowie Probleme aus der Abwasserbelastung der Grenzwasserläufe,
Mar. 10, 1971, BArch DK5/1498. The GDR was seeking at the same time to be
a participant at the upcoming 1972 Stockholm Conference, from which it was
barred on the basis of the Hallstein Doctrine. See Hünemörder, *Frühgeschichte*,
262–267.

79. "Ostpolitik: Salz in der Werra," *Der Spiegel*, Dec. 1, 1969, 27–28.

80. Vertrag über die Grundlagen der Beziehungen zwischen der Bundesrepublik
Deutschland und der Deutschen Demokratischen Republik [Basic Treaty], Dec.
21, 1972, Zusatzprotokoll II zu Artikel 7, Ziffer 9, in Presse- und Informationsamt
der Bundesregierung, Bulletin Nr. 155, Dec. 8, 1972, 1843–44.

81. Summary of events in Nds. Landtag, 9. WP. Niederschrift über die 15. Sitzung
des Ausschusses für Umweltfragen, Dec. 21, 1979, NLA HA Nds. 800 Acc. 2001/
090 Nr. 171.

82. Ministerrat der DDR, Arbeitsgruppe für Organisation und Inspektion beim
Vorsitzenden, May 30, 1975, BArch-SAPMO, Büro Mittag DY 3023/1434; Günter
Mittag to Erich Honecker, Jan. 14, 1976, BArch-SAPMO, Büro Mittag DY 3023/

1434. This source assesses the damage at VM 72.7 million. Later demands varied between VM 80 and 95 million. See also MfS, Information Nr. 588/75 über die Einbringung bzw. Lagerung von Schadstoffen [. . .] in der Nähe der Staatsgrenze der DDR, Aug. 21, 1975, BStU, MfS Z2421, fol. 01-04.

83. Since this practice was retained in the Thuringian mines, a veritable earthquake occurred in March 1989. The mine of the potash works Ernst Thälmann collapsed at the extent of 6.8 square kilometers and triggered seismic shocks that were felt all the way to Frankfurt/Main (West). See Eisenbach, "Kaliindustrie," 210–212; Karl-Heinz Baum, "Wie die DDR einst Hessen erschütterte," *Frankfurter Rundschau*, Nov. 2, 1996, 3; Ruck, "Die Kali-Industrie," 118–119.

84. Bonn response to GDR demands, transmitted by MinDirg Stern, BKAmt, June 21, 1976; Telegram of the [GDR] Auslandsvertretung (AV) Bonn, signed Baumgärtel, n.d.; Statement of the Government of the Federal Republic, June 30, 1977, all in BArch-SAPMO, Büro Mittag DY 3023/1434; West German explanation for the mine accident in BM Innerdt. Beziehungen, Aufzeichnung zum Stand der Verhandlungen über Massnahmen zur Reduzierung der Werraversalzung und Versenkung, Nov. 15, 1986, BayHStA StK/19611. See also Memo MinDir Weichert, BM Innerdt. Beziehungen, July 26, 1979, DzD VI.6, Doc. 37, 149–153.

85. The issue persists to the present day. See "Alarm am Monte Kali," *Der Spiegel*, Aug. 24, 2009, 42–44.

86. Mittag to Honecker, Jan. 14, 1976, BArch-SAPMO, Büro Mittag DY 3023/1434.

87. "Part of the wastewater that has been injected into the ground [. . .] moves subterraneously onto the territory of the GDR, thus sharing storing capacities in the GDR for this purpose." MUW, Vorschläge für das weitere Vorgehen im Zusammenhang mit der Beseitigung der Abwässer der Kaliindustrie, June 9, 1977, BArch-SAPMO, Büro Mittag DY 3023/1434.

88. Ministerrat der DDR. Arbeitsgruppe für Organisation und Inspektion beim Vorsitzenden, May 30, 1975, BArch-SAPMO, Büro Mittag DY 3023/1434.

89. MUW, Vorschläge für das weitere Vorgehen im Zusammenhang mit der Beseitigung der Abwässer der Kaliindustrie, June 9, 1977, BArch-SAPMO, Büro Mittag DY 3023/1434.

90. Presse- und Informationsamt der Bundesregierung, *Bulletin* Nr. 46, Apr. 30, 1980.

91. Mittag to Honecker, Apr. 18, 1979, BArch-SAPMO, Büro Mittag DY 3023/1434.

92. Memo MR Hulsch, Versalzung von Werra und Weser, hier: Stand der Verhandlungen mit der DDR, Feb. 4, 1980, NLA HA Nds. 800 Acc. 2001/090 Nr. 171.

93. Übersicht zu wirtschaftlichen Interessen der DDR in den Verhandlungen mit der Bundesrepublik Deutschland [. . .], May 27, 1977, DzD VI.5, Doc. Nr. 49, 180.

94. BM Innerdt. Beziehungen, Aufzeichnung zum Stand der Verhandlungen über Massnahmen zur Reduzierung der Werraversalzung und Versenkung, Nov. 15, 1986, BayHStA StK/19611.

95. Nds. Landtag, 9. WP, Niederschrift über die 23. Sitzung des Ausschusses für Vertriebene, Flüchtlinge und Aussiedler sowie Fragen des Zonenrandgebietes, Jan. 16, 1981, NLA HA Nds. 800 Acc. 2001/090 Nr. 173.

96. "Gesalzene Rechnung," *Der Spiegel*, Feb. 4, 1980, 72, 75. Running the pipeline would have cost an additional DM 15 million per year. See also Memo MinDir Weichert, BM Innerdt. Beziehungen, July 26, 1979, DzD VI.6, Doc. 37, 152; Nds. Ministerium für Ernährung, Landwirtschaft und Forsten to Governor, June 24, 1981, NLA HA Nds. 800 Acc. 2001/090 Nr. 173.

97. Overview of negotiations in BM Innerdt. Beziehungen, Aufzeichnung zum Stand der Verhandlungen über Massnahmen zur Reduzierung der Werraversalzung und Versenkung, Nov. 15, 1986, BayHStA StK/19611; kieserite issue in Memo MinDir Weichert, BM Innerdt. Beziehungen, July 26, 1979, DzD VI.6, Doc. 37, 152. Increasing kieserite production in West Germany was estimated to cost DM 80 million; the delivery of the GDR's annual share was calculated at DM 38 million.

98. On potash mining methods see Wittich, "Produktionsprozesse," 137–166, on flotation: 153–156; on ESTA: 156–158.

99. BM Innerdt. Beziehungen, Aufzeichnung zum Stand der Verhandlungen über Massnahmen zur Reduzierung der Werraversalzung und Versenkung, Nov. 15, 1986, BayHStA StK/19611.

100. Ibid.

101. The West German delegation informed their counterparts in October 1980 about the successful tests with the ESTA technology. See Bericht über das 3. Gespräch zu den mit dem Kaliabbau im Grenzgebiet zw. der DDR und der BRD zusammenhängenden Fragen am 17. und 18. Okt. 1980 in der Hauptstadt der DDR Berlin, Dec. 18, 1980, BArch-SAPMO, Büro Mittag DY 3023/1435.

102. von Berg, "Umweltschutzabkommen," 125–126.

103. Claus-Einar Langen, "Wo Ost-Berlin Schaden fürchtet: Deutsch-deutscher Deichbau interessanter als deutsch-deutscher Umweltschutz," *Frankfurter Allgemeine Zeitung*, June 20, 1980.

104. Bastian, *Greenpeace in der DDR*, 18–20.

105. Kurt Singhuber, Ministerium für Erzbergbau, Metallurgie und Kali, to Hans Reichelt, MUW, Aug. 29, 1988, BArch DK5/1498.

106. von Berg, "Zusammenarbeit," 609.

107. BM Innerdt. Beziehungen, Vermerk, Feb. 6, 1987, BayHStA StK/19611; Nonpaper, Sept. 14, 1988, BArch SAPMO, Büro Mittag DY3023/1436.

108. Mittag to Honecker, Nov. 29, 1988, signed "agreed" by Honecker on Nov. 30, 1988, BArch SAPMO, Büro Mittag DY3023/1436.

109. MinDirg Vogl, Bay. Staatsmin für Landesentwicklung und Umweltfragen, to Anneliese H., Lichtenberg, Dec. 18, 1979, BayHStA StK/19664.

110. Friederike Bauer, "Nach der Aufregung der Wende kehrt neue Normalität ein: Hof in Oberfranken—'ganz oben in Bayern,'" *Frankfurter Allgemeine Zeitung*, Apr. 27, 1993.

111. Metzger, *Waldsterben*, 135–201; von Detten, ed., *Waldsterben*, 138–151.

112. BMI, MR Kupfer, Ergebnisvermerk, Abteilungsleiter-Gespräch in Berlin (Ost), June 7, 1985, BArch 288/108. The memo contains a six-point priority list.

113. In 1982, the GDR emitted 4.73 million tons of SO_2, as compared with 3 million in West Germany. Based on the size of the country, the GDR emitted 60 percent more SO_2 than West Germany. See "Luftverunreinigung in der DDR: Die Emission von Schwefeldioxid und Stickoxiden," *DIW Wochenbericht* 30/85, July 25, 1985, 345. The gap widened significantly during the 1980s as East Germany's lignite dependency grew and West Germany increased the use of desulfurization technology. In 1983, the GDR deposited 196,000 tons of SO_2 in West Germany; 156,000 tons went in the other direction. Figures in Grosse Anfrage: Luftverunreinigung, saurer Regen und Waldsterben, BT, 9. WP, Drs. 9/1955, Sept. 7, 1982, 9.

114. Hünemörder, *Frühgeschichte*; Huff, *Natur und Industrie*, 176–177, 235–250.

115. On the GDR's unsuccessful efforts to engage the CSSR see Huff, *Natur und Industrie*, 225–235; on pollution in the northern Czech borderlands see Glassheim, *Cleansing*, 8–10, 113–122.

116. Alfred Dick, Bay. Staatsminister für Landesentwicklung und Umweltfragen to Hans-Dietrich Genscher, Foreign Minister, May 12, 1978, BayHStA, Bay. GrePo Nr. 631.

117. Strauss to Schmidt, Aug. 17, 1980, BayHStA StK/19664. See also Strauss to Schmidt, Feb. 8, 1980, BayHStA StK/19664; Kleine Anfrage: Grenzüberschreitende Luftverunreinigung aus DDR und CSSR, BT, 9. WP, Drs. 9/1569, Apr. 13, 1982.

118. Bernd Hummel, "Unmut an Zonengrenze über verpestete Luft: 'Volkseigene Dreckschleudern' vertreiben Touristen," *Die Welt*, May 30, 1984; Mayor Heinel, City of Lichtenberg to Franz Josef Strauss, Governor of Bavaria, June 29, 1986, BayHStA StK/19668.

119. Dr. Hans Heun, Mayor of Hof, to Franz Josef Strauss, Governor, May 5, 1986, BayHStA StK/19668.

120. Steiner, *Plans That Failed*, 172–175; Roesler, "Aussenwirtschaftspolitik," 565–566; Judt, *Kommerzielle Koordinierung*, 139–141.

121. Huff, *Natur und Industrie*, 181–182, 269, 272; Paucke, *Chancen für die Umweltpolitik*, 33–35. On Günter Mittag's department see Lepsius, "Reformunfähigkeit," 104–115.

122. *Chronik der Zellstoff- und Papierfabrik Rosenthal*, 23.

123. Bay. Staatsministerium für Ernährung, Landwirtschaft und Forsten to StK, Dec. 10, 1979, BayHStA StK/19664; Eiber, *Hof. Tor zur Freiheit*, 184–189.

124. Grenzpolizeiinspektion Hof to Landratsamt Hof, July 18, 1979; Bay. Staatsministerium für Landesentwicklung to StK, Dec. 18, 1979, both in BayHStA StK/19664.

125. Untersuchung der Belastung des Raumes Blankenstein/Saale durch SO2 (1980). Bearb. durch das Institut für Wasserwirtschaft Bereich Umweltschutz (Wittenberg), Leiter: Prof. Dr. Egon Seidel, VVS-B-392-7/81/3/3, BArch DK5/1905.

126. Western standards: Grenzpolizei Hof to MR Dr. Baer, StK, Aug. 11, 1980, BayHStA StK/19666; emissions: Bay. Staatsministerium für Landesentwicklung und Umweltfragen to Bay. StK, Oct. 2, 1984, BayHStA StK/19666. VEB Rosenthal produced cellulose in a magnesium-based sulfite process (as opposed to a calcium-based process), which the Bavarian Ministry acknowledged as "environmentally friendly."

127. Ministerium für Umweltschutz und Wasserwirtschaft, Weisung Nr. 36/81 (VS B161-17/81), Nov. 24, 1981, BArch DK5/1498.

128. *Chronik der Zellstoff- und Papierfabrik Rosenthal*, 25, 35. The Bleiloch dam collapsed ecologically around 1977. In 1978, VEB Rosenthal installed a water treatment plant with Swiss technology that provided primary (mechanical) and secondary (biological) treatment. It also invested in deep ventilation units to resuscitate the dam, yet to no avail.

129. Rennert and Fiehn, "Einführung umweltverträglicher Technologien," V13.

130. Wettestad, "Environmental Regimes," 682–688; Levy, "Tote-Board Diplomacy," 78–81; Rothschild, "Burning Rain," 186–188.

131. Darst, *Smokestack Diplomacy*, 91–102; Kajser, "Under a Common Acid Sky," 221–225; Brain, "Appearing Green," 458–461.

132. Wettestad, "Environmental Regimes," 685–686. The West German government passed the Large Combustion Plant Directive in 1983. It subsequently pushed the issue onto the agenda of the European Community, where a similar directive was implemented in 1988 (88/609/EEC).

133. The motives of various CLRTAP signatories and the effectiveness of the 1985 Sulfur Protocol have been widely discussed in the literature. Most western signatories pursued SO_2 reductions anyway, reached them accidentally as a result of changes in their energy policy, or surpassed the 30 percent goal for domestic political reasons. Some of them could be virtuous on the international stage at no additional cost. Even nonsignatories reduced their emissions, leading some scholars to discuss counterfactually if reductions would have been achieved even without the Stockholm process. See Levy, "Tote-Board Diplomacy," esp. 116–127; Connolly, "Asymmetrical Rivalry," 122–154; Kajser, "Under a Common Acid Sky," 233–235.

134. It is irrelevant that the GDR government never ratified the Helsinki signature, as Huff, *Natur und Industrie*, 270, points out. It was the highly visible public commitment at Munich in 1984 that mattered politically.

135. "Luftverunreinigung in der DDR: Die Emission von Schwefeldioxid und Stickoxiden," *DIW Wochenbericht* 30/85, July 25, 1985, 337–346; "Die DDR hat sich in Helsinki viel vorgenommen," *Frankfurter Allgemeine Zeitung*, July 26, 1986. See also "Zunehmende Luftverschmutzung in der DDR durch Renaissance der Braunkohle," *DIW Wochenbericht* 4/83, Jan. 27, 1983, 43–49.

136. Roesler, *Umweltprobleme*, 48–49; Huff, *Natur und Industrie*, 176–177; Hünemörder, *Frühgeschichte*, 264–265.

137. Darst, *Smokestack Diplomacy*, 100–102. The Soviet Union had insisted on contract language for CLRTAP that spoke of reducing "transborder fluxes" instead of mandating 30 percent reductions across the board. Soviet officials had no intention of letting any foreign body monitor their domestic emissions.

138. Huff, *Natur und Industrie*, 183, 249, 262–268.

139. Langstreckentransport vom SO_2 über die Staatsgrenze (1979): Bearbeitet durch das Institut für Wasserwirtschaft Bereich Umweltschutz (Wittenberg), Leiter—Prof. Dr. Egon Seidel, Verfasser [Rainer] Schenk, Ursula Andrasch, Hans-Jürgen Discher, BArch DK5/1755. The percentage relates to emissions per quarter.

140. Email correspondence with Prof. Dr. Rainer Schenk, Apr. 2016. Referenced with permission.

141. Aufzeichnung, Umweltschutzpolitik in der DDR, Feb. 9, 1983, BayHStA StK/19588. Reichelt announced the plan in an interview with the East German paper *Neues Deutschland* in early February 1983.

142. West German industry invested an estimated DM 13.5 billion to comply with the 1983 Large Combustion Plant Directive. The British technology purchased by the GDR cost some 40 million pounds and was bought with British loans. See "Emissionen von SO_2 aus Braunkohlekraftwerken in der DDR," *DIW Wochenbericht* 11/87, Mar. 12, 1987, 154–157; Huff, *Natur und Industrie*, 258–268.

143. Huff, *Natur und Industrie*, 269.

144. Ibid., 249, 264, 268, 270. Again, the GDR more or less followed the Soviet example. See Darst, *Smokestack Diplomacy*, 99–102.

145. Although talks about the salinization of the Werra started in the spring of 1980, the presence of UBA representatives at inter-German talks or on the international stage regularly led to ritualized protest. See *40 Jahre Umweltbundesamt*, 27, 134–135. Conversations about air pollution started in 1983 but were interrupted by the cancellation of the planned visit of Erich Honecker to Bonn in 1984 and resumed in 1985.

146. On the GDR's debt crisis see Steiner, *Plans That Failed*, 161–165, 172–175; Volze, "Devisenverschuldung," 151–177; Roesler, "Aussenwirtschaftspolitik," 558–572; Judt, *Kommerzielle Koordinierung*, 132–141, 158–166, 172–174; Maier, *Dissolution*, 59–72; Ahrens, "Debt, Cooperation, and Collapse,"161–176.

147. Mittag to Reichelt, Standpunkt und Vorschläge zur weiteren Entwicklung der Beziehungen zwischen der DDR und der BRD bzw. Westberlin auf dem Gebiet des Umweltschutzes, Mar. 20, 1984, BArch DK5/5756. The tightening grip of the GDR's liquidity crisis in the 1980s explains a whole cluster of environmental deals with West Germany that Günter Mittag's office either concluded, offered, or considered at the time. See Eckert, "Grenzgewässer," 93–96.

148. Honecker had planned a Bonn visit for 1984 but canceled it under pressure from the Soviet Union. See Oldenburg and Stephan, "Honecker," 791–805. In preparation for the visit, East and West German experts met three times in 1983 to discuss transboundary air pollution and desulfurization projects, but these meetings were discontinued due to the cancellation of the visit.

149. Information und Vorschläge zur Fortführung von Gesprächen zwischen der DDR und der BRD auf dem Gebiet des Umweltschutzes; confirmed by Honecker on May 7, 1985, BArch DK5/5756.

150. Information über das 5. Gespräch mit der BRD zu Fragen der weiteren Gestaltung der Beziehungen auf dem Gebiet des Umweltschutzes, n.d. [Nov. 27, 1985], BArch DK5/5756.

151. Marlis Menge, "Berlin: Dicke Luft," *Die Zeit*, Jan. 22, 1980; "Janz Berlin is eene Wolke," *Der Spiegel*, Feb. 25, 1985, 88–96.

152. "Markt vor der Tür," *Wirtschaftswoche*, Feb. 15, 1985, 18–20.

153. Christoph Derix, StaeV, Vermerk, July 2, 1986, BArch B288/109. This document addressed the possibility of a power plant for East Berlin at DM 160 to 220 million. The federal government had reservations about the proposal since it violated the Polluter Pays Principle, but West Berlin representatives argued "decidedly" for this solution. West Berlin's larger plans for East German power plants in Manfred Breitenkamp, Senator für Stadtwentwicklung und Umwelt, memorandum, Oct. 10, 1985, BArch B288/108.

154. The concepts "asymmetric vulnerability" and "asymmetrical rivalry" play a key role in the analysis of the Stockholm process, especially among political scientists and economists. See Wettestad, "Environmental Regimes," 680–681; Connolly, "Asymmetrical Rivalry."

155. Judt, *Kommerzielle Koordinierung*, 158–166; Steiner, *Plans That Failed*, 172.

156. "For Bavaria, it was a first that a minister from the GDR visited Bavaria in an official capacity for several days; it was also a first that the GDR established official contact directly with a federal state. Thus far, such encounters were only possible on the federal level," [MR Dr. Baer], Vermerk, Besuch des DDR-Umweltministers Dr. Reichelt in Bayern, n.d. [Oct. 1983], BayHStA StK/19755.

157. Ibid.

158. Vermerk, Besuch von Herrn Staatsminister Dick vom 14. bis 18. Mai 1984 in der DDR, BayHStA StK/19764.

159. Vermerk, Staatsministerium für Landesentwicklung und Umweltfragen, June 1, 1984, BayHStA StK/19668.

160. Bay. Staatsministerium für Landesentwicklung und Umweltfragen to Bay. StK, Oct. 2, 1984, BayHStA StK/19666.

161. Oldenburg and Stephan, "Honecker"; von Berg, "Umweltschutzabkommen," 127–128.

162. See the Introduction, note 1.

163. Information 19/83 über die Inbetriebnahme eines in Bau befindlichen Kohlekraftwerks der BRD in der Nähe der Staatsgrenze der DDR auftretende erhöhte Schadstoffablagerung der DDR und Vorschläge zum Vorgehen, June 30, 1983, BArch DK5/1498.

164. Voraus-Auszug aus der Niederschrift über die Ministerratssitzung, May 12, 1987, BayHstA StK/19611. The political wrinkle here was that Bavaria insisted that the federal government pay half the cost of any such deal, again as in the Röden agreement.

165. MR Dr. Baer, Vermerk, June 21, 1989, BayHStA StK/19670. The agreement was drafted in April 1989.

166. An influential publication was Peter Wensierski, " 'Wir haben Angst um unsere Kinder': Spiegel-Report über die Umweltverschmutzung in der DDR," parts 1–3, *Der Spiegel*, beginning July 8, 1985; published also as Wensierski, *Von oben nach unten.*

167. StaeV to BKAmt, BMU, BM Innerdt. Beziehungen, AA, Mar. 31, 1989, BArch B288/384: "[G]elegentlich entstand der Eindruck, dass die DDR auf diesem Wege letztlich die valutamässige Totalsanierung der Abwasserprobleme ihrer Elb-Industrien beabsichtigt."

168. Gemeinsame Erklärung des Stellvertreters des Vorsitzenden des Ministerrates und Ministers für Umweltschutz und Wasserwirtschaft der DDR [Reichelt] und des Bundesministers für Umwelt, Naturschutz und Reaktorsicherheit der Bundesrepublik Deutschland [Töpfer] über die Durchführung von Umweltschutz-Pilotprojekten in der DDR, July 6, 1989, in *DDR Umweltschutz: Ökologie statt Autarkie* (Bonn: Deutscher Industrie- und Handelstag, 1990); Förster, "Arzneimittelwerk," 26–27.

169. MUW, Vorschläge für das weitere Vorgehen im Zusammenhang mit der Beseitigung der Abwässer der Kaliindustrie, June 9, 1977, BArch-SAPMO, Büro Mittag DY 3023/1434.

170. Mittag, *Um jeden Preis*, 273.

171. *Chronik der Zellstoff- und Papierfabrik Rosenthal*, 33–35.

172. "'Kontrollbesuch': Zellstoff- und Papierfabrik Rosenthal GmbH—3 Jahre danach," *Zellstoff & Papier* 43:5 (1994): 77.

173. Zschiesche, "Umweltschutz in Ostdeutschland." Among the very few examples of those who tackle the issue are Chaney, "Chemical Landscape Transformed"; Lenz, *Verlusterfahrung Landschaft*, 197–207, 221–228; and Schwarzer, *Mondlandschaften*.

174. von Berg, "Verwirklichung," 903–906. The key documents that defined the starting position of the EnvU were the so-called *Eckwerte* papers: *Umweltpolitik: Eckwerte der ökologischen Sanierung und Entwicklung in den neuen Ländern* (Bonn: FedMin Env, Nov. 1990); *Ökologischer Aufbau: Eckwerte der ökologischen Sanierung und Entwicklung in den neuen Ländern* (Bonn: FedMin Env, Nov. 1991). Legal aspects in Kloepfer, *Umweltrecht*.

175. Scholars emphasize monitoring and accumulating scientific knowledge as among the main outcomes of the Stockholm process. See, e.g., Wettestad, "Environmental Regimes," 682–684; Connolly, "Asymmetrical Rivalry," 142; Levy, "Tote-Board Diplomacy," 115, with reference to the (reluctant) contribution of Eastern European countries. Rothschild, "Burning Rain," emphasizes British obstruction.

176. Rudolf Eickeler, "Die Zeiten der billigen Entsorgung sind vorbei," *Handelsblatt*, Feb. 15, 1990.

177. Thiemo Heeg, "Milliarden für die Umweltsanierung im Osten," *Frankfurter Allgemeine Zeitung*, Oct. 22, 2010; Radkau, *Ära der Ökologie*, 535.

178. Radkau, *Ära der Ökologie*, 522–523, 526–527. It is easier to locate key texts about German unification that ignore environmental themes. See, e.g., Rödder, *Deutschland einig Vaterland*; Ritter, *Wir sind das Volk*; Jarausch, ed., *Unified Germany*.

179. Marlise Simons, "West Germans Get Ready to Scrub the East's Tarnished Environment," *New York Times*, June 27, 1990.

180. ARGE Weser, *Reduktion der Salzbelastung*, 11.

181. The contract was leaked in 2014 and seemed to confirm that the Thuringian mines had been closed to save jobs in western mines. See the twelve-part series "Die Tragödie von Bischofferode" in *Thüringer Allgemeine Zeitung*, running from Feb. 22 to June 24, 2014; Martin Machowecz, "Hinterm Berg," *Die Zeit*, Mar. 27, 2014.

182. Müller von der Grün, "Unter einem Dach," 223–237.

183. Dr. Lübcke, Regierungspräsident Kassel, Wasserrechtliche Erlaubnis zur Einleitung salzhaltiger Abwässer aus dem Werk Werra [Philippsthal] in die Werra, Nov. 30, 2012.

184. Eisenbach, "Kaliindustrie," 219.

185. "K&S Studie: Fischart Groppe fühlt sich in salzhaltiger Werra wohl," *Handelsblatt*, June 3, 2014. The presence of the bullhead in the Werra was already well known. See Hübner, *Fließgewässerbewertung*, 53–55.

186. Based on the chemical classification of water quality by LAWA, the German working group on water issues of the federal states and the federal government represented by the federal environment ministry.

187. Ralf Euler, "Werra erst 2075 mit Prädikat 'Süsswasserqualität,'" *Frankfurter Allgemeine Zeitung*, Sept. 29, 2014; Euler, "Versalzene Suppe," *Frankfurter Allgemeine Zeitung*, Oct. 8, 2014. The Werra-Weser-Roundtable convened in 2008 and ended in late 2014.

188. "EU-Verfahren wegen Salzeinleitung in die Werra," *Handelsblatt*, July 18, 2012. The opponents document their activities at http://www.wasser-in-not.de/ (accessed Jan. 2018).

189. "Illegale Abfallentsorgung? Durchsuchungen erschüttern K+S," *Handelsblatt*, Sept. 9, 2015; "K&S soll bei Entsorgungsantrag getrickst haben," *Spiegel online*, Dec. 16, 2015; Andreas Macho, "Anklage gegen die K&S Manager," *Wirtschaftswoche*, Feb. 19, 2016.

190. "Der Topf ist voll," *Der Spiegel*, Nov. 4, 1992, 134, reports the size of the underground lake as 300 square kilometers. A publication by the Geological Survey in Hesse estimates the expanse of the underground saltwater distribution at 480 square kilometers. See Skowronek et al., *Salzabwasser*. The size of Lake Constance is 536 square kilometers.

CHAPTER 5

1. GK Nord, Aufklärungssammelbericht für den Zeitraum vom 20. Feb. 1982 bis 20. März 1982, BArch-MA, DVH 48/13646. A similar call was made a year later: "Nur Kraniche sind am Todesstreifen sicher. Selbstschussanlagen ersetzen Minen," *Braunschweiger Zeitung*, Apr. 13, 1983. See also Steffens, *Lebensjahre*, 135–136.

2. Cunningham, "Permeabilities"; Trouwborst et al., "Border Fences."

3. The activities of the European Green Belt are best traced on its website, http://www.europeangreenbelt.org/ (accessed Apr. 2018). See also Terry, Riecken, and Ullrich, *Green Belt of Europe*; Marschall et al., eds., *European Ecological Network*.

4. Havlick, *Bombs Away*, 1–11.

5. Brady, "Life in the DMZ"; Kim and Cho, "Ecological Resource Value"; Thomas, "Exquisite Corpses."

6. Bankoff, "Making Parks."

7. Davis, "Military Natures," 131.

8. Coates, "Borderlands"; McNeill and Engelke, *Great Acceleration*, 181–182.

9. The phrase is ubiquitous in Green Belt marketing materials and websites. See, e.g., http://www.erlebnisgruenesband.de/en/gruenes-band.html (accessed Apr. 2018). Accounts of the German Green Belt are frequently written by stakeholders, i.e., professional conservationists involved in its management and policy consultation. See, e.g., Frobel, Riecken, and Ullrich, "Naturschutzprojekt Deutsche Einheit"; Keil, "Sielmanns Vision"; Schlumprecht et al., "E+E Vorhaben."

10. See, e.g., "Das Grüne Band: Vom Todesstreifen zur Lebenslinie," BUND website, https://www.bund.net/gruenes-band/ (accessed June 2018).

11. "Because this was an area that had remained undisturbed for decades—nature essentially had been given a 40-year holiday! The species in the region used this

opportunity." Kai Frobel, quoted in "German Environmental Prize: From death zone to nature reserve," *Deutsche Welle*, Sept. 7, 2017, http://www.dw.com/en/german-environmental-prize-from-death-zone-to-nature-reserve/a-40399243 (accessed May 2018).

12. Larson, *Metaphors*.

13. Shears, *Ugly Frontier*, 9; Sepp Binder, "Die Narbe der Nation: Zwischen Touristen und Tretminen," *Die Zeit*, June 13, 1969, 8.

14. Bailey, *Edge of the Forest*, 13, 55.

15. "Agency" is a central, albeit contested paradigm in animal studies. See Krüger, Steinbrecher, Wischermann, eds., *Tiere und Geschichte*, 12–15; Flack, "Continental Creatures"; Specht "Animal History after Its Triumph," proposes abandoning the paradigm.

16. Term in Havlick, *Bombs Away*, 2.

17. The rough distinction of the terrain was established by East German border troops. See Erläuterung zum Plan der Hauptmassnahmen zur Verstärkung der Westgrenze der DDR, n.d. [1961], BArch-MA DVH 27/129422.

18. Sheffer, *Burned Bridge*, 97–163; Johnson, *Divided Village*, 65–88; Ritter and Lapp, *Grenze*; Stacy, *U.S. Army Border Operations*, 178–195; Rottmann, *Berlin Wall*; Lebegern, *Sperranlagen*; Schultke, *"Keiner kommt durch,"* 45.

19. The razed villages appear for the most part in local histories. See Hesse, *Befriedet*; Fuchs, *Billmuthausen*.

20. As a result of West German and international pressure, combined with West German loans as an incentive, Honecker agreed in 1983 to have the SM-70s removed. At the same time, the minefields were cleared as well. What looked like an important concession to the Federal Republic also relieved the GDR of expensive and dangerous maintenance work.

21. Sheffer, *Burned Bridge*, table in app. 3, 263–264. Wirsching, *Provisorium*, 605, points out that the number of escapes declined not only due to more intricate fortifications but also because alternatives to leaving the GDR opened up after 1975.

22. Behrens, ed., *Naturschutzgeschichte*, 1–3.

23. Ritter and Lapp, *Grenze*, 56.

24. Meldung Grenzpolizei Mellrichstadt, June 15, 1976, BayHStA StK/19535. The Special Task Force "Chemical Services" of the National People's Army used the herbicide Anforstan. See Büttner, ed., *Die "Chemiker" der NVA*, 241. The book is a hagiographic account written by former members of the unit.

25. Kdo. der Grenztrupppen, Abt. Aufklärung, Einsatzstudie: Herstellen von Tonbandaufnahmen von Gesprächen in unmittelbarer Nähe zur Staatsgrenze, June 19, 1963; Grenzbrigade, Unterabteilung Aufklärung, Bericht Oct. 3, 1963, both in BArch-MA DVH 32/117432.

26. Lohs and Martinetz, "Chemie des Todesstreifens," 18–19; the authors claim that the border troops deployed 10 to 50 kilograms of herbicides per hectare per year. See also BMU, AG Bodenschutz, Vermerk, Apr. 26, 1990, BArch B295/13831.

27. Müller-Wegener and Schmidt, *Bodenkontamination*; for Berlin see Litz, "Belastungssituation," 257–261.

28. Where the demarcation line formed a horseshoe bend (*Sack*) and the terrain proved difficult to patrol, the border authorities often opted for a simplification: the fence would not parallel the demarcation line but run from one tip of the horseshoe to the other, thus cutting off the interior of the loop. The land inside such a U-shaped bend was thus abandoned and barely patrolled.

29. BM Finanz, [monthly report on border incidents], July 29, 1963, and Aug. 26, 1963, both in PA/AA, B38/51.

30. Weber, "Vom 'Todesstreifen' zum 'Grünen Band,'" 660–661.

31. Ritter and Hajdu, *Innerdeutsche Grenze*, 48; Steffen, *Lebensjahre*, 136.

32. Franz, *Blaukehlchen*, 61–69; Theiss, "Lebensraum Grenzstreifen," esp. 6–7.

33. The threat of land mines to animals in war zones has long been the focus of animal rights groups. See Roberts and Stewart, "Land Mines"; on the consequences of modern warfare and weaponry more generally see Dudley et al., "War and Civil Strife."

34. Dieter Tasch, "Viele Minen sind des Wildes Tod," *Wolfsburger Allgemeine*, June 19, 1963; Landrat, County Herzogtum Lauenburg to Ministry of the Interior, Schleswig-Holstein, Nov. 2, 1964, LASH, Abt. 605/8401; Keil, *Postenhirsche*, 89–96, passim.

35. Interview with Ralf Maaß, Groß Molzahn, Oct. 23, 2010, I (1:13).

36. "Tiertragödie am Stacheldraht," *Braunschweiger Zeitung*, Bad Harzburg/Braunlage ed., Apr. 12, 1969.

37. "Für den Waidmann unerträglich: Ende der Tiertragödien an der Zonengrenze nicht abzusehen," *Göttinger Tageblatt*, Jan. 12, 1967.

38. Ohms, Zollkommissariat Braunlage (Harz) to Staatl. Forstamt Braunlage, Jan. 12, 1965, NLA WO, 13 A Nds Zg. 42/1996 Nr. 13; "Minen-Sperren im Oberharz halbierten den Rehbestand," *Herzberger Zeitung*, Jan. 11, 1968.

39. Bieder, Zollkommissariat Braunlage (Harz) to Staatl. Forstamt Braunlage, Apr. 13, 1967, NLA WO, 13 A Nds Zg. 42/1996 Nr. 13; "Minen-Sperren im Oberharz halbierten Rehbestand," *Herzberger Zeitung*, Jan. 1, 1968.

40. "Traurige Bilanz in der Bundesrepublik: Jeder sechste Hase wird vom Auto 'erschossen,'" *Braunschweiger Zeitung*, May 1, 1964. The article attributes the death of 50,000 roe deer, 100,000 hedgehogs, and 1 million songbirds per year to car traffic.

41. The National People's Army (NVA) maintained its own forest districts outside the regular forestry bureaucracy within the Ministry for Agriculture, Forests, and Food Supply. The NVA forests provided hunting districts for members of the armed forces. The borderlands, however, were not part of any NVA hunting district but were in a category of their own. Only members of the border troops could be part of a "hunting collective" in the borderlands. See Stubbe, *Jagd in der DDR*, 362–371, esp. 370–371.

42. Marie-Luise Scherer, "Die Hundegrenze," *Der Spiegel*, Feb. 7, 1994, 94–115, here 110. The practices of the "hunting collectives" were confirmed in an interview with Ralf Maaß, Groß Molzahn, Oct. 23, 2010, I (1:03). See also Dirlam, "Scharfenstein," 211; Eiber, *Hof: Tor zur Freiheit*, 198.

43. "Tiertragödien an der Zonengrenze nehmen ab. MGZ trennen den Rotwildbestand des Harzes: Biologisch positiver Austausch unterbunden," *Hannoversche Allgemeine Zeitung*, Feb. 10, 1970.

44. Rottman, *Berlin Wall*, 21; Lebegern, *Sperranlagen*, 50–52.

45. Cited in Sven Felix Kellerhoff, "Bei Gewitter detonierten die Minen im Todesstreifen," *Die Welt*, May 12, 2011. The testing took place in the Altmark region, today's Saxony-Anhalt. Despite precautions, 40 percent of the SM-70 explosions were triggered by deer. See Thoß, *Gesichert in den Untergang*, 183.

46. "Aufbau des Grenzhundewesens der DDR-Grenztruppe," *Zeitschrift des Bundesgrenzschutzes* 16:1 (Jan. 1989): 24. On target practice see Schultke, *"Keiner kommt durch,"* 72.

47. "Aufbau des Grenzhundewesens."

48. Ritter and Lapp, *Grenze*, 116.

49. Scherer, "Hundegrenze." Harz reference in Schultke, "Eiserne Vorhang," 99.

50. Scherer, "Hundegrenze." The Lankow Lake episode was also related during my conversation with Ralf Maaß, Groß Molzahn, Oct. 23, 2010.

51. "Verschmuste Bestie," *Der Spiegel*, Jan. 29, 1990, 84–85.

52. Blackbourn, *Conquest of Nature*.

53. Palis and Peitschner, *Drömling*; Baumann and Müller, "Naturpark Drömling"; Landesamt für Umweltschutz, ed., *Naturschutz in Sachsen-Anhalt* 30 (1993), esp. 4–18. See also Wasserwirtschaftamt Celle, Ergänzender Erläuterungsbericht, Feb. 5, 1974, 18–21, NLA HA Nds. 620 Celle Acc. 2001/170 Nr. 2.

54. Ackmann, "Gegenüber der Altmark," 78; Jorns, Kratz, and Pudack, "Drömling," 12–13.

55. Wasserwirtschaftsamt Celle, Wasserwirtschaftliche Grenzprobleme im Drömling, Apr. 5, 1977, NLA HA Nds. 620 Celle Acc.2001/170 Nr. 2.

56. Landkreis Gifhorn, Vermerk betr. Hannoverscher Drömling, Feb. 26, 1969, NLA HA Nds. 620 Celle Acc.2001/170 Nr. 2.

57. Rudolf Berndt, Entwicklungsplan für den Drömling als Großreservat für Naturschutz, -forschung und -beobachtung, Braunschweig, Dec. 10. 1968, quotations on pp. 5–6, NLA HA Nds. 620 Celle Acc. 2001/170 Nr. 2.

58. SPD Ortsverein Vorsfeld, [pamphlet,] *Rettet den Drömling*, n.d. [1988], BStU BV Magdeburg Abt. XX Nr. 3024; Jorns, Kratz, and Pudack, "Drömling," 17.

59. In 1961, a section of a fen called Giebelmoor was designated as a nature preserve (NSG). It was enlarged in 1979 and combined with the riparian forest of the Aller, reaching 313 hectares. In 1965, most of the western Drömling was put under landscape protection (LSG), which aims to preserve the appearance of the landscape but is less strict in its regulations than a nature

preserve. In 1988, the 600-hectare Vorsfelder Drömling was put under nature protection. In 1990, the 400-hectare nature preserve Kaiserwinkel became official. Since the 1970s, conservationists had tried to establish Kaiserwinkel as a preserve, which, aside from political bickering, proved problematic because of ongoing draining on the GDR side. The data on protected zones in Lower Saxony is available at www.naturschutzgebiete.niedersachsen.de/ (accessed Sept. 2015). For advocacy see BUND, DBV, eds., *Der Drömling: Stellungnahme der Naturschutzverbände zur Gefährdung eines Feuchtgebietes von internationaler Bedeutung* (Feb. 1988).

60. Kurzreferat Forstmeister Kuke, n.d., BStU BV Magdeburg Abt. XX Nr. 3024. The association was called Fördergemeinschaft Drömling.

61. MfS, Kreisdienststelle Klötze, Zwischenbericht zur OPK "Drömling," Feb. 3, 1989, BStU BV Magdeburg, Abt. XX Nr. 3884.

62. Chaney, *Nature of the Miracle Years*; Engels, *Naturpolitik*.

63. "Über 16,000 Menschen sagen 'Ja!' zu 'ihrer' Stadt an der Zonengrenze: Schulen, Wald und Industrie," *Lübecker Nachrichten*, Oct. 5, 1958.

64. On the confusing situation for fishermen see Steffens, *Lebensjahre*, 174–187. After 1978, East German authorities even built a wall on the shores of Lake Dassow. Rätzke, *DDR-Alltag*, 92–95.

65. "Wird Buchhorst Naturschutzgebiet?," *Lübecker Morgen*, Feb. 29, 1964. Buchorst Island has some 800 hectares. Further information on the Dassow Lake shore and Buchhorst nature preserves at http://unv.luebeck.de/naturschutz/arten_biotopschutz/schutzgebiete/dassower_see.html (accessed May 2016).

66. Buchhorst provides a good example of the fact that the persistence of biodiversity in the landscapes of Central Europe is rarely the result of noninterference but rather of extensive use such as grazing and seasonal mowing, i.e., of outdated agricultural techniques. The fact that Buchhorst was placed off limits in 1983 did not preserve its status. Instead, the non-use allowed invasive species such as giant hogweed and common reeds and shrubs to crowd out more sensitive flora. By 2011, only 80 of the 190 plant species identified in the early 1980s had survived. Conservationists subsequently recommended the introduction of goats for grazing. See Jürgen Lenz, "Naturschützer schlagen Alarm: Immer weniger Arten auf der Insel Buchhorst im Dassower See," *Ostsee Zeitung*, Jan. 14, 2011.

67. Brauneis, "Hessens Grenze," 336.

68. See the efforts on behalf of the eagle by the Permanent Mission of the Federal Republic in East Berlin, 1980–1982 in BArch B288/158; figures in Hauff, "Seeadlers *Haliaeetus albicilla*," 11; see also Standpunkt zu Verhandlungen mit der BRD über Zug, Bruterfolge und Schutzmassnahmen von Seeadlern, n.d. [May 1987], BArch DK1/28738. According to Hauff, 11, the heraldic interest in the white-tailed eagle was the result of a smart PR campaign on

the part of the conservationists. The federal heraldic symbol, however, is a generic eagle.

69. Petra Burghardt, "Thomas Neumann: Grünes Band oder Grüne Perlen?," in *Mehr Geschichte von Drüben* (Books on Demand, 2011), 58–69; on customs officers see "Zollstreifen haben auch ein Auge auf die Natur," *Lübecker Nachrichten*, Aug. 21, 1983.

70. The preserves are Ebenhöhe-Liebenberg, Sturzlieder Berg, Plesse-Konstein, Liebenberg-Hasenkanzel, Frankenloch bei Heldra, and Dreiherrenstein-Eschenberg. Interview with Wolfram Brauneis, July 13, 2009.

71. "Tod im Ei," *Der Spiegel*, Mar. 7, 1977, 204–206.

72. On the falcon program see Brauneis, Hammer, and Saar, "Auswilderung"; Stephan Börnecke, "Der Wanderfalke im Aufwind," *Frankfurter Rundschau*, Oct. 29, 2003; interview Brauneis, July 13, 2009; on Brauneis see "Eier im Nest: Wolfram Brauneis—ein Konditor rettet den Wanderfalken," *Spiegel Spezial*, Feb. 1, 1995, 106–107; Schreiber, "Brot des Konditors."

73. Beck and Frobel, "Letzter Zufluchtsort." See also Frobel, "20 Jahre Grünes Band," 5–6.

74. Christian Sebald, "Vom Todesstreifen zur Lebenslinie," *Süddeutsche Zeitung*, Aug. 12, 2009; Weiger, "Kai Frobel"; Phil McKenna, "The Boys Who Loved Birds," *The Big Roundtable*, Feb. 18, 2015, https://thebigroundtable.com/the-boys-who-loved-birds-cd6e117a608 (accessed Jan. 2018); interview with Kai Frobel, Nürnberg, July 20, 2009.

75. Frobel, Riecken, Ullrich, "Naturschutzprojekt Deutsche Einheit," 399; interview with Frobel, Nürnberg, July 20, 2009 (32:20). See also Irene Jung, "Der Vogel, der die Stille liebt," *Hamburger Abendblatt*, Apr. 21, 1984, 24, about land purchases in Lüchow-Dannenberg County for the protection of the crane.

76. Keil, "Sielmanns Vision." A segment of the 1988 show is embedded in a 2009 video: http://www.ndr.de/fernsehen/sendungen/expeditionen_ins_tierreich/expeditionen249.html (accessed Jan. 2018).

77. König, "Brutvogelbestand," 43–58, "first-name basis": 48.

78. Bernd Katzer to author, Mar. 4, 2013 and Apr. 13, 2013; cited with permission.

79. Original quote: "[F]ür jemanden, der sich z. B. mit Ornithologie oder Feldherpedologie beschäftigte [. . .] war jede Schicht wie eine Exkursion." Bernd Friedrich to author, Mar. 22, 2010; cited with permission. Friedrich, "Uhu"; see also Friedrich and Fahrenholz, "Avifaunistische Mitteilungen."

80. "The special status of the area under investigation does not allow for an exact description of landscapes, habitats and biotopes that the observed birds were found in." Katzer and Baeseler, "Ornithologische Notizen," 17. Katzer and Baeseler were both border guards. Baeseler to author, Feb. 21, 2013.

81. Dr. Bernd Nicolai, Director, Museum Heineanum Halberstadt, to author, Aug. 11 and 12, 2010; cited with permission.

82. Martin Görner, interview, Aug. 23, 2010, Artenschutzzentrum Thüringen in Ranis, Thuringia.

83. Görner and Schultheis, "Schwarzstorch." See also Pfeifer, "Schwarzstorch"; Jost, "Vorkommen."

84. Martin Görner, interview, Aug. 23, 2010, Artenschutzzentrum Thüringen in Ranis, Thuringia. Görner, a specialist on eagle-owls, was a member of the Institut für Landschaftsforschung und Naturschutz (ILN) Halle, Zweigstelle Jena from 1968 until 1990. The Institute was founded in 1953 as the central East German institution for nature conservation. Görner was suspended in 1990 amid claims that he had worked for the Stasi. His permit for the security strip, regularly renewed without much ado, might have contributed to the suspicions about him. He was thoroughly screened on the basis of records available at the office of the Federal Commissioner for the Records of the Stasi (BStU) and fully rehabilitated in 1992 by the Labor Court in Jena. His former employer, ILN, had to publish a note to that effect. See *Landschaftspflege und Naturschutz in Thüringen* 29:4 (1992): 112. On Görner, see the autobiographical note in Behrens and Hoffmann, eds., *Naturschutzgeschichte(n)*, 75–92, esp. 84–88. Unfortunately, Görner's annual reports about the security strip can no longer be located in the state archives. On the ILN see Behrens, "Institut."

85. Uwe Barschel (1944–1987) was a Christian Democrat and served as governor (*Ministerpräsident*) of the federal state Schleswig-Holstein from 1982 to 1987. He was considered a rising star within his party and most likely harbored ambitions to enter federal politics. His tenure as governor, indeed his entire biography, remains overshadowed by the scandal nicknamed Waterkantgate. He was accused of having spied on his political opponent, Björn Engholm (SPD), during the 1987 state election campaign. In a televised statement, he gave his word of honor that the accusations were unfounded. He resigned in October 1987 and was found dead on October 11, 1987, in a Swiss hotel. The circumstances of his death remain unclear to the present day.

86. Ministerium für Ernährung, Landwirtschaft und Forsten des Landes Schleswig-Holstein (MELF SH), *Landesprogramm zum Schutz der Natur und zur Verbesserung der Struktur an der schleswig-holsteinisch-mecklenburgischen Landesgrenze*, Kiel, Sept. 1985, quotation: 1; Lauenburgische Akademie für Wissenschaft und Kultur, Seminar vom Mai 1987 über das Landesprogramm, Seminarberichte Heft 1 (1987). I wish to thank Reinhard Schmidt-Moser of the Ministry for Agriculture and the Environment for providing the materials cited here. See also MELF SH, Kabinettsvorlage 47/1985, Apr. 10, 1985, LASH, Abt. 605/6483.

87. Pressemitteilung 2-9-85 zum Landesprogramm, LASH, Abt. 611/8391; Karsten Henke, "20 Millionen für den Schutz der Natur," *Lübecker Nachrichten*, Sept. 3, 1985; "Land will Fremdenverkehr und Naturschutz in Schwung bringen," *Kieler Nachrichten*, Apr. 17, 1985; Andreas Moser, "Das Naturschutzprogramm

findet grossen Anklang," *Lübecker Nachrichten*, May 4, 1985; "Bedrängte Natur soll Refugium entlang der deutsch-deutschen Grenze erhalten," *Flensburger Tageblatt*, Apr. 17, 1985.

88. Rede des MP Uwe Barschel zur öffentlichen Anhörung über den Entwuf eines Landesprogramms [. . .] am 2. Mai 1985 im Herrenhaus Steinhorst, LASH, Abt. 605/6484. Schaalsee Lake formed the link between the Lauenburg and Mecklenburg lake districts.

89. Handwritten note on a draft of Kabinettsvorlage 47/1985: "Die deutsch-deutsche Grenze soll durch den Naturschutz friedlicher werden," LASH, Abt. 605/6483.

90. Barschel to StS Hanns-Günther Hebbeln, Mar. 29, 1985, LASH, Abt. 605/6483.

91. The state of Schleswig-Holstein was deeply involved in the export of industrial and household waste to the Schönberg landfill in the GDR, just east of Lübeck. Schönberg was run by the GDR company Intrac; their western counterpart was the Hanseatische Baustoffkontor run by Adolf Hilmer. The highly profitable waste business was closely monitored by the Stasi. In January 1984, Hilmer transmitted a message from Schleswig-Holstein's environmental minister to his Stasi contact, IMB "Siegfried." The message conveyed the topics the minister wanted to address with the GDR, including the extension of the nature preserves Dassow Lake, Buchhorst, and Graswerder, as well as the opportunity for meetings of conservationists from both sides. The note vaguely implied economic incentives if the GDR proved amenable. On the assumption that the environmental minister would not use such a back channel without Barschel's knowledge, one may therefore say that Barschel engineered his "green border" initiative through Schönberg-related Stasi contacts. See BStU MfS AG BKK Nr. 2, fol. 134.

92. Potthoff, *Schatten*, 173–216; on ideological differences between Schmidt and Kohl's policies see Korte, *Deutschlandpolitik*, 479–484; on symbolic rhetorical shifts under Kohl see Wirsching, *Provisorium*, 591–594.

93. On Honecker's Bonn visit see Potthoff, *Schatten*, 257–272; Wentker, *Aussenpolitik*, 515–518.

94. Vereinbarung zwischen der Regierung der BRD und der Regierung der DDR über die weitere Gestaltung der Beziehungen auf dem Gebiet des Umweltschutzes [Umweltabkommen], *Bulletin* Nr. 83 (Sept. 10, 1987), 716–718. All attachments on working groups, etc., in BArch B295/21553.

95. Barschel to Kohl, May 14, 1985; Wolfgang Schäuble, BKAmt, to Barschel, June 21, 1985, both in BArch B288/162. Further preparatory work between federal and state agencies from 1983 in BayHStA StK/19738.

96. Hans Otto Bräutigam, Leiter StaeV, to StS Sönke Traulsen, MELF SH, May 24, 1985, including non-paper of July 19, 1984, LASH Abt. 605/6484; Oskar Fischer, GDR Foreign Minister, to Günter Mittag, July 23, 1984, BArch SAPMO DY3023/1435; the non-paper is also in BArch DK5/5756; on deliberately skirting: MELF to BKAmt, June 26, 1984, BArch B295/9105.

97. Landesamt für Naturschutz und Landschaftspflege Schleswig-Holstein, "'Lauenburg-Programm' zügig angelaufen," Dec. 1986; my thanks to Reinhard Schmidt-Moser (MELF SH, Kiel) for this document. However, the western shore of Schaalsee Lake was not designated as a nature preserve, only as a landscape preserve. The fact that the less potent category was applied reflects the assumption that the border was there to stay and would suffice to protect the lake.

98. Memo, Gemeinsame Projekte Bundesrepublik Deutschland/DDR auf dem Gebiet des Biotopschutzes, Feb. 11, 1986, LASH Abt. 605/6635.

99. Maps and materials on "Werra-Aue von Treffurt und Heldra" and "Heldrastein" in Sammlung Brauneis, Eschwege.

100. "Barschel will mit der DDR über Naturschutz an der Grenze reden," *Kieler Nachrichten*, Sept. 3, 1985; MfS Hauptabteilung XVIII, Information Nr. 262/85 über den am 9. 12. 1985 geplanten Besuch des [. . .] BARSCHEL, Uwe (CDU), aus der BRD, BStU MfS HA XVIII Nr. 19304, 8–14.

101. Sozialdemokratischer Informationsbrief Nr. 150/85, June 21, 1985, LASH Abt. 611/8391; "Weiss die DDR von nichts? Streit um grenzüberschreitenden Umweltschutz," *Schleswig-Holsteinische Landeszeitung*, June 22, 1985; "Streit um grenzüberschreitende Umweltinitiativen mit der DDR," *Kieler Nachrichten*, June 22, 1985.

102. Herbert Wessels, "Schaalsee soll deutsch-deutsches Naturschutzgebiet werden," *Hamburger Abendblatt*, Dec. 11, 1985; Barbara Borowsky, "DDR prüft Wunsch der Fischer," *Lübecker Nachrichten*, Dec. 13, 1985; "Barschel lobt Gesprächsbereitschaft der DDR-Vertreter in Sachen Umweltschutz," *Husumer Nachrichten*, Dec. 13, 1985.

103. Hans Reichelt, Information über ein Gespräch mit dem Ministerpräsidenten des Bundeslandes Schleswig-Holstein, Uwe Barschel, am 9. Dezember 1985, BStU Mfs HA XVIII Nr. 19304, 17–20.

104. The Stasi preapproved a list of nature preserves that West Germans and visitors from other capitalist countries were allowed to visit. Gen. Maj. Kleine, HA XVIII, Jan. 16, 1986, BStU MfS HA XVIII Nr. 21342.

105. Generalforstmeister Rüthnick to Hermann, Stellv. Minister für Umwelt und Wasserwirtschaft, June 30, 1988, BArch DK1/28734. According to Rüthnick's report, West German representatives were surprised by how openly their interlocutors addressed environmental damages; they were also said to have accepted the eastern view that industrial production and nature conservation were compatible.

106. Günter Mittag to Erich Honecker, Feb. 23, 1988, with attachment: Information über die Vorschläge der BRD zur Errichtung grenzüberschreitender Naturschutzgebiete und Grundsätze für das weitere Vorgehen, BArch SAPMO Büro Mittag DY3023/1445; see also Standpunkt zur Einrichtung von grenzüberschreitenden Schutzgebieten zwischen der DDR und der BRD, Aug. 31, 1987, BArch SAPMO Büro Mittag DY3023/1444.

107. Oberstlt. Wolsky, Vermerk, Abt. VIII, Jan. 21, 1988, BStU BV Magdeburg, Abt. XX Nr. 3884, fol. 88–90; see also Information über die Vorschläge der BRD zur Errichtung grenzüberschreitender Naturschutzgebiete und Grundsätze für das weitere Vorgehen, BStU BV Magdeburg, Abt. XX Nr. 3884, fol. 138–141.

108. For an overview of forestry as economic sector in the GDR see Huff, *Natur und Industrie*, 209–214.

109. Figures in Hausmitteilung, Rudolf Rüthnick to Peter Findeis, Stellv. Minister MLFN, Nov. 6, 1984, BArch DK1/24741. Other documents refer to twenty-two forest districts with holdings in the border area. Rüthnick was the highest forestry official in the GDR and the head of the Forestry Department within the GDR Ministry for Agriculture, Forests and Food Supply. For basic data on GDR forestry see Kurth, "Forstwirtschaft."

110. Vereinbarung über die Zusammenarbeit zur Gewährleistung der Planung, Organisation, Durchführung und Sicherung der Schädlings- und Unkrautbekämpfung im Schutzstreifen an der Staatsgrenze der DDR zur BRD und Westberlin zwischem dem Ministerium für Nationale Verteidigung und dem Ministerium für Land-, Forst- und Nahrungsgüterwirtschaft (MLFN), May 15, 1974, BArch DK1/24741.

111. Nelson, *Cold War Ecology*, 141–170, esp. 142–144, 161–167; Huff, *Natur und Industrie*, 211–213.

112. Staatlicher Forstbetrieb (StFB) Schleiz. Niederschrift über die Beratung zum Problem der Schneebruchaufarbeitung im Schutzstreifen des StFB Schleiz, July 5, 1980, BArch DK1/24741.

113. MLFN, Protokoll zur Kontrollberatung im Grenzgebiet des Bezirkes Magdeburg, June 29, 1983, BArch DK1/24741.

114. On the lack of maps and knowledge about forest stockings see VEB Forstprojektierung Potsdam, Plan zur Inventarisierung und Bewirtschaftung der Waldbestände im Grenzgebiet, Apr. 26, 1983, BArch DK1/24741.

115. Staatlicher Forstbetrieb (StFB) Schleiz. Niederschrift über die Beratung zum Problem der Schneebruchaufarbeitung im Schutzstreifen des StFB Schleiz, July 5, 1980, BArch DK1/24741.

116. Hausmitteilung Rüthnick to Minister Heinz Kuhrig, Apr. 24, 1976, BArch DK1/24741. The bark beetle invasion described in this document occurred in the forest districts of Wernigerode and Scharfenstein in the Harz Mountains.

117. Staatlicher Forstwirtschaftsbetrieb Schleiz, Oberforstmeister Fischer, to Rat des Bezirkes Gera, Mar. 31, 1986, BArch DK1/24741.

118. The agreement of May 1, 1982, referenced in Rüthnick to Lt. Gen. Baumgarten, Chef der Grenztruppen, Min. Nationale Verteidigung, July 20, 1983, BArch DK1/24741.

119. The documents refer to 1975 as the last time that regular forestry inventory work (*Forsteinrichtungsarbeiten*) was conducted in the security strip. See, e.g.,

VEB Forstprojektierung Potsdam, Director Dr. Bieberstein to Rüthnick, MLFN, July 11, 1983, BArch DK1/24741.

120. Theo Zehnter, President, Deutscher Bauernverband to Franz Josef Strauss, Governor of Bavaria, Apr. 9, 1984, BArch DK1/24741. Zehnter urges Strauss to contact East German authorities to clear their forests lest the snow breakage of 1981–1982 invite another bark beetle infestation, which would affect forests in Upper Franconia on the West German side.

121. Landforstmeister Purfuerst, Rat des Bezirkes Suhl, to Rüthnick, MLFN, June 29, 1984, BArch DK1/24741.

122. On the disintegration of forest management in the 1980s see Nelson, *Cold War Ecology*, 159–161; on the increasing pressure on forest productivity due to air pollution and calamities see Huff, *Natur und Sozialismus*, 214–218.

123. On the environmental costs of GDR agriculture see Buck, "Umwelt- und Bodenbelastung," 432; Heinz, *Mähdrescher*, 314–332; Schmidt, "Landwirtschaft und Naturschutz;"; Heinz, "Klassenkampf gegen Hecken."

124. "Rekultivierung oder Naturschutz?," *Lübecker Nachrichten*, Sept. 18, 1985. The article refers to a horseshoe bend east of Schaalsee Lake, the Valluhner Sack. For an example in Bavaria see Steffens, *Lebensjahre*, 29.

125. Landratsamt Rhön-Grabfeld, Landrat Dr. Steigerwald, to Bavarian StK, Aug. 8, 1989; Landesbund für Vogelschutz (LBV), Ornithologische Arbeitsgruppe Coburg (OAG) to Minister of the Environment, Klaus Töpfer, Aug. 30, 1989, both in BArch B295/21664.

126. Töpfer to Reichelt, Nov. 9, 1989, BArch B295/21664.

127. Rödder, *Deutschland einig Vaterland*, 279–289.

128. Wolfgang Röhl, "Ein Bericht und Bilddokumente von der Grenzöffnung Eckertal—Stapelburg/DDR am 11. November 1989," http://www. wolfgangroehl.de/Grenzoeffnung-Eckertal/Grenzoeffnung-Eckertal.htm (accessed Aug. 2017).

129. For a list of all 164 crossings that existed by June 1990 see Hermann and Sroka, eds., *Grenzlexikon*, 63–64. The number of cars in Mustin: "Katastrophale Verkehrslage in den grenznahen Städten," *Lübecker Nachrichten*, May 10, 1990.

130. "An der Grenze herrscht das Chaos: 70 Kilometer Autostau in Rudolphstein, 'Japanische Verhältnisse' in Zügen aus der DDR," *Süddeutsche Zeitung*, Nov. 18–19, 1989; Hannes Krill, "Wiedervereinigung findet im Stau statt," *Süddeutsche Zeitung*, Nov. 20, 1989.

131. Viola Roggenkamp, "Keine Bleibe für die töffelnden Kolonnen: Grossparkplatz stösst auf Ablehnung," *Die Zeit*, Dec. 29, 1989. References to Trabi exhaust are ubiquitous in the press coverage of late 1989.

132. "An der Grenze herrscht das Chaos," *Süddeutsche Zeitung*, Nov. 18–19, 1989; "Schaden im Schlagloch," *Der Spiegel*, Dec. 18, 1989, 82–84; Landrat Zeitler,

Landratsamt Coburg, Baumassnahmen an Kreisstrassen im Zusammenhang mit der Öffnung von Grenzübergängen zur DDR, July 20, 1990, BayHStA StK 19616; Bürgermeister Oskar Herbig, Mellrichstadt, to Bavarian StK, Dec. 1, 1989, BayHStA StK 19461.

133. Bund Naturschutz (BN) in Bayern, "Die Öffnung der Grenze: Chance für den Umweltschutz," press release 81/89 (Nov. 30, 1989), Archiv BN, Ordner GRE BN –Schr-PRÖ 1989–1997. The position of BN is reflected in Peter Schmitt, "Mit der S-Bahn von Selb nach Plauen: Warnung vor umweltschädlichem Strassenbau im Grenzgebiet," *Süddeutsche Zeitung*, Feb. 8, 1990; Bernd Meyer, "Todesstreifen als Lebenszone für seltene Tiere," *Süddeutsche Zeitung*, Apr. 23, 1990; Hannes Krill, "Attacke auf die 'Asphalt-Cowboys': Im Genzland soll die Bahn Vorrang haben," *Süddeutsche Zeitung*, Mar. 9, 1990. Insinuating an "anti-road construction dogma" among the environmentalists is Hans Jürgensen, "Verkehrsinvestitionen für die Zukunft," *Frankfurter Allgemeine Zeitung*, Nov. 14, 1990.

134. "DDR hebt Sperrzone an Grenze auf. Freier Zugang zu den Ortschaften im Schutzstreifen," *Süddeutsche Zeitung*, Nov. 14, 1989.

135. On the GDR's limited tourist capacity in 1990 see Baumann, "Innerdeutscher Tourismus"; Christoph Wendt, "Die Natur leuchtet in den Landesfarben: Vor dem Sommer in Mecklenburg," *Frankfurter Allgemeine Zeitung*, May 23, 1990, R7. See also "Hänschen Prahlhans: Die Westdeutschen [. . .] steuern als neues Urlaubsziel die DDR an," *Der Spiegel*, Dec. 18, 1990, 101–102.

136. Quotations in Dankwart Guratzsch, "Umweltschützer fürchten in der DDR einen Massenansturm von Touristen," *Die Welt*, Mar. 22, 1990. The article covers a town hall meeting in Berlin-Charlottenburg convened by the Friends of the Earth (BUND). See also Rudolf Braunburg, "Im Osten ist besser brüten," *Deutsches Allgemeines Sonntagsblatt*, Feb. 23, 1990; Theodor Geus, "Biotop oder Freizeitpark? Zur touristischen Entwicklung in Brandenburg," *Frankfurter Allgemeine Zeitung*, Apr. 9, 1992.

137. "Reservat für Wendehälse," *Der Spiegel*, Jan. 29, 1990, 81.

138. Jörg Bremer, "Spaziergänge im alten Sperrgebiet," *Frankfurter Allgemeine Zeitung*, Feb. 24, 1990, *Bilder und Zeiten* suppl., 5.

139. One such appeal was a home-made sign mimicking the BGS "Halt! Hier Grenze" signs that had lined the border on the western side. The imitation "Stop! Untouched Nature! We will NOT proceed here" stood in the border strip near Mödlareuth, Bavaria. Photo in Hermann, *Grenze*, 163.

140. Eckert, *Brocken*, 9–16, 118–127; Vollers-Sauer, "Goethes Harz"; Ude-Koeller, *Harzklub*.

141. Bindewald, "Brocken," 122–126.

142. But see Seelig, "Schwarzkehlchen," 120. This short report refers to observations in the summer of 1989.

143. Jörg Wunram, "Als auf dem Brocken die Mauer fiel," *NDR Info*, Dec. 3, 2014, http://www.ndr.de/kultur/geschichte/chronologie/Als-auf-dem-Brocken-die-Mauer-fiel,mauerfallbrocken100.html (accessed Jan. 2018); Björn Menzel, "Bennos Brocken," *einestages: Zeitgeschichte auf Spiegel Online*, Mar. 8, 2011.

144. Cejka, "Einbruch," 11; Stephan Börnecke, "Wenn erst die Bierdosen rollen ist der Uhu fort," *Frankfurter Rundschau*, Mar. 16, 1990. The number of hikers reported on the Brocken ranged from 3,000 to 15,000 per day.

145. Günther et al., "Aktuelles."

146. Johannes Leithäuser, "Erste Fahrt der Brockenbahn nach 30 Jahren: Proteste von Naturschützern—Die Hoffnung einer ganzen Region," *Frankfurter Allgemeine Zeitung*, Sept. 17, 1990.

147. "Aus ernster Umweltlage rasch Lehren ziehen," *Freies Wort* (Suhl), Mar. 6, 1990; Cejka, "Einbruch," 12; Gabriele Walkhoff, "Sporttourismus in der DDR macht Naturschützern Sorge," *Frankfurter Allgemeine Zeitung*, Sept. 26, 1990.

148. Until the mid-1990s, some 2,000 hectares, or 11 percent of the space relevant to the Green Belt, had been turned into fields. Frobel, "Naturschutzprojekt Deutsche Einheit," 400.

149. Stephan Börnecke, "Die Hohe Rhön—ein Reservat der Natur," *Frankfurter Rundschau*, Jan. 22, 1990; Stephan Börnecke, "Wenn erst die Bierdosen rollen ist der Uhu fort," *Frankfurter Rundschau*, Mar. 16, 1990. The HGON was pitted against the Interessengemeinschaft Heldrastein in this conflict. Founded in April 1990, the Interessengemeinschaft defined its goal as developing Heldrastein for hikers.

150. Justus de Cuveland, "Biotop im Brennpunkt: Dassower See," *Lübecker Nachrichten* Apr. 11, 1990, 19; Andreas Oelker, "Seltene Vögel verenden in Stellnetzen: Zwist um Fährlinie [. . .] spitzt sich zu," *Lübecker Nachrichten*, May 31, 1990.

151. Landesamt für Naturschutz und Landschaftspflege Schleswig Holstein, Schleswig-holsteinisch-mecklenburgischer   Grenzraum—Mögliche Konfliktpunkte zum Naturschutz, Jan. 10. 1990, BArch B295/21666; Gebhard and Braun, "Naturraum von der Wakenitz bis zur Ostsee."

152. Carl-Albrecht von Treuenfels, "Ungestörte Biotope an der innerdeutschen Grenze," *Frankfurter Allgemeine Zeitung*, Dec. 1, 1989.

153. Nina Valoni, "Besuch bei Mutter Kasewski," *Hamburger Abendblatt*, Nov. 18, 1989; "Eine Wanderung zu neuen Ufern," *Hamburger Abendblatt*, June 12, 1990. See also the reports in *Geo Special*, no. 2: DDR (Apr.– 11, 1990); *Merian Extra: DDR* (Jan.–Feb. 1990). These perceptions were grafted onto travel literature and impressions about the GDR published before 1989. See Doßmann, "Sehnsucht."

154. On the bathing area see BGS, Grenzlagemeldung, Jan. 11, 1990, LASH Abt. 611/8391; on the other developments see Carl-Albrecht von Treuenfels,

"Ungestörte Biotope an der innerdeutschen Grenze," *Frankfurter Allgemeine Zeitung*, Dec. 1, 1989, 11; Karl Hermann, "Trabanten gegen Reiherenten. Natur im Niemandsland," *Die Zeit*, Dec. 22, 1989; Nicola von Hollander, "Überleben—ein Grenzfall," *Hamburger Abendblatt*, Jan. 13, 1990; Klaus Brill, "Bedrohte Idylle im Schatten der Wachtürme," *Süddeutsche Zeitung*, Jan. 23, 1990; Cejka, "Einbruch," 10–11; and "Touristen Nervenkitzel auf dem Todesstreifen," *Frankfurter Rundschau*, Aug. 23, 1990.

155. "Grundstücke: Glücksspiel im Osten," *Der Spiegel*, Nov. 27, 1989, 133; "Schwarzhandel: Leben wie ein Direktor," *Der Spiegel*, Dec. 4, 1989.

156. Schleswig-Holsteinischer Landtag, 12. WP, 8. Sitzung, Feb. 21, 1990, 2917; Hinz to author, Mar. 11, 2011. Hinz photographed handwritten signs offering money for valuable leads on seashore properties.

157. "DDR-hungrige Touristen zerstören Öko-Reservate: Zwei Seeadler-Paare geflüchtet," *Kieler Nachrichten*, May 28, 1990; on clapping Cejka, "Einbruch," 11; on the helicopter see Stefan Scheytt and Oliver Schröm, "Hubschrauber am Adlerhorst: Die Einheit bedroht ein Stück Natur, das im Schutz der Teilung prächtig gedieh," *Die Zeit*, June 14, 1991.

158. Interview with Ralf Maaß, Groß Molzahn, Oct. 23, 2010, II (6:00).

159. On the shifts in the West German understanding of nature conservation see Chaney, *Nature of the Miracle Years*; Hasenöhrl, *Zivilgesellschaft*.

160. Horst Stern, "Das Gebirge der Seele: Naturschutz als Menschenschutz," *Frankfurter Allgemeine Zeitung*, Dec. 8, 1990, suppl. *Bilder und Zeiten*, 1.

161. Chaney, *Nature of the Miracle Years*, 213–242; Hasenöhrl, *Zivilgesellschaft*, 235–256.

162. Leibenath, "Biotopverbund."

163. For the basics on Natura 2000 see Rajal, *Natura 2000*. The EU became a player in environmental policy in 1973 when it issued the First Programme of Action of the European Communities on the Environment (OJ/C/112, Dec. 12, 1973). On the EC's growing involvement during the 1970s see Meyer, "Zivilgesellschaftliche Mobilisierung."

164. "[The] inter-German border strip with its adjacent areas is predestined to provide a major contribution to NATURA 2000." Referat N[aturschutz] 1, BMU, Vermerk (3. Entwurf), Zusammenarbeit im Bereich des innerdeutschen Grenzstreifens, Feb. 5, 1990, BArch B295/20498; Referat N[aturschutz] 1, BMU, Vermerk GUA-Sitzung am 20.3.1990, Mar. 15, 1990, BArch B295/20492.

165. Brandt most likely never said these words on November 10, 1989. The line nonetheless took on significant meaning after the fall of the Berlin Wall. See Rother, "Gesprochene Wort"; Günter Bannas, "In der Erinnerung zusammengewachsen," *Frankfurter Allgemeine Zeitung*, Oct. 14, 2014.

166. See the occasional reference to the project as "Nature Protection Project German Unity" in, e.g., Frobel, Riecken, and Ullrich, "Naturschutzprojekt Deutsche Einheit."

167. Stephan Börnecke, "Die Hohe Rhön—ein Reservat der Natur," *Frankfurter Rundschau*, Jan. 22, 1990; Stephan Börnecke, "Auenverbund Werra überwindet die Grenze: Ein bedeutendes Projekt im hessisch-thüringischen Naturschutz," *Frankfurter Rundschau*, Jan. 31, 1990.

168. Protokoll der Tagung hauptamtlicher und ehrenamtlicher Naturschutz in der Hansestadt Lübeck und angrenzenden DDR-Bezirken, Jan. 20, 1990, BArch B295/20491. The Federal Nature Conservation Act (NatSchG) allows for preliminary protection (*einstweilige Sicherstellung*) to secure an area for up to two years. During that time period, all required data must be provided to bring the decree for final protection into effect.

169. Facsimile of resolution in Frobel, Riecken, and Ullrich, "Naturschutzprojekt Deutsche Einheit," 400; Günter H., Kurzer zusammenfassender Bericht über die 1. Inoffizielle Zusammenkunft mit interessierten Gruppen aus der DDR auf Einladung des [BN] am 9.12.1989 in Hof "Eisteich," Archiv BN, Ordner DDR/BUND Thüringen/BUND Sachsen; "DDR-Umweltschützer brauchen westliche Hilfe," *Süddeutsche Zeitung*, Dec. 12, 1989; "Todesstreifen als grünes Band," *Frankenpost*, Dec. 11, 1989; "Naturschützer aus Ost und West einig," *Nordbayerischer Kurier*, Dec. 11, 1989.

170. Such requests in BArch B295/21665 and 21666.

171. This was a change not just in personnel but also in jurisdiction. The task of nature protection moved from the agriculture ministry to the environmental ministry. "Reichelt nach Kritik zurückgetreten," *Frankfurter Allgemeine Zeitung*, Jan. 11, 1990; Succow, "Erinnerungen," 64–66. The papers of the Central Round Table, esp. tenth meeting, Jan. 29, 1990, in BArch DA3, http://www.argus.bstu. bundesarchiv.de/DA3-26498/index.htm (accessed Jan. 2018).

172. See, e.g., Succow, Jeschke, and Knapp, eds., *Krise als Chance*; Succow, Jeschke, and Knapp, eds., *Naturschutz*; Knapp, "Nationalparke in der DDR," 4–9.

173. The GDR had no conservationist on the county level and only one in each *Bezirk*. In the ministry, there was also only one civil servant in charge of nature and landscape protection. One of the primary tasks of the new staff entering the ministry in the fall of 1989 was to build up a conservation bureaucracy from scratch. Succow, "Erinnerungen," 66; "Staatlicher Naturschutz wird verstärkt," *MNUW Umwelt Report* 1 (Apr. 1990): 21–22.

174. BMU, Vermerk, Deutsch-deutsche Zusammenarbeit im Naturschutz—Besprechung am 16.01.1990 im MNUW, Jan. 18 1990, BArch B295/20718; Landesbund für Vogelschutz in Bayern, Bund Naturschutz in Bayern, memorandum about the mapping of the border strip, hand-delivered to the ministers Töpfer (FRG), Dick (Bavaria), and Steinberg (GDR), June 23, 1990, Archiv BN, Ordner DDR PM // Artikel // PRÖ.

175. Übersicht über die Vorschläge für geplante Naturschutzgebiete im Grenzbereich der DDR/BRD, Feb. 13, 1990, BArch B295/21666; Ministerrat der DDR. Beschluss und Information über den Stand und die vorgesehene

Entwicklung von Biosphärenreservaten, Nationalparks und Naturschutzparks in der DDR, Mar. 16, 1990, BArch B295/21668.

176. "Am Geld wird 1990 kein sinnvolles und ausgereiftes Projekt scheitern." The state secretary in the Bonn environmental ministry wrote this line in the margins of a document about funding for nature conservation in the GDR's additional appropriations for 1990. Minister Töpfer added in green: "correct!" BArch B295/20492.

177. See, e.g., BMU, Vermerk, Deutsch-deutsche Zusammenarbeit im Naturschutz—Besprechung am 16.01.1990 im MNUW, Jan. 18, 1990, BArch B295/20718. In this memo, the East Germans are reported as wishing to create "nature parks." Adding to the confusion was the fact that the East Germans did indeed use the term "*Natur*schutz*park*" (nature protection park). Yet this term was deployed in conscious opposition to the West German "nature park" and contained an emphasis on nature protection (-*schutz*). Reichhoff and Böhnert, "Nationalparkprogramm," 201–202; Rösler, "Nationalparkprogramm," 565.

178. It was the ministry's department for nature protection that invited the nonprofit Association of German Nature Parks to join the discussion. Not surprisingly, its representatives soon realized that East German conservationists were not keen on talking to them. N5, BMU, Vermerk, Zusammenarbeit mit der DDR, hier: Naturparke, Feb. 7, 1990, BArch B295/21666.

179. Not free of rumors is the press release Deutscher Bund für Vogelschutz (DBV), "Welche Chance hat die 'Grüne Grenze'?," Feb. 12, 1990, BArch B295/21666; for the term "false labeling" (*Etikettenschwindel*) see Cejka, "Einbruch," 13.

180. Blab et al., "Naturschutzgrossprojekte des Bundes," 3–9.

181. MR Dieterich, N2, Vermerk, Gespräch von Herrn BM mit Natur- und Umweltschutzverbänden, Feb. 8, 1990, BArch B295/20718.

182. On the NPP's race against time see Müller-Helmbrecht, "Endspurt," 597–608; for the chronology also see Knapp, "Nationalparkprogramm."

183. Aktenvermerk Biosphärenreservat Rhön—gemeinsame Besprechung am 11. Apr. 1990 in Würzburg, BArch B295/20499; Protokoll Besprechung der für Naturschutz zuständigen AL des Bundes und der Länder am 24. und 25.04.1990, May 14, 1990, in Würzburg, BArch B295/20493; Stephan Börnecke, "Hohe Rhön wird Biosphärenreservat," *Frankfurter Rundschau*, June 12, 1990.

184. Bureaucracy: Landesamt für Naturschutz und Landschaftspflege Schleswig-Holstein, Jan. 10, 1990, BArch B295/21666; bickering: Schleswig-Holsteinischer Landtag, 12. WP, 8. Sitzung, Feb. 21, 1990, 2917–2927; preservation decrees: Ministerium für Land-, Forst- und Nahrungsgüterwirtschaft an Vors. des Rates des Kreises Hagenow, Nov. 22, 1989, Sammlung Neumann; Landesverordnung zur einstweiligen Sicherstellung des geplanten NSG [eight names], Mar. 28, 1990, BArch B295/20498; list of all preserves related to Schaalsee at http://www.schaalsee.de/inhalte/download/Uebersicht-der-festgesetzten-Naturschutzgebiete.pdf (accessed May 2018).

185. On the legal aspect see Reichhoff and Böhnert, "Nationalparkprogramm," 201–202; on the biosphere reserve see Jarmatz and Mönke, "Naturpark Schaalsee," 175–183.

186. "Nein aus Niedersachsen," *Der Spiegel*, Feb. 19, 1990, 14. The state's environmental ministry called the East German initiative "*vorpreschen*," implying that it was not well thought through. It advocated lengthy coordination with the stakeholders in tourism. Nds. MELF to BMU, June 28, 1990, BArch B295/20403. Contestations about the Harz National Park in Ude-Koeller, *Harzklub*, 237–250.

187. Wegener, "Hochharz," 649–657; Wegener, "Nationalpark Harz," 104–112.

188. Frohn, Rosebrock, and Schmoll, eds., *Natur*; for various historical case studies see Hasenöhrl, *Zivilgesellschaft*.

189. "Reservat für Wendehälse," *Der Spiegel*, Jan. 29, 1990, 81–82. The mayor of the small town Tettau in Franconia (West) even went on record saying that he would "machine-gun" down any conservationist trying to obstruct his road-building plans. See letter to the editor, "Neuer Schiessbefehl an der Grenze?," *Neue Presse*, Aug. 26 1991.

190. Baumann, "Naturpark Drömling," 191, 194; another reference to a former Stasi building in Caroline Möhring, "Die Insel Vilm ist noch ein kleines Paradies," *Frankfurter Allgemeine Zeitung*, Oct. 5, 1990.

191. Friedrich Karl Fromme, "Die DDR als Naturschutzgebiet?" *Frankfurter Allgemeine Zeitung*, Feb. 13, 1990.

192. Caroline Möhring, "Vor kurzem noch war es eine verrückte Vision—jetzt soll aus dem Todesstreifen ein Refugium der Natur werden," *Frankfurter Allgemeine Zeitung*, Aug. 25, 1990.

193. Bundestag Drucksache 13/1023, Mar. 30, 1995; Stehböck, "Abbau der Grenzanlagen"; agricultural use: Klaus Mandery to Hubert Weiger, June 25, 1991, Archiv BN, Ordner GRE BN Schr –PRÖ 1989–1997.

194. Press release PM 34/91, "Todesstoss für das Grüne Band?," Apr. 14, 1991, Archiv BN, Ordner GRE BN Schr –PRÖ 1989–1997. Further documentation in the same folder.

195. Methods discussed in Klaus Mandery to Hubert Weiger, June 25, 1991, Archiv BN, Ordner GRE BN Schr –PRÖ 1989–1997.

196. BMVtg to Hubert Weinzierl, Chairman BUND, July 22, 1991, and Sept. 30, 1991, Archiv BN, Ordner GRE BN Schr –PRÖ 1989–1997.

197. Extended search: Bundestag Drucksache 13/1023, Mar. 30, 1995; missing mines: Thomas Otto, "Grünes Band voller Gefahren," DLF-Magazin on dradio.de, Aug. 2, 2012; Saskia Döhner, "Minengefahr im Grenzstreifen," *Hannoversche Allgemeine Zeitung*, May 11, 2012.

198. Figure in BUND, Bund Naturschutz in Bayern, eds., *Handlungsleitfaden*, 7.

199. Michael Thumann, "Milliarden-Poker um den Todesstreifen," *Die Zeit*, Sept. 11, 1992; Frobel, Riecken, and Ullrich, "Naturschutzprojekt Deutsche Einheit," 401.

200. Horst Stern, "Ausverkauf der Natur," *Die Woche*, Nov. 14, 1997, 10–11; Martin Wunderlich, "Das Grüne Band: Bald ein Flickenteppich," *Berliner Morgenpost*, Oct. 31, 2000; Walter Schmidt, "Grünes Band wird versilbert: Das Natur-Refugium an der früheren innerdeutschen Grenze ist akut bedroht," *Frankfurter Rundschau*, Apr. 17, 2001.

201. For further details see Frobel, "20 Jahre Grünes Band," 8–9; text of coalition agreement in BUND, *Handlungsleitfaden*, 12.

202. BUND, *Dauereinsatz*, 30–31, 46–47.

203. Schlumprecht, "E+E Vorhaben 'Bestandsaufnahme Grünes Band,'" 407–414.

204. Beyer, *Grüne Band im Wandel*.

205. BUND, *Dauereinsatz*, 44–45.

206. Beck and Frobel, "Letzter Zufluchtsort," 24; Keil, "Sielmanns Vision."

207. Bankoff, "Making Parks," 82–86.

208. Havlick, *Bombs Away*, 85–93, 101–113; BUND, *Traces of the Past*.

209. Frobel et al., *Erlebnis Grünes Band*, 41, 154–155; see the "before-and-after" illustration in BUND, *Traces of the Past*, 20–21; on restoration ecology see Piechocki et al., "Renaturierung," 39–48; Havlick and Hourdequin, "Ecological Restoration," 1–10.

210. White, *Organic Machine*, x.

211. Purdy, *After Nature*, 14; see also Cronon, "Trouble with Wilderness," 69–90; Stahl, "Veranstaltete Wildnis," 84–95.

212. Havlick, *Bombs Away*, 92.

CHAPTER 6

1. Walter Sullivan, "Bonn Plans Disposal of Nuclear Wastes," *New York Times*, May 27, 1977.

2. Salander, "Concept." Salander was the head of the German Company for the Reprocessing of Nuclear Fuels (DWK), a company founded by the German electric power industry for the purpose of building the NEZ.

3. Radkau and Hahn, *Aufstieg und Fall*, 56–67. This is not to say that the use of nuclear energy was uncontroversial. See Gleitsmann and Oertzel, *Fortschrittsfeinde im Atomzeitalter?*

4. Brunnengräber, *Ewigkeitslasten*, 28–31.

5. Scott, *Seeing Like a State*; Herbert, "Europe in High Modernity."

6. Illing, *Energiepolitk*, 135–139.

7. The nexus was part of the Fourth Atomic Law of 1976. See Tiggemann, *Achillesferse*, 243–258; Issel, *Wiederaufbereitung*, 269–270.

8. Blowers, *Legacy*, 188.

9. The term "nuclear community" is well established in social scientific debates on nuclear siting processes and known to historians from the "atomic communities" in Kate Brown's depiction of Richland (US) and Ozersk (Soviet Union) in

Brown, *Plutopia*. The nuclear industry tends to call such places "communities with industry awareness" and refers to "community partnerships." See Di Nucci, "NIMBY," 126–127.

10. According to their own calculations, by 2013 the utility companies had invested 1.8 billion euros in the exploration of the Gorleben salt dome. See Moench, "Refinanzierung der Endlagersuche," 104. *Atomwirtschaft (atw)* was a journal of the nuclear industry.

11. Kretschmer, "Wackersdorf," 165–217; Gaumer, *Wackersdorf*.

12. Blowers, *Legacy*, 180; Issel, *Wiederaufarbeitung*, 117 n. 460.

13. Högselius, "Spent Nuclear Fuel Policies," 259–260.

14. The global state of the technology for nuclear energy production and waste management in the mid-1970s was reflected at a 1977 international conference convened by the International Atomic Energy Agency (IAEA), published as *Nuclear Power and Its Fuel Cycle: Proceedings of an International Conference, Salzburg, 2–13 May, 1977*, 8 vols. (Vienna: IAEA, 1977).

15. The boldness of the move has strong echoes in Carter, *Nuclear Imperatives*, 265; the competitive angle in the development of nuclear technology is highlighted in Milder, *Greening Democracy*, 22–25.

16. Radkau and Hahn, *Aufstieg und Fall*, 141–195, 285–288; Issel, *Wiederaufbereitung*, 89–106.

17. According to the historian Joachim Radkau, German nuclear engineers displayed a veritable breeder fixation that was rooted in the ambition to reach fuel autarky. Radkau and Hahn, *Aufstieg und Fall*, 51–52, 112–113, 143. See also Gross, "Decoupling," 527–528.

18. Radkau and Hahn, *Aufstieg und Fall*, 205–206; Alley and Alley, *Too Hot to Touch*, 97–99.

19. On the reinforcement loop between rising uranium prices and advocacy for the breeder technology see Högselius, "Challenging Chernobyl's Legacy," 192. American proponents of the breeder argued in similar ways. See Camp, "Clinch River Breeder Reactor Debate."

20. The storage problem was equally unresolved for nuclear waste from military use, which, however, is not the focus here. It is the consensus in the literature that the issue of long-term storage of high-level wastes had been neglected. See, e.g., Radkau and Hahn, *Aufstieg und Fall*, 206–207; Tiggemann, *Achillesferse*, 773. However, Möller, *Endlagerung*, 346–347, argues that West German efforts in the 1960s to provide final repository space were actually internationally ahead of their times.

21. Quotation in Rucht, *Von Wyhl nach Gorleben*, 57; on the common assumption see Alley and Alley, *Too Hot to Touch*, 89.

22. Flowers, "Nuclear Power," 26. See also "Wohin mit dem Atom-Müll? Ins Meer, unter die Erde, in den Weltraum? Noch grübeln die Forscher," *Die Zeit*, May 5, 1961.

23. Walker, *Yucca Mountain*, 1–50; the quotations are the titles of chaps. 1 and 2.

24. Böhm, "F+E für das Entsorgungskonzept," 186–190, highlights this "double function" of reprocessing.

25. Hamblin, *Poison in the Well*; Alley and Alley, *Too Hot to Touch*, 22–45; Tiggemann, *Achillesferse*, 123–133.

26. Stewart and Stewart, *Fuel Cycle to Nowhere*, 22–25; Brunnengräber, *Ewigkeitslasten*, 62–68; Tiggemann, *Achillesferse*, 134–141.

27. Walker, *Yucca Mountain*, 34; Alley and Alley, *Too Hot to Touch*, 10–11; Stewart and Stewart, *Fuel Cycle to Nowhere*, 26, 28–29.

28. Möller, *Endlagerung*, 146–153, 174–227. Although it was slated to be a site of scientific research, the Bonn bureaucracy began in 1968 to treat the Asse mine as a final repository for nuclear wastes to encourage further development of the nuclear energy sector. Radkau and Hahn, *Aufstieg und Fall*, 310, called the Asse a "chance purchase" (*Gelegenheitskauf*) of the federal government.

29. Brunnengräber, *Ewigkeitslasten*, 57–59. Issel, *Wiederaufarbeitung*, 122, reflects the contemporary view that after the acquisition of Asse, the industry did not expect problems with waste disposal.

30. Illing, *Energiepolitik*, 137–138; Gross, "Decoupling," 525–527.

31. Government proposal in Schmidt-Küsters, "Entsorgungssystem." See also Illing, *Energiepolitik*, 139–141; Tiggemann, *Achillesferse*, 234–239; Issel, *Wiederaufarbeitung*, 190–192.

32. Müller, "Moratorium," 65.

33. See, e.g., Am Emb Bonn to State Dept, Bonn Bonn Nr. 5762, April 6, 1976; Nr. 13987, Aug. 20 1976; Nr. 15741, Sept. 23, 1977, all in NARA RG 59, Central Foreign Policy Files, created 7/1/1973–12/31/1979, retrieved online via Access to Archival Databases (AAD): https://aad.archives.gov/aad/ (accessed June 2017).

34. In retrospect, industry representatives like to emphasize that politics forced them down the path of reprocessing irrespective of economic considerations. This position is evident in Issel, *Wiederaufbereitung*, e.g., 387. Issel was part of the KEWA team that undertook the assessments of possible sites for the NEZ before the Gorleben announcement.

35. Issel, *Wiederaufbereitung*, 128 n. 515.

36. Am Emb Bonn to State Dept, Nr. 15714, Sept. 23, 1977; Nr. 5929, Apr. 4, 1977; quotation in Nr. 6612, Apr. 11, 1978.

37. Schmidt-Küsters, "Entsorgungssystem," 341.

38. Alley and Alley, *Too Hot to Touch*, 93–97; Stewart and Stewart, *Fuel Cycle to Nowhere*, 44–47; Carter, *Nuclear Imperatives*, 98–119. The only commercial American reprocessing plant in West Valley, New York, operated from 1966 to 1971 and left behind waste problems unresolved to the present day.

39. Hagen, "Warum Wiederaufarbeitung?," 567; Am Emb Bonn to State Dept, Nr. 5929, Apr. 4, 1977. The telegram covers the conference discussions relating to reprocessing.

40. Kurt Becker, "Ist der Atomteufel aus der Flasche?," *Die Zeit*, Aug. 20, 1976.

41. Gray, "Commercial Liberties." Gray reports the projected volume of the transaction as DM 10 billion. On an earlier sale of a heavy-water reactor to Argentina see Radkau and Hahn, *Aufstieg und Fall*, 181–182.

42. Vermerk MR Klaus Stuhr to Dr. Hans-Joachim Roehler, Jan. 10, 1977, NLA HA Nds. 500 Acc 002/138 Nr. 3.

43. Blowers, *Legacy*, 184; see also Di Nucci, "NIMBY," 129. Although Bavarian authorities could have known better after the experiences at Wyhl and Gorleben, they decided to proceed the same way when they selected Wackersdorf as a possible site for a reprocessing center. See Gaumer, *Wackersdorf*, 58.

44. Blowers, *Legacy*, 184–186, 205.

45. See, e.g., Jürgen Voges, "Geheimprotokoll zu Gorleben: Kalter Krieg ums Endlager," *tageszeitung*, Jan. 11, 2010; Greenpeace, *Die Akte Gorleben* (May 2010), www.greenpeace.de/sites/www.greenpeace.de/files/Greenpeace_Dossier_Gorleben_052010_0.pdf (accessed June 2017). The smoking-gun character of the siting controversy significantly hindered historical research. See Tiggemann, *Achillesferse*, 34 n. 70, 37 n. 81, 38, 39 n. 92, 382 n. 22; Tiggemann in *Gorleben UA*, 600–601.

46. The metrology institute is the Physikalisch-Technische Bundesanstalt (PTB). The political interference with the PTB was first reported by the *tageszeitung*: Jürgen Voges, "Politischer Druck auf die Wissenschaft," *tageszeitung*, Apr. 18, 2009.

47. BT, 17. WP, Drs. 17/13700, May 23, 2013: Beschlussempfehlung und Bericht des 1. Untersuchungsausschusses nach Art. 44 GG (henceforth cited as *Gorleben UA*). Strictly speaking, the commission investigated why the Kohl government decided in July 1983 to explore only the salt dome in Gorleben as the site for the final storage of highly radioactive waste. However, the initial selection of Gorleben in 1977 as the site for the then-projected NEZ played heavily into the investigation.

48. On sources see *Gorleben UA*, 47–48; list of witnesses, 51–54. The witness interviews were highly politicized and should not be mistaken for oral history testimony.

49. Tiggemann, *Achillesferse*, 377–422, 590–596; Tiggemann, *Gorleben*. For the federal government perspective see Möller, *Endlagerung*, 293–314; for the industry perspective see Issel, *Wiederaufarbeitung*, 215–219; for a blow-by-blow account see *Gorleben UA*, 67–95.

50. Kernbrennstoffwiederaufbereitungsgesellschaft, or Spent Fuel Reprocessing Association. On the founding of KEWA see Tiggemann, *Achillesferse*, 264–268.

51. *Gorleben UA*, 68–74; quotation in facsimile document, 74.

52. Ibid., 78, II.1.c, cc.

53. Ibid., 89; Albrecht, *Erinnerungen*, 86–87.

54. AL RS [Sahl], Nov. 15, 1976, Vermerk, Betr. Ministergespräch Bund-Land Niedersachsen über Einrichtung eines Entsorgungszentrums in Niedersachsen, hier: Zusammenfassende Darstellung, BArch B106/65405 and 66356.

55. Soell, *Helmut Schmidt*, 782; [interview with Albrecht] "Wo man die Kernenergie kennt, da blüht den Grünen der Weizen nicht mehr," *Bonner Energie Report*, June 6, 1983, 18–21.

56. Schmidt's objections in Schmidt to Albrecht, Dec. 15, 1976; Schmidt to Albrecht, Jan. 28, 1977; see also Konow, BKAmt, to various ministries, Telex Nr. 2655–2657, Dec. 10, 1976; BMI, Abt. Reaktorsicherheit to Minister via StS Hartkopf, Dec. 14, 1976, all in BArch B106/65405. The material is summarized in *Gorleben UA*, 94–96, and evaluated, 287–288. See also Tiggemann, *Gorleben*, 53–55, 66–68.

57. The objections were also widely reported in the press. See, e.g., Dieter Tasch, "Bundesregierung: Atomabfall nicht an DDR-Grenze," *Hannoversche Allgemeine*, Jan. 26, 1977; "Atommüll soll an die DDR-Genze: Harte Bonner Kritik an Albrecht," *Hannoversche Allgemeine*, Feb. 23, 1977; "Bölling betont Bedenken gegen Entsorgungsanlage in Gorleben," *Tagesspiegel*, Feb. 24, 1977. See also Tiggemann, *Achillesferse*, 409–410; Tiggemann, *Gorleben*, 78–79.

58. Pressure from Hannover in Nds. Min Wirtschaft to BMI, StS Hartkopf, confidential, Jan. 17, 1977, BArch B106/65405; *Gorleben UA*, 80.

59. "Kuckucksei," *Hannoversche Allgemeine*, Feb. 23, 1977; Robert Leicht, "Albrecht gibt den Schwarzen Peter nach Bonn zurück," *Süddeutsche Zeitung*, Feb. 24, 1977; Peter Klinkenberg, "Der Trick des Ernst Albrecht," *Frankfurter Rundschau*, Feb. 24, 1977; Wolfgang Wagner, "Die Kröte," *Hannoversche Allgemeine Zeitung*, Mar. 1, 1977; "Druck abgeschüttelt," *Der Spiegel*, Mar. 14, 1977, 35–36.

60. BM Innerdt. Beziehungen, Vermerk, May 2, 1977, BArch B136/18826. The GDR representative was Michael Kohl, head of the Permanent Mission of the GDR in Bonn.

61. Albrecht, *Erinnerungen*, 88. See also [interview with Albrecht], *Bonner Energie Report*, June 6, 1983, 20; *Gorleben UA*, 95.

62. [Interview with Albrecht], *Bonner Energie Report*, June 6, 1983, 20.

63. Wirsching, *Provisorium*, 367–368.

64. Albrecht, *Erinnerungen*, 90–91; Patterson, "Gorleben Hearings," 11; Tiggemann, *Achillesferse*, 610–643.

65. Jost Schmidt, "Der Graf will seine Macht ausspielen," *Süddeutsche Zeitung*, Feb. 24, 1977; Viola Roggenkamp, "Der streitbare Graf von Gartow," *Die Zeit*, July 28, 1978. On the Bernstorff family, including the Gartow branch, see Conze, *Von deutschem Adel*.

66. *Gorleben UA*, 95.

67. Ibid.

68. Schmidt to Albrecht, July 6, 1977, BArch B136/18826.

69. Pressure from Hannover in Nds. Min Wirtschaft to BMI, StS Hartkopf, confidential, Jan. 17, 1977, BArch B106/65405.

70. Example: Josef Schmidt, "Gorleben nahe der DDR-Grenze für Entsorgungszentrum vorgesehen," *Süddeutsche Zeitung*, Feb. 23, 1977.

71. Tiggemann, *Achillesferse*, 421; Tiggemann, *Gorleben*, 78–79. Tiggemann did not use any GDR records.

72. Popp, "Persönliche Reminiszenzen," 55. Popp was head of the ministry's subdivision on energy policy.

73. Peter Mlodoch, "'Provokatorische Handlung der BRD': DDR-Position zu Gorleben," *Frankfurter Rundschau*, Mar. 16, 2010.

74. Information Nr. 513/74 über den Bau einer kommerziellen Grossanlage zur Wiederaufarbeitung bestrahlter Kernbrennstoffe in der BRD, July 31, 1974, BStU MfS HVA Nr. 109, 66–71.

75. Information A/2815/11/76, Vermutlich geplante "Entsorgungsanlage" der BRD an der Staatsgrenze zur DDR, Nov. 28, 1976, BStU HA XVIII Nr. 18910, 26–27.

76. Information Nr. 8/77 über BRD-Pläne zum Bau eines nuklearen Entsorgungszentrums in der Nähe der Staatsgrenze zur DDR, Jan. 24, 1977, BStU MfS HA XVIII Nr. 18910, 13–17.

77. Ibid., 15: "Für das taktische Vorgehen bei diesen Gesprächen wird empfohlen, die Regierung der DDR im Glauben zu lassen, dass es sich beim Standort Gorleben um einen unter vielen handelte und die Vorgespräche mit der DDR nicht unter dem Zwang einer bereits endgültig getroffenen Standortentscheidung aufgenommen werden."

78. Ibid., 17.

79. Compare Information Nr. 323/77 über Entscheidungen der BRD zum Standort Gorleben für das nukleare Entsorgungszentrum der BRD, May 23, 1977, BStU MfS HVA Nr. 64, 125–130, with AL3, Vermerk für die Sitzung des Kabinettsausschusses für die friedliche Nutzung der Kernenergie am 30. März 1977, Mar. 29, 1977, BArch B136/18826.

80. See HA XIII/8, Information zum Entsorgungszentrum Gorleben/BRD, Apr. 28, 1978, BStU MfS HA XVIII Nr. 18910, 146–147. Here, an IM reported on conversations with employees of the DWK company.

81. The Stasi had a broad interest in western technology. For background see Macrakis, *Seduced by Secrets*, esp. 23–47. For related Stasi activities in Bavaria see Neumeier, "Staatssicherheit [. . .] in Bayern," 357–364. In the files I consulted, reports pertaining to nuclear technology came from within, and related to, Siemens, DWK, Nuklear Chemie und Metallurgie (NUKEM), Kraftwerks Union (KWU), energy suppliers like the Hamburg Elektrizitätswerke (HEW) and Preussag, as well as federally funded research agencies such as the Karlsruhe Nuclear Research Center and various geological institutes such as the Bundesanstalt für Geowissenschaften und Rohstoffe (BGR). The fact that the Stasi wanted information from within these companies and organizations does not say anything about the quality of the information they obtained. Some of the Stasi efforts became public as Cold War spy stories. See "Orden im Müll," *Der Spiegel*, Sept. 28, 1981, 130–134.

82. See the section on anti-Gorleben protest later in the chapter.

83. The three IMs were "Rolf," "Rita Wirt," and "Sommer." The first two were contact persons; the latter was an "investigator." One worked in mechanical engineering, one for the police, and one in a handicraft business. One was recruited in the 1960s, the other two in the late 1980s. Information based on the respective MfS HVA Statistikbogen at BStU.

84. Obstl. Heyn, Vermerk über ein Gespräch mit dem Präsidenten des Staatlichen Amtes für Atomsicherheit und Strahlenschutz, StS Prof. Dr. Sitzlack, Feb. 18, 1977, BStU MfS HA XVIII Nr. 18910, 35–36.

85. HA XVIII/3, Information über eingeleitete staatliche Massnahmen im Zusammenhang mit dem geplanten Bau eines nuklearen Entsorgungszentrums der BRD, Feb. 14, 1977, BStU MfS HA XVIII Nr. 18910, 39–42.

86. These points appear frequently in Gorleben-related documents; fully developed in Günter Mittag to General Secretary of the SED Central Committee, Erich Honecker, Jan. 17, 1978, BArch SAPMO DY3023/1440.

87. Mittag to Honecker, Apr. 6, 1977, BArch SAPMO DY3023/1440.

88. Oskar Fischer, Min. Auswärtige Angelegenheiten, Mar. 31, 1977, BArch SAPMO DY3023/1440. This first approach conveyed that a private company had filed for a permit to explore Gorleben as a possible site for a reprocessing and waste storage plant. The activities of a private company, however, were said not to imply a final political decision about the site.

89. StaeV to BKAmt, Telex Nr. 644, June 24, 1977; StaeV, Vermerk Bräutigam, Feb. 2, 1978, both in BArch B136/18826.

90. See, e.g., BKAmt to StaeV, July 5, 1977, BArch B136/18826.

91. Vemerk des Stellv. Aussenministers der DDR Nier über ein Gepräch mit [. . .] Gaus, July 6, 1977, DzD VI.5 Doc. 63, 228–229.

92. Arbeitsstab Deutschlandpolitik, Vermerk, Feb. 2, 1978, DzD VI.5, 527–529, and GDR non-paper, Feb. 2, 1978, B136 Nr. 18826; "Gespräch zu Plänen der BRD bei Gorleben," *Neues Deutschland*, Feb. 4, 1978.

93. See the phrase "denkbar ungünstigster Standort" in, e.g., StaeV to BKAmt, Apr. 6, 1978, BArch B288/375.

94. First such draft of April 1977 from the Ministry of Coal and Energy in BStU MfS HA XVIII Nr. 18910.

95. See StaeV, Vermerk Feb. 12, 1981, BArch B288/103, which reviews the exchanges about Gorleben to date.

96. The SED considered stalling on conversations about the pollution of the Werra River yet again, this time not only with the customary reference to the Environmental Federal Agency (UBA) in West Berlin but also in retaliation for Gorleben. See Direktive für die Führung von Sondierungsgesprächen mit der BRD und für das weitere Vorgehen zu Fragen des Kaliabbaus im Werra-Kalirevier, Aug. 5, 1978, BArch SAPMO DY3023/1434.

97. ADN, "Sicherheitsinteressen der DDR beachten," Apr. 19, 1979, BArch B136/18826. The ADN report appeared in *Neues Deutschland*, Apr. 20, 1979, 2, as well as in other papers.

98. Arbeitsstab Deutschlandpolitik, Vermerk, Apr. 23, 1979, BArch B136/18826. Hans Otto Bräutigam advised against an open threat to the GDR and advocated for a more discreet warning. Only if the GDR escalated its protest against the Gorleben site would a public discussion of East German nuclear risks be deployed.

99. Abteilung BRD, Vermerk, Mar. 21, 1979, BArch SAPMO DY3023/1440. Overview of exchanges between FRG and GDR on Gorleben in Vorbereitung von Kontakten mit der DDR auf dem Gebiet der kerntechnischen Sicherheit, Aug. 4, 1980; Nukleare Entsorgung Gorleben, hier: Bisherige Gespräche/Demarchen zwischen beiden deutschen Staaten, Sept. 25, 1980, both in BArch B288/103.

100. Morsleben was located 6 kilometers east of Helmstedt (West) in the former rock salt mine Bartensleben. It thus lay within the East German security strip along the border. It is referred to as Morsleben, Bartensleben, or by the acronym ERAM (Endlager für radioaktive Abfälle Morsleben). Morsleben received its first load of nuclear waste in March 1978. On Morsleben see Reichert, *Kernenergiewirtschaft*, 293–300; Müller, *Kernenergie*, 259–265; Tiggemann, *Achillesferse*, 170–174; and the history workshop publication by Beyer, ed., *Morsleben*.

101. HA XVIII, Information über den Bau des Endlagers für radioaktive Abfälle (ERA) Morsleben/Kreis Haldensleben/Bezirk Magdeburg, Jan. 29, 1977, BStU MfS HA XVIII Nr. 18910, 21–25.

102. HA XVIII/3, Information über eingeleitete staatliche Massnahmen im Zusammenhang mit dem geplanten Bau eines nuklearen Entsorgungszentrums der BRD, Feb. 14, 1977, BStU MfS HA XVIII Nr. 18910, 41: " [. . .] jedoch muss in der nächsten Zeit auch damit gerechnet werden, dass abgebrannter Kernbrennstoff (hochaktives Material) eingelagert werden muss [. . .] [für das] zur Zeit trotz mehrfacher Versuche seitens der UdSSR keine Bereitschaft zur Rücknahme besteht." See also Reichert, *Kernenergiewirtschaft*, 290; Müller, *Kernenergie*, 253.

103. Siebold, Ministerium für Kohle und Energie, to Günter Mittag, Apr. 14, 1977, BStU MfS HA XVIII Nr. 18910, 70.

104. See, e.g., SAAS, Stellungnahme zum irreführenden Vergleich in den Massenmedien der DDR zur Abfallproblematik in Gorleben/BRD and Morsleben/DDR, Apr. 25, 1979, BArch SAPMO DY3023/1440.

105. HA XVIII/3, Information über eingeleitete staatliche Massnahmen im Zusammenhang mit dem geplanten Bau eines nuklearen Entsorgungszentrums der BRD, Feb. 14, 1977, BStU MfS HA XVIII Nr. 18910, 39.

106. Müller, *Kernenergie*, 264.

107. "Beratung zum Strahlenschutz mit BRD-Delegation beendet," *Neues Deutschland*, Oct. 15, 1988, 5.

108. Schildt, "Hörfunk- und Fernsehnation," 58–71.

109. See, e.g., HA XVIII/3, Auszug aus Treffbericht des GMS "Diplom," Geplante Entsorgungsanlage der BRD in Gorsleben [*sic*!], Apr. 22, 1977, BStU MfS HA XVIII Nr. 18910.

110. Peter Jochen Winters, "Die SED hat Angst vor dem Brokdorf-Bazillus," *Frankfurter Allgemeine Zeitung*, Feb. 24, 1977; Christel Sudau, "DDR-Kernkraftwerke: Grosses Schweigen über alle Pläne," *Frankfurter Rundschau*, Feb. 25, 1977; "Auch die SED fürchtet ihre Atomkraft-Gegner," *Der Abend* (West Berlin), Feb. 25, 1977.

111. Gaus, StaeV to BKAmt, Telex Nr. 644, June 24, 1977, BArch B136/18826. On secrecy around nuclear issues and the lack of a significant anti-nuclear opposition in the GDR see Stude, *Strom für die Republik*, 12–14, 143–151.

112. Arbeitsstab Deutschlandpolitik, Vermerk, Apr. 23, 1979, BArch B136/18826.

113. For technical aspects see Reichert, *Kernenergiewirtschaft*, 153–154, 159–161; Müller, *Kernenergie*, 27–130, 133; Högselius, *Greifswald*, 115–118; Stude, *Strom für die Republik*, 78–79.

114. These plants were preceded by a trial reactor at Dresden-Rossendorf. On the history of nuclear energy in the GDR see Reichert, *Kernenergiewirtschaft*; Reichert's findings are discussed in Radkau and Hahn, *Aufstieg und Fall*, 311–318. See also Müller, *Kernenergie*; Abele/Hampe, "Kernenergiepolitk," 29–89; Stude, *Strom für die Republik*.

115. Reichert, *Kernenergiewirtschaft*, 324–341. On the security perimeter see Müller, *Kernenergie*, 139–141.

116. Reichert, *Kernenergiewirtschaft*, 201–205, 245; Abele and Hampe, "Kernenergiepolitik," 57–58.

117. Reichert, *Kernenergiewirtschaft*, 147, 151–153, 246, and passim; Stude, *Strom für die Republik*, 20–24, 108–109, 152–157; for "ready for repair" see Abele and Hampe, "Kernenergiepolitik," 58.

118. Müller, *Kernenergie*, 133–148, esp. 142–144; Högselius, *Greifswald*, 20; Stude, *Strom für die Republik*, 98–106, 126.

119. The report referred to "psychological warfare" techniques employed by the KWU that were designed to systematically denigrate Soviet and East German nuclear technology especially in the Middle East in order to gain a market advantage with "secure" western technology. The source of the report was a KWU employee in Erlangen. See "Das Gross- und KKW-Geschäft, Status, Struktur und F/E der KWU-Konzerngruppe, 'Konkurrenzausspähung' einschl. Beobachtung und Analyse der Energiewirtschaft, Export- und Kooperationsmöglichkeiten in RGW-Länder im 1. Halbjahr 1979," June 1979, BStU MfS BV Gera Abt. XV Nr. 2037.

120. Reichert, *Kernenergiewirtschaft*, 289–290. Rumors about a nuclear deal of some kind between the GDR and the FRG circulated among East German nuclear scientists. See Information, Mar. 21, 1980, BStU MfS HA XVIII Nr. 18910, 221–222.

121. Nukleare Entsorgung Gorleben, hier: Bisherige Gespräche/Demarchen zwischen beiden deutschen Staaten, Sept. 25, 1980, BArch B288/103.

122. BMI, Ergebnisse des ersten Gesprächs [über Strahlenschutz] am 25.10.1983 im BMI, Oct. 2, 1983, BArch B288/103; instructions for GDR delegation in SAPMO Büro Mittag DY3023/1441; "Abkommen [. . .] über Informations- und Erfahrungsaustausch auf dem Gebiet des Strahlenschutzes," Sept. 8, 1987, published in *Bundesgesetzblatt*, no. 7, Feb. 23, 1988.

123. Michael Bothe, Goethe Universität Frankfurt, Gutachten über Rechtsfragen möglicher nachteiliger Auswirkungen der Nuklearanlagen in Gorleben auf dem Gebiet der DDR, Nov. 29, 1984, BArch B288/103.

124. Hänel, *DDR-Energiewirtschaft*, emphasizes that West German officials never developed a real interest in East German nuclear power plants until they inherited them in 1990.

125. Blowers, *Legacy*, 1–12, 233–238; Blowers, "Nuclear Waste"; Aldrich, *Site Fights*, 8–15, 26–33.

126. Cragin, *Nuclear Nebraska*; Alley and Alley, *Too Hot to Touch*, 202–203; Aldrich, *Site Fights*, 126–128. On Bure see Blowers, *Legacy*, 154–171.

127. Aldrich, *Site Fights*, 12–15. See also Ott and Smeddinck, eds., *Umwelt, Gerechtigkeit, Freiwilligkeit*.

128. Brown, *Plutopia*, uses the term "atomic community" for Richland-Hanford and Ozersk. Blowers, *Legacy*, studies Hanford, Sellafield, La Hague and Bure, and Gorleben to focus on communities that manage nuclear waste and contamination.

129. My definition emphasizes the link between a nuclear facility and community affluence. Blowers, *Legacy*, 3, uses the term to denote communities that are engaged with the legacy of nuclear power such as waste management and cleanup. My thrust is prospective; his is more retrospective. Since the initially planned facility never fully materialized, Blowers, *Legacy*, 182, does not consider Gorleben a nuclear community. Here, again, I argue prospectively.

130. OKD Paasche to Karl Schiller, BMWi, July 25, 1968, BArch B137/12604. The argument frequently resurfaces in other correspondence and news coverage about the county.

131. This process had been under way since the 1950s. Wehler, *Deutsche Gesellschaftsgeschichte*, 81–88; Schneider, "Wirtschaftsgeschichte Niedersachsens nach 1945," 827–851.

132. The remaining farms had increased in size. Schlumbohm, "Landwirtschaft"; see also Flügge, "Landwirtschaftlichen Betriebe."

133. Ausschuss [des Nds. Landtages] für Zonengrenzfragen, Vertriebene, Flüchtlinge und Kriegssachgeschädigte, Protokoll [. . .] Bereisung des

Landkreises Lüchow-Dannenberg, June 10, 1968, Archiv des Nds LT, PA2001/
06/ZVFK/014; Regierungspräsident Lüneburg, Ergebnis Niederschrift
[Entwicklungsmöglichkeiten Lüchow-Dannenberg], Oct. 31, 1969, BArch
B137/12604.

134. Regierungspräsident Lüneburg, Ergebnis Niederschrift [Entwicklung-
smöglichkeiten Lüchow-Dannenberg], Oct. 31, 1969, BArch B137/12604. The
slopes were to be built at the Kniepenberg, a hill with an elevation of 86 meters.

135. Missing out on the Transrapid test tracks meant missing out on a lucrative
tourist attraction. In retrospect, however, the county was spared a major catastrophe. In September 2006, twenty-three people were killed in an accident on
the test tracks in Emsland. Nds. LT, 8. WP, Drs. 822, May 1, 1975, and Drs. 924,
July 1, 1975; Niehaus, "Transrapid-Unfall."

136. Wolfgang Tersteegen, "Immer mehr Bürger verlassen Stadt und Dorf,"
Frankfurter Allgemeine Zeitung, Oct. 31, 1975.

137. Nds. LT, 8. WP, Drs. 738, June 23, 1975, and Nr. 896, May 1, 1975.

138. The term was "Demontage des Zonenrands." See Wolfgang Tersteegen, "Immer
mehr Bürger verlassen Stadt und Dorf," *Frankfurter Allgemeine Zeitung*, Oct. 31,
1975, 9; Helmuth von Schilling, "Ein verlassener Kreis wird noch verlassener,"
Hannoversche Allgemeine Zeitung, Nov. 1, 1975.

139. Egon Höhmann, Parl. StS, BM Innerdt. Beziehungen, to Heinz Kreutzmann,
June 6, 1978, BArch B137/12604. See also BM Innerdt. Beziehungen, Memo
on Lüchow-Dannenberg, Nov. 2, 1978, BArch B137/7064.

140. OKD Klaus Poggendorf to Chancellor Schmidt, Mar. 20, 1978, BArch B136/
18826.

141. Regierungserklärung der Nds. Landesregierung zum geplanten NEZ in
Gorleben, May 16, 1979, BArch B106/66391; full text also in "Die Sicherheit
von Gorleben," *Süddeutsche Zeitung*, May 17, 1979.

142. Discussion about locating the reprocessing plant in Dragahn, another village in
the county, did not emerge until November 1982.

143. Poggendorf to Schmidt, May 25, 1979, BArch B106/66391.

144. The state government in Hannover received a similar "wish list." The drafts of
the lists as well as the protocol of the county parliament (*Kreistag*) deliberating
them are in Kreisarchiv DAN, Bestand OKD/Landrat Nr. 215. The final wish
list for Bonn is in BArch B136/12604.

145. Schubert, *Hinterland für Berlin (West)?*, 264–268.

146. Vermerk über das Gespräch des Bundeskanzlers mit Vertretern des Landkreises
Lüchow-Dannenberg am 8. November 1979, Nov. 12, 1979; Poggendorf to
Gerhard Konow, BKAmt Dec. 4, 1979, both in BArch B137/12604.

147. BKAmt, Ref. 36, Vermerk über das AL-Gespräch am 13.12.1979 im
Bundeskanzleramt, Dec. 18, 1979, BArch B137/12604.

148. The wish list that the county submitted to *Land* authorities in the spring of
1980 had grown to twelve pages. Peer Steinbrück, BKAmt, to Dr. Gerlach,

BMWi, Apr. 22, 1980, BArch B137/12604. The original list of November 1979 still fit on three pages.

149. Handwritten notes about a meeting in Hannover on June 11, 1980, BArch B137/12604. See also Wolf J. Schmidt-Küster, BMFT to OKD Poggendorf, July 31, 1981, Kreisarchiv DAN, Bestand OKD/Landrat, 214/1.

150. Vermerk Moennich, Dec. 11, 1979, BArch B137/12604.

151. Nds. Wirtschaftsmin., StS to Abt. 2, Nov. 16, 1976, memorandum about a call from Dr. Carsten Salander, Preussen Elektra AG, on Nov. 12, 1976, NLA HA Nds. 500 Acc 2002/138 Nr. 1. That Langendorf was canceled became public knowledge only in 1980. See "Vorerst kein Kraftwerk in Langendorf," *Elbe-Jeetzel-Zeitung*, Aug. 23, 1980.

152. Sachstandsvermerk [zur] Verwaltungsvereinbarung über Finanzierungsfragen, Demonstrationsschadensregelung, Feb. 20, 1979 and attachment 2: Adolf Elvers, Nds. Min Finance, Ergebnis Besprechung 6. Feb. 1979, NLA HA VVP 65 Acc 76/90 Nr. 11, Handakten MP Albrecht. On the negotiations between Bonn and the DWK see Tiggemann, *Achillesferse*, 461–464.

153. Vermerk über das Gespräch des Bundeskanzlers mit Vertretern des Landkreises Lüchow-Dannenberg am 8. November 1979, Nov. 12, 1979, BArch B106/66401.

154. Poggendorf to Chancellor Schmidt, May 25, 1979, BArch B106/66391, requesting the federal payment of the first installment; Poggendorf to Nds. Min Finanz, Mar. 24, 1981, NLA HA Nds. 200 Acc 2005/070 Nr. 315, complaining about late payment.

155. The discussions about the consequences of Albrecht's decision are in BArch B106/66391; see also Tiggemann, *Achillesferse*, 464.

156. BMI, Dept. Head Nuclear Security to Deputy Dept. Head, via SecState Hartkopf, Feb. 13, 1981; see also Baum to Schmidt, Apr. 2, 1981, BArch B106/66391.

157. Ibid.

158. Within the county, the municipalities of Gartow and Gorleben accused Poggendorf of withholding their share and requested that Hannover wire them the money directly. See Samtgemeinde Gartow to Nds. Finanzmin., Sept. 17, 1981, and Jan. 18, 1982, both in NLA HA Nds. 200 Acc 2005/070 Nr. 315.

159. BKAmt, Ref. 36, Vermerk über das AL-Gespräch am 13.12.1979 im Bundeskanzleramt, Dec. 18, 1979, BArch B137/12604: "Das BMI bemerkte in diesem Zusammenhang, dass an die DWK mit der Frage nach ihrer Bereitschaft zu Zahlungen herangetreten werden sollte."

160. von Hardenberg, Bezirksreg. Lüneburg, to Nds. Sozialmin., Oct. 21, 1982, NLA HA Nds. 300 Acc 2002/041, Nr. 2.

161. Niedersächsisches Institut für Wirtschaftsforschung, *Ansatzpunkte*, 8. Poggendorf, *Gorleben*, 65, reports DM 126 million from 1980 to 1993, amounting to some 9.7 million per year over thirteen years.

162. StS von Wuerzen, BMWi, to OKD Poggendorf, July 29, 1980; Birgit Breuel, Nds. Wirtschaftsmin., to OKD Poggendorf, July 29, 1980, both in BArch B106/

66401. The documents contain the promised measures and investments by federal and *Land* authorities.

163. An example is the visit of a delegation from the municipality of Gartow in Bonn in April 1983 during which the Gartow representatives wanted to discuss a new wish list and the continuation of direct payments. See BMI, Abt. Reaktorsicherheit, Vermerk, Mar. 31, 1983; Gemeindedirektor Gartow to Dr. Ziegler, BMFT, Mar. 28, 1983, both in BArch B106/66392.

164. The Unabhängige Wählergemeinschaft (UAW) was founded in 1981. The Greens did not yet run in the county elections that year.

165. Tiggemann, *Achillesferse*, 457. For Poggendorf's justification of the monies see Poggendorf, *Gorleben*, 65–74.

166. Poggendorf's justification of the mailbox in Poggendorf to Horst Schröder, Member of Parliament, Oct. 19, 1982, Kreisarchiv DAN, Bestand OKD/Landrat Nr. 214/2.

167. Karl-Friedrich Kassel, ". . . und lebt verdammt nicht schlecht!" *Die Zeit*, July 10, 1992; Kassel, "Reichtum macht stumm," *Die Zeit*, May 8, 1992. The *Zeit* articles are based on a series in the local paper, *Elbe-Jeetzel-Zeitung*. The Green Party reprinted the series in 2009 (http://www.bi-luechow-dannenberg.de/?p=2115, accessed January 2018). The journalist Kassel moved to Dannenberg County in 1980 and pursues the issue of the Gorleben monies to the present day.

168. Masurek and Hachmöller, "Akteursnetzwerke," 64.

169. A list of the projects financed with the Gorleben monies in "Ausgleichszahlungen des Bundes für die nuklearen Entsorgungseinrichtungen bei Gorleben," n.d. [1995], Kreisarchiv DAN, Bestand OKD/Landrat Nr. 216; on the fate of some of the projects see Schulz, "Kommunal-Fusion," 17; on Poggendorf's reckoning with the "colorful coalition" that, in his view, had wrecked his legacy see Poggendorf, *Gorleben*, 245–260.

170. Quotation in Niedersächsisches Institut für Wirtschaftsforschung, *Ansatzpunkte*, 111.

171. Hahn and Pudemat, "Entwicklung."

172. Referenced in BT, 14. WP, Drs. 14/5634, Antwort der Bundesregierung auf die Kleine Anfrage [. . .] der Landesgruppe Niedersachsen, Mar. 22, 2001.

173. Overview in Rucht, "Anti-Atomkraftbewegung," 245–266. On Wyhl see Rusinek "Wyhl," 652–666; Milder, "Grassroots Activism," 191–211; Vandamme, *Basisdemokratie*, 61–74. Contemporary account, Rucht, *Von Wyhl nach Gorleben*, 74–98.

174. Tompkins, *Better Active*, 147–195; Milder, *Greening Democracy*, 147–151.

175. Am Emb Bonn to State Dept, Bonn Nr. 9987, May 27, 1980, Doc. Nr. C05291512.

176. Tompkins, *Better Active*; Milder, *Greening Democracy*; Kirchhof and Meyer, "Global Protest."

177. Tompkins, "Grassroots Transnationalism(s)," 118.

178. CIA, "The World Oil Market in the Years Ahead: A Research Paper" (Aug. 1979), 55, Jimmy Carter Presidential Library Atlanta, NLC-7-48-7-3-2. For an earlier contemporary assessment see Sweet, "Opposition to Nuclear Power."

179. Despite a focus on the transnational nature of anti-nuclear protest, few researchers address the role of the actual border. See Müller, "Skeleton," 68–89; Tompkins, "Grassroots Transnationalism(s)."

180. *UA Gorleben*, Protocol Nr. 66, Dec. 20, 2011, testimony pastor Gottfried Mahlke, 2.

181. The role of women in the anti-Gorleben protests awaits a historian who will give more than a mere mention, as in Vandamme, *Basisdemokratie*, 85; Tiggemann, *Achillesferse*, 732. For early work see Kirchhof, "Frauen."

182. Nds. Innenmin. to BMI and Interior Ministries of all federal states, Feb. 22, 1977, NLA HA Nds. 100, Acc 149/97 Nr. 110.

183. Telex, n.d. [Feb. 25, 1977], Erkenntnisse über den Hauptinitiator der Bürgerinitiative Umweltschutz Lüchow-Dannenberg H.W.; Bericht über die kriminalpolizeiliche Situation im Landkreis Lüchow-Dannenberg hinsichtl. der geplanten Errichtung einer Atomentsorgungsanlage, Sept. 9, 1977, both in NLA HA Nds. 100 Acc.2003/116 Nr. 71.

184. For the term see Vetten, "Gleich hinter Gorleben," 56. On the influence of Wyhl as a template for Gorleben see Vandamme, *Basisdemokratie*, 60, 74. On "bäuerliche Notgemeinschaft" see Blowers, *Legacy*, 198–199.

185. The article "Stadtflucht der Dichter," *Der Spiegel*, Feb. 4, 1974, 118, was conceived in the context of the protest against the Langendorf nuclear power plant.

186. Some key texts are collected in Kahrs, ed., *Wendland*. Resident intellectuals encouraged writing about the Wendland with the founding of the *Künstlerhof Schreyahn* in 1979, which offered writing retreats in the area beginning in 1981. See also Blowers, *Legacy*, 208.

187. Artistically, this image of "sleepy" borderlands is captured brilliantly in Wim Wenders's road movie *Im Lauf der Zeit* (*Kings of the Road*) (1976).

188. Renate Just, "Deutschland: Am schönsten, wo es am ärmsten ist," *Zeit Magazin* (Aug. 1986), 20.

189. Vetten, "Gleich hinter Gorleben," 38–60. See also Wolfram Runkel, "Das stille Ende," *Zeit Magazin*, Apr. 22, 1983, 36–42.

190. Vetten, "Gleich hinter Gorleben," 60: "Den Kranichen nachgucken, die von Pommern kommen. Welche Sensation das Wort Pommern enthält." The texts about the Wendland frequently liken its landscape to that of East Prussia.

191. Müller, *Another Country*, 73–74.

192. Thomas Schröder, "Ein Wochenende in der letzten Ecke," *Die Zeit*, May 16, 1975.

193. Just, "Deutschland: Am schönsten, wo es am ärmsten ist," 21.

194. Geisler, "'Heimat' and the German Left," 34–41; for contemporary reflections see Greverus, *Suche nach Heimat*. See also the 1981 literary anthology edited by Walwei-Wiegelmann, *Die Wunde namens Deutschland*. Stangel, *Die neue Linke* is relevant in this context but does not cover the 1980s.

195. On the link between "authentic" rural spaces and the anti-nuclear movement see Tompkins, *Better Active*, 116–120.

196. Wilkens, "Natur- und Landschaftsschutz;" Prof. Dr. Ewald Sprecher, Biology Dept., University of Hamburg, to Governor Ernst Albrecht, Feb. 17, 1977, NLA HA Nds. 800, Acc 2001/110 Nr. 162; Bernhard Grzimek, Zoolog. Gesellschaft Frankfurt von 1858, to Nds. Landesverwaltungsamt, Nov. 3, 1977, NLA HA Nds. 110N, Acc. 7/90 Nr. 39.

197. "Flugblatt Bürgerinitiative Umweltschutz Lüchow-Dannenberg" (call for demonstration on Mar. 12, 1977). The flyer highlights the ecological value of the prospective nuclear site. It urges demonstrators to stay on paved roads and not alienate farmers by tramping across their fields, since the farmers' support will be needed in the future. Flyer in NLA HA Nds. 100 Acc.2003/116 Nr. 71.

198. *Elbe-Jeetzel-Zeitung*, Mar. 26, 1977, cited in Halbach and Panzer, *Zwischen Gorleben und Stadtleben*, 25.

199. Tompkins, "Grassroots Transnationalism(s)," 124–125.

200. Kai Hermann, "'Albrecht, wir kommen,'" *Die Zeit*, Mar. 30, 1979; Buch, *Unruhe*, 330–349. Both Hermann and Buch were residents of Dannenberg County. On the symbolic value of the farmer and the tractor for anti-nuclear site fights see Tompkins, *Better Active*, 119–121.

201. The nuclear state refers to Jungk, *Der Atomstaat*, a key text for the West German anti-nuclear movement.

202. First mention of the Republic idea in "Stadtflucht der Dichter," *Der Spiegel*, Feb. 4, 1974, 118. Hermann, "'Albrecht, wir kommen,'" and Buch, *Unruhe*, 348, both report that the "Republic" was proclaimed during the tractor caravan to Hannover in March 1979. See also Tiggemann, *Achillesferse*, 605, 731.

203. Am Emb Bonn to State Dept, Bonn Nr. 11415, June 16, 1980, Doc. Nr. C05291510. See also Zint, *Republik Freies Wendland*; Kai Krüger, "Das Wehrdorf im Wendland," *Stern*, May 22, 1980, 20–26.

204. Am Emb Bonn to State Dept, Bonn Nr. 15470, Aug. 8, 1980, Doc. Nr. C05291608. The "embassy," a wooden structure with a sod roof on Kennedy Square, was tolerated by the Bremen Senate for a year before being cleared.

205. Am Emb Bonn to State Dept, Bonn Nr. 11415, June 16, 1980, Doc. Nr. C05291510; "Behindert, beschimpft, bedroht, geschlagen und ausgesperrt. 29 Journalisten berichten über ihre Erfahrung im Umgang mit der Polizei während der Räumung des Bohrplatzes 1004 in Gorleben," *Frankfurter Rundschau*, Aug. 19 and 20, 1980; Halbach/Panzer, *Zwischen Gorleben und Stadtleben*, 5–6; Rucht, *Von Wyhl nach Gorleben*, 140–141. See also Tiggemann, *Achillesferse*, 743–747; Tompkins, *Better Active*, 189–193.

206. Am Emb Bonn to State Dept, Bonn Nr. 11415, June 16, 1980, Doc. Nr. C05291510.

207. One group of protesters had congregated elsewhere in order to mislead the police into believing that a large demonstration was afoot. The distraction was staged to enable another group of protesters to cross the demarcation line. See Hertle, "Hart an der Grenze," 93–95.

208. "Stadtflucht der Dichter," *Der Spiegel*, Feb. 4, 1974, 118.

209. "Kernkraftgegner demonstrieren auf DDR-Gebiet vor Metallgitterzaun," *Tagesspiegel*, Jan. 28, 1982. See also "Kernkraftgegner auf DDR-Gebiet," *Hannoversche Allgemeine*, Jan. 28, 1982.

210. "Protest auf DDR-Gebiet beendet," *Süddeutsche Zeitung*, Jan. 29, 1982.

211. Hans-Helmut Kohl, "Protest im Zwischenraum deutsch-deutscher Wirklichkeit: Zeltlager vor dem Todesstreifen," *Frankfurter Rundschau*, July 6, 1983: "Warum die DDR Grenzer bislang solch einen Langmut bewiesen haben, weiss hier niemand."

212. "In Ost und West," *Braunschweiger Zeitung*, July 5, 1983; "Lästige Gäste," *Braunschweiger Zeitung*, July 7, 1983.

213. Vandamme, *Basisdemokratie*, 83–84; interplay between locals and external supporters during the site occupation in Tiggemann, *Achillesferse*, 729–736.

214. Tompkins, *Better Active*, 121–127.

215. "Grenzgänger," *Hannoversche Allgemeine*, July 4, 1983; "DDR-Haft wünschen wir keinem, auch nicht den Grenzbesetzern," *Hannoversche Allgemeine*, July 5, 1983; "Mal rüber," *Der Spiegel*, July 11, 1983, 76–77; Hans-Helmut Kohl, "Protest im Zwischenraum deutsch-deutscher Wirklichkeit," *Frankfurter Rundschau*, July 6, 1983.

216. The book issued for the tenth anniversary of the Gorleben protests simply ignores the 1983 occupation of the border strip as if it had never happened. Ehmke, ed., *Zwischenschritte*.

217. MfS, Zentraler Operativstab, Leiter Oberst [Gerhard] Grünberg to HA VI, Leiter [Heinz Fiedler], Aug. 21, 1981, BStU MfS HA VI, Nr. 3830. The memo bears the handwritten remark that the information was only FYI ("zur Beachtung") but did not request any action. HA VI was the Stasi department in charge of the border.

218. Grenzkommando Nord, Stellvertreter des Stabschefs für operative Arbeit, Schlussfolgerungen und Aufgaben für die Grenztruppen der DDR aus der Grenzverletzung einer Gruppe von Zivilpersonen aus der BRD am 27. Jan. 1981 im Sicherungsabschnitt I, Grenzregiment 24, BArch-MA, DVH 48/138758.

219. MfS HA I, Information Nr. 226/83 über eine widerrechtliche Besetzung des Territoriums der DDR [. . .], July 7, 1983, BStU MfS ZAIG Nr. 16268, fols. 55–57; further documentation can be found in the same file.

220. Further examples: "Friedenscamp von Atomkraftgegner vor dem DDR-Grenzzaun," *Frankfurter Rundschau*, Oct. 10, 1983, about an occupation in Philippstal in Hesse; "Protest auf CSSR-Gebiet, dann über Schirnding abgeschoben," *Frankenpost*, Apr. 9–11, 1984; "Robin Wood besetzt DDR-Gebiet bei Hof," *Neue Presse*, Dec. 29, 1988; Peter Schmitt, "Umweltprotest im Dreiländereck: Transparente verkünden in die DDR und die CSSR— 'Schadstoffe kennen keine Grenzen,'" *Süddeutsche Zeitung*, Dec. 29, 1988. The youth group of

the German Alpine Association occupied the border strip in April 1986 to protest the use of nuclear energy. Documented in BayHStA StK/19437.

221. Tiggemann, *Achillesferse*, 801–804, notes the increase of anti-CASTOR protests in the late 1990s and a decrease beginning in 2001. There was a moratorium on CASTOR transports between 1998 and 2001. See also Blowers, *Legacy*, 194–197; Rucht, "Anti-Atomkraftbewegung," 260.

222. It was actually a conscious strategy of external Gorleben opponents to take up registered residence in Dannenberg in order to strengthen resistance "from within" the county. Nds. Innenmin., Vermerk [für den StS und Minister], Apr. 28, 1978, NLA HA Nds. 100 Acc.2003/116 Nr. 72.

223. Reichardt, *Authentizität*, 57–71; Tompkins, *Better Active*, 131–136.

224. Reichardt, *Authentizität*, 459–480; "Landkommune," in *Wendland Lexikon*, vol. 2 (Lüchow: Köhring, 2008), 15. On the context of natural foods and farming in the 1970s and 1980s, see Treitel, *Eating Nature*, 265–280.

225. On the so-called Wendland Project see Peter Menke-Glückert, BMI, to Georg Redeker, Nds. State Commissioner for Environmental Protection, Feb. 11, 1980; Konrad Otto[-Zimmermann], "Ökologische Modellregion Hannoversches Wendland," Vortrag in der Evangelischen Akademie Loccum, Dec. 16, 1978, both in BArch B106/66401.

226. Brink, *Wendland-Kooperative*.

227. Andreas Maier, "Widerständiges Wendland," *Frankfurter Allgemeine Zeitung*, Sept. 12, 2012; Neukölln (pseud.), "Wendländische Schmonzette," 107–111.

228. Röhling, "Techniken," 40.

229. Achilles, "'Nuclear Power?,'" 121–124; Radkau and Hahn, *Aufstieg und Fall*, 353–364; Brunnengräber, "Atompolitische Wende," 13–32.

230. Kahl (Bavaria) 1961; Neckarwestheim II (Baden-Württemberg) 1989. On the core time period for nuclear energy see Radkau and Hahn, *Aufstieg und Fall*, 321–322.

231. Hocke and Renn, "Paralysis," 930.

232. "'Den Schiet wüllt wie hie ok nich hebben,'" *Der Spiegel*, Nov. 7, 1976, 102–110; Tiggemann, *Achillesferse*, 394–403.

233. Blowers, *Legacy*, 180.

234. This center–periphery paradox is the core argument in the Gorleben chapter in Blowers, *Legacy*.

235. Martina Wimmer, "Die Bernstorffs," *Greenpeace Magazin* 6 (2007).

236. Benjamin Piel, "Lüchow schafft das," *Spiegel online*, Oct. 13, 2015.

237. Zoé Sona, "Ökonazis im Wendland: Jung, naturverbunden, rechts," *tageszeitung*, May 13, 2015; Benjamin Piel, "Wendland: Nach dem Rechten schauen," *Die Zeit*, Sept. 27, 2015; Andreas Speit, "Wendland färbt sich grün-braun," *tageszeitung*, Sept. 16, 2016. For an overview see Amadeo Antonio Stiftung, ed., *Völkische SiedlerInnen*.

238. Arbeitskreis Auswahlverfahren Endlagersuche, or Committee on a Site Selection Procedure for Repository Sites.

239. Hocke and Renn, "Paralysis," 926.

240. Blowers, *Legacy*, 210–217; Hocke and Renn, "Paralysis," 927–928.

241. Blowers, *Legacy*, 217; Hocke and Renn, "Paralysis," 927.

242. Federal Site Selection Act on the Storage and Disposal of High Active Waste and Spent Fuel, *Standortgesetz* (StandAG 2013). For background see Smeddinck and Semper, "Kritik am Standortauswahlgesetz," 235–259.

243. Kommission Lagerung hoch radioaktiver Abfallstoffe, ed., *Abschlussbericht: Verantwortung für die Zukunft—Ein faires und transparentes Verfahren für die Auswahl eines nationalen Endlagerstandortes* (Berlin, July 2016).

244. Quotation in Hocke and Renn, "Paralysis," 928.

245. Brunnengräber and Mez, "Atomkomplex im Zerfall," 298–310; Schulz, "Fonds oder Rückstellungen?," 262–287; Andreas Mihm, "Aus dem Schneider beim Atommüll," *Frankfurter Allgemeine Zeitung*, June 23, 2017; "Weg für Atommüll-Staatsfonds endgültig frei," *Frankfurter Allgemeine Zeitung*, June 23, 2017.

246. Brunnengräber and Mez, "Atomkomplex im Zerfall," 306–307.

247. See https://www.wunderlandkalkar.eu/de (accessed July 2017).

248. See http://www.erlebnisbergwerk.de/de/index.html (accessed July 2017).

CONCLUSION

1. *Im Lauf der Zeit* (*Kings of the Road*), dir. Wim Wenders, 1976; Böttcher, *Nachglühen*; Rausch, *Restlicht*; Buddenbohm, *Marmelade im Zonenrandgebiet*.

2. Seidel and von Ehrlich, "Persistent Effects of Regional Policy," argue that the aid program was effective, as evidenced by increased income per capita and "economic density." By contrast, Erdmann, "Ende der Welt," points out that after a brief unification boom and with some regional exceptions, most of the former borderlands lapsed back into their previous underperformance vis-à-vis the rest of West Germany.

3. Ther, Europe after 1989, 260–287; Bösch, "Divided and Connected," 7–8.

4. Mingus, Remapping Modern Germany; Strubelt and Briesen, eds., Raumplanung nach 1945.

5. Gabriel et al., Deutschland 25.

6. Examples: Dingemann, Mitten in Deutschland; Kieling, Ein deutscher Wandersommer; Esser, Radtouren am Grünen Band; Scherzer, Grenz-Gänger.

7. Term in Gross, "Decoupling," 546.

8. Eckhart Lohse and Stephan Löwenstein, "Überrollt," *Frankfurter Allgemeine Zeitung*, Sept. 3, 2016; "Grenzöffnung für Flüchtlinge: Was geschah wirklich?" *Die Zeit*, Aug. 22, 2016; "Two Weeks in September: The Making of Merkel's Decision to Accept Refugees," *Spiegel online*, Aug. 24, 2016; see also the rather angry book by Alexander, Die Getriebenen.

9. On the fall of the Berlin Wall as a "global iconic event" see Sonnevend, Stories without Borders.

Bibliography

ARCHIVAL SOURCES

Bundesarchiv (BArch)

Koblenz

B102   Bundesministerium für Wirtschaft, BMWi (Federal Ministry for Economic Affairs)

B106   Bundesministerium des Innern, BMI (Federal Ministry of the Interior)

B135   Bundesministerien für besonderen Aufgaben (Federal Ministries for Special Tasks)

B136   Bundeskanzleramt, BkAmt (Federal Chancellery)

B137   Bundesministerium für innerdeutsche Beziehungen, (Federal Ministry for Inter-German Relations)

B288   Ständige Vertretung, StaeV (Permanent Representative Mission of the Federal Republic in East Berlin)

B295   Bundesministerium für Umwelt, Naturschutz und Reaktorsicherheit, BMU (Federal Ministry for the Environment, Nature Protection and Reactor Security)

B369   Deutsch-deutsche Grenzkommission—Vertretung des Bundesgrenzschutzes (German-German Border Commission)

Berlin-Lichterfelde

DK1   DDR Ministerium für Landwirtschaft, Forst- und Nahrungsgüterwirtschaft (GDR Ministry for Agriculture, Forestry, and Food Supply)

DK5   DDR Ministerium für Umweltschutz und Wasserwirtschaft (GDR Ministry for Environmental Protection and Water Management)

Stiftung Archiv der Parteien und Massenorganisationen der DDR im Bundesarchiv (BArch-SAPMO)

DY 30   Zentralkomitee der SED

DY 3023 Büro Mittag im ZK der SED

Freiburg—Militärarchiv (BArch-MA)

DVH 27	Deutsche Grenzpolizei Kommando der Deutschen Grenzpolizei
DVH 32	Kommando der Grenztruppen
DVH 36	5. Grenzbrigade (Kalbe in der Altmark)
DVH 38	7. Grenzbrigade (Magdeburg)
DVH 48	Grenzkommando Nord
DVH 49-4	Grenzregiment 23 (Gardelegen)
DVH 49-5	Grenzregiment 24 (Salzwedel)
DVW	Ministerium für nationale Verteidigung

Archiv der Behörde des Bundesbeauftragten für die Stasi Unterlagen, Berlin (BStU)

BV Magedeburg, Abt. XX	Staatsapparat, Kultur, Kirchen, Untergrund
BV Gera, Abt. XV	HVA Bezirksverwaltung
MfS HA I	NVA und Grenztruppen
MfS HA II	Spionageabwehr
MfS HA VI	Passkontrolle, Tourismus, Interhotel
MfS HA IX	Untersuchungsorgan
MfS HA XII	Zentrale Auskunft, Speicher
MfS HA XVIII	Volkswirtschaft
MfS HA XXII	Terrorabwehr
MfS HVA	Hauptverwaltung Aufklärung
MfS ZAIG	Zentrale Auswertungs- und Informationsgruppe
MfS ZOS	Zentraler Operativstab
AG BKK	Arbeitsgruppe Bereich Kommerzielle Koordinierung (KoKo)

Hessisches Hauptstaatsarchiv Wiesbaden (HHStAW)

Abt. 502	Hessische Staatskanzlei
Abt. 504	Kultusministerium
Abt. 507	Hessisches Ministerium für Wirtschaft und Verkehr
Abt. 508	Hessisches Sozialministerium
Abt. 509	Hessisches Ministerium für Landwirtschaft und Forsten
Abt. 531	Oberfinanzdirektion Frankfurt a. M.—Teilbestand
Abt. 654	Hessisches Landratsamt Hanau
Abt. 660	Hessisches Landratsamt Schlüchtern

Bayerisches Hauptstaatsarchiv, Munich (BayHStA)

Bayerische Staatskanzlei (StK)
Präsidium der Bayerischen Grenzpolizei

Niedersächsisches Landesarchiv Hannover (NLA HA)

Nds. 20	Landesministerium
Nds. 50	Staatskanzlei
Nds. 58	Landeszentrale für politische Bildung
Nds. 100	Innenministerium
Nds. 110	Landesverwaltungsamt
Nds. 120 Lün	Regierungspräsident Lüneburg Gesamtbestand
Nds. 200	Finanzministerium
Nds. 300	Ministerium für Soziales [MS], Frauen, Familie und Gesundheit
Nds. 380	Ministerium für Bundesangelegenheiten
Nds. 500	Ministerium für Wirtschaft und Verkehr
Nds. 600	Ministerium für Ernährung, Landwirtschaft und Forsten (MELF)
Nds. 620	Celle
Nds. 800	Umweltministerium
Nds. 1225	Lüneburg
Nds. 1050	Grenzschutzkommando Nord
VVP 65 Acc 76/90 Nr. 11	Handakten MP Albrecht

Niedersächsisches Landesarchiv Wolfenbüttel (NLA WO)

4 Nds Zg.	Behörden des Landes Niedersachsen— Bezirksregierung Braunschweig (Abt. Landwirtschaft, Umwelt, Forsten)
94N Nr. 438	Nachlass Conrady

Landesarchiv Schleswig-Holstein, Schleswig (LASH)

Abt. 605	Staatskanzlei
Abt. 611	Innenministerium
Abt. 741	Umweltministerium
Hauptzollamt Lübeck-Ost	

Politisches Archiv des Auswärtigen Amts, Berlin (PA/AA)

B 38	Berlin und Deutschland als Ganzes, 1959-1971
B 202	Gebietsfragen

Archiv der Hansestadt Lübeck (AHL)

Bestand 04.01-0 Zentralamt, Hauptamt
Bestand 02.05 IHK zu Lübeck

Stadtarchiv Helmstedt

Stadtarchiv Fulda

10 Kämmerei
19 Kulturamt

Schlagwortkarton "Fulda Gap"

Kreisarchiv Lüchow-Dannenberg, Lüchow

Bestand OKD / Landrat

Historical Archives of the EU, Florence (HAEU)

Historical Archives of the European Commission, Brussels (HAEC)

Historisches Archiv zum Tourismus, Berlin (HAT)

Archiv des Niedersächsischen Landtags, Hannover (Archiv des Nds. LT)

PA/AA05
PA/AA06

Drucksachen

The Jimmy Carter Presidential Library and Museum, Atlanta

National Security Council (NSC) Declassification Collection

National Archives and Records Administration (NARA)

*RG 59: Central Foreign Policy Files, electronic telegrams created 7/1/1973–12/31/1979
via Access to Archival Databases (AAD), https://aad.archives.gov/aad/;*

further telegrams up to 1980 obtained through a Freedom of Information Act request

Bund Naturschutz in Bayern (BN), Nuremberg

Sammlung Wolfram Brauneis, Eschwege

PRINTED SOURCES

Brecht, Bertolt and Paul Dessau. *Herrnburger Bericht: Gewidmet der Freien Deutschen Jugend anlässlich der 3. Weltfestspiele der Jugend und Studenten für den Frieden in Berlin*. Berlin: Zentralrat der FDJ, 1951.
Deutsche Einheit: Sonderedition aus den Akten des Bundeskanzleramtes 1989/90, special ed. 1. Edited by Hanns Jürgen Küsters and Daniel Hoffmann. Munich: Oldenbourg, 1998.

Deutscher Bundestag. 17. Wahlperiode: Beschlussempfehlung und Bericht des 1. Untersuchungsausschuss nach Artikel 44 des Grundgesetzes. Drs. 17/13700. May 16, 2013.

Dokumente zur Deutschlandpolitik (DzD). Commissioned by Bundesministerium des Innern and Bundesarchiv.

VI. *Reihe*, vol. 1 (1969–1970). Edited by Daniel Hofmann. Munich: Oldenbourg, 2002.

VI. *Reihe*, vol. 5 (1977–1978). Edited by Eberhard Kuhrt and Michael Hollmann. Munich: Oldenbourg, 2011.

VI. *Reihe*, vol. 6 (1979–1980). Edited by Michael Hollmann. Munich: Oldenbourg, 2014.

Die Kabinettsprotokolle der Bundesrepublik, vols. 1–10. Edited by the Bundesarchiv. Boppard/Rh.: Boldt, 1982–2000.

Kommission Lagerung hoch radioaktiver Abfallstoffe. *Abschlussbericht. Verantwortung für die Zukunft. Ein faires und transparentes Verfahren für die Auswahl eines nationalen Endlagerstandortes.* Berlin, July 2016.

Ministerium für Ernährung, Landwirtschaft und Forsten des Landes Schleswig-Holstein (MELF SH). *Landesprogramm zum Schutz der Natur und zur Verbesserung der Struktur an der schleswig-holsteinisch-mecklenburgischen Landesgrenze.* Kiel, Sept. 1985.

Ministerium für Naturschutz, Umweltschutz und Wasserwirtschaft (DDR). "Staatlicher Naturschutz wird verstärkt." *MNUW Umwelt Report* 1 (Apr. 1990): 21–22.

Sitzungsprotokolle des Auschusses für gesamtdeutsche Fragen des Deutschen Bundestages, 1949–1953. Edited by Andreas Biefang. Düsseldorf: Droste, 1998.

GOVERNMENT-SPONSORED PUBLICATIONS ABOUT THE BORDER

Die Auswirkungen der Ostzonen Grenze auf die anliegenden Gebiete der Bundesrepublik: Erkenntnisse und Vorschläge. Edited by the Arbeitsgemeinschaft der Grenzlandkammern. Braunschweig, Dec. 1950.

Berlin: Das britische Weissbuch zur Krise—Eine Darstellung der Ereignisse, die zur Überweisung der Berliner Frage an die Vereinten Nationen führte. Edited by Information Services Division, CCG(BE). Hamburg: Die Welt, 1948.

Brönstrup, Rolf. *Stacheldraht: Notizen und Mosaiken* (Schriften zur deutschen Frage Nr. 15). Edited by the Niedersächsischer Minister für Bundesangelegenheiten, Vertriebene und Flüchtlinge. Leer: Rautenberg, 1966.

Bundesministerium für Gesamtdeutsche Beziehungen. *Die Sperrmassnahmen der Sowjetzonenregierung an der Zonengrenze und um Westberlin.* Bonn, 1953.

Bundesministerium für Innerdeutsche Beziehungen. *Ratgeber Zonenrandförderung* Bonn 1983.

Bundesministerium für Innerdeutsche Beziehungen. *Soziale und kulturelle Fördermassnahmen der Bundesregierung im Zonenrandgebiet.* Bonn, 1987.

Bundesministerium für Innerdeutsche Beziehungen. *Zonenrandförderung—warum? wieviel? wofür? Die Bundesregierung zieht Bilanz.* Bonn, 1976.

Deutschland im Wiederaufbau: Tätigkeitsbericht der Bundesregierung für das Jahr [1950–1960]. Edited by Presse- und Informationsamt der Bundesregierung. Bonn.

Grenzland der Mitte: Dokumentarisches Bildwerk über Wirtschaft und Verkehr in Niedersachsen. Hannover: Steinbock, 1963.

Im Schatten der Zonengrenze. Edited by Bundesministerium für Gesamtdeutsche Fragen. Bonn, 1956.

Unmenschliche Grenze/Inhuman Frontier (in German, English, and French). Edited by Niedersächsische Landeszentrale für Heimatdienst. Hannover, 1956.

GOVERNMENT PUBLICATIONS FOR BORDER VISITORS
(IN CHRONOLOGICAL ORDER)

Wie lange noch? Edited by Bayerische und Hessische Landeszentrale für Heimatdienst. Wiesbaden, 1957.

Unmenschliche Grenze. Inhuman Frontier. Omänskliga Gränser. Edited by Niedersächsische Landeszentrale für Heimatdienst. Hannover, 1958.

Mitten in Deutschland: Mitten im 20. Jahrhundert, 2nd ed. Edited by Bundesministerium für gesamtdeutsche Fragen. Bonn, 1959 (eleven editions between 1958 and 1971).

In the Heart of Germany—In the 20th Century. Edited by the Federal Ministry of All-German Affairs. Bonn, 1960.

Die Zonengrenzfahrt. Edited by Hessische Landeszentrale für politische Bildung. Wiesbaden, 1964.

En el Corazon de Alemania en Pleno Siglo XX: La Frontera con la Zona. Edited by Ministerio Federal para Asuntos de Toda Alemania. Bonn and Berlin, 1965.

Zonengrenze Niedersachsen. Edited by Niedersächsischer Minister für Bundesangelegenheiten, für Vertriebene und Flüchtlinge. Hannover, 1966.

Zonengrenze Niedersachsen. Edited by Niedersächsischer Minister für Bundesangelegenheiten, Vertriebene und Flüchtlinge. Hannover, 1968.

Zonengrenze Bayern. Edited by Bayerischer Staatsminister für Bundesangelegenheiten. n.d. [1970s].

Studienfahrten an die Demarkationslinie. Edited by Bundesminister für innerdeutsche Beziehungen. Kassel, 1971.

Deutschland diesseits und jenseits der Grenze Niedersachsen. Edited by Niedersächsischer Minister für Bundesangelegenheiten. Hannover, 1982.

"Die Grenze": Schleswig-Holsteins Landesgrenze zur DDR. Edited by Innenminister des Landes Schleswig-Holstein. Kiel, 1985.

The Border Between Hesse and the GDR: Brief Information for Visitors. Edited by Hessendienst der Staatskanzlei. Wiesbaden, 1986.

Die Innerdeutsche Grenze. Edited by Bundesminister für innerdeutsche Beziehungen. Bonn, 1987.

MEMOIRS AND RECOLLECTIONS

Albrecht, Ernst. *Erinnerungen, Erkenntnisse, Entscheidungen. Politik für Europa, Deutschland und Niedersachsen.* Göttingen: Barton, 1999.

Bastian, Uwe. *Greenpeace in der DDR: Erinnerungsberichte, Interviews und Dokumente.* Berlin: Edition Ost, 1996.

Böckel, Herbert. *Grenz-Erfahrungen: Der kalte Kleinkrieg an einer heissen Grenze— Berichte und Erlebnisse eines "West-Grenzers."* Fulda: Parzeller, 2009.

Eiber, Alfred. *Hof: Das Tor zur Freiheit—Die deutsch-deutsche Grenze in der Region Hof: Eine Zeitreise durch die jüngste deutsche Geschichte von 1945–1990.* Weissenstadt: Späthling, 2017.

Mittag, Günter. *Um jeden Preis: Im Spannungsfeld zweier Systeme.* Berlin: Aufbau, 1991.

Seidel, Karl. *Berlin-Bonner Balance.* Berlin: Edition Ost, 2002.

Steffens, Heiko, Birger Ollrogge, and Gabriela Kubanek, eds. *Lebensjahre im Schatten der deutschen Grenze: Selbstzeugnisse vom Leben an der innerdeutschen Grenze seit 1945.* Opladen: Leske + Budrich, 1990.

Succow, Michael. "Persönliche Erinnerungen an eine bewegte Zeit." In *Naturschutz in Deutschland,* edited by Michael Succow, Lebrecht Jeschke, and Hans Dieter Knapp, 64–66. Berlin: Links, 2012.

[Wrangel]. *Abgeordnete des Deutschen Bundestages: Aufzeichnungen und Erinnerungen.* Vol. 14: *Olaf von Wrangel,* edited by Deutscher Bundestag. Boppard/Rh.: Boldt, 1995.

NEWSPAPERS, MAGAZINES, AND OTHER PERIODICALS

Aller Zeitung, Allgemeine Zeitung Uelzen Berliner Morgenpost, Bild Zeitung, Bonner Energie Report, Bonner Generalanzeiger, Bonner Rundschau, Braunschweiger Zeitung, Christian Science Monitor, Christ und Welt, Deutsche Zeitung, Deutsches Allgemeines Sonntagsblatt, Elbe-Jeetzel-Zeitung, Die Flüchtlingsstimme, Frankfurter Allgemeine Zeitung, Frankfurter Rundschau, Freies Wort, Fuldaer Zeitung, Fuldaer Volkszeitung, Geo, Greenpeace Magazin, Hamburger Abendblatt, Hannoversche Allgemeine Zeitung, Helmstedter Kreisblatt, Hersfelder Zeitung, Herzberger Zeitungen, Hessendienst, Hessenspiegel, Hessische Allgemeine Zeitung, Hessische-Niedersächsische Allgemeine, Husumer Nachrichten, Isenhagener Kreisblatt, Kieler Nachrichten, Kreisblatt für Helmstedt, Landeszeitung Lüneburg, Life magazine, Lübecker Freie Presse am Morgen, Lübecker Morgen, Lübecker Nachrichten, Merian, Mittelbayerische Zeitung, Neue Presse, Neues Deutschland, Die Neue Zeitung, Neue Zürcher Zeitung, Newsweek, New York Times, New York Times Magazine, Ostsee Zeitung, Die Parole, Der Spiegel, Staats-Zeitung, Stern, Tagesspiegel, tageszeitung, Die Welt, Wirtschaftswoche, Die Woche, Wolfsburger Allgemeine, Die Zeit, Zeit Magazin, Zeitschrift des BGS

INTERVIEWS

Karl Berke, Ilsenburg (Harz), July 5, 2013.
Wolfram Brauneis, Eschwege, July 13, 2009.
Kai Frobel, Nuremberg, July 20, 2009.
Martin Görner, Ranis, Aug. 23, 2010.
Lebrecht Jeschke, Greifswald, Feb. 26, 2013.
Ralf Maaß, Groß Molzahn, Oct. 23, 2010.
Hubert Weiger, Berlin, July 23, 2009.

LITERATURE

40 Jahre Umweltbundesamt, 1974–2014. Dessau: UBA, 2014.
"Die leidenden Landkreise an der Zonengrenze: Versuch einer komplexen Schilderung der Störungen und Schäden— Vorschläge für eine durchgreifende Hilfe." *Die Selbstverwaltung* 7:1 (1953): 1–8.
Abele, Johannes and Eckhard Hampe. "Kernenergiepolitik der DDR." In *Zur Geschichte der Kernenergie in der DDR*, edited by Johannes Abele, Gerhard Barkleit, and Peter Liewers, 29–89. Frankfurt: Lang, 2000.
Abelshauser, Werner. *Deutsche Wirtschaftsgeschichte: Von 1945 bis zur Gegenwart*. Bonn: Bundeszentrale, 2011.
Abelshauser, Werner. "Zur Entstehung der 'Magnet-Theorie' in der Deutschlandpolitik." *Vierteljahrshefte für Zeitgeschichte* 27:4 (1979): 661–679.
Achilles, Manuela. "'Nuclear Power? No, Thank you!': Germany's Energy Revolution Post-Fukushima." In *Environmental Sustainability in Transatlantic Perspective: A Multidisciplinary Approach*, edited by Dana M. Elzey and Manuela Achilles, 104–127. Basingstoke: Palgrave Macmillan, 2013.
Ackermann, Volker. *Der "echte" Flüchtling: Deutsche Vertriebene und Flüchtlinge aus der DDR, 1945–1961*. Osnabrück: Rasch, 1995.
Ackmann, Fritz. "Gegenüber der Altmark. Zur Geopolitik des Zonengrenzkreises Gifhorn." In *Im Schatten der Zonengrenze*, edited by Bundesministerium für Gesamtdeutsche Fragen, 75–78. Bonn, 1956.
Ahonen, Pertti. *Death at the Berlin Wall*. Oxford: Oxford University Press, 2011.
Ahrens, Ralf. "Debt, Cooperation, and Collapse: East German Foreign Trade in the Honecker Years." In *The East German Economy, 1945–2010: Falling Behind or Catching Up?*, edited by Hartmut Berghoff and Uta Balbier, 161–176. New York: Cambridge University Press, 2013.
Ahrens, Ralf. "Teure Gewohnheiten: Berlinförderung und Bundeshilfe für West-Berlin seit dem Mauerbau." *Vierteljahrschrift für Sozial- und Wirtschaftsgeschichte* 102:3 (2015): 283–299.
Akademie für Raumforschung und Landesplanung. "Gleichwertige Lebensverhältnisse: Diskussionspaper des Präsidiums der Akademie für Raumfoschung und Landesplanung." *Nachrichten der ARL* 2 (2005): 1–3.

Aldrich, Daniel P. *Site Fights: Divisive Facilities and Civil Society in Japan and the West.* Ithaca, NY: Cornell University Press, 2008.

Alexander, Robin. *Die Getriebenen.* Berlin: Siedler, 2017.

Allen, Jennifer. "Against the 1989/90 Ending Myth." *Central European History* 52:1 (2019): 125–147.

Alley, William M. and Rosemarie Alley. *Too Hot to Touch: The Problem of High-Level Nuclear Waste.* New York: Cambridge University Press, 2013.

Alwens, Ludwig. "Das oberfränkische Textilindustriegebiet: Grenzlandsituation und Strukturprobleme." In *Im Schatten der Zonengrenze*, edited by Bundesministerium für Gesamtdeutsche Fragen, 17–20. Bonn, 1956.

Amadeo Antonio Stiftung, ed. *Völkische SiedlerInnen im ländlichen Raum.* Berlin: A. Antonio Stiftung, 2014.

Amberger, Franz, ed. *Grenzenlos.* Straubing: Attenkofer, 2000.

Ambrosius, Gerold. "Der Beitrag der Vertriebenen und Flüchtlinge zum Wachstum der westdeutschen Wirtschaft nach dem Zweiten Weltkrieg." *Jahrbuch für Wirtschaftsgeschichte* 2 (1996): 39–71.

Amos, Heike. *Vertriebenenverbände im Fadenkreuz: Aktivitäten der Staatssicherheit, 1949–1989.* Munich: Oldenbourg, 2011.

Amos, Heike. *Die Westpolitik der SED, 1948/49–1961.* Berlin: Akademie, 1999.

Andresen, Uwe. "Finanzierung der Einheit." In *Handbuch zur deutschen Einheit, 1949–1989–1999*, edited by Werner Weidenfeld and Karl-Rudolf Korte, 368–383. Bonn: Bundeszentrale, 1999.

Angerer, Hanskarl. "Oberfranken—Land zwischen den Grenzen: Wirtschaftliche Probleme im Zonenrandgebiet." In *Oberfränkische Wirtschaft: Zum 125jährigen Bestehen der Industrie- und Handelskammer für Oberfranken*, edited by Chamber of Commerce of Upper Franconia, 34–42. Bayreuth: IHK, 1968.

Ante, Ulrich. "Some Developing and Current Problems of the Eastern Border Landscape of the Federal Republic of Germany: The Bavarian Example." In *The Geography of Border Landscapes*, edited by D. Rumley and J. V. Minghi, 63–85. London: Routledge, 1991.

Applebaum, Anne. *Iron Curtain: The Crushing of Eastern Europe, 1944–1956.* London: Allen Lane, 2012.

ARGE Weser. *Folgen der Reduktion der Salzbelastung in Werra und Weser für das Fließgewässer als Ökosystem.* Hildesheim: Wassergütestelle Weser, 2000.

Atapattu, Sumudu A. *Emerging Principles of International Environmental Law.* Ardsley, NY: Transnational, 2006.

"Aufbau des Grenzhundewesens der DDR-Grenztruppe." *Zeitschrift des Bundesgrenzschutzes* 16:1 (Jan. 1989): 24.

Bailey, Anthony. *Along the Edge of the Forest: An Iron Curtain Journey.* New York: Random House, 1983.

Baker, Frederick. "The Berlin Wall: Production, Preservation and Consumption of a Twentieth Century Monument." *Antiquity* 67 (1993): 709–733.

Balk, Reinhold. "Das war der eiserne Vorhang." In *Grenzenlos*, edited by Franz Amberger, 16–29. Straubing: Attenkofer, 2000.

Bankoff, Greg. "Making Parks Out of Making Wars: Transnational Nature Conservation and Environmental Diplomacy in the Twenty-First Century." In *Nation States and the Global Environment: New Approaches to International Environmental History*, edited by Erika Marie Bsumek, David Kinkela, and Mark Atwood Lawrence, 76–96. New York: Oxford University Press, 2013.

Barlösius, Eva. "Gleichwertig ist nicht gleich." *Aus Politik und Zeitgeschichte* 37 (2006). http://www.bpb.de/apuz/29548/gleichwertig-ist-nicht-gleich?p=all (accessed Jan. 2018).

Barnes, Trevor J. "Notes from the Underground: Why the History of Economic Geography Matters—The Case of Central Place Theory." *Economic Geography* 88 (2012): 1–26.

Bauerkämper, Arnd. "The Industrialization of Agriculture and the Consequences for the Natural Environment: An Inter-German Comparative Perspective." *Historical Social Research* 29:3 (2004): 124–149.

Baumann, Fred. "Der Naturpark Drömling." In *Naturschutz in Deutschland*, edited by Michael Succow, Lebrecht Jeschke, and Hans Dieter Knapp, 191–199. Berlin: Links, 2012.

Baumann, Fred and Helmut Müller. "Der Naturpark Drömling in Sachsen-Anhalt." *Naturschutz und Naturparke* 152 (1994): 9–17.

Baumann, Michael. "Innerdeutscher Tourismus." *Deutschland Archiv* 23:5 (May 1990): 750–756.

Beck, Peter and Kai Frobel. "Letzter Zufluchtsort: Der 'Todesstreifen'?" *Vogelschutz: Magazin für Arten- und Biotopschutz* 2 (1981): 24.

Becker, Anja. *Wie Gras über die Geschichte wächst: Orte der Erinnerung an der ehemaligen deutsch-deutschen Grenze*. Berlin: TU Berlin, 2004.

Behrens, Hermann. "Das Institut für Landschaftsforschung und Naturschutz (ILN) Halle (S.) und die deutsche Naturschutzgeschichte." *IUGR-Standpunkte* 5 (Nov. 2011): 1–18.

Behrens, Hermann, ed. *Naturschutzgeschichte und Naturschutzbeauftragte in Thüringen: Lexikon der Naturschutzbeauftragten*, vol. 4. Friedland: Steffen, 2015.

Behrens, Hermann and Jens Hoffmann, eds. *Naturschutzgeschichte(n): Lebenswege zwischen Ostseeküste und Erzgebirge*. Friedland: Steffen, 2013.

Behrisch, Arno. *Oberfranken im Würgegriff: Eine Zusammenfassung und Ergänzung der einschlägigen Denkschriften und Reden*. Hof, 1950.

Békési, Sándor. "Die topografische Ansichtskarte: Zur Geschichte und Theorie eines Massenmediums." *Relation*, N.F. 1 (2004): 403–426.

Bellin, Kurt. "Das Wasser." In *Das Hannoversche Wendland: Beiträge zur Beschreibung des Landkreises Lüchow-Dannenberg*, 21–27. Lüchow: Landkreis, 1971.

Bennewitz, Inge and Rainer Potratz. *Zwangsaussiedlungen an der innerdeutschen Grenze: Analyse und Dokumente*. Berlin: Links, 2012.

Berdahl, Daphne. *Where the World Ended: Re-Unification and Identity in the German Borderland*. Berkeley: University of California Press, 1999.

Berg, Michael von. "Umweltschutzabkommen Bundesrepublik Deutschland/DDR." In *Umweltschutz in beiden Teilen Deutschlands*, edited by Maria Haendcke-Hoppe and Konrad Merkel, 123–130. Berlin: Duncker & Humblot, 1986.

Berg, Michael von. "Umweltschutz in Deutschland: Verwirklichung einer deutschen Umweltunion." *Deutschland Archiv* 23:6 (June 1990): 897–906.

Berg, Michael von. "Umweltschutz in Deutschland: Zusammenarbeit zwischen den beiden deutschen Staaten." *Geographische Rundschau* 39:11 (1987): 606–609.

Berg, Michael von. "Zum Umweltschutz in Deutschland." *Deutschland-Archiv* 17:4 (April 1984): 374–383.

Berg, Wilfried. *Zonenrandförderung: Verfassungs- und gemeinschaftsrechtliche Grundlagen und Perspektiven*. Berlin: Duncker & Humblot, 1989.

Bernhardt, Christoph. "Zwischen Industrialismus und sanitärer Wohlfahrt: Umweltprobleme im Sozialismus am Beispiel der Wasserfrage in der DDR." In *Technik, Arbeit und Umwelt in der Geschichte*, edited by Torsten L. Meyer and Marcus Popplow, 367–380. Münster: Waxmann, 2006.

Bethlehem, Siegfried. *Heimatvertreibung, DDR-Flucht, Gastarbeiterzuwanderung: Wanderungsströme und Wanderungspolitik in der Bundesrepublik Deutschland*. Stuttgart: Klett-Cotta, 1982.

Beyer, Falk, ed. *Die (DDR-)Geschichte des Atommüll-Endlagers Morsleben*. Magdeburg: Landesbeauftragter, 2005.

Beyer, Stefan. *Das Grüne Band im Wandel: Biotopentwicklung im Raum Coburg*. Mitwitz: Naturschutzzentrum, 2011.

Bigley, James D. et al. "Motivations for War-Related Tourism: A Case of DMZ Visitors in Korea." *Tourism Geographies* 12:3 (2010): 371–394.

Bindewald, Hendrik. "Brocken. Der Kalte Krieg im Äther." In *Grenzziehungen, Grenzerfahrungen, Grenzüberschreitungen. Die innerdeutsche Grenze, 1945–1990*, edited by Detlef Schmiechen-Ackermann, Carl-Hans Hauptmeyer, and Thomas Schwark, 122–126. Darmstadt: WBG, 2011.

Bjarsch, Hans-Joachim. *Ein alter braunschweigischer Landkreis an der Grenze mitten durch Deutschland: Der Landkreis Helmstedt nach dem Zweiten Weltkrieg (1945–1990)—Eine Chronik*, part 1. Oschersleben: Ziethen, 2005.

Blab, Josef et al. "Naturschutzgrossprojekte des Bundes: Förderprogramme zur Errichtung und Sicherung schutzwürdiger Teile von Natur und Landschaft mit gesamtstaatlich repräsentativer Bedeutung." *Natur und Landschaft* 66:1 (Jan. 1991): 3–9.

Blackbourn, David. *The Conquest of Nature: Water, Landscape, and the Making of Modern Germany*. New York: Norton, 2006.

Blaive, Muriel. "Border Guarding as Social Practice: A Case Study of Czech Communist Governance and Hidden Transcripts." In *Walls, Borders, Boundaries*.

Spatial and Cultural Practices in Europe, edited by Janet Ward and Marc Silberman, 97–112. New York: Berghahn, 2012.

Blaive, Muriel, and Bertold Molden. *Grenzfälle: Österreichische und tschechische Erfahrungen am Eisernen Vorhang*. Weitra: Bibliothek der Provinz, 2009.

Blowers, Andrew. *The Legacy of Nuclear Power*. Abingdon: Routledge, 2017.

Blowers, Andrew. "Nuclear Waste and Landscapes of Risk." *Landscape Research* 24:3 (1999): 241–264.

Böhm, H. "F+E für das Entsorgungskonzept der Bundesregierung." *atw* 22:4 (1977): 186–190.

Böhm, Rudolf, Torsten Fiedler, Siegried Schäfer, and Rainer Wiesinger. *Zur Geschichte der Stadtentwässerung Dresdens*. Dresden: Selbstverlag, 2007.

Bölsche, Jochen. *Die deutsche Landschaft stirbt. Zerschnitten, zersiedelt, zerstört*. Reinbek: Rowohlt, 1983.

Bösch, Frank. "Divided and Connected: Perspectives on German History since the 1970s." In *A History Shared and Divided: East and West Germany since the 1970s*, edited by Frank Bösch, 1–44. New York: Berghahn, 2018.

Bösch, Frank, ed. *A History Shared and Divided: East and West Germany since the 1970s*. New York: Berghahn, 2018.

Böttcher, Jens. *Nachglühen*. Reinbek: Rowohlt, 2008.

Brady, Lisa M. "Life in the DMZ: Turning a Diplomatic Failure into an Environmental Success." *Diplomatic History* 32:4 (2008): 585–611.

Brain, Stephen. "The Appeal of Appearing Green: Soviet–American Ideological Competition and Cold War Environmental Diplomacy." *Cold War History* 16:4 (2016): 443–462.

Braun, Helmut. "Osthilfe, 1926–1937." In *Historisches Lexikon Bayerns*. http://www. historisches-lexikon-bayerns.de/artikel/artikel_44784 (accessed Jan. 2018).

Brauneis, Wolfram. "Das Grüne Band: Hessens Grenze zu seinem thüringischen Nachbarn—10 Jahre danach." *Ornithologische Mitteilungen* 52:10 (2000): 335–340.

Brauneis, Wolfram, Wilhelm Hammer, and Christian Saar. "Auswilderung gezüchteter Wanderfalken in Nordhessen: Eine Zwischenbilanz." *Deutscher Falkenorden* (1981): 23–27.

Braunschweig als Grenzland. Edited by the Chamber of Industry and Commerce in Braunschweig. Braunschweig: Westermann, 1949.

Briesen, Detlef and Wendelin Strubelt. "Zwischen Kontinuität und Neubeginn: Räumliche Planung und Forschung vor und nach 1945." In *Raumplanung nach 1945: Kontinuitäten und Neuanfänge in der Bundesrepublik Deutschland*, edited by Briesen and Strubelt, 15–54. Frankfurt: Campus, 2015.

Brink, Antje. *Die Wendland-Kooperative: Der Aufbau einer Erzeuger-Verbraucher-Gemeinschaft als Beitrag zu einer eigenständigen und ökologisch orientierten Regionalentwicklung im peripheren ländlichen Raum*. Hannover: Institut für Landschaftspflege und Naturschutz, 1986.

Brown, Kate. *Plutopia: Nuclear Families, Atomic Cities, and the Great Soviet and American Plutonium Disasters*. New York: Oxford University Press, 2013.

Brunnengräber, Achim. "Die atompolitische Wende." In *Problemfalle Endlager: Gesellschaftliche Herausforderungen im Umgang mit Atommüll*, edited by Achim Brunnengräber, 13–32. Baden-Baden: Nomos, 2016.

Brunnengräber, Achim. *Ewigkeitslasten: Die "Endlagerung" radioaktiver Abfälle als soziales, politisches und wissenschaftliches Projekt—eine Einführung*. Baden-Baden: Nomos, 2015.

Brunnengräber, Achim, ed. *Problemfalle Endlager: Gesellschaftliche Herausforderungen im Umgang mit Atommüll*. Baden-Baden: Nomos, 2016.

Brunnengräber, Achim and Lutz Mez. "Der staatlich-industrielle Atomkomplex im Zerfall." In *Problemfalle Endlager: Gesellschaftliche Herausforderungen im Umgang mit Atommüll*, edited by Achim Brunnengräber, 289–311. Baden-Baden: Nomos, 2016.

Buch, Hans Christoph. *Bericht aus dem Inneren der Unruhe. Gorlebener Tagebuch*. Reinbek: Rowohlt, 1984.

Buck, Hannsjörg F. "Umweltbelastung durch Müllentsorgung und Industrieabfälle in der DDR." In *Am Ende des realen Sozialismus: Beiträge zu einer Bestandsaufnahme der DDR-Wirklichkeit in den 80er Jahren*. Vol. 4: *Die Endzeit der DDR-Wirtschaft: Analysen zur Wirtschafts- Sozial- und Umweltpolitik*, edited by Eberhard Kuhrt et al., 455–497. Opladen: Leske & Budrich, 1999.

Buck, Hannsjörg F. "Umwelt- und Bodenbelastung durch eine ökologisch nicht abgesicherte industriemäßig organisierte Tier- und Pflanzenproduktion." In *Am Ende des realen Sozialismus: Beiträge zu einer Bestandsaufnahme der DDR-Wirklichkeit in den 80er Jahren*. Vol. 4: *Die Endzeit der DDR-Wirtschaft: Analysen zur Wirtschafts- Sozial- und Umweltpolitik*, edited by Eberhard Kuhrt et al., 426–446. Opladen: Leske & Budrich, 1999.

Buddenbohm, Maximilian. *Marmelade im Zonenrandgebiet*. Reinbek: Rowohlt, 2012.

BUND, ed. *Das Grüne Band: Dauereinsatz für eine Vision*. Nuremberg: BUND, 2015.

BUND, ed. *Traces of the Past along the German Green Belt*. Nuremberg: BUND, 2017.

BUND and Bund Naturschutz in Bayern, eds. *Das Grüne Band: Ein Handlungsleitfaden*. Nürnberg: BUND, Nov. 2002.

Bundesbeauftragter für die Stasi-Unterlagen (BStU), ed. *Hessen und die Stasi: Die Überwachung im "Operationsgebiet West."* Berlin: BStU, 2015.

Bundesbeauftragter für die Stasi-Unterlagen (BStU), ed. *Niedersachsen und die Stasi: Die Überwachung im "Operationsgebiet West."* Berlin: BStU, 2014.

Burghardt, Petra. "Thomas Neumann: Grünes Band oder Grüne Perlen?" In *Mehr Geschichten von Drüben*, edited by Petra Burghardt, 58–69. N.p., Books on Demand, 2011.

Bürkner, Hans-Joachim. "Probleme der Regionalentwicklung im niedersächsischen Zonenrandgebiet vor und nach der deutschen Vereinigung." In *Die Wirtschaft im geteilten und vereinten Deutschland*, edited by Karl Eckart and Jörg Roesler, 277–297. Berlin: Duncker & Humblot, 1999.

Büschenfeld, Jürgen. *Flüsse und Kloaken: Umweltfragen im Zeitalter der Industrialisierung, 1870–1918*. Stuttgart: Klett-Cotta, 1997.

Büschenfeld, Jürgen. "Der harte Kampf um weiches Wasser: Zur Umweltgeschichte der Kaliindustrie im 19. und 20. Jahrhundert." In *Mensch–Natur–Technik: Aspekte der Umweltgeschichte in Niedersachsen und angrenzenden Gebieten*, edited by Carl-Hans Hauptmeyer, 79–109. Bielefeld: Regionalgeschichte, 2000.

Büttner, Rolf, ed. *Die "Chemiker" der NVA und der Grenztruppen der DDR*. Berlin: Dr. Köster, 2012.

Butz, Michael-Andreas. *Rechtsfragen der Zonenrandförderung*. Köln: Heymanns, 1980.

Camp, Michael. "'Wandering in the Desert': The Clinch River Breeder Reactor Debate in the U.S. Congress, 1972–1983." *Technology and Culture* 59:1 (2018): 26–47.

Carbon, Claus-Christian and Helmut Leder. "The Wall Inside the Brain: Overestimation of Distances Crossing the Former Iron Curtain." *Psychonomic Bulletin & Review* 12:4 (2005): 746–750.

Carter, Luther J. *Nuclear Imperatives and Public Trust: Dealing with Radioactive Waste*. Washington, DC: Resources for the Future, distributed by Johns Hopkins University Press, 1987.

Cejka, Regine. "Einbruch ins Naturparadies." *Öko Test Magazin* 6 (1990): 10–13.

Chaney, Sandra. "A Chemical Landscape Transformed: Bitterfeld, Germany since 1980." *Global Environment* 10 (2017): 137–167.

Chaney, Sandra. *Nature of the Miracle Years: Conservation in West Germany, 1945–1975*. Oxford: Berghahn, 2008.

Christaller, Walter. "Some Considerations of Tourism Location in Europe." *Regional Science Association Papers* 12 (1963): 96–105.

Chronik der Zellstoff- und Papierfabrik Rosenthal. Blankenstein: ZPR, 2001.

Chu, Winson. *The German Minority in Interwar Poland*. New York: Cambridge University Press, 2012.

Clute-Simon, Elmar and Reiner Emmerich. *Das Haus auf der Grenze*. Bad Hersfeld: Ott, 1996.

Coates, Peter. "Borderlands, No-Man's Land, Nature's Wonderland." *Environment and History* 20:4 (2014): 500–516.

Coates, Peter, Tim Cole, M. Dudley, and Chris Pearson. "Defending Nation, Defending Nature? Militarized Landscapes and Military Environmentalism in Britain, France and the United States." *Environmental History* 16:3 (2011): 456–491.

Coates, Peter, Tim Cole, and Chris Pearson, eds. *Militarized Landscapes: From Gettysburg to Salisbury Plain*. London: Continuum, 2010.

Cohn, Jeffrey P. "The Environmental Impacts of a Border Fence." *BioScience* 57:1 (2007): 96.

Connolly, Barbara. "Asymmetrical Rivalry in Common Pool Resources and European Responses to Acid Rain." In *Anarchy and the Environment: The International Relations of Common Pool Resources*, edited by J. Samuel Barkin and George E. Shambough, 122–154. Albany, NY: SUNY Press, 1999.

Conze, Eckart. *Von deutschem Adel: Die Grafen von Bernstorff im zwanzigsten Jahrhundert*. Munich: DVA, 2000.

Conze, Vanessa. "'Unverheilte Brandwunden an der Aussenhaut des Volkskörpers': Der deutsche Grenz-Diskurs der Zwischenkriegszeit (1919–1939)." In *Ordnungen in der Krise: Zur politischen Kulturgeschichte Deutschlands, 1900–1933*, edited by Wolfgang Hardtwig, 21–48. Munich: Oldenbourg, 2007.

Cordova, Ana and Carlos de la Parra, eds. *A Barrier to Our Shared Environment: The Border Fence Between the United States and Mexico*. San Ángel, México: Communicación Objectiva, 2007.

Cragin, Susan. *Nuclear Nebraska: The Remarkable Story of the Little County That Couldn't Be Bought*. New York: Amacom, 2007.

Creuzberger, Stefan. *Kampf für die Eineit: Das Gesamtdeutsche Ministerium und die politische Kultur des Kalten Krieges, 1949–1969*. Düsseldorf: Droste, 2008.

Creuzberger, Stefan and Dierk Hoffmann. "Antikommunismus und politische Kultur in der Bundesrepublik Deutschland." In *"Geistige Gefahr" und "Immunisierung der Gesellschaft": Antikommunismus und politische Kultur in der frühen Bundesrepublik*, edited by Stefan Creuzberger and Dierk Hoffmann, 1–13. Munich: Oldenbourg, 2014.

Creuzberger, Stefan, and Dierk Hoffmann, eds. *"Geistige Gefahr" und "Immunisierung der Gesellschaft": Antikommunismus und politische Kultur in der frühen Bundesrepublik*. Munich: Oldenbourg, 2014.

Cronon, William. "The Trouble with Wilderness, or, Getting Back to the Wrong Nature." In *Uncommon Ground: Toward Reinventing Nature*, edited by William Cronon, 69–90. New York: Norton, 1995.

Cunningham, Hillary. "Permeabilities, Ecology and Geographical Boundaries." In *A Companion to Border Studies*, edited by Thomas M. Wilson and Hastings Donnan, 371–386. London: Blackwell, 2012.

Darst, Robert G. "Bribery and Blackmail in East–West Environmental Politics." *Post-Soviet Affairs* 13:1 (1997): 42–77.

Darst, Robert G. *Smokestack Diplomacy: Cooperation and Conflict in East–West Environmental Politics*. Cambridge, MA: MIT Press, 2001.

Davis, Jeffrey Sasha. "Military Natures: Militarism and the Environment." *GeoJournal* 69 (2007): 131–134.

Deisenroth, Norbert. "Entstehung, Zusammensetzung und Veränderung der Salzlagerstätte." In *Bunte Salze, weisse Berge: Wachstum und Wandel der Kaliindustrie zwischen Thüringer Wald, Rhön und Vogelsberg*, edited by Hermann-Hohmann and Dagmar Mehnert, 7–24. Hünfeld: Ulmenstein, 2004.

Delius, Friedrich Christian and Peter Joachim Lapp. *Transit Westberlin: Erlebnisse im Zwischenraum*. Berlin: Chr. Links, 1999.

Demand, Klaus. "IMNOS." In *Handwörterbuch der Raumforschung und Raumplanung II*, edited by Akademie für Raumforschung und Landesplanung, 1234–1239. Hannover: Jänicke, 1970.

Demshuk, Andrew. *The Lost German East: Forced Migration and the Politics of Memory, 1945–1970*. New York: Cambridge University Press, 2012.

Derix, Simone. *Bebilderte Politik: Staatsbesuche in der Bundesrepublik, 1949–1990*. Göttingen: V&R, 2009.

Detten, Roderich von, ed. *Das Waldsterben: Rückblick auf einen Ausnahmezustand*. Munich: Oekom, 2013.

Dicke, Klaus. "Zwei Jahrzehnte nach dem Mauerfall: Memorialkultur an der ehemaligen innerdeutschen Grenze." *Tel Aviver Jahrbuch für deutsche Geschichte* 40 (2012): 213–234.

Dienel, Hans-Liudger. "Ins Grüne und ins Blaue: Freizeitverkehr im West–Ost Vergleich—BRD und DDR, 1949–1989." In *Mobilität für alle: Geschichte des öffentlichen Personennahverkehrs in der Stadt zwischen technischem Fortschritt und sozialer Pflicht*, edited by H.-L. Dienel and Barbara Schmucki, 221–249. Stuttgart: Steiner, 1997.

Dingemann, Rüdiger. *Mitten in Deutschland: Entdeckungen an der ehemaligen Grenze*. Hamburg: Malik, 2014.

Di Nucci, Maria Rosaria. "NIMBY oder IMBY: Akzeptanz, Freiwilligkeit und Kompensation in der Standortsuche für die Endlagerung radioaktiver Abfälle." In *Problemfalle Endlager: Gesellschaftliche Herausforderungen im Umgang mit Atommüll*, edited by Achim Brunnengräber, 119–143. Baden-Baden: Nomos, 2016.

Dirlam, Heinrich. "Der Scharfenstein im Grenzgebiet 1952 bis 1990." In *Ilsenburg (Harz) im 20. Jahrhundert*, edited by Karl Berke, 211. Ilsenburg: self-published, 2013.

Dittrich, Erich. "Deutsche Notstandsgebiete 1951." *Sonderheft der Informationen des IfR* (Apr. 1952): 81–91.

Dittrich, Erich. "Die deutschen Notstandsgebiete: Eine Aufgabe der Raumpolitik." *Wirtschaftsdienst* 1 (1951): 29–36.

Dittrich, Erich. "Notstandgebiete in der Bundesrepublik." *Wirtschaftsdienst* 42:10 (1962): 431–436.

Doering-Manteuffel, Anselm. "Die innerdeutsche Grenze im nationalpolitischen Diskurs der Adenauer-Zeit." In *Grenzland. Beiträge zur Geschichte der deutsch-deutschen Grenze*, edited by Bernd Weisbrod, 127–140. Hannover: Hahn, 1993.

Dominick, Raymond. "Capitalism, Communism, and Environmental Protection: Lessons from the German Experience." *Environmental History* 3:3 (July 1998): 311–332.

Doßmann, Axel. "Sehnsucht nach einem stillen Land: Wie zwei Reporter der ZEIT im Jahr 1979 die DDR darstellten." *Zeithistorische Forschungen / Studies in Contemporary History* 5:2 (2008): 339–344. http://www.zeithistorische-forschungen.de/2-2008/id=4447 (accessed Jan. 2018).

Doßmann, Axel. "'Stimmungsbarometer der Ost-West-Beziehungen': Übertragungen auf deutschen Autobahnen um 1950." *Archiv für Mediengeschichte* 4 (2004): 207–218.

Douglas, Raymond M. *Orderly and Humane: The Expulsion of the Germans after the Second World War.* New Haven, CT: Yale University Press, 2012.

Dudley Joseph P. et al. "Effects of War and Civil Strife on Wildlife and Wildlife Habitats." *Conservation Biology* 16:2 (2002): 319–329.

Eckert, Astrid M. "Geteilt, aber nicht unverbunden: Grenzgewässer als deutsch-deutsches Umweltproblem." *Vierteljahrshefte für Zeitgeschichte* 62:1 (2014): 321–351.

Eckert, Astrid M. "'Greetings from the Zonal Border': Tourism to the Iron Curtain in West Germany." *Zeithistorische Forschungen / Studies in Contemporary History* 8:1 (2011): 9–36. http://www.zeithistorische-forschungen.de/1-2011/id=4455 (accessed July 2018).

Eckert, Astrid M. "West German Borderland Aid and European State Aid Control." *Jahrbuch für Wirtschaftsgeschichte / Economic History Yearbook* 58:1 (2017): 107–136.

Eckert, Astrid M. "'Zaun-Gäste': Die innerdeutsche Grenze als Touristenattraktion." In *Grenzziehungen, Grenzerfahrungen, Grenzüberschreitungen: Die innerdeutsche Grenze, 1945–1990,* edited by Detlef Schmiechen-Ackermann, Carl-Hans Hauptmeyer, and Thomas Schwark, 243–251. Darmstadt: WBG, 2011.

Eckert, Gerhard. *Der Brocken: Berg in Deutschland.* Husum: Husum Druck, 1991.

Ehmke, Wolfgang, ed. *Zwischenschritte: Die Anti-Atomkraftbewegung zwischen Gorleben und Wackersdorf.* Cologne: Volksblatt, 1987.

Eick, Jürgen. *Die wirtschaftlichen Folgen der Zonengrenzen: Versuch einer Theorie der volkswirtschaftlichen Entflechtung.* Hamburg: Union, 1948.

Eisch, Katharina. *Grenze: Eine Ethnographie des bayerisch-böhmischen Grenzraums.* Munich: Institut für Volkskunde, 1996.

Eisenbach, Ulrich. "Kaliindustrie und Umwelt." In *Die Kaliindustrie an Werra und Fulda: Geschichte eines landschaftsprägenden Industriezweigs,* edited by Ulrich Eisenbach and Akos Paulinyi, 194–222. Darmstadt: Hess. Wirtschaftsarchiv, 1998.

Engels, Jens Ivo. *Naturpolitik in der Bundesrepublik: Ideenwelt und politische Verhaltensstile in Naturschutz und Umweltbewegung, 1950–1980.* Paderborn: Schöningh, 2006.

Erdmann, Thorsten. "Am Ende der Welt: Entwicklungen des westdeutschen Zonenrandgebietes seit der Wiedervereinigung." *Deutschland Archiv online,* Nov. 18, 2013. http://www.bpb.de/geschichte/zeitgeschichte/deutschlandarchiv/170619/am-ende-der-welt-entwicklung-des-westdeutschen-zonenrandgebietes-seit-der-wiedervereinigung (accessed Jan. 2018).

Eriksson, Lindsay and Melinda Taylor. "The Environmental Impacts of the Border Wall Between Texas and Mexico." UT Working Group Briefing Papers, n.d. https://law.utexas.edu/humanrights/borderwall/analysis/briefing-The-Environmental-Impacts-of-the-Border-Wall.pdf (accessed Jan. 2018).

Esser, Stefan. *Radtouren am Grünen Band: In 32 Etappen von Tschechien bis zur Ostsee.* Munich: Bruckmann, 2011.

Eulitz, Walter. *Der Zollgrenzdienst.* Bonn: Stollfuss, 1968.

Fäßler, Peter E. *Durch den "Eisernen Vorhang": Die deutsch-deutschen Wirtschaftsbeziehungen, 1949–1969.* Cologne: Böhlau 2006.

Federau, Fritz. "Der Interzonenhandel Deutschlands von 1946 bis Mitte 1953." *Vierteljahrshefte zur Wirtschaftsforschung* 4 (1953): 385–410.

Fickel, Joerns et al. "Crossing the Border? Structure of the Red Deer (*Cervus elaphus*) Population from the Bavarian-Bohemian Forest Ecosystem." *Mammalian Biology* 77: 3 (2012): 211–220.

Fielitz, Uli and Marco Heurich. "Rotwild—ein Grenzgänger im Bayerischen Wald: Erforschung des Raum-Zeit-Verhaltens von Rotwild im Nationalpark Bayerischer Wald." *LWF aktuell* 44 (2004): 3–5.

Flack, Andrew J. P. "Continental Creatures: Animals and History in Contemporary Europe." *Contemporary European History* 27:3 (2018): 517–529.

Flowers, Brian. "Nuclear Power: A Perspective of the Risks, Benefits and Options." *Bulletin of the Atomic Scientists* 34:3 (Mar. 1978): 21–26, 54–57.

Flügge, Heinrich. "Die landwirtschaftlichen Betriebe im Landkreis Lüchow-Dannenberg seit hundert Jahren und ihre weitere Entwicklung." *Hannoversches Wendland* 5 (1974–1975): 107–122.

Foley, Malcolm and J. John Lennon. "JFK and Dark Tourism: A Fascination with Assassination." *International Journal of Heritage Studies* 2:4 (1996): 198–211.

Förster, Andreas. "'Akute Umweltgefährdung' im Arzneimittelwerk." *Horch und Guck* 21:76 (2012): 26–27.

Frank, Sybille. *Wall Memorials and Heritage: The Heritage Industry of Berlin's Checkpoint Charlie.* London: Routledge, 2016.

Franz, Corinna. "'Wir wählen die Freiheit!' Antikommunistisches Denken und politisches Handeln Konrad Adenauers." In *"Geistige Gefahr" und "Immunisierung der Gesellschaft": Antikommunismus und politische Kultur in der frühen Bundesrepublik,* edited by Stefan Creuzberger and Dierk Hoffmann, 145–159. Munich: Oldenbourg, 2014.

Franz, Dieter. *Das Blaukehlchen: Von der Rarität zum Allerweltsvogel?* Wiesbaden: Aula, 1998.

Friedrich, Bernd. "Der Uhu (*Bubo bubo*) wieder Brutvogel im Kreis Eisenach." *Fliegende Blätter* (HGON) 2 (1987);

Friedrich, Bernd and Peter Fahrenholz. "Avifaunistische Mitteilungen aus dem südwestlichen Teil des Kreises Eisenach." *Thüringische Ornithologische Mitteilungen* 38 (1988): 31–43.

Fritsche, Christiane. *Schaufenster des "Wirtschaftswunders" und Brückenschlag nach Osten: Westdeutsche Industriemessen und Messebeteiligung im Kalten Krieg, 1946–1973.* Munich: Meidenbauer, 2008.

Frobel, Kai. "20 Jahre Grünes Band—eine Bilanz." *Nationalpark* 145:3 (2009): 5–9.

Frobel, Kai, Liana Geidezis, Melanie Kreutz, et al. *Erlebnis Grünes Band* (Naturschutz und Biologische Vielfalt 113). Münster: Landwirtschaftsverlag, 2012.

Frobel, Kai, Uwe Riecken, and Karin Ullrich. "Das 'Grüne Band'—das Naturschutzprojekt Deutsche Einheit." *Natur und Landschaft* 84:9/10 (2009): 399–403.

Frohn, Hans-Werner, Jürgen Rosebrock, and Friedemann Schmoll, eds. *"Wenn sich alle in der Natur erholen, wo erholt sich dann die Natur?"* Bonn: BfN, 2009.

Fuchs, Norbert. *Billmuthausen: Das verurteilte Dorf.* Hildburghausen: Frankenschwelle, 1991.

Füsslein, Peter. *Die Grenzkommission: Ein Rückblick auf deutsch-deutsche Verhandlungen.* Bonn: Bouvier, 2015.

Gabriel, Oscar W., Everhard Holtmann, Tobias Jaeck, Melanie Leidecker-Sandmann, Jürgen Maier, and Michaela Maier. *Deutschland 25: Gesellschaftliche Trends und Politische Einstellungen.* Bonn: Bundeszentrale für Politische Bildung, 2015.

Gaumer, Janine. *Wackersdorf: Atomkraft und Demokratie in der Bundesrepublik 1980–1989.* Munich: Oekom, 2018.

Gebhard, Bettina and Matthias Braun. "Naturraum von der Wakenitz bis zur Ostsee: Konfliktbereich zwischen Naturschutz und Wirtschaftsentwicklung vor den Toren Lübecks." *Mitteilungen aus der Norddeutschen Naturschutzakademie* 5:3 (1994): 2–7.

Geisler, Michael E. "'Heimat' and the German Left: The Anamnesis of a Trauma." *New German Critique* 36 (1985): 25–66.

Gentzen, Udo and Karin Wulf. *Niemand wusste, wohin wir gebracht wurden . . . Zwangs ausgesiedelte von 1952 und 1961 berichten über ihr Schicksal.* Hagenow-Boizenburg: Museum der Stadt Hagenow, 1993.

Giesler, Walter. "Hände weg von der Zonenrandförderung." *Kurhessische Wirtschaft* 7 (1982): 323.

George, Klaus. "Neue Bedingungen für die Vogelwelt der Agrarlandschaft in Ostdeutschland nach der Wiedervereinigung." *Ornithologischer Jahresbericht Museum Heineanum* 13 (1995): 1–25.

Glassheim, Eagle. *Cleansing the Czechoslovak Borderlands: Migration, Environment and Health in the Former Sudetenland.* Pittsburgh: University of Pittsburgh Press, 2016.

Glassheim, Eagle. "Unsettled Landscapes: Czech and German Conceptions of Social and Ecological Decline in the Postwar Czechoslovak Borderlands." *Journal of Contemporary History* 50:2 (2015): 318–336.

Glatzel, Frank and Edeltraud Hundertmark. *Braunschweig—Großstadt am Zonenrand* (Kommunalpolitische Schriften der Stadt Braunschweig 18). Braunschweig, 1956.

Gleitze, Bruno. *Ostdeutsche Wirtschaft: Industrielle Standorte und volkswirtschaftliche Kapazitäten des ungeteilten Deutschlands.* Berlin: Duncker & Humblot, 1956.

Gnest, Holger. *Entwicklung der überörtlichen Raumplanung in der Bundesrepublik von 1975 bis heute.* Hannover: ARL, 2008.

Golle, Hermann. *Das Know-How, das aus dem Osten kam: Wie das westdeutsche Wirtschaftswunder von der SED-Politik profitierte.* Stuttgart: Hohenheim, 2002.

Gordon, Joseph S. "East German Psychological Operations: A 1965 Case Study." In *Psychological Operations: The Soviet Challenge,* edited by Joseph S. Gordon, 89–123. Boulder: Westview, 1988.

Görner, Martin and R. Schultheis. "Schwarzstorch (*Ciconia nigra*) wieder Brutvogel in Thüringen." *Landschaftspflege und Naturschutz in Thüringen* 21:4 (1984): 88–90.

Grady, Tim. "A Shared Environment: German–German Relations along the Border, 1945–1972." *Journal of Contemporary History* 50:3 (2015): 660–679.

Gray, William Glenn. "Commercial Liberties and Nuclear Anxieties: The U.S.–German Feud over Brazil, 1975–77." *International History Review* 34:3 (2012): 449–474.

Gray, William Glenn. *Germany's Cold War: The Global Campaign to Isolate East Germany, 1949–1969.* Chapel Hill: University of North Carolina Press, 2003.

Greverus, Ina-Maria. *Auf der Suche nach Heimat.* Munich: Beck, 1979.

Gross, Stephen G. "Decoupling and the New Energy Paradigm in West Germany, 1973–1986." *Central European History* 50:4 (2017): 514–546.

Grossbölting, Thomas and Christoph Lorke. "Vereinigungsgesellschaft: Deutschland seit 1990." In *Deutschland seit 1990: Wege in die Vereinigungsgesellschaft,* edited by Thomas Grossbölting and Christoph Lorke, 9–30. Stuttgart: Steiner, 2017.

Grosser, Dieter. *Das Wagnis der Währungs-, Wirtschafts- und Sozialunion: Politische Zwänge im Konflikt mit ökonomischen Regeln.* Stuttgart: DVA 1998.

Grüner, Stefan. *Geplantes "Wirtschaftswunder"? Industrie- und Strukturpolitik in Bayern, 1945–1973.* Munich: Oldenbourg, 2009.

Gruner, Wolf ed. *Die Verfolgung und Ermordung der europäischen Juden durch das nationalsozialistische Deutschland, 1933–1945.* Vol. 1: *Deutsches Reich, 1933–1937.* Munich: Oldenbourg, 2008.

Günther, Egbert et al. "Aktuelles zur Vogelwelt des Brockengebietes." *Berichte der Naturhistorischen Gesellschaft Hannover* 139 (1997): 289–298.

Hachtmann, Rüdiger. *Tourismus-Geschichte.* Göttingen: V&R, 2007.

Hagen, Manfred. "Warum Wiederaufarbeitung?" *atw* 22:11 (1977): 566–570.

Hahn, Barbara and Petra Pudemat. "Die Entwicklung des Landkreises Lüchow-Dannenberg nach der Öffnung der innerdeutschen Grenze unter besonderer Berücksichtigung des Verarbeitenden Gewerbes." *Neues Archiv für Niedersachsen* 1 (1998): 65–84.

Halbach, Dieter and Gerd Panzer. *Zwischen Gorleben und Stadtleben.* Berlin: AHDE, 1980.

Haller, Jörg. "'Die heilige Ostmark': Ostbayern als völkische Kultregion 'Bayerische Ostmark.'" *Bayerisches Jahrbuch für Volkskunde* (2000): 63–73.

Hamblin, Jacob Darwin. *Poison in the Well: Radioactive Waste in the Oceans at the Dawn of the Nuclear Age.* New Brunswick, NJ: Rutgers University Press, 2008.

Hänel, Michael. *Das Ende vor dem Ende: Zur Rolle der DDR-Energiewirtschaft beim Systemwechsel, 1980–1990* (Occasional Papers in German Studies 15). Edmonton, 1998. http://nbn-resolving.de/urn:nbn:de:0168-ssoar-461778 (accessed July 2018).

Harbutt, Fraser J. *Yalta, 1945: Europe and America at the Crossroads.* New York: Cambridge University Press, 2010.

Hartard, Susanne and Michael Huhn. "Das SERO-System." In *Umweltschutz in der DDR*, vol. 2, edited by Hermann Behrens and Jens Hoffmann, 309–334. Munich: Oekom, 2007.

Harvey, Elizabeth. "Pilgrimages to the 'Bleeding Border': Gender and Rituals of Nationalist Protest in Germany, 1919–1939." *Women's History Review* 9:2 (2000): 201–229.

Hasenöhrl, Ute. *Zivilgesellschaft und Protest: Eine Geschichte der Naturschutz- und Umweltbewegung in Bayern, 1945–1980.* Göttingen: V&R, 2008.

Haslinger, Peter. *Nation und Territorium im tschechischen politischen Diskurs, 1880–1938.* Munich: Oldenbourg, 2010.

Hauff, Peter. "Zur Geschichte des Seeadlers *Haliaeetus albicilla* in Deutschland." *Denisia* 27 (2009): 7–18.

Havlick, David G. *Bombs Away: Militarization, Conservation, and Ecological Restoration.* Chicago: University of Chicago Press, 2018.

Havlick, David G. "Logics of Change for Military-to-Wildlife Conversions in the United States." *GeoJournal* 69 (2007): 151–164.

Havlick, David G. "Opportunistic Conservation at Former Military Sites in the United States." *Progress in Physical Geography* 38:3 (2014): 271–285.

Havlick, David G. and Marion Hourdequin. "Ecological Restoration and Layered Landscapes." In *Restoring Layered Landscapes: History, Ecology, and Culture*, edited by David G. Havlick and Marion Hourdequin, 1–10. New York: Oxford University Press, 2016.

Hefele, Peter. *Die Verlagerung von Industrie- und Dienstleistungsunternehmen aus der SBZ/DDR nach Westdeutschland.* Stuttgart: Steiner, 1998.

Heide, Hans-Jürgen von der. "Zonenrandförderung—eine Bilanz." *Der Landkreis* 44:5 (1974): 162–165.

Heide, Hans-Jürgen von der. "Zonenrandförderung—fast 40 Jahre nach Kriegsende noch notwendig?" *Der Landkreis* 3 (1983): 114.

Heidemeyer, Helge. *Flucht und Zuwanderung aus der SBZ/DDR 1945/1949–1961.* Düsseldorf: Droste, 1994.

Heinz, Michael. "Klassenkampf gegen Hecken und Teiche: Flurbereinigung in der DDR." *Horch und Guck* 76 (2012): 32–35.

Heinz, Michael. *Von Mähdreschern und Musterdörfern: Industrialisierung der DDR-Landwirtschaft und die Wandlung des ländlichen Lebens am Beispiel der Nordbezirke.* Berlin: Metropol, 2011.

Heitzer, Enrico. *Die Kampfgruppe gegen Unmenschlichkeit (KgU): Widerstand und Spionage im Kalten Krieg, 1948–1959.* Cologne: Böhlau, 2015.

Heller, Winfried. "Grenzüberschreitende Beziehungen zwischen den alten und den neuen Bundesländern in Deutschland nach der politischen Wende: Welche Seite profitiert am meisten?" *Zeitschrift für Wirtschaftsgeographie* 38:1–2 (1994): 83–91.

Herbert, Ulrich. "Europe in High Modernity: Reflections on a Theory of the Twentieth Century." *Journal of Modern European History* 5:1 (2007): 5–21.

Hermann, Ingolf. *Die deutsch-deutsche Grenze von Posseck bis Lehesten, von Ludwigsstadt nach Prex.* Plauen: Neupert, 1996.

Hermann, Ingolf and Karsten Sroka, eds. *Deutsch-deutsches Grenzlexikon: Der Eiserne Vorhang und die Mauer in Stichworten.* Zella-Mehlis: Bürgerkomitee Thüringen, 2005.

Herold, Klaus. "Zonenrandförderung: Politische und wirtschaftliche Aufgabe." *Wirtschaft und Standort* 10 (1976): 2–3.

Hertle, Hans-Hermann and Maria Nooke, eds., *The Victims at the Berlin Wall, 1961–1989: A Biographical Handbook.* Berlin: ZZF and Stiftung Berliner Mauer, 2011.

Hertle, Wolfgang. "Hart an der Grenze." In *Geschichten aus der Friedensbewegung: Persönliches und Politisches,* edited by Andreas Buro, 93–95. Cologne: Komitee für Grundrechte und Demokratie, 2005.

Hesse, Janet. *Befriedet: Vergessene Orte an der innerdeutschen Grenze.* Hamburg: Edel, 2009.

Heurich, Marco et al. "Country, Cover or Protection: What Shapes the Distribution of Red Deer and Roe Deer in the Bohemian Forest Ecosystem?" *PLoS ONE* 10 (3) (2015). http://journals.plos.org/plosone/article?id=10.1371/journal.pone.0120960 (accessed Jan. 2018).

Hocke, Peter and Ortwin Renn. "Concerned Public and the Paralysis of Decision-Making: Nuclear Waste Management Policy in Germany." *Journal of Risk Research* 7–8 (2009): 921–940.

Hoerner, Ludwig. "Zur Geschichte der fotografischen Ansichtspostkarten." *Fotogeschichte* 7:26 (1987): 29–44.

Hoerning, Erika M. *Zwischen den Fronten: Berliner Grenzgänger und Grenzhändler.* Cologne: Böhlau, 1992.

Hoffmann, Dierk. "Binnenwanderung und Arbeitsmarkt: Beschäftigungspolitik unter dem Eindruck der Bevölkerungsverschiebung in Deutschland nach 1945." In *Vertriebene in Deutschland. Interdisziplinäre Perspektiven und Forschungsperspektiven,* edited by Dierk Hoffmann, Marita Krauss, and Michael Schwartz, 219–325. Munich: Oldenbourg, 2000.

Hoffrichter, Arne. "Arbeitskräftebedarf contra Wohnraummangel. Die Berliner Luftbrücke und das Problem der SBZ-Flucht 1948/49." *Deutschland Archiv Online*

(Feb. 2013). http://www.bpb.de/geschichte/zeitgeschichte/deutschlandarchiv/
hoffrichter20130214 (accessed Jan. 2018).

Hoffrichter, Arne. "Uelzen und die Abgelehnten: Das Flüchtlingsdurchgangslager
Uelzen-Bohldamm und die Folgen der SBZ/DDR-Flucht als lokales Problem
1949/50." In *Flüchtlingslager im Nachkriegsdeutschland. Migration, Politk,
Erinnerung,* edited by Henrik Bispinck and Katharina Hochmuth, 190–209.
Berlin: Links, 2014.

Högselius, Per. "Challenging Chernobyl's Legacy: Nuclear Power Policies in
Europe, Russia and North American in the Early 21st Century." In *The Politics
of Nuclear Energy in Asia,* edited by Yi-Chong Xu, 190–210. London: Palgrave
MacMillan, 2011.

Högselius, Per. *Die deutsch-deutsche Geschichte des Kernkraftwerkes Greifswald:
Atomenergie zwischen Ost und West.* Berlin: BWV, 2005.

Högselius, Per. "Spent Nuclear Fuel Policies in Historical Perspective: An
International Comparison." *Energy Policy* 17 (2009): 254–263.

Hübner, Gerd. *Ökologisch-faunistische Fließgewässerbewertung am Beispiel der
salzbelasteten unteren Werra und ausgewählter Zuflüsse.* Phil. Diss., University of
Kassel, 2007.

Huff, Tobias. *Natur und Industrie im Sozialismus: Eine Umweltgeschichte der DDR.*
Göttingen: V&R, 2015.

Huff, Tobias. "Über die Umweltpolitik der DDR: Konzepte, Strukturen, Versagen."
Geschichte und Gesellschaft 40:4 (2014): 523–554.

Hughes, Michael L. "'Through No Fault of Our Own': West Germans Remember
Their War Losses." *German History* 18:2 (2000): 193–213.

Hulsch, Jürgen and Gerhard M. Veh. "Zur Salzbelastung von Werra und Weser."
Neues Archiv für Niedersachsen 27:4 (1978): 367–377.

Hünemörder, Kai F. *Die Frühgeschichte der globalen Umweltkrise und die Formierung
der deutschen Umweltpolitik, 1950–1973.* Stuttgart: Steiner, 2004.

Hunter, William Cannon. "The Visual Representation of Border Tourism:
Demilitarized Zone (DMZ) and Dokdo in South Korea." *International Journal of
Tourism Research* 17 (2015): 151–160.

Illing, Falk. *Energiepolitk in Deutschland: Die energiepolitischen Massnahmen der
Bundesregierung, 1949–2015.* Baden-Baden: Nomos, 2016.

International Atomic Energy Agency (IAEA), ed. *Nuclear Power and Its Fuel Cycle:
Proceedings of an International Conference Salzburg, 2–13 May, 1977.* 8 vols.
Vienna: IAEA, 1977.

Issel, Wolfgang. *Die Wiederaufbereitung von bestrahlten Kernbrennstoffen in der
Bundesrepublik Deutschland: Technologische Chance oder energiepoitischer Zwang.*
Frankfurt: Lang, 2003.

Jahn, Dietrich. "Die Sanierung der Berliner Gewässer." *Stadt + Umwelt* (Aug. 1989):
28.

Jákli, Zoltán. *Vom Marshallplan zum Kohlepfennig. Grundrisse der Subventionspolitik in der Bundesrepublik Deutschland, 1948–1982*. Opladen: Westdeutscher, 1990.

Jakubec, Ivan. *Schlupflöcher im "Eisernen Vorhang": Tschoslowakisch-deutsche Verkehrspolitik im Kalten Krieg—Eisenbahn und Elbeschiffahrt, 1945–1989*. Stuttgart: Steiner, 2006.

Jarmatz, Klaus and Rainer Mönke. "Der Naturpark Schaalsee—heute Biosphärenreservat." In *Naturschutz in Deutschland*, edited by Michael Succow, Lebrecht Jeschke, and Hans Dieter Knapp, 175–183. Berlin: Links, 2012.

Jarausch, Konrad, ed. *Unified Germany: Debating Processes and Prospects*. New York: Berghahn, 2013.

Jaworski, Rudolf. "Grenzlage, Rückständigkeit und nationale Agitation: Die 'Bayerische Ostmark' in der Weimarer Republik." *Zeitschrift für bayerische Landesgeschichte* 41 (1978): 241–270.

Jeffery, Charlie. "German Federalism from Cooperation to Competition." In *German Federalism: Past, Present, Future*, edited by Maiken Umbach, 172–188. Houndmills: Palgrave, 2002.

Jílek, Tomá. "Spezifika der Bewachung der tschechisch-bayerischen Staatsgrenze zu Zeiten des 'Eisernen Vorhangs,' 1948–1989." In *Die tschechisch-bayerische Grenze im Kalten Krieg in vergleichender Perspektive: Politische, ökonomische und soziokulturelle Dimensionen*, edited by Markus A. Meinke, 47–53. Regensburg: Staatsarchiv, 2011.

Johnson, Jason B. *Divided Village: The Cold War in the German Borderlands*. Abindgon: Routledge, 2017.

Johnson, Jason B. "'Wild and Fearsome Hours': The First Year of US Occupation of a Bavarian County, 1945–1946." *German Studies Review* 41:1 (2018): 61–79.

Jones, Elizabeth B. "Fixing Prussia's Peripheries: Rural Disasters and Prusso-German State-Building, 1866–1914." *Central European History* 51:2 (2018): 204–227.

Jones, Philip N. and Trevor Wild. "Opening the Frontier: Recent Spatial Impacts in the Former Inner-German Border Zone." *Regional Studies* 28:3 (1994): 259–273.

Jorns, Annette, Reinhold Kratz, and Hansgeorg Pudack. "Der Drömling." *Kosmos: Damit Mensch und Natur Zukunft haben* 7 (1986): 12–13.

Jost, Otto. "Das Vorkommen des Schwarzstorches (*Ciconia nigra*) im Fuldaer Land." *Vogel und Umwelt* 3 (1984): 151–158.

Judt, Matthias. *Der Bereich Kommerzielle Koordinierung: Das DDR-Wirtschaftsimperium des Alexander Schalck-Golodkowski—Mythos und Realität*. Berlin: Links, 2013.

Judt, Tony. *Postwar: A History of Europe Since 1945*. New York: Penguin, 2005.

Jung, Hans-Ulrich and Markus Krüsemann. *Struktur- und Entwicklungsprobleme von niedersächsischen Städten im ehemaligen Zonenrandgebiet: Duderstadt, Helmstedt, und Uelzen*. Hannover/Göttingen: Institut für Regionalforschung, 2002.

Jungk, Robert. *Der Atomstaat: Vom Fortschritt in die Unmenschlichkeit*. Munich: Kindler, 1977.

Jureit, Ulrike. *Das Ordnen von Räumen: Territorium und Lebensraum im 19. und 20. Jahrhundert*. Hamburg: HIS, 2012.

Kahrs, Axel, ed. *Im Wendland ist man der Wahrheit näher: Klassische Reportagen über Lüchow-Dannenberg aus vier Jahrzehnten.* Lüchow: Alte Jeetzel, 2007.

Kajser, Arne. "Under a Common Acid Sky: Negotiating Transboundary Air Pollution in Europe." In *Cosmopolitan Commons: Sharing Resources and Risks across Borders,* edited by Nil Disco and Eda Kranakis, 213–242. Cambridge, MA: MIT Press, 2013.

Kaltenborn, Steffi. "Leben mit der Grenze: Die westlichen Kreise des heutigen Sachsen-Anhalt zwischen 1945 und 1990." In *Politik und Regieren in Sachsen-Anhalt,* edited by Hendrik Träger and Sonja Priebus, 55–70. Wiesbaden: Springer, 2017.

Kaminsky, Annette. "Konsumwünsche und Konsumverhalten der DDR-Bevölkerung in den achtziger Jahren im Spiegel der Studien des Instituts für Marktforschung der DDR." In *Revolution und Transformation in der DDR 1989/90,* edited by Günther Heydemann, Gunter Mai, and Werner Müller, 105–115, Berlin: Duncker & Humblot, 1999.

Karl, Helmut. "Entwicklung und Ergebnisse regionaler Wirtschaftspolitik in Deutschland." In *Handbuch der regionalen Wirtschaftsförderung,* edited by Hans H. Eberstein and Helmut Karl, A II, Lfg. 61 (Nov. 2008), paras. 1–59.

Katzer, Bernd and Matthias Baeseler. "Ornithologische Notizen aus dem Kreis Sonneberg." *Thüringische Ornithologische Mitteilungen* 24 (1978): 17–30.

Kegler, Karl R. "'Der neue Begriff der Ordnung,' Zwischen NS-Staat und Bundesrepublik: Das Modell der zentralen Orte als Idealbild der Raumordnung." In *Vom Dritten Reich zur Bundesrepublik: Beiträge einer Tagung zur Geschichte der Raumforschung und Raumplanung,* edited by Heinrich Mäding and Wendelin Strubelt, 188–209. Hannover: ARL, 2009.

Keil, Albrecht. *Postenhirsche und Minenkeiler: Jagd im Schatten der Zonengrenze.* Melsungen: Neumann/Neudamm, 2008.

Keil, Holger. "Sielmanns Vision direkt vor der Haustür." *Nationalpark* 145:3 (2009): 14–17.

Kieling, Andreas. *Ein deutscher Wandersommer: 1400 Kilometer durch unsere wilde Heimat.* Hamburg: Malik, 2011.

Kim, Kwi-Gon and Dong-Gil Cho. "Status and Ecological Resource Value of the Republic of Korea's De-Militarized Zone." *Landscape and Ecological Engineering* 1 (2005): 3–15.

Kind-Kovács, Friederike. "Memories of Ethnic Cleansing and the Local Iron Curtain in the Czech–German Borderlands." *Nationalities Papers* 42:2 (2014): 199–222.

Kirchhof, Astrid Mignon. "Frauen in der Antiatomkraftbewegung: Am Beispiel der Mütter gegen Atomkraft." *Ariadne: Forum für Frauen—und Geschlechtergeschichte* 62 (2013): 48–57.

Kirchhof, Astrid Mignon and Jan-Henrik Meyer. "Global Protest against Nuclear Power. Transfer and Transnational Exchange in the 1970s and 1980s." *Historical Social Research* 39:1 (2014): 165–190.

Klaphake, Axel. *Europäische und nationale Regionalpolik für Ostdeutschland: Neuere regionalökonomische Theorien und praktische Erfahrungen.* Wiesbaden: DUV, 2000.

Klapper, Helmut. "Gewässerschutz und Gewässernutzung im Spannungsfeld zwischen Ökologie und Ökonomie." In *Umweltschutz in der DDR.* Vol. 2: *Mediale und sektorale Aspekte,* edited by Hermann Behrens and Jens Hoffmann, 233–243. Munich: Oekom, 2007.

Klemmer, Paul. "Gemeinschaftsaufgabe 'Verbesserung der regionalen Wirtschaftsstruktur.'" In *Handwörterbuch der Raumordnung,* 366–369. Hannover: Akademie für Raum- und Landesforschung, 2005.

Klemmer, Paul. "Raumgliederung für die Zwecke der Gemeinschaftspolitik." In *Das Europäische System der statistischen Information nach 1992: Eurostat Mitteilungen—Sondernummer,* 87–99. Apr. 1989.

Kloepfer, Michael. *Das Umweltrecht in der deutschen Einigung: Zum Umweltrecht im Einigungsvertag und zum Umweltrahmengesetz.* Berlin: Duncker & Humblot, 1991.

Knapp, Hans Dieter. "Nationalparke in der DDR: Bausteine für ein gemeinsames europäisches Haus." *Nationalpark* 67:2 (1990): 4–9.

Knapp, Hans Dieter. "Das Nationalparkprogramm der DDR." In *Die Krise als Chance: Naturschutz in neuer Dimension,* edited by Michael Succow, Lebrecht Jeschke, and Hans Dieter Knapp, 38–52. Neuenhagen: Succow Stiftung, 2001.

Komlosy, Andrea. *An den Rand gedrängt: Wirtschafts- und Sozialgeschichte des oberen Waldviertels.* Vienna: Krit. Sozialwissenschaft, 1988.

Komlosy, Andrea. "Auswirkungen der Grenzöffnung 1989: Das Beispiel des Oberen Waldviertels." In *Der "Ostfaktor": Die österreichische Wirtschaft, 1989–2009,* edited by Dieter Stiefel, 247–292. Vienna: Böhlau, 2010.

Komska, Yuliya. *The Icon Curtain: The Cold War's Quiet Border.* Chicago: University of Chicago Press, 2015.

König, H. "Der Brutvogelbestand einer Kontrollfläche in der Lenzener Wische (Kreis Ludwigslust) im Jahre 1965." *Mitteilungen der IG Avifauna DDR* 2 (1969): 43–58.

Könker, Hermann. "Komplexe Standortmeliorationen." In *Umweltschutz in der DDR,* vol. 2, edited by Hermann Behrens and Jens Hoffmann, 45–58. Munich: Oekom, 2007.

"'Kontrollbesuch': Zellstoff- und Papierfabrik Rosenthal GmbH—3 Jahre danach." *Zellstoff & Papier* 43:5 (1994): 74–78.

Koop, Volker. *Kein Kampf um Berlin? Deutsche Politik zur Zeit der Berlin-Blockade, 1948–49.* Bonn: Bouvier, 1998.

Kopper, Christoph. *Die Bahn im Wirtschaftswunder: Deutsche Bundesbahn und Verkehrspolitik in der Nachkriegsgesellschaft.* Frankfurt: Campus, 2007.

Korte, Karl-Rudolf. *Deutschlandpolitik in Helmut Kohls Kanzlerschaft: Regierungsstil und Entscheidungen, 1982–1989.* Stuttgart: DVA, 1998.

Koshar, Rudy. *German Travel Cultures.* London: Berg, 2000.

Koshar, Rudy. "'What Ought to be Seen': Tourists' Guidebooks and National Identities in Modern Germany and Europe." *Journal of Contemporary History* 33:3 (1998): 323–340.

Krahulec, Peter. "Alternative Grenzlandfahrt." In *Fuldaer Stadt-Buch*, edited by Rainer Brembs, 303–304. Fulda: Zeitdruck, Dec.1985.

Krämer, Sonja Isabel. "Westdeutsche Propaganda im Kalten Krieg: Organisation and Akteure." In *Pressepolitik und Propaganda: Historische Studien vom Vormärz bis zum Kalten Krieg*, edited by Manfred Wilke, 333–371. Cologne: Böhlau, 1997.

Kraus, Josef. *Zu Konzeption und Praxis der Zonenrandförderung*. Phil. Diss., University of Munich, 1982.

Krenzer, Jürgen H. "Eßkultur und Agrarkultur: Kulinarisches und gastliches Ereignis." *Berichte zur ländlichen Entwicklung* 82 (2004): 39–44.

Kretschmer, Winfried. "Wackersdorf: Wiederaufbereitung im Widerstreit." In *Von der Bittschrift zur Platzbesetzung: Konflikte um technische Grossprojekte*, edited by Ulrich Linse et al., 165–217. Bonn: Dietz, 1988.

Krüger, Dieter, ed. *Fulda Gap: Battlefield of the Cold War Alliances*. Lanham, MD: Lexington Books, 2018.

Krüger, Gesine, Aline Steinbrecher, and Clemens Wischermann, eds. *Tiere und Geschichte: Konturen einer "Animate History."* Stuttgart: Franz Steiner 2014.

Kruse, Michael. *Politik und deutsch-deutsche Wirtschaftsbeziehungen von 1945 bis 1989*. Berlin: Köster, 2005.

Kufeke, Kay. "'Jeder, ob Genosse oder nicht, ist schon 'drüben' gewesen': Die Durchlässigkeit der innerdeutschen Grenze in Mecklenburg vor 1952." *Zeitgeschichte Regional* 15:2 (2011): 34–38.

Kufeke, Kai. "'. . . völlige Klarheit schaffen, dass es nicht noch einmal anders kommt': Die Durchsetzung des DDR-Grenzregimes in Mecklenburg, 1946–1961." *Zeitschrift für Geschichtswissenschaft* 64:6 (2016): 542–557.

Kühn, Cornelia. "'Kunst ohne Zonengrenzen': Zur Instrumentalisierung der Volkskunst in der frühen DDR." In *Das Imaginäre des Kalten Krieges: Beiträge zu einer Kulturgeschicht des Ost-West-Konfliktes in Europa*, edited by David Eugster and Sybille Marti, 187–211. Essen: Klartext, 2015.

Kurth, Horst. "Die Entwicklung der Forstwirtschaft in der DDR." *Allgemeine Forst Zeitschrift* 35 (1990): 892–897.

Laakkonen, Simo, Victor Pál, and Richard Tucker. "The Cold War and Environmental History: Complementary Fields." *Cold War History* 16:4 (2016): 377–394.

Lagrou, Pieter. *The Legacy of Nazi Occupation: Patriotic Memory and National Recovery in Western Europe, 1945–1965*. Cambridge: Cambridge University Press, 2000.

Langston, Nancy. "Thinking like a Microbe: Borders and Environmental History." *Canadian Historical Review* 95:4 (2014): 592–603.

Lapp, Peter Joachim. *Grenzregime der DDR*. Aachen: Helios, 2013.

Larson, Brandon. *Metaphors for Environmental Sustainability: Redefining Our Relationship with Nature*. New Haven, CT: Yale University Press, 2011.

Lasky, Jesse R., Walter Jetz, and Timothy H. Keitt. "Conservation Biogeography of the US–Mexican Border: A Transcontinental Risk Assessment of Barriers to Animal Dispersal." *Diversity and Distribution* 17 (2011): 673–687.

Lebegern, Robert. *Zur Geschichte der Sperranlagen an der innerdeutschen Grenze, 1945–1990.* Erfurt: LpB Thüringen, 2004.

Leendertz, Ariane. "Der Gedanke des Ausgleichs und die Ursprünge des Leitbildes der 'gleichwertigen Lebensbedingungen.'" In *Vom Dritten Reich zur Bundesrepublik: Beiträge einer Tagung zur Geschichte von Raumforschung und Raumplanung*, edited by Heinrich Mäding, Wendelin Strubelt, 210–225. Hannover: Akademie für Raumforschung und Landesplanung, 2009.

Leendertz, Ariane. "Ordnung, Ausgleich, Harmonie: Koordinaten raumplanerischen Denkens in Deutschland, 1920–1970." In *Die Ordnung der Moderne: Social Engineering im 20. Jahrhundert*, edited by Thomas Etzemüller, 129–150. Bielefeld: Transcript, 2009.

Leendertz, Ariane. *Ordnung schaffen: Deutsche Raumplanung im 20. Jahrhundert.* Göttingen: Wallstein, 2008.

Lehn, Patrick. *Deutschlandbilder: Historische Schulatlanten zwischen 1871 und 1990.* Cologne: Böhlau, 2008.

Leibenath, Markus. "Biotopverbund und räumliche Koordination." *Raumforschung und Raumordnung* 68:2 (2010): 91–101.

Lemke, Michael, ed., *Schaufenster der Systemkonkurrenz: Die Region Berlin-Brandenburg im Kalten Krieg.* Cologne: Böhlau, 2006.

Lemke, Michael. "Totale Blockade? Über das Verhältnis von Abschottung und Durchlässigkeit im Berliner Krisenalltag 1948/49." In *Die Berliner Luftbrücke: Ereignis und Erinnerung*, edited by Helmut Trotnow and Bernd von Kostka, 121–135. Berlin: Frank & Timme, 2010.

Lemke, Michael. *Vor der Mauer: Berlin in der Ost-West-Konkurrenz 1948 bis 1961.* Cologne: Böhlau, 2011.

Lenz, Gerhard. *Verlusterfahrung Landschaft: Über die Herstellung von Raum und Umwelt im mitteldeutschen Industriegebiet seit der Mitte des 19. Jahrhunderts.* Frankfurt: Campus, 1999.

Lèofgren, Orvar. *On Holiday: A History of Vacationing.* Berkeley: University of California Press, 1999.

Lepsius, M. Rainer. "Zur Reformunfähigkeit der DDR: Wirtschaftliche Entscheidungsstrukturen und der 'Bereich Mittag' im Zentralkomitee der SED." In Lepsius, *Institutionalisierung politischen Handelns: Analysen zur DDR, Wiedervereinigung und Europäischen Union*, 104–115. Wiesbaden: Springer, 2013.

Levy, Mark A. "European Acid Rain: The Power of Tote-Board Diplomacy." In *Institutions for the Earth: Sources of Effective International Environmental Protection*, edited by P. M. Hass et al., 75–132. Cambridge: MIT Press, 1993.

Liersch, Klaus-Martin. "Salz in Werra und Weser." *Geographische Rundschau* 39:11 (1987): 642–647.

Light, Duncan. "Gazing on Communism: Heritage Tourism and Post-Communist Identities in Germany, Hungary and Romania." *Tourism Geographies* 2:2 (2000): 157–176.

Lindenberger, Thomas. "Divided, but Not Disconnected: Germany as a Border Region of the Cold War." In *Divided, but Not Disconnected: German Experiences of the Cold War*, edited by Tobias Hochscherf, Christop Laucht, and Andrew Plowman, 11–33. New York: Berghahn, 2010.

Lindenberger, Thomas. "Grenzregime and Gesellschaftskonstruktion im SED-Staat." In *Die Mauer: Errichtung, Überwindung, Erinnerung*, edited by Klaus-Dietmar Henke, 111–121. Munich: dtv, 2011.

Lindenberger, Thomas. *Herrschaft und Eigen-Sinn in der Diktatur: Studien zur Gesellschaftsgeschichte der DDR*. Cologne: Böhlau, 1999.

Lindenberger, Thomas. "'Zonenrand,' 'Sperrgebiet,' und 'Westberlin': Deutschland als Grenzregion des Kalten Krieges." In *Teilung und Integration: Die doppelte deutsche Nachkriegsgeschichte*, edited by Christoph Klessmann and L. Lautzas, 97–112. Bonn: Bundeszentrale, 2005.

Litz, N. "Zur Kenntnis der Belastungssituation durch Herbizide im Bereich ehemaliger Grenzstreifen." *Nachrichtenblatt Deutscher Pflanzenschutzdienst* 43:12 (1991): 257–261.

Lohs, Karlheinz and Dieter Martinetz. "Die Chemie des Todesstreifens." *Spektrum der Wissenschaft* (Dec. 1991): 18–19.

Long, Bronson. *No Easy Occupation: French Control of the German Saar, 1944–1957*. Rochester: Camden, 2015.

Lotz, Christian. "Gestrichelte Linien und schattierte Flächen: Darstellungen von Teilung und Einheit in ost- und westdeutschen Landkarten, 1945–1972." In *Die geteilte Nation: Nationale Verluste und Identitäten im 20. Jahrhundert*, edited by Andreas Hilger and Oliver Wrochem, 53–69. Munich: de Gruyter, 2013.

Löytynoja, Tanja. "National Boundaries and Place-Making in Tourism: Staging the Finnish–Russian Border." *Nordia Geographical Publications* 36:4 (2008): 35–45.

Macrakis, Kristie. *Seduced by Secrets: Inside the Stasi's Spy-Tech World*. New York: Cambridge University Press, 2008.

Mahlke, Matthias. *Zukunft der Grenzmuseen: Sammlungen, Präsentationen, Konzepte, wissenschaftliche Forschung, Koordination*. Hannover: Leibniz University, 2012.

Maier, Charles S. *Dissolution: The Crisis of Communism and the End of East Germany*. Princeton, NJ: Princeton University Press, 1997.

Maier, Jörg. "Zweitwohnsitze im Freizeitraum: Erscheinungsformen und Auswirkungen in wirtschaftlicher und sozialer Hinsicht." In *Zweitwohnsitze in Fremdenverkehrsorten*. Arbeitsmaterialien zur Raumordnung und Raumplanung, no. 38, 1–12. Bayreuth, 1985.

Martin, Terry. *The Affirmative Action Empire: Nations and Nationalism in the Soviet Union, 1923–1939*. Ithaca, NY: Cornell University Press, 2001.

Masurek, Lars and Gerd Hachmöller. "Akteursnetzwerke und Regionalentwicklung im Schatten von Gorleben: Der Landkreis Lüchow-Dannenberg." *Raumforschung und Raumordnung* 60:1 (2002): 61–69.

McNeill, John R. "Observations on the Nature and Culture of Environmental History." *History & Theory* 42:4 (Dec. 2003): 5–43.

McNeill, John R. and Peter Engelke. *The Great Acceleration: An Environmental History of the Anthropocene since 1945*. Cambridge, MA: Harvard University Press, 2016.

McNeill, J. R. and Corinna Unger, eds. *Environmental Histories of the Cold War*. New York: Cambridge University Press, 2010.

Mehnert, Dagmar. "Der Aufbau des Kalireviers und die Jahre bis 1945." In *Bunte Salze, weisse Berge: Wachstum und Wandel der Kaliindustrie zwischen Thüringer Wald, Rhön und Vogelsberg*, edited by Hermann-Josef Hohmann and Dagmar Mehnert, 35–99. Hünfeld: Ulmenstein, 2004.

Meinke, Markus A. "Zweimal 'Eiserner Vorhang'? Die tschechoslowakisch-bayerische Grenze in vergleichender Perspektive zur innerdeutschen Grenze." In *Die tschechisch-bayerische Grenze im Kalten Krieg in vergleichender Perspektive: Politische, ökonomische und soziokulturelle Dimensionen*, edited by Markus A. Meinke, 55–68. Regensburg: Staatsarchiv 2011.

Melis, Damian von and Henrik Bispinck. *"Republikflucht": Flucht und Abwanderung aus der SBZ/DDR 1945 bis 1961*. Munich: Oldenbourg, 2006.

Metzger, Birgit. *"Erst stirbt der Wald, dann du!" Das Waldsterben als westdeutsches Politikum, 1978–1986*. Frankfurt: Campus, 2015.

Metzler, Gabriele. *Konzeptionen politischen Handelns von Adenauer bis Brandt: Politische Planung in der pluralistischen Gesellschaft*. Paderborn: Schöningh, 2005.

Meyer, Christoph. *Die deutschlandpolitische Doppelstrategie: Wilhelm Wolfgang Schütz und das Kuratorium Unteilbares Deutschland, 1954–1972*. Landsberg: Olzog, 1997.

Meyer-Braun, Renate. *Löcher im Eisernen Vorhang. Theateraustausch zwischen Bremen und Rostock während des Kalten Krieges, 1956–1961*. Berlin: Trafo, 2007.

Meyer-Rebentisch, Karen. *Grenzerfahrungen. Dokumentation zum Leben mit der innerdeutschen Grenze bei Lübeck von 1945 bis heute*. Lübeck: City of Lübeck, 2009.

Milder, Stephen. "Between Grassroots Activism and Transnational Aspirations: Anti-Nuclear Protest from the Rhine Valley to the Bundestag, 1974–1983." *Historical Social Research* 39:1 (2014): 191–211.

Milder, Stephen. *Greening Democracy: The Anti-Nuclear Movement and Political Environmentalism in West Germany and Beyond, 1968–1983*. New York: Cambridge University Press, 2017.

Mingus, Matthew D. *Remapping Modern Germany after National Socialism, 1945–1961*. Syracuse, NY: Syracuse University Press, 2017.

Mitdank, Joachim. "Blockade gegen Blockade: Die Berlin Krise 1948/49." *Beiträge zur Geschichte der Arbeiterbewegung* 36:3 (1994): 41–58.

Moench, Christoph. "Refinanzierung der Endlagersuche und des Endlagers für wärmeentwickelnde radioaktive Abfälle." *atw* 58:2 (2013): 103–107.

Mohr, Hans-Joachim. "Die Entwässerung landwirtschaftlicher Nutzflächen: Schwerpunkt der Meliorationstätigkeit, 1960–1990—ein kritischer Rückblick." In *Umweltschutz in der DDR*, vol. 2, edited by Hermann Behrens and Jens Hoffmann, 59–80. Munich: Oekom, 2007.

Möller, Christian. "Der Traum vom ewigen Kreislauf. Abprodukte, Sekundärrohstoffe und Stoffkreisläufe im 'Abfall-Regime' der DDR (1945–1990)." *Technikgeschichte* 81:1 (2014): 61–89.

Möller, Detlev. *Endlagerung radioaktiver Abfälle in der Bundesrepublik Deutschland.* Frankfurt: Lang, 2009.

Möller, Frank and Ulrich Mählert, eds., *Abgrenzung und Verflechtung: Das geteilte Deutschland in der zeithistorischen Debatte.* Berlin: Metropol, 2008.

Mörchen, Stefan. *Schwarzer Markt: Kriminalität, Ordnung und Moral in Bremen, 1939–1949.* Frankfurt: Campus, 2011.

Moss, Timothy. "Divided City, Divided Infrastructures: Securing Energy and Water Services in Postwar Berlin." *Journal of Urban History* 35:7 (2009): 923–942.

Muhle, Susanne. *Auftrag: Menschenraub—Entführungen von Westberlinern und Bundesbürgern durch das Ministerium für Staatssicherheit der DDR.* Göttingen: V&R, 2015.

Müller, Birgit. "The Skeleton versus the Little Grey Men: Conflicting Cultures of Anti-Nuclear Protest at the Czech–Austrian Border." In *Border Encounters: Asymmetry and Proximity at Europe's Frontiers*, edited by Jutta Lauth Bacas and William Kavanagh, 68–89. New York: Berghahn, 2013.

Müller, Jan-Werner. *Another Country: German Intellectuals, Unification and National Identity.* New Haven, CT: Yale University Press, 2000.

Müller, Susanne. *Die Welt des Baedeker: Eine Medienkulturgeschichte des Reiseführers, 1830–1945.* Frankfurt: Campus, 2012.

Müller, Werner. "Dorf am Eisernen Vorhang." In *Im Schatten der Zonengrenze*, edited by Bundesministerium für Gesamtdeutsche Fragen, 21–26. Bonn: 1956.

Müller, Wolfgang D. *Geschichte der Kernenergie in der DDR: Kernforschung und Kerntechnik im Schatten des Sozialismus* (Geschichte der Kernenergie in der Bundesrepublik Deutschland, vol. 3). Stuttgart: Schäffer-Poeschel, 2001.

Müller, Wolfgang D. "Moratorium für Kernkraftwerke?" *atw* 22:2 (1977): 65.

Müller-Helmbrecht, Arnulf. "Endspurt: Das Nationalparkprogramm im Wettlauf mit der Zeit." In *Naturschutz in den neuen Bundesländern: Ein Rückblick*, edited by Regine Auster and Hermann Behrens, 597–608. Berlin: VWF, 2001.

Müller-Wegener, U. and R. Schmidt. *Erfassung der Bodenkontamination und Altlasten auf Liegenschaften des Bundes—Teilvorhaben Grenzstreifen: Pflanzenschutzmittelgehalte im Grenzstreifen der ehem. DDR*, edited by Institut für Wasser-, Boden- und Lufthygiene des Bundesgesundheitsamtes. Berlin: Feb. 1994.

Müller von der Grün, Claus Peter. "Unter einem Dach: Die wiedervereinigte Kaliindustrie im geeinten Deutschland." In *Die Kaliindustrie an Werra und Fulda: Geschichte eines landschaftsprägenden Industriezweigs*, edited by Ulrich Eisenbach and Akos Paulinyi, 223–237. Darmstadt: Hess. Wirtschaftsarchiv, 1998.

Mund, Karsten. *Der Landkreis Helmstedt als Grenzgebiet, 1945–1952*. Phil. Diss., Technical University Braunschweig, 1993.

Murdock, Caitlin E. *Changing Places: Society, Culture, and Territory in the Saxon-Bohemian Borderlands, 1870–1946*. Ann Arbor: University of Michigan Press, 2010.

Nägele, Frank. *Regionale Wirtschaftspolitik im kooperativen Bundesstaat*. Opladen: Leske & Budrich, 1996.

Nass, Klaus Otto. *Die Vermessung des Eisernen Vorhangs. Deutsch-deutsche Grenzkommission und DDR-Staatssicherheit*. Freiburg: Centaurus, 2010.

Nelson, Arvid. *Cold War Ecology: Forests, Farms, and People in the East German Landscape, 1945–1989*. New Haven, CT: Yale University Press, 2005.

Neukölln, Ingrid (pseud.). "Wendländische Schmonzette." In *Die anti-Atom Bewegung: Geschichte und Perspektiven*, edited by Tresantis, 107–111. Berlin: Assoziation A, 2015.

Neumeier, Gerhard. "Die Aktivitäten des Ministeriums für Staatssicherheit der DDR in Bayern, 1950–1989." *Zeitschrift für Geschichtswissenschaft* 60:4 (2012): 349–369.

Niedersächsisches Institut für Wirtschaftsforschung. *Ansatzpunkte zur Verbesserung der Ausgabensituation der kommunalen Ebenen im Landkreis Lüchow-Dannenerg im Zuge einer Neuorientierung der Verwaltung*. Hannover: NIW, 2003.

Niehaus, Andrea. "Der 'positive' Schock: Über den Transrapid-Unfall von Lathen (Emsland) und seine Folgen." *Inklings: Jahrbuch für Literatur und Ästhetik* 25 (2007): 107–119.

Niemann, Hans-Werner. "Wirtschaftsgeschichte Niedersachsens, 1918–1945." In *Geschichte Niedersachsens*. Vol. 5: *Von der Weimarer Republik bis zur Wiedervereinigung*, edited by Gerd Steinwascher, Detlef Schmiechen-Ackermann, and Karl-Heinz Schneider, 455–623. Hannover: Hahn, 2010.

Nobel, Rolf. *Mitten durch Deutschland: Reportage einer Grenzfahrt*. Hamburg: Rasch & Röhring 1986.

Nonn, Christoph. *Die Ruhrbergbaukrise: Entindustrialisierung und Politik, 1958–1969*. Göttingen: V&R, 2001.

Nützenadel, Alexander. *Stunde der Ökonomen: Wissenschaft, Politik und Expertenkultur in der Bundesrepublik, 1949–1974*. Göttingen: V&R, 2005.

Oertzel, Günther. *Fortschrittsfeinde im Atomzeitalter? Protest und Innovationsmanagement am Beispiel der frühen Kernenergiepläne der Bundesrepublik Deutschland*. Berlin: Verlag für Geschichte der Naturwissenschaften und der Technik, 2012.

Offer, Michael. *Das Zonenrandgebiet nach der deutschen Einigung: Wirtschaftliche Entwicklung und regionalpolitische Implikationen*. Mainz: Forschungsinstitut für Wirtschaftspolitik, 1991.

Oldenburg, Fred and Gerd-Rüdiger Stephan. "Honecker kam nicht bis Bonn: Neue Quellen zum Konflikt zwischen Ost-Berlin und Moskau." *Deutschland Archiv* 28 (1995): 791–805.

Ortmeyer, August. "Regionalpolitik in Deutschland: Blick zurück und nach vorn." In *Ordnungspolitik als konstruktive Antwort auf wirtschaftpolitische Herausforderungen: FS zum 65. Geburtstag von Paul Klemmer*, edited by Hans-Friedrich Eckey, 129–141. Stuttgart: Lucius & Lucius, 2001.

Oschlies, Johannes. *Entrissene Heimat: Zwangsaussiedlungen an der DDR-Grenze 1952 und 1961 im Bezirk Magdeburg*. Magdeburg: Bürgerkomitee Sachsen-Anhalt, 2006.

Ossowski, Mirosław. "Ostpreußen in der deutschen Literatur nach 1945." In *Europa im Wandel: Literatur, Werte und Europäische Identität*, edited by Birgit Lermen and Mirosław Ossowski, 115–134. St. Augustin: KAS, 2004.

Ott, Konrad and Ulrich Smeddinck, eds. *Umwelt, Gerechtigkeit, Freiwilligkeit: Insbesondere bei der Realisierung eines Endlagers—Beiträge aus Ethik und Recht*. Berlin: BWV, 2018.

Owczarski, Rolf. *Und hellen Augenglanz las ich von ihrem Gesicht: Weihnachtsbasar des Kuratoriums Unteilbares Deutschland im Landkreis Helmstedt, 1965–1989*. Helmstedt: Landkreis, 2000.

Paasche, Wilhelm. "Die Zonengrenze und ihre Auswirkungen." In *Das Hannoversche Wendland*, edited by Wilhelm Paasche, 97–99. Lüchow: Landkreis DAN, 1971.

Paasi, Anssi. *Territories, Boundaries and Consciousness: The Changing Geographies of the Finnish–Russian Border*. Chichester: Wiley, 1996.

Palis, Gustav and Bernhard Peitschner. *Der Drömling: Vom Moor zur Kulturlandschaft*. Horb am Neckar: Geiger, 1998.

Park, Jinhee. *Von der Müllkippe zur Abfallwirtschaft: Die Entwicklung der Hausmüllentsorgung in Berlin (West) von 1945 bis 1990*. Phil. Diss., Technical University Berlin, 2003.

Parker, Bradley J. "Toward an Understanding of Borderland Processes." *American Antiquities* 71:1 (2006): 77–100.

Patterson, Walter C. "Gorleben Hearings." *Bulletin of the Atomic Scientists* 35:6 (June 1979): 11.

Paucke, Horst. *Chancen für die Umweltpolitik und Umweltforschung: Zur Situation in der ehemaligen DDR*. Marburg: BdWi, 1994.

Petschow, Ulrich, Jürgen Meyerhoff, and Claus Thomasberger, eds. *Umwelt-Report DDR: Bilanz der Zerstörung, Kosten der Sanierung, Strategien für den ökologischen Umbau*. Frankfurt: Fischer, 1990.

Petzina, Dietmar. "Standortverschiebungen und regionale Wirtschaftskraft in der Bundesrepublik Deutschland seit den fünfziger Jahren." In *Wirtschaftliche Integration und Wandel von Raumstrukturen im 19. und 20. Jahrhundert*, edited by Werner Abelshauser et al., 101–127. Berlin: Duncker & Humblot, 1994.

Pfeifer, Robert. "Der Schwarzstorch *Ciconia nigra* in Bayern: Ausbreitungsgeschichte, Verbreitung und aktueller Status." *Ornitholoigscher Anzeiger* 36 (Sept. 1997): 93–104.

Piechocki, Reinhard et al. "Renaturierung: Zum Naturschutz der Zukunft." In *Re-Naturierung: Jahrbuch Ökologie, 2015*, edited by Heike Leitschuh et al., 39–48. Stuttgart: Hirzel, 2015.

Pingel-Schliemann, Sandra. *"Ihr könnt doch nicht auf mich schiessen!" Die Grenze zwischen Lübecker Bucht und Elbe, 1945–1989.* Schwerin: Landesbeauftragte, 2014.

Pittaway, Mark. "Making Peace in the Shadow of War: The Austrian-Hungarian Borderlands, 1945–1956." *Contemporary European History* 17:3 (2008): 345–364.

Plück, Kurt. "Hilfeleistungen des Bundes für die Zonenrandgebiete." In *Im Schatten der Zonengrenze*, 107–112. Bonn: Bundesministerium für Gesamtdeutsche Fragen, 1956.

Plück, Kurt. "Innerdeutsche Beziehungen auf kommunaler und Verwaltungsebene, in Wissenschaft, Kultur und Sport und ihre Rückwirkungen auf die Menschen im geteilten Deutschland." In *Materialien der Enquete-Kommission "Aufarbeitung von Geschichte und Folgen der SED-Diktatur in Deutschland"* (12. Wahlperiode des Deutschen Bundestages), vol. 5:3, 2015–2064. Baden Baden: Nomos, 1995.

Poggendorf, Klaus. *Gorleben: Der Streit um die nukleare Entsorgung und die Zukunft einer Region.* Lüneburg: Nordlanddruck, 2008.

Popp, Manfred. "Die unklare nukleare Entsorgung: Persönliche Reminiszenzen und Reflexionen." In *Wohin mit dem radioaktiven Abfall? Perspektiven für eine sozialwissenschaftliche Endlagerforschung*, edited by Peter Hocke and Armin Grunwald, 53–62. Berlin: Edition Sigma, 2006.

Potthoff, Heinrich. *Im Schatten der Mauer: Deutschlandpolitik 1961 bis 1990.* Berlin: Propyläen, 1999.

Potthoff, Heinrich. *Die 'Koalition der Vernunft'. Deutschlandpolitik in den 80er Jahren.* Munich: dtv, 1995.

Puffahrt, Otto. *Bauernland in Not. 75 Jahre Wasser- und Bodenverband der Lüchower Landgraben-Niederung, 1915–1990.* Lüchow: Selbstverlag, 1990.

Puffahrt, Otto. "Grossflächige Entwässerungsmassnahmen im Landkreis Lüchow-Dannenberg." In *Gewässerentwicklung in der Kulturlandschaft*, edited by Christoph Ohlig, 75–83. Siegburg: Dt. Wasserhistorische Gesellschaft, 2005.

Purdy, Jedediah. *After Nature: A Politics for the Anthropocene.* Cambridge, MA: Harvard University Press, 2015.

Radkau, Joachim. *Die Ära der Ökologie: Eine Weltgeschichte.* Munich: Beck, 2011.

Radkau, Joachim and Lothar Hahn. *Aufstieg und Fall der deutschen Atomwirtschaft.* Munich: Oekom, 2013.

Rajal, Bernd D. *Natura 2000: Das Schutzgebietssystem der EU.* Vienna: Manzsche Verlagsbuchhandlung, 2004.

Rätzke, Dorian. *Zwischen Stacheldraht und Strandkorb: DDR-Alltag in der Lübecker Bucht.* Boltenhagen: Boltenhagen 2011.

Rausch, Jochen. *Restlicht.* Cologne: KiWi, 2008.

Readman, Paul, Cynthia Radding, and Chad Bryant: "Borderlands in a Global Perspective." In *Borderlands in World History, 1700–1914*, edited by Paul Readman, Cynthia Radding, and Chad Bryant, 1–23. London: Palgrave Macmillan, 2014.

Reichardt, Sven. *Authentizität und Gemeinschaft: Linksalternatives Leben in den siebziger und frühen achtziger Jahren*. Frankfurt: Suhrkamp, 2014.

Reichert, Mike. *Kernenergiewirtschaft in der DDR: Entwicklungsbedingungen, konzeptioneller Anspruch und Realisierungsgrad, 1955–1990*. St. Katharinen: Scripta Mercaturae, 1999.

Reichhoff, Lutz and Wolfgang Böhnert. "Das Nationalparkprogramm der ehemaligen DDR." *Natur und Landschaft* 66:4 (Apr. 1991): 195–203.

Rennert, S. and G. Fiehn, "Erfahrungen bei der Einführung umweltverträglicher Technologien in der Sulfitzellstoffabrik Blankenstein." *Das Papier* 46:10 (1992): V9–V15.

Renzsch, Wolfgang. *Finanzverfassung und Finanzausgleich: Die Auseinandersetzungen um ihre politische Gestaltung in der Bundesrepublik Deutschland zwischen Währungsreform und deutscher Vereinigung, 1948–1990*. Bonn: Dietz, 1991.

Riedel, Matthias. "Die wirtschaftliche Entwicklung in Niedersachsen, 1945–1950." *Niedersächsisches Jahrbuch für Landesgeschichte* 55 (1983): 115–138.

Ritter, Gerhard A. *Wir sind das Volk! Wir sind ein Volk! Geschichte der deutschen Einigung*. Munich: Beck, 2009.

Ritter, Gert, and Joseph G. Hajdu. "The East–West German Boundary." *Geographical Review* 79:3 (July 1989): 326–344.

Ritter, Gert, and Joseph G. Hajdu. *Die innerdeutsche Grenze: Analyse ihrer räumlichen Auswirkungen und der raumwirksamen Staatstätigkeit in den Grenzegebieten*. Cologne: Geostudien, 1982.

Ritter, Jürgen and Peter Joachim Lapp. *Die Grenze: Ein deutsches Bauwerk*. Berlin: Links, 2006.

Roberts, Adam M. and Kevin Stewart. "Land Mines: Animal Casualties of the Underground War." *Animals Agenda* 18:2 (1998): 35–36.

Rödder, Andreas. *Deutschland einig Vaterland: Die Geschichte der Wiedervereinigung*. Munich: Beck, 2009.

Roesler, Jörg. "Der Einfluss der Aussenwirtschaftspolitik auf die Beziehungen DDR-Bundesrepublik. Die achtziger Jahre." *Deutschland Archiv* 26 (Mai 1993): 558–572.

Roesler, Jörg. "System- oder konjunkturbedingte Unterschiede? Zur Umweltpolitik in der DDR und der Bundesrepublik in den 70er und 80er Jahren." *Deutschland Archiv* 39:3 (2006): 480–488.

Roesler, Jörg. *Umweltprobleme und Umweltpolitik in der DDR*. Erfurt: Landeszentrale, 2006.

Roggenbuch, Frank. *Das Berliner Grenzgängerproblem: Verflechtung und Systemkonkurrenz vor dem Mauerbau*. Berlin: de Gruyter, 2008.

Röhling, Klaus-Jürgen. "Techniken, Konzepte, Herausforderungen: Zur Endlagerung radioaktiver Reststoffe." In *Problemfalle Endlager: Gesellschaftliche Herausforderungen im Umgang mit Atommüll*, edited by Achim Brunnengräber, 33–54. Baden-Baden: Nomos, 2016.

Rommelspacher, Thomas. "Das natürliche Recht auf Wasserverschmutzung: Geschichte des Wassers im 19. und 20. Jahrhundert." In *Besiegte Natur: Geschichte der Umwelt im 19. und 20. Jahrhundert*, edited by Franz-Josef Brüggemeier and Thomas Rommelspacher, 42–63. Munich: Beck, 1989.

Rosenbaum, Adam T. et al. "The History of Dark Tourism." *Journal of Tourism History* 10:3 (2018): 269–295.

Rosenfeld, Martin and Robert Kawka. "Regionale Differenzierungen in Ostdeutschland: Die Wirtschaftslage ostdeutscher Kreise an der Grenze zu Niedersachsen." *Wirtschaft im Wandel* 1 (2003): 27–33.

Rösler, Markus. "Das Nationalparkprogramm der DDR." In *Naturschutz in den neuen Bundesländern: Ein Rückblick*, edited by Regine Auster and Hermann Behrens, 561–595. Berlin: VWF, 2001.

Roth, Werner. *Dorf im Wandel: Struktur und Funktionssysteme einer hessischen Zonenrandgemeinde im sozial-kulturellen Wandel—Eine empirische Untersuchung.* Frankfurt: Hassmüller, 1968.

Rother, Bernd. "Gilt das gesprochene Wort?" *Deutschland Archiv* 33:1 (2000): 90–93.

Rothschild, Rachel. "Burning Rain: The Long-Range Transboundary Air Pollution Project." In *Toxic Airs: Body, Place, Planet in Historical Perspective*, edited by James Rodger Fleming and Ann Johnson, 181–207. Pittsburgh: University of Pittsburgh Press, 2014.

Rott, Wilfried. *Die Insel: Eine Geschichte West-Berlins, 1948–1990.* Munich: Beck, 2009.

Rottman, Gordon L. *The Berlin Wall and the Intra-German Border, 1961–1989.* Oxford: Osprey, 2008.

Rucht, Dieter: *Von Wyhl nach Gorleben: Bürger gegen Atomprogramm und nukleare Entsorgung.* Munich: Beck, 1980.

Rucht, Dieter. "Anti-Atomkraftbewegung." In *Die sozialen Bewegungen in Deutschland seit 1945: Ein Handbuch*, edited by Roland Roth and Dieter Rucht, 245–266. Frankfurt: Campus, 2008.

Ruck, Hartmut. "Die Kali-Industrie an der Werra in Thüringen, 1945–1989." In *Bunte Salze, weisse Berge: Wachstum und Wandel der Kaliindustrie zwischen Thüringer Wald, Rhön und Vogelsberg*, edited by Hermann-Hohmann and Dagmar Mehnert, 101–134. Hünfeld: Ulmenstein, 2004.

Ruck, Michael. "Ein kurzer Sommer der konkreten Utopie: Zur westdeutschen Planungsgeschichte der langen 60er Jahre." In *Dynamische Zeiten: Die 60er Jahre in den beiden deutschen Gesellschaften*, edited by Axel Schildt and Detlef Siegfried. 362–401. Hamburg: Christians, 2000.

Rummler, Toralf. *Die Gewalttaten an der deutsch-deutschen Grenze vor Gericht.* Berlin: Arno Spitz, 2000.

Rusinek Bernd-A. "Wyhl." In *Deutsche Erinnerungsorte II*, edited by Etienne Francois and Hagen Schulze, 652–666. Munich: Beck, 2001.

Rutter, Nick. "The Western Wall: The Iron Curtain Recast in Midsummer 1951." In *Cold War Crossings: International Travel and Exchange across the Soviet Block, 1940s–1960s*, edited by Patryk Babiracki and Kenyon Zimmer, 78–106. College Station: Texas A&M University Press, 2014.

Sadeleer, Nicolas de. "Polluter Pays Principle." In *Essential Concepts of Global Environmental Governance*, edited by Jean-Frédéric Morin and Amandine Orsini, 155–156. London: Routledge, 2015.

Sälter, Gerhard. *Grenzpolizisten: Konformität, Verweigerung und Repression in der Grenzpolizei und den Grenztruppen der DDR, 1952–1965*. Berlin: Links, 2009.

Sälter, Gerhard. "Loyalität und Denunziation in der ländlichen Gesellschaft der DDR: Die Freiwilligen Helfer der Grenzpolizei im Jahr 1952." In *Der willkommene Verrat: Beiträge zur Denunziationsforschung*, edited by Michael Schröter, 159–184. Weilerswist: Velbrück Wissenschaft 2007.

Sälter, Gerhard, Johanna Dietrich, and Fabian Kuhn. *Die vergessenen Toten: Todesopfer des DDR-Grenzregimes in Berlin von der Teilung bis zum Mauerbau, 1948–1961*. Berlin: Links, 2016.

Sälter, Gerhard and Hans-Hermann Hertle. "Die Todesopfer an Mauer und Grenze: Probleme einer Bilanz des DDR-Grenzregimes." *Deutschland Archiv* 4 (2006): 667–676.

Sälter, Gerhard and Jochen Maurer. "The Double Task of East German Border Guards." *German Politics and Society* 29:2 (2011): 23–39.

Salander, Carsten. "The Concept of the German Electric Power Industry for the Disposal of Spent Fuel from Nuclear Power Plants." *Kerntechnik* 20:5 (1978): 229–237.

Sander, Hans-Jörg. *Das Zonenrandgebiet*. Cologne: Aulis, 1988.

Sahlins, Peter. *Boundaries: The Making of France and Spain in the Pyreenees*. Berkeley: University of California Press, 1989.

Sammartino, Annemarie H.. *The Impossible Border: Germany and the East, 1914–1922*. Ithaca, NY: Cornell University Press, 2010.

Satjukow, Silke. "Grenze 2000." *Aus Politik und Zeitgeschichte* 21/22 (2009): 18–25.

Sattler, Friederike. "Rheinischer Kapitalismus: Staat, Wirtschaft und Gesellschaft der Bonner Republik." *Archiv für Sozialgeschichte* 52 (2012): 688–692, 694–695.

Schaefer, Sagi. *States of Division: Border & Boundary Formation in Cold War Rural Germany*. Oxford: Oxford University Press, 2014.

Schanetzky, Tim. *Die grosse Ernüchterung: Wirtschaftspolitik, Expertise und Gesellschaft in der Bundesrepublik 1966 bis 1982*. Berlin: Akademie, 2007.

Schätzlein, Gerhard and Reinhold Albert. *Grenzerfahrungen: Bezirk Suhl—Bayern/Hessen zur Zeit der Wende*. Hildburghausen: Frankenschwelle, 2005.

Scherer, Marie-Luise. "Die Hundegrenze." *Der Spiegel*, Feb. 7, 1994, 94–115.

Scherzer, Ludolf. *Der Grenz-Gänger*. Berlin: Aufbau, 2007.

Schildt, Axel. "'Die kostbarsten Wochen des Jahres': Urlaubstourismus der Westdeutschen, 1945–1970." In *Goldstrand und Teutonengrill: Kultur- und Sozialgeschichte des Tourismus in Deutschland, 1945–1989*, edited by Hasso Spode, 69–86. Berlin: Moser, 1996.

Schildt, Axel. "Zwei Staaten—eine Hörfunk- und Fernsehnation: Überlegungen zur Bedeutung der elektronischen Massenmedien in der Geschichte der Kommunkation zwischen der Bundesrepublik und der DDR." In *Doppelte Zeitgeschichte: Deutsch-deutsche Beziehungen, 1945–1990*, edited by Arnd Bauerkämper, Martin Sabrow, and Bernd Stöver, 58–71. Bonn: Dietz, 1998.

Schindelbeck, Dirk. "Propaganda mit Gummiballons und Pappraketen." In *Propaganda in Deutschland*, edited by Gerald Diesener and Rainer Grieß, 213–234. Darmstadt: WBG, 1996.

Schlemmer, Thomas, Stefan Grüner, and Jaromir Balcar. "'Entwicklungshilfe im eigenen Lande': Landesplanung in Bayern nach 1945." In *Demokratisierung und gesellschaftlicher Aufbruch: Die sechziger Jahre als Wendezeit der Bundesrepublik*, edited by Matthias Frese, Julia Paulus, and Karl Teppe, 379–450. Paderborn: Schöningh, 2005.

Schlumbohm, Friedrich. "Landwirtschaft gestern, heute und morgen." *Hannoversches Wendland* 11 (1986): 125–127.

Schlumprecht, Helmut et al. "E+E Vorhaben 'Bestandsaufnahme Grünes Band': Naturschutzfachliche Bedeutung des längsten Biotopverbundsystems Deutschlands." *Natur & Landschaft* 77 (2002): 407–414.

Schmale, Angela. "Heimlich, still und leise: Die Grenzschleusen und 'Grenz-IM' des MfS." *Zeitschrift des Forschungsverbundes* 35 (2014): 80–90.

Schmidt, P. A. "Landwirtschaft und Naturschutz in der DDR." *Forstwirtschaftliches Centralblatt* 109 (1990): 378–402.

Schmidt, Wolfgang. *Integration und Wandel: Die Infrastruktur der Streitkräfte als Faktor sozioökonomischer Modernisierung in der Bundesrepublik, 1955–1975*. Munich: Oldenbourg, 2006.

Schmidt-Küsters, Wolf-Jürgen. "Das Entsorgungssystem im nuklearen Brennstoffkreislauf." *atw* 19:7 (1974): 340–345.

Schmoll, Friedemann. "Zur Ritualisierung touristischen Sehens im 19. Jahrhundert." In *Reisebilder: Produktion und Reproduktion touristischer Wahrnehmung*, edited by Christoph Köcke, 183–198. Münster: Waxmann, 2001.

Schneider, Karl-Heinz. "Wirtschaftsgeschichte Niedersachsens nach 1945." In *Geschichte Niedersachsens*. Vol. 5: *Von der Weimarer Republik bis zur Wiedervereinigung*, edited by Gerd Steinwascher, Detlef Schmiechen-Ackermann, and Karl-Heinz Schneider, 809–920. Hannover: Hahn, 2010.

Scholzen, Reinhard. *Der BGS. Geschichte, Ausrüstung, Aufgaben*. Stuttgart: Motorbuch, 2006.

Schregel, Susanne. *Der Atomkrieg vor der Haustür: Eine Politikgeschichte der neuen Friedensbewegung in der Bundesrepublik, 1970–1985*. Frankfurt: Campus, 2011.

Schreiber, Jürgen. "Das Brot des Konditors." *Natur: Das Umweltmagazin* 7:88 (July 1988): 34–39.

Schroeder, Klaus and Jochen Staadt. *Die Todesopfer des DDR-Grenzregimes an der innerdeutschen Grenze, 1949–1989: Ein biografisches Handbuch.* Frankfurt: Lang, 2017.

Schroers, Ralf. "Die Sackgasse (1962)." In *Die Wunde namens Deutschland: Ein Lesebuch zur deutschen Teilung,* edited by Hedwig Walwei-Wiegelmann, 63–73. Freiburg: Kerle, 1981.

Schubert, Ernst. "Von der Interzonengrenze zur Zonengrenze: Die Erfahrung der entstehenden Teilung Deutschlands im Raum Duderstadt, 1945–1949." In *Grenzland: Beiträge zur Geschichte der deutsch-deutschen Grenze,* edited by Bernd Weisbrod, 70–87. Hannover: Hahn, 1993.

Schubert, Markus. *Ein neues Hinterland für Berlin (West)? Die Regionen im Umkreis der Transitübergänge als neues Einzugsgebiet von Berlin (West).* Berlin: Spitz, 1987.

Schugg-Reheis, Claudia and Michael Bahr, *Grenzenlos: Thüringer und Franken schreiben über 45 Jahre Grenzdasein.* Coburg: Neue Presse, 1992.

Schultke, Dietmar. *"Keiner kommt durch": Die Geschichte der innerdeutschen Grenze, 1945–1990.* Berlin: Aufbau, 2004.

Schultke, Dietmar. "Wie mich der Eiserne Vorhang härtete." In *Die Grenze die uns teilte: Zeitzeugenberichte zur innerdeutschen Grenze,* edited by Dietmar Schultke, 72–111. Berlin: Köster, 2005.

Schulz, Claudia. "Fonds oder Rückstellungen? Atommüll als Private Good und Public Bad." In *Problemfalle Endlager: Gesellschaftliche Herausforderungen im Umgang mit Atommüll,* edited by Achim Brunnengräber, 262–287. Baden-Baden: Nomos, 2016.

Schulz, Martin. "Kommunal-Fusion als Mittel der Haushaltskonsolidierung." *Innovative Verwaltung* 28:5 (2006): 16–19.

Schwarzer, Markus. *Von Mondlandschaften zur Vision eines neuen Seenlandes: Der Diskurs über die Gestaltung von Tagebaubrachen in Ostdeutschland.* Wiesbaden: Springer, 2014.

Schwengler, Barbara. *Einfluss der europäischen Regionalpolitik auf die deutsche Regionalförderung.* IAB Discussion Paper 18. 2013.

Schwenke, Helmut. *Die Förderung und Entwicklung der Wirtschaft im Landkreis Lüchow-Dannenberg: Eine Betrachtung und Beurteilung regionaler Förderpolitik.* Phil. Diss., Free University Berlin, 1970.

Scott, James C. *Seeing like a State: How Certain Schemes to Improve the Human Condition Have Failed.* New Haven, CT: Yale University Press, 1998.

Seaton, Tony. "Thanatourism and Its Discontents: An Appraisal of a Decade's Work with Some Future Issues and Directions." In *Handbook of Tourism Studies,* edited by Tazim Jamal and Mike Robinson, 521–542. London: Sage, 2009.

Seelig, Klaus-Jürgen. "Schwarzkehlchen (Saxicola torquata)—Brutvogel auf dem Brockenplateau." *Ornithologische Jahresberichte Museum Heineanum* 13 (1995): 120.

Seidel, Tobias and Maximilian von Ehrlich. "The Persistent Effects of Regional Policy: Evidence from the West German Zonenrandgebiet." *Beiträge zur Jahrestagung des Vereins für Socialpolitik, 2014.* Evidenzbasierte Wirtschaftspolitik—Session: Agglomeration, Policy and Persistence, no. B14-V4. http://hdl.handle.net/10419/100515 (accessed July 2018).

Shears, David. *Ugly Frontier.* New York: Alfred A. Knopf, 1970.

Sheffer, Edith. *Burned Bridge: How East and West Germans Made the Iron Curtain.* New York: Oxford University Press, 2011.

Siemer, Josef. "Bevölkerungs- und beschäftigungspolitische Bestandsaufnahme im Zonenrandgebiet für die Jahre 1950 und 1957." *Bundesarbeitsblatt* 9:16 (1958): 424–433.

Skinner, Jonathan. "Introduction." In *Writing on the Dark Side of Travel,* edited by Jonathan Skinner, 1–28. New York: Berghahn, 2012.

Skowronek, Frank et al. *Die Versenkung und Ausbreitung von Salzabwasser im Untergrund des Werra-Kaligebietes.* Wiesbaden: Hessisches Landesamt für Bodenforschung, 1999.

Sluga, Glenda. *The Problem of Trieste and the Italo-Yugoslav Border: Difference, Identity, and Sovereignty in Twentieth-Century Europe.* Albany, NY: SUNY Press, 2001.

Smeddinck, Ulrich and Franziska Semper. "Zur Kritik am Standortauswahlgesetz." In *Problemfälle Endlager: Gesellschaftliche Herausforderungen im Umgang mit Atommüll,* edited by Achim Brunnengräber, 235–259. Baden-Baden: Nomos, 2016.

Soell, Hartmut. *Helmut Schmidt—1969 bis heute: Macht und Verantwortung.* Stuttgart: DVA, 2008.

Sonnevend, Julia. *Stories Without Borders. The Berlin Wall and the Making of a Global Iconic Event.* New York: Oxford University Press, 2016.

Specht, Joshua. "Animal History after its Triumph: Unexpected Animal, Evolutionary Approaches, and the Animal Lens." *History Compass* 14:7 (2016): 326–336.

Spicka, Mark E. *Selling the Economic Miracle: Economic Reconstruction and Politics in West Germany, 1949–1957.* New York: Berghahn, 2007.

Spode, Hasso. "Some Quantitative Aspects of 'Kraft durch Freude' Tourism, 1934–1939." *European Tourism and Culture: History and National Perspectives,* edited by Margarita Dritsas, 123–134. Athens: Livanis, 2007.

Spode, Hasso. *Wie die Deutschen 'Reiseweltmeister' wurden: Eine Einführung in die Tourismusgeschichte.* Erfurt: Landeszentrale, 2003.

Spoerer, Mark and Jochen Streb. *Neue deutsche Wirtschaftsgeschichte des 20. Jahrhunderts.* Munich: Oldenbourg, 2013.

Stacy, William E. *U.S. Army Border Operations in Germany, 1945–1983.* Heidelberg: Military History Office, 1984.

Stahl, Harald. "Veranstaltete Wildnis: Einige Überlegungen zum Konzept 'Natur Natur sein lassen' aus kulturwissenschaftlich-volkskundlicher Perspektive." In *Kulturwissenschaftliches Symposium Wald-Museum-Mensch-Wildnis,* 84–95. Grafenau: Nationalpark Bayerischer Wald, 2011.

Standley, Michelle A. "From Bulwark of Freedom to Cosmopolitan Cocktails: The Cold War, Mass Tourism and the Marketing of West Berlin as a Tourist Destination." In *Divided, but Not Disconnected: German Experiences of the Cold War*, edited by Tobias Hochscherf et al., 105–118. New York: Berghahn, 2010.

Stangel, Matthias. *Die neue Linke und die nationale Frage: Deutschlandpolitische Konzeptionen und Tendenzen in der Ausserparlamentarischen Opposition (APO)*. Baden-Baden: Nomos, 2013.

Starke, Heinz. "Die Entstehung des Zonenrandprogramms." In *Oberfränkische Wirtschaft: Zum 125jährigen Bestehen der IHK für Oberfranken*, 26–33. Bayreuth: IHK, 1968.

Steege, Paul. *Black Market, Cold War: Everyday Life in Berlin, 1946–1949*. New York: Cambridge University Press, 2007.

Stehböck, Martin. "Abbau der Grenzanlagen und Minennachsuche." *Mitteilungen aus der Norddeutschen Naturschutzakademie* 5:3 (1994): 24–30.

Steiner, André. "Die DDR-Volkswirtschaft am Ende." In *Revolution und Vereinigung, 1989/90: Als in Deutschland die Realität die Phantasie überholte*, edited by Klaus-Dietmar Henke, 113–129. Munich: dtv, 2009.

Steiner, André. *The Plans That Failed: An Economic History of the GDR*. New York: Berghahn, 2010.

Steinle, Matthias. *Vom Feindbild zum Fremdbild: Die gegenseitige Darstellung von BRD und DDR im Dokumentarfilm*. Konstanz: UVK, 2003.

Steinmetz, Heinrich. "Berlins Hinterland: Eine Studie über die Regionen im Umkreis der Transitübergänge als neues Einzugsgebiet von Berlin (West)." *Stadt + Umwelt* (July 1988): 41–42.

Stennert, Doris. "'Reisen zum Wiedersehen und Neuerleben': Aspekte des 'Heimwehtourismus' dargestellt am Beispiel der Grafschaft Glatzer." In *Alltagskulturen zwischen Erinnerung und Geschichte: Beiträge zur Volkskunde der Deutschen in und aus dem östlichen Europa*, edited by Kurt Dröge, 83–94. Munich: Oldenbourg, 1995.

Stewart, Richard Burleson and Jane Bloom Stewart. *Fuel Cycle to Nowhere: U.S. Law and Policy on Nuclear Waste*. Nashville, TN: Vanderbilt University Press, 2011.

Stiftung Aufarbeitung, ed. *Orte des Erinnerns: Gedenkzeichen, Gedenkstätten und Museen zur Berliner Mauer und innerdeutschen Grenze*. Berlin: Bundesstiftung Aufarbeitung, 2011.

Stivers, William. "The Incomplete Blockade: Soviet Zone Supply of West Berlin, 1948–1949." *Diplomatic History* 21:4 (1997): 569–602.

Stokes, Lauren. "The Permanent Refugee Crisis in the Federal Republic of Germany, 1945–2018." *Central European History* 52:1 (2019): 19-44.

Stoll, Klaus Hartwig. *Das war die Grenze*. Fulda: Parzellers, 1997.

Stöver, Bernd. *Zuflucht DDR: Spione und andere Übersiedler*. Munich: Beck, 2009.

Strubelt, Wendelin and Detlef Briesen, eds. *Raumplanung nach 1945: Kontinuitäten und Neuanfänge in der Bundesrepublik Deutschland*. Frankfurt: Campus, 2015.

Stubbe, Christoph. *Die Jagd in der DDR: Ohne Pacht eine andere Jagd.* Melsungen: Nimrod, 2006.

Stude, Sebastian. *Strom für die Republik. Die Stasi und das Kernkraftwerk Greifswald.* Göttingen: V&R, 2018.

Stunz, Holger R. *Das "hessische Salzburg": Festspiele in Bad Hersfeld.—Entwicklung, Strukturen und Ideologie einer Institution kultureller Repräsentation der frühen Bundesrepublik.* Munich: Grin, 2003.

Succow, Michael, Lebrecht Jeschke, and Hans Dieter Knapp, eds. *Die Krise als Chance: Naturschutz in neuer Dimension.* Neuenhagen: Succow Stiftung, 2001.

Succow, Michael, Lebrecht Jeschke, and Hans Dieter Knapp, eds. *Naturschutz in Deutschland: Rückblicke, Einblicke, Ausblicke.* Berlin: Links, 2012.

Sweet, William. "The Opposition to Nuclear Power in Europe." *Bulletin of the Atomic Scientists* 33:10 (Dec. 1977): 40–47.

Taylor, Joseph E., III. "Boundary Terminology." *Environmental History* 13 (July 2008): 454–481.

Terry, Andrew, Uwe Riecken and Karin Ullrich. *The Green Belt of Europe: From Vision to Reality.* Gland, CH: IUCN, 2006.

Theiss, Norbert. "Lebensraum Grenzstreifen." *Ornithologischer Anzeiger* 32 (1993): 1–9.

Ther, Philipp. *Europe after 1989: A History.* Princeton, NJ: Princeton University Press, 2016.

Thies, Heinrich. *Weit ist der Weg nach Zicherie: Die Geschichte eines geteilten Dorfes an der deutsch-deutschen Grenze.* Hamburg: Hoffmann & Campe, 2005.

Thomas, Julia Adeney. "The Exquisite Corpses of Nature and History: The Case of the Korean DMZ." In *Militarized Landscapes: From Gettysburg to Salisbury Plain,* edited by Chris Pearson, Peter Coates, and Tim Cole, 151–168. London: Continuum, 2010.

Thoß, Hendrik. *Gesichert in den Untergang: Die Geschichte der DDR-Westgrenze.* Berlin: K. Dietz, 2004.

Thumer, Ingrid. "'Grauenhaft: Ich muss ein Foto machen'—Tourismus und Fotografie." *Fotogeschichte* 12:44 (1992): 23–40.

Tiggemann, Anselm. *Die Achillesferse der Kernenergie in der Bundesrepublik Deutschland: Zur Kernenergiekontroverse und Geschichte der nuklearen Entsorgung von den Anfängen bis Gorleben, 1955–1985.* Lauf an der Pegnitz: Europa-Forum, 2010.

Tiggemann, Anselm. *Gorleben als Entsorgungs- und Endlagerstandort: Der niedersächsische Auswahl- und Entscheidungsprozess—Expertise zur Standortauswahl für das "Entsorgungszentrum," 1976/77.* Hannover: Nds. Min. für Umwelt und Klimaschutz, 2010.

Timothy, Dallen J. "Collecting Places: Geodetic Lines in Tourist Space." *Journal of Travel & Tourism Marketing* 7 (1998): 123–129.

Timothy, Dallen J. *Tourism and Political Boundaries.* London: Routledge, 2001.

Tompkins, Andrew S. *Better Active than Radioactive! Anti-Nuclear Protest in 1970s France and West Germany.* Oxford: Oxford University Press, 2016.

Tompkins, Andrew S. "Grassroots Transnationalism(s): Franco-German Opposition to Nuclear Energy in the 1970s." *Contemporary European History* 25:1 (2016): 117–142.

Trees, Wolfgang. *Schmuggler, Zöllner und die Kaffeepanzer: Die wilden Nachkriegsjahre an der deutschen Westgrenze.* Aachen: Triangel, 2002.

Treitel, Corinna. *Eating Nature in Modern Germany: Food, Agriculture, and Environment, c. 1870–2000.* New York: Cambridge University Press, 2017.

Trouwborst, Arie, Floor Fleurke, and Jennifer Dubrulle. "Border Fences and Their Impacts on Large Carnivores, Large Herbivores and Biodiversity: An International Wildlife Law Perspective." *Reciel* 25:3 (2016): 291–306.

Ude-Koeller, Susanne. *Auf gebahnten Wegen: Zum Naturdiskurs am Beispiel des Harzklubs e.V.* Münster: Waxmann, 2004.

Uekötter, Frank. "Entangled Ecologies: Outlines of a Green History of Two or More Germanys." In *A History Shared and Divided: East and West Germany since the 1970s,* edited by Frank Bösch, 147–190. New York: Berghahn, 2018.

Ullmann, Hans-Peter. *Der deutsche Steuerstaat: Eine Geschichte der öffentlichen Finanzen vom 18. Jahrhundert bis heute.* Munich: Beck, 2005.

Ullmann, Hans-Peter. "Die Expansionskoalition: Akteure und Aktionen in der bundesdeutschen Finanz- und Schuldenpolitik der 1970er Jahre." *Geschichte & Gesellschaft* 41:3 (2015): 394–417.

Ullrich, Maren. *Geteilte Ansichten: Erinnerungslandschaft deutsch-deutsche Grenze.* Berlin: Aufbau, 2006.

Urry, John. *The Tourist Gaze.* London: Sage, 2002.

Vandamme, Ralf. *Basisdemokratie als zivile Intervention: Der Partizipationsanspruch der neuen sozialen Bewegungen.* Opladen: Leske & Budrich, 2000.

Vetten, Horst. "Gleich hinter Gorleben: Entdeckungen im Landkreis Lüchow-Dannenberg, der vielleicht seltsamsten Ecke Deutschlands." *Geo,* no. 6 (1980): 38–60.

Vollers-Sauer, Elisabeth. "Goethes Harz." *Welfengarten* 4 (1994): 35–45.

Volze, Armin. "Zur Devisenverschuldung der DDR: Entstehung, Bewältigung und Folgen." In *Am Ende des realen Sozialismus: Beiträge zu einer Bestandsaufnahme der DDR-Wirklichkeit in den 80er Jahren.* Vol. 4: *Die Endzeit der DDR-Wirtschaft— Analysen zur Wirtschafts- Sozial- und Umweltpolitik,* edited by Eberhard Kuhrt et al., 151–177. Opladen: Leske & Budrich, 1999.

Wacher, Gerhard. "Probleme eines peripheren Industriegebietes unter besonderer Berücksichtigung der Zonengrenzlage, dargestellt am Beispiel Oberfranken." Paper presented at Konferenz über Fragen der regionalen Wirtschaft, Brussels, Dec. 6–8, 1961.

Wagner, Manfred. *"Beseitigung des Ungeziefers . . ." Zwangsaussiedlungen in den thüringischen Landkreisen Saalfeld, Schleiz und Lobenstein, 1952 und 1961.* Erfurt: Landeszentrale, 2001.

Waldeck, Winfried. "Die Bevölkerungsentwicklung im Landkreis Lüchow-Dannenberg nach der innerdeutschen Grenzöffnung, 1989–1994." In

Hannoversches Wendland: 15. Jahresheft des Heimatkundlichen Arbeitskreises Lüchow-Dannenberg, 1994–1997, 315–324. Lüchow: Selbstverlag, 2001.

Waldeck, Winfried. "Räumliche Strukturanalyse: Beispiel Lüchow-Dannenberg." *Praxis Geographie* 7:8 (1992): 44–49.

Walker, J. Samuel. *The Road to Yucca Mountain: The Development of Radioactive Waste Policy in the United States.* Berkeley: University of California Press, 2009.

Walter, Bernd. "Der Bundesgrenzschutz der Bundesrepublik Deutschland: Sonderpolizei von Anfang an oder ursprünglicher Streitkräfteersatz?" *Österreichische Militärische Zeitschrift* 43:5 (2005): 643–647.

Walther, Achim and Joachim Bittner, *Heringsbahn: Die innerdeutsche Grenze bei Hötensleben/Offleben/Schöningen zwischen 1945 and 1952.* Hötensleben: Mitteldeutscher, 2011.

Walwei-Wiegelmann, Hedwig, ed. *Die Wunde namens Deutschland: Ein Lesebuch zur deutschen Teilung.* Freiburg: Kerle, 1981.

Wandschneider, Gerhard. "Ein Pfahl im Fleische Deutschlands." In *Im Schatten der Zonengrenze*, edited by Bundesministerium für Gesamtdeutsche Fragen, 93–97. Bonn: 1956.

Weber, Rolf. "Vom 'Todesstreifen' zum 'Grünen Band': Dargestellt am Beispiel der sächsischen Grenze zu Bayern." *Naturschutz in den neuen Bundesländern: Ein Rückblick*, edited by Regine Auster and Hermann Behrens, 659–669. Berlin: VWF, 2001.

Wegener, Uwe. "Der Nationalpark Harz." In *Naturschutz in Deutschland*, edited by Michael Succow, Lebrecht Jeschke, and Hans Dieter Knapp, 104–112. Berlin: Links, 2012.

Wegener, Uwe. "Die Unterschutzstellung des Nationalparkes Hochharz." In *Naturschutz in den neuen Bundesländern—Ein Rückblick*, edited by Regine Auster and Hermann Behrens, 649–657. Berlin: VWF, 2001.

Wehler, Hans-Ulrich. *Deutsche Gesellschaftsgeschichte, 1949–1990.* Munich: Beck, 2008.

Weiger, Hubert. "Flurbereinigung und Naturschutz—Bilanz 1982: Nach wie vor negativ." *Natur und Umwelt* 62:2 (Apr. 1982): 3–6.

Weiger, Hubert. "Kai Frobel: Der Initiator des Grünen Bandes." *Nationalpark* 143:3 (2009): 44–45.

Weight, Ernst. "Standorte neuer Industriebetriebe in Franken und der Oberpfalz unter dem Gesichtspunkt von Nachbarschaft und Fühlungsvorteil." *Berichte zur deutschen Landeskunde* 23 (1959): 383–400.

Weitz, Eric D. "The Ever-Present Other: Communism in the Making of West Germany." In *The Miracle Years: A Cultural History of West Germany, 1949–1968*, edited by Hanna Schissler, 219–232. Princeton, NJ: Princeton University Press, 2001.

Wengst, Udo and Hermann Wentker, eds. *Das doppelte Deutschland: 40 Jahre Systemkonkurrenz.* Berlin: Links, 2008.

Wensierski, Peter. "Umweltprobleme in der DDR: Eine Einführung." *Geographische Rundschau* 39:11 (1987): 604–605.

Wensierski, Peter. *Von oben nach unten wächst gar nichts: Umweltzerstörung und Protest in der DDR.* Frankfurt: Fischer, 1986.

Wentker, Hermann. *Aussenpolitik in engen Grenzen: Die DDR im internationalen System, 1949–1989.* Munich: Oldenbourg, 2007.

Wentker, Hermann. "Bundespräsens in West-Berlin: Perzeption, Propaganda und Politik der SED-Führung." In *Hauptstadtanspruch und symbolische Politik: Die Bundespräsenz im geteilten Berlin, 1949–1990,* edited by Michael C. Bienert, Uwe Schaper, and Hermann Wentker, 241–262. Berlin: Bebra, 2012.

Wentker, Hermann. "Zwischen Abgrenzung und Verflechtung: Deutsch-deutsche Geschichte nach 1945." *Aus Politik und Zeitgeschichte* 1–2 (2005): 10–17.

Westad, Arne. *The Cold War: A World History.* New York: Basic Books, 2017.

Wettestad, Jørgen. "Designing Effective Environmental Regimes: The Case of the Convention of Long-Range Transboundary Air Pollution (CLRTAP)." *Energy & Environment* 10:6 (1999): 671–703.

Wiesemann, Bernd. "Bedürftige und Förderungswürdige: Mehr Differenzierung wäre besser." *Wirtschaft und Standort* 12 (1978): 27–28.

Wilkens, Horst. "Die Rolle des Natur- und Landschaftsschutzes in der Bundesrepublik: Das Beispiel Gorleben." *Natur und Landschaft* 53:6 (June 1978): 183–186.

Winiwarter, Verena. "Buying a Dream Come True." *Rethinking History* 5:3 (2001): 451–455.

Winterhoff, Herbert. "Das Verkehrswesen." In *Das Hannoversche Wendland,* edited by Wilhelm Paasche, 129–133. Lüchow: Landkreis DAN, 1971.

Wirsching, Andreas. *Abschied vom Provisorium: Geschichte der Bundesrepublik Deutschland, 1982–1990.* Stuttgart: DVA, 2006.

Wishlade, Fiona G. *Regional State Aid and Competition Policy in the European Union.* The Hague: Kluwer Law, 2003.

Withey, Lynne. *Grand Tours and Cook's Tours: A History of Leisure Travel, 1750–1915.* New York: Morrow, 1997.

Witt. "Die DL bei Uelzen." *Die Parole* 21:1 (Jan. 20, 1971).

Wittich, Hans-Jörg. "Kurze Darstellung der Produktionsprozesse eines Kaliwerkes mit Beispielen der technischen Entwicklung in der Kaliverarbeitung." In *Kaliindustrie an Werra und Fulda,* edited by Ulrich Eisenbach and Akos Paulinyi, 137–166. Darmstadt: Hess. Wirtschaftsarchiv, 1998.

Wolf, Stephan. *Hauptabteilung I: NVA und Grenztruppen (Handbuch),* edited by BStU. Berlin: BStU, 2005. http://www.nbn-resolving.org/urn:nbn:de:0292-97839421300423 (accessed Jan. 2018).

Wolfrum, Edgar. *Die geglückte Demokratie: Geschichte der Bundesrepublik Deutschland von ihren Anfängen bis zur Gegenwart.* Stuttgart: Klett-Cotta, 2006.

Wolfrum, Edgar. *Geschichtspolitik in der Bundesrepublik Deutschland: Der Weg zur bundesrepublikanischen Erinnerung, 1948–1990.* Darmstadt: WBG, 1999.

Wolfrum, Edgar. "Die Mauer." In *Deutsche Erinnerungsorte*, vol. 1, edited by Etienne François and Hagen Schulze, 552–568. Munich: Beck, 2001.

Woodward, Rachel. *Military Geographies*. Malden, MA: Blackwell, 2004.

Wössner, Barbara. *Die Deutschlandklausel im EG-Beihilferecht (Art. 87. Abs. 2 lit. c EGV)*. Hamburg: Kovac, 2001.

Wright, Patrick. *Iron Curtain: From Stage to Cold War*. Oxford: Oxford University Press, 2007.

Würth, Gerhard. *Umweltschutz und Umweltzerstörung in der DDR*. Frankfurt: Lang, 1985.

Zahra, Tara. *The Great Departure: Mass Migration from Eastern Europe and the Making of the Free World*. New York: Norton, 2016.

Ziegler, Astrid. *Regionale Strukturpolitik: Zonenrandförderung—ein Wegweiser?* Cologne: Bund, 1992.

Zierenberg, Malte. *Berlin's Black Market, 1939–1950*. Houndmills: Palgrave Macmillan, 2015.

Zint, Günter. *Republik Freies Wendland: Eine Dokumentation*. Frankfurt: Zweitausendeins, 1980.

Zschaler, Frank E. W. "Bundeshilfen für Berlin." In *Hauptstadtanspruch und symbolische Politik: Die Bundespräsenz im geteilten Berlin, 1949–1990*, edited by Michael C. Bienert, Uwe Schaper, and Hermann Wentker, 209–220. Berlin: Bebra, 2012.

Zschiesche, Michael. "Umweltschutz in Ostdeutschland: Versuch über ein schnell verschwundenes Thema." *Aus Politik und Zeitgeschichte* B27 (2003): 33–38.

Index

For the benefit of digital users, indexed terms that span two pages (e.g., 52–53) may, on occasion, appear on only one of those pages.

Note: Figures are indicated by *f* following the page number

Printed in the USA/Agawam, MA
June 25, 2020

756842.005